Fidel

By the same author
Twilight of Tyrants
The Cuban Invasion
(*with Karl E. Meyer*)
The Winds of Revolution
Dominican Diary
Latin America
The Bombs of Palomares
Portrait of Spain
Czechoslovakia Since World War Two
Innocents at Home
The US and the Caribbean
  (*editor*)
Compulsive Spy
The Energy Crisis
The Illusion of Peace
Diplomatic Immunity
  (*a novel*)

FIDEL
A Critical Portrait

Tad Szulc

HUTCHINSON
London Melbourne Auckland Johnnesburg

Copyright © 1986 by Tad Szulc

First published in Great Britain in 1987 by Hutchinson Ltd, an imprint of Century Hutchinson Ltd, Brookmount House, 62-65 Chandos Place, London WC2N 4NW

Century Hutchinson Australia (Pty) Ltd
PO Box 496, 16–22 Church Street, Hawthorn, Victoria 31122, Australia

Century Hutchinson New Zealand Limited
PO Box 40–086, Glenfield, Auckland 10, New Zealand

Century Hutchinson South Africa (Pty) Ltd
PO Box 337, Bergvlei, 2012 South Africa

British Library Cataloguing in Publication Data

Szulc, Tad
Fidel: a critical portrait.
    1. Castro, Fidel   2. Heads of state——
    Cuba——Biography
    I. Title
    972.41′064′0924   F1788.22.C3

    ISBN 0-09-172602-6

Filmset in Linotron Bembo Medium by Deltatype, Ellesmere Port
Printed and bound in Great Britain by Mackays of Chatham Ltd, Kent

Contents

List of Illustrations

Castro and supporters in the jungle
Emphasising a point during an inaugural speech, 16 February 1959.
With his son, Fidelito, at the Hilton, Havana.
With his brother, Ramon.
At breakfast in his Havana home, with Juan Orta, Celia Sanchez, and Fidelito, trying on his father's hat.
At a farm in Northern Chile.
The heady days of January 1959 when Batista was ousted.
Bienvenido Fidel.
The Baseball Fan
The historic meeting in New York on 23 September, 1960, with Nikita Krushchev.
In Nicaragua, January 1985.
In New York, October 1979.
In Havana, May 1986.

Introduction

President Fidel Castro Ruz of Cuba asked me the following question as we stood in his office after a long conversation shortly after midnight of 11 February 1985:

'Will your political and ideological viewpoint allow you to tell objectively my story and the revolution's story when the Cuban government and I make the necessary material available to you?' He added: 'We would be taking a great risk with you.'

This was at the end of five long meetings I had with President Castro at the Palace of the Revolution in Havana in preparation for writing this portrait, and we had touched on an immense variety of themes concerning him and his life story. My reply to President Castro's question was that I didn't think total objectivity existed, but I would commit myself to approach this project with the greatest possible honesty. I remarked that since we were both honourable men, his ideology and mine, differing in the most absolute fashion as they did, should not interfere with the writing of an honest book. President Castro said, 'You may paint me as a devil so long as you remain objective and let my voice be heard,' and we warmly shook hands.

I had my first conversations with Fidel Castro in 1959, shortly after his revolution had triumphed, and I was in Havana as a correspondent for the *New York Times*. In 1961 I accompanied him on a tour of the Bay of Pigs battlefield. I returned to Cuba in January 1984 to interview President Castro for *Parade* magazine, and the idea of this book was born during a long weekend we spent together in Havana and the countryside. I had reminded him then that there was no serious biography of him or comprehensive study of the revolution in existence, and that he owed it to history to remedy this lack.

We went on exchanging messages through Cuban diplomats in Washington during the balance of 1984, and we immediately agreed that this should *not* be an official or authorized biography or portrait. Instead it would be an independent project with collaborative support by President Castro and his associates as well as access to written materials of the revolution. I spent a month in Havana early in 1985, holding a series of meetings with President Castro, then my wife and I set up shop in a house we rented in Havana for six months between March and August (where we were visited by President Castro). Our understanding did not require that the manuscript be seen by President Castro before publication, and therefore it has not been vetted by him. I am certain that when he does read it he will disagree with many of my opinions and conclusions, but he will find my pledge of honesty to have been met. He knows, of course, that others may see him differently than he sees himself, and for me to be critical is no violation of his trust.

Clearly this is not a definitive biography, principally because President Castro is still alive and has not completed his labours. Perhaps only a later generation of historians can attempt a full-fledged biography of this extraordinary personage. This critical portrait, therefore, simply seeks to capture his personality and the story of his life as objectively as is possible at this stage. It is not meant to be a history of the Cuban revolution, or of Cuban–American relations, and this is why I will avoid discussing in depth the achievements and problems of the revolution. Nevertheless Fidel Castro and his revolution are inseparable, so his portrait has been sketched against the broader background of contemporary Cuban history.

To write it I interviewed scores of Fidel Castro's friends, associates and comrades-in-arms in addition to my conversations with him. I have listened to a great many Cubans who have insight into the very complex personality of Fidel Castro and into the process of the revolution. I was able to see President Castro in action on occasions ranging from receptions at the Palace of the Revolution to a tour of the prison on the Isle of Youth (formerly Isle of Pines) where he had spent nearly two years as a prisoner of the Batista regime. I revisited the Bay of Pigs, and my wife and I climbed the Sierra Maestra to Fidel Castro's wartime command post to gain a sense of the environment in which he fought; we inspected the landing spot of the *Granma* that brought him and his rebels from Mexico, and the nearby battlefield where Fidel Castro's revolution almost ended three days after it began.

Among Cuban personalities I have interviewed and who have made this book possible because of the time they sacrificed were Vice President of Cuba and Education Minister J.R. Fernández Alvarez; Pedro Miret Prieto, a member of the Political Bureau of the Communist Party and one of President Castro's oldest associates; Vice President Carlos Rafael Rodríguez; Culture Minister and Political Bureau member Armando Hart Dávalos; former Interior Minister and close comrade-in-arms Ramiro Valdés Menéndez; Faustino Pérez and Universo Sánchez who were with Fidel Castro at the moment of near disaster; Alfredo Guevara whose friendship with Castro goes back to the university and their first revolutionary experiences; former Political Bureau member and Transport Minister Guillermo García who was the first Sierra Maestra peasant to join the Rebel Army; Blás Roca, Secretary-General of the Communist Party, and Fábio Grobart, one of its founders in 1925; Melba Hérnandez who fought with Fidel in the Moncada attack and was among the first members of the revolutionary movement; Vílma Espín, President of the Cuban Women's Federation and member of the Political Bureau (and wife of Raúl Castro); and Conchita Fernández who was Fidel Castro's personal secretary during the first years of the revolution.

It is impossible to list here all the Cuban officials, friends and acquaintances in political and cultural fields who were of immense assistance in my research. Foreign diplomats served as important guides, and among them I wish to mention Clara Nieto Ponce de Léon, former ambassador of Colombia in Cuba and, during our stay, the director of the UNESCO office. In the Sierra Maestra, peasants who knew Castro during the war provided remarkable accounts of those days. Finally, our research and interviews in Havana were coordinated by Alfredo Ramirez Otero and Walfredo Garciga of the Ministry of External Affairs.

In the United States conversations with Jorge Dominguez of Harvard University, Nelson Valdés of the University of New Mexico, Wayne S. Smith who served as head of the US Interests Section in Havana, George Volsky who is a journalist in Miami and a leading expert on Cuba, and Max Lesnick, a university friend of Castro and now a publisher in Miami, were immensely useful. Numerous Cubans who knew Castro in boarding school and university, and are now exiled in the US, shared their recollections. My special gratitude is to The Hon. Ambler H. Moss, Dean of the Graduate School of International Studies at the University of Miami, and to Dr Jaime Suchlicki, Director of the Institute of Inter-American Studies at the University of Miami for superb research and intellectual support. Garbiela Rodríguez was a most intelligent and resourceful researcher. My wife Marianne lived through all of it: meetings with President Castro, entertaining Cuban friends in Havana, climbing Cuban mountains, organizing masses of material we brought back from Cuba, researching in Washington, and reading, improving and editing the manuscript.

At William Morrow and Company, my publishers, Lisa Drew was an editor with whom it was a joy to work. Morton L. Janklow and Anne Sibbald, my literary agents, were marvellously imaginative and encouraging. My British publishers, Century Hutchinson, made the great contribution of making this both available for English language readers outside the United States, with Paul Sidey, my editor there, pioneering this effort.

Thank you all.   T.S.
                                                    Washington, D.C.,
                                                        July 1986

PART ONE
The Man

Chapter 1

Advancing on his elbows and knees so slowly that his great bulk hardly seemed to move at all, the sweaty man in an olive-green uniform, horn-rimmed glasses on his unshaven face, slid carefully into the low canefield until he was entirely covered by a thick layer of leaves. In his right hand he clutched a telescopic-sight automatic rifle, a Belgian-made 30.06 calibre weapon, his only and beloved possession.

The tall rifleman was a thirty-year-old lawyer named Fidel Castro Ruz, Cuba's fiercest apostle ever of comprehensive social and political revolution, and now – at high noon of Thursday 6 December 1956 – he faced not only the imminent death of his dreams but his own death as well.

Cubans had known Castro for years as a loud and ineffectual plotter; a loser. To the outside world, and notably to the United States next door, he was at most just another Caribbean troublemaker – of whose existence the Eisenhower administration was in fact not even aware.

This American ignorance reflected their traditional attitude towards Cuba, the nearest thing the United States had to a protectorate in the Western hemisphere: Washington need not worry about Cuban politics and politicians because its proconsuls in Havana always kept them in line. The idea that within a few years Castro would establish the first Communist state in the Americas would have been dismissed as ridiculous had anyone suggested it in December of 1956.

At that moment, in fact, Fidel Castro and his absurdly small rebel group – eighty-two men who had landed four days earlier, on 2 December, from a yacht designed to carry no more than twelve on the southern coast of his native Cuban province of Oriente after an almost fatal voyage from Mexico – were completely surrounded by government troops. The exhausted and famished expeditionaries had been totally routed and dispersed at Alegría del Pío the previous afternoon in their first battle ashore. Now in the canefield, he had only two companions. As Castro remarked many years later, 'There was a moment when I was Commander-in-Chief of myself and two others.'

Nevertheless the notion of surrendering to the soldiers of the dictatorship of President Fulgencio Batista Zaldívar that he and his men had arrived to overthrow never occurred to Castro. The 26th of July Movement had been growing in the underground of Cuban cities since 1953, the time of that disastrous and bloody attack on the Moncada barracks in Santiago, the capital of Oriente, conceived and led by Castro. He then spent twenty-one months in Batista prisons preparing himself for the next strike at the dictator. Now Castro had returned from the Mexican self-exile that followed his imprisonment to launch a guerrilla war against the regime in the rugged chain of Sierra Maestra. The son of a tough Spaniard, he had the inner certainty of triumph that only visionaries feel when the odds are impossibly arrayed against them.

The last time I was in Havana to see Fidel Castro he was approaching his sixtieth birthday, and I found him in a philosophical mood. Among other notions, he believed firmly it was his natural destiny that well over a quarter of a century before, he should have scaled the heights and reached the apex of power. He was perfectly matter-of-fact in acknowledging that some leaders are destined to play crucial roles in the affairs of men, and that, yes, his was a case in point.

He then turned to his favourite theme that such leaders may affect 'subjectively' the objective conditions in a country. To Fidel this is an absolutely vital point in the 'correct' interpretation of the Cuban revolution, inasmuch as he had succeeded in proving wrong the classical theories of the so-called 'old' Cuban Communists. These Communists had insisted that a Castro-preached mass revolution in Cuba was impossible because the necessary 'objective conditions', as defined by Karl Marx, did not prevail; accordingly they had turned their backs on the *Fidelista* insurrection until its closing months. Unprecedentedly, the Communists in Cuba were therefore co-opted by Fidel Castro (who did not even belong to the Party) rather than the other way round.

Traditional Cuban Marxist–Leninists, with their thirty years' experience as a Moscow-directed party, with activities confined to the organization of protest labour strikes or 'popular front' alliances with 'bourgeois' politicians (including Batista in the 1940s), had not been able to bring themselves to believe that a single man's personality could trigger a national revolution.

Castro was not proposing a peasant revolution in Cuba but, as the centrepiece of his strategy, he did envisage guerrilla warfare expanding with peasant support from a mountains' 'focus' to engulf in time the whole island – a concept the ideology-minded Communists would not absorb. Consequently the 'old' party had secretly sent an emissary to Mexico in November 1956 to dissuade Castro from his publicly announced plans to land in Cuba that year. In fact, Communist attitudes towards Castro at that stage and afterwards describe an immensely fascinating and complicated relationship, a relationship – constituting the political backbone of the Cuban revolution – that has never before been fully disclosed.

In a way that neither 'old' Cuban Communists nor the United States were able to comprehend at the time – and Moscow and Washington may still not fully understand it even now – Fidel Castro built his revolution primarily on the sentiments of Cuban history. He tapped the deep roots of mid-nineteenth-century insurrections against Spanish colonialism, and then themes of nationalism, radicalism and social-justice populism. Whatever the actual timing of his personal allegiance to Marxism, Castro waited more than two years after victory before publicly identifying himself with socialism; this may have been tactical, but it also demonstrated his recognition of the feelings of the Cubans towards the revolution of the Sierra Maestra.

The two most worshipped political deities in socialist Cuba are José Martí, the great hero of the Independence Wars and one of the most brilliant thinkers in Latin America, and Karl Marx. Their portraits appear together everywhere (sometimes along with Lenin's) and it is beyond question that Martí – the man who always warned against United States ambitions in Cuba and the Caribbean was from the outset Castro's personal role model. And, too, it is Martí's, and not Marx's, bust that stands guard in every Cuban school, notably in the tiny schools the revolutionary regime built even in the most remote mountain areas. In his speeches Castro tells his audiences that the Cuban sense of history and nationalism was as crucial as Marxism in giving birth to the great revolution. In 1978, twenty years after his victory, he reminded his fellow Cubans and the world: 'We are not only Marxist–Leninists; we are also nationalists and patriots.'

Even with Castro ruling as the First Secretary of the Cuban Communist Party since 1965 it took nearly seven years after the advent of *Fidelismo* to fashion Cuba into a full-fledged Communist state. Fidel himself considered that the contribution his approach to the revolutionary strategy provided to scientific Marxism was entirely practical; notwithstanding his exceptional intellect he has added little of note to Marxist thought or theory. For, above all, Castro is a man of action.

The revolution has bestowed on Cuba extraordinary gifts of social justice and equality, advances in public health and education, and an equitable distribution of the national wealth, and Fidel Castro deserves total credit for this. Cuban and world history would have evolved differently had this single individual been less determined and, most importantly, less lucky.

Efforts to gain a sense of Fidel Castro as a human being are not easily rewarded. Castro's bearded face may be one of the best known in the contemporary world, his public views on every subject under the sun (he has opinions about everything from medicine to *haute cuisine*) have cascaded in the billions of words of the thousands of his speeches over these long years, but with the secrecy habit of a life-long conspirator, he is a master of self-concealment. A deeply moody introvert despite his external *persona* – and a man of surprising shyness in initial personal contacts – Castro is exceedingly selective about disclosing facts that, in his judgement, may negatively affect what he thinks should be his public image. Castro, a student of the past and a political virtuoso, understands the strategic importance of controlling history.

Recently Castro, the Jesuit-educated, self-proclaimed Marxist–Leninist, has been spending much time debating and dictating for publication an intellectual rationalization of the values shared in his view by Christianity and Marxism in implementing social justice. Since John Paul II's election to the papacy, Castro has praised him often for his concern with the poor in the Third World (Cuba and the Vatican never interrupted diplomatic relations, and Castro has attended private dinners with the apostolic pro-nuncio in Havana). A meeting between the two has been discussed, and the Cuban National Ecclesiastic Encounter was held in February 1986 as the most important Roman Catholic Church conference since the revolution.

The idea of a synthesis between his brand of revolutionary socialism and Christian religion is very much on his mind: intellectually, when he speaks in praise of the Theology of Liberation (the powerful concern for social justice current in the modern Roman Catholic Church in Latin America) and mystically, when he contemplates the nature of martyrdom. In lengthy conversations in 1985 with a Brazilian Dominican friar, Fidel observed that 'I am certain that upon the same pillars on which today reposes the sacrifice of a revolutionary, yesterday reposed the sacrifice of a martyr for his religious faith.' Given the explosive political tensions in Latin America, and the new road taken by the 'young' Church there, Castro is engaging in more than a theoretical exercise. It fits into his strategic Bolivarian concepts, but it also brings out his mysticism and his Jesuit-learned logic.

Castro's feelings towards his son Fidelito (who was five years old when his father divorced his mother) seem to have been unusually strong, when one considers that from the moment the boy was born, Castro senior was successively a plotter (while practising law without charging his impoverished clients), a political prisoner, an exile, a *guerrillero* and a chief of state. Castro attempted to see Fidelito under the most difficult circumstances, including having him illegally brought to Mexico while the rebel force was being trained. A Soviet-educated physicist, Fidelito, now Secretary General of the Cuban Nuclear Commission, married and with two children (though it is difficult to think of Castro as a grandfather), is increasingly in the public eye, being shown on national television presiding over scientific meetings and attending ceremonial receptions at the Palace of the Revolution. He looks exactly the way his father did at his age, in his mid-thirties.

It is no secret in Havana that Castro has at least one other adult child (and a grandchild) from a romantic liaison. But Fidel Castro is a very private person, and Cubans normally do not discuss his personal life, mainly out of respect. He never remarried, and since Celia Sánchez, his absolutely devoted friend and guerrilla companion, died of cancer in 1980, nobody has replaced her in Fidel's trust and affection. Unquestionably Celia was the most important woman – and very likely the most important human being – in his life. No other woman has had her name linked publicly to Castro since Celia's death, and probably none ever will. Living among palace courtiers, Fidel seems a very lonely man.

Fidel was the fifth of nine children of Ángel Castro y Argiz, a Spaniard owning large estates in Cuba; the first two children were born to his father's first wife. Fidel Castro and his younger brother Raúl, his designated heir as head of state and government and first secretary of the Communist Party, evidently have a special personal and political relationship – they shared all the revolutionary experiences – but they choose to spent little of their free time together (Raúl has a wife and children, and is very much a family man). They are said to have had violent disagreements in the past, now seemingly forgotten. Fidel's rapport with his older brother Ramon and his half-sister Lidia is pleasant but limited. A half-brother and two sisters in Havana see him very seldom. One sister has long lived in Mexico, and another sister – Juana – though during the Sierra war she was his devoted supporter, is now in self-exile in Miami, denouncing Fidel at every opportunity as a Communist dictator.

The fundamental question concerning Fidel Castro, the 1959 revolution and Cuba's transformation into a Communist state is whether this whole phenomenon was logically dictated by Cuban history or whether it represents an extraordinary political aberration primarily instigated by his overwhelming personality.

Though the ultimate answer is too complex to be reduced to clear-cut explanations, Castro's personal role in launching and guiding the revolution is certainly impressive. Lenin sat out the start of the Russian revolution in Zürich, risking no combat. Stalin showed his mettle mainly in holding up banks and trains, and serving time in Siberian prisons. Mao Tse-tung controlled vast swathes of territory and led large armies, yet neither in the initial period of building his Communist base nor during the 1934–35 Long March did he undergo the constant personal hardships Castro would face in Cuba. Yugoslavia's Marshal Tito operated out of well-protected headquarters, later enjoying American and British missions' support. Vietnam's Ho Chi Minh had been in prison, but when the anti-French uprising was launched he was not called upon to lead troops in the battlefield.

Fidel Castro's conditioning as a *guerrillero* is therefore an extremely significant element in understanding and defining his personality today. He cherishes the title of Commander-in-Chief and the laurel leaves of rank on his formal military uniform. The total militarization of Cuban society is a concept stemming from his formative experiences. He learned the very hard way, his Sierra war creating a siege mentality for this hostility-surrounded island where at least one half of the population is trained and organized for defensive combat. He also learned that to survive he must be absolutely and undeviatingly uncompromising.

Chapter 2

Fidel Castro's overwhelming concern that chilly Thursday in December 1956 was how to break out of the encirclement, reassemble the survivors of his battered expedition, and lead them to victory. This required abiding faith that he could succeed in what was by any reasonable standards a demented enterprise. The Batista regime had at its disposal a 50,000-man army with cannon and armour, an air force and a navy, and murderously efficient police force, both uniformed and secret.

Besides, President Batista also enjoyed full United States support, including access to American arms. Tanks and artillery were shipped regularly to Cuba from US ports, Batista aircraft could refuel and load explosive and napalm bombs at the US naval station at Guantanamo on the coast of Oriente, and in Havana a US military mission trained the Cuban armed forces. All of this was consistent with the fact that Cuba, in effect, had been an American fiefdom since Spain lost the island in the 1898 war, and that Washington discouraged any changes in the status quo.

Thus the Eisenhower administration was squarely behind Batista, Vice President Richard Nixon having visited him in Havana just a short time before Castro's December landing in Oriente. But neither Batista's firepower nor American backing impressed Castro; to him, defeats really were victories in disguise, forging men's spirits and honing their courage.

In the canefield, once he was safely concealed by the *paja* carpet of dry sugarcane leaves, only his face protruding from the field, Fidel Castro whistled very softly. Another olive-green-clad figure slithered silently into the cane from a thicket across a narrow pathway; this was Universo Sánchez Álvarez, a tough, big peasant from the northern Matanzas province who had served as Castro's bodyguard during the clandestine period of invasion preparations in Mexico. Universo carried with him a telescopic-sight rifle (as Castro did), but he was barefoot, having lost his boots in the retreat from Alegría de Pía, a serious problem for a fighting man. Then, the third fighter reached the haven of the thick cane-leaf blanket. He was Faustino Pérez Hernández, a Havana physician of slight build and one of the two chiefs of staff of the rebel expedition. Faustino wore combat boots, but he no longer had his weapon. Both men were thirty-six years old, six years older than Fidel, and the average age in the rebel group was twenty-seven; most of them reasonably mature individuals.

The three men, burying themselves under the *paja* , lay on their backs next to each other so that they could communicate in whispers. Castro cleared his throat and murmured triumphantly: 'We are winning . . . victory will be ours!' Universo and Faustino said nothing. Fidel Castro, Universo Sánchez and Faustino Perez constituted at that juncture the *entire* Rebel Army, the fighting arm of Castro's anti-Batista 26th of July Movement.

Actually, this Rebel Army would remain limited to the three men and two rifles for thirteen days, until at a Sierra peasant's house they encountered Raúl Castro, the chief of one of the routed expedition's three platoons, who had been wandering in the mountains with four companions.

Raúl's group had five rifles and ammunition – and Fidel Castro became so excited at the growth of his 'army' to eight men and seven weapons that he proclaimed in his most dramatic style: 'Now we have won the war . . . the days of tyranny are counted!' Four days later, seven more expeditionaries, including Argentine-born Ernesto 'Che' Guevara de la Serna, who had been slightly wounded at Alegría del Pío, joined the Castro force. Fidel was ecstatic.

But on that first Thursday in Cuba, Fidel, Faustino and Universo had concluded in a soft-whisper consultation that their safest course was to remain under the leafy canefield blanket. They had to elude the troopers of the Rural Guard, a heavily armed gendarmerie corps, including artillery, that had surprised and smashed the expeditionary forces the previous day, and now hunted for survivors.

Although the Batista government had already announced that Fidel and Raúl had been killed along with forty other rebels in combat on 5 December (a story instantly disseminated around the world by United Press International, a piece of journalism Castro never forgave), a confidential report from the Rural Guard squadron commanders to their Havana superiors that night admitted that 'Dr Fidel Castro' might have escaped. Batista obviously realized that Castro had to be found and killed, no matter what: the dictatorship's political credibility and its reputation for military effectiveness were at stake.

Consequently aeroplanes were summoned to assist in the search. By mid-morning of Thursday, low-flying aircraft had spotted three separate groups of rebels hiding under thick tree growth on a hill just above the Alegría del Pío battlefield. One of these groups was Fidel Castro's, and they were bombed and strafed by twin-engine B-26 light bombers.

The planes missed them on the first pass, and the three rebels raced towards the nearest canefield while the aircraft regrouped in the sky. The fugitives repeated their manoeuvre several times until reaching a thicket which Fidel thought looked the safest. They slithered to it on their bellies, and hid themselves under the dry large leaves that lay on the ground.

Castro's theory was that the Rural Guard and the aircraft would end their search of the area by evening, moving on to the next grid. This, he thought, would allow him, Faustino and Universo to leave the canefield that same night and begin marching towards the foothills of the Sierra Maestra to the east where he knew that friendly peasants would protect and aid them. Faustino and Universo dissuaded Fidel, however, from making a run for it right away; when he insisted on going, Universo said, 'Damn it, Fidel, democratically it's two against one, so we stay.'

In the meantime, from barely a few hundred yards away they could hear shouted military commands, the metallic sound of Thompson submachine guns shifted from shoulder to hand by the soldiers, and occasional bursts of automatic gunfire. A canefield immediately to the south of the three rebels was set ablaze to flush out whoever might be concealed there, and thick, blueish smoke spread quickly over the flatland. They desperately held back their coughing, fearful that the troopers might hear. A B-26 roared low over the burning field to strafe it.

Things were bad for Fidel and his companions. Apart from being trapped inside a canefield they were parched and starving. They had lost most of their supplies and equipment, including food, four days earlier, when *Granma*, their yacht, was shipwrecked at dawn on Sunday 2 December, several hundred yards from the coast. As the eighty-two expeditionaries advanced slowly inland they contacted the area's few peasants and charcoal men, who received them well, sharing simple food with the rebels. Castro and his men had their last hot meal on the evening of Tuesday, 4 December – they also bought sausage and biscuits from the locals – before moving on towards Alegría del Pío.

What gave them away to the Rural Guard was their hunger the following day. Having consumed their sausage-and-biscuit rations, the revolutionaries began breaking off sugarcane stalks as they marched, sucking them dry, then dropping the cane on the ground. Fidel did the same, cane juice being a high-energy nutrient. But Rural Guard troopers, searching for the expeditionaries (the Batista navy and air force had quickly located the half-sunk *Granma* off Los Cayuelos), spotted the trail of discarded stalks, following and then surrounding the Castro force and routing it on Wednesday 5 December. This was the disastrous result of inexperience in new terrain (Rural Guard soldiers, of course, instantly knew they had found their quarry), and it was a lesson Fidel would never forget.

Now he, Faustino and Universo carefully reached for stalks near them to suck the sugar syrup for nourishment. But the Batista forces would not go away, and during the three days and nights they would stay in that canefield (and two more days and nights in one further east), the rebels developed mouth sores from sucking the stalks. Every dawn to quench their thirst they licked the dew from the leaves, but this also caused mouth and tongue infections because of the leaf roughness. Occasional night rain served only to soak the ground – and the three men.

The first night in the canefield, Castro placed his rifle atop his body: the barrel fitted against his throat and the butt was lodged against his feet. He released the safety catch, curling his fingers around the trigger. 'I shall not – ever – be taken alive by the soldiers of tyranny while I sleep!' he announced in a dramatic whisper. 'If I am found, I'll squeeze the trigger and die.'

His two companions looked at each other with incredulity. 'Fidel, you are crazy,' Universo Sánchez told him. 'What you're doing is suicidal. There are land crabs here, and a crab could trip the trigger.'

Castro, who disliked being contradicted, answered in a sulking murmur: 'Fine. You do what you want. *I* am going to sleep like this.' And that was the way he slept every night under the sugarcane *paja* , the rifle barrel at his throat. Universo settled in, sleeping with his rifle cradled in his arms. Faustino had no weapon.

The only sacrifice of which Fidel Castro was not capable was absolute muteness. He has always been unable to refrain from talking. And he is not a man of small talk, so he is serious almost every time he opens his mouth. Pinned down in the canefield, he was furiously and excitedly thinking ahead, planning their escape, organizing in his mind a guerrilla army, preparing the victory and outlining revolutionary laws and measures. He spoke day and night in a controlled whisper, not really expecting answers or comments. This is how Faustino Pérez, the liberal and sophisticated physician, remembers Fidel's speeches-under-the-leaves:

'Discussing the possibility of continuing on to the Sierra Maestra, Fidel was already convinced that we would meet with our companions. We would go that same afternoon, he was saying, or the next day in the morning. Personally, I was thinking at that moment that perhaps it would be possible for us to arrange a truce, that is to say to get out of there, try to organize ourselves again, and try to return.

'But Fidel was already talking about the future combat actions in which we must engage in order to keep growing – in other words, what would actually happen afterwards was already clearly seen by Fidel at a time when there were just the three of us, knowing nothing about the others.

'To be able to speak we had to put out heads together, to talk in whispers, because we were certain that the army surrounded us. And in this whisper, speaking with the enthusiasm that characterizes him, Fidel told us his future plans. But not only plans for the future. For the first time I heard him speak amply about other things, about the meaning of life, about our struggle, about history, about all these things. And I can say to you that it was there that my deepest understanding of Fidel and my absolute confidence in Fidel became crystallized. Because there, in the canefield, he spoke about what glory signified.

'I remember that for the first time I heard him repeat the phrase of José Martí that "all the glory of the world fits inside a kernel of corn" – I'd known the quotation, but not in this context, not in the context of the meaning life has for a revolutionary, and how one may not fight for personal ambitions, not even for ambitions of glory. . . He spoke of the necessity and the satisfaction, at the same time, that a revolutionary has in fighting for others, in fighting for his people, in fighting for the humble ones. . .

'In the sequence of his ideas, what I'm telling you is what struck me the most (in Fidel). But there were many other things of which he spoke. About organizing the country, about the people of Cuba, the history of Cuba, the future of Cuba. And about the necessity of launching a revolution, a real revolution. We didn't speak of Marxism and Communism in those days, but of a social revolution, of a true revolution, in our country. . . '

And this is how Universo Sánchez, the peasant from Matanzas who shifted his lifelong allegiance from the Communist Party to the 26th of July Movement because he thought the Communists were not doing enough against Batista, recollects Fidel Castro's whispered oratory under the sugarcane *paja*:

'At one point Fidel started discussing – apparently to give Faustino and me some courage – what would be the revolution and the future. He talked of the revolutionary programme, he raised our spirits. And at no time did Fidel consider himself defeated. It was always a thing with him to talk about regrouping our people. I began to believe at one stage that Fidel was crazy. I said to myself, "Shit, he's gone crazy." You will see that my rifle has my name scratched on it with the tip of the bayonet because I thought that when they would kill me, my family would know it was I who was killed, and I wouldn't just disappear.'

Fidel's loquacity is a legend. But he can also be a superb listener, when he is interested in the subject or the speaker. And he is a great questioner, centring swiftly on the heart of the matter of a theme under discussion. One often does feel that he may be dying to speak out, but his courtesy and curiosity usually prevail – and Fidel will remain silent for very long minutes, fiddling with his cigar, lit or unlit (before he abruptly quit smoking late in 1985), or twisting his beard with his fingers between his chin and lower lip in a characteristic gesture of thoughtfulness.

Chapter 3

That within just over two years of the canefield drama the Castro revolutionary war in the Sierra Maestra, coupled with the urban struggles by the 26th of July Movement and militant university students' organizations, would force the collapse of the Batista regime is a matter of history. It is similarly part of the history of the twentieth century that Fidel Castro had lead Cuba through the greatest social revolution since Mao Tse-tung imposed Communism on China a decade earlier, immeasurably improving the human condition of millions of Cubans – there were six million in 1959 and over ten million in 1986. As a belatedly self-anointed Marxist–Leninist, Castro has organized Cuba as the first (and thus far the only) Communist country in the Western hemisphere, allying himself politically, economically and militarily with the Soviet Union. He has pursued these policies and alliances in defiance of seven successive United States presidents (Ronald Reagan being the latest in this period of nearly three decades), defeating an American-supported invasion attempt and, in conspiracy with Nikita Khrushchev, bringing the world to the brink of nuclear conflagration in 1962.

Fidel Castro has held power longer than any other important head of government except North Korea's Kim Il Sung and Jordan's King Hussein – and has remained a highly active and influential player in international affairs. His health appears excellent, and all the signs are that, barring assassinations, he will be present in the world arena for a very long time.

Evidently Castro's Cuba commands sufficient attention from the Soviet Union to receive over four billion dollars annually in economic assistance. This is enormous for a population of ten million in terms of the traditional foreign aid programme of the superpowers. There is an additional half-billion dollars in sophisticated military hardware, from computerized control-and-command systems to MiG-23 jets. To the

United States, which after twenty-five years is still committed to the idea that Castro must vanish, Cuba is a permanent nightmare as Washington worries about its influence in Africa, Central America, the Caribbean and even in its 'own' Puerto Rico.

To much of the Third World, which made him chairman of the Non-Aligned Movement for the 1979–83 term, Fidel Castro is a hero, and not only because Cuban troops are in Angola and Ethiopia to defend them from 'imperialism' and Cuban advisers are in Nicaragua for the same ostensible reason. The Third World perceives Castro as its advocate and at times its conscience. He believes passionately that other peoples in the Third World deserve the kind of dignity as nations and individuals that their revolution has granted to the Cubans. This is what he likes to talk about the most, hour after hour, with foreign visitors.

He insists that Cuban 'internationalism' transcends the estimated 40,000 combat troops and advisers involved in wars from Angola and Ethiopia to nearby Nicaragua because, in the Castro logic, a much greater and more lasting impact is made by tens of thousands of Cuban doctors, nurses, teachers and technicians assigned to countries on three continents. He says that some 1,500 Cuban physicians are assigned to Third World countries. Increasingly consumed by what he sees as Christian and Marxist parallels, he argues heatedly that 'if the Church has missionaries, we have the internationalists'. Castro makes a point of recalling that the Christian–Marxist nexus he proposes is not a sudden inspiration because in meetings with Chilean Christian leaders in 1971 and Jamaican churchmen in 1977 he had already urged a 'strategic alliance' between the two forces 'to achieve the necessary social changes in our countries'. He is taken sufficiently seriously for a delegation of United States Roman Catholic bishops to have gone to meet with him in Havana early in 1985 – Castro had a marvellous time dazzling the bishops with his familiarity with theology and liturgy – and to confer with the Cuban episcopate late that year, the first such meeting in the twenty-six years of the revolution.

In sum, Fidel Castro is a fascinating phenomenon in our century's politics: to the increasingly grey and dull Western world, a man of panache, a romantic figure, an ever-defiant, dizzyingly imaginative and unpredictable rebel, a splendid actor, a spectacular teacher and preacher of the many credos he says he embraces. But Castro makes other impressions as well. Though his personal popularity in Cuba is immense there is at least a group of Cubans to whom Castro looms as a ruthless and cunning dictator, a cynical betrayer of liberal democracy in the name of which he rallied millions of Cubans to his cause, a servile satellite of the Soviet Union, the idolized object of a personality cult which he needs as he needs the air he breathes, and the cavalier creator of fundamental economic policy errors at home.

Such is the complexity of Fidel Castro that he may indeed be *all* of the above things – the hero of humble mankind and, at the same time, the repressive Communist dictator. So much in life being a matter of perception, the multiple facets of Castro need not be mutually exclusive.

For himself, he does not mind appearing devious, or worse, if in his opinion this is 'historically justifiable', the most spectacular example being his public admission that he deliberately concealed his Marxist–Leninist orientation during the guerrilla war in order to avoid antagonizing 'bourgeois' and other potential supporters. The final truth about Fidel's Marxism may never be known – it is beyond prediction what he may say about it and himself in the future – but for a long time his Marxist performance was ideologically vague. He doubtless realizes that people have short memories, and that in Cuba there is already a whole generation, now moving into positions of power and responsibility educated by and under the Revolution (a word that is always capitalized in Cuba in print and in speech), to whom the past does not exist – except as a time of shame and scorn. For that is how, demonologically, Castro has defined the Cuban past, the political past in which he grew.

In seeking to portray Fidel Castro precisely, an imprudent proposition at best, a crucial element is that he thrives on contradiction and paradox. With cigar in hand (before he quit smoking in 1985) and a mischievous sparkle in his brown eyes, he has engaged in virtuoso performances with American television correspondents whose homework left much to be desired. In most instances he has the upper hand, rhetorically and intellectually, and delightedly he takes advantage of it.

Inasmuch as Castro conducts domestic government and Cuban world policies mainly by frequent public speeches or endless interviews (secret negotiations and decisions are reserved only for the most delicate situations), it is truly impossible to keep track of what he has said and when he said it. An educated guess suggests that the number of public speeches Castro has delivered as the 'Maximum Leader' since 1 January 1959, the day he assumed effective power, must exceed 2500 (some of them running five hours or more, and the record being around nine hours in 1959) but not all have been published, broadcast or telecast, and it is probably impossible to locate the text of every speech Castro has made.

An idea of the Castro speech-making pattern can be gained from the fact that between 1 January 1966 and October 1984 he delivered *130* very lengthy public addresses on public health and medicine alone, admittedly one of his top-priority topics.

Indeed, Fidel Castro's revolution – or, at least, the selling of this revolution to Cubans – might not have succeeded without the medium of television. From the first day, in fact, Castro has governed through television, the first such use of this technology in the exercise of government as distinct from in mere campaign politics. While he does have a natural rapport with his audiences and he frequently used this symbiotic emotional relationship in the first years of his rule, television was vital in carrying the face, the voice and the message beyond the meeting plaza to Cubans in their homes. Later, television became the regular channel of communication between Castro and the population.

By Latin American and even United States standards, the Cuban television service was quite advanced technically when Castro forced Batista's ejection early in 1959, and the number of receivers in the country was relatively high, especially in the cities. But what mattered most was that Castro, whose revolutionary strategy was always built on communication with the masses, instantly understood that he and television were made for each other. Actually, Cuba had traditionally used radio in politics and in the second and last year of the guerrilla war Fidel had installed a radio station – Radio Rebelde – at his headquarters atop the Sierra Maestra, rapidly turning it into a superb instrument of propaganda and the dissemination of coded operational orders. He often addressed Cuba over Radio Rebelde.

The switch to television was thus natural, and Castro's ideal on-camera presence and his rich dramatic gifts did the rest. The Cuban propaganda apparatus today is so well honed that the nation may be treated to a Castro speech carried live (always in its entirety) as well as to a number of taped re-broadcasts over the two national channels, sometimes over a period of days. Additionally, every public appearance by Castro is either carried live in special reports or as part of the regular television news programmes (the radio, of course, carries the Fidel sound as well).

It may be difficult to believe that Castro, who seems to adore public speaking, actually fears it before the first words are out. He told the Cuban magazine *Bohemia*: 'I confess . . . I suffer from stage fright when I speak in Revolution Square. . . It is not at all easy for me.' As a young man he forced himself to deliver speeches in front of a mirror in his room until he was satisfied they were adequate to encourage him to pursue a career in the law and politics.

Of course, Castro is fascinated by the art of public speech and has reminisced that as a high school student he began collecting speeches by Demosthenes, Cicero and other great orators of that age, but that he subsequently concluded that their oratory 'was too rhetorical and grandiloquent'. In the end Castro decided to practise until he had created his own style, fiery yet chatty. It is unlikely that there is another Communist ruler in the world nowadays who is capable of dissecting classical oratory.

Additionally, all the top Cuban revolutionary leaders engage in a permanent flood of oratory to keep rallying the nation behind Fidel, to demand new efforts, and confess past errors, so that daily existence in Cuba is like living in an echo chamber. But it is untrue to suggest that nowadays Castro's speeches turn off the Cubans. Firstly, there is still a sense of fascination with him and his oratory; secondly, nobody in a society as rigidly organized ideologically as Cuba – it is more so than Eastern European Communist countries – can afford *not* to know what the President of the Republic is saying. Ideological indoctrination is so important that the people must study his speeches as promptly as possible after delivery, and be able to explain, preferably in his words and slogans, the views he holds on domestic and foreign problems.

Castro has a limitless capacity for indignation and does not hesitate to display it privately or publicly. He would have a tantrum fit in the Sierra Maestra when a single bullet was wasted by a careless guerrilla, and even today, as President of Cuba, he will throw a fit – complete with the foulest language imaginable in Spanish – when he learns of a bureaucratic stupidity. His most senior associates fear the 'Fidel furies'.

On another level there is little doubt that Castro ordered the Mariel exodus of over 100,000 Cubans to the United States in the spring of 1980, as a gesture of supreme personal rage against the Carter administration for the attitude it had taken towards a wave of asylum-seekers in foreign embassies in Havana. Emotion remains a powerful factor in the Castro decision-making, and it is assumed in Cuba that he suspended an immigration agreement that had been signed with the United States in 1985 because the Reagan administration put into operation a hostile radio station named Radio Martí. Castro told friends, however, that he did not care about the broadcasts themselves; what he had resented was the use of the hallowed Martí name against the Cuban revolution.

It seems that Castro tends to court death. In 1981 he decided to sail to the Mexican port of Cozúmel aboard a high-speed launch, rather than to fly for a secret meeting with the President of Mexico, in order to test personally the degree of vigilance of the US Navy in the Yucatán Straits. The navy was patrolling the Gulf of Mexico to determine whether the Cubans were shipping arms to Nicaragua, and Fidel's idea of fun was to see whether it could catch *him*. He then flew home, having made his point, though this incident was not mentioned in the Cuban media. It is an intriguing thought what a US Navy Destroyer skipper would have done if he had discovered Fidel Castro aboard a heavily armed craft, escorted by two missile-carrying patrol boats, in international waters between western Cuba's San Antonio Cape and Cozúmel. The *guerrillero* laughs about it.

Chapter 4

Fidel Castro's success in war and peace, apart from his qualities of leadership and iron determination, is due in great measure to the supreme loyalty he was always able to command among his fellow revolutionaries, relatives and friends, as well as among the Cuban people after the victory. Three decades later the loyalty of the first companions, men *and* women, of the *Fidelista* revolution remains as absolute as it was in their youthful and ardent days. In this the old *Fidelistas* resemble a medieval religious and military order, like the Knights Templar in the times of the Crusades. Inevitably many have grown apart from each other, and ideological differences – sometimes very deep ones over the issue of Communism – have developed. Still, they share the seemingly unbreakable bond of loyalty to Castro as their historical leader. To them, Fidel can do no wrong. But why is it so?

There is a character in the play *Galileo* by Bertolt Brecht who declares 'unhappy the land that has no heroes', to which Galileo replies 'unhappy the land that has need of heroes'. In Cuba's case, both reflections are true: the country never had a triumphant hero (José Martí was killed before independence was attained), and its depressing history made it hunger for one. Clearly, Castro has satisfied this deep need.

And like 'The Incorruptible', Maximilien Robespierre, Fidel Castro speaks the language of the revolution, he is the voice of the deepest revolutionary principles of his time. From the very beginning his proven commitment to these ideals assured him of his following. In a corrupt nation under the Batista dictatorship, Fidel represented the values of honesty, political legality and social justice – and he was believed because of his impressive oratory and his willingness to challenge the system at great personal risk.

Aside from pure politics, Castro inspires widespread loyalty on the basis of human chemistry. An immensely attractive and contagiously energetic man, he is an unparalleled persuader. He can and has convinced scores of men and women of varying backgrounds and temperaments to participate in military actions about which they have been told nothing specific until the last moment (the assault on Moncada and the voyage of the *Granma* are cases in point). The army lieutenant who captured him in the mountains after Moncada was persuaded by Castro's courage to spare his life and, years later, joined Castro's victorious army. His courage is so great that it borders on the insane. At one point in the Sierra Maestra all his officers signed a petition asking him to stop exposing himself to hostile fire in the front line of every skirmish and battle.

Most vitally, Castro has always been concerned with the welfare of his people. He refused to take on the Moncada attack men who had wives and children (though he himself was a husband and father), endlessly inquired about the personal problems of his Sierra fighters and their families, meticulously supervised food allocations to assure that all shared equally (once he berated Universo Sánchez for being unable to account for every piece of hard candy with which he was entrusted), and established an iron rule that the *guerrilleros* must pay the peasants in cash for every ounce of rice and every chicken they took.

The peasants' loyalty to Castro had made his survival possible during this Revolution – there was a $100,000 prize on his head – and this loyalty grew even more when the rebels helped with harvest and started rudimentary schools and clinics for Sierra children. A priest who joined the guerrillas as a self-appointed chaplain, Father Guillermo Sardiñas, spent much of his time christening children of peasant families in the Sierra, a greatly appreciated gesture inasmuch as, according to Castro, there were neither churches nor priests in the mountains. As a result Fidel recalls that numerous families 'wanted me to be godfather of their children, and Father Sardiñas christened there scores and scores of peasant kids . . . which in Cuba is like being a second father'. He says: 'I have masses of godchildren in the Sierra Maestra, and many of them perhaps already are army officers or university graduates.'

Fidel has also told a Brazilian friar that he wore a cross on a chain around his neck during part of the war because a little girl had sent it to him from Santiago with a 'tender message'; he said: 'If you ask me whether this was a question of faith, I'd tell you, "no", it wouldn't be honest to say it was a question of faith; it was a gesture towards that girl.'

This loyalty to his supporters has stood the test of time, in truth growing with it. After the 1983 United States invasion of Grenada, for example, Castro made a point of visiting almost daily at a Havana hospital the Cuban soldiers and construction workers who had been wounded in combat. He brought them books (among them Tolstoy's *War and Peace* in a handsome Spanish edition), video cassettes, and plenty of conversation. These visits were not publicized, but the word got around that the commander-in-chief cared about his men.

Armando Hart Dávalos, one of the first organizers of the 26th of July Movement after the Moncada attack, says that from the group with whom Castro met secretly in Havana four weeks before leaving for Mexico in mid-1955 to prepare the invasion 'every single person either remains with the revolution today or is a martyr of the revolution'. Hart himself was soon caught by the Batista police and remained imprisoned until the revolution's triumph. Castro immediately named him Education Minister (Hart was twenty-nine years old at the time, four years younger than Fidel), and over the decades he has been one of the Maximum Leader's most trusted advisers.

Coming from the moderate political background that characterized the urban 26th of July organization, Armando Hart (who earlier belonged to a right-of-centre nationalist group) unhesitatingly followed Castro in the shift to Communism, and currently is a member of the Party's ruling Political Bureau as well as Minister of Culture.

Faustino Pérez, Fidel's canefield companion of Alegría del Pío, represents another dimension of Castroist loyalty. He had joined the Movement after Moncada (about the same time as Hart, proceeding from the same moderate anti-Batista faction), and he too had attended the clandestine Havana meeting prior to Castro's departure. He then followed him to Mexico, landed from the *Granma* as a deputy military commander, survived with Fidel the first month in the Sierra, and was dispatched to Havana to establish the contacts between the guerrillas and the urban 26th of July Movement.

As a leading city underground leader Faustino Pérez participated in planning the bitterly disastrous general strike in April 1958, a milestone event that triggered the fundamental break between pro-Communists and anti-Communists (and various intermediate factions) within the revolutionary movement.

Castro has a strong sense of loyalty towards old companions when, even in disagreement with him, they are careful not to engage in what he considers as betrayal. In the case of Pérez, a strange minuet developed between him and Castro. When the revolution triumphed, Pérez was named to the first revolutionary government, but as Minister for the Recovery of Stolen Property, and was never invited to join the inner circle. This was the brief period in 1959 when Cuba lived under an 'official' government headed by President Manuel Urrutia Lleó (whom Castro while still in the Sierra had designated to the presidency) and Fidel's hidden but *de facto* government was secretly negotiating with the 'old' Communists for the joint takeover of the republic in the name of the 'real revolution'.

After the first open crisis over the issue of Communism in the revolutionary regime had erupted in 1959, and after Castro ordered on 21 October the arrest on charges of treason of Major Huber Matos, a highly popular but outspokenly anti-Communist guerrilla commander, two of the moderate ministers resigned at a stormy cabinet meeting with Fidel on 26 November. One of them was Faustino Pérez, but he did so without audible protest, publicly denying that he was leaving over the Matos affair. Castro responded by personally guaranteeing his safety, as a demonstration of loyalty to a comrade-in-arms. In the ensuing years Pérez fought alongside Castro at the Bay of Pigs, worked in obscure government posts (in 1969 he supervised the construction of a hydro-electric power plant in the Stalinist tradition of relegating undesirable politicians from sight), and notwithstanding his distaste for Communism, he joined the Party when Castro organized it as the 'highest leading force of the society and of the state'.

In the 1980s Faustino Pérez was a member of the Party's Central Committee, the chairman of a National Assembly committee, and coordinator of the mass-membership organization in Cuba's local self-government system and it is quietly evident that Faustino Pérez retains sincere admiration and loyalty for Fidel Castro. Without being hailed as a 'hero of the revolution' by the official propaganda, Pérez is still a highly respected figure in Cuba.

Finally, Universo Sánchez, the other member of the Alegria del Pío canefield trio, faced no ideological soul-searching when the revolution acquired its Communist identity. Finishing the war with the rank of *commandante* (major), then the highest in the Rebel Army, Universo faithfully performed over the years a variety of military and civilian tasks. Though never qualifying for Castro's hard core political circle, he wound up his revolutionary career in his late sixties as head of environment protection programmes. He resumed his membership in the Communist Party when Castro reorganized it, presumably because all of Fidel's followers who wished to stay with the revolution were expected to be members. However, unlike many others, Universo Sánchez invariably makes a point of telling visitors that the old Communist Party did not fight Batista the way it should have done.

The revolution never fully recovered from the April 1958 general strike, protestations of total unity nothwithstanding. The strike had been opposed by the orthodox Communists, still very much at arm's length from Castro, and it was chiefly advocated by the liberal-minded groups in the 26th of July Movement who thought it would quicken Batista's fall. Fidel himself had first publicly supported the general strike (though begrudgingly), but then sided with Che Guevara and with the Communists in the cities, to denounce the failed stoppage. The

Communists, even though they traditionally favoured political strike strategy, were against the April stoppage because they were being almost entirely left out of it, and they feared the adverse effects on their future influence in Cuba. Nevertheless, allegations of actual Communist sabotage of the strike cannot be proved.

In the Florentine climate of intrigue rising within the revolution, Castro chose to turn against the strike organizers, but only after the strike had run its course. He had come to believe that the urban wing of the 26th of July Movement – know as the *llano* , which means lowlands – had been withholding arms and money from the Sierra guerrillas, who were seeking to use the general strike to capture overall control of the revolution. Fidel, who still becomes agitated discussing these events despite the passage of so many years, further believed (and probably accurately) that the urban organizations, with their 'bourgeois' origins, would try to block the profound social revolution he had in mind for after the victory, and that they would settle on Batista's overthrow without allowing the overhaul of the entire Cuban system.

That Castro was planning from the beginning to dismantle the old social order, established by the Spaniards and continued under United States supervision after Cuban independence in 1902, was not made clear to most people on the island (and beyond it) when he was fighting in the Sierra. Later, of course, Fidel had no compunction about admitting this publicly, explaining that the people simply had not been ready for the 'real' revolution.

To effect this 'real' revolution Fidel Castro required trustworthy and experienced allies, and the Communists were able openly to enter the picture during the last year of the national insurrection principally because of the convergence of a series of political situations.

To the extent that it is possible to reconstruct the revolution's internal battles, it is certain that Castro's growing suspicions of the 26th of July Movement in the cities, encouraged by Che Guevara as his Sierra letters to Fidel make clear, led him to the decision to form an alliance with the 'old' Communists and to create with them his own 'new' Communists. It is Castro who later would first use publicly the expression 'new' Communists. And although Castro had decided not to rely on liberal 'bourgeois' managers in the conduct of civilian affairs, except in the initial transition period, he is known to have concluded that among his most loyal Sierra fighters there were few with any of the sound political or administrative experience required to operate a future government. Furthermore, it quickly became a matter of revolutionary principle that the Batista armed forces be entirely destroyed (apart from a handful of professional officers ready to join the cause), since Castro's theory was that the destruction of the old army was a precondition for the establishment of a new national order. Further, he felt that the new revolutionary armed forces must from the outset be controlled by these 'old' Communists, and transformed into the principal 'new' Communist power base in the revolution.

Cuba's 'old' Communists had been running labour unions, sitting in parliament, infiltrating the university and publishing newspapers for nearly forty years, providing a pool of dependability and experience for Castro to draw on. Castro was especially attracted by their sense of discipline and their organization skills. Nevertheless, considering that he had never belonged to the 'old' Communist Party and that the Communists had opposed and vilified him as an adventurer after Moncada and even when he set foot in the mountains, it remains astonishing that Castro would suddenly regard them as dependable partners and mentors. Being Fidel, he doubtless assumed he could control them.

The overall conclusion to be drawn from all these events is that the historical decision that the revolution should lead to the establishment of socialism and then Communism in Cuba was not reached by Castro with utter finality until the late spring of 1958 – probably following the series of crucial political meetings held in the Sierra during May and June.

Numerous Cuba scholars and specialists abroad have argued either that Fidel Castro was a secret Communist since Moncada or earlier, or that he had been pushed into Communism a year or two after he won power by the hostility of the United States. Both views are suspect in the light of careful analysis of existing materials as well as of in-depth discussions with key Cubans who participated in the entire revolutionary process. Fidel always knew where he was going. He might adjust strategy and tactics according to changing political situations, but his dream of a sweeping revolution was not a Communist revolution as defined by *the* Cuban Communist Party.

Castro's bitterness towards the United Stated dating back to his student days when he was active in a variety of 'anti-imperialist' organizations in Havana, and aggravated by American deliveries of bombs and ammunition to the Batista air force at the US naval base in Guantanamo, must have been an extremely important factor in his decision to go the Communist route to fulfil his broad revolutionary programme. He must also have understood from the outset that this course would assuredly antagonize Washington and that, sooner or later, he would be forced to obtain Soviet assistance and support if his revolution were to survive. He had calculated correctly that the Russians, facing at the time the split with China, would help. In this manner Castro was able to define beforehand – from the Sierra – the relationships that would involve Cuba, the United States and the Soviet Union – before either superpower suspected what this Caribbean rebel had in mind.

Fidel's basic political attitude is best expressed in a private message to

Celia Sánchez, his closest Sierra companion, on 5 June 1958, right after Batista aircraft had hit the rebels with US-supplied bombs:

'I have sworn that the Americans will pay very dearly for what they are doing. When this war has ended, a much bigger and greater war will start for me, a war I shall launch against them. I realize that this will be my true destiny.'

Castro's insights, of course, proved to be entirely correct though not even he could have suspected that as early as 10 March 1959, which was only two months after he entered Havana, the National Security Council in Eisenhower's White House had already reviewed ways of bringing 'another government to power in Cuba'. The record of this review exists in the classified NSC archives, a generally unknown – but fundamental – element in the broad Cuban–American tragedy.

Meanwhile, however, the immediate upshot of the April general strike fiasco was that Castro was able to establish undisputed sway over all the revolutionary factions in Cuba, and – most specifically – to subordinate the National Directorate of the 26th of July Movement to his political and operational control. In this sense the final phase of the Sierra war did for Castro what the Long March in China in 1935 did for Mao Tse-tung: it proclaimed his absolute primacy among his country's revolutionary leaders.

Inevitably, Fidel's relationships with his fellow revolutionaries began to change. Loyalty, of course, is as elusive a political notion as treason, and Fidel Castro reserves for himself the right of defining both, naturally quite subjectively in terms of the persons involved. Castro, exploding in fury, delivered an incredible seven-hour prosecutorial summation before the revolutionary court in the trial of Major Huber Matos, claiming that Matos had committed treason because he had 'conspired' with some of his officers in the Camaguey province command to resign in protest against Communist infiltration. Matos, one of the best Sierra commanders, was sentenced to twenty years in prison. That he had first written Castro a private letter loyally beseeching him to act against Communism in order to protect democracy in Cuba was not an attenuating circumstance. In Fidel's eyes, Matos's actions constituted a treasonable conspiracy because they threatened to split wide open his revolutionary regime and armed forces, playing into the hands of the United States and other enemies of the revolution. In this sense Castro's definition of loyalty versus treason was purely practical and political on the grounds that the defence of *his* revolution overshadowed all other considerations.

Clearly Fidel is merciless with those he considers traitors, and to him any 'counter-revolutionary' is a traitor, an appallingly broad definition. Thus in the mid-1960s there were at least 15,000 'counter-revolutionaries' serving terms in Cuban prisons by Castro's own admission, a figure reduced to 3000 in 1977, and to around 500 in 1985, some of them re-sentenced for unclear reasons. In conversations with foreign visitors Castro says that there are no prisoners of 'conscience' in Cuba, but international organizations attempting to monitor the observance of human rights on the island report – with names – that a number of persons are imprisoned under an article of the Cuban Penal Code, which punishes those who 'incite against the social order, international solid-arity or the socialist State by means of oral or written propaganda, or any other form; make, distribute, or possess propaganda of the character mentioned in [this] clause'.

'Incitement' by 'oral . . . propaganda' is such an arbitrary concept that its rigorous (or capricious) application in Cuba nearly guarantees the absence of organized dissent in the Eastern European or even Soviet sense. And, indeed, no such dissent exists in Cuba as far as can be ascertained on the island. Castro occasionally releases political prisoners as goodwill gestures towards foreign governments, groups or indi-viduals (such as the group released in 1984 to the Rev. Jesse Jackson), but he has never defined the criteria under which he selects persons to be freed. Final decisions concerning crime and punishment in Cuba are Fidel Castro's personal province.

Strangely, for example, Castro has sought on at least two occasions to give a last chance to men who conspired to kill him – out of a sense of loyalty to former guerrilla fighters who played important roles in the war or out of his private notion of justice. Castro very seldom explains the motivations for his actions nor makes them public unless it is absolutely necessary. These two stories have never before been told.

The first one concerns *Commandante* Humberto Sorí-Marín, a lawyer who was Castro's judge-advocate at the Sierra headquarters and, simultaneously, was in charge of economic planning for the future. Sori helped to draft the revolution's first agrarian reform law while the fighting was still going on, and he became Agriculture Minister after the victory. To a lesser extent Sori participated in the drafting of a more radical agrarian reform law promulgated by Castro on 17 May 1959, but immediately came into conflict with Che Guevara who accused the Agriculture Minister of being exceedingly moderate. Rather than battle with the unbending Che, Sori submitted his resignation from the cabinet. Castro tried hard to dissuade him (though would not promise to keep Che off his back), but the lawyer left on 14 June 1959.

During the summer Sori began to plot against the regime, and fled to the United States. In 1960 he returned clandestinely, apparently with the aid of the CIA, to link up with anti-Castro armed groups in the Escambray mountains in central Cuba, and to try to assassinate Fidel. Sori was captured, suffering a bullet wound in a shoot-out with state security agents. Soon afterwards Sori's brothers Raúl and Mariano (Raúl had stayed in Cuba as a supporter of the revolution, and Mariano, who had left, returned from Miami exile) succeeded in arranging a meeting with Castro to plead for Humberto's life.

As Mariano Sori-Marín would learn from a witness later, Castro went to see Humberto in prison, and told him, 'Humberto, you have betrayed us, and anyone but you would pay with his life.' This was meant as encouragement to Humberto to ask Fidel for the clemency that he was prepared to grant, wanting simply to be asked. Sori, however, reacted violently, insulting Castro and telling him: '*You* are the traitor of the revolution!' Fidel departed, and Sori was executed on 20 Aril 1961, while Castro was leading his militias in defeating the invaders at the Bay of Pigs.

The other story is of Rolando Cubela Secades. A physician who led the Students' Revolutionary Directorate guerrilla forces in the war against Batista in the mountains of central Cuba, Cubela was recruited by the CIA in the early 1960s under the top-secret AM/LASH project (kept secret from even President Kennedy) to assassinate Castro and overthrow the regime. Cubela, who may have been the never-identified CIA's 'B-1' agent inside the Cuban government, enjoyed Castro's confidence and in the mid-1960s was named envoy to UNESCO in Paris.

Late in 1965 Cubela was contacted by the CIA in Paris and Madrid, and advised that special weapons had been smuggled for him to Havana to assassinate Castro, as Cubela had already agreed to so. But the Cuban secret service, one of the best in the world, learned of the plot. When Cubela arrived in Havana on a routine trip from Paris early in 1966 Castro summoned him to a meeting at the palace. According to witnesses, Fidel asked Cubela searchingly: 'Is there anything special that you want to tell me?' But the doctor replied in the negative. He was arrested as he was leaving the palace, and eventually he testified at his trial that he had planned to 'shoot Premier Castro with a high-powered telescopic rifle, and later to share in top posts of a counter-revolutionary regime'. Had Cubela confessed the plot to Castro, the trial might well have been averted. As it was, Cubela was sentenced to fifteen years in prison – a relatively mild sentence by Cuban revolutionary justice standards, which often led to executions, and even that sentence was reduced. Cubela now lives in Spain. Why did he receive such leniency?

Apart from questions of betrayal and counter-revolution, Castro quietly practises personal loyalty towards old companions, making sure that they live comfortably. In a great many instances nice sounding jobs have been created for aging or less than highly qualified individuals because Fidel feels they must be given a sense of self-respect and the assurance that the revolution is eternally grateful for their deeds. This causes no resentments: most Cubans understand it. In many cases, on the other hand, Castro has perhaps allowed his judgement to be clouded, naming old companions to ambassadorial posts, for example, where they wind up embarrassing Cuba before being hastily recalled.

On one occasion Fidel demoted an 'old' Communist from an important industrial post for revealing that the general manager of the establishment, who was a friend of Castro's from the days of Moncada, was 'sleeping at his office, drunk as usual'. Castro knew the friend was an alcoholic who had to be gently removed from higher positions, and he had stopped at the man's office to see how he was coming along. Hence his violent anger at the Communist, not an anti-Batista fighter, for the contemptuous slur against an old revolutionary.

Even within the Castro brotherhood there are profound, if subtle, nuances among the knights, flowing from the length of their service and, very humanly, from the nature of their direct relationship with Fidel and their own personalities. These factors define the present power constellation in revolutionary Cuba as they would elsewhere, except that among Cubans the personal element is particularly significant.

And while the top power structure in Cuba is reasonably well coordinated in terms of the overall management of the country, the fundamental problem among them remains Fidel Castro's psychological inability to let go of any power. The result is that all authority and responsibility continue concentrated in his hands, a state of affairs that paralyses all initiative on lower levels. His compulsive dedication to detail and the conviction that, no matter what the subject, he knows more about it than anyone else, have combined to make Castro an obstacle to an efficient development of both economy and society. Most Cuban managers in the totally state-owned economy simply have no courage to make decisions, fearing displeasure on high, and most likely punishment. Therefore, a mutually protective association of bureaucrats has come into being, and the bitter Havana joke is that Cuba does have a two-party system after all: the Communist Party and the Bureaucratic Party. The waste of resources and talent is staggering.

Castro, of course, bristles at any suggestion that he is a dictator and that all the decisions are made by him. In 1977 he told an American interviewer: 'I'm a leader, but I am very distant from having unipersonal power or absolute power.' He went on to say that though 'my personal power was very great' during the war, almost immediately afterwards the revolution moved to 'establish a collective leadership . . . a leadership group from among the most capable leaders'.

In January 1984 Castro was still insisting on the collective character of the Cuban leadership, and that the process of institutionalizing the revolution had been completed. This, he said, was achieved with the 1975 national referendum approval of the new Cuban constitution (which became effective in 1976). This created novel mechanisms such as the Popular Power local government system under the National Assembly, meeting twice a year for two-day sessions, which votes on proposed laws and supervises in theory their implementation. Still, it taxes the imagination to visualize a rejection by the Assembly of a Castro-proposal law. Nevertheless Castro told me that in the Communist Party's Political Bureau he held only one vote out of fifteen (the membership at that time), and had been overruled on occasion – though he cited no examples.

On the other hand, of course, it must be recognized that he is caught in a political image trap because he cannot publicly acknowledge that he does actually hold 'unipersonal power'. Such an admission would undermine the integrity of the institutions he has created, removing whatever semblance of independence or autonomy they may have. The real point, of course, is whether these institutions can survive Castro's death or incapacitation and how the issue of succession and Cuba's future is to be resolved. To be sure, it was Castro who named his brother Raúl his successor thus, in effect, attempting to impose succession.

The official media portray the Council of State and the Council of Ministers (both presided over by Castro) as the decision-making organs of the republic. But in November 1984, for example, an infuriated Castro went before the National Assembly to denounce the shortcomings of an economic development plan for the following year prepared by the Central Planning Board, and its parallel five-year plan. Overnight he established a 'Central Group' in the Council of Ministers, headed by Osmany Cienfuegos, to develop a new plan, for 1985 only – hardly the best way of running the economy. Not long thereafter Planning Board President Humberto Peréz Gonzáles, once considered the most promising new-generation technocrat, was 'liberated from his functions', the general euphemism for being fired.

In general, Castro insists on being posted on just about everything. Consequently, even relatively minor decisions may be delayed or postponed until the commander-in-chief can catch up with them. His frequent speeches confirm that he is abreast of all aspects of every problem in Cuba: he touches upon all of them as he preaches the virtues of hard work and the tremendous need to save resources. The printing of the Communist Party's official daily newspaper *Granma*, the voice of the regime, may be held up until dawn while Castro personally edits a lengthy policy speech he delivered extemporaneously the previous day, or a major policy editorial (he writes some of the page-one unsigned editorials, his style being unmistakable for its colour and subtle invective).

Fidel Castro's style of government is based on what he calls dialogue or rapport with the population. In practice this means oratorical hard sell of new policies or an insistence on the fulfilment of old ones. This is usually done through televised speeches delivered before large audiences who applaud Castro and reply affirmatively when he asks whether they approve of what he proposes (in this fashion Cubans, since 1959, have 'approved' executions of Batista-regime torturers, the military presence in Angola, multifarious social and economic sacrifices, and even the transfer of the port town of Moa from Holguín province to Guatanamo province in eastern Cuba).

Crowds have never said 'No' to Castro, and this technique of popular consultation was refined by Fidel at the outset of his rule. He says it is 'direct democracy', preferable to old-fashioned elections, and it remains his most powerful political weapon in any crisis – the recourse to the masses. Chants of 'Fidel, Fidel!' punctuate the mass rallies as he whips the audiences into a frenzy of enthusiasm.

Mass-circulation newspapers and magazines – as well as especially printed booklets of interviews granted by Castro to foreign radio and television networks and publications – are another facet of government-by-verbiage. After *Playboy* printed a long, boring Castro interview in August 1985, an expanded text in Spanish was published as a special pull-out section in *Granma*, but carefully avoiding any reference to *Playboy* as the magazine where it had first appeared. Instead, *Granma* provided only the names of the two American interviewers. Fidel Castro is still prudish, at least concerning his image at home

Chapter 5

Fidel Castro's personal life and activities are normally kept well out of public view in Cuba for reasons of privacy as well as security. Only his very frequent official performances are reported in the press and on the radio and television, and most Cubans are not even aware how Castro works or of whom his immediate entourage is composed.

Extraordinarily busy as he is at the Palace of the Revolution and elsewhere, with occasional around-the-clock schedules, nearly always surrounded by people, Castro nevertheless projects an overwhelming impression of loneliness. A bachelor for the thirty years since his divorce, with many of his closest friends and companions dead or simply no longer around, Fidel does not appear to have anyone near him to whom he can turn in full trust and with whom he can share great and small victories and defeats. Not even his brother Raúl qualifies for such intimacy. His ex-wife, Mirta, had tried to be a friend and companion, but Fidel never included her in his plans and ambitions. They are said to have been in love. She visited him in prison immediately after Moncada and then they briefly exchanged letters. But in 1954 he decided to divorce her for political reasons: her parents and brother were too close to Batista.

By nature Castro is secretive and tends to keep his counsel. In the past, however, a few human beings have been extremely close to him. The most important of them, as every Cuban *does* know, was Celia Sánchez, the doctor's daughter from an Oriente sugar mill who, for twenty-three years until her death from cancer, was Fidel's unconditionally devoted helper and adviser in war and peace – in fact, his conscience and alter ego.

Celia had a cramped and shabby apartment, decorated without the slightest taste, in a small building at number 1007 of a short block of Eleventh Street in a middle-class section of Havana's residential district of Vedado. It was the centre of their life and work; Fidel frequently slept there, and Celia worked in the untidy apartment as his chief aide as well as preparing hot meals in the minuscule kitchen – to be sent to him wherever he happened to be in Havana during the lunch or dinner hours. Even after she died in 1980, the apartment with chromos on the walls is still home to him. The street block continues to be cordoned off with iron chains and guarded by armed State Security troopers in olive green.

Celia who was Fidel's senior by five years, never married. With Castro, for all practical purposes she was the first lady of Cuba, quite beloved and respected on the island. Since her death she has been virtually canonized by the revolution, with hospitals and schools named after her. While she was the warm, very human and very Cuban symbol of the revolution, she was also the firm *compañera* who protected Castro from too much outside pressure and from himself. She was probably the only person in Cuba able to tell him to his face that he was making a bad decision, although she told others that 'Fidel is always right'. Celia kept Fidel's days and nights from turning into total chaos, found time in his schedule for other Cubans with problems that could only be solved at the top of the government, designed a spectacular public recreation park and restaurant in suburban Havana (the Lenin Park), preserved antiques and museums, and organized an oral history project of the revolution up to the victory in 1959.

At her death Celia was Secretary of the Council of State, with ministerial rank. Strikingly, a large number of outstanding Cuban women of various backgrounds, including those from the highest circles of pre-revolutionary Havana society, came forward from the very outset to play invaluable roles in helping and supporting Fidel. Many risked their lives for his cause and to this day are fiercely protective of Fidel and his good name, even if they have not seen him in years.

Then, there was Dr René Vallejo, a distinguished surgeon who had served with the American army in Europe in World War Two and joined Castro in the Sierra, remaining with him afterwards as personal physician, aide-de-camp and around-the-clock friend and companion. Vallejo, one of the most *simpático* early figures of the revolution, died from a sudden illness in 1969, when only forty-nine, leaving behind a crushed Fidel Castro. Like Celia, Dr Vallejo could never quite be replaced in Castro's life.

In a very special fashion there was Castro's friendship with Che Guevara, two years his junior, an unmatched relationship. Though Guevara, whom Fidel first met in Mexico during the conspiratorial period, came on the *Granma* expedition as a physician (he was listed on the roster as 'Lieutenant Ernesto Guevara, Chief of Health'), he quickly turned into one of the principal guerrilla commanders. In the absence of radio or telephone links during most of the mountain war, Castro and his officers communicated through written messages, carried by couriers (often women). From these papers, mostly preserved, it appears that the single greatest volume of exchanges was between Fidel and Che.

The two men were the only intellectual equals in the Sierra and, in addition to operational orders and reports, they wrote each other long political letters that serve to demonstrate the ideological evolution in the guerrilla, with Che emphasizing his radical leanings, and Fidel being more practical and pragmatic about the politics of the war. There were also personal touches. As the Batista offensive began in May 1958 Fidel wrote to Che: 'It's been too many days since we've talked, and that's a matter of necessity between us.' On another occasion, complaining that he was not receiving promised ammunition from the cities, he opened a letter by saying 'this is a complete fuck-up'. Admitting that Castro had been correct in warning him about an enemy attack, Che wrote: 'As so many other times, your excellency (isn't there a junior lieutenant-colonel rank?) was right and the army got as far as our beards.'

In the first years of the revolution Castro and Guevara were inseparable. Conchita Fernández, who was Castro's personal secretary, aiding Celia Sánchez during the initial period, recalls that Fidel and Che lunched together almost every day, sharing the hot meal sent by Celia from the apartment.

It will probably never be known what exactly caused Che Guevara's mysterious leave-taking from Cuba in 1965; was there, for example, a deep personal break between them as many mutual friends think? In any event, no one has taken the mystical Argentinian's place as Castro's intellectual partner. Carlos Rafael Rodríguez comes the closest to this in the present power group but, unlike Che, he shares no experience of conspiracy, war and danger.

Castro once told a visitor that 'I detest loneliness, total loneliness.' He added: 'Aristotle said that man was a social being, and it seems I belong to that species,' mentioning in a reminiscence the months spent in solitary confinement in the Batista prison as proof that 'the fact that I detest loneliness does not mean that I am not capable of standing it'. In the absolute sense of physical loneliness, Castro clearly does detest it because he chooses to be so seldom alone – the acolytes are always on hand. But of course the company he keeps nowadays tells a lot.

First there is the palace entourage, the court over which Fidel Castro presides in a manner sometimes bordering on the royal, being in demeanour something of a Spanish royal personage himself – Marxism–Leninism and olive-green military garb notwithstanding.

The entourage at the Palace of the Revolution is rather undistinguished. Basically it is a staff composed of officials attached to the Council of State, which functions as Cuba's principal state organ. Castro is President of Cuba because he is Chairman of the Council of State and all his and his staff's offices are in the Palace of the Revolution, a sprawling structure with a broad front staircase built by Batista for the Supreme Court and located in the centre of a closely-guarded and well-landscaped government complex on the Plaza de la Revolución. The palace adjoins the building of the Central Committee of the Communist Party. Raúl Castro's Revolutionary Armed Forces (FAR) Ministry, the Interior Ministry (MININT), and the party newspaper *Granma* are nearby.

The man who has taken over Celia Sánchez's reponsibilities as the Council's Secretary is Dr José M. Miyar Barrueco, commonly known by his nickname Chomy, and he must be the most overworked individual in Cuba. A physician who met Castro in the Sierra, Chomy was Chancellor of the University of Havana for a time after the revolution, then was summoned to the Palace to replace Celia; he later became a member of the Communist Party's Central Committee.

Chomy had his own office on the ground floor of the palace but he is night and day at Castro's beck and call, attending most of the official meetings as well as sessions with foreign visitors that often stretch into the dawn. Every time Fidel has a fresh idea, a question or a request – which is all the time – Chomy writes it down, then passes on pertinent instructions to appropriate officials. Only when Castro goes to sleep is Chomy – who has only six staff – free to attend to his paper work. He is responsible for organizing and reorganizing the schedule of the *Jefe* , and the direction of the council's historical division. He is also opposed personally to the publication of serious historical material about Castro and the revolution, and is a most effective watchdog of the archives. A harried, superficially affable man who is obsessed with photographing Fidel all the time with everybody, Chomy has limited intellectual and political powers, but he wields the power of the doorkeeper.

Heading Castro's personal 'Coordination and Support Group' at the palace is Government Minister José A. Naranjo Morales, known as Pepín, who fought in the Student Revolutionary Directorate guerrillas, later becoming governor of Havana province. Naranjo is a bureaucratic jack-of-all-trades, running political errands for Fidel and coordinating the preparation of background studies and information for him on all imaginable subjects. This Support Group – ten men and ten women, all carefully picked, free to cross all bureaucratic lines in the Party and government, and equipped with up-to-date computers – is informally called the Fidel staff, and its relatively young members are groomed for promotion later to important administration positions. The new head of the state radio and television network was recruited from the Fidel staff when Castro strongly (and deservedly) criticized the quality of Cuban television in an off-the-record chat with leaders of the Women's Federation early in 1985.

The most interesting men around Castro, however, are the less visible ones, and all come from State Security Services. General José Abrahantes

Fernández, who replaced Ramiro Valdés in December 1985 as Interior Minister, is still directly responsible for Castro's security, his Special Forces of State Security being the Praetorian Guard hand-picked to defend Fidel and the regime in the direst of dangers. It is organized along the lines of the Soviet KGB's uniformed security forces. But although Abrahantes, even as Interior Minister, plays a limited political role, two other Security-linked figures were exceedingly important in the foreign policy field.

One was José Luis Padrón González, whose title was President of the national Tourism Institute (which operates all the Cuban hotels), but who served Castro extensively as a discreet international emissary and negotiator, bypassing the Foreign Ministry. A former colonel in State Security (there are more Security-linked officials in Cuba than meet the eye), Padrón was part of the new revolutionary generation, seemingly being groomed for high leadership. Padrón first impressed Castro when helping to set in motion the Cuban military intervention in Angola in 1975 – he was rushed to Luanda to prevent the collapse of the Marxist Popular Movement for the Liberation of Angola (MPLA) in the civil war that followed independence from Portuguese colonial rule.

Early in 1986, however, Padrón mysteriously vanished from sight, losing his job and palace access, becoming a nonperson. It happens in Fidel's Cuba.

A notable Security person at the palace is Comandante Manuel Piñeiro Losada, long known in Cuba as Barba Roja (for his red beard, now white). Piñeiro, a member of the Communist Party's Central Committee, is head of its Latin American Department and, as such, the chief coordinator of all the Cuban operations in the hemisphere, from Nicaragua and El Salvador to Panama, Peru and Argentina.

Given Castro's ambitions for Latin American leadership, Piñeiro's position is extremely important. Piñeiro acquired his anti-Americanism (and his first wife, an American) when he studied at Columbia University in New York in the early 1950s, and was humbled and 'radicalized' by his defeat by a 'rich South American kid' in the elections for president of a student association. He was in the anti-Batista underground back in Havana where his apartment was an arms depository before the failed and horribly bloody attack on the presidential palace by young revolutionaries in 1957. Later he joined Raúl Castro's command in the Sierra, and wound up as military governor in Santiago.

When Ramiro Valdés, Che Guevara's deputy, became chief of the Rebel Army's G-2 Section (Security and Intelligence), Piñeiro was named number two. He presided over the revolutionary tribunal that sentenced Batista aviators to severe prison terms in 1959 (they had been acquitted under another judge, then re-tried on Castro's orders). He subsequently took over as head of G-2. He was Cuba's top political policeman under

Valdés until 1968, when a Soviet-imposed reorganization of the Security Services forced him out – and Castro put him in charge of Latin American affairs.

It is rare for Piñeiro not to be present at social functions at the Palace of the Revolution (usually standing near Castro with a small group of the top leadership), and it is not uncommon to find him in the middle of the night having a milkshake with friends in Chomy's downstairs office. Naturally, he has permanent access to Castro's third-floor office.

Dr Antonio Nuñez Jiménez – geographer, explorer, historian, ardent Communist and Vice Minister of Culture – also has full access to Castro, whose story he is slowly writing in multiple volumes. Nuñez Jiménez is regarded primarily as a personal companion – he accompanies Fidel on most of his trips around Cuba and shares vacations with him, but he does not fit (or choose to fit) into the palace entourage. Finally, there is Jorge Enrique Mendoza, the editor of *Granma*, a close ideological and propaganda adviser; he is an irascible, hardline, dogmatic Communist who knew Castro in the Sierra, serving as the Rebel Radio announcer in the final phase of the war.

Castro enjoys the friendship of many people who are personally and even ideologically attuned to him, but exercise no political influence. The foremost among them is Gabriel García Márquez, the mustachioed Colombian Nobel Prize laureate in literature, currently the greatest Latin American novelist. His worship of Castro is evident in an early brief portrait he wrote, titled 'My Brother Fidel', based on conversations with Castro's sister Emma. Castro's and García Márquez's friendship is so close that when the Colombian comes on one of his visits the two men often converse for eight or ten hours, then again over several days and nights. Former Colombian president Alfonso López Michelsen, who was brought to Castro's island by García Márquez in 1984, and was with them much of the time, says: 'Fidel is a reader of extraordinary avidity. . . Gabito (García Márquez's first-name diminutive) brings him five books and he stays for ten days, and the day he leaves, Fidel comments on the books one by one. They are not necessarily serious books, they are often simply agreeable books that a statesman might use to relax with.

Castro fascinates the world's intelligentsia. Among his visitors have been the French philosophers Jean-Paul Sartre and Simone de Beauvoir, the American historian Arthur M. Schlesinger Jr, the British novelist Graham Greene and the British actor Alec Guinness who along with Noel Coward had gone to Cuba a few weeks after the victory in 1959 to film *Our Man in Havana*. And in 1982 Castro greatly enjoyed a secret conference with Lieutenant-General Vernon A. Walters, a former

Central Intelligence Agency Deputy Director and an ambassador-at-
large when President Reagan sent him to Havana.

Soviet poet Yevgeny Yevtushenko met Castro in Havana in the early
days of the revolution (he had actually made a point of learning Spanish
beforehand), and his impressions of revolutionary Cuba were vivid. In
his autobiography Yevtushenko tells the story of two Cuban plotters,
one of them a realist and the other an abstract artist, who argued furiously
while waiting for orders to attack the Batista palace, then 'went to fight
for the future of their country, and both were killed'. Yevtushenko
added: 'I very much wish this story were known to those dogmatists who
write off all modern artists as lackeys of bourgeois ideology.' This was, of
course, during the relative liberalization in the Soviet Union that
accompanied the de-Stalinization process, and Yevtushenko found it
useful to cite revolutionary Cuba as an example of new freedoms.

Elsewhere in the autobiography he writes that it was on the same
evening in Moscow when he spoke publicly about Cuba that he read for
the first time his famous poem 'Babi Yar' about the place where the Nazis
had massacred thousands of Jews during the war. Then Yevtushenko
reports that a white-haired old man, leaning on a stick, came up to him
afterwards to say: 'What you've said about Cuba and what you've written
about Babi Yar are one and the same. Both are the Revolution. The
Revolution we once made, and which was afterward so betrayed, yet
which still lives and will live on. I spent fifteen years in one of Stalin's
concentration camps, but I am happy that our cause, I mean the cause of
the Bolsheviks, is still alive.'

Perhaps the greatest danger facing Fidel Castro after all these years in
power is that of intellectual and political isolation. In this sense the deaths
of Che Guevara and Celia Sánchez were terrible blows to him. For one
thing, nobody now dares to contradict him. Today's immediate
entourage is essentially fawning and sycophantic, and of his top advisers
no more than three or four are first rate.

Furthermore, the personality cult around Castro is continually
enhanced. This is a very touchy subject with him. He angrily denies that
such a cult even exists, but in fact Fidel Castro lives bathed in absolute
adulation by the propaganda organs of the regime, expressed through the
use of all his titles – Commander-in-Chief, President of the Councils of
State and Ministers, and First Secretary of the Communist Party, in every
single printed or broadcast reference to him, sometimes every few
paragraphs. Editorials and speeches invariably speak of his wisdom and
genius, and the 1976 Cuban constitution proclaims the decision 'to carry
forward the triumphant Revolution . . . under the leadership of Fidel
Castro'. Quotations from Fidel are printed everywhere, even at the
bottom of every page in the Havana telephone directory

Every public act by Castro, no matter how routine, is printed on the first pages of newspapers and is the lead item on the evening television news. A shot of Fidel benignly waving from a balcony is part of the introduction to the news. Books and articles about the history of the revolution are adoring in every mention of Fidel. The first volume of Antonio Nuñez Jiménez's planned history of the revolution is a hymn to Fidel Castro. He is usually called Comandante-en-Jefe in normal conversations and nobody in his right mind, even in private, ever criticizes him. It is hard to believe that a man of Castro's immense intelligence does not realize that all this in fact adds up to an incredible cult of personality.

Furthermore, the progressive militarization of Cuban society which was resumed in earnest during the early 1980s emphasizes even more Castro's role as commander-in-chief, and the slogan, painted on walls and repeated in countless public pronouncements every day is 'Commander-in-Chief! Give the Orders!' and 'Commander-in-Chief! The Rearguard is Secured!'

Not surprisingly, Cubans regard themselves as a besieged society, constantly under the threat of an armed attack by the United States. The Bay of Pigs, the US military intervention in the Dominican Republic in 1965, the Grenada invasion in 1983, the CIA's Contras operations against Nicaragua, and the steady flow of warnings by the Reagan administration that it will go to 'the source' of all Central American affrays – i.e. Cuba – have given Castro sufficient reason to emphasise defence as the nation's first task. Inevitably, however, this phenomenon leads to the existence of a permanent situation of national emergency in which the *military* leader of the ten million Cubans must be supreme.

Castro has access to all forms of data and information but, in the absence of useful interlocutors, he lacks the opportunity to discuss this with anyone else. His favourite expression is 'Let us analyse it', and he engages aloud in the analytical process, sometimes for hours, in front of a visitor or his staff.

Castro's hunger for information is gargantuan. He carefully reads Cuban newspapers and magazines daily and receives around-the-clock copy from tickers of US and European news agencies as well as from Cuba's own *Prensa Latina* . Dish antennae at the palace pick up US radio and television broadcasts day and night, and in 1985 for a half-million dollars annually the government purchased the extensive computerized financial service of the Reuter's news agency of Britain (US restrictions on any commercial dealings with Cuba prevented buying a similar American service).

Castro also goes over the daily dispatches from Cuban embassies abroad, and reads reports from what he calls with a wink 'our special services'. From overseas he receives a steady stream of clippings, special publications, reports and books – some are translated or summarized for him, others he reads in full (Castro has a good command of written English, but hesitates to speak it). In the summer of 1985 he read and virtually memorized a study of US trade protectionist practices prepared by the Japanese chamber of commerce. His interests are so wide that almost any topic can inspire him to learn more about it, especially if it deals with economic development, agriculture, public health and education.

Castro amuses himself by extrapolating startling conclusions from data available to him, mainly to make a dramatic debating point. Talking about Latin America's huge external debt, he informed his audience on one occasion that he had figured out 'with pencil and paper' not only what citizens in the region owe per capita, but also how much of the debt corresponds to an acre of arable land. Such unusual statistics tend to impress his listeners, and Castro has also worked out how many pounds of sugar a Caribbean nation has to export in order to import a tractor from the 'capitalists', emphasizing that the cost of the tractor in terms of sugar keeps growing astronomically. This is the sort of language that Latin Americans understand and makes very effective anti-capitalist propaganda for Cuba – balance-of-payment statistics otherwise are mere abstractions to the hemisphere's millions of poor people.

When Castro is away from Havana, which happens frequently, helicopters deliver to him twice à day batches of publications, news agency cables, diplomatic reports, and everything else required to keep him fully informed. Even when he spends a few days at his fishing hideaway in the Caribbean he religiously follows the routine of studying all these materials.

Conversing with a friend from Washington, Castro showed curiosity about the briefing practices at the White House, inquiring how much information President Reagan was being given and how often. He offered no comment upon being told that American presidents usually have only one relatively short daily foreign policy and Intelligence briefing, but he seemed surprised.

Visitors from abroad (and chiefly from the United States) whom Castro sees in astounding numbers and at astounding lengths, often find themselves under third-degree interrogation. When a Texas oilman and self-made millionaire was brought by a Texas congressman friend of Castro to dine at Fidel's tiny fishing retreat, he was questioned in detail about his Horatio Alger history – and about offshore drilling. A wealthy rice broker from Arkansas, accompanying an Arkansas congressman, was debriefed about planting techniques, Cuba still being a rice importer and hoping to augment its domestic production. Another American was quizzed about Reagan's tax policies (and told firmly that sales taxes would be more acceptable to Americans than higher income taxes). A newswoman who had just visited Mexico was asked about Mexican poppy-plant eradication (Cuba forbids all drugs, but Castro admits that during the war he tolerated the planting of marijuana by some Sierra peasants because it was their only cash crop; now it is prohibited). A Texas pilot was expected to advise Fidel on the best private jet aircraft.

Castro's informality can startle Americans. When the Texas oilman (who had a beard) alighted on the fishing cay from the Cuban air force helicopter late at night, he almost collided with a tall bearded figure all in dark blue: sweatsuit, windbreaker, sailing cap and sneakers. The man in blue said, '*Bienvenido* to Cayo Piedra', and when the congressman began to introduce the oilman, Fidel broke in, saying, 'We've just met, we had a collision softened by our beards.'

Fidel's curiosity about people is so boundless, especially when it comes to Americans, that during a recent six-month period he met with a delegation of US Roman Catholic bishops; a score of congressmen; the daughters (on separate occasions) of Robert F. Kennedy and Nelson Rockefeller; a half-dozen book publishers; two television network correspondents (and crews); interviewers from a leading US newspaper and from a men's mass-circulation magazine (in the latter case for some thirty hours of taped conversation); a middle-level and pronouncedly hostile US State Department official who had not expected to be received by Castro during his business visit; a famous jazz musician; a number of businessmen; and several marine biologists.

In the same period he received the presidents of Algeria and Ecuador; the Secretary-General of the United Nations; numerous foreign cabinet ministers; leaders of Latin American political, labour, press and journalism organizations (these groups came to Havana to attend conferences on hemisphere economies, with Castro present at the day-long sessions); and Japanese and Mexican businessmen interested in trade with Cuba.

With his prodigious memory Castro appears to recall everything he has read, heard and seen in the past half-century. It is more than the *memoria technica*, as the Romans called the memorizing technique of ancient orators, because he can play infinite variations on his themes before his audiences, never forgetting facts and figures. As a law school student, Castro completed the last two years in one year, studying day and night and destroying all the materials he had learned by heart – so that he would be forced to depend on his memory.

In relaxed conversation or improvised speeches, he ranges easily from references to obscure Roman laws on debt moratoria to Victor Hugo's critique of Louis Bonaparte, the Little Napoleon, from tales of the Spanish conquest to quotations from Abraham Lincoln and José Martí, from a forgotten passage from Lenin to a line from Curzio Malaparte. In a written battlefield order in the Sierra he once lapsed into Latin to urge a *manu militari* solution in a tight spot.

At home or abroad Castro keeps incredible hours. The punishment is self-inflicted, but he seems to thrive on unpredictable schedules. His only recent concession to orderly behaviour is public punctuality. Whereas in the past he would be hours late arriving at a meeting, or delivering a scheduled speech, he is now exactly on time. At the Communist Party Congress in February 1986 he berated delegates for being a few minutes late for a 9 a.m. session, charging that if Communists are unable to arrive at a conference on time, they are probably incapable of running the country.

Castro seems to get by on very little sleep. Even under the best circumstances he does not go to sleep before three or four o'clock in the morning, yet he looks fresh and rested at nine o'clock the next day. When in Havana, Fidel may sleep (at dawn or for a daytime nap) at almost any location: in the Eleventh Street apartment, in the small bedroom behind his office on the third floor of the Palace of the Revolution, at his new and very private villa in the suburbs west of Havana (he experiments with enormous hydroponic tomatoes in the Garden there), or maybe in a friend's home.

In the first year of the revolution Castro used as home and office not only the twenty-third floor of the Habana Libre Hotel (formerly the Havana Hilton); but also the apartment kept by Celia Sánchez on Eleventh Street; a spacious house that a rich friend lent him, overlooking the sea on a hill in the fishing village of Cojimar five miles east of the city; and a house in the Miramar residential section. This was why it was so hard for people to locate him in those days. Conchita Fernández, his former secretary, recalls that he raced all the time, carrying papers, reports and notes in a briefcase, from one place to another in his motorcade of Oldsmobiles (the black Mercedes Benzes came later) with gun-toting, *barbudo* guards. He usually worked while being driven around, reading or dictating memoranda or ideas to Conchita who came along in the car. 'He never rested, not in the car, not anywhere else,' she recalls.

Conchita also remembers days when Castro would arrive at his INRA office at eight o'clock in the morning on some occasions, 'and would leave only three or four days later . . . not stopping in the morning, not in the afternoon, not at night, not at dawn. . . At best, he'd say, "I'll rest on the couch for three or four hours, and you wake me up at such and such time", and ten minutes later he was back in my office to read the correspondence.'

Twenty-five years later Castro's life may be more orderly and more elegant, but he has not changed very much in behaviour or attitudes. He has de luxe Soviet helicopters with interior wood panelling at his disposal as well as a fleet of Mercedes Benz limousines (he usually travels in a motorcade, with two limousines carrying Security guards), but he also has a weakness for Jeep-like vehicles. He enjoys driving the Soviet *gazik* vehicles during countryside outings and being driven in them around Havana suburbs; the drives remind him of the Sierra, which he often describes as the happiest time of his life. Occasionally he switches from *gazik* to limousine or the other way around (all the cars moving in armed convoy). On these drives he does not seem overly concerned for his security, occasionally even stopping at red lights.

As head of state Castro enjoys a degree of luxury and privilege, yet on a modest scale as compared with rulers elsewhere, including those in Communist countries. The most spectacular displays of luxury are the receptions he offers for visiting dignitaries on the ground floor of the palace, inviting as many as a thousand guests to eat and drink in a huge area decorated with rare ferns and plants from the Sierra Maestra. As a rule Castro strolls with the guest of honour, introducing him or her to his friends. The best meats, fish and lobster are served along with aged Cuban rum (Isla de Tesoro) and occasionally Chivas Regal whisky is available. All of this is a great treat in a country still plagued with shortages, particularly of quality food. But these are not caviar-and-champagne feasts, they end early without drunkenness, and Cubans do not seem to begrudge their Maximum Leader this form of official entertainment (the press reports in detail the holding of such receptions).

On such occasions – as well as at major conferences or National Assembly sessions – the fastidious Castro, his hair well-trimmed, wears the brown formal uniform of commander-in-chief, with his single star on a black and red diamond rank insignia and laurel leaves. The shirt is white, and the tie is black. The rest of the time, he prefers his perfectly tailored whipcord olive-green campaign uniform. Though open-necked, the uniform is quite heavy and Castro also wears an undershirt beneath the front-zippered tunic. To feel comfortable in this attire he has the palace air-conditioning system turned to the point where his aides, in Cuban style *guayaberas* or sports shirts, seem to be freezing.

Sometimes Castro chooses to wear olive-green fatigues, keeping his cap on his head even when sitting in his own office or at a friend's house. He always wears black combat boots, and army orderlies rush over to tuck the trousers inside the boots if they slip out. The orderlies also clean mud or dirt from the boots when he returns to the office.

Because of the Sierra Maestra legend and his dedication to olive-green uniforms, Fidel's image is still that of the *guerrillero*, careless about dress. But he has always been extremely conscious of his appearance: as a university student leader and budding politician running for elective office Castro preferred dark suits and ties to the *guayaberas* worn by most Cuban men, and it was in a good suit that he returned from prison to Havana, left for exile in Mexico, and planned the voyage of the *Granma*.

Photographs of the period show Castro looking quite tall and elegant, a kerchief in his jacket pocket, a pencil-line moustache over his upper lip. He looked for all the world like the scion of a Cuban millionaire family (even when, after prison, he owned only one suit), knowing that he would have more dramatic political effect than if he were just one more youth in a casual shirt. A picture taken with his son Fidelito, a few hours before leaving for the Moncada assault in 1953, shows him dapper and fashionable. The tailored campaign uniforms of today are consistent with Castro's pre-revolutionary dress code.

Fidel is quite near-sighted, and his vanity does not keep him from wearing horn-rimmed glasses when necessary. He wore them in the Sierra and at the Bay of Pigs and one of the few billboard pictures of Fidel portrays him during the battle wearing a brown beret and his glasses. A superb marksman, Castro wears his glasses when shooting; he has devised a system allowing him to aim with *both* eyes open, because this is more accurate through the glasses.

Fidel Castro is a curious combination of *hidalgo* courtliness and innate beautiful manners, especially towards women, and of outright rudeness and the peremptory treatment of subordinates. He may spit on the floor and use filthy language when only men are present. He swears easily, when playing chess or dominoes, being a master at both. He has regal carriage, but he nevertheless allows morsels of food to be caught in his beard when he eats.

Castro is a literary perfectionist, to the point of pedantry. He spends hours correcting and editing his speeches and other writings to achieve stylistic excellence; his pages are a labyrinth of inserts, arrows, interlines and squiggles in tiny script. Sometimes he does his editing in a fast-moving car, which drives his secretaries, much as they are used to his handwriting, to sheer despair. Fernández, the vice-president, recalls the occasion when Fidel began drafting in his limousine a letter to a foreign head of state, and had the driver go round in circles for four hours until he had finished, as he did not wish to have his concentration broken by stopping to go up to his office.

The rare times Castro really appears to relax is with a few companions or visitors at Cayo Piedra, a small volcanic cay in the Caribbean, ten miles south of the Cuban coast, where he flies in his helicopter to engage in his favourite sport of underwater fishing. The cay, once the site of a lighthouse, has a four-room rustic caretaker's house with a verandah and pergola, and this is Fidel's real home. Visitors are put up in a modern guest house on the other side of the cay (there is a collection of José Martí's works, but no Marx or Lenin, at the guest house), and all the meals are served aboard a barge tied to the wharf. Cayo Piedra has a pool where Castro swims every morning against the clock.

Most of the day is spent fishing off one of the two large powerboats (always escorted by two naval missile launches), with Fidel in his wetsuit diving deep with his speargun. A champion diver, he invited Jacque-Yves Cousteau, the famous explorer, to join him off Cayo Piedra during the Frenchman's stay in Cuba to study marine life there. After his dives Fidel is given eyedrops and nosedrops by his physician. Turtles are bred off the cay, and fresh turtle soup is served at dinner before the baked red snapper and lobster speared personally by Castro.

Informal meals with Castro usually follow the same pattern: first, there is a long cocktail hour with light banter – usually about the day's fishing or hunting – and occasional serious conversation, then dinner in a very small group, lasting sometimes until long after midnight. That is one of Fidel's favourite settings for a good discussion, at which he most brilliantly explains revolutionary Cuba to foreign visitors, dazzling even right-wing Republican congressmen from the US. He tends to grant formal interviews in his office, a relatively sparsely-furnished L-shaped room with bookcases behind his desk, and there he usually sits on a sofa under a modern Cuban mural. Camilo Cienfuegos looks down from a portrait on another wall. Fidel's reasonably orderly desk carries a large transistor radio (telephones are on an adjoining small table), cassette tapes, piles of documents, a jar containing his favourite hard candy, and until recently, boxes with long and short cigars. He increasingly favoured the short ones until he suddenly decided to quit smoking some time in October of 1985. Castro announced this event in a pre-Christmas interview with Brazilian television, and such evidently remains the fascination with him that the story made TV newscasts from the United States to Japan, and was printed prominently in newspapers and magazines worldwide. In his announcement he said: 'I reached the conclusion long ago that the one remaining sacrifice I must make for public health is to stop smoking; I haven't really missed it that much.' Given his proven willpower, the chances are that Castro, who began smoking at the age of fifteen, will stick to his decision. He explained that 'if someone had forced me to quit, I would have suffered . . . but since I forced myself, it worked.'

Years before, Castro had launched a vast anti-smoking campaign to persuade Cubans that tobacco, which had made the island so famous, was a danger to their health. Television, radio, billboards, magazines and newspapers were mobilized for the campaign (pregnant mothers saw televised sketches, for example, of how smoking can affect the foetus), and the price of cigarettes was raised to nearly $2 per pack. Anyone returning to Cuba after a long absence is immediately struck by the extent to which Cubans have ceased to be a nation of chain-smokers. Castro's own 'last sacrifice' was the ultimate weapon in the campaign, demonstrating that he now practises what he preaches.

If Fidel did away with his personal trademark of the cigar, he made it absolutely clear that the other symbol – the beard – stays on. He explained, as he had done in the past, that he and his companions grew their beards in the Sierra simply because shaving was too much trouble. Subsequently the *barbudo* cult grew, and Castro acknowledged that 'the beard became a symbol of the guerrilla'. But, typically, he also noted that beards 'have a practical advantage' because 'if you calculate fifteen minutes a day to shave, that is five thousand minutes a year spent shaving', and the time can be spent better reading or exercising. Nevertheless, he has strongly discouraged other Cubans, even in the highest ranks, from wearing guerrilla beards. Clearly he prefers his beard to be his personal mark of distinction.

Occasionally, Castro will talk about his foreign travels and the people he has met. He visited the Soviet Union more than a half-dozen times (not all his trips are necessarily publicized), Eastern Europe twice, and Vietnam once. He stayed away from China mainly because Cuba was firmly on the Soviet side in the Sino–Soviet feud and he acquired deep contempt for Mao Tse-tung whom he never met (he criticizes Mao for having allowed himself 'to become a God', but of Stalin he says only that 'during Stalin's time a personality cult developed and abuses of power did take place').

Fidel, the most widely travelled Communist chief of state in the world, has been several times in Africa, mainly in Algeria whose independence the Cubans championed after their revolution, and in Angola and Ethiopia where he dispatched combat troops in the mid-1970s – and where they remained a decade later. He has been to India, but the only time he touched the ground in Western Europe was during a one-hour stopover at Madrid airport.

With all his responsibilities and obligations, Castro still tries to be a free soul, to act on the spur of the moment, to do the unexpected. His decision to attend the inauguration of his revolutionary protégé, Nicaraguan President Daniel Ortega Saavedra in January 1985 was taken at the last moment when he discovered that no other head of government would be present (he took along Gabo García Márquez, only telling him when he was aboard the plane that they were flying to Santiago).

The commander-in-chief as a rule no longer attends diplomatic receptions (except at the Soviet Embassy, now a huge modernistic compound on the sea in uptown Havana), but he may suddenly turn up at dinner at an ambassador's residence, invited or self-invited. The first embassy Fidel ever visited was that of Brazil in 1959, and at that time he was still carrying his rifle (he checked it at the door) wherever he went.

Appearing unexpectedly one night at the French Embassy and staying until four o'clock in the morning in conversation with visiting parliamentarians, Fidel sent over the next day a case of Cuban scotch-type whisky, which is not, however, the greatest contribution to the pleasures of drinking. But Castro, the perfect dilettante, also plans to produce Camembert-type cheese and *pâté de fois gras* in Cuba and has already become a theoretical expert on force-feeding geese.

Although a revolutionary and a *guerrillero*, Castro is clearly far from being an ascetic. He had always been partial to good food and cooking, and in May 1958, as the great Batista offensive was opening, he dispatched a desperate note to Celia Sánchez in the Sierra headquarters, reporting that 'I have no tobacco, I have no wine, I have nothing. A bottle of rosé wine, sweet and Spanish, was left in Bismarck's house, in the refrigerator. Where is it?'

Cuisine in many forms has preoccupied Fidel since youth and, curiously, spaghetti was always among his favourite dishes. Manuel Moreno Frajinals, Cuba's leading historian who befriended the young Fidel in the late 1940s, still at the university, remembers his frequent visits at the family's apartment to discuss politics and grab a meal. On one occasion Castro arrived just as the maid was frying plantains. Smelling them, he rushed to the kitchen, telling the girl: 'Let me show you how to fry them properly.' When Moreno Frajinals' wife, who is an architect, asked, 'Do you think you know everything?' Fidel replied: 'Almost everything.'

In prison on the Isle of Youth (then called the Isle of Pines), Fidel continually attempted to cook spaghetti on a small electric plate in his solitary cell; guiding visitors through the prison, he never fails to recount how many hours it took for the spaghetti to be ready. His sister Emma says he went on to cook spaghetti in the Sierra for his fellow fighters. Conchita Fernández tells that Castro often dined in the kitchen of the Habana Libre Hotel (where he also granted all-night interviews), and that he frequently tried to show the cooks how to properly prepare the red snapper. He has definite views on preparing lamb chops. He believes that *confit* of duck should be made in a bain-marie, and he is partial to grilled fish.

Castro also holds powerful opinions on the intellectual aspects of sport: having played both basketball and baseball of almost professional quality, he once provided a visitor with a learned explanation of why basketball is the thinking man's game (there is no telling where a conversation with Fidel may lead). His theory is that whereas basketball requires strategic and tactical planning as well as speed and agility – thus preparing a man for guerrilla war – baseball poses no such needs (the whole subject came up when Castro forcefully denied a rumour then circulating abroad that he had once hoped to play for the majors in mainland baseball).

The complexities of Fidel Castro's personality are immense, and therefore no future change of course by him can ever be ruled out, should he become convinced that it is in the interest of Cuba, the revolution and himself. Naturally, these three sets of interests will overlap for as long as Castro dominates the Cuban scene. And one is tempted to think that his personal destiny was to achieve this domination.

PART TWO

The Young Years 1926–52

Chapter 1

Slightly more than thirty years after the tragic poet José Martí, the Apostle of Cuban independence, was killed in combat with Spanish troops in 1895, Fidel Alejandro Castro Ruz was born at a *finca* in the province of Oriente, barely twenty-five miles from the Dos Ríos battlefield. In terms of history three decades are a short period – they already roughly equal the span of Castro's own revolution – and in this sense his life has been intertwined from the outset with the struggles and symbolisms of Cuba's past.

As the island's greatest thinker and patriotic hero, Martí always was Castro's role model, and in landing with his rebels on the shores of Cuba to dislodge tyranny, Fidel was fulfilling his hero's destiny. Martí, the leader of the Cuban Revolutionary Party, had launched its final war of independence with a proclamation from his New York headquarters on 29 January 1895, and he came ashore in a rowboat on the Oriente coast two months later to join the guerrillas fighting the Spaniards. The Apostle was killed on 19 May astride a white horse, weeks after coming home to Cuba from exile. He was only forty-two, a slim sad-faced man with a bushy, pointed moustache and a half-goatee, and almost constantly in poor health.

It was therefore only natural for Fidel Castro to seek the most complete personal identification with Martí's martyrdom and, quite predictably, soon after the victorious revolution he made a pilgrimage to Playitas, the beach where the historic landing occurred on 2 April 1895. The pilgrimage produced an hour-long colour documentary, exhibited in cinemas and on television, showing Castro in battledress standing dramatically alone on the small horseshoe-shaped stretch of white sand, narrating the tale of Martí's sacrifice.

The parallels between 1895 and 1956 are many. Martí, after countless attempts to overthrow Spanish rule, concluded that a revolution in Cuba could only succeed from an expanding guerrilla warfare; Castro came to the same conclusion after the failure of his assault on the Moncada army barracks in 1953. Martí likewise understood the immense personal risks involved in leading a revolution, writing to a friend on the eve of his death that 'every day I am in danger of giving my life for my country and for my duty'; Castro would pledge before embarking on his invasion that 'we shall be free or martyrs'.

The tragic poet was convinced that even if he died, the liberating revolution would triumph. Sons of Spaniards, both Martí and Castro represent a very special strain of Iberian mysticism and romanticism, combined with a powerful dose of New World nationalism. Moreover, the real Cuban issue to both Martí and Castro was a revolution in depth, not just changes in the political status quo but a social revolution.

Martí wrote that government has a duty to provide education to the people because 'to read is to walk'. One of Castro's first major revolutionary undertakings after 1959 would be an island-wide crash literacy campaign. The earlier Cuban opposed, however, radical social transformations. His biographer M. Isidoro Méndez, a pre-revolution-ary historian, found Martí to be a 'social republican', believing in 'prudent socialism' without extremism.

Appearing many decades later on the Cuban political scene and in a totally changed world, Castro's extremism in social change, his rejection of direct-vote elections as the keystone of political life that Martí had urged in the nineteenth century, seems a stark and telling difference in their political platforms. This ideological difference surely stems from their distinct temperamental and psychological makeups. Martí, the classical democrat, essayist in three languages, and lyrical patriotic poet, believed in civilian government with the consent of the governed. Castro on the other hand is the quintessential Spanish military *caudillo*, wrapped today in a Marxist–Leninist mantle of convenience, offering the intel-lectual rationalization that 'real' revolution is impossible under an elective system, and that Communist authoritarianism is the necessary instru-ment for its implementation. He is thereby proving unwittingly the sad theorem that 'without power, ideals cannot be realized; with power, they seldom survive'.

While Martí and Castro would disagree on the means of achieving their ends, Castro is truly Martí's direct philosophical and political heir in his views on radicalism, agrarian reform, racial equality and social justice. Castro and Martí also share fears of the United States and its intentions towards Cuba. North American aspirations to annex or even buy Cuba (as Louisiana was purchased) go back to the early days of the last century. The American consul in Havana wrote in 1833: 'In the fullness of time, when Cuba and Spain and we should all be of one mind –

without discussion, or revolution, or war – Cuba would doubtless be added to the Union.'

Martí, having spent long years in the United States in forced exile from Spanish Cuba, had nightmares over an American grab of his island from Spain as the outcome of the independence war then under way. In the letter he penned the day before he died Martí said that he was battling the Spaniards for Cuban independence in order to impede 'the extension of the United States through the Antilles'. He wrote that in the United States he had lived 'inside the entrails of the monster', and he was concerned with American 'economic imperialism', remarking that 'the disdain of a formidable neighbour who does not really know us is the worst danger to our America'.

José Martí's days had coincided with the time of America's Manifest Destiny. Even twenty years before the independence war, the US economic presence in Cuba was already weighty. Cuban trade with the United States was six times larger than with Spain and, as Martí saw it, there seemed an economic and geographic inevitability about the island coming under complete American political domination.

In fact, no annexation of Cuba ever occurred formally, yet the fears of the nineteenth-century patriots were fully realized when the United States declared war on Spain in 1898 after the battleship *Maine* blew up in Havana harbour from unknown causes. This conveniently provided the *casus belli* for an open conflict with Madrid – for which Americans were spoiling anyway. As Theodore Roosevelt and his Rangers charged up San Juan Hill in Santiago and other American forces were landing elsewhere along the Cuban coasts, the exhausted Spaniards were quickly defeated (they had already been fighting the merciless Cuban guerrillas for three years). Later that same year the United States and Spain signed the Paris peace treaty, transferring *control* over Cuba to Washington. At the same time the United States also acquired Puerto Rico, the Philippines and Guam.

When Cuba came under outright United States military occupation, the island was made wholly dependent on its northern neighbour, and even the educational system was thoroughly Americanized in flagrant disregard for the local culture and language. As in Puerto Rico with the Puerto Ricans, the idea was to prepare Cubans to some day become good Americans. Inevitably, the four-year occupation established the foundations on which to make Cuba at least a de facto United States protectorate in the Caribbean for the next sixty years.

This protectorate status was engineered through the forcible insertion of the so-called Platt Amendment in the Cuban constitution, drafted with American blessings as a prelude to the grant of independence, as well as through the enforcement of trade and investment arrangements allowing United States interests completely free rein in Cuba. The amendment,

devised by Senator Orville H. Platt as part of a United States Army
appropriations bill, authorized the president to 'leave the government' of
Cuba to its own people, with the proviso that the Cuban constitution
recognize that 'the United States may exercise the right to intervene for
the preservation of Cuban independence, the maintenance of a government adequate for the protection of life, property, and individual
liberty. . .' The Cubans, given the choice of accepting the Platt
Amendment in their new constitution or possibly remaining for ever
under military occupation, engaged in fervent debates before capitu-
lating.

On 20 May 1902 Cuba was proclaimed an independent republic, the
last colony in the Americas to achieve this. Even so, this independence
was farce and fiction; Leonard Wood, the last governor-general, wrote
President William McKinley that 'there is, of course, little or no
independence left in Cuba under the Platt Amendment'. A year later
Senator Chauncey Depew declared: 'The day is not far distant when
Cuba, resembling the United States in its constitution, laws and liberties
. . . will have from five to six million people who are educated upon
American lines and worthy of all the rights of American citizenship.
Then, with the initiative from Cuba, we can welcome another star to our
flag.'

No such initiative ever came; instead, continuous, internal political
unrest resulted in a second United States military occupation lasting from
1906 to 1909, the landing of marines to protect American interests and
citizens in 1910, and another landing in 1917 to persuade Cuba, given the
island's strategic importance astride the sea-lanes, to enter World War
One. To protect American properties in Oriente from labour unrest and
sabotage, the marines remained in Cuba until *1923* – three years before
the birth of Fidel Castro. Throughout this period it was apparent that the
American government held Cubans in deep disdain. Small wonder, then,
that the young republic grew up with a paralysing inferiority complex,
and an anti-American sentiment to which Castro and his generation
became heir.

Though the Platt Amendment was removed by Franklin D. Roosevelt
in 1934, under his new Good Neighbour policy for Latin America, the
United States' political and economic stranglehold over Cuba would not
be broken until the great Castro revolution. This is why the defeat of the
Batista dictatorship in 1959 meant to Fidel and his *barbudos* the true
achievement of Cuban independence – independence for which José
Martí died sixty-four years before, and which was refused Cuba by the
Americans in 1898 and 1902. This historical dimension of the revolution
would elude the United States, however, along with any comprehension
that Cubans had lived all these years in the shame of being, as Castro
called it, a 'pseudo-republic'.

A large sugarcane-and-cattle estate, the Manacas *finca* is located in the municipality of Birán in the Mayarí region of the northern Oriente province coast. It is about twenty-five miles south of the Bay of Nipe and roughly the same distance east of Dos Ríos, the spot where José Martí was killed in a Spanish ambush in 1895.

It was at Manacas that Fidel Alejandro Castro Ruz was born on 13 August 1926, and by the time he was ready to attend the local elementary school he was already imbued with the Martí legend. This was part of every Cuban childhood, especially in the proud and ever-rebellious Oriente province. The revolutionary tradition in the area of Fidel's birth would again be emphasized when his brother Raúl Castro, leading his Rebel Army column from the Sierra Maestra to the Sierra Cristal in the north-east to establish the guerrilla war's Second Front, marched past the Birán house in April 1958. Raúl would make a point of mentioning this in his lengthy report to Fidel on the progress of his operations in the Mayarí region, the youngest brother being probably the most family-minded of the vast Castro clan.

The head of this clan was Ángel Castro y Argiz, an emigré to Cuba from his native village of Áncara, near the town of Lugo in the north-western Galicia region of Spain. He had arrived in Cuba a destitute thirteen-year-old orphan. Born around 1874, as a child he lived with an uncle in the Galicia *pueblo* in Spain's poorest and bleakest corner. Seven or eight years before the last Cuban War of Independence, Ángel, increasingly maltreated at home, sailed to join another uncle, one who had settled on the faraway Caribbean island. Castro has claimed on at least one occasion that his father had been sent to Cuba to fight as a Spanish soldier when the Independence War erupted in 1895, that he was repatriated after the war but, having liked the island, came back as a penniless emigrant in the first years of this century. This account is vague, and probably inaccurate; at least two of Fidel's sisters admit they have never heard about Ángel Castro's military experiences.

Significantly, Fidel Castro seems to know astonishingly little about his father's background and this must be either a conscious or a subconscious expression of his negative attitude towards Don Ángel, for reasons that may be deeply personal, political, or both. In a 1985 interview with the Brazilian Dominican friar, Frei Betto, Castro admitted: 'I do not know much what were [my father's] first years, because when I had the opportunity to ask all this, I didn't feel the curiosity that I may feel today to know what were his first steps. . .'

Considering that Fidel was thirty years old when his father died, he would surely have had ample occasion to ask questions – had he cared. Elsewhere in that interview, Castro volunteered the comment that although his father had the political ideas of a landowner he was a most

noble man because he never turned down an appeal for help. This, Fidel
said, 'is very significant'. Compared with his frequent warm and personal
references to his mother, the comment about his father seems forced and
supercilious.

Ángel Castro's uncle lived in the town of Santa Clara in central Cuba
where he had a brickmaker's business. Ángel was put to work there
(naturally, there was no time or opportunity for him to go to school), but
after some five years he evidently tired of the uncle's bricks, for he struck
out on his own. He moved east, probably walking most of the way and
for reasons no longer remembered in the family, he chose the Mayarí
zone in Oriente to try his luck. He never talked much about his youth; he
died in 1956 at the age of eighty-two, his past shrouded in oblivion, but he
must have arrived in the area just as the end of Spanish rule was
approaching and the American era was about to begin.

Mayarí is a region of fertile land, ideal for planting sugarcane and
tobacco, and for raising cattle. Its principal town, also named Mayarí,
lies on the river of the same name, and the Bay of Nipe beaches and its
fishermen are only four miles away. Some time after young Ángel Castro
reached Mayarí the once sleepy town of wooden houses dating back to
the early nineteenth century was transformed into a commercial centre of
activity fuelled by American capital.

At the end of the overlapping Cuban Independence War and the
Spanish-American war, the devastated country had been thrown wide
open to United States investments, the safety of which from trouble-
making Cubans was guaranteed by the military occupation. Across Cuba
these investments more than tripled in six years, from $50 million in 1898
to $160 million in 1906, chiefly in land. And lush and rich Oriente was the
preferred province. In 1899, for example, the Cuban-American Sugar
Company bought 70,000 acres in Chaparra on the north coast, and only a
year later the property accounted for 10 per cent of Cuba's sugar harvest.
At the same time the United Fruit Company and its subsidiary, the Nipe
Bay Company, purchased 240,000 acres in the Mayarí area – a veritable
private fief carved out of Cuba.

Speaking with enormous indignation about the economic consequences of the Cuban 'independence', Fidel Castro noted in a bitter
anniversary speech in 1968, one century after the first insurrection against
Spain, that 'in 1901 someone named Preston bought 75,000 hectares
[185,250 acres] of land in the Bay of Nipe zone for 400,000 dollars, that is
for less than six dollars per hectare of this land'. He added: 'The forests
that covered all these hectares with precious woods, and that were burned
in the furnaces of the sugar mills, were worth many times, incomparably
many times, this sum of money . . . they came with bulging pockets to a
nation impoverished by thirty years of war to buy the best land of this
country for less than six dollars the hectare.' Until the revolution

nationalized them in 1959, the United Fruit Company's Preston and Boston properties in Mayarí remained Cuba's main foreign-owned sugar mills and estates.

By the time Castro was born in 1926, American investments in Cuba exceeded $1.6 billion. Today this total investment would be equivalent to $3 billion. With the collapse of world sugar prices in 1920 (following the Dance of the Millions of the previous years when prices were ten times higher, and fantastic fortunes were made by Cubans), United States interests could and did pick up the pieces cheap. Foreign banks controlled 80 per cent of the sugar production; American companies gained monopolies in all the Cuban railways, electric power supply and telephones; and Cuban deposits in United States-owned banks on the island soared from 20 per cent in 1920 to 69 per cent in 1921, as most Cuban banks disappeared, unable to compete with the political power and resources of Yankee bankers.

Cuba's president in 1926 was Gerardo Machado, an American-supported friend of big business (Washington forced him out later, however, when he turned into a despotic dictator and the country's economic stability was threatened by the rising rebellion against him). He was as corrupt as his predecessors who ran the pseudo-republic in cahoots with the 'better classes' of Cuban society.

But among the new Cuban generation a new sense of anti-American nationalism was beginning to develop. Not only were the Cubans saddled with the Platt Amendment and the United States economic domination but they could also watch American military interventions by the marines in Mexico and Nicaragua. The Cuban Communist Party was created clandestinely in Havana just a year before Fidel Castro was born. Cuba had begun to stir.

The Mayarí region where Fidel grew up featured probably a greater American presence and control than any other place in Cuba. The United Fruit Company, a Boston-based corporate giant with operations throughout Latin America, maintained special housing in Mayarí for its American (and few Cuban) employees, hospitals, schools (for the children of the sugar-producing elite), stores stocked with American foodstuffs, a post office and, later, swimming pools and a polo club. In addition to the Rural Guard, a United States-trained Cuban gendarmerie, the company was protected by its own armed police force that assured order and kept out undesirable Cubans.

In Cuba thousands upon thousands of cane-cutters and mill workers lived with their families in miserable *bohíos* (shacks) on the estates during the four months of the annual *zafra* (harvest), usually earning less than a dollar a day (sometimes only forty or fifty cents, without food). In the year's remaining months – the sinister dead time in Cuba – there was simply no work, and the *guajiro* (peasant) families had to survive as best they could. This then was the social environment that Fidel Castro remembers from his childhood, and it awakened him politically as he matured.

When Ángel Castro first came to Mayarí there were occasional jobs available on the new railway the United Fruit Company had built between its mills and the port of Antilla on the Bay of Nipe, and he was briefly employed as a labourer laying down track. He was probably about twenty-five years old when he decided to start his own business as an itinerant pedlar among cane-cutters and woodsmen up and down Mayarí.

It was beautiful country, the classical Oriente landscape with clusters of tall palm trees rising proudly amidst green canefields and meadows, then deep woods extending far beyond in the direction of the sierras in the south. Rivers faithfully irrigated the fields. As the war ended and foreign capital poured in, the chimneys of new sugar mills over Oriente began to punctuate the skyline. More and more there were cattle grazing in the pastures with *guajiros* in big straw hats mounted on their tough little horses guarding the herds.

Selling lemonade he prepared every morning and transported in small barrels was Ángel Castro's first mercantile enterprise. With a donkey cart he toured the fields and woods of Mayarí, serving lemonade to the thirsty men. With his first tiny profits he started buying wholesale a variety of merchandise, peddling it from *finca* to *finca* in the ranch countryside. Fidel says he remembers having heard his father then organized a group of local workers, whom he paid to cut trees for new sugar-planting fields and for burning wood in the furnaces of the big mills. He apparently had a work contract with an American sugar company. As Spanish immigrants, and especially the *gallegos*, the poorest and the most determined of all, have always done, Ángel Castro worked incessantly to earn and save as much as possible. Somewhere along the line he learned how to read and write.

Probably in 1910, when he was thirty-five or so, Ángel began leasing land from the United Fruit Company in the Birán area, thirty-six kilometres south-west of the town of Mayarí, putting the proceeds from his sugar sales into the acquisition of parcels of land. Thus he became a *colono*, planting sugarcane for sale to the company's mills, a practice the corporation encouraged because this tied the small farmers closer to it. He employed his first farmhands, and gradually became Don Ángel Castro, the increasingly affluent landowner in Oriente.

About that time Ángel Castro married his first wife María Argota. She is thought to have been an elementary school teacher in the Mayarí area though virtually nothing else is known about her. They had two children, Pedro Emilio and Lidia, the latter born in 1915. In 1985 both of them lived in Havana, rarely seeing their famous half-brother, but in quiet comfort assured by him. Lidia, who eloped as a very young woman to marry an army officer and became widowed within a few years, devoted the rest of her life to Fidel, helping him immeasurably during his imprisonment and the Sierra war. Pedro Emilio was a minor politician prior to the 1952 Batista coup, then reverted to his real interest – Latin and Greek studies.

There is something of a mystery about the first Señora de Castro, and about the circumstances of Ángel Castro's second marriage. All the published accounts about the Castro family are extremely sketchy (Fidel likes to keep it that way), but they coincide in affirming that María Argota de Castro died shortly after her second child was born. Juana Castro, Fidel's younger sister, insists however that her father either divorced or simply left María (this point is unclear, since actual divorces in rural Catholic families in Cuba in the 1920s were most uncommon). Juana Castro says also that this first wife lived very long, dying well after the revolution.

Ángel Castro's second wife, the mother of Fidel and his six sisters and brothers, was Lina Ruz González, a woman easily twenty-five years younger than the Birán landowner. She appears to have been born in the westernmost province of Pinar del Río, and her daughter Emma once described her as 'a Cuban for a long time', presumably meaning that her parents were not first-generation immigrants from Spain. Juana says her mother was from 'the most humble origins', but it is unknown when and why she had come to Oriente. According to most published versions Lina worked as a cook or a maid in the Castro household while María Argota de Castro was still in residence.

Fidel says that his maternal grandparents had moved 'one thousand kilometres in a cart' from Pinar del Río to Oriente at the start of the century, with Lina and their other children. The grandparents were extremely poor and according to Fidel, Lina's father and his two brothers drove ox carts transporting cane from the fields to mills. It is unknown what happened to Grandfather Ruz, but Fidel recalls that his maternal grandmother lived about one kilometre from the Birán house and that she had even gone to Havana with Lina after the revolution in 1959.

Castro, who has rich memories of his mother, has often told of his mother being 'practically illiterate' until, as an adult, she taught herself to read and write. Both his mother and grandmother, he says, were deeply religious, 'the religiousness coming from ancient family tradition'. Because there were no churches or priests in the Bira region Fidel's mother's devotions were performed at home, and during the Sierra war both women made endless promises to God and the saints for the lives and safety of Fidel and Raúl. The day the revolution triumphed, Señora de Castro, her head covered by a black mantilla, knelt at the altar at

Santiago Cathedral to thank God for her sons' survival and victory. Castro recalls that when his mother and grandmother told him of the promises and their faith, he listened to them with interest and respect. 'Although I had a different concept of the world, I never discussed these problems with them, because I saw the strength, the encouragement, the consolation they derived from their religious sentiments and their beliefs.' Castro later remarked in all seriousness: 'The fact that we completed our struggle alive must have, doubtlessly, expanded her faith.' Of his father he says in a peculiarly detached fashion: 'I saw him more preoccupied with other subjects, with the political thing, the daily struggle . . . rarely, almost never, I heard him expound on religion. Perhaps he was sceptical in matters of religion. That was my father.' It seems almost as if Fidel resented his father for not sharing his mother's religious faith in his own destiny.

Some accounts by foreign writers claim that Ángel's and Lina's first three offspring – Ángela, Ramón and Fidel – were born out of wedlock during the period when Lina worked as a maid and cook for the household. All three have chosen, not surprisingly, not to discuss this publicly. It is entirely possible that the first wife simply decided to walk out and that the family subsequently let her slip into oblivion (although Pedro Emilio and Lidia went to live with her somewhere, at least for a time).

In any event, Ángel Castro and Lina were married in church after Fidel's birth in a ceremony arranged by Bishop Enrique Pérez Serantes, a friend of the groom and who, many years later, would be instrumental in saving Fidel's life from Batista soldiers. Ángela, Ramón and Fidel were baptized in church afterwards, with the proper surnames of Castro Ruz. There is nothing to suggest that Fidel's alleged illegitimacy has ever caused him the slightest problem in the tolerant Cuban society.

At the time of Ángel Castro's first marriage the two-storey hilltop frame house on piles of the Birán *finca* had already been partly built. It was quite large, with most of the bedroom windows facing the sierras in the south, and with the cattle and the dairy barn under the building. Upon Ángel's arrival in 1899 the village of Birán had had some 530 registered inhabitants, but it was growing rapidly by the time the Castro children were born. Marcané was the nearest town of any importance, having both a school and a doctor. All of this territory lay within the confines of the United Fruit Company empire.

Castro believes that his father built the house on wooden piles with space underneath for cattle and fowl because it was the architectural style of well-off landowners in Galicia; Ángel Castro had been born in a humble one-storey stone house in his Spanish village, and was eager to enjoy the prosperity he had earned through his hard work in the new country. Fidel has saved a photograph of the Galicia house, and he shows it to visitors to underscore his family's early poverty.

When Castro was a child the house was expanded to include an office for his father and later a cow barn was erected some hundred yards from the main building, followed by a small slaughterhouse and a repair shop. In time Ángel Castro built a store and a bakery. Eventually, Castro claims, the tiny post office and the small rural school were the only structures in Birán not belonging to his father. Near the house there was a cockpit where every Sunday during the harvest there were cock fights; Castro tells that 'many humble people spent there their scarce earnings [on betting]; if they lost, nothing was left to them and if they won, they spent it immediately on rum and *fiestas*'.

Manacas, the Castro *finca*, became in time a 26,000-acre domain (1920 acres belonged to Don Ángel and the rest was rented permanently) with some three hundred families living and working on the property. Many of these people were indigent Haitian cane-cutters brought to Cuba from the nearby island of Hispaniola to work the sugarcane fields. The cane was sold by the *finca* of the United Fruit Company's nearby Miranda mill. Don Ángel also grew fruit, raised cattle and owned forests in Pinares de Mayarí where his sawmill processed lumber for sale in big volume. A small nickel mine belonged to him as well (the Bay of Nipe zone is very rich in nickel and other minerals).

Ángel Castro played with gusto the role of the landed Spanish–Cuban patriarch, an imposing figure almost six feet tall, in a wide-brimmed hat covering his completely shaved head. Either his wife or one of his daughters would use a hand-clipper to keep his head hairless and shiny. Until the age of forty he had a beard, then shaved that off, too.

Don Ángel was an incredibly hard worker. Even as a rich man he rose at dawn every day to take breakfast personally to cane-cutters and planters in his fields. On the eve of Christmas and other major holidays he would sit at an outdoor table in front of the warehouse abutting the main residence to distribute vouchers to the workers for feast food as a present from the master. Despite this beneficent aspect the Castro children also remember Don Ángel as a man of an extraordinarily violent temperament, given to unpredictable explosions – traits he passed on in full to his son Fidel.

Chapter 2

Everything about Fidel Castro seems to be controversial, even the exact date of his birth. There has been for years a lively disagreement among writers on Fidel as to whether he was born in 1926 or 1927. The commander-in-chief himself swears that 1926 is the correct year – he once said laughingly that he actually wished he had been born a year later so that 'I would have been an even younger chief of government, thirty-one years old and not thirty-two, when we won the revolution'. Even the Soviet press gave the wrong date in a lengthy biography published in 1963, and the error was maintained in Cuban newspapers reprinting it. This confusion seems to have stemmed from a change made in his school records when he lost three months of classes because of post-append-ectomy complications. In any case, when he was born at 2 a.m. on 13 August, weighing ten pounds, Castro was named after Fidel Pino Santos, a very wealthy Oriente politician and friend of Don Ángel. The origin of the middle name Alejandro has been forgotten, but Fidel has used it as his nom de plume in anti-Batista newspaper articles after the 1952 coup, as his code name in clandestinity, and as his nom de guerre in the Sierra.

Fidel is both dramatic and mystical about the circumstances of his birth. He told Frei Betto, the Brazilian Dominican friar: 'I was born a *guerrillo*, because I was born at night, around two o'clock of the dawn. . . It seems that night might have had an influence in my *guerrilla* spirit in the revolutionary activity.' By the same token, he attached great importance to the number twenty-six in a very Cuban tradition of superstition and spiritism. The year of his birth was 1926, he points out that he was twenty-six years old when he launched his conspiracy against Batista in 1952 (Fidel also notes that fifty-two is the double of twenty-six). The assault on Moncada, the date having been chosen by Castro, was 26 July 1953, and his revolutionary movement became known as the 26th of July Movement. His friends say that Castro often picks the 26th day of the month for major decisions and acts: in 1962, for example, he chose 26 March to deliver a crucial speech that served to destroy the challenge against him by the so-called Sectarians of the Communist Party.

The choice of the first name for the future leader of the revolution was prophetically and politically felicitous: Fidel comes from the Latin word for 'faithful', and has a good, solid ring to it. In a nation where popular leaders are often known and called by their first names and with Castro always orchestrating mass rallies, it is hard to imagine crowds chanting rhythmically the name of, say, Felisberto, Dagoberto or even Ernesto. With *Fidel* he had a phenomenal political head start.

His name is a matter of pride to him, and he remarks: 'I'm entirely in agreement with my name, for faithfulness . . . I have always been a man of faith, confidence and optimism.' Castro also observes that 24 April is the day of his saint – the day of San Fidel – and that this was the date 'of my saint, because there is a saint called San Fidel; even before me there was another saint, I want you to know that'.

The question of whether his parents were married when he was born is not mentioned in Castro's rare and incomplete versions of his childhood, but he has gone to great lengths to make clear that while he was named after Fidel Pino Santos, this local millionaire never actually became his godfather. Confusingly, however, Castro also says that the reason he was not christened until he was five or six years old (he is not certain) was that it had been impossible to bring to Birán both the priest assigned to the region and the very busy Fidel Pino Santos.

Castro has said that because he had not been christened, other children in Birán called him 'the Jew'. Though he did not know at the time what Jew meant, he realized it conveyed a pejorative connotation related to his not having undergone baptism. There is a black-beaked bird in Oriente known as Judío (Jew), and Fidel at one point thought that for some reason he was being called *that*. With his selective memory it is interesting that he remembers so well his trauma as an unchristened child. He was finally christened at the cathedral in Santiago, where he was then living and going to school.

Myth-making official propaganda rejects a portrayal of the Castro family as nouveau riche and of Fidel's father as an uneducated man. Although the truth would not seem incompatible with the Cuban rags-to-riches tradition of generations of immigrants, particularly in the new revolutionary age of the common man, the Castro biography republished in the official newspaper *Revolución* from the Soviet press, which had to obtain its data from Cuba, describes a young Fidel 'spending hours in the company of his father, who tells him the tales of Independence and epic narrations of Troy and other ancient wars and their legendary heroes.' Russian readers may well accept this, but it is entirely improbable. Don Ángel was clearly a man of natural intelligence, interested in politics and public affairs, a careful reader of Havana newspapers to which he subscribed at the *finca* , but he was also a devoted radio listener and, in his old age, a breathless fan of televised wrestling. Overall a person of few words and a no-nonsense mien.

Fidel's childhood appears to have been very pleasant and basically happy, certainly a privileged childhood even by the standards of affluent Cuban landowners of the day. The Castro children seem to have received much love from their parents, despite Ángel's outbursts of violence, and clearly they were spoiled. The seven children of Lina were close despite age gaps, and Juana Castro, the fifth of them, says that Raúl was their mother's favourite (as well as hers) because he was 'tender and loving.' But although there is no question that Fidel was the most assertive, the one who always knew how to get his way, it is difficult to attribute his sense of rebellion to any childhood rejection or a hostile home environment.

Family album photographs show Fidel at the age of three, looking most serious and composed in an elegant little boy's suit with short pants and a jacket with a large round collar. His hair is carefully parted on the right side, and he holds a book in his left hand. His big brown eyes stare hard at the camera. In another picture Fidel sits atop a wall, between his older sister Ángela and brother Ramón who are standing on the ground. Looming over them, he dominates the scene.

At the age of four Fidel entered the public grammar school in Marcané that Ángela and Ramón were already attending. There were fifteen or twenty pupils at what Castro once called a kindergarten, and he had learned to read and write before he was five years old. His parents decided after his fifth birthday that he should transfer to Santiago, the capital of Oriente, to study under the very disciplinarian Marist brothers. As Castro recalls it, his parents simply lost patience with his disorderly behaviour at the Marcané school. It appears that although responding well to acts of kindness and special attention directed at him, from a very young age Castro had to have his way and rejected all form of authority. When he could not have his way he struck back with violence – against his parents, teachers, siblings and playmates.

Fidel's happiest moments were spent outdoors climbing hills, swimming in the Birán river, riding horses and, when he grew a little older, hunting with a shotgun and a pack of four dogs. He was a natural athlete. While still living at the *finca* and then during summer vacations at home from schools in Santiago and Havana, his passion for physical activities conditioned him for the future hardships of guerrilla life in the Sierra.

He learned to shoot with his U-type shotgun, and according to the brief section of his youth in the biography published in *Revolución*, he liked to practise on the *finca's* hens, 'and if one of his sisters threatened to tell their mother on him, he would convince them to shoot, too, so that they couldn't say anything'. The *Revolución* biography further reports that no matter what he did – play, swim, study or work at home – 'he never wants to lose and almost always arranges to win'.

His sisters recall that Fidel once organized a baseball team in Birán, his father having let him order bats, gloves and other equipment (baseball is Cuba's national sport). Characteristically, Fidel's preferred position was that of pitcher, though his very fast ball had little control. And he was a poor sportsman; when his side was not winning, Fidel would simply halt the game and go home. He may have learned this sort of reaction from his father: the sisters remember that one of Don Ángel's favourite games was dominoes, which he played every night with one of his employees or with his wife, but when an argument developed or he was losing, he would grab the board and hurl it to the ground below the verandah where they sat. Then, there would be no domino games for a week or so.

Fidel Castro himself is the foremost authority to the fact that he has always been given to tantrums, devious, manipulative, violent and defiant of all authority. In one of the few autobiographical interviews he has ever granted, in 1959 with Carlos Franqui, then editor of *Revolución*, Castro revealed this complicated personality frankly and at great length. (This conversation has never been published in Cuba).

Fidel says of the Birán school that 'I spent most of my time being fresh . . . I remember that whenever I disagreed with something the teacher said to me, or whenever I got mad, I would swear at her and immediately leave school, running as fast as I could. . . One day, I had just sworn at the teacher, and was racing down the rear corridor. I took a leap and landed on a board from a guava-jelly box with a nail in it. As I fell, the nail somehow stuck in my tongue. When I got back home my mother said to me: "God punished you for swearing at the teacher." I didn't have the slightest doubt that it was really true.' In Castro's self-portrait between the ages of four and six, he acknowledges: 'I had one teacher after another, and my behaviour was different with each one.' He adds: 'With the teacher who treated us well and brought us toys, I remember being well-behaved. But when pressure, force or punishment was used, my conduct was entirely different.'

Fidel's behaviour was presumably tolerated because his father was wealthy and influential in the area. Certainly he recalls that in general 'everyone lavished attention on me, flattered me, and treated me differently from the other boys we played with when we were children'. These other children, he remarks, 'went barefoot while we wore shoes; they were often hungry; at our house there was often a row at table over getting us to eat'.

Fidel Castro has often said that his sense of social consciousness was born at the little country school in Marcané and at the Birán *finca* where he studied and played with the children of the poor. This is substantiated in a lengthy personal letter written by Castro to a woman friend from his prison cell on 24 January 1954, when he was serving the sentence for the Moncada attack: 'My classmates, sons of humble peasants, were very poor. They learned poorly the first letters, and they soon left school, even if they were intelligent. They drowned, then, in a hopeless sea of ignorance and poverty. Today their children will follow them shouldering the burden of social fatalism. I, on the contrary, *could* study, I continued to study. . . Nothing has changed in twenty years. . .'

He is not certain whether he was moved to the school in Santiago 'because I caused too much trouble at home or because my teacher convinced my family that it would be a good thing to send me away'. He and his older sister Ángela travelled by train to Santiago, clear across Oriente to the south coast, and a new phase began in his life. He remembers how 'extraordinary' the big city appeared to him – 'the station with its wooden arches, the hubbub, the people' – and that they went to stay that evening at the home of the sister of the school teacher from Birán and her Haitian husband who soon thereafter would become Fidel's godparents. Fidel recalls: 'I remember that I wet the bed on the first night.'

In this version of his young years as given to Carlos Franqui in 1959 Castro was dispatched to Santiago to be enroled in the Marist brothers' La Salle school, a private establishment for children from affluent families. But in more recent interviews, granted in 1985, a wholly different story emerges. Now Fidel claims that he did not attend school at all during the first two years in Santiago when he lived with his godparents, the Hibberts. Instead, according to this account, his godmother taught him at home, and the studies were confined to memorizing the four arithmetic operations from the back cover of a booklet (he says he did so well that even now he can still add, subtract, multiply and divide as rapidly 'as a computer') and improving his orthography and handwriting; there were no other books in the Hibbert household.

Castro now appears to feel very resentful about that entire period, portraying himself as a victim of a situation mysteriously concocted by his parents and the Hibberts. He used expressions like, 'when they sent me away to Santiago – I was very small – I suffered such need and had so much work. . . I went hungry and I was the target of injustice'. He goes on to complain: 'I was the victim of exploitation by this family that was paid by my parents to have us there.' Yet it is hard to understand *why* Fidel's parents would have allowed such a state of affairs, or why it took his family so long to realize how badly he was treated in Santiago.

Without further explanation Fidel tells of having entered La Salle in his third year in Santiago as a first-grade day student (in the Franqui version he says he was immediately in 'the first grade' at that school) and of having to make up for the lost years. He still lived with the Hibberts, returning home for lunch ('then, there was no more hunger') and enjoying 'having professors, classes, companions with whom to play, and many other activities denied me when I was a lonely student learning arithmetic from the back of a booklet.'

But Fidel was soon unhappy again. His life was 'very dull'. While, for example, boarders at La Salle were taken to the beach or out for walks on Thursdays and Sundays, Fidel as a day student was left behind. He began to despise the Hibberts. As he tells it, he was six or seven years old when he took matters into his own hands, 'engaging in my first rebellion', to compel his godfather to let him be a boarder, too. One day, when Hibbert spanked him for some infraction, Fidel proceeded to 'rebel and insult everybody, disobey all orders, shout, and say all the words that were forbidden'. Castro says: 'I behaved so terribly that they took me straight to the school and enroled me as a boarder; it was a great victory for me.' He was one of thirty boarders; two hundred boys were day students. It cost his father $30 per month.

At La Salle the boys had to observe a strict dress code, wearing suits and ties. Even so, there is a group photograph of the school's second grade with Fidel sitting in the front row, tie loosened, and a look of bored contempt on his face. Yet there is nothing in his recollections to indicate that he felt unhappy being away from his parents at such a young age. He does say: 'On our first holiday we went home for a three-month vacation; I don't think I've ever been happier; we hunted with slingshots, rode horseback, swam in the rivers, and had complete freedom during those months.' But not a word about his family.

When Fidel completed the third grade, his older brother Ramón and his younger brother Raúl joined him at La Salle, where a special grade was created for the three of them to be together – incongruous, surely, since Ramón was ten, Fidel was eight and Raúl was four. Castro explains that it was made possible because the family was rich.

His stay at the Marist school was punctuated by battles for his rights, and Castro goes out of his way to draw a picture of himself as an uncompromising and violent boy. He recalls, for example, beating up a schoolmate – the teacher-priest's 'pet' – in a fight that followed a boat-ride argument. That evening the priest summoned Fidel away during a solemn chapel service to ask him what had happened and, without awaiting an explanation, 'gave me a slap that just about numbed one side of my face. . . I spun round, and he slapped my other cheek. . . When he let go I was in a complete daze, I felt painfully humiliated.' Castro continues: 'I promised myself never to let it happen again. We were playing ball one day, and I was with somebody when the priest came up to me from behind and hit me on the head. This time I turned on him, then and there, and started to hit him with my fists and bite him. I don't think I hurt the priest much, but the daring outburst became a historic event in school.'

In what Fidel calls 'a decisive moment in my life' Ángel Castro decided during the boys' summer holidays after the fourth grade that they would not go back to school. The father had not only received reports from La Salle that his three sons did not study and 'were the three biggest bullies who had ever gone there' (Fidel says it was 'an unfair report but they believed it at home'), but he had also discovered that they cheated by obtaining solutions to math problems from an answer book.

Ramón Castro was delighted to end his formal education because he preferred his life in Birán, the fields, the animals, the farm machines. Little Raúl, unable to speak up for himself, 'was packed off to a military school run by a sergeant who gave him a very hard time'. As for Fidel, he was determined to go to school. As he tells the story, 'I remember going to Mother and explaining that I wanted to go on studying; it wasn't fair not to let me go to school. I appealed to her and told her that if I wasn't sent to school I'd set fire to the house. . . So they decided to send me. I'm not sure if they were afraid or just sorry for me, but my mother pleaded my case.'

Fidel was learning quickly that uncompromising stubbornness was a powerful weapon. This may have been the most important lesson he drew from his young years at the *finca* and at the Santiago schools, and he never forgot it. Now, having in effect blackmailed himself back to school, Castro was enroled at the age of nine in the fifth grade of the much better Dolores boys' school in the centre of the city. It marked the beginning of his Jesuit education, one of the most significant influences in his life. Fidel says that Dolores 'was a school that set very high standards; I had trouble keeping up'. He claims also that he had changed schools at his own demand, refusing to stay at La Salle after the teacher had slapped him.

Fidel was receiving from Birán a twenty-cent weekly allowance, spending ten cents on Sunday movies, five cents for ice cream afterwards and five cents for the comic book *El Gorrión – The Sparrow* – which he bought on Thursdays. But his allowance was cut off if he failed to get the highest marks. Therefore, 'I decided to take steps to protect my interests.'

He did so by informing his teachers that he had lost the report card with his marks, so he was given another one. 'From then on,' Fidel says, 'I would put my own grades in the old book and take that one home to be signed – with very good grades on it, of course'. At that time he seems to have begun cultivating a more angelic demeanour so that he must have been above all suspicion. A photograph from that time shows him with a half-smile at the camera as he sits on a wooden bench at the long school dining table. He wears the Dolores uniform of white trousers, dark blue jacket, shirt and tie, and a white Sam Browne belt; the Jesuits favoured a military atmosphere, and there was even a band with which, as another photograph shows, Fidel marched under a Cuban flag and a Dolores pennant.

But again, he found himself a day student, staying with a merchant's family he deeply disliked; his sister Ángela, attending a girls' school in Santiago, was his only friend in the hostile house.

After turning ten, Castro developed appendicitis, eventually spending three months at the Colonia Española Hospital in Santiago when the scar would not heal properly. But, as usual, he used the time well, and he enjoys recounting the experience: 'I made friends with all the other patients. I am telling this because I think it shows I already had an ability to relate to other people; I had a streak of the politician. When I wasn't reading comic books, I spent my time visiting other patients. . . I had been impressed by operations like the one I'd been through. . . Some people thought I might make a good doctor, because I used to play with a Gillette razor blade, and "operate" on lizards – lizards that usually died, of course. Then I would enjoy watching how the ants carried them off, how hundreds of ants working together could carry the lizard and move it to their heap.'

Back at school there was a black woman teacher, known as Professor Danger. She had been tutoring his sister and saw great potential in him. Fidel says that he never had 'a guide who would help' him in his youthful rebellions but 'that black professor in Santiago was the nearest to being a preceptor'. She was, Castro adds, 'the first person I knew who stimulated me, who gave me a goal, who was able to make me enthusiastic about studying'.

Back at the merchant's home, Fidel, now in the sixth grade, was increasingly resentful. For one thing, he was angry that when he came home from school he was shut up in a room for hours to study 'when all any boy wants is . . . do nothing, listen to the radio or go out'. So he refused to work, letting instead his imagination 'fly off to events in history, and to wars'. Castro says that he liked history 'very much, and particularly the stories of battles. . . I even used to invent battles.' The hours he was locked up, he recalls, 'were a kind of military training. . . I'd start off by taking a lot of little scraps and tiny balls of paper, arranging them on a playing board and setting up an obstacle to see how many would pass, and how many wouldn't. There were losses, casualties. I played this game of wars for hours at a time.' Finally, when he could not stand his guardian's home any longer, he told the merchant's family 'all to go to the devil', and became a boarder at Dolores that same afternoon. Fidel does not explain whether his parents had any say in it. He was then barely eleven years old, yet he says that 'from then on I became my own master and took charge of all my own problems without advice from anyone. . . I played soccer, basketball, jai alai, all kinds of sports. All my energy went into them.' He explains that 'I suffered from my teachers' lack of even the most elementary understanding of the psychology of educating boys', but that 'I'm not blaming my parents, who were ignorant people without a proper education; they left us in the hands of others they believed were treating us properly, but we had a hard time of it'.

It would appear that Castro's view of his parents was principally one of contempt. Still, he went on for years using them to his advantage, accepting financial aid from them even as late as the preparations for the *Granma* invasion in 1956. Although his sister Juana believes that Fidel respected his father, very clearly there was no warmth between them. Fidel's threat at the age of nine to burn down the house if he were not allowed to return to school was probably his first major confrontation with Don Ángel. But by the age of thirteen, while his father paid the Dolores bills, Fidel was using the summer vacations not only to drive the *finca* tractors (one of his preferred pastimes), but also to try to organize the sugar workers against him. At eighteen, studying at an expensive Jesuit college in Havana, he fought with his father repeatedly over the family's 'capitalism', accusing him of 'abusing' the workers 'with false promises'.

The last time Fidel saw his father was early in 1953, before Moncada. He was in Mexico when Don Ángel died from a ruptured hernia in October 1956. A person who has known Fidel Castro from childhood says that he had 'no tenderness for anybody, not even for his wife', and that he is 'a passionate but not a caring or tender man, living outside all human problems except his own'. But this is a very harsh judgement, and it is not necessarily borne out by other accounts of Fidel's behaviour.

In the sixth grade at the Dolores school, Fidel was joined by Ramon and Raúl, their father having again changed his mind about educating all his sons. Raúl, who hated school, remembers: 'For me, it was a prison. School for me, it was prayer, the necktie, the fear of God. But what really killed me was the prayer. We prayed from morning till night. But Fidel was different. He dominated situations. He succeeded in everything. In sports, in studies. And, every day, he would fight. He had a very explosive character. He challenged the biggest and the strongest ones, and when he was beaten, he started it all over again the next day. He would never quit.'

Juan Rovira, who was Fidel's classmate at Dolores (and is now an exile in Miami), recalls him as a sports hero and a student with a phenomenal memory. Rovira says: 'Everybody was very enthusiastic about Fidel when there was a basketball game with La Salle, or when there was a track meet, because he ran so well. His athletic abilities were fantastic. When it came to work Fidel didn't stand out so much, but when the exams came, he studied a lot. Boarders were allowed to rise early, at four o'clock in the morning, to study. Besides, he had a prodigious memory – he wrote down everything exactly the way he had read it, and it looked as if he had copied it, but he had it all engraved in his memory. And so he got good grades.'

Castro's familiarity with mountains first came when he was at Dolores. The boys were taken on outings by school bus to climb mountains, sometimes to El Cobre, to Gran Piedra, or even the foothills of Sierra Maestra. Fidel recalls that 'I also loved to take off along the rivers when they were swollen, cross them, and hike awhile before coming back. The bus always had to wait for me. . . I did not imagine that mountains would one day play such an important role in my life!'

His determination to distinguish himself knew no limits. When a Santiago radio station sponsored a poetry contest, with parents requested to vote for the best poem, Castro entered. José Martí, his hero, had been a great poet, but this was a gift which Fidel totally lacked. He admits that in the contest his poems 'weren't the best, but I had made friends with all the boys. . . Almost all the kids asked their parents to vote for me; as a result, letters were sent in . . . that went something like this, "Elpidio's poem to mothers is very beautiful and very touching, but our vote goes to Fidel. . ."'

Chapter 3

On an October morning in 1941 Fidel Castro's knees were shaking, and he was perspiring profusely from nervous tension. Now sixteen years old, he was standing before Father José Rubinos, the director of the Avellaneda Literary Academy, to deliver from memory a ten-minute speech that would mark the birth of his professional political life.

If it pleased the demanding Father Rubinos, the speech would mean acceptance in the academy, the school of oratory at Belén College, an exclusive Jesuit high and preparatory school in Havana. He had turned sixteen in August, vacationing in Birán after completing the four years at Dolores, and had persuaded his parents to let him attend Belén because he regarded it as the best school in the country. It was also 'a centre of great prestige for the cream of the cream of Cuban aristocracy and bour-geoisie'. Castro always knew what was good for him.

Studying in Havana and leaving behind the provinciality of Oriente was a tremendous step towards a professional career, Fidel being the first in his family to be given such an opportunity. Belén, above all, was the road to the university, Castro's next planned move. It was his first time in Havana, and the bustling, cosmopolitan, vital, sensual and explosively loud capital city on the north coast, ever-mysterious in its promise of ideas and experiences, was a totally new world to the gangling and still rough-cut youth from the sugarcane countryside. Fidel arrived by train from Santiago, with 'a lot of money to buy clothes and other articles . . . and to pay tuition, purchase books . . . and for other expenses'. Tuition and board cost $50 monthly which, Castro says, was 'very cheap', considering Belén's ample facilities, but out of reach for the children, for example, of a school teacher whose salary was $75 a month.

Fidel did not know a soul in the city, but inevitably he was determined to make his mark as soon as possible. José Ignácio Rasco, his schoolmate at Belén and later at Havana University, recalls that on that October day at Avellaneda Academy, Castro 'was desperate because he worried that his nerves wouldn't let him pass the all-important test'. In the end, however, Castro was able to satisfy Father Rubinos and was accepted into the academy. Nobody remembers what he actually said, but the test (it was elective, not compulsory) was another victory over himself. In Cuba one cannot succeed politically without being a first-rate public speaker, and already at the age of sixteen Fidel was overwhelmingly attracted by the craft of politics and power – little as he knew about it.

Castro is recognized today as one of the great orators of his time, yet Rasco (who has lived in exile in Miami since 1980, having broken with Castro soon after the revolution over the issue of Communism) remembers that before delivering his first public speech as a university student five years after the agony of Avellaneda, Fidel had spent a week at his house, writing, rewriting and memorizing the address before practising his delivery in front of a mirror.

In Fidel Castro, astounding tenacity accompanied the timidity. Rasco emphasizes that as a student Fidel had immense powers of concentration as well as his phenomenal memory working for him. Frequently, distracted by other matters that interested him more, he would fall behind in his studies – then recover spectacularly.

Castro's tenacity was physical as well. Fidel had made up his mind to be Belén's best baseball pitcher, but because he had a muscle problem in his throwing arm, he practised sometimes until eight o'clock in the evening at the school's sports grounds, long after the catcher had tired and left. Rasco tells the story of Fidel bragging one day that he could succeed in anything he wanted to do, and when challenged by a student named Cabella, he bet him that he could hurl himself on a bicycle, head first, against a brick wall. Not surprisingly, he was knocked out by the impact, and he had to spend three days recovering at the school's infirmary.

During the four years Castro spent at Belén, he was by far the outstanding athlete. As several of his former schoolmates point out, however, Fidel was principally a solo rather than a team player. He was a track star, a table tennis champion, a pitcher in baseball and, as he explains it now, a 'thinker' in basketball – the de facto team captain.

Enrique Ovares who knew Castro very well at the university because of their many common political involvements, says that the Belén basketball team 'became famous because Fidel made famous everything he touched'. Ovares, an architect who now lives in exile in Florida, cannot be accused of being a Castro propagandist: he spent seven years in a Cuban prison after 1960 for anti-revolutionary plots. He reminisces that Castro's dedication was so great that 'he went to all the practice sessions, and if it was required to shoot fifty baskets, Fidel would shoot a hundred'.

Fidel also maintained his love for mountain-hiking, and he says that after the first outings by the Belén boy-scout troop 'the teachers determined that I was outstanding, and they kept promoting me until one day they made me the chief of the school's boy scouts, "the general of the explorers", as they called it'. He remembers organizing and leading an expedition to climb Guajaibon Peak, the tallest mountain in western Cuba, taking five days instead of the scheduled three because the ascent was so difficult.

In the context of Cuban society in the 1940s both the politically conservative, long-established rich families and those who had just acquired wealth – such as Spanish immigrants – were expected to send their sons to Jesuit schools. This was not necessarily because Catholicism was deeply engrained in them but rather because these were the best educational establishments. To attend a Jesuit school carried a social and snob cachet as well – girls from good families went to convent schools like the Sacred Heart or the Ursuline Sisters.

Affluent but liberal parents preferred non-religious private schooling for their offspring, often military academies for the boys. Middle-class or poorer families' children attended schools known as *institutos*, or technical and vocational schools. Peasants and other truly poor Cubans seldom could send their sons (much less daughters) to study beyond local grade school. In this sense, social stratification in Cuba was established in childhood and children on all levels knew instantly their place in society. For the now rich Castro family it was logical for the sons to go first to Dolores in Santiago, then to Belén in Havana.

Even though his family had accumulated wealth, however, Fidel Castro is eager to avoid any impression that he came from an aristocratic or upper-class bourgeois background. He makes the accurate observation that in privileged schools like Belén the students were divided into two groups – 'not so much by money, although money was the basic fact, but by social category, the homes where they lived, the traditions'.

He remarks that while the Castro's perhaps had adequate resources to rise socially, they never did so because they lived in the country rather than the town: 'We lived there among the people, among very humble workers . . . where animals were under the house, the cows, the pigs, the chickens and all that.' Fidel may be exaggerating the simplicity of his origins, but he is correct in portraying the status of Cuban rural class culture.

It is striking that so many years after his victorious socialist revolution and his supposed evolution into a fully fledged Marxist–Leninist, Castro still finds it necessary to engage in essentially gratuitous protestations about his social origins. He is defensive about his parents' affluence, offering the disclaimers that they 'worked every day under hard conditions' and had 'no social life', even though he willingly accepted parental financial support well into adulthood. Clearly he is determined to erase any suspicion that a bourgeois taint might lurk somewhere in his background. In any event, 'bourgeois' is an obscene word in Castro's lexicon, a word he almost fears, and it is a theme to which he constantly returns.

As the leading educational centre of the Cuban establishment elite, Belén was located on a large tract of land in the mainly residential Alturas de Belén (Bethlehem Heights) district of Havana, off Fifty-first Avenue. The school had originally functioned in cramped quarters in Old Havana, but the new building had comfortable accommodation for its 200 boarders (out of a total of 1000 students), several baseball and basketball fields and courts, a running track and even a swimming pool. After the revolution Belén was turned into the Military Technical Institute, a university-level technological centre for the armed forces in which Fidel's old room remains unchanged as a shrine-like showplace maintained by the Museum of the Revolution.

Discipline at Belén was strict, but Castro seemed to have no problems with it. The boys wore uniforms, were awakened at 6.30 to attend Mass at 7 (Mass and prayer and periodic religious three-day retreats were the only aspect of Belén life which Fidel now says he disliked), then breakfast, and classroom. Castro was given the responsibility for the main reading room where pupils studied between dinner and bedtime: he had to make sure that windows and doors were locked and lights turned off after the study period, but he often stayed on alone for hours to read for exams.

Castro tells that he made 'many friendships' with fellow students, and that 'without realizing it, or trying for it, I began to acquire popularity among them as a sportsman, athlete, explorer, mountain-climber, and as a person who, after all, had good grades'. He also says that 'perhaps during that time, some unconscious political qualities were emerging' in him. They must have been very unconscious indeed, since Fidel never developed political or any other following at the school and no Belén companion of his ever joined in Castro's later revolutionary activities.

Fidel and the other boarders were allowed to go out on weekends if they had relatives in Havana or were invited to friends' homes. But Castro seems to have rated few such invitations. His father was relatively rich yet in class-conscious Cuban society this did not automatically grant him entrée in old-money Havana circles, and behind his back he was occasionally called guajiro (peasant).

In his third year at Belén, Fidel, then age eighteen, was proclaimed Cuba's 'outstanding collegiate athlete', but in the classroom he did well only in the subjects that interested him: Spanish, history, geography and agriculture. Curiously, Fidel was fascinated by the Bible: the story of Moses, the crossing of the Red Sea, the Promised Land and 'all the wars and battles'. He says: 'I think it was in sacred history that I first heard about war, that is, I acquired an interest in military arts. . . It interested me fabulously, from the destructions of the walls of Jericho by Joshua . . . to Samson and his Herculean strength capable of tearing down a temple with his own hands. . . Jonah, the whale that swallowed him, the punishment of Babylon, the Prophet Daniel, they were marvellous stories.' Then, he says, came the New Testament where 'the whole process of the death and crucifixion of Christ . . . produced an undeniable impact both on the child and on the youth'.

At the same time, however, Castro also remembers his education in sinister terms: in a 1961 speech, he said, 'I lost many years of my life in obscurantism, superstition and lies.' Again, this is how Castro goes on re-creating his own myth.

Fidel Castro's stay at Belén – autumn of 1941 to spring of 1945 – straddled the Second World War and coincided with Fulgencio Batista's first presidency over Cuba. This former army sergeant, for seven years the power behind the throne in Cuba as the country's military chief, now emerged as a democratic leader.

Batista's political career began on 4 September 1933, when he led a coup by army non-commissioned officers to establish the armed forces as the conservative arbiter in Cuban politics.

The crisis of the 1930s in Cuba stemmed from the move by President Machado, initially supported by the United States, to prolong his four-year term in office by another five years. First elected in 1926, two years later Machado organized a phony election with himself as the only candidate receiving a new term to run from 1929 to 1935. Machado's manoeuvre triggered a violent five years of opposition, bringing together revolution-minded students, the young Communist Party, and moderate traditional political leaders. The United States ignored this state of affairs almost until the end, even though the Platt Amendment was still in force and Washington could have legally intervened. But so long as their economic interests were not in jeopardy, the United States paid no attention.

Starting a tradition that Fidel Castro would continue a quarter of a century later, revolutionary students and young professionals along with worker and peasant leaders formed the spearhead of the anti-dictatorial movement. From the university sprang the Student Directorate, which would be reborn during the Castro revolution, and the militant youth of the day became known as the Generation of 1930, profoundly national-istic and social-justice conscious. The anti-Machado struggle produced its heroes and martyrs: in January 1929 Julio Antonio Mella, a student leader and Secretary General of the illegal Cuban Communist Party, was assassinated in Mexico by agents of the dictatorship; in September 1930 the police killed Student Directorate leader Rafael Trejo during an anti-

Machado street demonstration. From thereon, Cuba was plunged into virtually permanent violence.

Only in 1933, when American businessmen and investors finally became concerned about the Cuban economy and their stake in it, did the United States government awake to the island crisis. President Roosevelt dispatched Benjamin Sumner Welles, his top diplomat in Latin America, to mediate between the Machado regime and the opposition groups. Protesting against the belated Welles effort, however, the Directorate and its allies saw in the anti-Machado battle the opportunity to bestow on Cuba real independence, free her of American influence, and to put into practice Martí's original teachings of freedom and justice. Thus Martí was the model and hero of the revolutionaries even back in the 1930s, a fact that goes far to explain subsequent Cuban history.

Machado was forced to resign on 12 August 1933 under the pressure of a revolutionary general strike on one hand and United States demands on the other. The strike was successful despite a last-minute decision by the Communist Party to withdraw its support on the unconvincing grounds that the strike might lead to an armed United States intervention and a patched-together agreement between the Party and Machado. The Communists, who seemed to have forgotten Mella's murder, were too late to save Machado, but this incident provided the first example of the extraordinary political flexibility of the Cuban Communist Party – if not necessarily of its wisdom.

Acting on Welles's advice, the traditional political parties and the army joined in handing the presidency to Carlos Manuel de Céspedes, whose father had led the first Independence War in 1868. But the Student Directorate and other radical groups, desiring a fully fledged revolution, were not satisfied with the simple disappearance of Machado. This is where Fulgencio Batista, the stenographer-sergeant, entered the scene. Non-commissioned officers headed by Batista rebelled against the army command on the night of 4 September, taking over power in Cuba in order to hand it to a five-man civilian commission named by the Student Directorate. President Céspedes had lasted three weeks.

The new president was Dr Ramón Grau San Martín, a professor of physiology and the idol of the students after his arrest, along with other university professors, by the Machado regime in 1931; they had been charged with sedition. Grau lacked political and administrative experience, but he was fully in tune with the rising wave of nationalism and radicalism among Cuban youth. As Jaime Suchlicki, an exiled Cuban historian, wrote about those intoxicating days, 'with Grau, the Generation of 1930 was catapulted into power' and the 'students held Cuba's destiny in their hands'. The guiding spirit in this revolution was Antonio Guiteras, twenty-five-year-old Interior Minister, who pushed for social and economic reform, and the abrogation of the Platt Amendment.

While the Communist Party now backed the government, it did not dominate it, and neither Grau nor Guiteras approved of the establishment of soviets in the sugar mills by Communist workers.

Nevertheless this was a situation the United States would not tolerate and the Cubans were reminded once more that nothing could be set in motion on the island without American blessing. This applied particularly to the Grau reforms. In discreet contact with Fulgencio Batista and his military commanders, the United States pushed for Grau's overthrow. Washington had never recognized the Grau regime, and early in January 1934 thirty US Navy warships encircled Cuba, sending a clear signal that no more Cuban nonsense would be permitted – and that the marines were ready to land. The Grau revolution had lived for 100 days. On 14 January Batista's army ousted Grau, Carlos Mendieta became the provisional president, instantly recognized by the United States, and from then on Cuba was run by a succession of five stooge presidents manipulated by Batista – until he was ready to run for president himself in 1940. Two years after Grau's fall Antonio Guiteras was killed by the police when he attempted to flee Cuba after failing to launch a fresh revolutionary movement. Together with the Communist leader Julio Antonio Mella, Guiteras came to symbolize the Generation of 1930 for the contemporaries of Fidel Castro. And Batista symbolized all the evils of the past.

Batista's presidency was a crucial period for Cuba. Nevertheless, Fidel was a totally apolitical student up to the time of his graduation from Belén shortly before his nineteenth birthday. As a teenager he had written a letter to President Roosevelt congratulating him on his 1940 re-election, declaring his support for democracy and his opposition to Nazism, and asking for a twenty-dollar bill. Fidel may have simply hoped for a signed reply from FDR, but all he received was a note of thanks from the Department of State and an expression of regret that the money could not be sent.

Although Castro's concern for social justice may well have been awakened when he was a youth among the poor peasantry of Birán, there was certainly nothing in the environment of his Jesuit college to encourage it. In fact Belén was the intellectual centre for the preparation of Cuba's future right-wing leaders. Most of the teachers were Spanish priests of extreme rightist persuasion, having come to Cuba after the end of the Spanish Civil War in 1939 and the victory of the Franco Nationalists. Often they represented the strain of Spanish anti-American nationalism and neither forgave nor forgot that the United States had wrested the island away from Spain in 1898. And, of course, right-wing and left-wing nationalisms and populisms tend to blur.

Castro himself has little to say about the Belén faculty politically apart from observing that without exception the teachers' ideology was 'rightist, Francoist, reactionary', and that at that time there were no 'leftist' Jesuits in Cuba. He remembers that at Belén Communism was considered 'a very bad thing', but, although he observed the rightist philosophy of his professors, 'I didn't question it much; I was in sports. . . I tried to advance my studies.'

Coexisting with rigidly rightist Spanish Jesuit teachings at Belén were groups favouring liberal Christian social trends in Cuban politics (now they would be described as Christian Democrats), and these groups made serious efforts to attract the apolitical Fidel Castro. José Ignácio Rasco, who launched a fully-fledged Christian Democratic movement in Cuba in the 1950s, believes that Fidel stayed away from such groups only while he still harboured his Roman Catholic faith. He thinks Castro lost his faith suddenly at the university.

Rasco's version is naïve, and Fidel must be believed when he says that he never had religious faith. Later, he declares, 'I had another type of values: a political belief, a political faith that I had to forge alone through my experiences, my reasoning and my emotions.' But it sounds like mere self-aggrandizement when he says that 'nobody inculcated me with political ideas . . . unhappily, I had to be my own teacher all my life.'

Castro's Belén schoolmates who remember him the best are convinced that from the outset the Jesuits had an eye on him as a leader to be formed by them, and then to have a great destiny in Cuban politics. Father Rubinos, the head of the oratory academy who was regarded as the ideologue of Belén, centred his attention on Fidel as the most intelligent student in the college, the best athlete and the leading outdoorsman. In the end the Jesuits failed to mould him; Castro is grateful for their intellectual influence, but contemptuous of their efforts to bring him into the fold.

Twenty years earlier the Jesuits had the same plans for Eduardo (Eddy) Chibás, the son of an Oriente millionaire, and a Dolores and Belén student of extraordinary promise. Instead Chibás took the revolutionary role in Cuban politics, first against the Machado dictatorship, then against the corrupt Batista-manipulated puppet presidents of the 1930s and Cuba's quasi colonial status. By the time Fidel Castro reached Belén, Eddy Chibás had become a famous opposition politician and the nearest figure in the young Cuban history to the incorruptible José Martí. In the years to come, Chibás would be Castro's political mentor and protector – and Castro his worthy successor. In its own fashion Belén was the school of great Cuban leaders.

Though Cuba was enjoying the first period of even reasonably represent-ative democracy in its history, vested economic interests and corruption continued to exist, and the country still could not risk antagonizing the

United States and the American investors. The Platt Amendment had been abridged after the fall of the Grau regime in 1934, but the 'empire' as Martí called it, had not relinquished its decisive voice in Cuban affairs.

In any case Fulgencio Batista was a constitutional president, governing with the backing of the armed forces, and conservatives, and the Communists – an unprecedented coalition. There was an elected congress where all voices could be heard, and there was a free press. In 1940 elections were entirely clean, and Cubans hoped that, finally, a new era had dawned. It was Batista himself who proposed the free elections, preferring to be president in name as well as in fact after seven years of ruling Cuba from behind the scenes in Camp Columbia, the Havana military headquarters. Unquestionably the struggle between Britain and Germany for the survival of democracy in the world, even though the United States was not yet formally in the war, was crucial to Batista's decision to act in a democratic fashion. And in the meantime the former sergeant had succeeded in becoming a very rich man.

To win the presidency Batista defeated Ramón Grau San Martín whom he had forcibly overthrown in 1934. But this time Grau was no longer the radical professor. He had reverted to the classical model of Cuban presidents and politicians whose overwhelming interest was pomp and wealth. Batista, on the other hand, chose to present himself as a candidate with advanced social and economic ideas, earning the leftist support Grau once had.

Batista's election to the presidency followed the drafting of a new Cuban constitution early in 1940. The constituent assembly that produced it had been freely chosen in probably the first such exercise of the vote in the history of the republic. This constitution was remarkably progressive by Cuban and Latin American standards of the day, including clauses proscribing latifundia and thus opening doors to an agrarian reform (which Fidel Castro would in fact institute twenty years later), establishing new social welfare provisions, and limiting the presidency based on democratic elections to a single four-year term.

The behaviour of the Communist Party at this juncture is extremely important not only historically but in the context of future revolutionary developments in Cuba and of Fidel Castro's complex relations with the Communists. In fact, the seeds of Communist Cuba were planted in 1940 when Castro was still at Dolores College in Santiago, and the men with whom he would form his alliance after the 1959 revolution were already seasoned organizers and politicians.

Cuban Communism has deep roots. A Communist Republic of Cuban Soviets was formed in Havana in August 1920, by a handful of admirers of the Russian revolution of 1917, but obviously it was no more than a gesture. In 1922 a Communist Association was organized in Havana by Carlos Baliño, then seventy-four years old and a remarkable figure in

Cuban history who had been an associate of José Martí in the Cuban Revolutionary Party in New York (he lived as a worker in the United States much of his life), was the founder of the Socialist Workers' Party in 1904, and was probably the first serious Cuban Communist militant.

Communist Associations appeared throughout Cuba, and in August 1925 Baliño and several others called a congress to give birth to the Cuban Communist Party. The party was founded by the seventeen delegates attending the congress, including Baliño, Julio Antonio Mella (a student leader), and Fábio (Abraham) Grobart, a Polish-born apprentice tailor in his early twenties who had arrived in Cuba three years earlier – speaking only Yiddish – to escape the persecution of Communists in his homeland. In 1986 Grobart, well into his eighties, was the only surviving founder of the party, a superbly lucid politician and a treasure trove of Cuban Communist lore. He had tears in his eyes when Fidel Castro awarded him a medal on the sixtieth anniversary of the party's foundation; at the party's Third Congress in February 1986 it was Grobart who introduced Castro to the delegates.

Though illegal, the Cuban Communist Party functioned in a brilliant and disciplined fashion, its influence vastly exceeding its numbers. Intellectuals, artists and labour leaders formed the backbone, making it possible for the Communists to occupy key positions in national life. Rubén Martínez Villena, one of the leading Cuban poets of this century, was an early party leader; there was general public mourning when he died after an illness while still young. Among party militants and sympathizers was the outstanding painter Wilfredo Lam; poets and writers Nicolás Guillén (in 1985 still president of the official Writers' Union though in his eighties), Alejo Carpentier (a distinguished Cuban novelist who died after the revolution), Juan Marinello (who was the party's president in the 1940s and a member of Castro's Politburo in the 1970s), Raúl Roa Garcia (who served until his death as Castro's fire-breathing foreign minister), Pablo de la Torriente Brau, and Emilio Roig de Leushenring; and the leading Cuban economists Jacinto Torras and Raúl Cepero Bonilla. In truth there were few creative personalities in Cuba since the 1930s who were not of the left, or the extreme left.

Communist leaders, not always admitting to their political persuasion, have dominated the powerful Cuban labour unions since the early 1930s, organizing political strikes and exercising a considerable influence on the economy. Following the directive issued in Moscow by the Seventh Conference of the Communist International (Comintern) the Cuban party adopted the policy of cooperation with non-Communist parties in 'popular fronts'. In Cuba this meant collaboration with Fulgencio Batista.

In a move that Fidel Castro may have found inspiring many years later, early in 1938 the Communists first created the Revolutionary Union

Party (PUR) to serve as a legal front for some of their activities while the illegal party continued its own clandestine operations. The PUR then helped to organize the Popular Revolutionary Block (BRP) with other opposition parties arrayed against the candidacy of ex-President Grau, promising their support to Batista in the 1940 elections. Straight-facedly, the Communist Party's central committee announced in mid-July of 1938 that Batista was no longer 'the centre of reaction' and that all efforts should be made to force him to keep 'progressive' promises.

This was a neat piece of political footwork, as a result of which the government of President Federico Laredo Brú (a Batista puppet), aware of the Communist strength in the labour union, rushed to nail down the party's support by legalizing it in September 1938, thereby ending the thirteen years of its illegal existence. The Communists stayed with Batista, continuing to build up their power. In January 1939 they merged the PUR with the real Communist Party to produce the Communist Revolutionary Union Party (PURC), and launched the Cuban Workers' Confederation representing, a half-million workers, under Communist leadership. In 1959 and 1960 Fidel Castro, working with the same Communist leaders, imitated this twin manoeuvre when he proceeded to unite all the revolutionary groups and to join with the Communists in controlling the labour confederation.

When Cubans voted for the Constituent Assembly in 1940 the Communist Party had only 90,000 members, and was able to win only six seats. The six Communist representatives succeeded, however, in attracting a disproportionate amount of attention by submitting their own draft constitution emphasizing the 'anti-imperialist' struggle (for propaganda purposes, never expecting their proposals to be adopted), and by persuading the assembly to allow radio broadcasts of their sessions. Thus Communists won access to the nationwide audience, another lesson that would not be lost on Fidel Castro.

In the presidential elections the Communists rode in on Batista's triumph, winning ten seats in the Chamber of Deputies, eighty municipal assemblymen throughout the island, and the mayoralty of the town of Manzanillo in Oriente – the first time Cuba had had a Communist mayor. The party justified its support for Batista by stressing the importance of his commitment to a liberal constitution and his programme of building schools, hospitals and roads. But party discipline prevailed – as it would prevail again and again in the future.

Batista naturally welcomed Communist support because of the party's power in organized labour, and this alliance became even smoother after the Nazis invaded the Soviet Union in 1941 and the Russians became the allies of the western democracies. Batista established diplomatic relations with Moscow and gave Juan Marinello, the party president, a seat in the cabinet; subsequently Carlos Rafael Rodríguez, the party's chief intellectual and now Fidel Castro's closest adviser, took that cabinet seat.

Marinello's and Rodríguez's membership in the Batista cabinet does not appear in official post-revolutionary histories of the Communist Party (though Fábio Grobart, the octogenarian party founder and a man of great intellectual honesty, mentions it in a monograph on Marinello). Fidel Castro says in one of his accounts of contemporary Cuban history only that the Communist Party 'had a certain influence' in the Batista government. Cuban political memories are, indeed, selective. Both the party's pro-Batista phase and its role in the revolution when it refused to go along with the *Fidelista* vision of history are very lightly passed over.

Acting on Moscow instructions in 1944 the Communists engaged in still another 'tactical manoeuvre'. With the end of the Batista term and the rise in anti-Communist sentiment the party changed its name to the Socialist Popular Party (PSP), thus doing away with the uncomfortable word, 'Communist'. Although the PSP delivered twice as many votes in 1944 as in 1940 it could not prevent Ramón Grau's election. Marinello, however, was elected to the Senate and the party retained its hold on the labour confederation through the presidency of Lázaro Peña, a member of the PSP leadership. Generally, however, Cuban workers elected Communists as their leaders not because of Peña's and the others' ideology but because of the high quality of their union performance. And after 1944 the Communists as a whole came under growing pressure in Cuba.

As part of the war effort, Batista's Cuba had granted military bases to the United States, (in addition to the big Guantánamo naval base in Oriente secured in 1902), emphasizing once more the island's immense strategic importance. Batista also agreed to the sale of Cuba's entire 1941 sugar crop to America for less than three cents a pound, a very low price. Like so many thoughtless American policies towards Cuba, this was one more reason for resentments to rise among the new generation. At Havana University, for example, an 'Anti-Imperialist League' was organized even before the war ended, not because of any specific American acts, but on general principle.

Economic relationships between the two countries were regulated by the 1934 Reciprocal Trade Agreement, which gave the United States total control over the insular market. The agreement was the quid pro quo for the abrogation by the Roosevelt administration of the already embarrassing Platt Amendment of 1902. Although both moves in fact stemmed directly from the overthrow of the threateningly radical first Grau regime by the Batista army, as far as most thinking Cubans were concerned Cuba still had to live with its 'historical fatalism', the feeling that Cubans could never do anything with their own country without North American approval.

The extent to which the adolescent Fidel Castro was aware of all these Cuban political pressures is most uncertain. There is nothing in the record and nothing in the recollections of his former teachers and fellow students to suggest the slightest curiosity on Fidel's part in Cuban and world politics. In fact, Castro would say later that he was a political illiterate until he entered university.

In any case, Belén gave Fidel Castro an extraordinary send-off. The basketball coach and teacher Father Francisco Barbeito wrote in the school's year book: 'Always Fidel distinguished himself in all the subjects related to letters. He was *excelencia* [in the top ten of the graduating class] and *congregante* [a student who regularly attended prayers and religious activities] and a true athlete, always defending the banner of the *Colégio* with pride and valour. He has known how to win the admiration and affection of all. He will make law his career, and we do not doubt that he will fill with brilliant pages the book of his life.'

Castro may not have been number one in the graduating class, but it is remembered that he received the biggest and warmest ovation from his fellow students when he was handed his diploma. The life of Fidel Castro would progress from ovation to ovation.

Chapter 4

If, as he says, Fidel Castro was politically illiterate before he entered university, his literacy in this field developed with lightning speed. Enroling in October 1945 in Havana University's Law School (a student then entered directly the faculty from which he hoped to graduate in his chosen profession), Castro almost immediately plunged into politics. He had just turned nineteen during the summer vacations in Birán and the savage environment he found at the university forced him into active involvement.

The political situation at Havana University reflected the overall state of affairs in Cuba, inevitably accentuated by youthful passions and their manipulation by professional politicians. Ramón Grau San Martín, the physician who had headed the short-lived radical junta in 1933–34, was elected to the presidency in 1944 as the candidate of the oppositionist *Auténtico* party (claiming it stood for the ideals of José Martí), principally because Batista let him win. In the postwar democratic climate Batista chose not to put up a military-supported successor, retiring to Daytona Beach, Florida, to continue building his personal fortune while keeping an eye on Cuban politics. Grau, increasingly shifting to the right and forgetting his dedication to social reform, allowed his regime to wallow deeply in corruption and chaos.

Corruption and brutal political rivalries led throughout the island to a generalized violence that Grau could not or would not stem. Havana University turned into a battlefield peopled with armed gangs whose origins went back to the anti-Machado Action Groups of the 1930s, and whose leaders now sought a new generation of recruits. It was impossible for politically conscious students to stay away from these confrontations. Even so, it was extremely difficult to define the programme or ideologies of the different factions roaming the university 'hill' in the centre of Havana and the broad expanse of stairs leading down from the faculty buildings – the famous *escalinata* where most of the political rallies were held.

Under these circumstances Fidel Castro, the new law student, had a wide choice of allegiances both ideologically attractive and politically useful. There are reasons to believe that he did a certain amount of shopping around at the outset, avoiding for a time becoming clearly identified with any of the factions. His instinct for elusiveness was already asserting itself, allowing him to maintain his freedom of action as long as possible.

Since Castro was not a member of the Communist Party it is very hard to reconstruct precisely his political profile during his university years. Essentially, he was engaged in creating a reputation for himself as rapidly and as dramatically as possible, exhibiting both his flair for the spectacular and his attraction to the limelight. Castro has said almost nothing about his university period, apart from his accounts of his conversion to Marxism. However, on a visit to his alma mater immediately after his revolutionary victory in 1959 he described Havana in his day as more dangerous than the Sierra Maestra. Like most activist students in those days he never ventured anywhere without a gun.

Castro is remembered on the campus as a serious and very intense young man, over six feet tall, powerfully built and very excitable and violence-prone. Though his face was still boyish he was a presence that could not be ignored. While most students wore *guayaberas* or sport shirts appropriate to Havana's heat and humidity, Fidel often made a point of wearing a dark wool suit and a necktie as if to set himself apart from the crowd by an aristocratic elegance. It was all part of his myth-building, and he would say in 1959 that 'I was the Quixote of the university, always the target of cudgel blows and gunfire' in the midst of the waves of gangsterism.

Aside from myth creation Fidel Castro was an extremely attractive young man, appealing to women and men alike. His almost Greek profile, his tall Spanish *hidalgo* carriage, his piercing brown eyes, his physical courage in university melees and his powers of persuasion quickly pushed him to the front of popularity. Fidel's athletic prowess, particularly as a high-jumper and 400-metre track runner, added to his reputation. Social backgrounds did not matter at the university as they had done at Belén, allowing Castro to take full advantage of his talents. Now he had to address himself to the active practice of university politics, and to become known beyond the students' *escalinata* in Havana.

At that time Havana University was composed of thirteen schools, ranging from law to medicine and architecture, and each school annually elected its president. The University Students' Federation (FEU) was the mainstay of student political activity and had a great deal of influence in

Cuban politics. The president of the FEU and other top officials were elected by the presidents of the thirteen schools. The presidents of the individual schools were elected by delegates from each year (say from the four years of the law school or the six years of the architecture school), and the 'year' delegates were chosen by delegates from each course who had to be selected by the students attending the courses. Basically this was a very democratic procedure, but all these elections were part of the larger Cuban political process which everybody, from the government to the Communists and the gangster groups, tried to influence to his personal advantage with votes, money and muscle.

Because the university was autonomous – neither the police nor the army could enter the campus – this Sacred Hill in the heart of Havana was a sanctuary for politicians of all persuasions, and for gangster groups which inevitably called themselves revolutionary to improve their image. Shoot-outs on and off the campus and brutal beatings were routine occurrences and it was truly impossible to establish anyone's political identity with complete assurance. This was particularly true of Fidel Castro as he battled his way through the jungle of university and Havana politics.

Castro fought hard for an elective post in the FEU, but the only time he succeeded was when he was chosen a delegate from one of the courses in the first year of law school in 1945, shortly after he entered the university. This was the lowest elective position in the FEU structure. Evidently Fidel was never able to muster enough support to win him the presidency of the law school – if he had it would have made him a member of the federation's governing body and opened the way to the chairmanship of the FEU. The student elected president of the law school that year was Baudilio Castellanos, a childhood friend from Birán and a personal friend to this day.

The most plausible explanation of Castro's failure to be elected to any significant university post is that he was constitutionally unable to be a team player – in politics as in sports – and that therefore none of the politically-organized student groups wanted to risk supporting him. He was too unreliable. Ironically, even the Communists at the university, including his best friends, refused to back him in elections, notwithstanding their personal admiration for him.

That Fidel Castro was too independent for the Communists is confirmed in considerable detail by Alfredo Guevara who is one of the most intriguing figures in Cuban revolutionary politics, and one of the men most trusted by Castro over the forty years of their friendship. Alfredo Guevara (no kin to Argentina's Che Guevara), presently the Cuban ambassador to UNESCO in Paris, has spoken freely of his university time with Castro.

Guevara entered Havana University at the same time as Castro, but enroled in the school of philosophy and letters. Guevara and his friend Lionel Soto were of humble social origins (Guevara's father was a Havana railway locomotive engineer) and had graduated from a school where they directed an anarchist-minded student association. But at the university they began to develop their ideas into what Guevara calls 'socialism', and soon both became members of Communist Youth (JC).

Guevara picked the philosophy school because women were in the majority among the students, and he calculated correctly that he could be elected president there more easily than elsewhere. The law school adjoined the philosophy school, and almost immediately he began hearing of a student next door named Fidel Castro. He therefore marched over to the law school, finding Fidel in the patio, surrounded by students listening to him. Guevara's interest was in 'leadership' affairs, and he introduced himself to Castro who impressed him greatly. But, Guevara has said, 'at that moment I had prejudices against Fidel, because I [was] a poor student from the Havana institutes, and he came from a religious school . . . from Catholic priests. For me in those days, a religious school and a man of religion were the same thing. . . .' Despite this Guevara felt that 'here I have found a boy who will be either a José Martí or the worst of the gangsters, because I saw in him a man of action, and for me the image of men of action was one of gangsters fighting. . . The problem was that we tried to organize political meetings the way we had done at school, having one person speak, then another, and another, so that we could capture the meeting in the end. But Fidel would start speaking on his own after everything had been organized, and he changed everything.'

This was evidently an early indication to the Guevara Communist group that Castro could not be trusted and thus should not be supported politically. In the 1947 FEU elections, as we have already seen, it was Guevara who beat Castro for the post of Federation secretary, when Fidel ran with the Catholics against the Ovares ticket.

Curiously, this did not interfere with the formation of a personal friendship between the two men. Havana University was, after all, a small place, and outstanding students tended to gravitate towards each other even if they differed ideologically. Enrique Ovares, an anti-Communist, says that in the 1940s 'it was the era of hatred against Nazism and falangism and more or less all the Cuban political leaders were people of the left. . . The kids at the university were full of ideals, and one really believed that all these things proposed in theory by the socialists and the Communists could be achieved. . . .'

A strong friendship developed between Guevara and Castro, and in 1959 Alfredo Guevara was part of a secret task force that allowed Fidel Castro to assume full control of the new revolutionary government, still filled with independents, and then to move Cuba towards Communism (he also ran the cinema industry and served as vice minister of culture).

After the revolution's victory in 1959, having succeeded in controlling the Communists instead of being controlled by them (and a powerful Party faction would attempt again to impose itself in 1962 and 1968 before being smashed), Castro made full use of his Communist university friends. Although none of them participated in any of the great *Fidelista* revolutionary actions – the Party did not support them at the time – they were afterwards given important assignments. Knowing they had no other place to go after 1959, and believing in their organization skills, once he had made the basic decision to go that route, Castro recruited the university Communists to set in motion Cuba's transition to Communism. As for the top party leadership, when these older men were brought into the 1959 political picture they were, with a few exceptions, merely decorative.

Available evidence, therefore, indicates strongly that Castro became a convert to Marxism in his own way and in his own good time. Castro himself says that he became familiar with the ideas of Marx, Engels and Lenin in his third year at the university, which would have been in 1948 or 1949. He acknowledges that he patronized the Communist Party's bookstore on Havana's Carlos III Street (today Avenida Salvador Allende), and there is no reason to doubt his remark that 'if Ulysses was captivated by the songs of the siren, I was captivated by the incontestable verities of the Marxist literature'.

Even so, while at the university he carefully refrained from using words like 'Marxism' or 'socialism' in public speeches; conversely, he never attacked socialism or Communism in his political pronouncements.

Alfredo Guevara is right in emphasizing that he saw Castro as a man of action, and there was plenty of action for Fidel outside the confines of university politics. Despite his efforts at the university Fidel wound up as a political loner, a role which proved to be much more compatible with his personality and which would become his strength in the wider political arena.

The lethal realities of Havana politics, in and out of the university, were established by two powerful gangster groups whose origins went back to the violence surrounding the Machado dictatorship in the early 1930s. One was the Socialist Revolutionary Movement (MSR), founded in 1945 by Rolando Masferrer, a Spanish Civil War veteran on the Republican side who had broken away, with several friends, from the Cuban Communist Party. The other was the Insurrectional Revolutionary Union (UIR), headed by Emilio Tró, a veteran of both the Spanish war (where he fought alongside the anarchists) and World War Two during which he served with the US Army in the Pacific, participating in the

Guadalcanal campaign. Because the only thing the MSR and the UIR had in common was greed for power and political economic influence, they were natural enemies, permanently involved in mutual killings. They each opposed the government of President Grau, and Grau - unwilling or unable to put an end to such political gangsterism – preferred to temporize, even attempting at times to buy off the two organizations. Inevitably this did not work.

The MSR claimed it stood for an anti-Communist 'revolutionary socialism', whatever that meant, that would also oppose United States imperialism and Grau's *Auténtico* party. Its other stated objective was the overthrow of the bloody dictatorship of Rafael Leónidas Trujillo Molina in the Dominican Republic (a 1930 creature of the United States and the marines who were occupying the country at the time). The anti-Trujillo stance gave the MSR a certain respectability, attracting to its leadership such men as the exiled writer Juan Bosch who was later elected President of the Dominican Republic in 1962, after Trujillo's assassination. Basically, however, the MSR was an association of gunmen and much of its power was concentrated at the university where Manolo Castro, an engineering student and an associate of Masferrer, was FEU president for five years.

The UIR's official objective, on the other hand, was simply to rid Havana's streets of 'assassins', presumably meaning the MSR.

The great conflict between the two organizations erupted early in 1947, when President Grau committed the folly of naming the UIR's Emilio Tró and the MSR's Mario Salabarría to be majors in the National Police, a desperate effort to neutralize the gangs. Tró was also made chief of the National Police Academy, and Salabarría was appointed head of the Investigations Department of the National Police. Thus Grau managed to start a war within the police apparatus as well. Grau's other idea was to name Manolo Castro to be the National Sports Director. This post prevented Manolo Castro from running for re-election as FEU president in 1947, opening the federation instead to a succession struggle (won by Enrique Ovares and lost by the slate which included Fidel Castro) in which the MSR and the UIR were naturally deeply involved.

The war between the MSR and the UIR directly affected Fidel Castro because in order to survive, politically as well as physically, he had to manoeuvre skilfully between the two gangster organizations. This was his first taste of real infighting, and Fidel instantly demonstrated a talent for concealing his true position and playing both sides against each other, an ability universally acclaimed as political genius.

Even today it is impossible to determine accurately Castro's relationships with the MSR and the UIR, possibly because they were of such shifting nature, especially in terms of personal ties with leaders on both sides. Fidel is known to have developed a good relationship with MSR's Manolo Castro when the latter was winding up his presidency of the Student Federation, but Fidel was never seriously identified with this movement. In 1946 he was even accused, but without proof, of wounding with a gunshot an obscure UIR student activist named Lionel Gómez to please Manolo Castro.

At the same time, however, according to contemporary accounts, Castro had also aligned himself with the UIR while completing his first year at the law school in the spring of 1946. Jesús Diegues, a UIR leader, told an exiled Cuban historian in a letter many years later that Castro 'used us for his own political battles within the university without ever really identifying [publicly] with UIR'. It has also been said that Fidel went to the UIR when the MSR rebuffed him. A published report claims that Castro was present when President Grau swore in Emilio Tró, the UIR chief, as director of the National Police Academy, but there is no further corroboration. In the end, it seems impossible to ascertain the truth.

Meanwhile Fidel's first outside political performance came in the spring of 1946, before he had turned twenty. The occasion was a meeting at the home of Carlos Miguel de Céspedes, a rightist politician running for mayor of Havana with ties to the Machado dictatorship and hoping for the support of the Student Federation. He invited Manolo Castro, then FEU president, to negotiate student backing, and Manolo insisted on bringing along three colleagues from the university, tactlessly including Fidel Castro who in previous weeks had led law school students in a violent attack on a group of youths, described as Nazi-Fascists, trying to hold a meeting on the campus.

Céspedes, according to an article published in *Bohemia* magazine in June 1946, outlined his campaign plans and asked for comments. When Fidel's turn came he started out by saying that he would support the candidate – and here the hosts broke out in smiles – but on three conditions. He made the classical Fidel pause, and said that the first condition was that all the young revolutionary leaders killed by rightist regimes be brought back to life; that Céspedes and his friends return to the national treasury all the money they had 'stolen from the people'; and that history be set back by a century. Dramatically Fidel announced that 'if these three conditions are met, I shall immediately sell myself as a slave to the colony into which you want to turn Cuba'. Then he rose and marched out of the mansion. This speech, not generally known, is vintage Castro rhetoric: the powerful Cuban nationalism, the belief in Cuba's betrayal by one and all since the Wars of Independence, and the thundering protest against the exploitation of the poor by the rich, all these continue to be Fidel's fundamental themes forty years later.

At the university Castro joined the newly formed Anti-Imperialist

League and the FEU's committee for the independence of Puerto Rico, as a great many other students did. Given deep nationalist sentiments surfacing among young Cubans during and after the war, and the concurrent exacerbation of resentments against the United States for the role it had played in Cuba since 1898, it was not particularly surprising that a man like Fidel should have become a member of such organizations. It did not at all define him as a Marxist. When it comes to anti-imperialism he had been consistent from his student days as a *Cuban* perhaps more than as a Marxist, which is a subtle point not often appreciated in the United States.

Fidel crowned his first full year at university with his début as a public speaker on 27 November 1946. He was in his second year at law school (academic years straddle calendar years), he had just turned twenty, and was already sufficiently well known to rate front-page treatment in the next day's newspapers. The occasion was the seventy-fifth anniversary of the execution of eight medical students by Spanish colonial authorities as punishment for their independentist activities. Traditionally the ceremony was organized by Havana University, and held before the martyrs' elaborate grave at the sprawling Colón cemetery in the Vedado district.

Castro naturally paid tribute to the memory of the medical students, but then quickly launched into a tirade against the Grau government, denouncing the president's unconstitutional plans to try for re-election in 1948, accusing the regime of exploitation, and appealing to Cubans to abandon their apathy and rise against those who allowed them to starve to death.

This was the speech Fidel had carefully rehearsed at the home of his fellow student, José Ignácio Rasco, and it evidently made a great impression, especially when he attacked 'the presidential tolerance for some ministers who steal public funds and for the gangs that invade the inner circles of the government'. In rhetoric that would become familiar to Cubans in the years and decades to come, Fidel proclaimed that 'if Machado and Batista assassinated and persecuted decent persons and honourable revolutionaries, Doctor Grau now has killed all the hopes of the Cuban people, transforming himself into a scourge for the entire nation'.

Castro had hit on the great populist formula of Cuban speech-making, and he would never really deviate from it. Though he was the last speaker at the lengthy ceremony he was quoted in the newspaper *El Mundo* in its lead article on page one, ahead of much better-known political speakers. The newspapers, referring to him as Fidel *de* Castro, failed to explain on whose behalf he had spoken – it may have been in the name of the law school – but it did not truly matter because for all practical purposes a new star had ascended the firmament of contentious Cuban politics. And Fidel was not yet legally of age.

Chapter 5

Nineteen forty-seven was for Fidel Castro the year of definitive political commitment, the year he launched in earnest his political career, and the year of great romantic political adventure and immense personal peril. Following up on his cemetery speech the previous November, Castro was one of the thirty-four signatories of a declaration against President Grau's re-election by the central committee of the FEU, which he helped to draft as a delegate of the law school. Among the signatories were Federation President Enrique Ovares, Law School President Baudilio Castellanos (Fidel's childhood friend), and his future brother-in-law Rafael Díaz-Balart.

The declaration, issued on 20 January 1947, had a *Fidelista* ring to it (though admittedly his companions had a similar penchant for rotund oratory), affirming that 'the ideas of re-election, extension of the period in power, or even the imposition of candidates can be found only in the sick minds of traitors, opportunists and the consistently insincere'. It pledged 'to fight Grau's re-election even if the price we have to pay in the struggle is our own death – it is better to die on your feet than to live on your knees'. As Cuban scholars have noted, Castro would often use this slogan about life and death, a phrase appropriated from Mexico's revolutionary leader Emiliano Zapata.

Now a believer in maximum public exposure and confrontation, and full of ideas, Fidel shortly thereafter organized a trip by law students to the Isle of Pines to inspect a new prison there. Built according to blueprints for a high-security prison in Illinois, it had become known in Cuba as 'the model penitentiary', but Castro found there execrable food and brutal treatment of inmates, and nearly started a free-for-all with the guards. Returning to Havana, he publicly chastised the prison administration, and, of course, made the newspapers. Ironically, it was in this model penitentiary at the Isle of Pines that Batista would incarcerate Fidel and his rebel companions seven years later.

Castro realized from the very beginning of his political life that in order to succeed he had to operate on a variety of levels, often simultaneously. He had already become visible in politics in and out around the university – from the FEU to the 'revolutionary' gangs – and he had learned the value of well-mannered confrontation. In the spring of 1947 he decided to penetrate the world of traditional politics as well.

An opportunity came when Senator Eddy Chibás, the voice of anti-Grau opposition and the immensely popular champion of the Cuban common man against governmental corruption and exploitation by the rich, moved to form his own political party. Chibás, whose battle-cry was his famous slogan 'Dignity against Money', was regarded as a future president and as the most honest and idealistic Cuban leader since José Martí. He was elected to the Senate at the age of thirty-seven and now, as he was launching his Cuban People's Party (PPC), he was just forty years old. Grau's determination to seek re-election, which Castro denounced in his January speech, triggered Chibás into leaving the official *Auténtico* party.

Fidel, who knew the Chibás legend from Belén college, was already a sufficiently important name in Cuban politics to be among the hundred or so citizens invited to the historic meeting on 15 May 1947 when the PPC was officially born. The record shows that this meeting was attended by six senators, ten congressmen, numerous mayors, experienced politicians, academics, businessmen and industrialists.

Fidel Castro, not yet twenty-one years old, was the only university student asked to come that afternoon to the headquarters of the Youth Section of the *Auténtico* party from which Chibás was breaking away. It is an exaggeration to say that Castro was a founder of the PPC, but he certainly was present at its creation, and his association with Chibás would be invaluable in the years to come. The PPC quickly became known to the public as the *Ortodoxo* party because it claimed to stand for orthodoxy in its loyalty to the principles of Martí, a notion that fitted perfectly with Castro's own sense of Cuba and personal destiny.

What Castro achieved by joining the *Ortodoxo* party was to give himself the option of pursuing his long-term political ambitions through establishment politics, and to position himself to take the best advantage of any success it might gain. Being an *ortodoxo* and dedicating much time to the Orthodox Youth Section, Fidel committed himself full time to a political life and involved himself in its chaos and violence.

There is no real contradiction between Castro's very practical decision to play politics from the inside through the new party and what he has described as his revolutionary instincts and his evolution towards Marxism. Even at this young age Fidel had enough sense and political radar to know that revolutions are not accomplished overnight and that the proper climate must exist for them to occur (his study of the French Revolution and his readings of Marx surely helped him to understand it). Obviously he was unable to predict that Fulgencio Batista would launch a coup d'état five years later and thereby create the revolutionary climate he would need – at this time he had the notion that he could propagate the ideas of social revolution through the media (whose darling he was becoming) and through a seat in the Congress to which he already aspired. Should some kind of revolutionary conditions develop, however, as was always possible in Cuba, Fidel says that he would have instantly shifted into its vanguard.

Moreover, Castro was compromising neither his image nor his principles by joining the *Ortodoxos*. Chibás and the new party were not only the most powerful opposition instrument in Cuba, but they projected liberal and socially progressive views far to the left of President Grau's ossified *Auténtico* politicians. Chibás himself was a romantic figure, full of panache, a man who challenged political opponents to sword duels when he felt aggrieved. Most of Cuba came to a standstill on Sunday evening when Eddy Chibás made his fiery weekly radio broadcast.

It suited young Castro in 1947 to give the deliberate impression, still persisting among many Cubans, that he was Chibás's favourite disciple and, in time, his chosen political successor. He campaigned hard for Chibás in the senator's unsuccessful bid for the presidency in 1948, and it is to Fidel's credit that he publicly warned Chibás that the young people would abandon him if he continued to seek alliances (which he did) with rich landowners in Oriente. Castro was important enough for Chibás to answer from the rostrum in Santiago that, 'No, *compañero* Fidel Castro, you may forget your doubts. . . Chibás would be incapable of defrauding the devotion of the masses. . . The day Chibás senses an extinction of the citizens' love, he will shoot himself in the heart.'

Privately, as fresh evidence from interviews and written materials shows, Chibás and Castro rather resented each other, the former fearing Fidel's ultimate rivalry, and the latter seeing the senator as an obstacle to his future advancement. Eddy's brother, Raúl Chibás, who replaced him as the *Ortodoxo* chief when Eddy committed suicide in 1951, says that 'I do not recall my brother ever talking to me about Fidel', but that at the outset there were people in the new party who did not wish Fidel to join it 'because they considered him a negative element . . . he was a fourth-rate figure'. Raúl Chibás was in the Sierra with Castro and joined him in drafting the first guerrilla manifesto to the nation, and so is a credible witness and not a Fidel detractor (though he is now in exile in the United States).

To Castro the association with Chibás and the *Ortodoxos* must have been exceedingly important and, except for the clash during the 1948 presidential campaign, he accepted the senator's leadership. The *Ortodoxos* was the only political party Fidel ever joined. But Raúl Chibás's revelations, and the fact that Castro stopped mentioning Eddy after the victory of the revolution, suggest strongly that the two men simply used each other, with no love lost between them. Fidel would use Eddy most spectacularly in the aftermath of the senator's self-inflicted death.

So completely was Fidel Castro politically engaged in 1947 that he simply had no time to study at the law school or to enjoy any of the social life of glittering Havana with its bars, restaurants, hotels, casinos, theatres, cinemas, nightclubs, brothels, beaches and swimming pools.

Castro had passed the exams at the end of his first year of law school with little problem, but by 1947 he was so involved in extracurricular activities that he did not even present himself at the final exams. As he tells it, he audited third- and fourth-year courses without being a regular student, which complicated his standing as a law school course delegate in the FEU.

Fidel's single-mindedness about politics affected his personal life as well. He simply never went out evenings or weekends, except to attend political meetings or to visit fellow students or other young people he wanted to convince of his ideas. No sooner had he joined the *Ortodoxo* party than he began to build a personal following within the youth section through a group called Orthodox Radical Action (ARO), which, under Fidel's influence, recommended seeking power through revolutionary rather than electoral means. ARO and Castro published a mimeographed pamphlet, the *'Acción Universitaria'*. This had only limited impact, but ARO and Castro's network of young political friends would eventually form the embryo of the *Fidelista* movement.

His social life was also controlled by the time and interest available; certainly not by money (he received enough from home for recreation) or standing in society (which was irrelevant among students). Max Lesnick, who was head of *Ortodoxo* youth and a friend of Castro at the university (he is now exiled in Miami, but remains well informed about events in Cuba), says that he never saw Fidel at any of the dancing and drinking spots patronized by students in the capital. 'I've never seen Fidel dance, and I don't know anybody who has,' Lesnick says, adding that this was very unusual in Havana where young people in the 1940s were as devoted to dance and music as they were to politics.

Lesnick also recalls Fidel's awkwardness and timidity with women. On one occasion, he says, he and Fidel were at the *Ortodoxo* party headquarters on Prado Avenue in Havana when three 'very pretty, very well-dressed young women' walked in to ask a question. According to Lesnick, Castro was most popular among women students, yet 'behaved with incredible shyness'. Lesnick says: 'The man who was capable of discussion with a youth, an old man, a politician or a student, froze in front of these girls.'

At the university, Lesnick says, Fidel had no girlfriends, except for Mirta Díaz-Balart, a philosophy student whom he knew from Oriente and whom he married in 1948. Lesnick remembers that 'at that time politics were Fidel's obsession, and he would never miss a meeting in order to take a girl out or go to a dance'. But, his friends say, he was not practising chastity, either.

Violence went on rising in Havana in the spring and early summer of 1947; on 26 May, for example, an MSR leader named Orlando León Lemus was wounded by a gunshot, and rumours spread that he would be 'finished off' for using his alleged revolutionary credentials for personal gain, which accusation was true of most of the gang *pistoleros* . The MSR's action squad responded by machine-gunning in the streets members of the rival UIR organization.

In July Enrique Ovares, backed by the MSR and the Communists, was elected FEU president (to replace Manolo Castro, the new national sports' director), beating the slate on which Fidel ran for the Federation's secretary general. As it happened, the UIR was supporting this ticket, leading the MSR leadership to conclude that Castro was beyond any doubt identified with their enemy. From that moment on Fidel was persuaded that the MSR was out to murder him, and he increased this risk by public attacks on political gangsters.

He wrote denunciatory anti-gang articles in the student newspaper *Saeta* (*The Arrow*) which he had helped to launch with Communist friends in 1946. This was the first regular publication to print Castro's editorials. He kept up his attacks when one of the principal speakers at the inaugural session of the University Constituent Assembly on 16 July. Castro was among the main movers behind the effort to provide Havana University with a charter guaranteeing its freedoms and modernizing its educational methods, and he was at the end of the speakers' table in the university's auditorium in the company of the chancellor, several deans and the FEU president to address the 891 delegates. This was Fidel's first fully fledged political speech (longer and more formal than at his cemetery appearance in the previous November), and it is believed to have been the first time he appeared in a photograph in Havana newspapers and was identified in the caption.

Fidel started by paying tribute to the 'pleiad' (classical education and allusions were a must in Cuban political speech-making) of student martyrs, such as Communist Party co-founder Julio Antonio Mella, murdered in the defence of a 'progressist university movement'. Praising dead heroes, Castro knew then as he knows now, is the best way to strike an emotional chord in his audience, preparing it for the real message the speaker wishes to convey.

He charged that false leaders – he had Fulgencio Batista and President Grau in mind – had been leading students in recent years toward 'indifference and pessimism'. The university, Castro said, must not be a place 'where ideas are traded as if they were merchandise', and 'a shameful environment of collective cowardice'. He took on the gangs, especially the MSR when he urged students to 'unmask the merchants who profit from the blood of martyrs', and he was inviting even more hostility by describing the Grau government 'as a tyranny that has descended over our nation'. This was the classic structure of a Castro speech, manipulating audience moods, awing the crowd with flashy oratorial imagery and establishing his absolute authority as a speaker whose words must be obeyed. Fidel had not altered this basic technique over the decades, obviously because it works. In the university auditorium he received tremendous applause after his speech, and his credentials as an orator were now firmly set.

In the meantime the Grau government and the MSR, the political gang in cahoots with it, reached the conclusion that they had had enough of Fidel Castro, now the most outspoken and increasingly popular critic of the regime and its friends. Since he could be neither co-opted nor corrupted, he was given an ultimatum: to abandon his anti-government and anti-gangster stance or to leave the university altogether. The warning was sent by Mario Salabarría, the top associate of MSR's founder Rolando Masferrer, and who had been named secret police chief by Grau earlier in 1947. Salabarría had an assassin's reputation, and Castro, who had referred to him as the 'owner of the capital', recognized that reprisals against him might well go beyond his simple removal from the university.

Fidel decided to go away alone to a beach near Havana to consider his situation, and to make up his mind. As he recalled it later, 'This was the moment of great decision. Alone, on the beach, facing the sea, I examined the situation. If I returned to the university I would face personal danger, physical risk. . . But not to return would be to give in to the threats, to admit my defeat by some killer, to abandon my own ideals and aspirations. I decided to return, and I returned – armed.'

This was one of the first significant turning points in Castro's life. He knew that if he had capitulated, in a country where masculine qualities like physical courage have an exaggerated weight, his career as a politician and revolutionary leader would be instantly finished. It was in Fidel's nature, as his entire life demonstrates, to accept challenges and take high risks in the name of principle. But it was also in his introvert's nature to isolate himself at the start of a crisis and to make the great decisions in solitude. He would do this on many future occasions, and emerge renewed and strengthened from these retreats, ready to do battle. Moreover, Fidel would discover that disappearances from public view also had the value of keeping his foes off balance, wondering where he was and what he would do next.

Fidel Castro could never leave well alone. As soon as he emerged from the Salabarría confrontation he volunteered for the next adventure, an invasion of the Dominican Republic to oust the Trujillo dictatorship. The expedition was being organized by a group of Dominican exiles led by Juan Rodríguez García, a millionaire, and the writer Juan Bosch, the future Dominican president, supported and financed by both the Grau government's top officials and Masferrer's and Salabarría's MSR. All in all, it was a blend of political opportunism and economic greed, touched by a very respectable idealism, and was recurrent in the Caribbean in those days.

To recruit Cuban idealists for the invasion the planners had to turn to Havana University where the MSR, always seeking an idealistic and revolutionary image, held sway. In practice this meant that Masferrer, Salabarría and Manolo Castro controlled the recruitment. If Fidel were to join the Dominican adventure he would have to be accepted by the MSR chiefs, and be given guarantees that their gunmen would not assassinate him in the training camps. He remained convinced that the MSR was out to get him. Therefore he needed a truce, or a deal, with his enemies.

Fidel was anxious to participate in the invasion because it was both a matter of revolutionary honour, as he saw it, and of political limelight. To have helped to overthrow the hated Trujillo would have been a badge of honour for a young leader like Fidel. Contemporaries confirm that most students of that generation were powerfully motivated against Trujillo, and that it was 'normal' for Castro to volunteer.

Early in July Castro still had to complete several exams to graduate from the third year of law school, but when he learned of the Dominican project, he says that, 'I considered that my first duty . . . was to enrol as a soldier in the expedition and I did so'. The implication is that this was the reason he failed to take the exams and thus lost his standing as a regular student along with his freshly gained position as president of the law school. This is one of the many convoluted episodes in Castro's history. He explains that while someone else had been elected earlier in 1947 to the presidency of the law school – it was a student named Aramís Taboada (who was imprisoned in the early 1980s in Cuba for allegedly defending a 'counter-revolutionary' at a trial) – the student majority rejected this president and named Castro instead. This version is not borne out elsewhere but at least one Havana newspaper late in 1947 referred to Fidel as the law school president.

Fidel recounts that at the time he was chairman of the university's Committee for Democracy in the Dominican Republic, and while he was not among the organizers of the expedition, he was close to exiled Dominican leaders and was duty-bound to sail with them. He does not tell, however, the troubles he had in being permitted to join the anti-Trujillo force.

Enrique Ovares, the new FEU president and an organizer of the invasion with the rank of *comandante,* says that he negotiated Castro's participation with the MSR chieftains. Ovares and Castro had friendly relations from their school days, their university political differences notwithstanding. Ovares said: 'Fidel came one day to my house in Vedado, and we sat in the garden. "It's not possible that they will deny me the opportunity of offering my life to do away with the Trujillo dictatorship. . . But I cannot go because they will kill me there, because you know that Masferrer will kill me." So I asked Fidel if I, as president of the FEU, all of whose students must be accepted [in the expedition], insist that he goes, would he go? Fidel said: "If you guarantee my life, I shall go." So I went to see Manolo Castro [the outgoing FEU president and MSR leader], who was a friend of mine, and I told him there was a problem with Fidel Castro. Manolo Castro replied: "Fidel is a shit, but he is right. I am going to speak to all these people and Fidel will go to the training camps." '

Because Manolo Castro was one of the chief advocates of the invasion, along with the incomparably corrupt Education Minister José M. Alemán and army Chief-of-Staff General Genovevo Pérez Dámera (the latter two saw profit and power in the Dominican Republic after Trujillo was overthrown), Fidel received his guarantees. Late in July he was sent to Holguín in the north of Oriente to receive his first experience of basic military training at the local polytechnic institute. On 29 July Fidel and his companions were driven to the port of Antilla on Nipe Bay (near the Birán family home), and placed aboard four vessels to sail to Cayo Confites, an islet north of the coast of Camagüey province, adjacent to Oriente.

The expeditionary force totalled around 1200 men who spent fifty-nine days on Cayo Confites under blistering sun and a permanent mosquito assault, ostensibly undergoing additional military training but basically doing nothing because the invasion leaders could not make up their minds. Fidel says that he was named lieutenant in charge of a squad, then promoted to company commander when word was received from Havana late in September that the whole campaign was being called off. It is not entirely clear why this happened. Castro says simply that 'contradictions between the civilian government and the army' forced the cancellation. But there is evidence that Cuban and international politics intervened to dismantle the expedition.

Soon thereafter, Emilio Tró Rivera, the head of the UIR, the rival political action group with which Fidel had strong ties, was assassinated in Havana on 15 September by MSR hit men as a new wave of violence swept the capital. Tró was also director of the National Police Academy, and police agents under the secret police chief Salabarría had failed to kill him in a previous attempt on 2 September. UIR gunmen murdered an MSR-connected policeman on 12 September, and Salabarría ordered Tró's arrest. Three days later Salabarría's men located Tró dining at the home of a suburban police chief. At the end of a three-hour fusillade during which several bystanders were killed Tró was dead, riddled by bullets (the Cuban press reported that there were sixty-four political assassinations and a hundred assassination attempts in Cuba during Grau's 1944–48 term).

The Grau government's official version links, not very credibly, Tró's murder and the cancellation of the Cayo Confites expedition. In a press briefing on 29 September the army spokesman explained that while investigating Tró's death, military investigators found clues that led them to the América ranch near Havana, belonging to Education Minister Alemán, where 'fantastic quantities' of arms and ammunition were discovered along with documents concerning plans for the Dominican invasion. The army then learned that the expedition's headquarters were at the Hotel Sevilla on Havana's Prado Avenue, close to the presidential palace. With this knowledge in hand the army acted to prevent the invasion.

As the invasion preparations were widely known from the outset, with the education minister and the army chief of staff behind it, this story seems unlikely. The truth appears to be that Trujillo complained to Washington that he was about to be invaded, and the United States quietly convinced the Grau regime to call off the invasion. After the Cuban Army and Navy rounded up most of the expeditionaries (General Pérez Dámera now being committed to regional law and order), the State Department expressed its satisfaction that a 'threat to peace' had been removed.

Castro was on Cayo Confites when Tró was killed, though he was probably then unaware of it. He says that when orders came to cancel the invasion some men deserted, but his battalion sailed anyway. They were twenty-four hours away from landing, he recalls, when 'we were intercepted and everybody was arrested'.

Most likely, the vessel – a small coastal freighter the men had nicknamed *Fantasma* (*Ghost*) – was boarded by a Cuban Navy unit and ordered to turn back (other expeditionaries were arrested by the army on Cayo Confites), but Fidel escaped detention. 'I did not let myself be arrested – more than anything else, as a question of honour: it shamed me that this expedition should end by being arrested.' Therefore, when the

Fantasma sailed back west, Fidel jumped from the deck in front of the Oriente fishing port of Gibara, and swam south-west along the coast for eight or nine miles in waters supposedly full of sharks to reach Saetía at the mouth of Nipe Bay. According to one published version, Fidel actually went in a small boat he lowered at night from the ship, but he says flatly that he swam all the way, and there is is no reason to doubt it.

From Saetía Castro went to Havana (it is not known whether he stopped at home in Birán to rest and change his clothes) in an immense hurry to return to his political battles and the university. He says he wasted August, September and October in Cayo Confites, again missing his law school exams. Once back in the capital, he went to the apartment of his sister Juana – he had no other place to stay – and instantly plunged into the Havana in-fighting. He had reached legal maturity, turning twenty-one on the desolate and frustrating Caribbean cay, and now he craved action.

Castro wasted no time. He had swum from the ship to Saetía at dawn on 28 September, and on 30 September he was already delivering an anti-government speech at the university. The occasion was the anniversary of the killing of a student during the Machado dictatorship, but Fidel used it to blame the Grau government for having betrayed the cause of Dominican liberation and to urge, once more, the resignation of the president. As a child Fidel had learned that permanent attack is not the only route towards victory – even if he had not yet defined his ultimate objective – and he now adopted the principle of one of his French Revolution heroes, Danton, acting 'with audacity, always audacity. . .' Audacity has always been Fidel Castro's most distinctive trait.

His intense political involvement inevitably interfered with systematic studies, so he chose not to enrol officially for the continuation of the third year at the law school, not wanting to fail at exams. Instead, he signed up to audit third- and fourth-year classes. Despite this carefully considered change in his student and political status Castro claims that 'at a certain moment, without seeking it, I became the centre of that struggle against the Grau government'.

Fresh from the Cayo Confites experience, Castro used every opportunity to harass the regime and its principal figures. Havana was turning into a permanent battlefield in the closing months of 1947. At the demonstration on 30 September Fidel's principal target was Education Minister Alemán, for his role in the Cayo Confites episode as well as his corrupt practices and his private corps of armed thugs. In the Senate the opposition submitted a censure motion against Alemán. His response was the unhappy idea of having his followers organize a public show of 'adhesion' on 9 October but a scuffle developed in the crowd and a high school student named Carlos Martínez Junco was shot dead by one of the minister's bodyguards.

The boy's death triggered a near revolt, particularly when Alemán proceeded with his plans to hold the self-congratulatory meeting in front of the presidential palace – where Grau was then foolish enough to come out on the balcony to praise his education minister. Within hours thousands of students, carrying the coffin of Carlos Martínez Junco, marched on the palace, shouting demands for Grau's and Alemán's resignations, shaking their fists at the balcony as they filed past. Fidel Castro was in the first row of the demonstrating students.

When the student mass reached the *escalinata* – the vast stretch of stairs on the university campus – Castro addressed them in an outpouring of emotion. He blamed Grau for the boy's death, saying that 'there is no culprit of these tears and this grief other than President Grau'. Noting that the following day, 10 October, Cuba would be commemorating the anniversary of the first independence war in 1868, the history-conscious Castro accused Grau of commemorating it 'with the criminals of this government . . . as a joyful feast with lights and champagne while we students cannot celebrate because we must bring here, to bury him, the cadaver of one of ours, of a student assassinated by the new thugs. . . '

A forty-eight hour general strike by students, supported by labour unions, followed to demand Alemán's resignation, and demonstrations went on for several weeks with Fidel Castro always present, always visible, always audible, and usually in charge. Senator Chibás, the chief of the *Ortodoxo* party, chose to leave the street demonstrations to Fidel, his youth leader, working himself in the Senate for the approval of the anti-Alemán motion. In his weekly radio address on 12 October he lashed out at the regime's murderers. Now there was no question that Chibás and the young Castro were Cuba's most important opposition leaders, each concentrating on his own public though Fidel lacked the older man's stature.

Inevitably the MSR and the regime's police were out gunning for Castro. Salabarría had been arrested by the army after the Cayo Confites fiasco (ten $1000 bills were found inside his shoes), but Rolando Masferrer remained firmly in control of his gangsters. Numerous attempts were made at the university to ambush Fidel, but each time he escaped. One day Evaristo Venéreo, a lieutenant of the campus police, tried to disarm him. Castro pointed his gun at the policeman, saying coldly: 'If you want it, try to grab it by the barrel.' Venéreo surprised Fidel by challenging him to a pistol duel in a deserted corner of the university sports stadium; Castro accepted at once, his honour being at stake, but he took the precaution of bringing along a group of armed friends. This was fortunate because the lieutenant had posted policemen in the bleachers to ambush Fidel; they were spotted and fled together with

Venéreo as the students shouted insults. Castro said later: 'It was a miracle that I came out of that alive.'

A feverish imagination was part of Fidel Castro's political arsenal – as he would demonstrate to the nation in the first days of November with the October disturbances barely over. He had devised a plan he thought could lead to a mass popular uprising and Grau's overthrow, a premature expectation perhaps but one that was successful in creating a national scandal of vast proportions. In this, again, Fidel had the genius to summon Cuban history as inspiration for the masses while he attempted to stage his coup. His chosen instrument in this case was La Demajagua bell, the Cuban equivalent of the US Liberty Bell, which Carlos Manuel de Céspedes rang at his estate near the Oriente port of Manzanillo to mark the opening shot in the 1868 independence war. For many decades the bell had been entrusted to Manzanillo as part of a national shrine.

Actually it was the Grau government that first became interested in the bell for a mix of historical and political reasons, a common Cuban phenomenon. Grau's idea was to bring La Demajagua (named after the Céspedes sugarcane estate) to Havana to make it ring, as it had done eighty years before, at the following year's anniversary commemorations; Grau was still thinking about re-election in 1948, and it struck him that the bell would toll well for him.

Unexpectedly, however, the Manzanillo municipal council not only refused to let the bell go to Havana, but virtually expelled Grau's emissary. The reason was, most probably, that Manzanillo had a radical political tradition based on the sugar-mill workers living around it and the industrial workers in town, and that it was a centre of opposition to Grau. Moreover, Manzanillo had Cuba's first Communist mayor in history, in the person of Francisco (Paquito) Rosales, elected in 1940. Batista's agents were to murder him in 1958.

Hearing that Manzanillo had turned down Grau's request for the bell, the ever-inventive Fidel Castro conceived the idea of having Havana university students bring the bell to the capital – he knew that the municipal council would agree to it – and organize a mass gathering at which the bell would be rung, and crowds would then descend on the presidential palace and demand Grau's resignation.

Fidel, outlining his concept to his Communist friend Alfredo Guevara (who was also the FEU's secretary general), was fully confident that it would work and that Grau's overthrow would be achieved. The next person brought into the scheme was Lionel Soto, also a Communist at the university, and a friend of both Guevara and Castro. Finally, FEU President Enrique Ovares was informed (it was necessary because of the role the university was to play in Fidel's scenario), and he too liked the idea.

Ovares confirms that the plan, presented to him by Fidel and Alfredo

Guevara, aimed at a confrontation with the government. He says that he agreed to accompany them to Manzanillo, but the plotters decided that Lionel Soto would go instead of Guevara. Max Lesnick, a fellow student and head of the *Ortodoxo* party youth, recalls that several party leaders, including Senator Chibás, contributed around $300 to cover the expenses of the Manzanillo trip.

To extract maximum political effect from their enterprise Fidel and his companions spread the word that they were bringing the venerable bell, and thousands of students awaited the train's arrival in Havana on 5 November (two Manzanillo citizens came along to keep an eye on their treasure). A large open car carried the 300-pound bell from the railway station to the university in a triumphal parade lasting over two and a half hours. There is a contemporary photograph of a very youthful-looking Fidel Castro in his dark striped suit and a flowery necktie, his right arm around the bell, and his left hand clutching a ceremonial candle holder.

At the university Castro addressed the cheering crowd from the convertible, declaring that Manzanillo patriots had refused to surrender the symbol of Cuban independence to 'puppets at the orders of foreigners'. But, he said, 'The liberators of yesterday have faith in the student youth of today and continue their labour of independence.' La Demajagua was placed in the Gallery of Martyrs next to the office of the chancellor of Havana University for safekeeping while the students spent much of the night on the campus, planning the great anti-Grau demonstration the next day. The following morning, when the chancellor's office was opened, the students discovered that the bell had been mysteriously removed. The police who had surrounded the campus all night (together with a hundred MSR gunmen), denied any knowledge of the bell's theft.

Enrique Ovares recalls that Fidel, Alfredo Guevara and several other student leaders appeared at his house early in the morning to apprise him that the bell was gone. Ovares said that as FEU President he would deliver a written accusation to the university chancellor on the grounds that *he* was responsible for La Demajagua (the elderly chancellor later challenged Ovares to a duel because he felt insulted). Fidel rushed to a radio station to charge the regime with stealing the bell while thousands of students began gathering at the university. Around noon Castro was on the campus, grabbing the microphone to shout: 'Let the rats stay here; we are going to denounce this robbery', and to lead thousands of students to the nearest police station to make a formal complaint.

In the early afternoon Fidel returned to Ovares's house, but several police officers he had named in his broadcast as culpable followed him, brandishing their guns. Ovares and his mother convinced the policemen to leave. Fidel was subsequently accused of cowardice for hiding in the house, but Ovares says: 'Fidel is an intelligent man; why would he want to leave the house? To commit suicide?'

At night a mass rally was held at the campus (though the chancellor had decreed a seventy-two hour suspension of classes to prevent disorders) and Fidel wasted no time in delivering a slashing attack on President Grau. He accused him of breaking his promises to look after the restoration of the 'national dignity', and to help the neglected peasants and their hungry children, saying that 'the faith has been lost'. Castro warned Grau that the students for whom 'the deception was the most terrible' were there to proclaim that 'a young nation can never say, "We surrender" '.

In a passage that would become a Castro theme in all the years to come he spoke of a 'betrayed revolution', the nationalist revolution that Grau had promised to Cuba, with peasants still without land, and 'the country's wealth in foreign hands'. Then he moved on to what would be another *Fidelista* rhetorical discovery and weapon: the power of statistics. He had already mastered the need for homework, his prodigious memory providing the means for conveying his knowledge comprehensively to his audiences. In this instance Fidel was able to inform his listeners that in the three years or so that Grau had been in power his government had been given 256 million pesos (the peso being equal to the dollar), but public health was awarded only 14 million pesos and public works 112 million pesos while defence – meaning the armed forces – gained 116 million pesos. Castro was always obsessed with the need for huge investments in public health, which he was able to assign when he took power, but this was the first time he raised the issue publicly.

The threat of 'militarism' was another Castro concern, and he warned his university audience of the growing power of the military – more than five years before Batista's coup. And he urged students to become militant in the battle for national unity of the people 'to obtain its true independence, its economic liberation, its political sovereignty, its political liberties . . . the definitive emancipation of our nation'.

Some scholars of the Castro revolution consider the 6 November 1947 speech at the university as Fidel's coming of age as a political thinker and as his first coherent attack on the status quo from a leftist perspective. This is debatable, inasmuch as Castro himself concedes that his evolution towards Marxism was then still developing. There is no question, however, that at this juncture Fidel had created a distinctive political style that he would nurture for the rest of his life.

As to whether Castro was alone on that occasion in expressing leftist and nationalist views, the centrist newspaper *El Mundo* reported in its front-page article on the university rally that this was not so. Practically all the student speakers, it said, 'made special references to "Yankee Imperialism" '. This is an important point: in 1959 the American government and public opinion were, by and large, under the impression that Cuban nationalism and anti-Yankee sentiment were essentially Castro inventions. Hence the surprise of the true meaning of the *Fidelista* revolution when it finally came.

Several days after the Havana disturbances La Demajagua was delivered to President Grau by parties unknown, and immediately sent back to Manzanillo. It marked the end of this particular incident, but young Fidel Castro had achieved new fame as Cuba's most promising rising political star, and his increasingly controversial ascent would continue in the new year.

Chapter 6

For Fidel Castro 1948 was a breathless year, politically and personally. He was asserting his political identity, engaging in immense activity, and acquiring new responsibilities.

Around him Cuba was disintegrating, socially and politically, the island having lived in a revolutionary environment since the insurrection against the Machado dictatorship in September 1930.

Cuba had the outward trappings of a democracy, advanced social legislation, and a progressive social and political instrument in the form of the 1940 constitution. But the frustrations of a nation sharply divided by the huge wealth of a minority and the quite abysmal poverty of the majority – peasants and urban and rural salaried workers – had created a state of affairs in which Cuba was in reality essentially ungovernable. The urban middle class was too small and divided to provide a solid political centre.

Tolerating political violence and corruption on a grand scale, President Grau had abdicated not only national leadership but also his elementary responsibility for the maintenance of day-to-day law and order. He then compounded the national resentments and divisions by his unconstitutional decision to seek re-election to a second term in 1948. The advent of a new generation, represented by the leadership and the rank and file in the University of Havana (and even in secondary education schools), constituted a direct challenge to the putrid status quo, and conditions were perfect for the emergence of a challenger such as Fidel Castro, a believer in a 'true' Cuban revolution.

Elsewhere in postwar Latin America similar pressures were gathering. In Argentina Juan D. Perón had taken power in 1945 to launch a populist and nationalist movement in the name of social justice, producing a militaristic and fascistoid dictatorship while managing to remain a hero of the masses. Perónism was a phenomenon in which Fidel Castro at the northern end of Latin America was developing a special interest. In 1948 in Peru the army had smashed a revolt by the nationalist and socially committed APRA movement, one of the few wholly original revolutionary movements in Latin America, eschewing classical socialism and Marxism. During the same year in Venezuela, a nation belonging emotionally as much to the Caribbean as to South America, a tyranny had fallen and been replaced by a democratic and socially radical government. And next door in Colombia a vicious civil war with deep social undertones was in progress.

In Cuba the political and social tensions of the era were accentuated and magnified by the island's physical smallness, and revolution as a way out of the fundamental national crisis was the talk in 1948. Cuba's disturbing relationship with the United States was an added dimension in the bitter Cuban search for identity.

For years unbridled political gangsterism had flourished in the guise of 'revolutionary' movements and organizations, rendering the word 'revolution' meaningless. By 1948, however, the whole question of the unfinished Cuban revolutions, and Cuba's partial independence, became the subject of most serious public debate, even by the spokesmen of mainstream political and ideological currents.

The rightist *Diario de la Marina* in Havana agreed editorially that Cuban youth must find ways to channel its demands, but protested against attempts to bring together 'workers, peasants and students' because it smelled of 'Communist' inspiration. Summing up the Cuban establishment's total incomprehension of the reality, the editorial remarked that 'among student, proletarian and agrarian youth there is not necessarily any community of origins and interests'. Francisco Ichaso, a well-known right-wing polemicist, wrote that a minority in Cuba had convinced itself that one of the safest and most profitable endeavours is 'what they call revolution', using the young to activate it.

At the other end of the political spectrum, Raúl Roa García, a professor at Havana University (who would become Fidel Castro's ideologically radical foreign minister in 1959), argued that it was wrong to claim, as the rightists did, that the 1940 constitution 'had concluded the revolution' in Cuba. Though the 'colonial structure' had been removed, Roa wrote, the constitution was 'a road, not a goal'.

As for Fidel Castro he was now obsessed by revolution. Manuel Moreno Frajinals, a noted Marxist historian who befriended young Fidel at the university that year, recalls that every conversation with him dealt with 'deep revolution'. Castro frequently visited the Moreno Frajinals household, and the historian says 'even then, Fidel was determined to lead a revolution, he was convinced it would happen, and everything he did was in preparation for it. . . He talked incessantly about the revolution.' Castro, he says, also realized early that access to, if not control of, the communications media was vital, and while still at the university he wooed newspapers, magazines and radio, all of which were highly developed in Cuba. In fact Fidel lost no opportunity to be as visible as possible.

On 22 January 1948 in Manzanillo, a Communist labour stronghold in Oriente, Jesús Menéndez Larrondo, a black union leader of sugar workers, a Communist and a member of the Chamber of Deputies, was killed by an army captain. Invoking his parliamentary immunity Menéndez had refused to submit to arrest and was summarily shot. He had been arrested and briefly detained the previous October along with hundreds of leftist labour leaders as part of the campaign by Labour Minister Carlos Prio Socarrás to rid the unions of Communist control. Menéndez had been warned that he was on the army's death list.

General Pérez Dámera, the army chief of staff, publicly commended the captain for his actions as a model example to his fellow officers 'so that every time a similar situation occurs, similar action is to be taken'. The Grau government evidently no longer had any contact with political reality. The Menéndez assassination came as a tremendous shock to public opinion, the labour leader had been very popular, and his casket was placed on display at the National Capitol; tens of thousands of Cubans filed past to pay him homage.

Two weeks later Castro was back in the limelight. On 11 February a student demonstration was held in the centre of Havana to protect against police brutality toward students in Guantánamo in Oriente, and a streetcar was burned during the riot. The police charged the students, chasing them back to the university, but Commander José Caramés, the police chief of the university district, personally raced up the escalinata on the campus, pistol in hand. Before his men could convince him to leave the campus he had pistol-whipped a student with a limp, and a serious confrontation was narrowly averted with armed students.

Clearly a violation of the university's autonomy had occurred when the police entered the grounds, so Fidel Castro called for a peaceful protest demonstration the following day. In Havana, however, there was no such thing as a peaceful demonstration. While a group of young people deployed a .50-calibre machine gun atop the escalinata in the event of a new police invasion, Fidel and a fellow student led a student march into town, carrying a huge Cuban flag and signs proclaiming, 'We protest against the violation of university autonomy!' Singing the national anthem the students reached police barricades at an intersection and began shouting, 'Out with Caramés, Down with Grau – The Assassins!'

Riot police moved in on the students with clubs in their hands, and Fidel was among the first to be hit. Headlines in the next day's newspapers announced that he had been 'injured' (this was the first time he made the headlines). News stories said he had 'suffered a grave contusion' on the head, and had been taken to the Calixto García hospital to be X-rayed. Castro's injury turned out to be superficial and he refused to remain at the hospital. None the less he had publicly shed his first blood for the revolution, and that was all that counted. The police released students who had been arrested, and Caramés was suspended pending an investigation. It was a most successful day for Castro and his cause.

An event of extraordinary gravity was the assassination in Havana on 22 February, ten days after the university riots, of Manolo Castro, the national sports director and founder of the MSR organization. Manolo was shot by unknown assailants in front of a cinema of which he was a co-owner, after being called out to the street on some pretext.

The general assumption was that Manolo Castro had been killed in retribution for the death of Emilio Tró Rivera in September 1947, chief of the rival UIR political gang and head of the National Police Academy. His actual assassins were never found, however. Manolo Castro was a very important politician and he had received numerous death threats in the previous weeks and months. He was uncertain who exactly wanted him dead, but he went to the extreme of asking Communist friends from his university days for help. There was nothing they could do.

The MSR immediately accused Fidel Castro of murdering Manolo Castro, probably because the MSR group under Rolando Masferrer (from whom Manolo Castro had protected Fidel on Cayo Confites) was determined to do away with Fidel as his most dangerous political rival.

Tiempo en Cuba, a publication belonging to Masferrer, happened to have printed a few weeks before the Manolo Castro death an article seeking to link Fidel with university gangsters. The day of the assassination a nephew of Masferrer publicly charged Fidel. Within three days, on 25 February, Fidel and three fellow student leaders were arrested in a car on the Havana seaside boulevard at 11 p.m. by policemen in a cruiser. The reason given was the investigation of the Manolo Castro death.

The four student leaders indignantly denied any involvement with the murder and Fidel testified that he had spent the afternoon of the assassination day at El Dorado café with friends whom he named, and that he spent the night at the Plaza Hotel. He told the investigating judge that when he saw his name the next day in the newspapers mentioned in connection with Manolo Castro, he instantly went to the nearest police station to offer testimony, but the officer in charge sent him away because there were no orders for his arrest.

The latter is an important point because over the years numerous published reports have created the impression that Cuban authorities had actually issued a detention order against him, and the myth has survived. The arrest on 25 February was entirely on the initiative of the officer in the police cruiser. The four men were submitted that night to a paraffin test to determine whether any of them had recently fired a weapon, and the investigating judge ordered them released on 'conditional liberty' at 2 a.m. – whereupon Fidel immediately held a press conference at the police station.

He charged that Masferrer 'wants to take over the leadership of the university to make it serve his personal interests', but 'we have not allowed him to do so, in spite of the coercion and violence practised against us'. Fidel said that Masferrer 'wishes to incite action against us, using Manolo Castro as a pretext; in other words, he wishes to profit from the death of a friend. . .' Fidel Castro's reputation in this context is also defended by FEU ex-president Enrique Ovares, now in exile in Miami following lengthy imprisonment in Havana after the revolution. Ovares says: 'Fidel had absolutely nothing to do with the Manolo Castro thing. If you have to attack Fidel, attack him with the truth. Fidel has done terrible things. But why is it necessary to invent? This is the problem that bothers me about people who write [about Fidel]. If there is sufficient truth, why should one lie?'

Fidel's innocence in this crime was no guarantee, however, that Masferrer or others would not try to kill him, and so he decided it would be wise to vanish from sight for a time. His sister Lidia, Alfredo Guevara and Mario García Inchaústegui helped him to hide and lead a semi-clandestine life. But, as usual, a new project suddenly materialized to capture Castro's attention, and, most conveniently, provided him with an opportunity to leave Cuba for a time. It would quickly turn into Fidel's greatest adventure to date.

The new project was an 'anti-imperialist' association of Latin American students, a concept that had initially been proposed by the Perón regime in Argentina. Castro embraced it with total enthusiasm. The congress was designed to organize a Latin American Students' Association, heavy on nationalism and anti-Yankeeism, and a preparatory session of hemisphere student leaders was to be held in the Colombian capital of Bogotá early in April.

As happens so frequently with events in the life of Fidel Castro, contradictory versions exist concerning his exact role in the preparations for the Bogotá meeting and the entire background of the effort to create the Latin American student body. Specifically, it is unclear where and how the idea of the 'anti-imperialist' association was really hatched and developed: by the Perónists aided by Fidel Castro, or by Fidel Castro aided by the Perónists?

It is a matter of record that Perón had been actively seeking to spread the influence of Argentina under the guise of his *Justicialismo* (social justice) politics throughout Latin America. Usually covertly, Perónist funds flowed to labour unions, journalists, specific publications and student groups, to convert them to pro-Argentine sentiments and to the Perón doctrine: the general saw himself as a world figure, and his movement as a Third Force in international affairs.

This effort had been much less than successful, but in 1948 the Argentinians were still investing money in it. The notion of an anti-imperialist students' association was probably born in Buenos Aires, but it is unknown why the Perónists turned almost exclusively to Cuban students to set the operation in motion. Senator Diego Molinari, who was chairman of the Argentine Senate's foreign affairs committee, at least one cabinet minister and several lesser lights appeared in Havana at the start of 1948, to meet with Cuban student leaders and persuade them to help organize the association. By most accounts, Argentina agreed to pay all the expenses.

The Argentine proposal was well received in Havana by all student segments. Perón seemed to offer them a way out of isolation and into a community of nationalist solidarity. That Perón had nationalized British and American utilities, that he was at odds with the United States (which had futilely tried to undermine and oust him), and that he was portraying Argentina as a victim of British colonialism for retaining the Falkland Islands in the South Atlantic only served to enhance his prestige. Young Cubans were prepared to overlook Perón's military dictatorship, and the Socialist Youth studiously ignored the anti-Communist aspects of *Justicialismo*. Nationalism and anti-Americanism were the common denominator. Interestingly, just at the time when the law student in Havana, Fidel Castro, was coordinating plans with Perón's envoys for the congress, Ernesto Guevara de la Serna, the future Che of the Cuban revolution, was already a Perón supporter as a nineteen-year-old second-year student at the medical school at the Buenos Aires University. It is most unlikely that Guevara knew then of Fidel's existence, but clearly revolutionary sympathy existed between the radical youth of Latin America and the Perónists.

As a student leader Castro claims he took it upon himself to represent Cuban students despite his 'conflicts' with the leadership of the FEU and the fact that, not being officially enroled in the university at that stage, he could not act as a federation official. In this Castro version he became the central figure in setting up the congress because 'I represented the great majority of the students who followed me, regarding me as the leader.' He says that 'the idea of organizing the congress was mine', and that 'I conceived the idea' that this congress be held in Bogotá simultaneously with the planned conference of Western Hemisphere foreign ministers, 'called by the United States to consolidate its system of domination here in Latin America'. The students were to meet, he explains, on the basis of 'anti-imperialist' principles.

In this fashion Fidel Castro apparently planned to create an open confrontation with the United States and the Organization of American States in a Latin American capital, an impressively ambitious undertaking for a twenty-one-year-old Caribbean revolutionary unknown beyond the confines of Cuba. And although Fidel never considered any of his ideas to be unattainable, in this instance he could not possibly have foreseen that the Bogotá congress would turn into such an explosive event – the reasons for this were purely coincidental to his purpose. Still, Castro's political career is built from historical events over which he had no control whatsoever, but which cleared the way for his success and advancement.

The way Fidel tells the story, both the Perónists and the FEU were almost marginal in the preparation of the Bogotá congress. He himself was the main inspirational and organizational presence. Fidel does tend to interpret history in this manner. Some of his companions, however, have slightly different recollections. Four Cuban student leaders in fact went to Bogotá for the congress; Enrique Ovares, as FEU president, was one of them; others were Alfredo Guevara, the FEU's Communist secretary general, Rafael del Pino, Fidel's friend; and Fidel himself.

While Castro may overstate his personal commanding role in preparing the congress, he was unquestionably its spokesman. On 15 March, three weeks after the problems resulting from Manolo Castro's assassination, Fidel issued a declaration from his hiding place in Havana to outline the plans for the congress.

'We hope that this act will initiate a movement of major proportions that will find support in all Latin America, especially among university students, united under the banner of anti-imperialist struggle,' he said. He then announced that preparatory sessions for the congress would be held in Bogotá early in April, during the inter-American ministerial conference there 'in order to support accusations against colonialism that various Latin American countries will present'. Always the strategist, Fidel noted that 'it will be easier to make such accusations if we come in on a wave of protests'.

On 19 March, Castro drove to Havana's Rancho Boyeros (today José Martí) airport to catch a plane for Caracas, his first stop en route to Colombia. But the police detained him before boarding and he was taken before a judge on the ground that he was attempting to violate the conditional liberty on which he had been released four weeks earlier, during the murder investigation. Happy to capitalize on the incident, Fidel informed the judge that he was carrying out a mission designed to 'strengthen the bonds of friendship' among Latin American students. Taking the offensive, he demanded that the authorities issue a public statement concerning plans by armed thugs in Havana to assassinate him.

The judge promptly let his prisoner go, erasing all charges, but Castro first told newsmen that he had been victimized by those determined to obstruct his student activities and 'to create for me an unfavourable situation before public opinion'. He left for Venezuela the next day, full of indignation and surrounded by fresh publicity.

In Caracas Castro and Rafael del Pino met with university students who agreed to send a delegation to the Bogotá congress, visited the editors of the government newspaper, and made a courtesy call at the home of Venezuela's President-Elect Rómulo Gallegos, a noted poet and novelist. The Venezuelan military dictatorship had been overthrown by a revolution led by young intellectuals and officers of the left-of-centre persuasion.

From there, the two Cubans arrived in Panama in the wake of demonstrations against United States control of the Canal Zone, and Castro remembers visiting a Panamanian student who had suffered what turned out to be permanent injury as a result of the riot. Students in Panama similarly agreed to send representatives to Bogotá.

Even from afar he kept watching politics in Cuba. Presidential elections were to be held on 1 June, and Castro, as a member of the oppositionist *Ortodoxo* party, supported the candidacy of Senator Eddy Chibás. But he disagreed with Chibás refusal to make a pact with the Communists. Although the Popular Socialist Party (the Communist Party's current name) had its own candidate in Juan Marinello (the former Batista cabinet minister), it had offered to throw its backing to Chibás to help prevent a government victory. On 31 March Castro issued a statement for the Cuban press approving this move by the Communists – perhaps as a last-ditch means of bolstering Chibás's chances, since he was then last in the polls – but Chibás firmly rejected any such alliance.

Castro's public support for a pact with the Communists raises again the question of when he actually became a Marxist or a Communist – and whether his membership of the *Ortodoxo* party was not a cover. There is no absolute proof one way of another but even anti-Communists among his fellow university students reject the notion that Fidel was a 'hidden' Communist.

During the events of Bogotá and subsequently, Castro was widely charged with being part of a Communist conspiracy to sabotage the foreign ministers' conference. Fidel would be deeply involved in the violence that surged in Bogotá, but this was more a display of adventuresome youthful nationalism than a proof of Communist militancy. Again it is Ovares who rises in Castro's defence, insisting that 'I was there and I have not the slightest notion that he was a Communist.

'These are lies,' Ovares says about reports that Castro had met with Communists and received at the time a letter from the Cuban

Communist leader Blás Roca. 'The Communist was the one who was with me, and this was Alfredo Guevara.'

Castro arrived in Bogotá with Rafael del Pino on 31 March, staying at the small, three-storey Claridge Hotel downtown. FEU's Enrique Ovares and Alfredo Guevara flew in from Havana the next day, going to the San José boarding house, near the Claridge, because it was even cheaper. On 1 April the Cuban group met with Colombian and foreign student delegates at the university to organize the work of their congress. But there is a dispute as to who presided over the meetings. Ovares insists that he was named chairman because he was the president of the Cuban FEU, which was the organizer of the Bogotá congress. The meeting was very small because the Argentinians never came, and there was only a scattering of Venezuelans, Colombians, a few Mexicans and a Guatemalan. Ovares says that to 'pacify him' Fidel was named the emissary to call on Jorge Eliécer Gaitán, the immensely popular leader of the 'progressive' wing of the Colombian Liberal Party, to invite him to attend the student congress.

Castro has a very different version. He says that 'different progressive and leftist forces of Latin America' were present at the student sessions and that 'the congress was organized' because of steps taken by him. He recognizes that he could not officially represent Cuban students because he was no longer an FEU leader, 'but I spoke with considerable vehemence, I explained all that I had done, how I had done it, and why. . . I have to say that the students supported me almost unanimously after I made my presentation, even a bit passionately – as was to be expected at that time and at their age.' Fidel goes on to explain: 'I was presiding over the meeting. I said that . . . what interested me were the struggle and the objectives of this struggle. . . The students applauded enthusiastically when I spoke, and they supported the idea that I remain the organizer of this event.' The students then passed a resolution condemning the conference of American foreign ministers that was to be inaugurated in Bogotá on 3 April.

This was the Ninth Inter-American Conference, and the United States delegation was headed by Secretary of State George C. Marshall, underscoring the importance of the occasion for Washington. The previous year the foreign ministers had drafted the so-called Rio Pact (they had met near Rio de Janeiro in Brazil) of mutual defence, and now in Bogota they were to debate and sign the Charter of the Organization of American States, meant to replace the old Pan American Union as the hemispheric instrument of collective policies.

The Cold War was already well under way – President Truman had already proclaimed his 'doctrine' for defending Greece and Turkey from Communism, and the Marshall Plan to reconstruct Western Europe had been launched in 1947. Inevitably, therefore, to young Latin Americans the Inter-American Bogotá conference loomed as a United States scheme to assert its total domination over the region. There was little awareness that in the previous month, March of 1948, Communists had liquidated representative democracy in Czechoslovakia through a bloodless coup d'état.

In Bogotá the students set out to harass the foreign ministers. One evening, Fidel, a Cuban companion he does not identify, and a Colombian student scattered anti-imperialist leaflets at a Bogotá theatre during a gala performance for the visiting dignitaries, and soon afterwards Fidel found himself arrested by the Colombian police. He recalls that they were arrested at their hotel, being taken to 'tenebrous' offices in 'sordid' buildings, and interrogated by detectives. Evidently he was able to talk their way out of this predicament, because they were released within a few hours. Talking himself out of tight spots, including situations when his life was at stake, is an art Fidel had mastered from childhood.

On 7 April Castro visited Jorge Gaitán with Rafael del Pino, being taken to his office by Colombian 'Liberal students'. At that stage Colombia had for over two years been split by a savage civil war between the traditionally rival Conservative and Liberal parties, with thousands of dead in cities, towns and villages. In 1948 Colombia's president was Mariano Ospina Pérez of the Conservative Party and the country was on the brink of a fratricidal catastrophe.

A few days before the conference of the foreign ministers whom the Colombian government had so imprudently invited to its tinderbox capital (and also before the arrival of the Cuban students), Gaitán had led 100,000 demonstrators in a March of Silence to protest against police violence and brutality, and had delivered his soon-to-be-famous Speech in Favour of Peace. Receiving the Cubans, Gaitán gave them the text of the speech, explained the Colombian political crisis to them, and, according to Castro, agreed to close the student congress with an address by himself to the delegates at a mass rally.

The next day Castro went to a Bogotá court to observe Gaitán in action as a lawyer, defending a police lieutenant charged with killing a Conservative politician. This was a major cause célèbre in Colombia, with the proceedings broadcast over the radio network. Fidel found Gaitán to be 'brilliant' in the courtroom. He says he gained 'a really good impression of Gaitán. . . he was a virtuoso orator, precise in language and eloquent . . . also he was identified with the most progressive positions in the country against the Conservative government.' Gaitán invited Castro to meet with him again on 9 April. In terms of Fidel's political maturing, knowing Gaitán was crucial; again, events favoured him.

Meanwhile Fidel had another curious encounter in Bogotá. Alfredo

Guevara recalls that at a meeting with students at the National University he and Castro were introduced to a youth whose name was Camilo Torres. At the time Torres meant nothing to the Cubans. But this was the young Colombian revolutionary who first became a Roman Catholic priest and then the famous chief of a guerrilla force that for years would fight the army in the Andes. Father Torres was killed in the 1960s, and he now belongs to the pantheon of Latin American revolutionary martyrs and heroes. The ever-loyal Alfredo Guevara says: 'It is sad that great human beings do not carry a distinguishing mark on the forehead, because then one would have understood at that moment that it was *the* Fidel Castro and *the* Camilo Torres who stood there.'

Fidel's appointment with Gaitán on 9 April was for two o'clock in the afternoon. He says he had lunch at the hotel, then went out on the street to take the short walk to Gaitán's office. But, Castro says, suddenly 'there appeared people running frantically in all directions . . . people who seemed crazed. . . People shouting, "They killed Gaitán! They killed Gaitán" . . . Angry people, indignant people, people telling what had happened, spreading the word like gunpowder.'

Gaitán had just been shot and killed on the pavement in front of his office building, and although his assassin, identified only as one Juan Roa, was instantly lynched by the crowd, Bogotá – and indeed all Colombia – ignited like a revolutionary volcano. The presence of the American foreign ministers at their conference fuelled official suspicions that the assassination had been planned by radical students to trigger a revolution and deal a terrible blow to the Organization of American States, but nothing was ever uncovered to corroborate this. Castro, who witnessed and participated in the Bogotá street battles says flatly that 'nobody organized [the events of] 9 April. . . I can assure you that it was a completely spontaneous explosion that nobody could have organized. . . What 9 April completely lacked was organization . . .'

The *Bogotázo*, as that urban revolt is now known, became Fidel Castro's real baptism as a revolutionary, and obviously had an enormous impact on him, his thinking, and his future planning. It was the most important single event of his life up until then, and was unquestionably one of his major experiences, providing him with a unique opportunity to observe revolution at close quarters – and to learn from it.

His own account of his activities during the five days of the *Bogotázo* is the most complete in existence, and those who were then in contact with Castro accept it as accurate. Fidel told his Bogotá story over long hours of conversation with the Colombian journalist Arturo Alape in 1981, cautioning him that after thirty-three years he might have forgotten certain details. Still, his memory is so excellent that the interview transcript reads like a marvellously vivid adventure tale.

The first thing Castro recalled after the news of Gaitán's death had fired up the city is the sight of a man in a little downtown park trying to break up a typewriter he had somehow obtained, but having a terrible time of it. Fidel says he told the man, 'Hey, give it to me,' and 'I helped him, grabbed the typewriter, threw it high up in the air, and let it fall.'

Castro decided to go to the National Capitol where the ministerial conference was being held, but he increasingly came across people smashing 'windows and things'. This, he said, 'began to disturb me – because even then I had very clear and precise idea of what a revolution is and what things should not happen. . . I began to see signs of anarchy. . . and I wondered what Liberal Party leaders were doing.'

He saw the congress building invaded by a furious crowd, people carrying clubs and other weapons, and watched office furniture being hurled out of the windows into the square. Castro, who was with Rafael del Pino, then went to the boarding house where they found Ovares and Guevara. From there Fidel saw a huge crowd rushing down one of the main avenues in the direction of a police station. It was at this instant that Castro made up his mind to join the revolution in Colombia.

'I join the leading ranks of this crowd,' he said. 'I see there is a revolution erupting, and I decide to be part of it. . . I have no doubt that the people are oppressed, that the people who are rising are right, and that the death of Gaitán is a great crime.' At the police station policemen were aiming their rifles at the crowd, but not firing, and Castro says many of them were joining the rebels. Entering the police station, the only weapon Fidel would still find there was a tear-gas shotgun so he grabbed it along with twenty or thirty gas cartridges.

'I don't have a rifle,' Castro continued, 'but I do have something that at least can fire, this shotgun with a huge barrel. But here I am in a suit, not dressed for a war. I find a cap without a visor, and I put it on. And my street shoes are not fit for a war. . . I climb to the second floor and enter the officers' room. There I start looking for clothes, and more weapons, and I start putting on a pair of boots. An officer runs in and, I'll never forget it, in the middle of all this chaos, he wails, "Oh, not my boots, not my boots. . ." '

In the courtyard Castro came upon an officer trying to organize a police squad, and he forcibly swapped his tear-gas shotgun for the officer's regular rifle and bullets. He replaced his cap with a beret and put on a policeman's jacket. Now the armed crowd, with policemen and soldiers in its midst, rushed off in another direction like a raging torrent with Castro in the vanguard. Several cars with students he knew from the university drove by, and Fidel learned from one of them that a student group had taken over a radio station in the city, and was now being attacked. He immediately led a group to the aid of the besieged students, but the confusion, the firing and the rioting were too much for them.

And, Fidel remarked critically, 'There are people who have been drinking, arriving with bottles of rum.'

Castro said that it was unclear at that stage whether the army, like much of the police, had joined the uprising. Suddenly he came across a battalion paraded in front of the War Ministry. 'Possessed by revolutionary fever myself,' Fidel recalled, 'and trying to attract the greatest number of people to the revolutionary movement, I jump on a bench to harangue the soldiers to join the revolution. Everybody listens, nobody does anything, and there I am on the bench with my rifle, delivering my harangue.'

From the War Ministry Castro and several companions resumed their walk to the radio station (he remembers that his wallet with all the money he had was stolen from him at that moment), but suddenly they came under heavy rifle fire, barely managing to hide behind some benches. Again unable to reach the radio station, he resolved to take over a nearby police station with his fellow students.

'It is assumed that I must be the one to take the police station because I am the only one who has a rifle,' Castro recounted. 'This really is suicidal. . . But, luckily, that station had already been taken in a [police] uprising . . . and they receive us in a friendly fashion.' He sought out the police station commander, who was also the leader of the rebel policemen, and explained that he was a Cuban student organizing a congress in the city. Thereupon, Fidel says, 'The police commander names me as his aide.'

The two of them got into a Jeep to go to the headquarters of the Liberal Party, and Castro said he was delighted because he had been concerned all day over the lack of any proper organization. He added: 'Everything I'm telling you about the things that happened that day is absolutely accurate.' At the party headquarters the police chief procured a second Jeep and they returned to their station. At night Fidel and the police chief drove again to the party headquarters, each in his Jeep, but the officer's vehicle broke down, and 'I carry out the quixotic act' of giving him 'my own Jeep'. Castro and a few students were left behind in the street, finally meeting with a squad of rebel policemen with submachineguns, and making their way to another police station, also in revolutionary hands. But, he said, he did not have a cent for a cup of coffee.

This was the Fifth Police Division station, and Castro says it had some four hundred policemen and civilians. The confusion in organizing the station's defences was enormous, but he was eventually assigned a post on the second floor. What bothered Fidel most that night was the looting in Bogotá streets, with 'people carrying away a refrigerator on their backs, or a piano', and he says that 'unhappily, because of lack of organization, because of the local culture, because of the great poverty . . . many people carried away all they could. . . Through lack of political preparation and other factors, the city was looted. . . I was very disappointed that instead of seeking a political solution, many people chose to loot.'

Seeing the rebel force kept inside the police station, Castro took it upon himself to tell the division chief and his officers that 'the entire historical experience demonstrates that a force that remains in its barracks is lost'. He cited Cuban military experiences to urge the police chiefs to dispatch their forces into the street, assigning them an attack mission against government positions. Fidel was heard out amiably, but no decisions were made although he kept insisting that 'a revolutionary force that stays inside is lost'.

'I had learned some military theory from my studies of the history of revolutionary situations,' Castro said, 'of the movements that occurred during the French Revolution, the taking of the Bastille, of the Cuban experience – and I saw clearly that this was an insanity. . . They were waiting for an attack by government forces.' Castro also criticized the rebel policemen for beating up pro-government policemen they had captured: 'This disgusted me.'

He had realized, Fidel said, that he did not really know why he was there alone ' in a mousetrap', foolishly awaiting an attack, but decided to remain at the police station 'because I reasoned that, well, the people here are just like the people in Cuba, people are the same everywhere, and this is an oppressed, exploited people. I had to convince myself: they had had their principal leader assasinated, this uprising is absolutely just, I am going to die here, but I am staying.'

Castro finally persuaded the police chief to assign seven or eight men to him to patrol the hill behind the station from where the army could attack them. At one point the patrol ordered a civilian car near the station to stop, suspecting that it was driven by a government spy. But the man in it was with two prostitutes, taking them to have sex. 'Can you imagine,' the prudish Fidel Castro asks indignantly, 'the city burning, the war erupting, and this man driving around Bogotá with two prostitutes?'

On the morning of 11 April, a Sunday, word circulated that an agreement was being reached between the government and the Liberal opposition. Fidel recalls that he still had his improvised uniform with a beret, his rifle with nine bullets, and a sabre. Within hours an accord was announced, and the rebels were asked to surrender their weapons. Castro wanted to keep the sabre, but it was not allowed. He believed that the peace agreement was a 'betrayal' (one of his favourite words) of the people: certainly, once the rebels had given up their arms, government forces 'began to hunt down the revolutionaries all over the city'.

Fidel returned downtown, finding Ovares and Guevara at the boarding house where they had sat out the rebellion. But the owner was a Conservative, and he starting abusing Gaitán and the Liberals. Castro lost his patience, became 'exalted', and contradicted the man by defending the Liberals. This was a half-hour before the 6 p.m. curfew, and the owner threw out the three Cubans – who reached the safety of a downtown hotel with only five minutes to spare. But, Fidel added, 'it was immature of me to have engaged in polemics with the owner at twenty-five minutes before six o'clock.' No lesson is ever lost on Castro.

At the hotel the Cubans ran into an Argentinian diplomat they knew, and persuaded him to drive them to the Cuban Embassy (diplomatic cars being exempt from the curfew). Fidel recalls that they were very well received at the embassy 'because we were already famous and everybody was looking for the Cubans'. The Cuban students remained at the embassy until 13 April, when they were flown home to Havana aboard an official Cuban aircraft that had come to Bogotá to fetch bulls. Castro thought it was pleasantly ironic that they were saved by the Cuban government they so strenuously opposed.

Summing up his Bogotá experience, Castro says: 'The spectacle of an absolutely spontaneous popular revolution has to have exercised a great influence on me.' And, he says 'Remember that I was twenty-one years old then, and I think what I did there was really noble. . . I am proud of what I did. . . I think that my decision to stay there that night, when I was alone and it all seemed like a great tactical error, was a great proof of idealism. I was loyal until the last moment. . . I was disciplined and I stayed although I knew it was dangerous. . . I behaved with principle, with correct morality, with dignity, with honour, with complete altruism. . .'

Castro claims that furthermore the Bogotá experience led him to 'extraordinary efforts to create political conscience in Cuba . . . to assure that in the triumph of the revolution there would be no anarchy, no looting, no disorders . . . that people would not take justice into their own hands. . . Bogotá's greatest influence was on the Cuban revolutionary strategy, on the idea of educating the people during our struggle.'

Nevertheless, Fidel admitted, 'My presence there was accidental, and our congress had nothing to do with what happened.' In fact, the Bogotázo ruined the organization of the congress. The plan for an anti-imperialist students' association was never revived by the Cubans or the Argentinians.

The return of Fidel Castro and his Cuban associates from Bogotá made the front pages of Havana newspapers. Despite contradictory reports about his activities in Colombia and charges that he was part of a Communist conspiracy, Fidel's image at home gained very considerably. At twenty-one he was now an international as well as national figure in the eyes of many Cubans. True to his life pattern, he had lucked out once more; as he said himself, he materialized 'accidentally' in the midst of the Colombian civil war.

Back in Cuba Castro immediately threw himself into the presidential electoral campaign, now in its closing phase. Though he was veering towards Marxism he maintained his strong support for the candidacy of Senator Chibás – presumably because he felt that the *Ortodoxo* party offered the best solutions for the Cuban crisis, and because he was not ready to break with the traditional political process. Notwithstanding his revolutionary propensities he was also a practical politician, and he must have seen no advantage whatsoever in becoming formally identified with the weak (if loud) Communist Party.

Fidel spent several weeks in May campaigning for Chibás, chiefly in their native Oriente province, and national newspapers duly reported his presence along with *Ortodoxo* congressmen and mayors. Campaigning for Chibás, however, Castro was careful to preserve his personal reputation for independence, often being more outspoken than the candidates on social issues, and even being critical in public of the senator over his friendship with very wealthy landowners. It was one more major political experience for the young Castro.

On 31 May, the eve of the elections, Fidel described the contest as 'a decisive battle' between Chibás's 'idealism' and the 'vested interests' of the candidates of the Grau government. Eddy Chibás may have been the conscience of young Cuba, but on 1 June he was demolished at the polls by Grau's Labour Minister Carlos Prío Socarrás, with the Liberal Party's Ricardo Nuñez Portuondo, a conservative, coming in second. Chibás beat only the Communists' Juan Marinello.

After the defeat Castro turned to his long-range political interests, including his radical ARO group within the *Ortodoxo* party, driving all over Havana behind the wheel of his second-hand green Buick, and in less than a week he was embroiled in a new problem.

A university police sergeant named Oscar Fernández Caral was shot in front of his house on 6 June, and before dying he supposedly identified Castro as his assassin, and an unnamed witness corroborated it. Fidel in this instance learned of these charges from the newspapers, and went into hiding again, believing that once more the campus gangsters and their friends in the police were out to kill him. After he had issued protests the witness retracted the accusation, telling newsmen that he had been bribed by the police to name Castro. But early in July an effort was made to reopen the case, and Fidel informed the judge that he had no intention of appearing in court 'to help in the government's unforgivable attempt to implicate myself in something of which I am completely innocent'. Castro went on to tell the judge that if his arrest were ordered 'some police agents' might take advantage of the opportunity to assassinate him. Predictably, nothing further happened.

He spent a short vacation in Birán, saw his parents, and returned to Havana early in September to resume his law studies, still on an auditing basis. Simultaneously he engaged in new research into Marxism and socialism. Then, on 8 September, Grau's outgoing government authorized the Havana bus company to increase fares, and the next day Communist labour and student leaders were the first to protest through street rallies and speeches.

By the afternoon of 9 September, the FEU and university students had joined the fray, capturing eight buses, decorating them with Cuban flags, and driving them to the campus. Castro, who could not, of course, stay away from this latest confrontation, joined Alfredo Guevara and Lionel Soto in warnings that serious clashes would occur if people violated the autonomy of the university. The buses, however, vanished overnight from the campus, and this particular incident ended abruptly. But the fare increases were cancelled.

President Prío was inaugurated on 10 October 1948, a national holiday, opening a period of corruption and mismanagement in Cuba that would exceed even Grau's. Fidel Castro, however, succeeded in ignoring this occurrence, at least for a while. Two days later, on 12 October, he married Mirta Díaz-Balart, the pretty, dark-haired philosophy student he had met several years earlier through her brother Rafael who was at the law school; the two men were friends.

The Díaz-Balart family was, like the Castro's, from Oriente, and the wedding took place at their home in Banes, not far from Birán. The Díaz-Balarts were wealthy, very well-connected politically in Santiago and Havana, and, except for Rafael, less than enthusiastic about Mirta's marriage to the twenty-two-year-old Fidel. They disapproved of his politics, and, most likely, of his family background.

Virtually nothing is known of the circumstances of this marriage, except that it was fated to be destroyed by politics within five years. By all accounts Mirta was deeply in love with Fidel, and his friends say that she was the only woman in whom he had been interested as he divided the bulk of his time between his studies and politics. Yet this does not explain why Fidel and Mirta were married so young, particularly when Castro was still in law school and all his free time consumed by revolutionary dreams.

Fidel and Mirta travelled to the United States for their honeymoon, an interesting choice given Fidel's anti-American sentiments. In any event, the young Castro's remained on the mainland for several weeks, including a New York stay where Fidel apparently gave some thought to trying for a scholarship at Columbia University. It is said that it was in a New York bookshop that Castro purchased a number of books by Marx and Engels, including *Das Kapital*.

Chapter 7

A political career and a professional career, both in earnest, were Fidel Castro's most urgent priorities. He realized that his frantic activities in so many directions had interfered with his larger purposes and now he had to concentrate on systematic Party work and on law courses. But his ideological preoccupations never left him.

Castro would say later that at the time of Bogotá 'I was almost a Communist, but not yet actually one,' which is one of those obfuscating phrases he delights in throwing out. He would complain that it was 'a great calumny' to blame the Colombian or the Cuban Communist parties, or the international Communist movement, for the uprising. As far as he was concerned, 'the whole people fought' in Bogotá. And after so many years there is still no reason to doubt his basic conclusions.

Back in Havana, however, he must have been shocked to discover that the Cuban Communist Party sharply criticized his 'adventurism' in participating in the Bogotá street fighting. The Communist Alfredo Guevara had been in Bogotá with Fidel in his capacity of FEU official, but he never stirred out of the boarding house during the disturbances; obviously Guevara knew the party line, while impulsive Fidel did not.

Whether Castro seriously regarded himself as 'almost a Communist' or not in the aftermath of Bogotá, the Communists distrusted him absolutely and would do so until the eve of his revolutionary victory *ten* years later. Castro's intricate ideological positions and his manoeuvrings after Bogotá suggest quite plainly that he drew a fundamental distinction between Marxism, socialism and Communism on the one hand, and the traditional Cuban Communist parties on the other. This is a point, as so many other points about Fidel, that the United States and the Soviet Union alike have had difficulties in grasping for a quarter of a century.

Meanwhile Fidel Castro, if somewhat incongruously, settled down to married life. Their home was a room in a small, inexpensive hotel at 1218

San Lázaro Street in downtown Havana, one block from the university. While convenient for Fidel it must have been confining for Mirta, although she still attended some classes at the philosophy school, and went on seeing her friends and family. Fidel was rarely in attendance. If he was not studying or politicking at the university he was at the *Ortodoxo* party headquarters at 109 Paseo de Prado, the lovely, broad avenue linking the seaside Malecón boulevard at the harbour with the National Capitol, for meetings with opposition politicians. Castro always cultivated pivotal *Ortodoxo* figures to keep open his electoral options, and at that time he was already thinking of running for office. The rest of his day and night hours were consumed by other political meetings, occasional involvement in street disturbances if they were politically profitable, and voracious reading.

Fidel and Mirta lived in the hotel for a full year, presumably because they could not afford to rent a house or an apartment. His allowance from Don Ángel in Birán was around 80 pesos ($80), which was probably just enough for the hotel room and the service that came with it, including some meals. Not working, he had no other income. Mirta's family were quite wealthy, but chances are that the proud Fidel did not let his in-laws help to support him, and his wife must have been loyal enough to agree. She was accustomed to great comfort, yet she did not appear to mind the hotel life with Fidel – her love for him compensated for all the deprivations. And Mirta would endure more sacrifices in the near future.

In his fourth year at law school, Castro received high grades in courses on labour legislation, and only passing grades in property and real estate, which may have been a clue to his interests.

In Havana political violence of all sorts continued, with Fidel Castro in the thick of it. The Havana bus company again demanded a fare increase, which the Prío government approved on 20 January. The FEU at a university meeting split over whether students should return to the bus-fare battle in the streets. The FEU's Struggle Committee was for it, but the leadership opposed student action, fearing a campus invasion by the police. The pro-fight faction led by Fidel insisted that the FEU's prestige was involved in the protest. On 24 January thousands of students gathered on the campus, preparing to march downtown. But police cars surrounded the university, policemen firing guns at the students. With Castro in the vanguard, students responded with a barrage of stones and tomatoes. Then the student committee printed 50,000 leaflets (it was Castro's idea) urging *habaneros* to boycott the buses.

In March 1949 an incident occurred in Havana that added to the bitterness against the United States, an incident that Cubans in general and Fidel Castro in particular never forgot – explaining why anti-

American sentiment tended to rise rather than diminish with the passage of time.

This was the desecration of the statue of the revered José Martí in Havana's Central Park on the evening of 11 March by a group of inebriated United States Navy sailors on shore liberty. At least one sailor urinated against the base of the statue, and another sat on Martí's sculpted head. An infuriated crowd gathered quickly, and the sailors were saved just in time by the police who took them to a station. Presently the US naval attaché and a Shore Police patrol arrived at the station to take the sailors back to their ship. There was no effort by the Cuban authorities to lodge any charges against the men.

Word of the profanation spread instantly throughout Havana and there was immediate reaction by students led by Fidel Castro. He and a number of students appointed themselves as a guard of honour, standing by the Martí statue all night as a patriotic gesture, and making plans for an anti-American demonstration the following day. The student protest in front of the American Embassy on 12 March was directed by Castro and his friends Baudilio Castellanos, Alfredo Guevara and Lionel Soto, the university's principal activists.

The American Ambassador in Havana, Robert Butler, who fully understood the gravity of the Martí incident, came out to speak to the students and apologize for the sailors. Just then police riot squads commanded by Havana's new police chief Colonel José Caramés (who the previous year as university district police commander had broken up the bus-fare demonstration), attacked the students with extraordinary brutality. Fidel was beaten up. Caramés's actions were presumably intended to show the United States how efficiently Cuban authorities could protect the embassy, but contemporary accounts indicate that Butler himself was taken aback by this violence.

The ambassador then drove to the Foreign Ministry to deliver official United States apologies to Foreign Minister Carlos Hevia, but the students followed him. Finally Butler had the opportunity to try to explain the incident, reminding the students of his country's friendship for Cuba, in the name of which, he said, the United States had helped win independence for the island in 1898. Given the history of Cuban–American relations, the military occupation and the imposition of the Platt Amendment, that was not the most felicitous way of pacifying the students; they made this clear by shouting Butler down. Although the ambassador then went to the Central Park to place a wreath at the Martí statue this, too, was seen as provocative: what the Cubans wanted was the sailors punished at least by the US Navy. Castro, Guevara and Soto made the rounds of Havana newspaper offices delivering a statement, published the next day, charging that it was 'shameful for Cuba' to have a police chief who instead of preventing American sailors from desecrating

Martí's monument, chose instead 'to attack those who defended our honour'. Cubans have declared that the incident will never be forgotten: in his post-revolution picture on the modern history of Cuba, *Viva la República*, the cinema director Pastor Vega has included old newsreel footage of the demonstrations, with a very clear explanation of what happened that day.

Though Castro took advantage of every conceivable public situation to demonstrate his political involvement and assert his leadership aspirations, the Martí statue events being a perfect example, he devoted much of his time to regular political activities on many fronts. He had to build up a reputation beyond that of a patriotic or socially-inspired agitator. Consequently he made an effort to become known in the impoverished, working-class districts of south Havana, visiting homes, stores and repair shops on the miserable, narrow streets. Castro also wangled invitations to speak on the COCO radio chain several times a month, preaching social justice and honesty in politics, and clearly wishing to remain identified with Eddy Chibás who, despite his defeat in the presidential elections, remained very popular, planning to run again in 1952. In May, for instance, Chibás issued a documented report on Batista's personal enrichment during his presidential term, attracting great attention throughout the country. Fidel knew the senator was a political virtuoso, that his 'honesty' campaign was having a growing impact on President Prío's corrupt administration, and he believed Chibás would win the presidency in the end. Therefore he watched the master closely, studying his techniques and preparing to adapt them for his own future use.

On another level Castro was active in the University Committee for the Struggle against Racial Discrimination. In a country as racist as Cuba (even poor whites thought themselves better than the blacks and mulattos in Cuba's heavily mixed society), opposition to discrimination was not a popular cause, but Castro embraced it from the outset. There is every reason to believe that Castro was always personally opposed to racial discrimination, and he realized that the kind of mass political or revolutionary movement in Cuba that he was already urging could never develop without major support from non-white Cubans. Events would prove him right. Nevertheless, despite his efforts, Castro has not been able even a quarter of a century after the revolution to eradicate visceral racism among white Cubans. As a radically mixed Latin American society, Cuba most resembles Brazil, and in spite of the existence of severe anti-discrimination laws in both countries the whites have not, by and large, shed their sense of superiority. It comes out in casual remarks, jokes, and subtle societal attitudes.

On 1 September 1949, with the birth of Fidel Castro Díaz-Balart, immediately known as Fidelito, Fidel Castro became a father. At the time of Fidelito's arrival his parents still lived in the hotel room on San Lázaro Street, and it was many months before they could arrange to move to a small, modest apartment on Third Street. Although in the affluent residential district of Vedado, only one block from the sea and across the street from the Fifth District police station, the new Castro residence was still very far from luxurious. Fidel still basically depended on the allowance from his father. He was too busy in politics to earn money in the evenings after his university classes and Mirta had to watch every peso. All the furniture for the apartment, simple as it was, had to be bought on an instalment plan.

About the same time, Fidel persuaded his parents to let his brother Raúl come to Havana. Raúl had done so badly at the Belén college that Don Ángel made him come back home and work in the farm office with Ramón, the eldest brother. Fidel thought that Raúl, being highly intelligent (his Belén problem had been his hatred of discipline and particularly of prayer), should be given another chance. Consequently, Raúl returned to Havana late in 1949, hoping to be ready to enter the university the following year. This move would have important implications on the *Fidelista* revolutionary future.

In the meantime corruption and gangsterism were soaring in Cuba under Prío, the violence rising again, both in and out of the university. Justo Fuentes, a top FEU leader, was killed in April, by unknown gunmen. Castro was threatened innumerable times (some of his friends think his apartment facing the police station was rented as a security precaution for his family and himself). Finally Eddy Chibás went on the radio late in September to charge that corrupt members of Prío's administration controlled the political gangs shooting it out in Havana streets,

Prío's response was to solve the violence problem with what Cubans called The Gangs' Pact, and which, in effect, meant that the president secretly bought all the gangsters. It was a much more creative idea than simply to put the gangs on the payroll: Prío's concept was to negotiate a peace pact with the principal organizations, spreading government appointments (with attendant payments and shake-down possibilities) among them on the condition that there would be no more violence. Moreover, none of the gangsters would be charged with crimes or arrested.

This was virtually turning Cuban government over to the gangs, and the students, supported by the main opposition political parties, were the first to publicly denounce the secret pact. To this end the *Ortodoxo* party youth section and the Socialist Youth (a branch of the Communist Party) joined in organizing the 30th of September Committee, so named because the student leader Rafael Trejo had been killed by the Machado dictatorship on that date in 1930. In this committee Fidel Castro would soon play a crucial and dramatic role.

Fidel was not among its founders, and had not been considered for membership because of his earlier ties with UIR. The principal leaders of the new student committee were Max Lesnick, a university student and national director of the *Ortodoxo* Youth, and Alfredo Guevara, still president of the philosophy school and university representative of the Communists' Socialist Youth. Between them Lesnick and Guevara controlled student politics in 1949, because they represented the most cohesive and best-organized political entities in Cuba, and they got along personally extremely well.

Castro had a pleasant relationship with Lesnick and, of course, Alfredo Guevara had been with him in Bogotá (even if, as alleged by mutual friends, Guevara had criticized Castro behind his back for his revolutionary fervour in Colombia). Other Communist leaders in the group were Lionel Soto and Antonio Nuñez Jiménez. Although he had closer personal links with the three Communists, Fidel chose to approach Lesnick first to be invited to join the 30th of September Committee. Lesnick, now exiled in Miami, recalls how Castro instantly turned into the hero of the new movement, and what happened subsequently:

'Fidel came to see me at the university to say that he wanted to join the committee. Well, it seemed absurd to me: Fidel who was involved with the gangs, the 30th of September Committee could not welcome him. . . I told him, "Look Fidel, I cannot decide alone on this," and he asks me to propose his name to the committee. There were ten or twelve of us who were important [in the committee], but, fundamentally, it was Alfredo Guevara and I.'

Lesnick agreed reluctantly and Fidel met with him and Guevara at Lesnick's apartment on Morro Street, near the presidential palace, to request his admission. Max Lesnick continues: 'Alfredo and I then start coming up with impossible conditions. No member of the committee may be armed when he goes to the university, and Fidel always carries a pistol. Fidel says, "Well, I won't carry it any more." The second condition is the endorsement of the [*Ortodoxo*–Communist] pact, which demands that all those covered by the Gangs Pact must be denounced, and their official posts revealed. So Fidel says, "Well, I'll sign the document," Then Guevara asks who should be chosen to make the denunciation before the FEU, and he answers, "I shall do it." '

In the closing days of November a meeting attended by thirteen presidents of Havana University schools and 500 students was held late in the afternoon in the Martyrs' Gallery on the campus. In the words of Max Lesnick 'Fidel takes the floor and delivers a demolishing denunciation of the whole gangster process.'

Fidel then proceeded to name all the gangsters, politicians and student leaders profiting from Prío's secret Gangs Pact, and the effect was stunning. With his network of friends and acquaintances in the Havana political world he had no trouble procuring detailed information on this subject. Castro had to realize that he was embarking on an extremely dangerous venture, but he had evidently made his classic risk calculation – a blend of intellectual analysis and pure instinct – that his challenge would succeed, that he would be cleared once and for all of gangsterism accusations, and that his political stature would rise significantly. It was not bravura but an act of deliberate courage. Hardly had Castro finished speaking before automobiles loaded with armed thugs began to appear around the university.

'The problem now,' Max Lesnick says, 'was to get Fidel out of there alive. I had a red convertible, and I told him that I would drive him out. It was seven o'clock in the evening. . . I didn't do it out of courage, but figuring that if Fidel is seen in the open car next to me, the gangsters wouldn't dare to shoot. It would be too much of a scandal to attack a well-known *Ortodoxo* leader's car.'

The ploy worked. Lesnick took Fidel to his Morro Street apartment, hiding him there for fifteen days 'because he would be killed if he went out in the street'. The Havana newspapers prominently displayed Castro's speech, and he was an inviting target. It is not clear what, if anything, Mirta – still in the hotel room with their three-month-old baby – was told about her husband's whereabouts and plans. As a rule Fidel never discussed his political activities with her.

The rest of this story has never been publicly told, presumably because Castro wished it kept quiet. Having agreed with his friends that he should leave Cuba until tempers cooled, Castro decided to go to New York. The decision was wise, but Castro may have feared that a secret departure from the country under such circumstances could be regarded as a cowardly act, and he did not desire any taint on his reputation.

While his trip was being prepared Fidel spent the time in Lesnick's apartment reading, listening to the radio, talking and being bored. According to Lesnick, one day Fidel grabbed a broomstick, and pointing it from his bedroom window at the north terrace of the presidential palace, he said to Lesnick's grandmother: 'You know, if Prío steps out on that terrace to make a speech, I could get him from here with a single bullet from a telescopic-sight rifle . . .' But Fidel has always had an unusual sense of humour.

It was Lesnick and a mutual student friend named Alfredo (Chino) Esquível who drove Castro to the railway station in Havana in mid-December; there Fidel and Chino boarded a train for the city of Matanzas, then another train to Oriente and the Castro home in Birán. Apparently Fidel was able to obtain enough money from his father to finance his trip to the United States. Castro then flew to Miami, and on to New York where he remained for three or four months. Virtually nothing is known about this trip except that he lived in a room in a brownstone on 155 West 82nd Street in Manhattan. It is unclear whether Mirta with or without the baby joined him for any part of the New York stay or how he supported himself, though he most likely received money from home.

In any case, Castro had ample opportunity to read and think and even to write. He improved his knowledge of English, but even so one has the impression that somehow Fidel was not able, not then and not later, to grasp fully the nuances of American attitudes. In the future this shortcoming may have had an unfortunate effect on some of his policy decisions.

Three months before this self-imposed exile in September 1949 Mao Tse-tung's Communists had achieved ultimate victory in the long civil war with the United States-supported nationalists, a milestone in the history of great modern revolutions. The struggle that led to the creation of the People's Republic of China that year had immense relevance to Castro's own revolutionary interests – from ideology to guerrilla warfare – yet he seemed to ignore it, and Mao certainly never was a military model for him. Strangely, this lack of apparent interest in Communist and revolutionary events abroad (except where Cuba is directly involved as in Nicaragua or Angola) is part of a pattern. He rarely refers to them, and during the 1950s he is not known to have publicly spoken of the Chinese experience, the Vietnamese victory over the French at Dien Bien Phu, or the anti-regime uprisings in Poland and Hungary.

Castro had resolved to graduate from law school during 1950, and through the spring and summer in Havana he lived day and night with his books. Rather than attend classes, he prepared himself by reading voraciously, absorbing in less than six months a normal two-year work load. His willpower and superb memory helped him greatly. His friends were astounded that he had so totally removed himself from all political activity and feared that in staying away from meetings and discussions he might be forgotten. He knew he would not be. Though he could spare very little time for his family he evidently doted on Fidelito, and right after his return from New York he took the baby's photographs, sending prints to grandparents in Birán and Banes. His brother Raúl was in Havana about to enter the university, and his youngest sister Emma came through the city en route to private school in Switzerland.

September 1950 saw Fidel Castro graduated from the University of Havana with the titles of Doctor of Law, Doctor of Social Sciences and Doctor of Diplomatic Law; the Cuban system permitted a student to work for multiple degrees. Fidel says that during his crash study programme he completed forty-eight out the fifty required courses on his own, a record that no other student had matched during a comparable period. Being short of the fifty course, Castro was not eligible for the scholarship abroad that he had thought of pursuing. But by this time Fidel says he was too impatient with the political 'realities' at home to pursue the scholarship notion, deciding instead to dedicate himself to politics and a law practice.

In terms of conventional politics, Castro recalls, his ties with the *Ortodoxo* party remained 'strong' as he graduated from the university 'although my ideas had advanced much more'. This party, he says, was able to give a voice to much of the discontent of the Cuban masses over unemployment, poverty, and the lack of housing, schools and hospitals. As an *Ortodoxo* youth leader Fidel was not 'preaching socialism as an immediate goal,' he says, but campaigning against 'injustice, poverty, unemployment, high rents, low salaries, expulsions of peasants [from the land they tilled] and political corruption'. In his opinion, looking back nearly thirty-five years, this was a programme for which Cubans were much better prepared, the phase during which a start had to be made in moving the people in a 'genuinely evolutionary direction'.

Castro had never alluded publicly to his Marxist–Leninist evolution and persuasion until he declared himself a Communist in a speech in December 1961, and over the ensuing years he has maintained a high degree of imprecision about the stages of his socialist conversion, blurring considerably (though surely deliberately) his whole educational process. But he is consistent in stating with complete candour that he had concealed the socialist character of his political programme until he thought Cubans were ready for it and he himself felt sufficiently in control of the country to reveal it.

After graduating Fidel Castro decided to go immediately into law practice, but to concentrate on political cases and what his friends would call the lost causes of litigations on behalf of the poor. To proceed in this fashion was a conscious political move on Fidel's part, consistent with both his professed beliefs and his political-revolutionary ambitions. It would have been easy for him, particularly through the Díaz-Balart marriage connection, to seek partnership with influential firms and lawyers, and to rapidly command a lucrative practice, but Castro chose another route.

The partners Fidel selected for his law office were Jorge Aspiazo Nuñez de Villavicencio, a former bus driver, nine years older than Castro, who graduated in the same class with him, and Rafael Resende Viges, another fellow student with a background of poverty. Jorge Aspiazo, now retired in Havana, recalls that Fidel met with him and Resende on the *escalinata* of the university one afternoon in September to propose the partnership. Aspiazo, who had voted against Fidel for class delegate in their first year in the law school because he suspected him of being a 'rich boy', soon became a friend, though to this day he remains apolitical. Resende, the same age as Fidel, was also a friend. Later he would swerve to the right, joining the Batista camp and ultimately emigrating to the United States.

As Aspiazo recalls it they selected quarters consisting of a small reception room and a tiny private office on the second floor of a rundown building at 57 Tejadillo Street, in Old Havana. This was the capital's banking and business area in the narrow streets and small squares of colonial structures near the harbour, and most law offices were located there. The ancient Rosario building where Castro and his partners went to rent space was almost entirely occupied by law firms.

The monthly rent was $60 (the Cuban peso and the dollar being then at par), and the owner, José Alvárez, insisted on the first month's payment and a month's security, for a $120 total. However the three young lawyers had only $80 between them and it took persuasion for Alvárez to agree to settle for that. They also talked him into lending them some furniture, including a desk and a single chair so that they could start working. They bought a typewriter on hire purchase.

Aspiazo says that their first professional arrangement was with a wealthy Spanish immigrant who owned a wholesale lumber business which sold materials to local carpenters. A typical Fidel proposition, the deal was that the Gancedo firm would provide the lawyers with free lumber to build their office furniture, and in return they would collect overdue bills from carpenters who had purchased wood from the Spaniard.

This was collection-agency work, but that is not the way Fidel conducted it. Instead, Aspiazo recounts, Fidel summoned Gancedo's debtor carpenters to the office and asked them for a list of people who owed *them* money for their services. The lawyers then spent their time collecting on behalf of the carpenters, and whenever they succeeded Fidel would call his client to say that they had money for him. But Aspiazo says that when the carpenter asked Castro to pay, for example, $20 to the lumber merchant, Fidel would often reply, 'No, you need this money now, and our client does not'.

On one occasion Castro and Aspiazo went to collect from a carpenter in the Lawton district of Havana, one of the poorest, but the man was away. Aspiazo says that the carpenter's pregnant wife asked them to wait, stepping into the kitchen to make coffee for them, and Fidel asked his partner to lend him five pesos, placing the bank note under a plate on the table. When the wife served them coffee Fidel told her the carpenter should not worry about his debt to Gancedo, and should come by their office only when he could.

Aspiazo adds that they never paid the lumber company a cent. After sending bills for their furniture materials 'they got tired and never collected from us'. But the law firm did poorly in collections itself because Fidel insisted that most of its work be *pro bono publico* – or a free public service. They represented stall owners at the municipal market in Havana, peasants in Havana province who were being expelled from farms, students involved in riots – just about every poor person who had a legal problem turned to Aspiazo, Castro & Resende. In their three years of partnership (which ended, in effect, when Castro left to lead the attack on the Moncada barracks in 1953), they earned a total of 4800 pesos, of which 3000 pesos were for one case and 1800 pesos for another. They also sued the American-owned Cuban telephone company on behalf of the subscribers for lower rates, and the court actually found in their favour, but by that time Castro was already in prison.

Whether from the viewpoint of his law firm or himself, Fidel had a total disdain for money. Theoretically his allowance from Birán was designed to support his family but, as his friends say, Fidel often gave it away the moment it arrived; it was enough even for a casual acquaintance in his political circle to ask for a loan for Castro to produce the money.

On his graduation from law school Fidel received a brand-new Pontiac sedan as a present from his father. Shortly thereafter a friend borrowed it for a trip out of town, wrecking the Pontiac in an accident and suffering serious injuries. At the hospital, where he rushed as soon as he heard about the accident, Fidel met his friend's father, a powerful and rich conservative politician who told him that he would pay for the car. Castro replied: 'You are wrong. Your son is dying. How can you be concerned about the car? You don't have to pay anything; you should worry about your son.' Three years later the politician would intervene with his friend Fulgencio Batista to assure that Castro received decent treatment in prison; he may even have saved Fidel from assassination by his jailers.

When his old friend Baudilio Castellanos visited Havana, Fidel invited him to lunch at home. On Castellano's arrival, however, Castro – who was alone – suggested they drive first to the municipal market where he went from stall to stall, picking rice, potatoes and *malanga* (an edible root, popular among poor people in Cuba), but without paying for anything. Castellanos remarked on it, and Fidel said, 'Oh, I never pay here . . . they are my clients, and they pay my fees with food.' Thereupon they drove back to the apartment on Third Street where Fidel cooked the lunch.

Fidel's financial recklessness continually distressed Mirta. One day, when Castro was out of Havana, she telephoned Jorge Aspiazo in tears, begging him to come over immediately. At the apartment Aspiazo found all the furniture gone, and Mirta weeping on the floor with Fidelito in her arms. The store, she told him, had repossessed all their furnishings, including the baby's crib, because Castro had failed to make the instalment payments. Aspiazo somehow obtained enough cash for a downpayment for new furniture; when Fidel returned the next day and looked around the apartment, he remarked in surprise, 'Christ, this is not *my* furniture. . . ' He took Aspiazo's resolution of the problem for granted.

Very soon Castro had his first opportunity to act as his own attorney in court. This came as a consequence of his arrest on 12 November 1950, in the southern port city of Cienfuegos, for participating in an anti-government student demonstration. After a year-long hiatus, Castro was back in the public view, his name again in the newspapers.

Not that Castro had been forgotten. Alfredo Guevara recalls that in Havana even strangers asked him 'How is Fidel?' and word of his 'public defender' reputation was spreading. Still, he needed a national event, and Cienfuegos seemed to fill the requirement. High school students there had called a 'permanent strike' to protest against the ban on their organizations and associations by Education Minister Aureliano Sánchez Arango and Interior Minister Lomberto Díaz, and to Fidel this was a matter of principle worth a good fight.

Castro and his companions were arrested by soldiers at the student rally even before he could begin speaking, and they were taken to jail and hit with rifle butts. For the next four hours students, army and police fought in the streets, and as an account of the Cienfuegos events published after the revolution put it quite accurately, 'the objective that brought Fidel . . . had been achieved; the protests of the people against the regime were much more violent than if the meeting had been peaceful'.

From Cienfuegos Castro and Benavides were taken during the night to the provincial capital of Santa Clara and locked up in the prison there, but Senator Chibás had gone on nationwide radio to denounce the arrests, and a demonstration erupted in front of the prison during the morning. The two men were released conditionally, but before returning to Havana Fidel issued a thundering denunciation of 'the executioners of the people', printed in full in Cuban newspapers

In mid-December, Castro and Benavides returned to Santa Clara for their trial, and Fidel informed the court that as he was a lawyer he intended to conduct his own defence. When it developed that he needed an attorney's black robe and black cap to be allowed to address the judge – as well as five pesos in fees – a collection was taken up at once among the audience, and Castro rose to speak. Always believing that offence is the best defence, he delivered a roaring accusation of the government for 'strangling the liberties' of Cuba, claiming that the regime and the army should be judged at the trial – not him and Benavides. The presiding judge heard Fidel out, and pronounced his verdict: 'Not Guilty.' It was a victory that Castro still often and fondly recalls.

Increasingly, as before, Castro was gaining access to public opinion through the press and radio. Ramón Vasconcelos, the editor of the outspoken daily *Alerta* (and formerly a Prío cabinet minister), had become a friend, opening his newspaper's pages to Fidel's fiery articles. In June 1951, for example, Castro published a lengthy defence of workers' rights, citing the cases of 900 employees illegally dismissed by a canning company and of peasants deprived of land. He concluded by stating that 'justice for Cuban workers and peasants' must be the nation's principal goal. He also had frequent access to the Voice of the Antilles radio station, constantly attacking the Prío government on issues of corruption and denial of justice in Cuban society.

On the evening of Sunday 5 August 1951 Senator Eduardo Chibás shot himself in the abdomen during his weekly programme from radio station CMQ, attempting to commit public suicide. He died eleven days later.

The reasons for Chibás' suicide at the age of forty-three have never been fully understood. He shot himself with a .38 Colt Special revolver, a powerful weapon, at the end of a speech urging Cubans to 'awaken' in the name of 'economic independence, political liberty and social justice'. En route to the hospital he whispered, 'I am dying for the revolution. . . I am dying for Cuba. . .'

But this explains little. The senator was a passionate and popular figure, the leading candidate for the presidency in the 1952 elections and a man seemingly happy in his personal and family life. His brother Raúl, who was also his closest political associate, says thirty-four years later: 'I still do not find an answer. . . I think that in part it was disillusion because it is very easy to become disillusioned in politics if things are not going well, if people turn their backs on one. . . He must have felt a little lonely, and that many people who should have helped him, did not help him. They were not cooperating. . . Possibly he felt he was no longer useful, and that he could be more useful making an example of himself. . .'

Raúl Chibás was unquestionably referring to the serious dilemma his brother was facing that Sunday when he was unable to produce the promised proof of his long-standing allegations that Education Minister Aureliano Sánchez Arango was guilty of corruption and self-enrichment on a colossal scale. The senator's accusations for more than a month over ' the radio were Cuba's greatest political sensation, and on the appointed day the nation breathlessly awaited Chibás documentation. But, surprisingly, he failed to mention the subject, shooting himself as the climax of his appearance. It is generally believed that the group of congressmen who held the documents of proof against the minister and who had promised them to Chibás, betrayed him at the last moment. Having spent his political life preaching honesty and truth, Chibás could not face the fact that he would break his word to the people. This assessment is privately shared by Fidel Castro.

In any event Chibás' death completely altered the Cuban political scene, removing not only a powerful candidate for the presidency but also a man who was the nearest thing to Cuba's conscience. Most importantly perhaps, the Chibás suicide paved the way for Batista's coup d'état the following year; Raúl Chibás and many other Cubans are convinced that Batista would not have risked the coup if Eddy were alive: the influential senator would have instantly become the leader of a powerful anti-dictatorship movement.

For Fidel Castro the death of Chibás had many implications. He could not yet foresee the Batista coup in the vacuum that had been created, but he understood probably better than any other politician in Cuba that the whole situation had changed, and was now sufficiently uncertain to bring about the revolutionary climate he so earnestly desired.

In terms of *Ortodoxo* party politics Fidel was too young to aspire to replace Chibás as the top leader, and this never entered his calculations. He did perceive, however, that without Chibás dictating policy, younger and more independent-minded *Ortodoxos* could be diverted to his revolutionary line. There were no commanding personalities in the party who could replace the senator when it came to influence over the young. At the same time, Fidel spared no effort to show himself as an absolutely loyal and heart-broken disciple of the dead leader. It would be unjust to portray Castro as simply an opportunist: he must have had some liking and admiration for Chibás even though they disagreed on much in politics, and even though today the Castro regime has erased his memory.

As Chibás lay dying for eleven days, Castro was near the door of Suite 321 at Havana's Medical Surgical Centre around the clock. When Chibás's body lay in state at the university's *Aula Magna* (Hall of Honour), Fidel stood by the bier as part of the honour guard for the twenty-four hours preceding the funeral. A photograph published in Cuban newspapers and magazines shows him standing in the front row, the fourth from the casket, staring at the floor. He wears a grey suit and a tie; most of the other politicians there are in *guayaberas* (this is also the first photograph showing Castro with a pencil-line moustache).

Raúl Chibás and Castro led the victorious campaign to place Chibás body on display at the university instead of at the National Capitol. They argued that his political career had begun at the university, whereas the Capitol could be seen as a symbol of the corruption the senator had always denounced.

The senator was to be buried the following day, 17 August, at Havana's Colón cemetery, the funeral cortege from the university led by the military. According to his friends Max Lesnick, Fidel conceived the idea of diverting the procession before the burial to the presidential palace where Chibás's body would be placed in the presidential chair, and be symbolically proclaimed Cuba's president. Lesnick says that Castro nearly convinced the officer commanding the escort of the gun carriage transporting the body to take the procession to the palace, but in the end reason prevailed, with the officer realizing that he could trigger a mass uprising – which was presumably what Fidel had in mind. He never lacked ideas.

His next idea, less than a month after Chibás's death, was to formally charge two National Police officers with the death of a worker, a member of the *Ortodoxo* party, during a riot back on Sunday 18 February. In his attorney's capacity Castro presented the charges against Major Rafael Casals Fernández and Lieutenant Rafael Salas Cañizares before a Havana criminal court. The latter was also involved in violence against students during the Martí statue incident in 1949. The case attracted wide attention, and the government tried futilely to move it to military jurisdiction. In the end the officers were placed on conditional liberty under 5000-peso bail, but not acquitted (the case was dropped after the Batista coup, and Castro would have to contend again with Lieutenant Salas Cañizares).

A curious political episode involving Fidel Castro and Fulgencio Batista appears to have occurred some time after Chibás's death. Batista, who ended his elected presidential term in 1944, returned to Cuba from his Florida home in 1950 to re-enter politics – hoping to be president again. He founded the Unitary Action Party (PAU), whose principal ideological aim was to restore him to the presidency, and began to gather and buy support. Before dying, Chibás claimed that the Communists were supporting Batista in the fear that the *Ortodoxos* would steal the social justice thunder from them, and that they could resume the pleasant cooperation they had with Batista in 1940–44, when a Communist served in the cabinet.

This is quite plausible, and it was probably in the light of this situation that Batista supposedly expressed his interest in meeting Castro about whom he had been hearing a great deal – including Fidel's attacks on him. According to at least three separate and credible versions, the meeting was arranged through Fidel's brother-in-law Rafael Díaz-Balart, who headed Batista's youth organization in PAU, and a mutual friend named Armando Vallibrende who had known Castro through the UIR political gang in the 1940s. Fidel was taken to Batista's luxurious Kuquine estate, not far from Havana, and received by the general in the baronial splendour in which he lived. In the private office there was a large painting of Batista as sergeant along with busts of famous historical personages, a solid-gold telephone, the telescope Napoleon used on Saint Helena, and the two pistols the emperor had in Austerlitz.

According to one version, Batista confined the meeting to general conversation, taking the measure of Castro and avoiding politics.

Another version has it that they did discuss politics, and that Fidel told Batista that he would support him if he ousted Prío in a coup d'état. If this were the case Castro was probably testing the older man, and Batista became afraid that Castro had somehow learned of his secret plans for a coup the following year and was acting as *agent provocateur*. To Fidel's extremely logical mind it would make perfect sense that Batista might attempt a coup, particularly with the rapid disintegration of the Prío regime and Chibás's death, and he was simply seeking a confirmation. Batista, however, terminated the meeting abruptly – never suspecting the grief the young man would cause him in the future.

Castro's line was to increase his attacks on both Prío and Batista as he stepped up his efforts to run for the chamber of deputies from Havana province as an *Ortodoxo* in the June 1952 elections. Robert Agramonte, a traditional Cuban politician from a famous family, had replaced Chibás as the *Ortodoxo* presidential candidate, inheriting the senator's one-hour Sunday radio spot on CMQ. Fidel thought, however, that the party's youth (represented by himself) should share in the CMQ time, and managed to obtain ten minutes' air time on CMQ from Agramonte for his own pronouncements. Castro was also given time on Radio Álvarez, another Havana station, and *Alerta* went on publishing his occasional articles.

Towards the end of 1951 Fidel was managing three major separate but related political enterprises: he was representing thousands of poor Havana urban dwellers whose homes the Prío government was planning to raze to build a huge civic square in the centre of the city; he was investigating Prío's personal misdeeds as president; and he was campaigning vigorously to represent a Havana district in the congressional elections. Nobody seems to recollect anything about Castro's family life at that time, except that he saw his brother Raúl quite often, mainly because he was at the university and increasingly active in politics; he had not yet formally joined the Communist Party's Socialist Youth, but he was very close to the Communists.

The area that the government wanted to level in mid-town Havana was a twenty-hectare district known as La Pelusa, a miserable slum. To defend its inhabitants Fidel first convinced them that their rights would not be ignored, then instructed them at street rallies what to say to government inspectors, and went to court to demand that the Public Works Ministry indemnify each homeowner (or shack-owner) for the property to be razed. The ministry finally agreed to pay a 50-peso compensation in each case, which was not unreasonable, but the payments were never made because Batista soon ousted Prío and cancelled the agreement. Batista then expelled the area's residents and proceeded with building the civic square. Today it is Castro's Revolution Square.

To investigate Prío in depth, Fidel mobilized not only his law firm partners but friends from the *Ortodoxo* party's Youth Section as well, notably a young man named Pedro Trigo from Havana province. Between September 1951 and January 1952 Castro and his investigators came up with impressive evidence against the president. Fidel had learned the Chibás lesson that accusations without proof are self-defeating. On 28 January 1952, stressing that the date marked the anniversary of José Martí's birth, Castro presented the indictment of Prío to the Court of Accounts (a federal administrative tribunal), summing it up in five specific charges. Each one began with the words, 'I ACCUSE the President of the Republic'. The charges specified that Prío had received bribes in return for granting amnesty to a friend serving a prison term for child molestation, and then appointing him nominal owner of presidential farms; violated labour laws by forcing workers into twelve-hour shifts under military foremen; insulted the armed forces 'by turning soldiers into labourers and peons and forcing them to slave labour'; contributed to unemployment 'through the substitution of paid workers by obligatory labour from soldiers'; and betrayed national interests by selling farm products at prices below their market value.

The enormously detailed accusation, full of names and figures, was published the next day in its entirety in *Alerta* under the headline, 'I ACCUSE' (Castro having read Emile Zola) and broadcast over The Voice of Antilles radio station. Prío, Cubans were told, had constructed 'ostentatious palaces, swimming pools, airports, and a whole series of luxuries' and acquired 'a chain of the best farms and most valuable lands in the vicinity of Havana'.

Never quitting when ahead, Castro issued a second indictment of Prío on 19 February 1952, this time charging that the president was paying 18,000 pesos monthly to political gangs and *pistoleros* and keeping 2000 gangsters in public jobs, the price of the 1949 Gangs Pact negotiated by him and denounced by Castro at that time. Fidel also charged that in four years Prío's land holdings rose from 67 to 810 hectares. All these revelations stunned Cubans, and Jorge Aspiazo, who was Fidel's principal law partner, remarked later that 'friends were assuring us that Fidel would not last more than a week'.

Castro succeeded in so shaking up the Cuban political establishment that his own *Ortodoxo* party was scared to have him as a candidate, especially now that the fiery Chibás was dead. Playing it safe, Roberto Agramonte, the party's presidential candidate, simply omitted Castro's name from the *Ortodoxo* electoral list issued in February. Agramonte had underestimated, however, Fidel's determination to have his own way. This was where Castro's gift for planning ahead paid off. It was still possible for one or more districts in Havana province to select him at their local party assemblies as the congressional candidate and the poverty-stricken Cayo Hueso district of Havana where Fidel had begun his door-to-door campaign in 1951, was perfectly willing to pick him. Then came the rural district of Santiago de las Vegas also, where Castro had been investigating Prío; Jorge Aspiazo says that the dwellers from Le Pelusa (where Fidel had been fighting for the rights of the homeowners about to be dispossessed) collected coins in tins in the streets to raise enough money to rent a bus to take them to Santiago de las Vegas to attend a Castro rally and support his candidacy.

Now a candidate, Castro engaged in what by Cuban standards was a political *blitzkrieg*, rich in new techniques. Jorge Aspiazo says that in December 1951 Fidel inaugurated a new radio programme on the Voice of the Air station that within two months had attracted 50,000 regular listeners, according to the ratings. Max Lesnick, who as chief of the *Ortodoxo* party's Youth Section monitored it closely, recalls that Fidel had mounted 'a fabulous campaign', obtaining franking mail privileges from five friendly congressmen plus a list of 100,000 names. Then, Lesnick says, Castro had 100,000 envelopes addressed and sent to every *Ortodoxo* party member in Havana province with a personal message in blue ink, signed by him. He had cut a stencil for the messages, but the workers and the peasants did not know it. 'This had never happened in Cuba before,' Lesnick adds, 'Previously political leaders simply went to rallies to deliver their speeches.' Raúl Chibás, himself a candidate for senator, says that Fidel 'had his own group that followed him, his own organization within the party'. This was Castro's Radical Orthodox Action (ARO) faction inside the party, the young rebels who were the forerunners of his revolutionary movement and whom the older leaders had always tried to neutralize. Conchita Fernández, who had been Eddy's and Raúl Chibás's secretary, also ran for congress from Havana province, and she recalls how Castro often appeared at the end of her rallies to speak in her support. On the day his first anti-Prío indictment was published Fidel appeared in the township of San Antonio de Río Blanco, just as the small crowd was dispersing after hearing Conchita. But, she says, he summoned the people back by shouting and waving a copy of *Alerta* with his exposé and the photographs of Prío's *fincas* which he had taken from the nearby house of a friend. 'And within five or ten minutes,' Conchita recalls, 'that park was full because he had such magnetism and people simply had to listen to him.' Conchita, who had known Fidel since he was a student leader in 1947, and always admired him (she would become *his* secretary after the revolution in 1959) says that crowds applauded Castro 'deliriously' because he spoke the truth, 'and he didn't care if the next day someone shot him.' Thus the Castro legend was being created with the young candidate delivering as many as four hour-long speeches in four different localities in one night.

At that stage the Communists withdrew their support from Batista (they had no presidential candidate of their own for 1952), realizing that the *Ortodoxos* could win even without Chibás; they were also impressed by Castro's possibilities as a congressman. Consequently they proposed an electoral pact in all the Senate and Chamber of Deputies races, and even after their offer was turned down they announced that they would vote for certain *Ortodoxo* candidates anyway.

The general assumption early in 1952 was that Castro would be elected to the Chamber of Deputies with the votes of the Havana province proletariat, urban and rural. Max Lesnick, the *Ortodoxo* youth chief, says that there was not 'the slightest doubt' about his victory, adding: 'I knew the influence he had among all the young people in the party, the most sincere people in the party, and the working people.'

The elections were never held because of the Batista coup, but it is nevertheless interesting and useful to speculate on how Castro would have acted in the congress, reconciling the representative system with his revolutionary ideas. The next question concerns whether Castro might have advanced all the way to the presidency through the electoral system, or if he in fact needed the Batista dictatorship in order to create the revolutionary climate leading to his ultimate victory.

Many Cubans think that without a coup Castro would have served as a congressman for the four years until 1956, then run for the Senate, and made his pitch for the presidency in 1960 or 1964. Given the fact that Cuba wholly lacked serious political leadership, and given Castro's rising popularity, such a scenario is not implausible. In that case, it would appear that he was fated to govern Cuba – no matter how he arrived at the top.

Castro himself said in a 1965 interview with an American visitor that even before the Batista coup 'I already had some very definite political ideas about the need for structural changes. . . I had been thinking of using the parliament as a point of departure from which I might establish a revolutionary platform and influence the masses in its favour. . . Already then I believed that I had to do it in a revolutionary way.'

Fidel then told the interviewer: 'Once in parliament, I would break party discipline and present a programme embracing practically all the measures that . . . since the victory of the revolution had been trans-formed into laws,' knowing that although it would never be approved, it would rally the population around it for subsequent action. And, he said, 'I already definitely believed in the need for seizing power by revolution.' Ten years later Castro told Lionel Martin that he had always realized that the Cuban problem could not be resolved through parliament, and that his plan had been to 'break institutional legality' at the proper moment and proceed to take power. His parliamentary resources and immunity, he remarked, would have helped him 'to move about more easily and to conspire more freely'.

Whatever Fidel Castro had in mind as a candidate including plans that may never have worked out, it is unquestionable that the Batista coup and the end of the electoral process in 1952 saved him the 'political phase' of his secret and seemingly improbable dreams of revolution and the conquest of power.

Castro's suspicions that Batista was preparing a coup may have been reinforced early in February 1952. Raúl Chibás recalls that around that time he ran into Fidel on the stairs of the Havana house of Roberto Agramonte and a conversation ensued about various perils ahead. He says that suddenly Castro asked him if 'I had any news about a conspiracy, that Batista was conspiring and thinking of a coup d'état'. Chibás replied that he had not heard anything; in retrospect, he thinks that Fidel 'had soldiers, army people, working in his campaign, and that was how he learned about the plot'. He saw Castro again the following week, and Fidel was even more certain that a coup was in the works.

One version maintains that Castro had been told of unusual activity, involving comings and goings by military officers and civilians at Batista's Kuquine estate. So he hid outside the estate, the story goes, photographing all this traffic a day or two before the coup, but by then it was too late to be of any use. According to another account, President Prío had received a letter from a woman in Oriente, reporting a military conspiracy. But when the chief of staff of the army asked the head of his bureau of investigations to look into it, the officer advised his superiors that there was nothing to it; the military Intelligence officer was of course a Batista agent.

At dawn on 10 March 1952 Fulgencio Batista strutted into the army's Camp Columbia in Havana with his officers, to be warmly greeted by the troop commanders. This was the coup that, meeting no resistance, ousted Carlos Prío Socarrás from the presidency. It was quick, silent, bloodless, surgically precise and wholly cynical. The next day, already proclaimed chief of state, he moved to the Presidential Palace that he had left eight years earlier as constitutional president.

PART THREE
The War 1952–58

Chapter 1

As directed and inspired by Fidel Castro, the Cuban revolution was born directly from the Batista coup d'état. Batista's rule was so widely hated that it brought more unity to Cubans than any event since the Machado dictatorship twenty years earlier, unity which Batista himself failed to understand and which would serve as the main trigger for the revolution. But even with Batista on the scene the great revolution could be set in motion only through the leadership provided by Fidel Castro, then a twenty-five year old Havana lawyer not yet taken too seriously by the Cuban political establishment but already known for his dedication to rebel causes, his oratorical gifts and his single-mindedness. The events between 1952 and the last days of 1958, when the guerrilla army achieved military victory and captured political power, show that while Batista opened the door to this historical revolution it was Castro who would inevitably march through it.

In Castro's mind, however, the ousting of Batista was only the first tactical objective in his revolutionary enterprise. The strategic objective, which he chose not to reveal until the successful completion of the first phase, was the social revolution that ultimately turned Cuba into a Marxist–Leninist state, today financed by the Soviet Union, but in the final analysis still moulded by Fidel Castro.

At that time Castro was the only individual in Cuba who knew exactly where he was going politically. Nobody else, neither in the old nor the new generation, had any sense of direction, let alone historical vision. Looking back over nearly forty years of Castro's adult life, analysing his evolving opinions, listening to his old friends and companions and, above all, observing the societal transformation of Cuba, it seems evident that he possessed this vision in the way that history bestows only upon a chosen few. Fidel often contradicts himself over causes or the nature of past events or his role in them, yet the record shows his absolute consistency in working for a revolution. He had talked social revolution and had prepared himself for it long before the Batista coup. His Bogotá experience four years earlier was no more than a stage in his revolutionary development. To get rid of Batista was simply another stage. His life goal was all-embracing social revolution.

Castro's opening military challenge to Batista, sixteen months after the dictatorial takeover, was the assault on the Moncada army barracks in Santiago and a simultaneous attack in Bayamo, the other stronghold in Oriente, by rebels of the still unnamed Movement. Fidel personally led the charge on Moncada, barely escaped death, then defied Batista in the courtroom, and vanished for a year and a half to a prison cell where he tranquilly planned the next challenge while devouring hundreds of books on politics, history, philosophy, economics and literature. Prison was, in effect, his postgraduate school in humanist studies. It also turned out to be a considerable political asset as a nationwide campaign to grant him and his companions amnesty made Fidel even more famous than the assault itself.

In the history of the Cuban revolution the 1953 attack on Moncada is revered as the equivalent of the launching of the first war of independence in 1868 and José Martí's uprising against Spain in 1895, both of which likewise failed in their immediate time. But Moncada is the cornerstone of modern Cuban history, and Fidel Castro's courtroom oration in justification of the assault – *History Will Absolve Me* – is regarded as Cuba's real declaration of national independence, *the* great revolutionary manifesto, and something akin to the Scriptures, all three magnificently fused together. It is also the most cited text in Cuba, constantly analysed and interpreted, its dogmatic verities never questioned, but new insights into Fidel Castro's mind and heart devoutly discovered and deepened with the passage of years.

With the dominance of His Majesty King Sugar, as the Cubans called their principal product, unbalancing the economy and pushing un-employment to frightening levels, the social conditions during the Batista years were fuel for an explosion, sooner or later. While the luxury Havana Hilton hotel and a casino for rich Americans were being built in the capital, the average farmhand in 1952 had only 108 days of work at $1 per day, and 64 days in 1955. The rest was dead time, with no employment of any kind. Social justice had to be the clarion call for any leader. It would be powerfully sounded in Castro's Moncada oration, and it has remained the justification for every revolutionary act after his victory, including the permanent imposition of a politically and intel-lectually oppressive state apparatus.

Fidel Castro set out to organize his unnamed Movement (much later, it would formally become the famous 26th of July Movement, complete with black and red flag and stirring hymn), in the dawn of Monday 10 March 1952, virtually within minutes of learning that Fulgencio Batista and his officers had occupied the Columbia army camp in Havana, thereby deposing Carlos Prío Socarrás from the presidency. In Cuba in those days the real power resided at Columbia, and Batista, who had no chance of being elected to a new presidential term, resolved to seek it there. A general election was scheduled for 1 June, with Castro a candidate for the Chamber of Deputies from the capital's poorest workers' *barrios*, but the coup put an instant halt to all electoral processes. Fidel, who never trusted 'liberal bourgeois democracy' anyway, was delighted with this turn of events, violently denouncing Batista for 'a brutal theft of power'. It had been just brave talk for Castro to say that he would use his congressional seat as a revolutionary platform. Batista's coup was a gift from heaven, putting Castro seriously and promisingly in the business of revolution. From the first day of the new regime he dedicated himself to plots, plans, manoeuvres, seductions, feints and attacks and to the creation of a conspirational revolutionary movement, in a systematic and brilliant manner.

The sixteen-month period of preparation was rich in drama, as classic Castro acts of defiance added to his public image as Cuba's 'pure' leader of the new generation. His strategy was to operate simultaneously on two levels: the invisible level of conspiracy, and the visible level of constant street and courtroom protests against Batista. These two levels were complementary: Fidel's public performance facilitated recruitment for the conspiracy and the growth of the conspiracy helped to create a blindly loyal following for his public performance.

Melba Hernández, a lawyer who is seven years older than Castro (the age difference might have been important when they met in 1952) and one of the two women who participated in the Moncada assault, says of his impact on people: 'I think this happens to everybody: from the moment you shake hands with Fidel, you are impressed. His personality is so powerful. When I gave my hand to this young man I felt very secure, I felt I had found the way. When this young man began to talk, all I could do was listen to him. . . Fidel spoke in a very low voice, he paced back and forth, then came close to you as if to tell you a secret, and then you suddenly felt you shared the secret. . . .'

This may sound sycophantic, but Castro certainly did persuade enough carefully-selected men and women to accept his guidance at any cost, for them to be able rapidly to organize his movement. Pedro Miret Prieto, then an engineering student from Santiago (he had attended the same La Salle boys' school as Fidel, though they had not met there) and the man who personally gave secret military training to each Moncada fighter, says that on the day he first encountered Castro, six months after the Batista coup, he decided immediately to follow him, realizing that 'all the other politicians would do nothing' against Batista, but Fidel would act. And this story is repeated over and over again as today's aging revolutionaries recall meeting Castro in their youth. Obviously it was an unforgettable emotional experience.

But Castro also had his eye on an even wider audience. And an example of how his method worked for him there is the account by Ramiro Valdés Menéndez, once one of Cuba's most powerful men and until 1986 the Interior Minister, of how he joined the Movement. The son of a poor family in Artemisa, a town in Havana province with unusually strong radical and anarchist traditions, when the Batista coup came Valdés was a twenty-one-year-old truck driver's helper with virtually no formal education. But he was interested in politics, and through a friend in the *Ortodoxo* party youth, Valdés arranged a meeting with Castro because he had listened to him on the radio and now wanted to see whether this was a leader to be followed.

They met in Havana in the heat of July at the *Ortodoxo* party headquarters, and as Valdés recalls it, 'there was Fidel in his striped winter dark blue suit, and there we talked . . . and there I enroled in the Movement.' Valdés was entrusted with organizing a ten-member secret cell in Artemisa – and each of the ten was to recruit the next ten-member cell, and so on, under Castro's compartmentalized conspiracy structure. Thereafter Valdés was with Fidel at Moncada, in prison, in Mexico, in the Sierra and in the revolutionary government. Valdés's experience of seeking out Castro was repeated by scores of others as the Movement acquired its own life. In time Fidel's rebels acquired the honour of being called The Centennial Generation – the generation launching a revolution on the year of the hundredth anniversary of Martí's birth. This, too, was a marvellous touch of *Fidelista* mythology.

Castro was able to move smoothly into the leadership of young *Ortodoxo* party members and sympathizers wanting to challenge Batista chiefly because there was nobody else. There had not been the slightest effort to resist Batista's coup on 10 March. President Prío fled the country, and traditional political leaders either exiled themselves or proved to be pathetically ineffectual. Although Castro was prepared to support any anti–Batista move with his tiny band of followers, and certain wealthy old–line leaders were quick to promise money, arms and action from abroad, he and his friends were repeatedly disenchanted and irritated by the arms that were to be delivered always *mañana* and *mañana*. A few idealists in Cuba did attempt to conspire, only to be caught instantly by the secret police.

Cuban Communists, the only ones with a professional organizational structure, were just as ineffectual after the Batista coup as all the other traditional political parties. As in the 1940s they were probably not above cutting a deal with Batista to maintain their key positions in the labour confederation or, at least, remain neutral. In the 1950s Moscow-directed Communist parties were much less confrontational and adventurous than one might expect. Moreover, Batista himself may have toyed with the idea of some modus vivendi with the Communists, since he allowed the Communist daily *Hoy* to be published for a time even after the Popular Socialist Party was declared illegal.

In any event the last thing Castro wanted at that juncture was an alliance with the Communists. In a 1981 conversation Fidel put it very plainly: 'Although I had a Marxist–Leninist orientation I still didn't enrol in the Communist Party. Instead we created our own organization and we acted within that organization. Not because I had prejudices against the Communist Party, but because it was very isolated, so that from within its ranks it would have been very difficult to carry out the revolutionary plan I had conceived.'

To organize a revolutionary movement single-handed, starting from nought, is an endeavour so ambitious that it verges on absurdity. Yet Fidel, moving from hideout to hideout in and around Havana in his battered old carmelite brown Chevrolet sedan (his latest car), had succeeded by the end of the year in both creating the insurrectional nucleus and expanding it into an armed movement.

Ironically, the United States reaction to the Batista coup revolved around the entirely irrelevant Communist question. On 24 March, two weeks after the deed, Secretary of State Dean Acheson wrote to President Truman in a secret memorandum that 'while Batista when President of Cuba in the early 1940s tolerated Communist domination of the Cuban Confederation of Workers, the world situation with regard to international Communism has changed radically since that time, and we have no reason to believe that Batista will not be strongly anti-Communist'. This conclusion, plus the fact that most Latin American governments had recognized the Batista regime by 1 April (Dictator Trujillo in the Dominican Republic being the first), led the United States to do likewise. In those days many Latin American governments were dictatorial, and democracy was not a hemisphere issue in any of the capitals, including Washington. Further, the United States also did not wish to endanger its special economic relationship with Cuba at a time when the island's economy was in dire straits, and huge American interests were beginning to suffer.

Finally, Ambassador Willard L. Beaulac, a highly competent career diplomat, advised the State Department that in the absence of any meaningful opposition to Batista, the United States might as well accept him. But the State Department had forgotten the role of revolutionary students in triggering the overthrow of the Machado dictatorship two decades earlier, and there is nothing to indicate that the Embassy or the

State Department were at all aware of the Generation of 1930 or of Fidel Castro. He may have been big in Artemisa, but not in Washington.

The hard core of Fidel Castro's Movement consisted of no more than eight or ten persons until the middle of 1952, when it began to gain recruits more rapidly. This nucleus was formed by members and sympathizers of the *Ortodoxo* party, Communists from the Popular Socialist Party being excluded both because of Castro's early decision not to join it and because of the Communists' own reluctance to submit to his leadership.

Actually the Communists did attempt to influence his tactics and behaviour in their own favour immediately after the Batista coup, and Fidel rebuffed them. Alfredo Guevara, the Communist Party's chief representative at the university, was the instrument for this approach. In an interview in Havana in 1985 Guevara maintained that on instructions from Socialist Youth (the party's youth organization), he contacted Castro as soon as he could – Castro had gone into hiding the morning of the coup – to urge him to return to the university as a student 'to become the great figure at the university'. The Communists' idea was to build anti-Batista opposition, slowly and on their terms, using Fidel and the university as the leading edge in their strategy. Guevara also acknowledged that the party had lost control of the Student Federation and was having a hard time regaining it.

According to Guevara the reason for Fidel's refusal to go along with the Communists was that while the Popular Socialist Party had in mind 'a struggle of the masses', which meant political unity in opposing the dictatorship, 'Fidel had the idea of direct action, that is of popular insurrection'. Guevara added that the next time he saw him, Fidel had already acquired a clandestine radio station and was engaged in preparing for Moncada.

Fidel's refusal to subordinate himself to the Communists did not mean he had no contacts with them or avoided participating in public protest activities with them and other opposition groups. But the only member of Fidel's Movement who was an active Communist, his young brother Raúl who had formally joined the Socialist Youth in June 1953, was excluded from all secret policy planning and decision-making, never being part of the Movement's 'General Staff'. (Luciano González Camejo, a middle-aged worker, was the only other Communist to take part in Moncada, but he joined the Movement late and his ideological persuasion had apparently been overlooked.) Raúl devoted most of his energies to university demonstrations, often carrying the Cuban flag in the front row of marchers, his short figure almost dwarfed by it.

Castro had resolved to stay away from the university even before Guevara made his proposal. Contrary to published reports he was not among the mass of students gathered at the university in mid-morning to demonstrate against Batista (Raúl, however, was there). Fidel thought that he might be arrested, and he also concluded that there were more important things to do politically than to shout 'Death to Batista!'

Late the previous year Castro and his family had moved from the tiny apartment on Third Street to a larger one on the second floor of a building at 1511 Twenty-third Street, also in the residential Vedado section, but in a less elegant neighbourhood. Still, the rent was about the same, and Fidel was as broke when the coup came as he had been before. At one point during the conspiracy, when Fidel was once more in hiding (he would vanish when the Batista secret police put on the heat, reappear, hide again, and so on), he and Pedro Trigo, an *Ortodoxo* textile worker and one of the first Movement members, happened to be driving in the evening past the Castro apartment building on Twenty-third Street, so they stopped and went upstairs. They encountered disaster. The electricity had been cut off because the bill had not been paid and the apartment was in darkness. Three-year-old Fidelito had a throat infection and a high fever, and the best Castro could do was to arrange for the child to be taken to the Calixto García hospital to be looked after by a friendly physician. He also borrowed five pesos from Pedro Trigo, giving it to his wife to buy supplies. Actually, Castro had a hundred pesos in his pocket, but this was money he had collected that day for the purchase of weapons, and he felt he could not use it, even for family sickness. Subsequently Fidel's friends took it upon themselves to make sure that his rent, services and furniture instalments were paid.

Another time Castro could not find his old car in front of the *Ortodoxo* party offices downtown where he had left it. It had been repossessed by a representative of the finance company from which Fidel had bought it. As a friend tells the story, that was the darkest day ever for Castro. Deprived of his car he walked over to the café where he often had a cup of coffee and smoked a cigar. He told the owner that he was also hungry because he had missed lunch, but had no money on him. Since he already owed the café five pesos, the owner refused him further credit. Fidel thereupon began walking home, a distance of three miles. Crossing Central Park he stopped to look at newspaper headlines, but did not have the five cents to buy a newspaper. The vendor shouted at him, 'Keep moving, keep moving. . . . Don't just stand there. . . . '

At his apartment he collapsed onto the bed in deep depression, falling asleep. Awakening late in the afternoon Fidel, as his friend tells the story, had overcome his depression and was again full of fighting spirit. Later, he would laugh when recounting these incidents, and the way his friends had assumed the responsibility for paying his bills, and 'they would even give me something to take care of my food'. He would say he was the 'first paid professional member of the Movement'.

Nothing is remembered, however, about his wife Mirta. Until the divorce in 1955 she must have suffered in silence the daily hardships and Fidel's continual absences. After the coup the situation became still more untenable when her brother, Rafael Díaz-Balart, was named Vice Minister of the Interior in the Batista government, the ministry in charge of public order and the secret police. Now the brothers-in-law were in opposing camps.

Fidel had slept at home the night of the coup, but he fled at dawn to the apartment of his sister Lidia, five blocks away. He left behind Mirta and Fidelito as well as his brother Raúl who was staying with them at the time. Fidel's instincts were correct, and secret policemen did appear at the apartment in mid-morning looking for the brothers (they also missed Raúl who had gone to demonstrate at the university).

Normally Castro spoke on the radio every day in the early afternoon for a fifteen-minute political chat (or harangue), but he knew he would be arrested if he turned up at the studio on the day of the military takeover. His immediate concern was to be kept fully informed about events, and several of his friends offered their services. One of them, René Rodríguez, had been told by Mirta that Fidel was at his sister's house, and he reached him there. Castro asked Rodríguez to visit the university numerous times that day and to keep him posted on student movements.

From the university Rodríguez brought FEU President Alvaro Barba to confer with Fidel at Lidia's house. Then Rodríguez went to the residence of Roberto Agramonte, the *Ortodoxo* party presidential candidate, to check on the mood among the leaders. When Rodríguez reported that Agramonte and his colleagues were thinking of nothing more drastic than passive resistance to Batista – and that they had no message or marching orders for him or the party youth, Fidel exploded in rage, shouting that the *Ortodoxo* leaders were cowards and worse. That night Castro decided he was no longer safe at Lidia's apartment and moved to the Hotel Andino, which was a boarding house downtown where he had once lived. On the morning of 11 March Rodríguez, who was making the arrangements, went with Castro to the home of Eva Jiménez, an *Ortodoxo* party youth militant, in the middle-class section of Almendares. Eva had bought enough food for several days, and gave her maid the week off. Castro was wearing dark glasses, which he never normally used (because he was near-sighted he needed clear, prescription spectacles, but he disliked them), and the two men took a bus to Eva's place. Fidel had a five-peso bill Lidia had given him, but the driver had no change and, in the end, a stranger on the bus paid the 16 cents for their fare.

Unbeknownst to Fidel that day another safe house had been provided for him. This was the luxury apartment where Natilia (Naty) Revuelta lived in Vedado with her husband, a leading Havana heart specialist.

Naty, an attractive blonde educated in the United States and France had revolutionary sympathies and friendships in the *Ortodoxo* party, and had heard a lot about Fidel Castro. The day of the Batista coup she delivered keys to her apartment to several prominent *Ortodoxo* leaders in case they needed a haven from the secret police, with the specific request that one of the keys be given to Castro. But in the confusion of the March events the key did not reach Fidel until later. Afterwards Naty Revuelta became a very important person in Fidel's life, one of an extraordinary contingent of beautiful and/or highly intelligent women who, in effect, dedicated their lives to him and his cause – and without whom he might not have succeeded.

Castro spent two days and nights at Eva Jiménez's apartment, drafting and redrafting in longhand (no typewriter was available) on a kitchenette table a proclamation against the Batista takeover under the heading of 'Not a Revolution – A Dull Thud!' The proclamation was written strictly on his own behalf, and on 13 March Fidel dispatched Rene Rodríguez and Eva Jiménez to the newspaper *Alerta* , which had published his articles in the past, to ask its editor to print his broadside. However, Ramón Vasconcelos, the editor, turned it down on the ground that anti-Batista opposition was 'unrealistic'. Because press censorship had been established Fidel's envoys made no effort to contact other newspapers.

But Castro was determined to circulate his proclamation, and he sent Rodríguez to contact a friend who lived above a pharmacy in downtown Havana and had a mimeograph machine in his apartment. Raúl Castro and Antonio López Fernández, a six-foot-six worker whom Fidel had befriended during his electoral campaign and was known as Ñico, mimeographed 500 copies of the proclamation to be distributed in the streets as soon as possible.

The opportunity to do so came on Sunday 16 March when Fidel left his refuge clad in a white *guayabera* and drove to the Colón cemetery to join *Ortodoxo* leaders and students who had gathered at the grave of Eddy Chibás as they had done every sixteenth of the month since his death the previous August. The *Ortodoxo* party leaders' speeches were so tepid that Fidel could not restrain himself, and raised his right arm to shout, 'If Batista grabbed power by force, he must be thrown out by force!' As policemen approached menacingly, the tall figure was encircled by his friends to protect him. *Alerta*, which had refused to publish his manifesto, reported Castro's cemetery outburst, commenting that his words were 'well received by the crowd . . . demonstrating again the sympathy he enjoys among the masses of the party'.

Finally distributed at the cemetery, the mimeographed proclamation charged that 'there is nothing in the world as bitter as the spectacle of a people that goes to bed free and awakens in slavery', that there is 'infinite happiness in fighting oppression', and that 'the fatherland is oppressed, but some day there will be freedom'. Castro ended by quoting from the Cuban national anthem: 'To live in chains is to live sunk in shame and dishonour. To die for the fatherland is to live!'

As far as Castro was concerned, he now was personally at war with the Batista dictatorship. In his proclamation he urged 'courageous Cubans to sacrifice and fight back'. Looking back at these events twenty years later Fidel told the American journalist Lionel Martin that he had launched his campaign 'a bit as a *guerrillero*, because in politics one must also be a guerrillero. . . .' Once embarked on his war, Castro would never give up. On 24 March, a week after the Colón cemetery occurrences, he presented in his capacity as attorney a brief to the Constitutional Court in Havana, accusing General Batista of violating the Constitution by his military coup. He then went on to list punishment for such acts as prescribed by the penal code, concluding that therefore 'Fulgencio Batista's crimes have incurred punishment deserving more than one hundred years' imprisonment.'

Castro's goal in presenting this brief was not so much to attract new attention to himself (*Alerta* published a report on it the following day), and certainly not to obtain a legal satisfaction from the court, but to establish a fundamental revolutionary principle for future action. Specifically, he set out to proclaim the concept of revolutionary legitimacy, making the point that 'if, in the face of this series of flagrant crimes and confessions of treachery and sedition [Batista] is not tried and punished, how will this court try later any citizen for sedition or rebellion against an illegal regime, the product of unpunished treason?' Knowing perfectly well that the court would never try Batista, Fidel was carefully building the legal base for his planned revolution, justifying it beforehand as a *legal act* against an *illegal regime*. This would grant full legitimacy to the revolutionary government he would instal in 1959. To the highly legalistic Latin American mind, formal legality is paramount.

Fidel gave up his actual law practice, such as it was, in the aftermath of the Batista coup, but his law firm stayed in business and, on his instructions, proceeded to conduct additional legal battles against the dictatorship. Jorge Aspiazo, his former partner, says that Fidel had him sue three Batista cabinet ministers in criminal court for defrauding the State Unemployed Persons' Fund through the naming of 'imaginary persons' to public posts, 'firing' them, and collecting themselves unemployment payments. The case wound up in the Supreme Court, which threw it out.

But Castro kept up the barrage. On 6 April the newspaper *La Palabra* (closed by the regime after its first issue) published another ferocious attack by him on Batista along with Fidel's poetic warning that 'the seed of heroic rebellion is being sown in all our hearts' and that 'faced with danger, heroism is strengthened by generously shed blood'. Castro always understood that revolutions demand romanticism and rhetoric.

On clandestine fronts Castro kept equally busy. Operating from different safe houses and from the *Ortodoxo* party offices on the Prado (strangely, the regime allowed political parties to go on fuctioning although the congress was closed and all elections cancelled), Fidel had literally hundreds of meetings and interviews with prospective Movement members between the time of the March coup and the start of May when a new phase in his campaign would begin. According to Jorge Aspiazo he often drove out into the countryside at night to meet in a field with local *Ortodoxo* members from rural sections of the party.

Historically it is relevant that the Castro Movement was born almost entirely from the rank and file of the *Ortodoxo* party, the reformist and radical but essentially establishment organization founded by Senator Chibás in 1947. Great numbers of working-class and middle-class Cubans, including sugar workers and mountain farmers, had become powerfully attracted to Chibás and his party as a new and 'clean' phenomenon in the country. The now aging Communist Party, on the other hand, seemed unable to penetrate what should have been its natural constituency among the workers and, also typically, its strength was chiefly among intellectuals, students, and labour-union leadership. The claim that Cold War propaganda against Communism was responsible for this state of affairs is not credible.

In fact, young *Ortodoxos* (and even middle-aged ones) from modest backgrounds were much more revolution-minded than the Communists. They had no use for Communist ideological discipline, and they admired Castro. Fidel, who himself had joined the *Ortodoxo* party in 1947, used the intervening years to develop wide contacts, especially inside the youth section and the Radical Orthodox Action (ARO) faction he had organized. Despite the animosity of older party leaders, Castro expanded his contacts and loyalties in the course of his electoral campaign. When the Batista coup came on 10 March 1952, and Fidel made his decision to fight 'independently', he already had a potential revolutionary network. Now his task was to turn it into an actual revolutionary instrument.

At a chance meeting at the Colón cemetery Castro was introduced to Abel Santamaría, a twenty-four-year-old accountant at a Havana Pontiac dealer's office. It seems as if cemeteries play a major part in Cuban politics, and this stems from an old tradition of using the anniversaries of dead personages, even of such heroes of the past as Céspedes and Martí, as an emotion-laden pretext for political demonstrations that the police under any regime would hesitate to break up. On this particular occasion the Batista government had forbidden May Day labour celebrations, so many opposition militants went on 1 May to the grave of Carlos Rodrígues instead. Rodrígues had been killed by the police during the Prío presidency, and Castro had been the attorney who had taken two key police officers to court on murder charges. Now Castro was at the cemetery as a revolutionary gesture, and he was presented to Santamaría by Jesús Montané Oropesa, an accountant at the General Motors office whom he met shortly before the coup when he unsuccessfully tried to swap his ailing car for a better one. Since March Montané, Santamaría and a few other friends had been looking for ways of fighting Batista.

Castro and Santamaría, a tall, light-haired man from Las Villas province, hit it off immediately, and their 1 May encounter was a turning point for the incipient Movement. For one thing they shared rural origins: Abel was born at the Constancia sugar mill where he worked until coming to Havana at the age of nineteen and Fidel was from the Oriente sugar fields. That Castro came from a landowning family and Santamaría was the son of workers made no difference. Besides Abel, along with Montané, was an *Ortodoxo*. Abel lived with his sister Haydée (she was called Yéyé) in an apartment near Castro's home, and their first long conversation took place at the Santamarías. It produced a lasting relationship between the two of them, with Fidel acting as the chief of the Movement and Abel as his deputy. It was the less spectacular, but more cool-headed Abel, who would be crucial in giving shape to the Movement.

In the weeks and months that followed, the Movement grew. Montané joined the nucleus with his friend Boris Luís Santa Coloma, also an accountant (an exiled Cuban scholar wrote in all seriousness that the accountancy backgrounds of so many key Cuban revolutionaries deserve to be analysed); Melba Hernández, the *Ortodoxo* lawyer who was so impressed with Fidel and her friend Elda Pérez did likewise. Melba brought in Raúl Goméz García, a twenty-three-year-old poet and teacher; Fidel added his friends Pedro Trigo and Ñico Lopés. By mid-year this was the core of the Movement.

From the outset Castro's authority was undisputed, and he ran his Movement like a military organization. Melba Hernández, who was the closest to Fidel and the Santamarías during the whole preparatory period, recalls it as 'militancy twenty-four hours a day', and as a life of extraordinary discipline, which also required a complete change in the social relationships of all the Movement members.

Melba, nowadays honoured as a Heroine of the Revolution and still very active politically although in her seventies, says that Castro demanded a series of compromises from the revolutionaries. First, she says, 'we had to hate the regime that oppressed us, which was easy, then to repudiate that society that lived from corruption, and to take the decision to fight against it'. To be able to fight the corruption, great temptations had to be resisted, she recalls, 'and because this was a clandestine movement it had very rigid discipline, very strict discipline and secrecy, complete discretion, and militant behaviour. . . This is how we were being educated, and a militant would be expelled from the Movement for the violation of any of these rules. As the Movement grew', she recalls, 'the groups of young people who already belonged to the Movement met every Sunday. It was like a test. For example, they would be summoned for 5.05 p.m. If someone wasn't there at exactly that time, we would examine the situation and then the person would be admonished, or punished, or expelled. Indiscretion, any kind of indiscretion, no matter how small, was cause for expulsion.'

Additionally, Melba Hernández says, the Movement's General Staff, composed of Fidel Castro, Abel Santamaría, Haydée Santamaría and Melba, met once a week to discuss the activities and behaviour of all the members (some published accounts state erroneously that only Fidel and Abel formed the General Staff). Fidel and Abel conferred regularly with the Military Committee and the Political Committee. The two of them headed both committees; each committee had four other members. But only Fidel and Abel had the power to select recruits and to make all the strategic and tactical decisions. The Movement was organized into cells ranging in membership from ten to twenty-five persons, and their orders came from the General Staff or from one of the committees, depending on the subject and its importance. It was a totally vertical structure without political groups or delegated functions, a principal difference between the Castro Movement and Communist or other political revolutionary parties. Fidel had intended it, in effect, as a *caudillist* structure designed solely to win the war.

Whatever Castro's inner ideological convictions were at that stage he was determined to keep his Movement from ideological identification with Marxism–Leninism. Melba Hernández says: 'In our ranks in that period there was never talk about Communism, socialism or Marxism–Leninism as an ideology, but we did speak of the day when the revolution would come to power, that all the estates of the aristocracy must then be handed over to the people and must be used by the children for whom we are fighting.' Melba makes a point of noting that 'the problem of workers exploitation was not discussed', but 'we did talk about the workers' wages, the abuse of the workers, the abuse of the peasants'. And Fidel and Abel insisted on 'the importance of the inclusion of women in the revolutionary struggle'.

In a 1977 interview with the Soviet Communist Party theoretical journal *Kommunist*, Castro said that 'during all that period I maintained contacts with the Communists' but 'one could not ask them to have confidence in what we were doing'. He explained that it 'would have been difficult for a party educated in a classical form, with its plans, its concepts' to have faith in the Movement. This whole issue remains very sensitive among Communists, and Castro must have had that in mind when he spoke to the Moscow publication.

Mario Mencía, the only serious historian of the Cuban revolution working in Havana, has written that though Castro had a 'Marxist orientation' since his student days, 'he avoided any [public] identification with iron willpower, even in his declarations'. Mencía finds that while early on Castro 'had a revolutionary project under way which pointed towards socialism', he faithfully followed José Martí's precept that to achieve one's goals 'one must conceal [them]' because to 'proclaim them for what they are would raise difficulties too great to allow them to be reached.'

After Pedro Miret, the engineering student and the arms expert, met Castro in September 1952, and agreed to train Movement members for military purposes, the internal discipline became even stricter. As Melba Hernández recalls it, constant personal control over the members was their leaders' great preoccupation, and at the weekly meetings Castro and Santamaría analysed the behaviour of each revolutionary during the previous seven days, including their personal lives, and often 'criticism was made . . . leading to expulsion'. But Fidel and Abel also practised self-criticism, a familiar Marxist concept.

Jesús Montané, the accountant who was in the first revolutionary nucleus and nowadays is a key member of the Politburo, recalls that 'in our Movement it was absolutely forbidden to drink alcohol,' and those who had the drinking habit, 'could not be militants'. Montané says that 'the lives of these revolutionaries were guided by the most absolute austerity and morality'.

The Movement's principal headquarters were at the Santamarías' apartment at Twenty-fifth and 'O' streets in Vedado (it is now a national shrine), but the plotters also used the apartment of Fidel's sister Lidia three blocks away, the apartment of Melba Hernández's parents (who were fervently pro-revolutionary) on Jovellar Street in downtown Havana, and an office on Consulado Street just off the seaside Malecón boulevard, provided by a secret member of the organization who worked for a rich businessman. The office on Consulado, Melba says, offered the best 'camouflage'.

As usual, propaganda was foremost on Fidel's mind. Before they met him the Santamarías and Montané had published irregularly a mimeo-graphed publication called *Son Los Mismos (They Are the Same)* to attack Batista, the name indicating that the military regime was as bad as all previous ones. But as soon as they joined forces Fidel proposed that the publication be renamed *El Acusador (The Accuser)*, and he began to edit it with Abel and the young poet Raúl Goméz García. *Son Los Mismos* went on being printed simultaneously for some weeks, then it was dropped altogether. At the university the Communists printed their publication *Mella* for which Fidel had written in the past, and continued to do so occasionally in the later period.

Now, however, Castro signed his articles Alejandro, which was his middle name and which he also used as his code name in the Movement and later in Moncada and the Sierra. Raúl Gomez, the poet, signed his articles 'The Citizen', another sign of the influence of the French Revolution on the *Fidelistas*. The Movement's publications were produced on an ancient mimeograph machine purchased by Abel Santamaría and Montané for 75 pesos; to avoid discovery by the police the copying machine was constantly moved from place to place by a friendly Spanish taxi driver, and Montané said later it spent most of the time in the trunk of a car parked in front of the Detroit bar on Twenty-fifth Street.

But Castro wanted to be on the air as well. A few days after he met Santamaría, he convinced him to come in his car (Fidel's latest vehicle was virtually unusable) with Montané to visit a physician in Colón, 150 miles from Havana, whose name he had received from a Movement member. The physician was Dr Mario Muñoz Monroy, and at the age of forty-one he was an ardent revolutionary, ready to follow Fidel. As it happened, Dr Muñoz was a light-aircraft pilot and a ham radio operator as well, and what Fidel wanted from him were *two* ham transmitters to announce an anti-regime demonstration that was being planned by the university for the following week. He wanted two transmitters in case one failed, and the enthusiastic doctor was miraculously able to provide the first one in time to broadcast the rally on 20 May, as the Free Airwaves of the Resistance and National Liberation Movement, on the 40-metre band.

The name of the Movement was invented by Fidel for the occasion, and the broadcast was barely heard, but *Son Los Mismos* was able to report the existence of the underground radio, which was one of the main objectives in having the transmitters. Castro believed correctly that different types of propaganda feed on each other; also Dr Muñoz's stations were forerunners of the Rebel Radio that Fidel would instal in the *Sierra* six years later. As Montané recalls it, Castro produced new ideas for the Movement all the way to and from Colón in Abel's car.

Anti-Batista opposition also took shape in the National Revolutionary Movement (MNR) formed on 20 May 1952 by Rafael García Bárcena, a well-known professor of psychology, sociology and philosophy at the University of Havana and the national War College. García Bárcena had founded the *Ortodoxo* party with Chibás in 1947, and now he attracted to his MNR young middle-class opponents of Batista – such as Armando Hart, Faustino Pérez and Juan Manuel Márquez, all of whom later joined the Castro movement. In Santiago, the MNR recruits were Frank País, who would become a hero of the war, and Vilma Espín, now Raúl Castro's wife.

Fidel took a noncommittal stance towards the MNR – he distrusted middle-class liberals who relied on the conquest of power through military coups – and also towards the Liberating Action (AL) organized in July by a politician named Justo Carrillo. He concentrated on his own Movement. At that time, Pedro Miret was busying himself training MNR members in the use of arms at the university; he had not yet met Castro. Justo Carrillo was trying to infiltrate groups of young army officers.

On 16 August a huge rally was held at the Colón cemetery to commemorate the first anniversary of Senator Chibás's death, and Fidel had his associates print 10,000 copies of the third issue of *El Acusador* , an enormous run for a mimeograph publication, to be distributed there and in Havana streets. As Alejandro, Castro had written two fiery articles for it: one criticizing the *Ortodoxo* party for the cowardice of its leadership, and proclaiming that 'the movement is revolutionary and not political', the other accusing Batista of being an 'evil tyrant'. In his best style of political invective Fidel informed the dictator that 'the dogs that lick your wounds every day will never conceal the stench emanating from them', and that 'when history is written . . . it will speak of you as it speaks of plagues and epidemics. . .'

But this was the end of *El Acusador* . Even before the cemetery rally began the secret police had found the mimeograph machine at the apartment of Joaquín Gonzáles, a Movement member. The agents smashed the machine and seized the publication copies they found there, about one-half. As they approached the cemetery with *El Acusador* copies, Abel Santamaría, Elda Pérez and Melba Hernández were arrested. In the ranks of the Movement's directorate only Fidel and Haydée Santamaría escaped arrest. Elda and Melba were released later that day and were able to find Fidel and tell him of their jailed companions.

The next day Castro and Melba appeared at the Castillo del Principe prison in their capacity as attorneys to seek freedom for Santamaría and González. At the prison they were stunned to see most of their other companions in detention, too: Montané, the poet Raúl Goméz and all the others. It was only then that Castro realized that the Movement had been betrayed by an infiltrated police informer, and that arrests had been carried out methodically the previous day and night.

Castro spent the day arguing for the release of his companions and then devoted days and nights trying to track down the 'traitor' – who was never discovered. This effort, however, prevented him from going to the hospital where Fidelito again had to undergo emergency surgery. He was only able to see his son back at the apartment, days later. Several days after the arrests the Military Intelligence Service – the murderous SIM – tracked down one of the Movement's two radio transmitters.

These setbacks did nothing to discourage Fidel. Strangely, his companions were released within a few days, and during the first week of September he presided over a clandestine meeting of new Movement members in Old Havana. He told them: 'All those who join the Movement will do so as simple soldiers; any post which they might have had in the *Ortodoxo* party will not matter here. The fight will not be easy and the road to be travelled will be long and arduous. We are going to take up arms against the regime.'

The next day Fidel and Abel were arrested in Castro's brown Chevrolet sedan on a Vedado Street by a patrol car. At the police station they and the car were searched, but nothing incriminating was found, and they were let go. This was Fidel's first arrest as the secret Movement's head, making him even more careful about all his moves.

In due course a tragic anniversary was once more the occasion for a revolutionary act: 27 November was the eighty-first anniversary of the execution by the Spaniards of the eight nationalist medical students, and Castro and student leaders gathered after dark at the university for an anti-Batista rally. Fidel and his companions brought along the second radio transmitter which Dr Muñoz had supplied to broadcast the demonstration. But the police cut off electric power to the university, preventing the holding of the rally.

It was one more disappointment, and it marked the end of the first phase of the Movement's revolutionary activities. But the evening was not wasted altogether. In the darkness of the campus *escalinata* Fidel was introduced by his friend Jorge Valls to Naty Revuelta, the rich and beautiful revolutionary wife of the heart specialist, the woman who back in March had tried to send him a key to her apartment to hide from the police. A romance was born that evening.

Chapter 2

The hundredth anniversary of the birth of José Martí fell on 28 January 1953, and for Fidel Castro this was an extraordinary opportunity for spectacular revolutionary gestures. Clandestine military training had acquired momentum in the closing months of 1952, and despite the fact that Castro had practised extreme caution in his personal appearances the celebration of Martí's centennial could not be ignored.

The Movement was in its second phase: planning and preparation for actual revolutionary action had begun. By this time Fidel had cut himself off from any direct identification with the training operations. He never went to the university grounds where Pedro Miret conducted secret exercises, and most of the new recruits were unaware that Castro was the man who headed the Movement; he, of course, knew who each individual was and what he was doing.

As a basic rule Castro believed the he and his fighters should not call unnecessary attention to themselves. They had been involved in university demonstrations from the previous 27 November, but now the *Fidelistas* lay low, staying away from continuing university affrays during December and the start of January 1953. On the other hand, Castro was a committed public figure and he understood that it might be harmful politically for his absence to be noted. Fidel had to walk a thin tightrope, a situation aggravated by his penchant for acting on impulse.

On 13 January Castro chose to attend a Havana meeting of the leadership of the *Ortodoxo* party to hear a proposal to form an alliance with other political parties to oppose Batista. The session collapsed in chaos when the most prominent of the *Ortodoxo* walked out in protest against what they suspected would be the end of what was left of their party's independence after the coup. Stomping out, Fidel shouted, 'Let's get out of here. . . You can't count on these politicians to make a revolution.' This was Castro's final contact with traditional politics in Cuba.

About the same time Communist and other extreme leftist students formed a committee to erect a statue to Julio Antonio Mella, a university leader and co-founder of the Cuban Communist Party in 1925, who was assassinated in Mexico in 1928. The idea was to consecrate the memory of Mella and thereby make the Communist leader a national hero. By placing the statue in the street outside university buildings, they would also expand the territory of campus autonomy where the authorities could not legally enter.

The committee was organized by Fidel Castro's old Communist friend Alfredo Guevara, and on 10 January the Mella statue was unveiled. For tactical reasons Fidel made a point of not attending but his brother Raúl was present. There was a certain political ambivalence in the relations between the two brothers (who personally were quite close, with Raúl living for varying periods with Fidel and Mirta). Fidel insisted on keeping him out of the Movement at that time, but kept him informed of its progress. That Raúl was involved with the Communists evidently did not trouble Fidel, and he may have been developing the notion that it would be useful to have his younger brother become something of a link; Alfredo Guevara could not discreetly play that role.

On the morning of 15 January students discovered that during the night the white marble bust of Mella had been splashed with black paint, and quickly a crowd of angry youths began to gather. By noon thousands of students were marching down Havana streets, hanging Batista in effigy, and battling with the police who began firing on the demonstrators. It was the biggest riot since Batista's assumption of power, and in mid-afternoon the youths decided to march on the Presidential Palace. The police fought back with tear gas and bullets, and a twenty-one-year-old student named Rubén Batista Rubio was fatally wounded.

After dark, groups of students, among them Alfredo Guevara and Raúl Castro, returned to the university to regroup and to await a police attack. Thirty other students, who formed a protective cordon around the Mella statue, were arrested and taken to police stations. At the Third Police Station, a student named Quintín Pino suddenly saw a familiar figure entering the precinct around midnight, and he cried to his companions, 'Hey, here comes Fidel. . .' Castro, who had meticulously avoided the riot in which Raúl had fought all day, now chose to appear as attorney, obtaining the release of the thirty students before dawn. Politically this had more value than hurling stones at the police.

University tensions and disorders went on until the week of the Martí anniversary celebrations, an occasion on which the Batista regime and its opponents battled over the proprietorship of the Apostle's memory. The government launched the celebrations with a reception at the Presidential Palace on the evening of 25 January, and the festivities continued with a formal session in front of the National Capitol (where parliament had functioned before the coup) on the night of 27 January.

Counter-celebrations were simultaneously set in motion by radical opposition groups, ranging from the University Students' Federation (FEU) and *Ortodoxo* and Socialist (Communist) Youth, to the Women's Martí Centennial Civic Front, the latter a very new entity. The FEU organized a Martí Congress for the Defence of the Rights of the Youths, with Raúl Castro acting as a key member of the founding commission. The congress produced a permanent committee, with Flavio Bravo, the chairman of Socialist Youth (and a full-time Communist organizer), as one of its fifteen vice presidents, and Raúl Castro as one of the ten permanent secretaries, personally responsible for propaganda. Fidel Castro had no part in the congress but, inevitably, he was caught up in its aftermath.

The evening of the youth Martí congress, 26 January, the police raided a house in the Hàvana suburb where about twenty women belonging to the Civic Front were preparing to distribute the following day a leaflet condemning the regime for collecting additional taxes to pay for the anniversary celebrations. The women were pushed into a waiting police van to be taken to the headquarters of the investigations section, but they shouted and sang inside the vehicle, and their voices were recognized by three occupants of a car that happened to pass them at the entrance to the bridge over the Almendares river. The three men were Fidel Castro, Aramís Taboada and Alfredo (El Chino) Esquível; all three were lawyers and all three belonged to the secret Movement.

'Let's turn around and follow them,' Fidel said, and the three attorneys reached the investigations office close behind the police van. Castro announced that he was the women's legal representative and, as one of them said later, 'He didn't move from there until the last one of us left the police office at dawn.' But Castro's grand revolutionary gesture was yet to come. Fidel Castro and his Movement were to celebrate the Martí centennial by staging a public parade of his clandestine 'army' the following evening.

The Movement's 'army' had begun to take shape at both the university and in the countryside in the early autumn of the previous year when Castro had decided to act 'independently', and met Pedro Miret, the engineering student who undertook to mould the Movement into a military weapon. At the outset Miret and others at the university were engaging in sporadic weapons training, mostly in the basement of buildings, but because silence had to be maintained the guns could not be fired – except occasionally at the sports stadium. The instruction therefore centred on arms handling, assembling and disassembling, and crawling with rifles in hand. When Miret began to train the first volunteers (he taught almost anyone who asked, before he had joined Fidel's Movement), all he had was an ancient Halcon submachinegun, one M-1 rifle, one Springfield rifle, one Spanish-made Mendoza rifle, two Winchester shotguns and a few pistols.

Miret's operation changed totally after he met Castro on 10 September 1952. Fidel had heard about him, and sent Ñico López, his *Ortodoxo* worker friend, to ask Miret to train 'a little group' he had. Miret, then a fourth-year student, was disenchanted by the old-line political organiz-ations for whom he was then training young men, and after meeting with Fidel he devoted himself completely to the Movement. When Fidel formed the Movement's Military Committee shortly thereafter, Abel Santamaría, Miret, José Luís Tasende who worked in a refrigeration plant, Ernesto Tizol, a chicken farmer, and Renato Guitart, a young man from Santiago where he worked at his father's small trading firm, were the members.

Most of Fidel's recruits were poor workers from Havana and nearby. They spent their Sundays (and their few extra cents for bus fares) at the university, learning the mechanism of a weapon that, as Miret once said, could not even fire. Most of them had never set foot in a primary school, let alone a university, and they had to overcome a sense of social inferiority when dealing with students.

The recruits came to the university in cells of ten or fifteen men, each cell being given an exact hour and place to report for training. First, the groups stopped at a Havana high school to receive the password for the day. Tasende and Tizol usually checked the identity of the recruits at the entrances before letting them enter.

Security precautions were so strict that men from different cells were forbidden to talk to one another, and names were never given or exchanged. Castro himself not only avoided ever being present at training sessions, but he even concealed his relationship with Miret. When messages had to be exchanged or plans coordinated, Ñico López, Tasende or Tizol would act as contacts between Castro and Miret. By the same token Miret never went to places where he could run into Fidel, Abel or other senior Movement members. Armando Hart, later one of Castro's most trusted companions and still a Politburo member after the 1986 reshuffle, remembers that after meeting Fidel for the first time at the *Ortodoxo* party headquarters in Havana, he was asked how his military training at the university was coming along. For months Hart could not figure out how Castro knew about it because he had no idea that Miret, who had invited him to undertake military instruction, had links with Fidel.

To build his Movement Castro says he travelled 40,000 kilometres in his car during the fourteen months between mid-1952 and the Moncada attack contacting groups and individuals all over Cuba so that the revolutionaries would be equipped and ready to strike. Given the Movement's lack of funds this was a miracle of improvisation and secrecy. Fidel said: 'We succeeded in recruiting 1200 men, and I spoke with each one of them. I organized every cell, every group.' Miret estimates that from September to December 1952 between 1400 and 1500 trainees passed through his hands (not all of them remained in the Movement) divided among 150 cells. But because the Movement was woefully short of weapons at the time of Moncada, the attackers were selected from only the twenty-five cells in Havana and Pinar del Río provinces. Even in these cells members knew only each other, and in one instance in the town of Artemisa two young workers who were close friends discovered only on the eve of the Moncada assault that they belonged to different cells of the same Movement.

Artemisa, with its working-class and anarchist traditions, was one of Castro's best recruitment pools. It produced 250 volunteers and some of the best sharpshooters of the Movement, among then Ramiro Valdés, the future interior minister. When Pedro Miret decided early in 1953 that field training was required as well, the rebels practised in rural areas around Artemisa and in Havana province.

Assisting Miret in training the rebels was a United States Army veteran from the Korean war named Isaac Santos, known as Professor Harriman to the volunteers. It was Castro who discovered Harriman at a friend's house, learning that he had been instructing another anti-Batista faction and that he was an expert in hand-to-hand combat. Harriman ran a tough commando course and he taught the *Fidelistas* how to use a compass and orient themselves in any terrain. Eventually, however, the rebels suspected him of being a plant of American Intelligence services, and he was eased out before Moncada. He was seen in a Batista prison in 1953, exhibiting signs of torture, suggesting that the suspicions of treachery may have been unjust.

When the Martí centennial came in January 1953 Fidel Castro already had a rebel army of sorts, and he decided to show it off, a risky gesture, but for him a typical one. To compete with the Batista celebration at the National Capitol on the night of 27 January, university students' organizations, the new youths' rights committee, the women's Civic Front, high-school groups and young workers had planned a huge torchlight parade across Havana, and this is where the *Fidelistas* chose to first present themselves to the country.

They did so by fielding a 500-member contingent that marched in the parade in military formation behind Fidel Castro, chanting, 'Revolution! . . . Revolution! . . . Revolution! . . .' The flaming torches they carried were armed with large iron nails at the top, potentially lethal weapons in the event of an attack by riot police. The *Fidelistas* had spent all morning constructing the nail torches at the Calixto García Hospital and at the university stadium. Late in the afternoon, Abel Santamaría and José Luis Tasende organized the rebels into marching units; when night fell Castro arrived to assume command of his troops. Raúl Castro marched behind his brother as did Melba Hernández and Haydée Santamaría, the two women founders of the Movement, and most of the General Staff.

Presumably because of the presence in Havana of distinguished foreign guests the regime did not interfere with the parade; the police made no move to halt the parade, ignoring the chants of 'Revolution' and 'Liberty', and there was no violence. The next morning, the actual Martí anniversary day, thousands of young people paraded again through Havana, this time from the university to Martí's monument in Central Park and, again, Fidel led his perfectly drilled units, the men marching arm in arm. Melba Hernández recalls that the *Fidelistas'* martial appearance caused a 'sensation', but that she also heard people in the streets saying, 'Here come the Communists'. At the same time neither the crowds nor the authorities seemed to realize that the highly disciplined detachments marching behind Castro in the two successive parades were actually under his command, that they belonged to an organized movement, and that they had received military training.

Fidel and his associates give no rational explanation for their decision to participate in the Martí parades as a large group that could so easily be identified by the police and the SIM as a revolutionary organization, thereby inviting its own destruction. This act threatened all the painstaking security measures taken over long months to prevent the Movement's public identification with Castro, and it is a mystery how the secret police failed to draw the obvious conclusions from the spectacle of Fidel marching at the head of his columns.

Though it certainly demonstrated the bravado on which Castro thrives – the temptation to flex his muscles in public for the first time may have been too great to resist – he may also have calculated that the Batista regime, unaware of the Movement's existence, would think nothing of the presence of Fidel and his friends among the parading protesters. Asked about the risks, Pedro Miret says: 'We were certain that nobody would know who we were', and that at the time the government saw only the traditional political parties as enemies: 'We were nothing to them, we did not exist.' Besides, Miret says, the plotters held the authorities' professional competence in low esteem.

Castro remained in public view during most of February, even though he and his closest associates were already actively engaged in preparation of targets for military revolutionary action. On 8 February Castro published in the mass circulation weekly *Bohemia* an article denouncing the destruction by the police of the studio of the Havana sculptor Manuel Fidalgo. Among the works destroyed were small busts of Martí with the inscription 'For Cuba that Suffers' (a Martí quotation) and death masks of Senator Chibás. Fidalgo sold most of his works to raise funds for Castro's Movement, and Fidel made the sculptor's unexplained disappearance after the police raid sound ominous. The article was printed with photographs taken by Fernando Chenard, a professional photographer who had come to the Movement from the Communist Party. It was the first time since the Batista coup that the Cuban press published an article signed by Castro.

On 13 February Rubén Batista Rubio, the youth shot by the police during the Mella statue disturbances the month before, died at a Havana hospital, and this triggered another protest. Castro, who had been at his bedside almost every day, helped to lead a silent funeral procession by some 30,000 persons from the university to the cemetery on 14 February. Riots broke out all over Havana after the burial, automobiles were set ablaze, and the police fired on the students. The next day formal charges of promoting 'public disturbances' were lodged by the secret police against 'Doctor Fidel Castro', who was described as an *Ortodoxo* youth leader. The government eventually dropped the case without bringing it to trial.

There were more disturbances in Havana in February and March, including some on the first anniversary of the Batista takeover, but Castro and his Movement concentrated principally on their military preparations. Mario Mencía, the leading historian of the Cuban revolution, believes that after the events of 14 February Castro had made a 'tactical change' in the revolutionary movement. During the first year, he writes, the nascent Movement took advantage of every opportunity to publicly defy the Batista regime. In the second year, however, Castro's policy shifted to the avoidance of any situations interfering with the Movement's principal goal of direct action. Mencía observes that this 'revolutionary agitator' knew how to adjust to changing circumstances.

For these reasons Castro remained neutral when another anti-Batista faction engaged in an attempt to overthrow the regime through a civilian-military coup. The MNR, the Nationalist Revolutionary Movement, had been organized the previous year by Rafael García Bárcena, a liberal university professor with links to young army officers. Drawing its following from among middle-class students, intellectuals and professionals, it had no particular ideological tendencies. Its ranks included, however, a number of lawyers, doctors and other professionals who later joined Castro in the 26th of July Movement. García Bárcena's aim was to lead about fifty men, armed with pistols and knives and daggers, on the army's Camp Columbia in Havana and to seize it with the support of pro-MNR officers inside the installation. Then, the professor believed, a popular uprising would follow and Batista would fall. In fact this was of course a very unconvincing plan, depending as it did on the improbable success of an attack by a small group of civilians on Cuba's largest military base and on the ability of a handful of young officers to assume the command of government troops.

Castro was aware of this enterprise, planned initially for 8 March, and then postponed to 5 April, and considered it pure adventurism. The idea of organizing an army, seizing the barracks and ousting Batista in twenty-four hours 'seemed absurd'. Subsequently, Castro was accused of fearing García Bárcena as a rival. But when Professor Bárcena outlined his plot and asked for his backing early that spring, Castro claims that he told the professor he was willing to 'analyse' the plan with him, and that he had enough men and weapons to participate in such an action if he felt it had any chance of success. However he felt that the MNR leaders must halt immediately their plot discussions with every politician on the island. García Bárcena ignored this advice, and Castro remarked later that the conspiracy had been bound to fail because 'it was the best advertised action in the history of Cuba', and consequently the Movement could not risk becoming involved.

There were, of course, deep ideological differences between the two leaders. In the end, however, the whole argument became academic when the MNR was betrayed from inside its ranks (as Castro had warned), and on the morning of Easter Sunday, 5 April, the police raided the house in Havana where García Bárcena and his followers were preparing to launch their coup.

Seventy persons were arrested in the MNR's revolutionary fiasco, and fourteen were tried for subversion in a trial lasting nearly two months, attracting great public attention. García Bárcena, defended by the young lawyer Armando Hart (who was an MNR member but had not been arrested), was sentenced to a two-year prison term. There were more disturbances in the streets of Havana and other cities, but General Batista appeared satisfied that the only serious threat to his rule had been removed.

Equally, Batista experienced no fears over the 'Montreal Pact' signed in a Canadian hotel on 2 June by leaders of the internally divided traditional political parties, proposing his removal and the return to constitutional government. Although the pact failed to issue any call for armed rebellion against Batista, concerns developed within the Movement's leadership that whatever funds were available to Cubans abroad for the purchase of arms might flow to the followers of the political parties on the island rather than to the *Fidelistas*. Indeed, according to one published version, Castro had agreed to be a regional coordinator for an armed uprising financed by the Montreal group under the overall command of Juan Manuel Márquez, an *Ortodoxo* politician in Havana. But this would have been a wholly implausible role for Fidel. Later, however, Márquez became one of Castro's closest associates (and one of the first to die after the *Granma* landing in 1956).

Understandably, perhaps, Cuban revolutionaries at that time were entirely consumed by domestic politics, hardly aware of great world events. Though Cuban students had opposed the United States over the Korean War in 1950 and 1951 (Castro being among the most outspoken critics of American policies), they seemed to have lost interest in it now that the armistice was approaching. On 5 March 1953 Josef Stalin died at the Kremlin, but there is no record of any reaction to it among the 'old' Cuban Communists or among the self-proclaimed young Marxists such as Fidel Castro.

And the only interest the United States had in Cuba at that juncture was to announce publicly its support for Batista's proposal to revise the 1943 Electoral Code (Batista periodically talked about elections) so that, in effect, Communists under any disguise would be kept out of any future elections. But Washington failed to use this as an opportunity to insist that Batista actually set an election date; the assumption was that the Havana regime was firmly in control, and nobody had any idea that Fidel Castro and his Movement even existed.

At the start of Easter week Fidel Castro motored to Oriente, stopping briefly in Santiago, Palma Soriano and several other spots. This was a perfectly normal holiday trip for a Havana lawyer whose family home was in Oriente, and there was no reason for anyone to suspect that Castro was actually surveying the terrain for the attack on Batista which he was preparing. Furthermore, Fidel had selected this particular week for travel because he knew that García Bárcena's conspiracy was planned to erupt on Easter Sunday, and he wanted the whole Movement leadership to be away from Havana. Abel and Haydée Santamaría took Melba Hernández to their native Las Villas province, and Jesús Montané went to see his parents on the Isle of Pines.

The idea of seizing an army base through an attack by several hundred armed men was devised by Fidel late in 1952, when Pedro Miret had completed the first stage of the volunteers' military training. He had settled on the Moncada army barracks in Santiago, Cuba's second-largest military installation, as his target, some time between January and March 1953.

The dilemma facing Castro was that he could not start a revolution without arms, and the Movement had no funds with which to purchase them. Fidel could barely support himself and his family; they were essentially subsidized by friends in the Movement. As there was no real source of money for this secret organization in Cuba nor any prospects from abroad, Castro concluded that if they could not buy arms, they had to steal them. In a pep talk to his companions in the first weeks of January 1953 Fidel summed it up: 'There are places where there are more than fifty

M-1s; there are places where there are one thousand oiled rifles, well-kept rifles. . . There is no need to buy them, there is no need to bring them, there is no need to oil them, there is no need to do anything; the only thing that needs to be done is to capture them. . .'

The risk involved was once again overridden by Castro's self-confidence. Attacking Moncada in Santiago would serve two purposes: obtaining quantities of modern weapons and establishing a major military base which could become a centre around which a national revolution would grow. Castro was able to remind his companions that the Cuban armies in the Independence Wars started out as guerrillas, equipping themselves with weapons obtained from assaults on Spanish fortresses. During the uprising in Bogotá in 1948, too, crowds obtained weapons from the police stations they attacked.

In a 1966 speech Castro explained the military aspects of his Moncada strategy: 'We did not expect to defeat the Batista tyranny with our handful of men. But we did think that this handful of men could seize weapons with which to begin arming the people; we knew that a handful of men would be sufficient not to defeat that regime, but to unleash that force, that immense energy of the people, that, yes, would make possible the defeat of that regime.' The central political aspect of the Castro strategy, he said, was a rejection of the traditional notion that 'revolutions can be made with the army or without the army, but never against the army'. Nobody back in those days, Castro said, would even think of a revolution against the army, yet his entire philosophy rested on the belief that the army must be destroyed to clear the ground for a 'real' revolution. Castro's master plan, then, called for the capture of arms by his revolutionary handful in order to defeat the Batista regime *and* destroy its army, and only then to proceed to the great revolution.

For reasons that Castro describes as 'accidental', the Moncada assault failed. He has never accepted intellectually the possibility that his concept or planning might have been faulty. Moreover, it will never be known if the great revolution would have indeed leaped ahead with the capture of the barracks. Castro evidently believed that favourable conditions already existed in Cuba so that Moncada could trigger a nationwide rebellion, but in retrospect this seems not necessarily a correct assessment. Besides, it was doubtful that Batista would be deserted by the bulk of the armed forces even if Moncada fell, and therefore Castro would have had to fight for survival against the dictator's superior firepower. Ironically, it was his early defeat, combined with his spectacularly defiant stance afterwards, and the birth of the 26th of July Movement, that helped to create a revolutionary climate on the island. When he launched the Sierra war three years later, the revolutionary conditions had come into being, making his enterprise much more plausible. Speaking in general terms long after the fact, Castro declared: 'It is an error to think that [revolutionary] conscience must come first, then the struggle.' On the contrary, he said, 'The struggle must come first and, inevitably, behind the struggle will come with rising impetus the revolutionary conscience.' This worked for Castro in an exceptional fashion during and after the Sierra war, but might well have failed if he had found himself sitting inside Moncada with his handful of men and no adequate support in the country at large. This is why the Communists refused to support him for such a long time and, ultimately, he triumphed only by means of an incredible series of gambles and unparalleled self-confidence.

At his trial after the assault, Castro explained that he had expected to take Moncada by surprise and without any bloodshed, in part because he did not think the government would ever anticipate an attack in Santiago; the coup tradition was to try to seize Camp Columbia in Havana. Asked by the prosecutor what he had proposed to do if he had captured Moncada, Fidel said: 'We counted on the help of all the people of Cuba, which we would have obtained if we could have communicated by radio. . . The people would have responded if we had succeeded in contacting them. Our plan was to take Moncada and then broadcast the last speech of [Senator] Chibás over all the radio stations of the city. We would have read our revolutionary programme to the people of Cuba; our declaration of principles touched on all the aspirations of generations of Cubans. At that time, all the opposition leaders would have supported us, joining the Movement throughout the republic. With the entire nation united, we would have overthrown the regime. . .'

In the meantime Fidel Castro ordered the acceleration of his forces training. Military training conducted by Pedro Miret, Harriman, Tasende and Tizol in university basements and atop roofs was now moved to farms and fields to allow actual firing and combat practice; after January 1953 there was no more military activity on the campus.

The *Fidelistas* trained wherever they could. They used the small farm where Pedro Trigo (one of the first Movement members) and his wife lived in the south-eastern suburb of Calabazar and the farm belonging to another friend in Catalina de Güines, not far from Havana. In all at least fifteen different field locations were used for training, sessions being switched from one place to another for security reasons. The trainees came usually in small groups by bus, often getting off individually at different points, then following instructions to reach their final destination. Sometimes an unknown person – for example a tall (or short) man in a sports shirt with blue (or red) squares had to be spotted and asked for instructions.

Oscar Alcalde, who owned a laboratory and worked part time as a Finance Ministry inspector, joined the Cerro Hunting club where he regularly brought Movement members as guests (but never twice the same ones) to practise target shooting with shotguns. Alcalde had to pay (thirty) or forty pesos each time for bullets and additional pesos for tips to avoid problems with club employees. The club was also used for final firing practice with .22-calibre sports rifles by those selected to participate in the Moncada attack (although they were never told where they would be going). There were fake mobilizations and emergency drills, and the military commanders winnowed out one by one those among the volunteers who were not considered fit for combat.

Castro attended field training sessions very rarely, but when he came he displayed his meticulous nature. On one occasion during training at a farm near Los Palos in Pinar del Río province, a tiny metal part was lost from a damaged rifle, and in the rain and gathering darkness Castro searched in tall grass until he found it; turning to the volunteers he said, 'Perseverance will give us our victory.'

Castro was aware of the vital importance of every weapon in the Movement's small and antiquated arsenal, and he kept track of individual bullets as well as rifles. Modern weapons were not only expensive but difficult to obtain. One day Pedro Miret and Oscar Alcalde, the treasurer, almost fell into a secret police trap when they went to buy ten old Thompson submachineguns from a man who claimed to be a Spanish Republican refugee, but was actually a military Intelligence agent. The contact had been made through a third party, and the Movement security was so solid that the police had not identified the prospective buyers beforehand; Miret and Alcalde fled when they realized they were being surrounded by plain-clothes men in identical blue shirts at the spot where the transaction was to occur.

Miret says that the military committee finally decided to arm the *Fidelistas* with relatively cheap and easy to find .22-calibre rifles and hunting shotguns. Still, it was on surprise and not firepower that they relied. In the end the arsenal included sawed-off Winchester shotguns, automatic Remington shotguns and several semi-automatic .22-calibre Browning rifles – plus the old M-1, the Springfield and the Spanish submachinegun that Miret had treasured all along. Ernesto Tizol was in charge of purchasing most of the shotguns because he owned a chicken farm, and could make it appear plausible. In other cases, Movement members falsified order forms from businesses where they had friends. Fidel received a Luger pistol purchased for 80 pesos, and he carried it at Moncada. In Santiago Renato Guitart was able to buy a number of shotguns and rifles, and 5000 bullets.

Raising funds for the purchase of arms, ammunition, food and everything else needed to equip the little army was a constant pre-occupation. More and more Movement members and their families had to be supported because they were too busy with the revolution to be able to work. At his trial Castro told the court that 16,480 pesos had been donated by individual volunteers, most of whom died at Moncada or were murdered by the army and the police afterwards. The best estimate is that overall the Movement was able to collect up to 40,000 pesos during its entire pre-Moncada existence, an amount so small that the prosecutors refused to believe it.

There was a tiny trickle from the sale of the works of the sculptor Fidalgo (who reappeared late in May when he had failed in his attempt to escape police by sailing to New York as a stowaway) and impressively generous donations from individuals in and around the Movement. Jesús Montané contributed his entire 4000-peso severance pay when he quit his accountant's job; Oscar Allende gave 3600 pesos from mortgaging his laboratory; Tizol mortgaged his chicken farm; the photographer Chenard gave 1000 pesos; and Pedro Marrero sold all the furniture from his apartment, except for the bedroom furniture which Castro would not let him dispose of. Abel Santamaría sold his car. Naty Revuelta, the beautiful society wife of the heart surgeon, turned over her 6000-peso savings.

Naty Revuelta also joined a group of Movement women who worked endless hours at the apartment of Melba Henández's parents sewing uniforms from material bought cheaply from a nearby department store, making military caps and sewing noncommissioned officer's stripes on the sleeves of a dozen uniforms. Castro had decided the rebels would wear Cuban Army uniforms to conceal their identity until the last moment. His idea was to buy two or three hundred uniforms, and Pedro Trigo located a medical corps corporal named Florentino Fernández Léon who detested Batista and was willing to do the purchasing from soldiers he knew in Havana. But he was able to buy only one hundred uniforms by June, and Castro decided to have the Movement sew the additional ones he needed. As usual, nothing was left to chance, no detail was overlooked.

Fidel Castro arrived in the Oriente town of Palma Soriano on 3 April to confer with a local dentist named Pedro Celestino Aguilera, the chief of one of the Movement's cells in eastern Cuba. Aguilera briefed Castro on the political situation in the region, emphasizing the widespread opposition to the Batista dictatorship. Castro thanked him, told him he would be in touch, and departed without saying what he was planning to accomplish in Oriente.

Having already selected Moncada as the attack target on the basis of information from Movement contacts in Santiago and on the basis of his own conclusions, Castro began dispatching secret emissaries to study the area in detail. Oscar Allende went to Santiago in May to observe the change-of-guard pattern and timing at the fortress downtown. Lester Rodríguez, a senior Movement member, followed him to concentrate on every detail of the small area between a nearby courthouse and the barracks, a stretch of street through which some of the attackers would drive. And so on.

During his April tour of Oriente, accompanied by Renato Guitart, Castro instructed Ernesto Tizol to buy a small farm on the road between Santiago and Siboney Beach where Fidel used to go as a high-school student. He, Guitart and Tizol spent a day walking up and down the road until they agreed on the farm they deemed suitable. Then they went to swim at the beach. Castro calculated that the farm would be the perfect spot to concentrate his forces on the eve of the attack, and to have a place to fall back on in case of need. The farm was ten miles from downtown Santiago and Moncada, and seven or eight miles from the Sierra Maestra foothills in the other direction. In the event of a disaster at Moncada, Castro's plans contemplated a retreat to the Gran Piedra mountains nearby, which he knew well from his schoolboy climber's days. Tizol was instructed to say to the owner that he was buying the farm to raise chickens as well as to have a vacation place not far from the sea. After initial hesitation the owner sold El Siboney farm to Tizol.

In June Abel Santamaría departed for El Siboney to prepare the farm to receive clandestine arms shipments. Before Abel left Havana Castro told him to assume the overall command of the Movement if anything happened to him. Abel did not tell his sister Haydée where he was going; the reasoning was that in case of detention it was better for her not to know her brother's whereabouts. Fidel instructed her to move to Melba Hernández's apartment.

While Abel and Tizol worked at the farm in secrecy, other Movement members in Oriente were instructed by Castro to buy furniture and a refrigerator for El Siboney, to rent mattresses for the men who would arrive later, and to rent rooms for others in hotels and boarding houses in Santiago and Bayamo. Castro was planning a simultaneous attack on Bayamo army barracks on the western approaches to the Sierra Maestra. After his visit to Palma Soriano he went to the manganese mines of Charco Redondo to establish contacts with the miners. Charco Redondo was just outside of Bayamo, and it was to serve as a support area during the attack on the barracks. The master plan was rapidly turning into military reality.

On his way back to Havana from Oriente Fidel stopped overnight at the Birán farm to see his parents and to borrow 140 pesos from his brother Ramón. Fidel had asked him for a larger amount, without saying that it was intended for the Movement, but Ramón refused. This was the last time Fidel saw his father: he would be too busy to see Don Ángel before departing for Mexico two years later, and the old Spaniard would die before his son could return in triumph.

Chapter 3

Fidel Castro's great adventure, after fourteen months of conspiracies and preparations, finally began on the evening of Friday 24 July 1953, in the suffocating heat and humidity of summertime Havana. Having completed all the last-minute arrangements, delivered updated sets of instructions to those staying behind, and made his farewells to the very few persons who mattered to him personally, Castro climbed in a rented 1952 blue Buick sedan with a cream-coloured roof for the long road journey to Oriente and what he called his encounter with destiny.

Castro, Abel Santamaría and the rest of the Movement's military committee had picked Sunday 26 July as the date of the planned dawn attack on Moncada and Bayamo. They were the only six men in the whole organization who knew the place and the date of the action. Some time in May, but just before Fidel left for Santiago, the entire battle plan was reviewed one more time. Castro, Pedro Miret, José Luís Tasende and Ernesto Tizol, the four members of the military committee still in Havana, went over every operational detail.

As a security precaution Castro slept at a different home every night in the weeks preceding the departure for Oriente, rarely appearing at his latest apartment on Nicanor del Campo avenue in the Nuevo Vedado where he had moved with Mirta and Fidelito some months earlier. His movements around the city avoided any pattern or routine. On that last Friday he shifted from using a black Dodge to a blue Buick (rented that morning for $50 for a weekend 'vacation at Varadero beach'), with a young black Movement member from Oriente as his driver. The responsibility for driving Castro had been given to Teodulio Mitchel on the eve of the trip to Santiago although Fidel had met him only a week earlier. Mitchel was an ex-soldier, and for the past year or so a truck driver in his native Palma Soriano where Dr Anguilera, the local dentist, recruited him into his Movement cell. The idea was that Castro's driver should be someone from the area who knew the territory and was known there himself, and Anguilera had sent Mitchel to Havana to meet Fidel. They hit if off instantly and Castro bought Mitchel a meal of steak with fries, to mark the start of a friendship. For at least forty-eight hours his life would be in Mitchel's hands, based on Fidel's instinct for whom he could trust.

In the preceding weeks Castro had gradually dispatched key personnel to Oriente, starting with Abel Santamaría, and in the last week he had begun moving the bulk of his force, travelling in small groups or individually by train, bus and car. Haydée Santamaría and Melba Hernández, the only two women in the combat ranks of the Movement, went separately by train to Santiago, on 21 and 22 July respectively. They each carried weapons in their suitcases; Melba had rifles in a florist's box. Larger shipments of arms and ammunition along with the uniforms had been sent to La Siboney during June and July through a variety of means. The last purchase of weapons was made in Santiago two days before the attack.

Raúl Castro was away during these preparations. Working very closely with the Communists at the university (though not yet a Party member) and notably with the Socialist Youth's chief Lionel Soto, Raúl left Cuba in February as a member of the Cuban delegation to the Communist-sponsored Fourth World Youth and Student Festival in Vienna. Then he went on to Bucharest, spending a month in Rumania, continuing his discovery of Communist Eastern Europe with leisurely visits to Budapest and Prague, 'visiting factories', which he followed with a nine-day stay in Paris. Raúl sailed home, arriving in Havana on 6 June. Part of his European tour was financed by his parents who gave him $500 after his sister Juana had talked them into it.

As a result of his absence Raúl played no role whatsoever in the moulding of the revolutionary movement. This may have been because Fidel clearly wished nobody in the Movement with direct links to the Communists (the few ex-Communists in the Movement had resigned from the party), or else because the Communist leadership found Raúl to be more useful as a university leader; his close brotherly ties with Fidel were an additional plus. Actually, Fidel wanted Raúl to participate in the Moncada coup de main as a plain 'soldier', but he kept him in the dark about all the plans until the last moment. Raúl, who formally joined the Communists' Socialist Youth after returning from Europe, said later that when he received word on 24 July to leave Havana immediately for an unknown destination, he failed to inform the Socialist Youth. 'In not advising it,' he said, 'I surely committed an error, but I had belonged to the party only for a month and a half, and I didn't have a very keen sense of obligation [to it].' Still Raúl almost missed the Moncada assault altogether.

On his return to Havana in early June Raúl had been arrested along with two Guatemalans he had befriended during the crossing (another member of the shipboard group was a Soviet citizen who was not allowed to disembark in Havana, and whom Raúl later called 'my first Soviet friend') on charges of carrying subversive propaganda. The Guatemalans were released when Guatemalan diplomats intervened, and placed back aboard the liner. Raúl was the only one to remain imprisoned.

Melba Hernández, who went to the Castillo del Principe prison as an attorney to try to free Raúl, says that she found him 'very enthusiastic' about his European trip. The police had confiscated his diary, and the chief of secret police investigations told Melba that Raúl had written in it that 'the socialist world is a paradise'. She was unable to obtain his release because he had now been charged with 'public disorder' and had to stand trial. The next day Fidel obtained from a judge a provisional liberty warrant. The case never came up: Raúl would be already in a Santiago prison for participating in the Moncada attack when the date of his court appearance for public disorder rolled around.

Raúl was unable to undergo even a minimum of military training in the short time remaining before Moncada. Nevertheless he seemed to doubt the success of any armed action by the Movement because he thought the group was too small. Perhaps he was taking the orthodox Communist view of *putsch* conspiracies, but when his friend José Lúis Tasende asked him whether he would come along if the Movement launched an operation, Raúl replied, 'Yes, I shall come. . . In the Movement there is my brother and my best friends: you, Miret, Juan Almeida. . . ' Robert Merle, the French historian who had written widely about Moncada, believed that 'at the decisive moment sentimental fidelity overcame ideological loyalty'.

Raúl was sharing a boarding house room with Pedro Miret when Tasende came to tell him that 'we are taking the train tonight'. Suffering from an awesome hangover after attending a late party the previous night, Raúl summoned his energy to meet Tasende later that afternoon to pick up a shipment of weapons and to board the train. Sixteen other *Fidelistas* under Tasende's command were travelling on the same train, but they pretended not to know each other. Raúl received his ticket from Tasende who sat next to him, and saw that Santiago was the destination. 'Moncada?' he asked. 'Yes,' Tasende replied softly. They arrived in Santiago in the afternoon of the next day.

Between 120 and 130 men travelled from Havana and Pinar del Río provinces to Oriente between 23 and 25 July, a typical feat of Fidel logistics. In addition to buses and trains, fifteen automobiles were used in this deployment, Fidel going in one, Pedro Miret in another, and so on. Each departure followed a precise timetable, which included stopovers and arrival times. The cars were borrowed or rented from travel agencies.

The overwhelming majority of the volunteers had no idea where they were going until reaching their destination, but the discipline was so great that except in one or two instances no questions were asked, nothing was questioned. On Castro's insistence, save for himself only men who did not have children were chosen for the revolutionary mission; there were to be no orphans.

Fidel Castro had always demonstrated the most acute interest in the personal lives and welfare of his fellow revolutionaries. Melba Hernández recalls, for example, that shortly before the departure for Oriente, Castro suddenly realized that Gildo Fleites López, one of the most active Movement members, had been engaged for years to a girl whom he had known from childhood and that he might die at Moncada without a chance to marry her. 'Therefore,' says Melba, 'Fidel organized rapidly here in Havana a wedding with all the requirements of the law, a wedding with a veil and with everything that a girl dreams about. Gildo had his honeymoon with Paquita. Gildo fell, he did not return.' In Mexico, three years later, Castro decided that Arturo Chaumont, one of the rebels selected for the *Granma* expedition, should marry his woman companion Odilia Pino so that she would not become a spinster in the event of his death during the landing. As Melba tells the story, neither of them had actually planned marriage, but Fidel kept insisting that 'we must marry them'. His companions began to complain that Castro was interfering in people's private lives, but Melba says that he conducted the project like a military campaign. In the end Fidel prevailed, and money was somehow found not only for a church wedding but for a honeymoon in Acapulco and a cash wedding gift from the Movement. Three months later Arturo Chaumont was captured by the Batista troops, never to be seen again. Says Melba Hernández: 'Fidel has this preoccupation with giving his friends a bit of happiness. . . '

Even though the specific mission had never been discussed during the long months of preparations there were vastly more volunteers than equipment to arm them. In the end Fidel and the military committee determined that 135 attackers would be required for Moncada and thirty for Bayamo, and the chiefs of the individual cells were ordered to select their best men to meet the necessary numbers. The volunteers were told only to bring casual clothes for an extended absence.

The Wednesday before the attack Castro had supervised the drafting by the poet Raúl Gómez García of the Moncada Manifesto that was to be issued to the nation when the rebels attacked in Santiago and Bayamo. Late that day he went to the apartment of his friend Naty Revuelta in an exclusive section of Vedado to give her the text of the Manifesto to be retyped in a number of copies for him to take along to Santiago and others to be distributed by her to principal political leaders and editors in Havana the moment he seized Moncada.

Naty, the green-eyed blonde who had been devoting most of her time to Fidel's cause, and upon whom he had learned to rely, had already selected and purchased the records that the revolutionaries planned to play in their moment of victory over Santiago radio stations: the Cuban national anthem, independence wars hymns, Chopin's triumphant A-flat *Polonaise* and Beethoven's *Heroic Symphony*. The great sound of patriotism and revolution, the blood-quickening music, the Chibás farewell speech, the appeal for the creation of armed people's militias, and the Manifesto would be the spark for the national uprising against Batista. The Manifesto, signed by 'The Cuban Revolution', first invoked the memory of Jose Martí, charging that the 'true revolution' ignited by him and continued by subsequent generations had been undermined by Batista's 'treacherous coup' to bring 'the crimes of blood, dishonour, unlimited lust and theft of the national treasury'. It then proclaimed: 'Before the chaos into which the nation has fallen, the determination of the tyrant, and the godless interests of the men who support him, the youth of Cuba who love freedom and man's dignity stand up in a gesture of immortal rebellion, breaking the insane pact made with past corruption and present deceit.'

In the document Castro offered Cuba a nine-point programme with the first point stating: 'The *Revolution* declares itself free from the shackles of all foreign nations.' This sense of priorities presumably conveyed his nationalism (if not his anti-Americanism), but it also was the nationalism of his generation, and no Marxist connotations should be read into it. If nothing else, Castro himself insists that at that stage he carefully concealed his Marxism. The Manifesto also called for 'definitive social justice' and 'respect for workers and students', but such phrases had been employed by Cuban politicians for a half-century. In terms of representative democracy (meaning democratic elections), Castro declared the 'Revolution's . . . absolute and reverent respect for the constitution of 1940', which Batista had suspended with his 1952 coup. In other words, the Moncada Manifesto was hardly a call to the barricades, and one might even wonder in retrospect whether it would have been sufficient to set the country aflame.

In any event Castro was confident that he and the young poet had produced an inspiring text, and one of his great errands on his last day in Havana – Friday 24 July – was to pick up retyped copies of the Manifesto from Naty Revuelta. With Teodulio Mitchel driving him Fidel started the day meeting Movement members at the apartments of the Santamarías and Melba Hernández's parents for quick conferences. Next he rushed to the south-east suburbs to pick up two platoon leaders, to the vicinity of the airport to locate a cell chief, and then to Santiago de las

Vegas for the same purpose. Back in Havana Castro stopped again at the Santamarías' home to pick up extra arms, and at the apartment of his sister Lidia to hand instructions to a group just arrived from Artemisa. Tauntingly, he also visited the secret police headquarters to inquire about a 'client', on the theory that he would sense if there were suspicions about him. Apparently he sensed nothing.

When night fell Fidel was racing again along the airport route to contact an aviation radio specialist whose services he required in Santiago. Except for minutes of catnaps, he had not slept, and had eaten virtually nothing, in the past forty-eight hours, too busy and too charged up to be able to relax. Because the blue Buick ignored a stop sign, Castro and Mitchel were stopped by a police cruiser, and fined on the spot after Fidel calmly informed the police that they were en route to the airport to meet family members. Had the highway patrolmen decided to take them to a police station, which was often done in such traffic cases, Fidel's revolution might have been thrown completely off schedule. He always seemed to live on the brink.

Returning to the city, Castro met briefly at a bar with the dentist from Palma Soriano, then drove two blocks to his own apartment. There he told Mitchel that he was going upstairs 'to kiss my son . . . God only knows when I'll be able to do it again.' A photograph in official Cuban archives shows Castro with Fidelito, then nearly four years old. Castro is pointing at something in the distance with his extended right arm and index finger, his son appearing pleased and amused. Castro wears a suit and a tie, there is a kerchief in his breast pocket and, shot in profile, he looks a perfect Latin matinée idol. The caption says that in the picture Fidel is saying goodbye to his son, but it seems too posed, and one suspects that the photograph may have been taken some time before for future historical purposes.

Castro is not known to have said anything to Mitchel about taking leave from his wife, and it is extremely unlikely that he gave Mirta the slightest indication of his plans or of the reason for kissing his son goodbye. Again she remains the unseen figure in the Castro family drama. At the apartment Fidel put on a white *guayabera* and, as one of his friends said later, his only baggage for the trip was an extra *guayabera* and a volume of selected works of Lenin.

Castro's last stop was Naty Revuelta's apartment on Eleventh Street in Vedado. There he picked up the original of the Manifesto and several copies as well as the records she had bought for the planned revolutionary broadcast from Santiago. Naty was the only person not in the top leadership of the Movement to have advance knowledge of the Moncada attack: not only had she obtained the records and typed the Manifesto but now Fidel instructed her to hand deliver copies to the heads of the *Ortodoxo* party, including Raúl Chibás, the brother of the late Senator

Chibás, and the publishers of the weekly *Bohemia* and two main daily newspapers. Naty was to take the Manifesto to their homes at five o'clock in the morning of Sunday 26 July. Then, Fidel said goodbye to her.

It was already late in the evening when Castro and Mitchel finally took the Central Highway that runs east from Havana to Oriente. In Matanzas, two hours later, they happened to come across another Movement automobile, and Castro chatted for a few minutes with its occupants. He repeated the warning he had given earlier that all the drivers must observe the speed limit and avoid being stopped by the police (but which he himself had forgotten), and the blue Buick headed for Colón where they stopped at the home of Dr Mario Muñoz. The physician was preparing to leave for Santiago to join the assault teams.

Castro and Mitchel had breakfast early in the morning in El Cobre, then stopped in Santa Clara, the provincial capital of Las Villas, to find an optician. Fidel, who always remembered everything, had left behind his spectacles at the Melba Hernández apartment in Havana, and he did not want to lead the attack on Moncada half-blind (in those days he seldom wore his glasses in public). Although it was Saturday the optician agreed to make a pair for Fidel while he waited.

They reached Bayamo around six o'clock in the evening of Saturday 25 July and Castro went to the Gran Casino inn to talk with the twenty-five men who were to attack the army barracks there the next dawn. They had arrived in groups by train and automobiles earlier in the day, and Fidel reviewed with them all the details of the battle plans. After leaving Bayamo at 10 p.m. the Buick was stopped at an army checkpoint near Palma Soriano. This was where Teodulio Mitchel proved his real value. As a soldier approached the car to check the passengers' documents and search the trunk, Mitchel recognized him as a friend from their home town, greeting him by name. 'Is that you, Mitchel?' the soldier said. 'Go on through.'

At midnight Castro and Mitchel arrived in Santiago, in the midst of wild celebrations at the annual *Oriente* carnival. In Cuba carnival is in July, and Santiago was always famous for its music and dancing in the streets, day and night, from Friday until Sunday night. It was for this reason that Fidel had chosen the dawn of Sunday 26 July for the attack. He assumed correctly that most of the garrison would be away from Moncada on weekend passes and that the guard would be lax. This strategy, too, may have come from Martí as he had chosen Sunday 24 February 1895 to launch the anti-Spain uprising because it was pre-Lent carnival time.

The two men had coffee in a shop downtown, and drove on to La Siboney. The farmhouse was completely dark, and the blue Buick was challenged by Jesús Montané who stood guard in the shadows. Inside,

Fidel found 118 men of his Rebel Army and Melba and Haydée. Most of
the men had gathered at the farm in the course of the afternoon, directly
from Havana via Santiago or after an overnight stop there, and they were
exhausted from lack of sleep and the heat. Melba and Haydée, who earlier
had fixed a chicken-with-rice meal for the men, ironed the 120 army
uniforms for the *Fidelistas* ; they were in the only room with a light.

Abel Santamaría briefed Castro on the state of readiness, and Fidel
insisted on returning to Santiago at two o'clock in the morning for one
final mission there. Abel went with him as some of the men at the farm
tried fitful sleep, or just chatted in low voices and smoked. In the early
evening, weapons had been brought out from dry wells on the property
where they had been hidden; the automobiles were concealed inside
especially-built wooden chicken runs. Fidel's foray to Santiago was to
find Luís Conte Agüero, a well-known radio commentator and *Ortodoxo*
politician who had a house in the capital of Oriente; he wanted to tell the
radio man about the impending assault and persuade him to coordinate
the revolutionary broadcasts. However, Conte Agüero had stayed in
Havana that weekend, and the disappointed Fidel was back at La Siboney
at 3 a.m. It was his fourth consecutive night without sleep, but he was
bursting with energy.

Additional men arrived and the final count was 131 fighters, including
Dr Muñoz, Melba and Haydée, and Fidel himself. Castro ordered the
men to change into the light brown army uniforms, suddenly discovering that even the largest uniform available was too small for him. He
worriedly inspected himself in a mirror in the half-dark room, concerned
that he might not look convincingly soldier-like at the moment of attack
– a potential security problem.

Though detailed plans had been worked out beforehand, Castro
discovered at La Siboney that Abel Santamaría, whom he had not seen in
long weeks, insisted on leading the main assault group instead of letting
Fidel do so. The original plan had provided for Castro to attack the
fortress itself while Lester Rodríguez would move on the courthouse
across the street, and Abel would capture the nearby hospital. Fidel
wanted Abel at the hospital because it seemed the safest place, and he had
been designated as his successor at the head of the Movement if Castro
was killed. But Abel pleaded with Fidel, 'Don't be like José Martí,
exposing yourself needlessly,' and Castro answered, 'My place is at the
head of the fighters. It can't be anyone else.' In the end Fidel ordered him:
'It is decided: you will go to the hospital.'

The next argument was with Melba and Haydée. They informed
Castro that they intended to participate in the attack. 'No,' said Fidel.
'You've done enough. You will stay at the farmhouse.' It was Dr Muñoz,
wearing a doctor's white coat on Castro's instructions, who solved the
dispute, proposing that the two women accompany him and Abel in the

takeover of the hospital. It was a civilian hospital, not guarded by soldiers, and Melba and Haydée would be useful to him as nurses.

At four o'clock in the morning Castro assembled the rebels in the darkened house to outline the plan of attack; only the military committee members had known until that moment that it was Moncada they were to assault. There was an instant of terrible fear of discovery when one of the men accidentally fired a shot from his rifle, but there was nobody in the area to hear it. After explaining the operation which, he promised, would last no more than ten minutes, Fidel said:

'In a few hours you will be victorious or defeated, but regardless of the outcome . . . this Movement will triumph. If you win tomorrow, the aspirations of Martí will be fulfilled sooner. If the opposite occurs, our action will set an example for the Cuban people, and from the people will arise young men willing to die for Cuba. They will pick up our banner and move forward . . . You know already the objectives of our plan; it is a dangerous plan, and anyone who leaves with me tonight will have to do so willingly. There is still time to decide. Those who are determined to go should move forward. The watchword is not to kill except as the last resort.'

A rebel asked Castro what should be done with prisoners, and Fidel replied, 'Treat them humanely; don't insult them. Remember that the life of an unarmed man must be sacred for you.' Suddenly one of the four university students in the group told Castro that they had decided not to go because they thought the armament was not adequate for the mission. With withering indignation Castro ordered them placed in the bathroom under guard. Then the radio expert from Havana airport announced he would not engage in 'illegal' actions; he, too, was taken to the bathroom. Now Fidel had 121 men and two women to launch the revolution.

Fidel Castro says that when he embarked on the Moncada enterprise 'there was [only] a small group of those with the greatest responsibility and authority who already had a Marxist orientation'. Recalling these events in conversations in 1985, Castro emphasizes that the 'qualities we did require from the companions were, in the first place, patriotism, revolutionary spirit, seriousness, honourability, disposition to fight . . . and agreement with the goals and risks of . . . armed struggle against Batista'.

Castro's definition of the ideological make-up of the Moncada rebels is entirely consistent with the recollections by scores of early Movement members that when the attack was being prepared, political instruction centred on the Martí tradition – never on Marxism–Leninism. It is also borne out by the political backgrounds of the Moncada group. According to Mario Mencía, the historian of the revolution, out of 148 participants in the Moncada and Bayamo actions, there were only two Communist

Party members: Raúl Castro, who had joined the party six weeks earlier and had no voice in any Movement decisions, and the sugar worker, Luciano Gonzáles Camejo. Castro and Abel Santamaría considered themselves as serious students and adherents of Marxism, but the overwhelming number of their followers held essentially moderate social-justice views in terms of the Cuban experience.

As Castro has repeatedly stressed he recruited Movement members among young working-class followers of the *Ortodoxo* party of Senator Chibás, a party which had stood for social justice, social-welfare legislation for the overwhelmingly poor Cubans and for anti-Communist nationalism. Castro may have assumed that once exposed to widespread and victorious revolutionary processes these *Ortodoxo* workers and peasants would be propelled towards socialism, relinquishing their traditional distrust of anything identified with Marxism. He has often charged that this antipathy towards Communism was due to cold-war 'imperialist propaganda', but the record shows the Communists' historical inability to attract masses. On the other hand, when Chibás founded the *Ortodoxo* party hundreds of thousands of workers who normally ignored political affiliations rushed to join him – probably because of his enormously appealing personality.

In any event, of the *Fidelista* army only the leaders had intellectual backgrounds. Four of them had university degrees: Fidel Castro and Melba Hernández as lawyers, Mario Muñoz as a doctor, and Pedro Celestino Aguilera as a dentist. Raúl Gómez García, the poet, Pedro Miret, Raúl Castro, Lester Rodríguez and Abelardo Crespo were occasional university students. The bulk of the Movement members had only elementary school education, and many lacked even this background. Though lacking university degrees, five members were public accountants, including Abel Santamaría and Jesús Montané – two top rebel leaders. No more than twenty rebels earned more than 200 pesos monthly. The largest group were construction workers (carpenters, painters, bricklayers and so on), then came farm workers, cooks and waiters, office workers, drivers, shoemakers, mechanics, bakers, milkmen, ice delivery men, street vendors and self-employed persons (travelling salesmen, for example). And there were many unemployed young men in the revolutionary ranks. The oldest fighter was Manuel Rojo Pérez, a fifty-one-year-old peasant.

In December 1961, when Castro announced to the world his allegiance to Marxism–Leninism, he noted that he had been asked whether at the time of Moncada he thought the same way as now, and added: 'I thought very similarly to how I think today. This is the truth.'

Before her suicide in 1980 Haydée Santamaría reminisced about her brother Abel, assassinated at Moncada, being encouraged by Castro to study Marxism more intensively when they were organizing their revolutionary movement. But Haydée added that even at the risk of 'being impolitic' she had to say that Abel had refused to join the Communist Party because he knew he could not enjoy there the political freedom he had in the *Ortodoxo* party. After Moncada, however, at El Siboney farm, the army found a copy of the first volume of a two-part Spanish edition of Lenin's *Selected Works* with Abel's name flourishingly written across the cover; the Batista regime used it as evidence that the assault was a Communist plot, and newspapers printed photographs of an army lieutenant at the farm, a rifle in his right hand and the captured Lenin book proudly displayed in his left hand.

There is therefore remarkable consistency in Castro's descriptions between 1961 and 1985 of his own, his friends' and his Movement's ideological evolution. In his own case the emphasis is on his steady advance both in the ideological content of his thought and in its public disclosure. His principle was to proceed one step at a time, strategically and tactically. At Moncada Fidel Castro wished to be seen as the defender of Cuban democracy and social decency from the ravages of the Batista rule. Subsequently, he chose to espouse Marxism–Leninism publicly. To his critics he has practised crude deception; in his own eyes he deserves plaudits for brilliant revolutionary strategy.

Looking back at *Fidelismo's* trajectory it is evident that, even for the initial purpose of ousting Batista, Castro had organized a revolutionary movement totally lacking in internal democracy. From the outset the Movement was dominated from above by a few individuals (Fidel and Abel Santamaría, then Fidel alone after his friend was killed at Moncada) with the conviction that its military programme could be unfolded.

In the intervening years Castro has demonstrated further consistency in his political behaviour: once he had imposed Marxism–Leninism as the official Cuban doctrine he proceeded to bring to power the Communists who were his university friends but had never participated in any of his revolutionary actions, often promoting them at the expense of veteran *Fidelista* fighters. From the university Communist network Lionel Soto Prieto, who took Raúl to Eastern Europe, served for long years as Cuban ambassador to the Soviet Union, and at the Third Congress of the Communist Party in 1986 was named to the key post of Secretary of the Central Committee; Flavio Bravo Pardo, once secretary general of Socialist Youth, is a Central Committee member and chairman of the National Assembly; Alfredo Guevara, who was Castro's first Communist friend, commutes between Paris and Havana as a 'cultural ambassador', as close as ever to Fidel and Raúl. And from the ranks of the 'old' Communists, the Party leaders and guiding lights before and during Batista's time, most have held Politburo and Central Committee posts as long as their advancing age and health permitted. At the Third Congress in 1986 it was the octogenarian Fábio Grobart, the only surviving co-founder of the Cuban Communist Party in 1925, who officially introduced Fidel Castro to the delegates.

When Fidel Castro outlined his plan for the attack on Moncada he assured his followers gathered in the darkness of El Siboney that with the element of surprise in their favour the attack itself would be short and swift. He refrained from explaining what would happen afterwards. At his trial, too, he said only that he was certain the the people of Cuba would rise to support him and liquidate the dictatorship. While Castro may have deliberately avoided sharing his strategic concepts there is considerable evidence that his plans for the next revolutionary phase were extremely detailed and ambitious.

Thus Pedro Miret, a member of the Movement's Military Committee, emphasized in a conversation in Havana in 1985 that the assault on Moncada was specifically designed to 'isolate the region of Oriente, which could have been easily isolated'. This would have been possible at the time, Miret said, because there were no adequate communications among Havana and regional military commands and facilities; such communications were established after Moncada. Castro, who was a born strategist, reasoned that for army reinforcements from Holguín, a city in the north of Oriente province where at least a regiment was stationed, to reach Santiago and try to retake Moncada and the city it would have been necessary to come down the Central Highway. But this mountain highway led through Bayamo, and this was the reason for the effort to secure the Bayamo barracks simultaneously with the capture of Moncada. Then the revolutionaries would blow up the bridges over the Cauto river, which flows through Bayamo, cutting off the Holguín–Santiago highway there. Theoretically the southern part of Oriente province would then be sealed off by the rebels, creating, in effect, a 'liberated zone', a concept to which Castro returned in launching the Sierra war at the end of 1956.

As he had said, Castro assumed widespread popular support after taking Moncada in the historically rebel Oriente province, and he hoped for armed 'people's militias' to emerge to bolster his revolutionary power. Moreover, nestling between the Caribbean sea and the mountains, Santiago would be relatively easy to defend; it had only one major land access route. A study of the Moncada operation by the Historical Section of the Political Direction of the Revolutionary Armed Forces, issued in 1973, confirms that Castro's strategy was to make 'a rebellion erupt in a region, try to keep it alive, call a general strike, and gain time for a popular mobilization that would raise the struggle to a national level'. Since Santiago was Cuba's second-largest military centre, located at the opposite end of the island from Havana, that made the plan even more enticing. After removing arms from Moncada and Bayamo barracks (Moncada had 4 heavy machine guns, 10 submachineguns, 865 Springfield rifles and 471 revolvers, which would have been plenty to equip a major rebel force), Castro would abandon the buildings to avoid being attacked from the air. There were no anti–aircraft guns at either location, but the rebels would have spread throughout the areas they controlled, never presenting a single target to aircraft.

The Moncada study suggests that if the Batista regime did not collapse immediately, the Castro forces would engage in irregular war in the mountains and fields as the independence fighters had done in the nineteenth century. The closeness to the mountains would allow a rapid transition to guerrilla war if the conflict became prolonged. The official study concludes that the Castro blueprint was excellent, but allows itself the remark that 'the weak aspect of the project was the reliance on the exclusive result of a single action, making the rest of the plan depend on it'. If the attempt to capture the barracks failed, the study says 'the whole plan would fail'. But, it adds, this was 'the only possibility open' to the rebels, so 'they had to follow it'.

This conclusion amounts to the judgement that for Fidel Castro there are risks he is always willing to take, no matter how extraordinary, because such is his nature and his instinct. It is reminiscent of the comment about Prussia's Frederick the Great (whose life Castro had studied) by an American historian that the king was a romantic, 'and part of Frederick's romanticism was surely the ability to envision ultimate victory when all rational calculation indicated it was clearly impossible'.

Castro had instilled his faith in victory in his men. In the darkness of El Siboney, a few minutes before five o'clock in the morning of Sunday 26 July, the young Cubans sang in whispers the national anthem. They were ready to go.

Chapter 4

The Moncada barracks are an ugly sprawl of buildings in the shape of an irregular rectangle, occupying a six-hectare area of high ground in downtown Santiago. They were originally built as a fortress by the Spaniards, and reconstructed after a fire in 1938. Named for General Guillermo Moncada of the Liberation Army in the independence wars following the establishment of the Cuban republic, they served an essentially internal security function, since an external attack on Santiago was wholly unlikely.

At the time of the assault at dawn on 26 July 1953 Moncada was the headquarters of Infantry Regiment No. 1, known as the Maceo Regiment (General Antonio Maceo was a hero of the last independence war), and its normal complement was 402 men, of whom 288 were privates. A 26-man Rural Guard squadron was also stationed there. Castro's calculation was that on a carnival night the barracks would contain less than half of the total number: the missing men on general holiday leaves, those remaining asleep or drunk. For the attack, Fidel would have seventy-nine men to take Moncada, the rest of the force being assigned to related targets in the fort's immediate vicinity, and a separate detachment having been deployed in the town of Bayamo. His plan was designed in such a manner that it had to succeed totally, or fail totally.

The Moncada compound was divided into two main parts. The eastern portion of the rectangle was a firing range, the western portion was the fort proper, and this constituted the main objective of the rebel operation. The fort's perimeter was formed by yellow thick-walled, two-storey crenellated barracks buildings on its east side where the official entrance to Moncada headquarters was located, as well as along the south and north sides for a half-block each. The other half-blocks on the northern and southern flanks and the entire length of the western side of the compound were protected by high walls and fences; officers' and enlisted men's clubs were behind in the south-west inside the fort's perimeter, and exercise fields in the north-west.

The fort could be penetrated through the main entrance into the command building with its guardroom, but such a frontal attack would have been foolhardy. There were gateways on the west side of the compound and on the east side; they were inconveniently far from the centre of the fortress, however, obliging the attackers to cover much terrain in the open. Castro therefore chose Gate No.3, in the south-eastern corner of the fort, directly south of the headquarters building entrance. Automobiles could enter the fort through this gate to reach the courtyard, with the rebels then storming the structures from inside the compound and seizing them.

For insurance Castro had decided to occupy the Palace of Justice (the Santiago courthouse), a three-storey building one block south of the compound's southern perimeter line, to provide covering fire on the courtyard area inside. Small houses and bungalows of the regimental officers and non-commissioned officers filled the block between the fort and the courthouse. The military hospital was next to the courthouse, but Castro did not think it a useful firing position. He did order, however, the occupation of the Saturnino Lora civilian hospital, a two-storey building with single-storey wards in the back, that looked down on the compound's western wall and could provide additional cover for firing across the street.

Having studied the Moncada layout and security for months, Castro concluded that the fort could be rushed through Gate No.3 after the commando team in the lead automobile had disarmed the three guards in front of two blockhouses with firing slits in the sides, and lifted an iron chain across the roadway to let the other commando cars into the courtyard. Once inside the rebels were to run up the stairs of the buildings, disarm the sleeping soldiers (killing them only if they resisted with weapons), take over the fort's radio transmitter and then fan out through Moncada with freshly captured army weapons. This was the plan and Castro saw no flaws in it; his scouts had even determined the exact times at which a two-man army patrol passed Gate No.3 during its nocturnal rounds along the perimeter. The assumption was that the patrol would adhere to its schedule.

The sixteen automobiles with Fidel Castro and his 121 attackers, including Haydée Santamaría and Melba Hernández, began departing from El Siboney at 4.45 a.m. The first car was a 1950 Pontiac driven by Abel Santamaría; the commando team that was to disarm the guards was in the fourth car, a 1950 Mercury; and Fidel drove the fifth car, a brand-new 1953 Buick. The automobiles would take their assigned places in the attack column en route to Santiago because it was easier to organize the caravan on the highway than in the dark confinement of the farmhouse yard.

All the men wore brown Cuban Army uniforms with black neckties, wide-brim campaign hats or visored caps, and knee-high boots or leggings. (Haydée and Melba were in slacks and blouses.) The only difference between them and genuine Cuban soldiers lay in their arms. Whereas the Maceo Regiment's troopers carried modern .30-calibre New-Springfield rifles, the *Fidelistas* were equipped with an assortment of hunting shotguns, .22-calibre semi-automatic sports rifles, a few .44-calibre Winchester sawed–off rifles, a single M-1 rifle and a single Browning submachinegun. All the same, pathetic or brave, the rebels were superbly trained in the use of their weapons.

To avoid being identified in the event of premature capture the rebels carried no documents of any kind on them. Castro and a group of older-looking men (many in the force were barely over twenty years old; Raúl Castro was twenty-two and appeared younger) wore sergeants' stripes on their sleeves to exact even more respect from Batista soldiers; this was a highly respected rank, Batista himself having led a sergeants' rebellion in the 1930s that handed him power over Cuba. Fidel had shaved off his moustache a day or so before the assault, possibly in order not to be recognized.

There was no sign that the regime had any advance notice of the coming attack. When Castro had reached El Siboney the previous night he learned to his immense frustration that Colonel Alberto del Río Chaviano, the commander of the Oriente Military District to which the Maceo Regiment belonged, had even opened Moncada to the public on Friday the 24th as part of the carnival celebrations. 'What a lost opportunity!' he kept muttering angrily, imagining the ease with which he could have taken over the fort had he known of Chaviano's plans in advance.

At this peak of the summer the rest of Cuba was completely tranquil. General Batista was spending the holidays at the luxury Varadero beach resort, and had been aboard his yacht *Marta II* off the coast for the last few days. Near his home town of Banes in Oriente, however, 150 peasants had been arrested by the Rural Guard for putting up squatter homes on land belonging to the Santa Lucia sugar mill, and the story was published in the newspaper *Alerta* on Sunday 26 July – just as the *Fidelistas* converged on Moncada to launch a revolution to depose Batista and bring social justice to the country.

But everything began instantly to go awry for them. The third car to leave El Siboney was a black 1948 Chevrolet driven by Mario Dalmau and bringing five other men, including team commander Raúl Castro. (At the last moment Fidel made his brother the chief of one of the three detachments at Moncada, albeit the smallest.) On the way to their target, the Palace of Justice, they made a wrong turn, winding up at a downtown square in the opposite direction, and finally arriving at the courthouse several minutes after schedule, when the fighting had already begun.

The sixth car, carrying Boris Luís Santa Coloma (Haydée's fiancé and member of the Movement's Civilian Committee), and seven other fighters, had a flat tyre right after leaving the farmhouse. Boris and three others were able to transfer to companions' vehicles, but four men had to be left behind for lack of space, and the car was abandoned. Now the force was reduced to 118 combatants and 15 automobiles.

The four university students who had decided hours earlier not to participate in the operation, and were ordered by Fidel to be the last to leave the farm (en route for home in their car after detention in the bathroom), disobeyed him and managed in the darkness to start in the middle of the motorcade. As they approached Santiago they turned left on the Central Highway in the direction of Havana, and the car behind them containing eight rebels assumed that this was the way to Moncada and followed. The driver realized his error only far past Santiago. When the eight men returned to the city it was already too late to fight. Thus the total assault contingent that finally struck the fort area was down to 110 persons, including Fidel Castro, and 14 vehicles. In a 1959 interview with Carlos Franqui, the editor of *Revolución*, Castro said: 'The best-armed *half* of our troops was delayed at the city gates and so was not present at the vital moment. . . Our reserve division, which had almost all our heavy weapons – except for those with the advance party – made a wrong turn, and completely lost its way in a city that was unfamiliar to them.' This is completely misleading: Castro had not been denied the best-armed half of his troops, but only twelve men. Raúl and his five-man team were a few minutes late, yet in position at the courthouse during the battle. Abel Santamaría with twenty-three rebels, including the two women and Dr Mario Muñoz, reached the civilian hospital precisely on time.

The whole operation did suffer a delay when the motorcade had to halt at the narrow bridge over San Juan river to let a Jeep go by with two innocent hunters leaving town for a day in the countryside. Then Fidel, swearing savagely, had to stop his Buick just before the turn-off to the barracks to let the advance party's car manoeuvre into position in front of him.

The time for the attack on Moncada had been set for 5.15 a.m., but it probably was a few minutes later when the commando vehicle, a Mercury, braked at Gate No.3 to force the entry into the courtyard and open the way for Fidel's Buick and the rest of the motorized column. The commando team hit at once. Because the movement operated on the principle that leaders must always personally lead armed actions, this eight-man commando was composed of two Military Committee members, Renato Guitart and José Luís Tasende; Civilian Committee member Jesús Montané; the three best cell leaders, Ramiro Valdés, Pedro Marrero and José Súarez; and the two outstanding marksmen, Carmelo Noa and Flores Betancourt (whose brother was in the Bayamo detachment).

According to plan, Guitart shouted imperiously at the three army sentinels at the gate, 'Clear the way, the general is coming!' and the men, seeing his sergeant's stripes, drew up to attention. Montané, Valdés and Súarez took the Springfield rifles away from the stunned soldiers while Guitart and four others removed the iron chain over the entrance and rushed up the outside stairs of the barracks building to occupy Moncada's radio communications centre and prevent contact with Havana and Holguín.

Fidel, armed with his huge Luger pistol, slowed the Buick as he drove past the Military Hospital on his left, about 150 yards before Gate No.3. This was so that he and his six companions could decide what to do about the two-man army patrol, armed with submachineguns, that had suddenly materialized in front of them, and now tensely watched the action at the gate. They were either ahead of time in their appointed round or the *Fidelistas* were critically behind schedule. Simultaneously a real army sergeant appeared in the street, examining the situation suspiciously. For all practical purposes the battle of Moncada was lost by the rebels at that precise moment because they no longer had the element of total surprise in their favour.

'At that moment,' Fidel Castro told French historian Robert Merle in 1962, 'I had two ideas in mind. Because each of the men of the army patrol had a submachinegun, I feared that they would start firing on our companions who were busy disarming the sentinels. I also wanted to prevent their fire from alerting the rest of the barracks. I conceived, then, the idea of surprising them and taking them prisoner. This seemed easy because their backs were turned to me. . .'

All these events lasted seconds, perhaps minutes, as Fidel drove slowly towards the patrol, readying his Luger carefully, opening the door on his side, then suddenly accelerating the Buick at them when they turned and pointed their Thompsons in his direction. The Buick hit the kerb with its left front wheel and the engine stalled. The army sergeant shifted his body, aiming his revolver at Fidel, but he was brought down by rifle fire from the rebel vehicle behind the Buick. Fidel and Pedro Miret, who rode with him in the Buick's front seat, somehow found themselves on the ground behind their car, with a soldier firing at them from a window of the Military Hospital on their left. Bullets whizzed past Fidel's face and he covered his ear with his hand as if he had been deafened. At that moment alarm bells went off with shrieking fury throughout the barracks.

The entire action was over in less than a half-hour. Ramiro Valdés,

Jesús Montané and Jose Súarez were the only rebels who actually succeeded in entering the fort, and for a few minutes they had as captives some fifty half-dressed soldiers whom they found on cots along the walls inside the courtyard. But other soldiers, rifles and revolvers in hand, began appearing from all over the barracks, firing at the three rebels. Soon the three were separated, each fighting his way out of the building. Valdés and Montané remember bringing down several soldiers with their bullets. All three ultimately escaped to the street.

Now soldiers were firing massively at the retreating *Fidelistas* trapped in the short twenty-foot-wide street between Gate No.3 and Garzon Avenue behind them. Fire came from the roofs and windows of the barracks about them, from the Military Hospital and, in diagonal trajectory, from a .30-calibre heavy machine gun mounted atop a tower on the firing range 600 feet away. The rebels were an excellent target for the machine gun, the emplacement of which was a painful surprise for them (they were also unaware that a .50-calibre heavy machine gun was on the roof of the officers' club, neutralizing Raúl Castro's small group at the Palace of Justice).

Renato Guitart, the member of the Military Committee who had been in charge of most of the arrangements in his native Santiago, was killed in front of Gate No. 3 along with Pedro Marrero, Carmelo Noa and Flores Betancourt. They were the first rebel fatalities of Castro's revolution.

Fidel Castro knew that he had irretrievably lost the Moncada battle the instant his Buick stalled outside the fortress and the alarm bells began clanging, but he still tried desperately to regroup his men to a second attack. He stood in the middle of the street, barely visible in the half-light of the dawn and the thickening gunsmoke, shouting commands and encouragements of '*Adelante, muchachos! Adelante!* . . . ' (Advance, boys! Advance! . . .) But the men could not hear him, and the spirit of the attack was quickly lost. To give them a clear example, Fidel climbed back in the Buick, trying to start it up, but it was in vain. Furious beyond words, he attempted once more to regroup his troops, waving his Luger in the air. Most of the rebels were hiding behind the low fences of the bungalows across the streets, pinned down by withering fire from Moncada.

Yet Fidel still stood his ground. Spotting two soldiers setting up a heavy machine gun on the roof of the fort, he fired at them with his heavy pistol, then fired again at other soldiers taking up positions above. His companions were yelling, 'Fidel, Fidel! . . . Get out of there!. . . Get out! . . . ' but he seemed oblivious to their cries and to the hail of bullets around him.

Pedro Miret, then the Movement's principal military expert (after Fidel), believes that it was impossible to regroup the attackers because 'they faced a situation that had not been anticipated'. Reminiscing about the battle, he says that the plan called for all the automobiles to enter the courtyard behind Fidel's car, for Fidel to lead the men up the main staircase to occupy the Moncada command post, and then for others to spread out through the barracks. But when this failed there was little Fidel could do 'as he urgently tried to organize everything in the midst of a firefight'. Miret thinks that the critical moment was the accident of the sudden encounter with the army patrol. After the rebels were thrown back, he says, he attempted to deploy a defensive line to cover the retreat, and Fidel was 'again organizing everybody'. But, Miret adds, 'We had lots of people who never heard real gunfire and, especially, never heard a .50-calibre machine gun, which is very impressive.'

In the end, Miret says, Fidel 'decided to leave' with as many men as he could, and they became separated. Miret does not admit it, but he and two others seem to have stayed behind deliberately to cover the departure of the Castro group; he wound up inside the Military Hospital, beaten, left for dead, rescued by a doctor, put in bed, nearly murdered by army Intelligence agents in the hospital, and, finally, put on trial. It was in prison that he next saw Fidel.

Meanwhile Fidel was in an absolute fury at himself as he concluded that it had been a serious error to attempt the capture of the army patrol. The resulting series of clashes had led to the sounding of the alarm in the barracks and the end of his chance at Moncada. With his companions falling dead or wounded a new attack was out of the question, and there was no alternative but to become resigned to defeat and to pull back.

Satisfied that all the surviving rebels had left the vicinity of Moncada, Fidel got into the last vehicle to depart from the scene, a car containing six others, including one with a serious thigh wound. But as the automobile started, Fidel saw one of his men on foot, trying to escape from the gunfire. He ordered the car to stop, stepped out to make room for the other man, and proceeded to retreat, walking backwards and firing at the barracks. As he was turning the corner of Garzon Avenue behind the Military Hospital and out of the field of direct fire, the automobile of the rebel taxi driver from Artemisa came in reverse from Gate No. 3, picking up Castro and three additional companions.

The first idea occurring to Fidel at that point was that the simultaneous attack at Bayamo might have succeeded and that he should try to join the contingent there. But he also decided that the five of them in the car could start by capturing the small Rural Guard post at El Caney, a few miles north of Santiago, and secure the rearguard for Bayamo. If the action at Bayamo had failed, Fidel reasoned, they would go up the mountains to continue the struggle – as the Movement's plans had anticipated – and El Caney would be the best place to regroup.

The driver of the car, who was unfamiliar with the Santiago region, either misunderstood Castro's instructions or simply had no desire to go to fight in El Caney. Thus instead of going north he turned east on the road leading to El Siboney farmhouse, meeting the four rebels who had been left behind before dawn when Boris Luís Santa Coloma's car had a flat and could not continue. Fidel no longer insisted on doubling back to El Caney, and he stopped a passing private car, ordering the two occupants to take these four to El Siboney. But the first rebel vehicle had now caught up with him, so the private car continued on its way. Not quite three hours had elapsed since Fidel Castro had left the farmhouse to conquer Moncada – and Cuba.

In Havana, Naty Revuelta had left her Vedado apartment at five o'clock in the morning, as instructed, to distribute copies of the Moncada Manifesto to political leaders and newspaper publishers. Several of them were not to be found at home; others were unreceptive. A publisher sent his son-in-law out to meet Naty in his living room and tell her that they just had heard on the radio the news of a failed armed coup in Santiago. Naty was gently but firmly pushed out of the apartment. And she knew then that if she were stopped by agents of SIM, the military Intelligence service, with copies of the revolutionary document in her handbag, she faced imprisonment, or worse.

From the high terrace of the Palace of Justice, Raúl Castro and his men had witnessed the débâcle in front of Gate No. 3, but they could be of no real help. Strategically they were in an excellent spot, but their weapons were inadequate to give Fidel covering fire, and the terrace anyway quickly became a target for the Moncada heavy machine guns. Seeing Fidel's group retreat and the shooting die down, Raúl concluded that they had better leave, before being surrounded. Downstairs they ran into five armed policemen but were able to get past them into the car driven by Mario Dalmau. They fled in a hail of bullets. Only Lester Rodríguez, whose home was in Santiago, went on foot to his parents' house. The courthouse team suffered no casualties. Raúl ordered Dalmau to drive to the coast.

Occupying the civilian hospital, across the street from the western side of the Moncada compound, Abel Santamaría could not see what was happening at Gate No. 3, so he was unaware of Fidel's retreat. But soldiers from the barracks were now firing heavily at the hospital, and Abel realized that he was being encircled. Thinking that by fighting as long as possible he could aid Fidel's group, he decided to stay at the hospital until he ran out of ammunition. He told his sister Haydée and Melba Hernández that 'we are lost', and that they should try to escape and that they might survive because they were women. Abel added: 'Don't take risks. . . Someone has to live to tell what happened here.'

But Haydée and Melba did not even try to escape. The firing did not stop until around eight o'clock in the morning, when Abel and his men had no more bullets. But the army waited a further full hour before daring to enter the hospital building, and the two women spent the time helping the nurses to feed screaming babies in the maternity ward; the babies had been in the midst of a battle for nearly three hours. In the meantime other nurses put hospital gowns on the rebels and made them appear to be bedridden patients to protect them from the soldiers. Abel's head was bandaged over one eye, and he was put to bed in the ophthalmolagy section.

It was the rebels' bad luck that the Moncada civilian press chief, Señor Carabia Carey, happened to be at the hospital during the siege, undergoing some form of treatment, and he betrayed the *Fidelistas* to the army, adding that two rebel women were also hiding in the building. Melba and Haydée saw Abel being pulled out of bed and beaten with rifle butts, his face bloody. In the late morning the women were escorted to Moncada, and as they crossed the street they witnessed Dr Mario Muñoz being hit by rifle butts on the head, then shot in the back. A mild-mannered physician with a small moustache and spectacles, he died on his forty-fifth birthday. The press chief Carabia was arrested after the revolution, serving a thirty-year prison term. He then was allowed to leave for the United States.

In a hallway in the Moncada headquarters building Haydée and Melba saw a young man, his face so smashed by rifle-butt blows as to be beyond recognition, thrown on the floor by soldiers. Then they left him sitting on a bench, and the youth had the strength to scribble on a piece of paper, 'I was taken prisoner – Your son.' Melba realized it was meant for his mother, then she looked into his eyes and knew he was Raúl Gómez García, the young poet who had drafted the Moncada Manifesto, had written a stirring poem at El Siboney, and who was to have read the Movement's victorious proclamations over the radio. Then a soldier shot him dead.

The soldiers referred to the rebels as 'Koreans', an allusion to North Korean Communists who had invaded South Korea three years earlier. Haydée and Melba heard them brag about beating to death a very tall and tough rebel who tried to fight them with his fists, who had then been tied up and tortured by army interrogators. When a soldier mentioned that the rebel wore black and white shoes, Haydée realized it was her fiancé, Boris Luís. Boris had been unable to procure boots to fit him. He died without saying a word to his interrogators. Later Haydée was told by a soldier that Abel was being tortured, and a sergeant brought her her brother's gouged-out eye as proof. Abel died in torture later than Sunday. All the men in Abel's detachment were subsequently murdered by the army, except a young teacher who had succeeded in hiding.

Ramiro Valdés, one of the three attackers who actually penetrated

Moncada, extricated himself from the battle and climbed into one of the rebels' cars, dragging with him Gustavo Arcos, a friend who had been shot in the belly. Arcos had travelled in Fidel's car from the farm to Moncada, then became separated from him in the affray. The car had four flat tyres, but Valdés drove on the rims, succeeding in getting Arcos to a physician's home a few blocks away.

Nearly ninety miles north-west of Santiago, the Bayamo rebel action was over in less than fifteen minutes. Twenty-seven men had been assigned to the operation there, but only twenty-two actually took part in the attack on the army barracks. Led by Raúl Martínez Arará, an early Movement member, the detachment divided into three squads, rushing the structure from the back because it was the only side protected by barbed wire instead of a wall.

The rebels, moving at 5.15 a.m. in complete darkness, crossed an open field between the street and the barbed-wire fence. But they discovered to their surprise that the gate in the fence, open during the day, was padlocked at night. Attempting to climb over the fence, the men stumbled over some empty tin cans, alerting the soldiers. A dog barked, horses in the stable kicked the sides of their stalls, and a guard shouted at them to halt. Hiding behind bushes, the *Fidelistas* began firing on the barracks with their sports rifles and shotguns, but the soldiers countered with machine gun fire – and it was all finished.

Martínez Arará ordered the retreat and the men raced to their cars or just down the street on foot. Twelve rebels died at Bayamo (including Mario Martínez Arará, the commander's brother, who was tortured to death). The other ten succeeded in escaping. Among them were the commander, Fidel's friend Ñico López, the black poet Agustín Díaz Cartaya who weeks earlier had composed a revolutionary march that would become famous later as the '26th of July March', and Teodulio Mitchel, the truck driver who had brought Fidel from Havana to El Siboney only six hours earlier (he had rushed to Bayamo to fight as soon as he had dropped Fidel off).

By noon of Sunday 26 July there were twenty exhausted conspirators back at El Siboney farmhouse, three of them wounded. Twenty more appeared by mid-afternoon, just as Fidel Castro was preparing to leave for the mountains to resume the war, this time leading a guerrilla band.

Within hours of reaching the farm he announced that he was going to set up guerrilla operations in the Gran Piedra Sierra, a mountain chain running diagonally to the sea north-east of Santiago. Gran Piedra lay some ten miles from the city, and its highest peak, also called Gran Piedra, was over 3000 feet. Fidel asked for volunteers, and nineteen agreed to go – though one of them named Emilio Hernández, changed his mind within minutes of starting the march because his new shoes hurt.

The next day this nineteen-year-old boy was captured and murdered by the army; the official announcement said he was killed fighting at Moncada.

Fidel's column included Jesús Montané, the Movement's treasurer Oscar Alcalde, José Súarez and Israel Tápanes who had fought at Gate No. 3, and Juan Almeida, the black bricklayer's apprentice who began working at the age of eleven and would become one of the top guerrilla commanders, and young Reinaldo Benítez who had a festering bullet wound in his leg. An old black woman in a shack above Siboney sent her grandson as a guide with the Castro group, and next day they reached the village of Sevilla Arriba. Looking down at Santiago bay at their feet, Fidel raised his arms, and in his best fighting style proclaimed to his little band 'Compañeros, today it was our turn to lose, but we shall return.'

Further uphill the men came across a hut, but the black peasant refused to sell Fidel any of the chickens he was raising there; this was one time when Castro's powers of persuasion failed. But the peasant led them to his brother's house a distance away, and the rebels feasted on a pig the man killed for them. Fidel, according to a published account, talked with him about peasants' oppression by local landowners. Then he gave the man a nickel-plated pistol, saying, 'When they come to question you, open fire with this pistol . . . don't believe in anyone. Defend what is yours.'

At another peasant's house Fidel listened to the radio speech by General Batista with his version of the events of 26 July. The dictator had rushed back to Havana from his yacht on the afternoon of the Moncada attack, setting up operational headquarters at Camp Columbia. His Council of Ministers declared a state of emergency in Cuba, and suspended a provision of the Prison Code under which wardens are held responsible for the lives of the prisoners.

This seemed to be intended to legalize the decision taken by Batista and General Francisco Tabernilla, the army chief of staff, to murder the *Fidelista* prisoners being caught by the military in and around Santiago – even in hospital beds – and even as far away as Havana, which a handful had succeeded in reaching. Over a period of four days, starting on 26 July, sixty-one men were thus assassinated, including Abel Santamaría and Boris Luís Santa Coloma, who first were horribly tortured, the poet Raúl Gómez García, José Luís Tasende who was a member of the Military Committee, and Dr Muñoz. In seventy-two hours Fidel lost many of his best friends. Only eight had died in combat, among them Gildo Fleitas whose wedding Castro had organized in Havana the month before, the other sixty-one having been assassinated. The army and the police suffered nineteen fatalities in the fighting and had twenty-seven wounded. The final *Fidelista* death toll was sixty-nine, and only five wounded rebels were allowed to survive.

But the regime needed to make the outcome of Moncada seem a great victory, so in his report to the Santiago Court of Justice Colonel Chaviano (a dandified officer who had cowered under his desk at the command post during the battle) claimed that between four and five hundred men, 'equipped with the most modern instruments of war', had attempted to overthrow the regime. In tune with official propaganda, Chaviano reported that the attackers used knives 'to open the abdomens of three innocent patients' in the Military Hospital, and in firing on the troops they employed dum dum bullets in their automatic Remington rifles.

Batista charged that the attack was planned, organized, financed and armed by anti-regime groups exiled abroad, notably by former President Carlos Prío overthrown in the March 1952 coup. Such a propaganda line served to justify the subsequent repression and declaration of martial law. It is also entirely possible that it had not occurred to the dictator that an uprising like Moncada could have been so secretly orchestrated by a young troublemaker from Havana University and a group of his penniless followers. Listening to these accusations over the radio, Fidel Castro said, 'They wedded us to a lie, and forced us to live with it.'

In Santiago the army command sought to prevent newsmen from seeing too much of the barracks on the afternoon of the attack, but a photographer succeeded in taking pictures of a number of *Fidelistas* tortured to death and still lying in hallways and passages. Marta Rojas, a young reporter for the weekly magazine *Bohemia*, hid the photographs under her brassiere as she flew to Havana that evening. The gruesome photos were published five days later, shocking the nation and unleashing a wave of sympathy for the rebels.

On 28 July, as Fidel and his men were climbing the Gran Piedra mountains, civic leaders were meeting in Santiago under the chairman-ship of Archbishop Pérez Serantes (who twenty years earlier had prevailed on Fidel's father to have the boy baptized) to try to halt any further executions. Word that rebel prisoners were being killed had spread in the city, and the group decided that the archbishop should persuade Colonel Chaviano to guarantee the lives of any new prisoners. Both the archbishop and the colonel knew that Fidel Castro was at large in the mountains and their agreement, as far as Monsignor Pérez Serantes was concerned, specifically assured that if Castro were taken he would be kept alive. Additionally the archbishop published the next day a declaration, titled 'Enough Blood!' outlining the new accord with the army.

As a result of the archbishop's statement, thirty-two *Fidelistas* came out of hiding to surrender to the authorities, and they were treated without undue violence while locked up at the Santiago jailhouse. Before the intervention of the Roman Catholic Church, Haydée Santamaría and

Melba Hernández had been moved from Moncada to the jail on the dawn of 28 July and during the trip in a Jeep a soldier burned Haydée's bare arm with the red-hot tip of his cigar. Later that week even *Fidelista* leaders who emerged from their hideouts, including Dr Aguilera and Ernesto Tizol, were given full protection.

But the rebels who were the most wanted, namely Fidel and Raúl Castro, were not surrendering. They had to be taken, and the archbishop was increasingly concerned about their fate. He did not entirely trust Colonel Chaviano and his officers, and he had already travelled to Manzanillo, a city near Bayamo, to escort personally a *Fidelista* prisoner captured there. On 29 July, a Wednesday, Raúl Castro was arrested at a roadblock near the township of San Luís as he walked towards Birán and his parents' *finca*. He had fled by car from the Palace of Justice where his brother had stationed him during the uprising, but soon realized that he was safer on foot, and in two days and nights covered the distance from the south to the north of Oriente. The Rural Guard has detained Raúl simply because he had no identity documents, and at the local police station he insisted that his name was Ramón Gonzáles. But the lieutenant who interrogated him suspected that he was lying and locked him up in the tiny jail.

The next morning a travelling salesman came through San Luís, and the lieutenant summoned him to try to identify his prisoner. In the Oriente countryside most people know each other, and the man said, 'This is Raúl, the son of old Ángel, and the brother of Fidel Castro.' Raúl was transferred to Santiago and Moncada the same afternoon, spending the night at the barracks, certain that he would be shot. But Colonel Chaviano was not looking for a confrontation with the Church, so Raúl was sent to the jail, which was rapidly filling with his companions.

For Fidel Castro, Wednesday and Thursday were bad days. He ordered a halt for the Thursday night in a canyon. His band was in terrible shape. Reinaldo Benítez could hardly move because of his leg wound. Jesús Montané, who was flat-footed, dragged himself behind the others. The heat was suffocating, and they had no food. Suddenly a shot rang out: one of the rebels had accidentally fired his rifle and the bullet went into his shoulder. On Friday 31 July Fidel allowed the group to split up. Five men, including Montané and the two injured rebels, started back to Santiago, and were arrested en route. But Castro and thirteen of his followers were determined to stay in the Sierra. In fact Fidel had developed the notion of returning to the coast and moving east to Sierra Maestra.

Archbishop Pérez Serantes, meanwhile, had become so preoccupied with the fate of Fidel Castro and the other missing revolutionaries that he had taken to the road in a car to look for them; he must have been a strange sight, an elderly priest in a black cassock, a cross and chain around his

neck, stopping every few hundred yards in the wet heat of the equatorial
forest road, calling out to the rebels.

On the evening of Friday 31 July Fidel and his companions stopped at a
hut on a hillside for an overnight rest. They had been moving south
slowly towards the coast, but it was turning into an impossible
undertaking. Five more men had abandoned Castro, leaving nine. They
were almost entirely out of food. Behind the hut they spotted a young
peasant, crouching over a wood fire on which he was boiling a pot of rice.
Without a word the rebels moved in behind the peasant, took his spoon
away from him and began to eat his rice.

'Do you have more food?' one of the men asked. The peasant said he
did not, but would guide them to the farm of his employer, two hours
away. The farm was near the Siboney road, and Fidel recognized the
owner as an old acquaintance and learned from him of the archbishop's
efforts. He was also told of Chaviano's guarantees, and this convinced
Fidel that only he and the two other Movement leaders – Oscar Alcalde
and José Súarez – should attempt to cross over to the Sierra Maestra. The
others, he said, should surrender. In the meantime they returned to the
hillside hut to spend the night.

It was there that at dawn of Saturday 1 August a sixteen-man Rural
Guard squad led by Lieutenant Pedro Manuel Sarría Tartabull came
upon Castro and his sleeping companions and opened submachinegun
fire on the hut. The army had been tipped off that Fidel might be in the
area and Sarría was dispatched to look for him on the vast Mampriváestate, which included the mountain farm. The fire flushed out the rebels,
and Sarría cried, 'Cease fire! . . . I want them alive! . . . ' One of the
soldiers called Castro an 'assassin' for killing soldiers at Moncada, but
Fidel, with automatic rifles fixed on him and his eyes burning with rage,
yelled back, 'It is you who are assassins . . . it is you who kill unarmed
prisoners . . . you are the soldiers of a tyrant!' A corporal shouted to
Sarría, 'Lieutenant, we'll kill them!' Sarría, a tall, black fifty-three-
year-old professional officer, raised his arm. 'No,' he roared. 'Don't kill
them! I order you not to kill them! I am in command here. . . You can't
kill ideas . . . You can't kill ideas!'

Eventually the soldiers calmed down. They tied the hands of their
prisoners. Fidel, who did not realize then that he and Sarría had met once
at the university in Havana, insisted that his name was Rafael González.
He was deeply tanned by the Sierra sun, and he hoped the lieutenant
would believe him, especially because he had heard the official radio
announce his own death.

Later as Sarría's detachment escorted the *Fidelistas* to the road, Castro
whispered to him, 'Yes, I am who you think I am. . .' Then he asked,
'Why didn't you kill me? You would have received a nice promotion, a
promotion to captain.' Sarría replied: '*Muchacho*, I am not that kind of

man.' Fidel said, 'But if you spare me, they will kill you.' And the black lieutenant told him quietly, 'Let them kill me. . . It's a man's own ethics that must decide what he will do.'

Fidel Castro's life was spared also by the fact that Rural Guard Lieutenant Luís Santiago Gamboa Alarcón was in bed with flu in the Moncada barracks on the night of 31 July–1 August when Squad No. 11 was dispatched to look for the rebels in the hilly countryside above Siboney. Gamboa was a tough officer, wholly devoted to the regime, and it is certain that he would have killed Castro without the slightest hesitation upon finding him, aware that Colonel Chaviano wanted the rebel chief dead – no matter what he had promised the archbishop. Later, during the Sierra war, Gamboa was promoted to captain after executing six peasants in Oriente whom he suspected of aiding the revolution. In January 1959, after a quick trial, he was among the first Batista officers to be shot by a revolutionary firing squad. Gamboa's illness that night gave Lieutenant Sarría the command of the squadron. On the day of the attack Sarría had also intervened inside Moncada to prevent soldiers from executing two rebel fighters captured in the street. Many years later he told an interviewer in Havana that he had spared Fidel's life not because he sympathized with him, but 'because he was a human being. . . I love the profession of arms, and where I am in command, I believe that no crimes should be committed.'

Sarría's courage had especially been demonstrated by his determination to control his soldiers at the psychologically risky moment when Fidel, Oscar Alcalde and José Súarez were captured. All the Rural Guard troopers had happened to be black, as was Sarría, and the three prisoners were white. In the complex world of power relationships in Cuba, and especially in Oriente, black and mulatto soldiers tended to identify with Batista – himself a mulatto. To them whites with guns in their hands were automatically law-breakers who deserved to be killed. Additionally, in their privileged military position the soldiers suffered no racial discrimination, so Batista was their hero. Thus when they flushed out the three white rebels, the soldiers' first cries were 'They are white . . . they must be killed', and Lieutenant Sarría had to summon all his authority to halt what would have been, in effect, racial murders.

Acting on a hunch, Oscar Alcalde then told the lieutenant he was a freemason, a fairly widespread affiliation in Cuba, wondering aloud whether Sarría might not be one, too. When Sarría nodded Alcalde said, 'From freemason to freemason, and because you have saved our lives, I will tell you where we have hidden our weapons – they are thirty feet from the hut, under bushes.' Sarría needed to strengthen his authority over the troopers, and the find of the arms cache – eight rifles and three pistols – made him look good before the soldiers. Alcalde had thought this would be the case.

As to Fidel, he was chastizing himself for the 'terrible error', as he said later, of having slept inside the hut. He knew that as a rule military search parties never fail to go into huts, shacks and houses, but it had been 'so tempting to sleep under a roof because it had rained and the soil was wet'. They were exhausted after living on fruit for six days and nights in the mountains. Castro said that until his rude awakening 'we slept and slept deliciously'. Thereafter, however, Castro ensured that during the nearly two years in Sierra Maestra, 'even when rains came down in a deluge, we always slept in hammocks strung between trees, or rolled in a blanket on the ground'.

As Sarría and his squad and prisoners neared the Siboney road, firing broke out, and the lieutenant ordered them to drop to the ground. Sarría's point men had spotted five rebels, including the black Juan Almeida, hiding in the tall grass off the road, and began to shoot at them.

This time, the situation was saved by Archbishop Pérez Serantes. That Saturday he had gone out again in his Jeep to look for the rebels, leaving Santiago with a driver and two friends – but no military escort. A peasant they met on the road told them that a group of rebels had surrendered further ahead, and the archbishop left the Jeep to look for the men on foot. He reached the place where Almeida and the four others had been surrounded, just as the soldiers were about to shoot them. On the run, the monsignor lifted his cassock to jump over a fence, interposing himself between the rebels and the troopers, shouting, 'Don't kill them. . . I have guarantees from the authorities!'

The soldiers were furious over his intervention, ordering him to leave, insulting him, with one trooper chanting, 'I'm going to kill me a priest, I'm going to kill me a priest!' Devotion to the Church and its servants is superficial among poorer Cubans, and now Sarría had to impose his authority to save the archbishop. The five new prisoners had their hands tied, and Fidel, Alcalde and Súarez presently joined them. Sarría commandeered a flatbed truck to transport the prisoners to Santiago, placing Castro between the driver and himself in the cab. The archbishop, unaware of the events of the past hours, walked over to the lieutenant to warn him: 'These prisoners are under my protection. I have given guarantees to them.' The lieutenant replied: 'Monsignor, you should tell that to Colonel Chaviano, not me.' Fidel, who became concerned that the word would spread that he had surrendered to the archbishop, broke in to say loudly, 'I have nothing to do with the Monsignor; I was captured, and it was you, Lieutenant, who captured me.' Politically, Castro had to avoid the impression of surrender.

The army command in Santiago had been advised by telephone from the farm that Castro and seven companions had been seized, and presently Sarría's truck was stopped by truckloads of soldiers under the command of Major Andre Pérez Chaumont, the deputy to Colonel

Chaviano. Pérez Chaumont, a small man who was known in Oriente for vying for elegance with Chaviano and was nicknamed Beautiful Eyes, informed Sarría: 'I came to take delivery of the prisoners.' Sarría looked down at him, saying, 'No, these are *my* prisoners; I'm taking them to Moncada.' The major then proposed that Sarría keep all the others, if he delivered Castro to him. The two officers argued sharply for several minutes, Sarría being certain that Fidel would be killed if he turned him over to Pérez Chaumont. But the archbishop pulled up in his Jeep, and the major gave up his efforts to pull rank.

Instead he ordered the lieutenant to take the prisoners to the Santiago city jail rather than Moncada, thus depriving him of the prestige among the military of having personally brought in Fidel Castro. This was fine with Sarría: at Moncada, Castro would have been in the hands of Chaviano, Pérez Chaumont and Captain Manuel Lavastida, the Santiago chief of SIM. It was SIM and its head, Colonel Manuel Ugalde Carillo, who had ordered and carried out the murders of the captured *Fidelistas*.

At the city jail, however, Colonel Chaviano was already awaiting Fidel Castro, and Sarría had no choice but to surrender his prisoner. But once at the jail, very much in public view, Fidel was protected. As to Sarría, he remained in the army, was tried by a court martial in 1957 for refusing to fight the rebel army in the Sierra Maestra, and was kept under house arrest until the revolution triumphed. Sarría was promoted to captain in the new *Fidelista* army, and was regarded as a hero of the revolution. When he died in Havana in 1972 at the age of seventy-two, Castro attended the solemn funeral, and Pedro Miret delivered the oration to recall that 'we owe Captain Sarría eternal gratitude for having saved the life of Fidel and his companions.'

From the moment he arrived at the Santiago jail, an ancient two-storey structure downtown, Fidel Castro was an instant celebrity. Keeping calm, he behaved with humour and defiance. When Colonel Chaviano, immaculate in a fresh uniform, his waxed moustache bristling, met him in the jail office, the commander had a group photograph taken. Standing under a portrait of José Martí, Fidel – unshaven, in dark slacks and a white short-sleeved sports shirt towered over Chaviano, Pérez Chaumont and Major Rafael Morales Alvárez. He seemed like the guest of honour.

Sitting on a bench with his fellow rebels as he awaited a meeting with Chaviano later that morning, Castro glanced at the local newspaper *Ataja* with a huge front-page headline: 'DEAD! FIDEL CASTRO!' At Chaviano's office in the jail Fidel was allowed to sit across the desk from him, his hands untied, for what became a Castro speech rather than an interrogation. The official army communiqué said that Castro 'affirmed that he was responsible for the entire subversive movement. . .'

Rather than simply 'confessing' his deeds, Fidel made a point of narrating in detail how and why he had organized the Movement, emphasizing his certainty that if the Moncada attack had worked the people of Oriente would have risen in his support. Chaviano allowed a summary of his declaration to be given to the press, and let newsmen interview his prisoner. He even held a news conference to discuss his 'interrogation' of Fidel. Newspapers and magazines throughout Cuba reported widely and amply Castro's words; the Moncada defeat began to turn into the seeds of a future victory.

Incredibly, Chaviano proposed that Castro repeat his story over the radio so that the whole nation could learn, the colonel reasoned, how dangerous the subversive movement smashed by the army had been. Fidel was delighted, and as he told Robert Merle ten years later: 'Imagine the imbecility of these people! They ask me to take the microphone and to defend my viewpoint before them . . . who as a result of their crimes are morally disarmed before me! Obviously, I took the microphone. . .' Castro then said to Merle, laughing 'And at that minute, the second phase of the revolution began.' In that broadcast over station CMKR, Fidel proclaimed, 'We came to regenerate Cuba.'

To be sure, the Movement suffered very serious losses in men. Three out of six members of the Military Committee, including Abel Santamaría, were killed. Over one hundred rebels were killed, murdered or arrested. But many key persons had survived, and Fidel found most of them at the Santiago jail: Raúl Castro, Jesús Montané, and Haydee and Melba. Up to then Fidel had not even known they were alive. At the same time he discovered that Raúl had become the chief of the rebels at the jailhouse; a photograph shows him standing at attention in front of some thirty men in the unmistakable stance of a leader. Now Castro assumed his own leadership position, greeting each rebel with words of praise for having attempted with him to 'take the sky by surprise'.

In the meantime the Castro's in Birán were informed that their sons were safe and well treated, the word reached Naty Revuelta in Havana, and Archbishop Pérez Serantes telephoned Mirta in Havana to assure her that her husband was well. This was probably the first time in nearly five years of marriage that Mirta was told anything about her husband's activities, and she appeared to be grateful for the call. She had been very worried about Fidel since she heard about the abortive Moncada attack, and she wanted to be in touch with him. Her brother, Rafael Díaz-Balart, now Acting Minister of the Interior in the Batista cabinet, had gone to Santiago immediately after the events of 26 July, but it is unlikely that he would have served as a link between Fidel and Mirta, mostly because Castro would not have wanted it.

The day after Castro's capture, on Sunday 2 August, President Batista flew to Santiago to tour Moncada, receive reports from Chaviano and other officers, award the Honour Cross to the flag of the Maceo Regiment and salute the troops as they marched past him inside the fortress. The people of Santiago, however, were in attendance at the solemn mass for the dead at which Archbishop Pérez Serantes officiated at the cathedral. Starting at seven o'clock in the morning thousands of them filled the cathedral to hear the requiem and, on the way out, to kiss the archbishop's ring. He was the other hero of Santiago.

Also that day Fidel Castro and all the other Moncada prisoners were transferred to the Boniato Prison, some five miles north of Santiago, to await their trial. Fidel celebrated his twenty-seventh birthday in Boniato Prison twelve days later, but he was too busy planning his next move in the war against Batista to reflect much on it. Not only had he to prepare his trial defence but he had decided to issue as rapidly as possible a complete account of the Moncada events, including the insistence that the Movement was independent of conventional Cuban political groups. The regime was alleging that the uprising had been directed by the *Ortodoxo* party and the Communists, and key leaders of both parties had been arrested all over Cuba. By coincidence top communist leaders were in Santiago the weekend of Moncada for a birthday celebration; to Batista this was proof of their involvement in the conspiracy.

New names, soon to be famous, began to be associated with Castro's Movement. Manuel Urrutia Lleó, the chief judge of the Santiago Summer Court and the future president of revolutionary Cuba had undertaken an inquest on 27 July designed to identify the Moncada victims. Humberto Sorí-Marín, representing the National Lawyers' Association, visited Castro in prison to discuss his defence; later Sorí-Marín would be the rebel army's judge advocate, the author of the agrarian reform law and a minister of agriculture under Castro – before being executed in 1960 for conspiring *against* the revolution.

Working round the clock (and letting his moustache grow again), Fidel wasted no time in organizing the rebel prisoners politically and educationally, demanding books and other materials from outside. Raúl and Pedro Miret, the latter recovered from his battle wounds, became his principal collaborators. Letters came to the Boniato cell from all over Cuba, including from Naty Revuelta in Havana. Lina Castro, Fidel's and Raúl's mother, and their older sister Lidia came to visit them in prison as did Fidel's wife, Mirta.

Castro was in high spirits: he was fighting again, his head brimmed with plans, conspiracies and denunciations. The disaster of Moncada already lay behind – if not forgotten, certainly not perceived by him as a crippling defeat. It was on that defeat, rather, that Castro was now building his next great offensive.

Chapter 5

At Boniato Provincial Prison Fidel Castro was Prisoner No. 4914 in Case 37–053, awaiting trial before the Provisional Tribunal of Santiago for his participation in the assault on the Moncada army barracks on 26 July 1953. After the sentence he would become National Men's Reformatory Prisoner No. 3859. But he certainly was not an anonymous prisoner hidden behind a mug-shot number. In fact this was when Fidel Castro first became really famous in Cuba, when he became the centre of nationwide sympathies (and General Batista's wrath) and the recognized leader of anti-dictatorship opposition.

But the Batista regime still failed to realize what it had on its hands. This prisoner was more politically dangerous behind bars, in the glare of public attention, than he had been as the obscure and penniless revolutionary plotter just weeks earlier. And Batista did not suspect, either, how Fidel Castro was preparing to take advantage of the new situation, his supercharged mind constantly generating tactics, manoeuvres and strategies to expand his struggle.

In the hilltop prison Castro was held in solitary confinement in a small first-floor cell, while the other Moncada prisoners shared cells in the adjoining block. The two blocks were separated by a corridor, and Fidel and his companions could not see or talk to each other. Melba Hernández and Haydée Santamaría were in a cell on the same floor. Theoretically Castro was isolated from his group, but ways were rapidly devised for communication among them in the fifty-one days between his arrest and his trial.

The rebels were charged under Article 148 of the Social Defence Code, which provided for a prison sentence of between five and twenty years for 'the leader of an attempt aimed at organizing an uprising of armed persons against Constitutional Powers of the State'. Castro's defence strategy had two main objectives: first, to obtain acquittal for the majority – some seventy-five – of the Moncada and Bayamo assailants on the ground that they were not 'leaders' in the uprising; and, second, to use the trial as a forum in which to accuse Batista and the military of having imposed an illegal dictatorship in Cuba, and of having massacred unarmed rebel prisoners after the abortive attack.

Realizing that he would inevitably be found guilty, Castro had concluded that the trial should be turned into the most profitable affair possible for the Movement and himself. The initial step was to establish exactly and in the greatest detail what had happened to each of the rebels now detained in Boniato before, during and immediately after the assaults on the army barracks. Castro had lost contact with most of his troops when the combat began in Santiago, and he had not seen any of the survivors (except his own companions on Gran Piedra) until entering the prison. To lay the groundwork for his courtroom battle he had to have the maximum information.

As Pedro Miret recalls, he and Raúl Castro took upon themselves the task of interviewing every single Moncada prisoner in their group, 'hearing each one's version of what he did'. In this fashion, Miret says, 'We were able to collect a mass of information that we passed on to Fidel, so that when he delivered his statement [to the court] he had all the most up-to-date material.' During the seven weeks the defendants spent in Boniato, Castro was fed this material through messages given him in quick whispers by fellow prisoners as they passed the bars of his cell, or even by friendly guards, and through tiny scribbled messages thrown inside the cell. Having become the hero of common criminals serving time in Boniato, he had their support; thieves and murderers were turned into secret revolutionary messengers. And with his formidable memory Fidel was able to build in his mind detailed files on at least seventy-five Movement members.

With this data in hand Castro was in a position to identify the prisoners most likely to be acquitted. With Pedro Miret and Raúl acting as his delegates, he prepared all his companions for the trial. His plan was that the leaders, the hard-core rebels, including himself, should confess their participation in the attacks, but the majority could safely deny this. They were completely unknown men, and the authorities probably could not prove their guilt. Many of them, for example, had been arrested from Santiago, often simply on suspicion (several already murdered by the military on suspicion had not actually been involved in the conspiracy at all).

It was Castro who decided which of the prisoners should confess and which of them should not. Miret says the criterion was that 'of courtroom probability'. Each prisoner was told what Castro recommended, but this 'was not an obligation, certainly not an order'. The prisoners were free to do what they thought best, but in the event all of them followed his advice. Castro, who wanted as many men as possible acquitted to help rebuild the Movement, made a point in the courtroom of personally identifying who had and who had not participated in the uprising. As a practical matter neither the prosecution nor the judges could challenge Castro's careful selection and they went along with him. It was an extraordinary judicial situation in which the chief defendant, in effect, instructed the court as to who should be sentenced with him.

Miret and Raúl Castro also used their time in Boniato to organize a small library for their fellow prisoners from books requested by them from friends and relatives on the outside. And they also held daily classes for the group in subjects they knew best: history, language, physics and mathematics. The idea was to maintain the men's unity and discipline, not to let them lapse into depression or self-pity, and to whip them into good psychological shape for the coming trial. Fidel always believed in physical and intellectual discipline, and in improving the education of the rebels at every opportunity. Because the *Fidelistas* already were a highly disciplined military organization they gladly participated in this prison 'school'. Miret and Raúl Castro, as the only university students, were the logical leaders in this endeavour.

Fidel too discovered that prison offered a magnificent chance to engage in his favourite occupation of reading. Until Boniato he never had had enough time to read as much as he would have wanted. In his first letter to Mirta, three weeks after his imprisonment, he asked for Júlian María's *Philosophy In Its Texts*, the works of Shakespeare and García Morente's *Preliminary Lessons of Philosophy* as well as 'any novels that you think might interest me'. In September, while awaiting trial, he wrote his older brother Ramón that he was 'taking advantage' of the time in prison: 'I read a lot and I study a lot.' And Castro added 'It seems incredible; hours fly by as if they were minutes, and I, with my restless temperament, spend the day reading, barely moving a finger.'

Castro also showed concern for his family, perhaps greater than at any previous time. He exchanged letters with Mirta until he broke with her a year later, expressing preoccupation over Fidelito's welfare and future. But they were not love letters, not even emotional letters, Fidel simply signing them, 'Kisses for the *niño* and for you.' On 18 August he wrote her from Boniato: 'I don't know whether you are in Oriente or in Havana . . . I have heard very little about you; only that you were in Santiago after my detention, and also that you came to the prison to bring me clothes that were delivered to me. . . I am well; you know that prison bars cannot break my spirit, my determination, or my conscience. . . Be calm and courageous. Before all else, we must think about Fidelito. I want him to go to the school you have chosen. . . When you come, bring him with you; surely, they will let me see him.'

On 5 September Castro wrote to Ramón that he had learned from

Mirta's letter that Fidelito had spent a week in the family *finca* , remarking that 'he very much likes the countryside and animals. . . On the first of the month, he became four years old. . . Mirta wants to send him to school, I mean private school; we shall see whether this is possible.' Two weeks later he informed Ramón that Mirta had placed Fidelito 'in a kindergarten almost across the street from the house. . . She sent me some photographs, and I can see that he has grown a lot in recent months.'

But Fidel wanted his parents to understand his situation as well. 'It is necessary for you to make my parents see that prison is not the horrible and shameful thing they taught us it was,' he wrote to Ramón. 'That is true only when a man goes there for acts that dishonour him. . . When the motive is high and noble, then prison is a very honourable place.' In another letter to Ramón he mentioned that his father had sent him a telegram inquiring whether Fidel and Raúl needed clothes, and that he replied at once that they had all they needed from Mirta. He said he planned to write to his parents later that day, adding: 'Do they understand that I am imprisoned for doing my duty?' Then he thanked Ramón for the cigars his brother had sent him, asking for more boxes 'because the last one is almost finished, and it is often necessary to give cigars to people who help us. . .'

The trial of Fidel Castro and his companions opened on Monday 21 September 1953 at the Santiago Palace of Justice, overlooking the Moncada barracks. It was held before the three-judge Provisional Tribunal of Santiago, one of a network of special political courts whose sentences could not be appealed. The Chief Judge was Adolfo Nieto Piñeito-Osorio and the prosecutor was Francisco Mendieta Hechavarría; both were respected jurists.

It was a mass trial. The 122 defendants were represented by 22 lawyers, there were 6 forensic medicine specialists, dozens of relatives and friends, and about 100 rifle-wielding soldiers. They were crowded into a courtroom 45 by 15 feet and, the humid heat of Santiago notwith-standing, the doors and windows were closed as a security measure. Chief Judge Piñeito-Osorio described it as 'the most significant trial in the history of Republican Cuba', and despite the national state of emergency the people were well aware that Fidel Castro was being tried. Six journalists, including Marta Rojas from the Havana weekly *Bohemia* were allowed inside – although they would not be allowed to publish their accounts (their presence, however, would later directly help Fidel Castro as well as assist in the creation of the historical record).

Hours before the trial started armoured army units cut off the streets around Moncada and the Palace of Justice. About one thousand soldiers with automatic weapons lined the route from Boniato Prison to the courthouse. The prisoners arrived in buses, at the back door of the Palace of Justice. Fidel Castro was transported alone, under heavy guard in an army Jeep. He wore his old, striped dark blue wool suit, a white shirt, a red print necktie, and black shoes and socks. His wife had sent the suit at his request (he wrote her asking for it to be dry-cleaned first and sent with a belt), and now Fidel was sweating profusely in the morning sun. His new moustache was well trimmed and his hair neatly combed. The prisoners, all of them handcuffed, were taken to the library of the Palace of Justice where for the first time they had the opportunity to talk, however briefly, with their lawyers.

As the prisoners entered the courtroom there was a chorus of whispers: 'This is Fidel! This is he!' until the chief judge gavelled for silence. Before taking his seat Castro raised his manacled hands towards the judges and addressed them in a clear, loud voice: 'Mr President . . . I want to call your attention to this disgraceful fact . . . What fairness can there be in this trial? Not even the worst criminals are held this way in a place that calls itself a hall of justice. . . You cannot judge people who are handcuffed. . .'

The chief judge sided with him. He declared a recess until handcuffs were removed from all the prisoners, and warned the captain of the army escort that he would not ever allow prisoners to be brought handcuffed into his courtroom. Fidel had easily won the first round, and suddenly there was a new mood in the Tribunal of Justice. That Castro and his principal associates would be found guilty under Article 148 was taken for granted from the outset – in the light of the confessions they had volunteered, the judges would have no choice. What had changed was the atmosphere in which the proceedings would unfold. Chief Judge Nieto Piñeito-Osorio and Judge Juan Francisco Mejías Valdivieso were thought to sympathize with the accused, and the third judge, Ricardo Díaz Olivera, although he was believed to be pro-Batista, seemed to be behaving in a similarly benign fashion. Furthermore, the prosecutor did his job, and no more. In the end Castro and his companions were given astounding latitude. Repeatedly they made accusations against the regime rather than defending themselves. After the trial Captain Lavastida, the SIM chief in Santiago told one of the defence lawyers that politically the government had lost the case: the public was for the defendants, even the judges were for the defendants, he said. And in Santiago, Castro also had going for him the Oriente tradition of rebellion and freedom wars.

Clearly Batista had failed to understand the political implications of what was occurring before the three judges; there is no indication that he tried to exercise pressure on them to control the rebels' behaviour. It must be admitted, however, that the Cuban judiciary had jealously guarded its independence from interference by the government, and the Santiago judges would go on maintaining this stance even during the most climactic moments of the Sierra war.

The central intention behind Castro's courtroom appearances was to establish the principle of legitimacy for the Movement's attack on the army barracks, arguing that the rebels had the *right* to try to overthrow Batista because he was an usurper who had gained power through a military coup and violation of the constitution. With an absolutely straight face Castro reminded the court that, immediately after the coup, acting as attorney, he had brought charges against Batista before a special court in Havana and had demanded up to one hundred years in prison for the dictator. Fidel did not attempt to defend himself and his companions from the charges of instigating an uprising; rather he confirmed the charges and proudly justified their actions. By the end of the first day before the Provisional Tribunal of Santiago the accused had become the accuser.

Castro then proceeded to play a dual role: the first was that of the indignant defendant delivering political and revolutionary lectures in his replies to the prosecution. When Prosecutor Mendieta Hechavarría asked him about the participation of certain other defendants he declared: 'These young people, like me, love the freedom of their country. They have committed no crime unless it is considered a crime to wish for our country the best there is . . . Isn't this what they taught us in school?'

Fidel's second role, even more successful, was acting as his own attorney. It was his right as a lawyer, and it gave him the opportunity to cross-examine his accusers, including the Moncada commander, Colonel Alberto del Río Chaviano, and to heap more insults on the dictatorship. Castro paid the five pesos with which attorneys were required to purchase the courtroom licence, becoming an officer of the court. Then he went through the dramatic ritual of donning attorney's black robes when he acted as lawyer, and then taking them off when he returned to his defendant's bench. In Cuban courts judges and lawyers had to wear robes, and that first day a robe large enough for Fidel could not be found, forcing him to work in one several sizes too small. On his lawyer's table he placed a copy of the Social Defence Code and a volume of Martí's works.

Castro produced a further moment of drama when he was asked who was the 'intellectual author' of the attacks on army installations on 26 July. The question was fundamental in the trial because the law prescribed punishment for leaders of an armed assault against the state, and because in the Cuban legal tradition the notion of the 'intellectual author' of a crime, the person who inspired it, was as important as that of the person who physically carried it out. To this question Castro answered calmly: 'The only intellectual author of this revolution is José Martí, the Apostle of Our Independence.' Now he was turning the proceedings in the suffocatingly hot Santiago courtroom into a trial by history.

To each defendant the prosecutor confined himself to the single question of whether he (or she) had participated in the assault. The rebels who responded with a 'yes' then went on with accounts of atrocities by the Batista forces against their companions. Baudilio Castellanos García, Fidel's childhood friend and law school colleague, defended forty-six of the rebels, the bulk of the accused (including Raúl Castro), and his statements and questions meshed perfectly with the overall Castro strategy. Between them Castro and Castellanos established for the court's benefit which of the accused had participated in the attacks and which, in effect, should be acquitted. Under Castro's secret selection system each rebel knew beforehand how to answer. Raúl and Miret had done their job well.

And, one by one, the accused went on to stun the courtroom with horror tales: the beatings by the soldiers, the tortures, the summary executions of captured rebels, the brutalities and the insults. The day after the Moncada attack the Santiago 'summer court' (judges on the bench in the criminal tribunal substituting for vacationing regular justices) had ordered autopsies on thirty-four bodies found in the vicinity of the barracks – before the authorities had had time to carry out their plan to bury them in a common grave at the Santa Ifigenia cemetery. The autopsies described 'unidentified' individuals with smashed skulls and other signs of violent death by beatings or point-blank gunshots, and were entered in the trial records in Case 37-053, enormously damaging the government's political image.

Surprisingly, it was Prosecutor Mendieta Hechavarría himself who through persistent questioning of Haydée Santamaría brought out the story of what the army had done to her fiancé Boris Luís Santa Coloma and her brother Abel before killing them. Haydée testified that after the soldiers had occupied the civilian hospital and captured her and Melba Hernández a guard approached her to say that Boris was in the next room and 'to tell me that they had cut off his testicles' to make him talk (Jesús Montané had testified earlier that an army officer had approached him in the Moncada detention area, holding in one blood-covered glove a rotting ball of flesh and in the other a razor, saying: 'You see this? If you don't talk, I'll do the same thing to you I did to Boris. I will castrate you.' About her brother, Haydée said, 'They gouged out one of his eyes.' An army witness then confirmed that Abel's eyes had been removed with a bayonet.

At the end of the testimony about army brutalities presented by scores of defendants and after his own statement on the subject in his capacity as defendant, Castro assumed his role of attorney. In his black robes, he requested the court to collect and isolate all the testimony on the army's

treatment of the prisoners and the killings from the record of the
Moncada trial so that it could form the basis for subsequent trials for
assassination and torture which he proposed to seek against Batista
regime officials. To Fidel Castro's own surprise the court agreed. Thus
Castro now was formally both a defendant and an accuser.

It is interesting to note that in the course of the Moncada trial the
Communists chose not to show any support for the *Fidelista*. Two top
leaders of the Popular Socialist Party, Joaquín Ordoqui Mesa and Lázaro
Peña, were arrested in Santiago on the day of the attack, and charged
under Article 148 along with Castro's rebels and a half-dozen well-
known opposition politicians. Asked whether they had conspired with
others concerning an insurrection against the government, Ordoqui and
Peña denied it, truthfully declaring they had come to Santiago, as they did
every year, for the birthday celebrations of the party's Secretary General
Blás Roca. The two Communists said they had no contacts with
opposition political parties and no advance knowledge of the Moncada
assault. They restated that Cuban Communists had opposed the Batista
coup, but they volunteered no expressions of sympathy or solidarity with
Castro and his revolutionaries, and their Popular Socialist Party actually
denounced the Castro uprising, presumably because the party's (and
Moscow's) policy was to oppose any initiatives it did not control,
especially when they were not in conformity with the dogma. Both men
were acquitted.

Meanwhile, after five days of the trial, the Batista regime finally
concluded that the situation was getting politically out of hand and that
Fidel Castro could no longer be tolerated in the courtroom. His dual-role
performance was too damaging and embarrassing to the government,
and the Provisional Tribunal was clearly not disposed to curb him. Not
wishing to confront the court directly, Batista let the army take matters
into its own hands; this opened the way for another spectacular episode in
the Castro drama.

When the court convened on Saturday 26 September and the routine
roll-call of the defendants got under way, and the name of Fidel Castro
was called, there was silence – the first time, the second time, the third
time. The principal defence lawyer, Baudilio Castellanos, rose to tell the
court that Castro was not answering because he was not present; he had
not been brought to the Palace of Justice that day. The chief judge said the
trial must proceed, but Castellanos jumped to his feet to demand that the
court determine first why the principal defendant was absent. When the
chief judge summoned the army officer in charge of guarding the
prisoners he was handed a letter from the office of Colonel Chaviano, the
Moncada commander, explaining that Castro could not be brought to the
courtroom because he was ill at Boniato Prison; a medical certificate was
appended to the letter. A court official read the communication aloud.

Castro, the certificate said, was suffering from a 'nervous crisis'.

There was commotion, and a woman's voice shouted: 'Fidel is not ill!' It was Melba Hernández who had risen from the defendants' bench and marched toward the judges, removing a scarf from her head. She extracted a folded envelope from her hair and handed it to the chief judge, announcing: 'This is a letter from Doctor Fidel Castro.' Returning to her seat Melba whispered to Haydée: 'Now they can't kill him. . .' Castro and his friends had again beaten their enemies to the punch.

Some time earlier Fidel and his principal associates had reached the conclusion that there was a plot afoot to kill him in prison. His food would be poisoned, he believed, so for some weeks he ate only what was sent to the rebels from the outside by families and friends, or purchased through the ever-helpful ordinary prisoners. He would not even smoke prison cigars. Whether or not the Batista regime had actually set out to kill Fidel is impossible to prove. However, Lieutenant Jesús Yanes Pelletier, the prison's military supervisor, was removed from his post shortly after Castro's arrival at Boniato, supposedly for refusing to obey orders to poison him. (Yanes later became a captain in the Rebel Army, and chief of the Castro bodyguard.) Besides, Fidel has always had a keenly developed sense of the dangers facing him; as his former Interior Minister Ramiro Valdés says: 'He can smell the risks in the air. . . This Fidel is a sorcerer, a sorcerer. . .'

In any event Castro's suspicions were confirmed, at least in his mind, when he was informed on the evening of 25 September that he would not be taken to court the next day because he was thought to be ill. The secret network inside the prison was activated at once. As his companions and the common prisoners strolled back and forth in front of his cell, as they did every evening, Castro whispered that he would be writing an urgent letter that had to be delivered to the court the next day. Then he proceeded to write it on paper held inside a magazine he pretended to be reading. Leonel Gómez Pérez, a prisoner who had mistakenly been charged with participation in the Moncada operation, was assigned the task of receiving the letter from Fidel and passing it on.

Leonel had the habit of reading a book as he walked up and down the prison corridor, and therefore the guards paid no attention when he did it that particular night, not noticing as he came closer and closer to the bars of Castro's cell. When the guard in the corridor looked away for a moment, Fidel threw the letter through the bars so that it would land inside Leonel's book. Leonel kept walking for a while longer, then calmly returned to his cell block. He gave the letter to one of the *Fidelistas* who, in turn, had it delivered to Melba Hernández by one of the common prisoners. Melba folded it into a tiny square and concealed it in her hair.

In his letter to the court Castro, describing himself as his own attorney, charged that all possible means were being used to prevent him from being present at the trial so that he could not expose 'gross official falsehoods' about the events of 26 July and make known 'the most outrageous massacre in the history of Cuba'. He insisted that he was not ill and that the court was being told unprecedented lies, and he complained that he had been kept illegally incommunicado for fifty-seven days, 'without being allowed to see the sun, talk with anyone, or see my family'. Fidel informed the court that he had learned with certainty that 'my physical elimination, perhaps under the pretext of an escape attempt, or through poisoning, is being planned', and that 'the two girls' (Melba and Haydée) faced the same danger because 'they are irreplaceable witnesses to the massacre of 26 July'.

Castro then demanded his immediate examination by the dean of the medical school of Santiago, the assignment of a court officer to the prisoners while being transported between Boniato and the Palace of Justice, and the delivery of copies of his letter to the Supreme Court and the Cuban Bar Association. He named Melba Hernández (herself a lawyer) as his representative in court, and concluded: 'I would rather lose my life than sacrifice any part of my rights or my honour in order to keep it. Even at the bottom of a grave a just principle is more powerful than an army!'

The three judges agreed to order an independent medical examination of their famous defendant, and despite the army command's opposition two distinguished physicians undertook it, finding Castro in perfect health. On the basis of their report the court requested his return to the trial. But the Boniato wardens still refused to let Castro leave the prison, and the judges gave in. This was their compromise with the regime: they ruled that Castro's case was to be separated from the main trial, to be tried separately afterwards. Fidel never again set foot in the Palace of Justice. At Boniato he was transferred to a cell on the ground floor, far away from his companions. Melba and Haydée were also punished: they were removed from the other *Fidelistas* and placed in a cell from which, in the words of the military warden, 'you won't even be able to see the sky'.

Castro's transfer to a remote cell revived concern among his companions that he might still be an assassination target, and at the next session of the court, on 28 September, Raúl Castro rose to announce loudly: 'I fear for the life of my brother! They have mounted a conspiracy to assassinate Fidel, and I propose that you suspend this trial. . . ' Raúl was ordered to sit down and shut up, but the chief judge reassured him at the same time that when the court had received Fidel's letter two days earlier, 'it took all measures necessary for the protection of the defendant'.

The trial continued for another week, with a parade of witnesses drawn from among army and police officers as well as hospital nurses. Their testimony demolished the charges originally presented by Colonel Chaviano that the rebels used 'modern arms', hand grenades, and knives and daggers to behead the soldiers, and that they had murdered patients in their beds in the civilian and military hospitals. Both defence and prosecution forced out denials or admissions of 'I really don't know' from the government's own witnesses, each one rendering the proceedings even more embarrassing for the regime. Finally, on 5 October, the court convened to conclude the trial. In suitably bizarre fashion Prosecutor Mendieta Hechavarría first announced that, as Castro had recommended, he was dropping charges against all the political parties' leaders, including the Communists, who were among the defendants, and against the *Fidelistas* whose links with the insurrection could not be proved. This left twenty-nine rebels to be judged. These the prosecutor praised in his summation for 'acting with honour, for having been sincere and very courageous, proper in their confessions . . . and noble in their attitudes'. He said he 'sincerely applauded' their integrity in admitting their guilt. It was an astonishing spectacle. Eventually the prosecution virtually apologized for being forced by the rebels' confessions to ask the court to sentence them to prison terms under the provisions of Article 148. On 6 October the chief judge handed down the sentences: Raúl Castro, Pedro Miret, Ernesto Tizol and Oscar Alcalde – the top leadership group – were each given thirteen years in prison. Twenty other men received ten-year sentences, and three men got three-year sentences. Melba Hernández and Haydée Santamaría were sentenced to seven months' detention at the women's prison at Guanajay, west of Havana. Relatively speaking, the sentences were not heavy: the maximum imprisonment under the law was twenty years.

Still undecided, however, was the fate of Fidel Castro in his cell at Boniato Prison and of Gustavo Arcos, the man who had been in Fidel's car at Moncada and was now recovering from his wounds at the Colonia Española hospital. No date was set for their trial, and the rebels again began to worry that Fidel could be in danger. Twenty-six prisoners were placed aboard an army aircraft on 13 October; to their surprise they were flown to the Isle of Pines, which lies immediately south of the Cuban coast, where the men were taken to the island prison while Melba and Haydée continued on to Havana, en route to Guanajay. The court had specified that the men would be held at La Cabaña fortress in Havana, but the regime decided otherwise; the Isle of Pines was more remote from civilization.

Fidel Castro's trial lasted exactly four hours on 16 October and he was sentenced to fifteen years in prison. The trial was held in virtual secrecy in a small nurses' lounge, a room measuring twelve feet by twelve feet, in the Nurses' School at the Saturnino Lora civilian hospital, the building captured by Abel Santamaría's detachment on 26 July. Short as it was, the trial produced Fidel Castro's defence speech which immediately became known as *History Will Absolve Me*, and remains to this day the fundamental document of the Cuban revolution, the most venerated scripture of the rebel movement.

The decision to hold the trial in a hospital room was taken in order to perpetuate the official fiction that Castro was too ill to attend the main proceedings in the Palace of Justice (though he still had to be transported the admittedly shorter distance from Boniato to the hospital). To add credibility a wounded rebel and a prisoner who had nothing to do with the whole affair were also brought to the nurses' lounge. Fidel could not resist remarking that it was risky 'to banish justice to a hospital room, guarded by men with bayonets on their rifles, because the people might conclude that our justice is ill'.

The surroundings were, indeed, absurd. A human skeleton hung inside a glass case, and one wall was adorned with a picture of Florence Nightingale. Enough desks and chairs had to be packed into the hot, airless room to accommodate the three judges, the prosecutor, the secretary of the court, three lawyers, six journalists and three defendants (the wounded rebel was on a stretcher on the floor). Two army officers and twenty armed soldiers assured security. The room had a single barred window, and the morning heat was debilitating.

Fidel Castro, wearing his heavy dark blue wool suit, arrived hand-cuffed with his military escort at exactly nine o'clock, and the proceedings began. There is no official transcript or record of the trial, and all the descriptions are based on the recollections of those present. Castro delivered his speech extemporaneously, and Marta Rojas and the other journalists took copious notes, but the official text of *History Will Absolve Me* was later reconstructed from memory by Fidel and put on paper.

By then Fidel had spent seventy-five days in solitary confinement, and he had lost so much weight that his watchband kept slipping off his wrist but he was in fine form. Asked the ritual question whether he had participated in the Moncada attack, Castro replied: 'Affirmative.' When the prosecutor inquired whether the purpose was to overthrow the government, Castro said: 'It could not have been any other.' The prosecutor said he had no other questions. Then Colonel Chaviano and other military officers testified about the Moncada events, repeating earlier charges. Castro again requested permission to act as his own attorney, and a young mulatto lawyer named Eduardo Sauren lent him a black robe; it was too small and kept bursting at the armpits whenever Fidel raised his arm to make an oratorical point. Cross-examining Major Pérez Chaumont, the Moncada deputy commander, Castro charged that two additional members of his Movement had been murdered by the

Rural Guard and, as before, he insisted that the army killed many captured rebels, wanting no prisoners. And this was the end of the proceedings.

Prosecutor Mendieta Hechavarría chose not to deliver a summation, speaking for barely two minutes to ask the court to apply the maximum punishment to Fidel Castro, as the principal leader of the insurrection, under the terms of the Social Defence Code. Castro looked up to say matter-of-factly: 'Two minutes seem to me to be a very short time in which to demand and justify that a man be locked up for a quarter of a century.' The maximum sentence could be twenty-six years in the case of a top organizer of an insurrection. Then Castro announced that he insisted on delivering his own defence, and the chief judge authorized him to proceed. Standing behind a small table Fidel had a sheaf of notes, a copy of the Social Defence Code and his book of Martí quotations.

He spoke for two hours, one half of the time allotted to his trial. Held overnight at Moncada, he had kept his cellmate awake until dawn while he practised his delivery, and it was a stunning *tour de force* of memory, erudition and patriotic and revolutionary emotion. Evidently he had meditated deeply in his prison cell, and this masterful piece of oratory - it is really much more than a speech – is transformed by his superb command and love of the Spanish language into a great work of literature. But just as he claimed that José Martí was the intellectual author of the Moncada attack, Martí was equally clearly the inspirer of this oration. As it happens, Martí's first great piece of political writing was an essay on 'The Political Prison in Cuba', published when he was eighteen years old, after serving time at hard labour for conspiring against Spain, and it was a perfect literary model for Fidel. In the copy of the Martí book before him at the trial, Castro had underlined twenty-nine major passages, and he directly quoted the Apostle fifteen times in his discourse.

Castro, opening his oration in low and slow tones, first reviewed the 'illegalities' surrounding his trial and his thesis that insurrection against a tyrant was legitimate. Then he traced the history of his Movement, discussed the reasons for the defeat at Moncada, denounced the tortures and killings of his companions, and stressed governmental corruption in Cuba, and the unfair treatment of army soldiers (from the beginning, Fidel always sought to attract the 'honest' military to his side). But the brunt of his attack was aimed at Batista: 'Dante divided his hell into nine circles; he put the criminals in the seventh, the thieves in the eighth, and the traitors in the ninth. What a hard dilemma the devil will face when he must choose the circle adequate for the soul of Batista. . . ' He called him in Latin *Monstrum Horrendum!*

Next Castro turned to the Movement's political programme, the appalling social-economic conditions prevailing in Cuba and the revolutionary laws the rebels would have proclaimed had they won at Moncada: a return to the 1940 constitution, agrarian reform, restitution of stolen goods and resources, education reform, profit-sharing for the workers and public housing policies.

'I bring in my heart the doctrines of Martí and in my mind the noble ideas of all men who have defended the freedom of the people,' Castro said. 'We have incited a rebellion against a single illegitimate power which had usurped and concentrated in its hands the legislative and executive powers of the nation . . . I know that I shall be silenced for many years. I know they will try to suppress the truth by every possible means. I know that there will be a conspiracy to force me into oblivion. But my voice will never be drowned; for it gathers strength within my breast when I feel most alone.'

To Fidel the struggle for the people meant 'the *six hundred thousand* Cubans who are out of work and who want to earn their daily bread honestly . . . the *five hundred thousand* farm workers who live in miserable huts, who work four months and go hungry the rest of the year . . . the *four hundred thousand* industrial workers and labourers whose retirement funds have been stolen . . . the *one hundred thousand* small farmers who live and die working land that is not theirs, contemplating it as Moses did the promised land, only to die before owning it . . . the *thirty thousand* self-sacrificing and devoted teachers and professors who are so badly treated and poorly paid . . . the *twenty thousand* debt ridden small merchants, ruined by economic crises . . . the *ten thousand* young professions [who] leave school with their degrees, only to find their careers at a dead end . . . To these people, whose road of anguish is paved with deceit and false promises, we say, "Here you are, now fight with all your might so that you may be free and happy." '

Reaching into his impressive memory Castro built history's case to justify taking up arms against tyrants: he noted that Charles I and James II were dethroned for despotism; cited the Civil War in Britain, and the French and American revolutions; the hardly-won independence of European colonies in Latin America; and he summoned up the spirit of freedom and defiance of Stephanus Junius Brutus of ancient Rome, St Thomas Aquinas (in *Summa Theologica*), John of Salisbury, Martin Luther and John Calvin, the Scottish reformers John Knox and John Paynet, Montesquieu (in *The Spirit of the Law*), Jean-Jacques Rousseau (in *The Social Contract*), John Milton, John Locke, Thomas Paine, the seventeenth-century German jurist John Althusius, the French revolutionary jurist Léon Duguit, Honoré de Balzac, and, of course, José Martí.

But, Castro said, 'So great is the outrage done to this nation that it looked as if the apostle Martí was going to die in the year of his birth's centennial. It looked as if his memory would be extinguished for ever.

But he lives. He has not died. His people are rebellious, his people are worthy, his people are faithful to his memory. Cubans have fallen defending his doctrines. Young men, in a magnificent gesture of reparation, have come to give their blood and to die at the side of his tomb so that he might continue to live in the hearts of his countrymen. O Cuba, what would have become of you if you had let the memory of your Apostle die!'

And Fidel Castro concluded: 'As for me, I know that jail will be as hard as it has ever been for anyone, filled with vicious threats, with vileness, with cowardly brutality; but I do not fear this, as I do not fear the fury of the miserable tyrant who has snuffed out the lives of seventy of my brothers. Condemn me, it does not matter. *History will absolve me!*'

Castro finished, and the three judges and the prosecutor consulted in whispers in the crowded room for a few minutes. The chief judge ordered 'the defendant, Doctor Castro Ruz' to be kind enough to stand, then announced: 'In accordance with the request of the prosecutor, this court has imposed on you a sentence of fifteen years in prison . . . The trial has been concluded.' Fidel put out his hands to be handcuffed, and when a soldier had trouble doing so he suggested that the officer of the guard put the manacles on him, because of the man's greater experience. 'And be careful with my watch,' he added. Walking out of the nurses' lounge, Fidel turned to Marta Rojas, the young reporter, to ask: 'Did you get it all? Do you have all the notes?' As Castro left the hospital under heavy guard, people in the street cheered him.

A week later the last of the rebels, Gustavo Arcos, was sentenced to ten years in prison at a special trial held at the Colonia Española hospital where he lay wounded. And about the same time General Batista incongruously announced that presidential elections would be held in Cuba on 1 November 1954, more than a year away. As for the Eisenhower administration, it named Arthur Gardner, a financial expert and an admirer of General Batista, as the new United States ambassador in Havana.

Undeniably the *History Will Absolve Me* discourse is an important milestone in Fidel Castro's career. The problem, however, is how it should be interpreted. Since the formal implantation of Marxism–Leninism in Cuba the official version is that 'history' is decidedly an 'anti-imperialist' document, forged with the tools of Marxist dialectics and Leninist inspiration (apart from the Martí inspiration). Castro himself is prepared nowadays to accept this interpretation of his 1953 thoughts – even though at the time the Communists failed to reach the same conclusion.

In the end one is left with the impression that Castro was keeping his options open when he dramatically addressed the court in October 1953, and that his ideas evolved in a firm Marxist–Leninist direction much later. It is an empirically and historically flawed notion to assert that history pointed Cuba irreversibly towards Communism. Perhaps more to the point, the Castro oration very soon overshadowed the Moncada defeat, allowing him to build on the terrible experience of 26 July and to become the revolutionary hero of Cuba. It is a good example of words being mightier than arms.

In any event Fidel Castro was selected by the Havana weekly *Bohemia* as one of the twelve most outstanding world figures of 1953, along with such personalities as the Shah of Iran (overthrown that year and restored to the throne by the CIA), the Pugilist Kid Gavilan, Costa Rican President José Figueres, Queen Elizabeth (crowned in 1953), and the Soviet KGB Chief Lavrenti Beria (shot after Stalin's death). This was very heady company for an imprisoned twenty-seven-year-old Cuban revolutionary, but Fidel would have had no doubt that he belonged there. Even before he was flown from Santiago to the prison on the Isle of Pines he was busy planning future actions against Batista. It never crossed his mind that he might actually spend the full fifteen years of his sentence behind bars.

Chapter 6

Fidel Castro's Rebel Army was born in the men's prison on the Isle of Pines where he and twenty-five companions were confined by the Batista regime for one year and seven months. Of this group, fourteen men (including Fidel) were to be aboard the yacht *Granma* when she sailed from Mexico at the end of 1956 to launch the war in the Sierra Maestra; seven were officers in the invading force. In 1986 five of the Isle of Pines prisoners, headed by Raúl Castro, were still among Fidel's closest associates. Two of them were Comandantes de la Revolución, a title bestowed on only three Sierra commanders.

The Moncada and Bayamo attacks had shown Castro's men to be a contingent of militarily inexperienced and ill-trained idealists with inadequate weapons and flawed intelligence about the enemy. Politically and ideologically the 26th of July rebels were immature and essentially vague about their long-range objectives. There was much naïveté in that first brave enterprise, and the Movement had been virtually unknown in Cuba up to that time.

The Moncada trial, with the wide public recognition it gave Castro and the *Fidelista* (press censorship mattered little on an island where word of mouth disseminated news with lighting speed), and the experience of imprisonment that followed, represented a great turning point in the history of the revolution. On one level the fate of the Isle of Pines prisoners became a national issue – they were the object of a great outpouring of sympathy and the Batista regime became held in increasingly low esteem – and Castro was able to take advantage of this situation by creating a political organization from his prison cell. He understood the absolute necessity for central, unquestioned authority in the leadership of the Movement, and for skilled propaganda to help the organization grow. As he wrote from the Isle of Pines to a friend: 'The propaganda and organization apparatus must be so powerful that it will totally destroy all those who try to create cliques, or to rise up against the movement.' Castro remained faithful to this principle in prison, in exile, in the Sierra war, in the hour of revolutionary victory, and in later beating down a challenge by old-line Communists.

But Fidel also knew the value of the moral imperative in politics. He had been an attentive student of von Clausewitz's writings, and his approach to the creation of his great revolutionary instrument was inspired by the Prussian military genius; in warfare 'the physical seems little more than the wooden hilt, while the moral factors are the precious metal, the real weapon, the finely-honed blade'. Specifically, Fidel's objective was to endow his Movement with such moral strength, combined with the natural Cuban penchant for patriotism, history and nationalism, that in time it would be greater than the physical and economic power at Batista's command.

Thus the trial and prison became the crucible in which Castro would perfect himself and his men. Under him they would constitute the hard core of revolutionary leadership, the vanguard of the Movement. This called for their political education and discipline and, ironically, the Batista prison provided ideal conditions for him to hone his future Rebel Army. Castro had concluded that in order to succeed his revolution required its own army, an army that believed in the revolution, and had rejected the idea of a political solution for Cuba that would seek to change the government with the support of the existing military establishment. His plan now was to destroy the Cuban armed forces and replace them with *his* Rebel Army. In retrospect he agrees that, harsh and frustrating as was his imprisonment, it offered him and the Movement a unique opportunity to create the revolutionary framework. Without the prison experience the *Fidelista* revolution might never have soared.

Imprisonment on the Isle of Pines was useful for Fidel Castro because it provided him with still more symbolism. The island had been José Martí's first place of exile from Havana. Moreover, the Isle of Pines bitterly reminded the Cubans of the worst aspects of American imperialism. Under the 1901 Platt Amendment which had defined the terms of Cuban independence after the Spanish–American war, the island was 'omitted from the proposed constitutional boundaries of Cuba, the title thereto being left to future adjustment by treaty'. Both the United States government and American businessmen therefore treated the Isle of Pines as a colony; only in 1926 (the year of Fidel's birth) did the United States finally cede sovereignty over it to Cuba under the Hay–Quesada Treaty.

Twenty-three rebel prisoners landed at the island's Nueva Gerona airport on 13 October, a week after their sentencing in Santiago, to begin serving their terms at the model penitentiary. Actually, there are published discrepancies concerning the number of prisoners brought to the Isle of Pines. Twenty-nine rebels, including Melba and Haydée, were sentenced on 6 October, which left twenty-seven men in that group to be transported to prison. But Mario Mencía, the revolution's chronicler, lists only *twenty-six* prisoners on the Isle of Pines, including Fidel Castro and Abelardo Crespo (the wounded prisoner who was tried together with Fidel in the hospital), in his authorative account on the confinement of the rebels. While Fidel and Crespo arrived in Nueva Gerona four days after the group, for some unknown reason three men sentenced in Santiago with the others never appeared on the Isle of Pines, although their names are included in the warden's report on 13 October. It seems that twenty-five is therefore the correct number for the men finally held in the prison there. The only one of them familiar with the Isle of Pines was Jesús Montané, a member of the Movement's Civil Committee, who was born there; his parents still lived in Nueva Gerona.

The Isle of Pines is a roundish island, just over two hundred miles in circumference, laying some fifty miles south of the coast of the province of Havana. Farming had been its chief economic activity, but the model penitentiary rivalled agriculture when it was built by the Machado dictatorship in 1931. The prison consists of four huge five-storey circular structures, each designed to hold 930 prisoners, and a half-dozen other large buildings. One of them is a hospital, and the Movement prisoners were installed in its southern ward, known as Building One. They were all housed in a rectangular hall with metal beds set in two rows; the ward had three showers, two toilets and a sink for the twenty-five. A barred door led to a cement-floored inner patio where the prisoners could exercise. They had access to volleyball, table tennis and chess. The prison's advantage over Boniato was that they were all together. Thus their conditions were not the worst possible – most probably because the Batista regime wished the minimum of adverse publicity.

When the first group of rebels reached the model penitentiary (it was so described because it was modelled after a prison in Joliet, Illinois, then a monument to modern penology), they had no news about Fidel and feared that he might have been sent to another prison, or even killed. None the less their spirits remained high. Pedro Miret, the weapons expert, became the acting chief of the group, assisted by Israel Tápanes and Raúl Castro, and they wasted no time getting organized. There was a bookcase in their ward, and all available books were assembled in a ward library named after Raúl Gómez García, the young poet killed at Moncada. One prisoner was named to conduct outside purchases for the group and keep track of individual accounts, and another man was in charge of distributing supplies to the cooperative the men had formed. Then there were regular political meetings chaired by Miret, and the beginning of the rebels' prison school. A ten-article list of regulations set forth the system of the meetings, including this provision: 'Wounding expressions may not be used in the debate, and it is absolutely prohibited to justify mistakes by claiming that the critic would have made the same, a similar or some other kind of mistake.'

Recalling the prison days, Pedro Miret says that the prisoners had immediately decided to establish a more rigid daily discipline than the penitentiary's schedule. 'If we were ordered to get up at 6 a.m., we would get up at 5.30,' he says. 'By being stricter than the prison regulations we were able to do almost whatever we wanted. To the authorities we seemed very quiet prisoners, so they left us alone. They were so ignorant that they never realized what education could do for us.'

Fidel Castro joined his companions on the Isle of Pines on 17 October, hugging and embracing them in the ward. In the evening he sat on his bed in the first row, almost at the entrance to the bathroom, and brought his men up to date on the final events in Santiago, including his hospital trial and his History discourse. Fidel's prison file – now he was Prisoner No. 3859 – contained photographs showing the well-trimmed moustache, and noted that he 'had education', and that he had a long scar, apparently from appendicitis surgery, on his abdomen, and another scar on his left thigh.

With Fidel back with his companions he was at once elected chief of the group, and prison life picked up in momentum. In addition to the library, which grew to over 500 volumes (including 100 belonging to Fidel), the men organized the Abel Santamaría Ideological Academy as the prison 'university' to teach philosophy, world history, political economy, mathematics and languages, as well as Spanish-language classics. The academy functioned in the patio with men sitting at the wooden tables where they normally ate. They had a small blackboard. There were nearly five hours of classes a day, with Fidel teaching philosophy and world history on alternate days, and public speaking twice a week; Pedro Miret lectured on ancient history (he remarked later that they were amnestied in the midst of the medieval period); and Montané instructing in English. Montane wrote later: 'From the outset Fidel told us that our imprisonment should be combative, and we should acquire rich experiences from it, experiences that would help us continue the struggle once we were freed.'

Castro also read aloud to the group, everything from Napoleon Bonaparte's infantry attack on Hugomont to José Martí's pleas to the Spanish Republic for freedom for Cuba. Castro and Miret wrote to friends and relatives asking for books. Raúl Roa García helped them further by publishing in the weekly Bohemia a book-request letter from Miret; censorship had been lifted, and this letter called additional political attention to the prisoners. Miret believes that their library had four volumes of José Martí, most of the important works on the French Revolution, and a complete collection of Lenin, Marx and Engels – suggesting that the education of the Fidelistas now was taking a pronounced ideological slant. And Fidel wrote to a a friend: 'What a formidable school this prison is . . . from here, I can complete my vision of the world and the sense of my life.'

In his first letter from the Isle of Pines to his brother Ramón, Fidel informed him that the prison censors had refused to deliver to him a registered letter from Ramón 'because it touched on subjects not permitted by censorship . . . which greatly surprises me.' But he urged his brother not to form a negative impression from this: 'The people running the prison are much more decent and well-organized than those in Boniato.' Prisoners were not robbed or exploited, and 'men here are much more serious . . . there is discipline, but there is no hypocrisy . . . I don't want to tell you, brother, that we are in paradise; there still are many things we need which have not yet been obtained, but it seems there is goodwill on the part of the authorities, and everything will work out eventually.' The prisoners were allowed to receive visits once a month, and Castro's letter to Ramón indicated that Mirta was planning to fly from Havana to see him at the prison. He urged his brother to come with Mirta.

By December Castro was again on the offensive. In an immensely long letter to his friend Luís Conte Agüero, the radio commentator, Castro retold the massacres suffered by his rebels at Moncada, and asked: 'Why have the barbaric mass tortures and murders . . . not been denounced? That is the inescapable duty of the living. To fail to carry it out will cause a stain that will never be erased.' Castro also informed Conte Agüero that as a result of the denunciations he had made during the Santiago trial the court there had accepted three lawsuits by him against Batista and three of his top commanders 'as the men who ordered the killing of prisoners'. He added that the court in Nueva Gerona on the Isle of Pines, in the jurisdiction of which he now belonged, had also accepted the lawsuits. In the strange world of Cuba a rebel chief serving a prison term for insurrection against the regime was able to sue for murder the head of state he had tried to overthrow. Indeed, various Cuban courts were still hearing depositions in these cases at the time of Castro's amnesty.

Fidel then went on to say that triumph at Moncada would have meant the transfer of power to the *Ortodoxo* party in the spirit of the 'true ideas of Chibás'. This was the first and the only time he proposed such a course. He repeated from the History discourse the revolutionary laws the new government would have promulgated, and now there was not the slightest whiff of Marxist thinking. Fidel clearly sought *Ortodoxo* support as he prepared his rebel army. Moreover, he wanted the letter to be issued by Conte Agüero as 'The Manifesto of the Nation', with a subtitle taken from Martí: 'Message to a Suffering Cuba'. He also asked that this manifesto be handed to his wife Mirta for publication in the Havana

University publication, *Alma Mater*. Interestingly, Fidel was increasingly seeking Mirta's help in his political endeavours. She tried her best, but the manifesto was published only much later, and then only as a small pamphlet.

Christmas was approaching, but Fidel told Conte Agüero that 'needless to say, we shall not celebrate Christmas, we shall not even drink water, to show our mourning. . . Make this known, because I believe in that way our objective will be seen as more noble and humane.' Meanwhile he continued his voyage of intellectual discovery, becoming fascinated with Napoleon III (the despised 'Little Napoleon'), reading both Victor Hugo and Karl Marx on this topic. He wrote to a friend in Havana that much as Hugo's *Les Misérables* had stimulated him, 'I grow a little tired of his excessive romanticism, his verbosity and the sometimes tedious and exaggerated heaviness of his erudition.' But he found that 'on the same topic of Napoleon III, Karl Marx wrote a wonderful work entitled *The Eighteenth Brumaire of Louis Bonaparte . . .* Where Hugo sees no more than a lucky adventurer, Marx sees the inevitable result of social contradictions and the conflict of the prevailing interests of the time. For one, history is luck. For the other, it is a process governed by laws.' Again there was relevancy to it in terms of Castro's current interests: Napoleon III had seized power through a coup (or a putsch in modern language), and Fidel saw it as an evil act in the context of his own Cuban perceptions.

Castro's reading list at the end of 1953 did seem to confirm that prison was a fantastic university and that his own tastes defied definition: there was Thackeray's *Vanity Fair*, Ivan Turgenev's *Home of the Gentry*, a biography of the Brazilian Communist leader Luis Carlos Prestes, the Dean of Canterbury's *The Secret of Soviet Strength*, a modern Russian novel by a young revolutionary, A. J. Cronin's *The Citadel*, and Marx's *Das Kapital*, Somerset Maugham's *The Razor's Edge*, four volumes of the *Complete Works of Sigmund Freud*, and seven Dostoevski novels, including *Crime and Punishment*. Castro's reading led him to the conclusion that Julius Caesar was a 'genuine revolutionary' in the context of Rome's 'intense class struggle'. Looking through Fidel's comments on his studies in history, literature, science and politics, one sees how his methodical mind subordinates all texts to his private interpretation (or prejudice), thus confirming what he had already decided has been the irrefutable course of history. Seeing such certainty about past history, it is easier to understand Castro's similar certainty about *future* history and the role he sees foreordained for him to play in it.

While he waited for the next great swing of history, however, he had to cope with the immediate reality of Cuban politics – as represented by the announcement in January 1954 by Ramón Grau San Martín that he would run against Batista in the promised presidential elections in November. This annoyed Castro immensely: he felt that no responsible politician should dignify Batista's elections with his rival candidacy (which Batista would surely rig for him to lose), and he personally despised Grau for the gangster politics during the 1944–48 term. But most disconcerting of all was the new illegal Communist Party's decision to support Grau (who had persecuted the Communists during his last presidency) against Batista (whom the Communists had supported in 1940, but whom he outlawed in 1952). It seemed to make no sense for the Communists to play any part whatever in the Batista electoral farce, but again Castro refrained from open criticism of the Communists.

After Christmas he fell foul of Batista, with the most disagreeable consequences. On Saturday 12 February 1954 the general came to the prison to inaugurate a new power plant, about sixty yards from Castro's hospital ward. As soon as Castro became aware of his archfoe's presence, he gathered the men and proposed that they sing together and as loudly as possible the Movement's revolutionary hymn. Shortly before the attacks on the army barracks Castro, always on the alert for propaganda possibilities, had commissioned the hymn from Agustín Díaz Cartaya, a young black self-taught composer who belonged to a Havana clandestine cell of the Movement, and what Díaz Cartaya wrote turned out to be one of the great battle songs, certainly Cuba's best. Its stanzas urged 'Forward, all Cubans, may Cuba ever prize our heroism; we're soldiers united, fighting so that our country may be free'; they damned 'cruel and insatiable tyrants', and they ended on the triumphant note of *Vive la Revolución!* It was first called 'The Freedom March ', but after the assault Díaz Cartaya (who was captured in Havana after escaping from the Bayamo strike) was asked to add a stanza about the death of 'our comrades in Oriente', and the song was renamed the '26th of July March'. It is played to this day at great revolutionary rallies, and it is the musical theme of Radio Havana's world service.

Now, Fidel could not resist the temptation of baiting Batista, and the twenty-six men under the window of the hospital ward burst into song. At first the general thought the hymn was a tribute to him by prison inmates, but as soon as he made out the lyrics he exploded in fury and left the prison. The next morning guards removed four *Fidelista* leaders from the ward; each was placed for two weeks in a tiny individual cell in the hospital's mental patients' section. That same afternoon Fidel was taken away from the group and put in permanent solitary in a fifteen by twelve-foot cell by the door of the hospital, across the corridor from the prison morgue. Then Díaz Cartaya was locked up in an isolation cell, the guards beating him with ox-pizzle whips; on 15 February he was beaten so severely that he was finally left unconscious on the floor of his cell.

Castro and his companions paid a heavy price for their brief act of defiance. Fidel himself would remain in his separate cell until he was released from prison under the amnesty fourteen months later (his brother Raúl was allowed to join him six months before they left the Isle of Pines). The others were deprived in their hospital ward of newspapers and mail, their radios, and for a time of outside visitors. Though Castro was able to maintain communication with his companions in prison and the outside world through a chain of amazingly inventive clandestine contacts – and to go on directing the Movement – he no longer had direct contact with his group. He could no longer teach them and before very long the Ideological Academy quietly folded. The *Fidelistas* were now busy in the intricate prison conspiracies required to support Castro's organization and propaganda efforts.

All things considered, Fidel was not particularly uncomfortable in his cell. It was large enough for him to pace up and down, and it had a toilet and a shower. He had a bookcase and a small hot-plate, and the metal hospital bed was equipped with mosquito netting. The big problem was light: in the daytime a weak light seeped through a window high up on the wall. He had no artificial light for forty days and strained his eyes trying to read at night with a tiny oil lamp. Later, electric light was installed in the cell, and he wrote to a friend that enforced darkness was the 'most absurd of all the human barbarianisms I can conceive'. After two months in solitary, Fidel told a woman friend in Havana in a letter: 'You can't imagine how this solitude devours energy; sometimes I'm exhausted . . . when one is fatigued by everything, there is no refuge from boredom . . . Days elapse in lethargy . . . I always try to do something, I invent my own worlds, and I think and I think, but this is precisely why I am so exhausted. How they do shrink me as a human being. . . ' Frequent rainstorms flooded his cell, and often he had to put his beloved books inside suitcases to protect them from the water.

On 20 February 1954 Melba Hernández and Haydée Santamaría were released from the women's prison at Guanajay after serving five months of their seven-month sentences. For Fidel Castro this was an event of immense importance: Melba, the skilled lawyer and one of the key personages in organizing the Moncada attack, would now become his trusted agent on the outside. From the original leadership group Melba was the only one to whom Fidel could now turn – all the others were either dead or imprisoned. Moreover, prison had made her even more combative. Leaving the prison, she spoke freely to waiting newsmen, and Havana radio stations (temporarily free of censorship because of the Batista electoral campaign) were able to broadcast her words: 'We went to Moncada moved by a sacred love for freedom, and we are ready to give our lives for its principles.' Clearly, however, the regime was attaching no importance to the opinions of a woman just out of prison.

It did not seem to pay any attention, either, to the increased activities of Mirta on behalf of her imprisoned husband, of Lidia, Fidel's revolutionary-minded older sister, or of Naty Revuelta who not only corresponded with him openly but also served as a clandestine communications channel. In the history of the Cuban revolution and in Castro's success, women have played a role that may well have been decisive, a fact that a great many Cubans do not fully appreciate even today.

Mirta and Fidelito were permitted to visit Castro several times (he wrote to a friend in June 1954 that 'I have now spent more than three thousand hours completely alone, except for the briefest moments I have spent with my wife and my son'), and they used these meetings for the exchange of operational messages for the establishment of a revolutionary network. During June, Mirta attended a tribute at Havana's Theatre of Comedy for the *Ortodoxo* radio commentator Luís Conte Agüero, going on stage to read a letter from Fidel, praising his friend and denouncing Batista as a 'tyrant' and 'despot'. But Fidel had also written about his life in solitary: 'I only have company when some dead prisoner, who may have been mysteriously hanged or strangely assassinated . . . is laid out in the small mortuary facing my cell.'

When Fidel sent his first letter of instructions through a secret channel to Melba Hernández on 17 April he told her that 'Mirta will give you the means of communication with me every day if you want it'. Having insisted that 'propaganda cannot be abandoned even for a minute because it is the soul of all the struggle', Castro advised Melba that 'Mirta will speak to you about a pamphlet of decisive importance because of its ideological content and its tremendous accusations, to which I want you to pay the greatest attention'. He urged her to maintain the 'most absolute secrecy' about the communications channel he had set up with Mirta. He also reported that Mirta had told him in prison 'about the great enthusiasm with which all of you are fighting . . . I only feel an immense sadness, being absent.'

Castro's communications system both within the prison and with the outside functioned perfectly. Most of his secret messages were written with lemon juice, serving as invisible ink, between the lines of open letters he wrote to friends and relatives in Havana, which the prison censor passed. When the heat was applied to the sheets of white paper, the brown tracing of lemon juice writing stood out. As part of the system he was receiving large numbers of lemons along with other foods sent him from the outside, and his appetite for lemons was never questioned by the jailers. Fidel also tells of placing tiny scraps of paper covered with nearly microscopic writing inside false bottoms of wooden match boxes. The boxes were switched back and forth between Fidel and other rebels and visitors as they kept lighting up cigars and cigarettes, and this too went unnoticed by the wardens. Pedro Miret has reminisced about the means used by his fellow prisoners to keep in touch with Fidel and with the outside. Their hospital ward was about 150 yards from Castro's cell, he says, with one outside patio used by the whole group of prisoners for exercising – while Fidel had a separate patio with a wall and the roof of the hospital building between them.

'In our patio, we often played with rag balls, which we made ourselves,' Miret says, 'and every once in a while we would deliberately make the ball land on the roof. One of the prisoners would then ask permission to climb up on to the roof, supposedly to recover the ball, and would throw it to the other side and [Fidel] would pick it up.' Written messages were concealed inside the rag balls, and Castro hurled rag balls back to his companions over the walls with *his* messages. Again, the warders never discovered the system.

At one point Miret and Raúl Castro found a *Petit Larousse* dictionary in the prison library, and came upon the deaf-and-mute code set out in it. Miret says it took them a month to learn the hand signals but when, after six months of separation, Raúl was allowed to join his brother in his cell, the code served its purpose. Though the barred doors of Fidel's and Raúl's cell and those of the hospital ward were at a considerable distance, Pedro Miret and Raúl managed to signal to each other by using the code. 'It was very difficult,' Miret says, 'but it worked.' Later Raúl perfected a system of using fingers for letters of the alphabet to make the dialogue easier, Miret recalls, and even today the younger Castro playfully addresses him with hand signals.

Food was a message-delivery device as well. Miret says that the prisoners sometimes cooked a dish and had a guard take it over to Fidel in his cell. On one occasion a guard realized what was happening, 'but Fidel spoke with him and persuaded him to continue passing the messages'. Mashed potatoes were a favourite delivery medium, but cigars were the best for sending lengthy pieces of information. Miret and the others learned how to unroll and re-roll cigars with great expertise – they were cigars the prisoners received from the outside as presents – to insert the messages inside. To send out messages, on visiting days prisoners would go to meet their families with lit cigars, putting them out before the fire had burned down too far, and passing the cigars to the relatives during an affectionate embrace. Still another method was for the prisoners to carve matchbox holders in wood and pass them on to visitors with messages hidden inside the holders.

The entire text of Castro's *History Will Absolve Me* discourse was smuggled out of prison by such means. Fidel spent several months reconstructing from memory what he had said before the judges in the Santiago hospital lounge, and he proceeded to commit it to paper in tiny, barely legible writing. He completed it in June. *History* was the pamphlet of 'decisive importance' that Mirta had mentioned to Melba Hernandez on Fidel's instructions, and now they all faced the tremendous task of getting it out, transcribing and publishing it. This mass of material, adding up to fifty-four closely printed book pages, was sent out in part as lemon-juice interline writing in letters by Fidel and others, and in part inside cigars. Miret says it took three months to smuggle out the entire text.

Melba and Lidia coordinated this remarkable editorial enterprise. The two women and Haydée Santamaría first ironed the letters to bring out the lemon-juice writing. Then the manuscript was typed by five persons working separately, including Melba and her father Manuel Hernández, at the family apartment. Next the typewritten pages were taken to Lidia's apartment to be collated. But meeting Fidel's subsequent instructions proved impossible. He had written to Melba in mid-June that 'at least 100,000 copies should be distributed within four months' throughout the island, with mailings to 'all journalists, lawyers and doctors' offices and teachers and other professional groups'. Castro had somehow calculated that it would cost only $300 to print each batch of 10,000 copies, completely underestimating the problems involved, but insisting that it must be done because 'the material contains our programme and our ideology, without which nothing great may be expected'. The next day he wrote: 'our immediate task . . . is not to organize revolutionary cells to build our ranks – that would be a grievous error – but our task now is to mobilize public opinion in our favour, to spread out ideas and win the people's backing.'

For this reason he was anxious to publish *History* in a mass printing. But the lack of money and the need to produce the pamphlet clandestinely limited the print orders to only 27,500 copies, and it was not until the end of the year that even this number could be distributed. The public impact was limited.

Publishing *History* was not the only task with which Melba was charged. Castro ordered her to travel to Mexico to establish contacts with Movement members exiled there, notably with his university friend, Lester Rodríguez. Fidel was very disturbed by the possibility that other opposition groups, especially the wealthy faction headed by the ousted president Carlos Prío, might achieve success and attract others to its banner. This would naturally undermine Castro's ambitions, and Melba's mission in Mexico was to persuade his friends abroad not to follow Prío. In May, Batista had granted amnesty to the ex-president and the other signatories of the 1953 Montreal Pact, but this excluded 'those who took part in the attack on the Moncada garrison', and Fidel had every reason to feel threatened politically.

The isolation also began to tell on him. Apart from a few visits in the early part of 1954, by Mirta and Fidelito, and an unexpected one in April from Waldo Medina, a Havana judge whom he had known at the university, Castro saw nobody but the prison guards. This monotony was broken on the five occasions when he was taken to the court in Nueva

Gerona, the capital of the Isle of Pines, to testify in the criminal cases he had brought against government officials for the killings at Moncada. But the prison director overrode instructions from Interior Minister Ramón O. Hermida to let the Castro brothers appear before courts in Santiago and Havana, leaving Fidel deeply embittered.

Having completed the *History* text and issued secret instructions to Melba and other Movement members, he turned again to his reading marathon. He reported in a letter to Havana that he fell asleep finishing Kant's *The Transcendental Aesthetics of Space and Time*, remarking that 'of course, space and time disappeared for a good while from my mind'. He complained in another missive that 'I have nothing at all about Roosevelt's New Deal', and that 'I mainly want information on him: in agriculture, his price-raising policies for crops, the protection and conservation of soil fertility, credit facilities, the moratorium on debts and the extension of markets at home and abroad; in the social field, how he provided more jobs, shortened the workday, raised wages and pushed through social assistance to the unemployed, the old and crippled; and, in the field of the general economy, his reorganization of industry, new tax systems, regulation of the trusts and banking and monetary reforms.'

Five years later, when his revolution triumphed, his policies covered every single point in the New Deal legislation which he had studied in prison. In the meantime Fidel wrote to a friend: 'I can't stop thinking about these subjects, because – sincerely – I would revolutionize this country from end to end with joy . . . I am convinced that one could make all its inhabitants happy. In such a cause I would be disposed to bring upon myself the hatred of a thousand or two men, among them my parents, half of my friends, two-thirds of my colleagues, and four-fifths of my former college companions!'

Two major revolutionary events occurred in the world during the spring of 1954, leaving varying degrees of impression on Fidel. In May, France's colonial rule in Indochina crumbled with the victory of the Vietminh Communists and nationalists at Dien Bien Phu. There is nothing in Castro's writings at the time to suggest any great interest in this Communist guerrilla triumph, militarily or ideologically.

On 17 June, however, a right-wing military force organized and financed by the Central Intelligence Agency and the United Fruit Company invaded Guatemala to overthrow the leftist regime of President Jacobo Arbenz Guzmán. Arbenz had begun nationalizing American-owned agricultural land, imposing advanced social legislation and giving free vent to anti-American sentiment. The CIA intervention in Guatemala, the first such act in Latin America since the 1930s, had an enormous impact on Castro, confirming all the Martí warnings and corroborating the 'historical fatalism' theory that nothing might happen in the region without the permission of the United States. In the long run the Guatemalan intervention may have marked Castro more deeply than Marxist and Leninist theories. In his prison cell Fidel was photographed reading a magazine report on Guatemala. Later, he would have first-hand accounts of the Guatemala affair: one from Ñico López, his early Movement companion and Bayamo fighter who exiled himself to Central America, and the other from the Argentinian physician, Ernesto Guevara, who had been working under Arbenz. Castro and Guevara were to meet before long.

On the evening of Saturday 17 July 1954 Fidel Castro suffered a devastating blow. Listening to the radio newscast, he heard an announcement that the Interior Ministry had terminated the employment of Mirta Díaz-Balart, his wife. He had never realized she was employed by the ministry, or received sinecure payments from it. Publicly as well as clandestinely supportive of her imprisoned husband and his cause, Mirta was believed to be totally loyal to Fidel, notwithstanding her family ties with the government. In fact Castro at first refused to believe that she had accepted ministry money. The very evening of the broadcast he wrote her that she should immediately enter a libel and defamation suit against the interior minister, suggesting that perhaps someone else was forging her signature to collect the payments.

Mirta's parents were alive, but she and Fidelito were apparently being supported by the Castro family and by several wealthy friends of Fidel. It made no sense to him that his wife would betray him, and he said in a letter that same night to Luís Conte Agüero that this was 'a machination against me, the worst, the most cowardly, the most indecent, the vilest and intolerable'. He wrote that Mirta was too intelligent to allow herself to 'be seduced by her brother, consenting to be on the government payroll, no matter how hard was her economic situation . . . She has been miserably calumnied.' Castro asked Conte Agüero to find out the truth from her brother Rafael, but centred his wrath on Interior Minister Hermida, saying that 'only someone as effeminate as Hermida, in the last stages of sexual degeneration', could turn to such behaviour of 'inconceivable indecency and lack of manhood'. This reference, correct or not, is the first recorded expression of his anti-homosexual obsession. He told Conte Agüero that 'now wrath blinds me and I almost cannot think', but that Conte Agüero should take whatever measures he considered convenient, and that he was ready to challenge his brother-in-law to a duel. 'The prestige of my wife and my honour as a revolutionary are at stake,' he wrote, 'let them see me dead a thousand times rather than having me suffer impotently such an offence!'

But Fidel was wrong. His sister Lidia informed him four days later that Mirta had indeed been on the Interior Ministry's payroll, and Castro instantly initiated divorce proceedings against her. There is no known explanation for her behaviour. Mirta, who the following year married an *Ortodoxo* politician named Emilio Nuñez Blanco, had never publicly discussed her personal life, and Fidel himself is reticent to this day about what happened. She left for the United States with Fidelito immediately after the break with her husband, and presumably they never saw each other again (she has lived in Spain since the revolution, and now she visits Fidelito quietly, and his children in Cuba, whenever she desires). In any event, Castro answered Lidia with a brief note: 'Do not be concerned with me; you know I have a steel heart.'

On 26 July, the first anniversary of Moncada, Interior Minister Hermida and two other cabinet ministers unexpectedly visited Castro in prison, giving a display of courtesy and cordiality that bewildered him. But that same day in Havana the police violently dispersed a university commemoration, organized (on Fidel's orders) by Melba and Haydée. The central fact was that Castro was now regarded by the government to be important enough politically to receive personal apologies from three cabinet ministers; Hermida flattered him by saying that no man in Cuba had a clearer political reputation than Castro, and telling him, 'Don't be impatient: In 1931 and 1932 I, too, was a political prisoner.'

Nevertheless Fidel remained shattered by Mirta's betrayal, as he saw it. He wrote to Conte Agüero: 'I live because I have duties to fulfil . . . In the many terrible moments I have had to suffer in this year, I have often thought how much more pleasant it would be to be dead. I consider the 26th of July [Movement] to be very much more important than myself, and the moment I know that I can no longer be useful to the cause for which I have suffered so much, I will deprive myself of life without hesitation, especially now that I no longer have a personal cause to serve.'

In the divorce battle between their lawyers Fidel demanded that the first condition be the return of Fidelito to Cuba and his enrolment in a school he chose for his son, now five years old. He wrote to his sister Lidia: 'I refuse even to think that my son may sleep a single night under the same roof that shelters my most repulsive enemies, and may receive on his innocent cheeks the kisses of those miserable Judases . . . To take this child away from me, they'll have to kill me . . . I lose my sanity when I think about these things.' Castro continued to insist on having Fidelito's custody when he left prison, telling his lawyers that if a court ruled against him, 'it would reaffirm my determination to fight until death to live in a more decent republic'. In 1955 he issued an ultimatum for Fidelito to be a boarder in a Havana school by 1 April, or he would block the divorce. Fidel's and Mirta's divorce decree was in fact granted the next year, by which time he had already left Cuba, but the struggle over Fidelito would continue for years – until Castro was in a position to win it.

Meanwhile Castro had become Cuba's most famous political prisoner and, increasingly, a factor in national politics, proving that an isolation cell can be the stepping stone to respectability and leadership. Early in June the newsweekly *Bohemia* published a lengthy interview with Fidel, illustrated with seven photographs showing him in his cell and in the prison library. This was the first time he received such massive national exposure, and in the interview he minced no words about the crimes of Batista, and his own revolutionary plans. The Hermida visit had resulted in a major crisis over Castro in the Batista cabinet, and the government now handled him with kid gloves.

In August, when Raúl was allowed to join Fidel in the cell, he reported that their cell was considerably enlarged, that they were given a large patio, that prison personnel took over cleaning chores, and that 'we don't have to get up until we want to . . . we have plenty of water, electric light, food and clean clothes – all free . . . we don't even pay rent'.

This was his political assessment: 'Our moment is coming. Before, a handful of us seemed enough; now, we must join with the people. Our tactics will be different. Those who view us simply as a group will be sadly mistaken. We will never have a group mentality or group tactics. Now, moreover, I can dedicate myself body and soul to my cause. I will put all my energy and time into it. I will begin a new life. I am determined to overcome all obstacles and fight as many battles as may be necessary. Above all, I see our path and our goal more clearly than ever. I haven't wasted my time in prison, for I've been studying, observing, analysing, planning and training the men. I know where the best of Cuba is and how to look for it. When I began, I was alone: now there are many of us.'

Castro was thinking about creating a national movement to replace the pre-Moncada secret army, and he was intrigued by the proposal which Conte Agüero sent him in August for establishing 'a civic movement, that is becoming a pressing need'. He replied quickly that he agreed on the need, but, most pointedly, he warned against a situation in which multiple opinions and interests would have to be accommodated. He believed as ever in revolutionary unity under his command, and he told Conte Agüero that the first step would still have to be the release of the 26th of July prisoners. 'A perfectly disciplined nucleus . . . will be tremendously valuable in terms of training cadres for insurrection or civic organization,' he wrote. 'A great civic and political movement must have the necessary strength to win power, by peaceful or revolutionary means; otherwise it will run the risk of having that power snatched away. . . '

Students of the Cuban revolution have questioned whether at that stage Castro was applying Leninist or Caudillist principles to the organization of a vertical revolutionary movement; a simpler answer is that he was holding out for absolute leadership – without which he correctly believed nothing could be accomplished in Cuba.

Fidel Castro had just turned twenty-eight years old and, still in prison, he loomed as a major national political leader. When former president Grau, now again a candidate for office against Batista, spoke at a rally in Santiago in October, the crowd began chanting Fidel's name; Grau's response was that as soon as he was elected, he would declare a full amnesty, including the 'boys of Moncada'. But he soon realized he could never defeat Batista's machine and pulled out of the race. Meanwhile amnesty for the Isle of Pines prisoners was turning into a nationwide campaign, and Batista knew he could not ignore it.

Running unopposed, Batista was elected as 'constitutional' president on 1 November 1954, a result that plunged Cubans into deep depression. But the United States, which could not – or would not – appreciate the intricacies of Cuban politics and the rising revolutionary potential, rushed to embrace the dictator again. After all, he had fully supported the Guatemalan operation. Accordingly, Vice President Richard Nixon came to Havana in February 1955 to toast Batista at a black-tie palace reception, being followed soon by CIA Director Allen W. Dulles, the author of the intervention in Guatemala. Neither of them had ever heard of Fidel, but before long the young Cuban would cost Dulles his career.

The pro-amnesty campaign was launched early in 1955 by a committee of the prisoners' mothers', entitled, 'Cuba, Freedom For Your Sons'. It soon became transformed into the Relatives' Amnesty Committee for Political prisoners; Fidel's sister Lidia was a militant leader; a young architecture student from Santiago, Vilma Espín, became involved in the effort; and Celia Sánchez, the daughter of a revolution-minded doctor at an Oriente sugar mill, organized deliveries of canned meat, chocolate bars and other delicacies to the men on the Isle of Pines. All these woman would be crucial both to the revolution and to Fidel's life.

Castro inevitably had dramatic ideas to enhance the amnesty effort. On 1 January 1955 he instructed Ñico López and Calixto García, who had escaped from Bayamo and exiled themselves first in Central America and then in Mexico, to present themselves to Cuban emergency courts as 'Moncada fighters'. This, he wrote, would force the re-opening of the basic Moncada trial, 'and we would rouse the nation against Batista just when on 24 February, he is about to assume power'. Fidel's idea was to make López and García the subject of a huge propaganda campaign, and he sent them public statements for their signature, to be given to principal radio stations and newspapers on the eve of their return to Cuba. Then, the two men would be met by journalists for interviews, although 'you will doubtless be arrested immediately'. Castro urged López and García to talk other rebel exiles into surrendering to Cuban courts for trial as well, 'but make sure it appears as your own idea; I don't want to put any moral pressure on them . . . If anybody else decides to follow in your footsteps and return before 24 February the government will go crazy just when it wants to make a show of political normality at all costs, and this might become a decisive factor in forcing it to sign the amnesty.' The two men, however, failed to return before the amnesty.

Batista was obviously feeling the growing pressure to grant Castro's contingent amnesty, but he was also sufficiently concerned about leftist activities in the country to accept United States advice and create a special Intelligence agency to combat Communism, under the name of BRAC. On Batista's inauguration day as constitutional president an impressive group of traditional political leaders, editors and intellectuals signed a 'Public Appeal', demanding 'liberty for the political prisoners and guarantees for the return of all those in exile'. On 10 March, the third anniversary of the Batista coup, amnesty bills were presented to both chambers of the Cuban Congress, and the regime made it known it would give them its blessings if the *Fidelistas* promised not to attempt fresh insurrections.

Castro replied with a statement, signed by all his fellow prisoners, rejecting the conditions. He wrote: 'The Pharisees once asked Christ whether or not they should pay tribute to Caesar or the people. The Pharisees of all times have used that trick. Today, they are trying either to discredit us in the eyes of the people or find a pretext for keeping us in prison. I'm not interested in persuading the regime to grant the amnesty . . . Today, we are more than political prisoners; we are hostages of the dictatorship . . . The regime commits a crime against our people and then holds us hostages . . . Our personal freedom is an inalienable right as citizens. . . We can be deprived of these and all other rights by force, but no one can ever make us agree to regain them by unworthy compromise. We won't give up our honour in return for our freedom.'

Fidel knew he had a winning hand and that he could wait for an amnesty on his terms – which meant no terms at all. He had also learned José Martí's counsel that a revolutionary must always be patient. In April, pro-amnesty demonstrations occurred in Havana and other cities, and the Cuban press, now free of censorship, was openly in favour of an amnesty, denouncing the regime for keeping the Moncada men in prison. Angered by Castro's defiance the regime retaliated: the penitentiary's administrative council sentenced Fidel to thirty days in solitary for illegally sending out his statement, published in *Bohemia* magazine, against a conditional amnesty. The press now seized on this act to attack the government. Batista finally had to accept Castro's terms in order to prevent a major crisis.

On 3 May the Congress approved the Amnesty Bill, and Batista signed it on 6 May 'in honour of Mother's Day'. On Sunday 15 May 1955, exactly at noon, Fidel Castro and all his companions were freed from the Isle of Pines prison – less than two years after the assault on Moncada.

And he came out fighting. A now famous photograph shows him with his right arm raised in a salute as he walks out of the prison's administration building with Raúl, Juan Almeida and Armando Mestre, and followed by the others. He wears his old grey wool suit (he had sent the dark blue suit of the trial back home) with an open-collar white shirt; he had written to Lidia earlier, telling her not to waste money on a new *guayabera* and slacks.

From the prison Fidel was driven to the home of his companion Jesús Montané, and then to the Isle of Pines Hotel in Nueva Gerona to hold his first press conference and sign autographs; as he had so often emphasized, propaganda must never stop.

In the evening the ex-prisoners boarded the steamer *El Pinero* for the crossing to the fishing port of Batabanó on the mainland. Their friends on the island shouted farewells as the vessel left, and some three hundred supporters greeted them on arrival at five o'clock on the Monday morning. The crossing gave Fidel his first opportunity in fifteen months to confer with his prison companions, and they used these first hours to plan the launching of the 26th of July Movement as a revolutionary organization of the masses. But Castro also found time to draft the 'Manifesto of the People of Cuba from Fidel Castro and the Combatants', declaring that their war was just beginning:

'As we leave prison . . . we proclaim that we shall struggle for [our] ideas even at the cost of our lives.   Our freedom shall not be a cause to feast or rest, but to battle for a nation without despotism or misery . . . There is a new faith, a new awakening in the national conscience. To try to suppress it will provoke an unprecedented catastrophe . . . Despots vanish, peoples remain. . . '

The document was published in the Havana mass circulation daily *La Calle* on the morning of the arrival of the Isle of Pines prisoners at the capital. When their train entered the station a crowd broke into the national anthem. and Castro was carried on the shoulders of his admirers through to the street. Now Fidel wore a white *guayabera* and grey slacks, and was carrying a two-metre-wide Cuban flag that had been handed to him as he stepped off the train. Speaking to journalists Castro announced that he would remain in the country, and become active again in the *Ortodoxo* party. This was part of his short-term strategy: the *Ortodoxos* were well organized and well disposed towards him (the Moncada rebels had been mainly recruited from among young *Ortodoxo* militants), and they provided a natural base for the creation of the 26th of July Movement. Nor did Castro wish to antagonize the army as he returned to the political scene; he went out of his way to praise the army officer in charge of security at the island prison (whom he had warmly embraced as he left the penitentiary).

Castro's blueprint for the new Movement included other young anti-

Batista activists, and he wasted no time in contacting those who had been released from Havana prisons under the terms of the general amnesty. Among these men Castro found two recruits who would very soon play key roles: Armando Hart Dávalos and Faustino Pérez Hernández, a lawyer and a physician.

Naturally, his sister Lidia (with whom he went to stay in Havana), Melba and Haydée had been among the first whom Fidel greeted and embraced, as was Naty Revuelta. Raúl Castro, who had rented a room downtown with Pedro Miret, travelled to Birán late in May to spend a week with his parents, but Fidel was too busy with his conspiracy to go to Birán.

Though Castro had declared on his return from prison that he would devote himself to legitimate *Ortodoxo* party politics, he knew that armed struggle was inevitable. He said to his followers, and they immediately began organizing the 26th of July Movement. At the same time he embarked on a public campaign designed to make him intolerable to Batista; he believed in self-fulfilling prophecies. He said he and his associates would serve as guinea pigs to test Batista's promise of constitutional guarantees for the opposition, adding: 'I have been informed that acts of aggression are being prepared against me ar 1 my companions.'

Meanwhile violence once more exploded in Havana, with assassinations, bomb bursts, fires and beatings. Students fought the Batista police, and the authorities responded in kind. Castro jumped into the fray with articles in *La Calle* and *Bohemia* denouncing the regime, and with fiery radio broadsides. When Pedro Miret was arrested on vague charges Fidel issued a statement charging that 'amnesty is a bloody hoax', and rushed to court to defend him. The regime banned Castro from access to the radio, so he raised the level of his accusations in the press. At every opportunity Fidel reminded Cubans of the massacre of his men on 26 July, and when Colonel Chaviano, the Moncada commander, published his own version of events ('we did our duty'), Castro lashed back with a savage *Bohemia* article under the headline, 'Chaviano, You Lie!' But also, in an attempt to divide the military, he paid tribute in another article to army officers whose conduct he described as gallant.

Making his home with his sister Lidia who fed him and every day washed his only *guayabera* shirt, Fidel was in perpetual motion, in an ecstasy of revolutionary activity. As if to make up for the twenty-two months behind prison bars, he delivered speeches, wrote articles, and constantly held meetings with his followers. Armando Hart and Faustino Pérez, who had belonged to the short-lived moderate National Revolutionary Movement (MNR), now became a channel for recruiting MNR activists for the 26 of July. One evening several friends listened to Fidel's account of the battle of Moncada – and to his rousing conclusion that 'now I have enough experience; next time, with new resources, we shall not fail.'

As he went on defying Batista, Castro was increasingly concerned about his safety, and in the first days of June his brother Raúl, Ñico López (who had just returned from exile in Mexico) and Jesús Montané, all of them armed, moved into Lidia's apartment to protect him. After a week or so, however, Fidel decided that he should not sleep two nights in a row in the same place, and he kept moving among the homes of various friends. But he never ceased attacking Batista.

The severe beating of Juan Manuel Márquez, an opposition leader, and the killing of Jorge Agostini, a former naval officer who had just returned from exile, marked the beginning of open warfare between Batista and the Castro-led opposition. Castro accused the government of murdering Agostini, and the same night seven bombs exploded in Havana; Castro said they were the work of Batista's agents. The authorities countered by accusing Raúl Castro of having placed a bomb in a cinema, and Fidel in turn charged before the emergency court in Havana that the regime was planning to murder him and his brother. He also called for a strike in support of railway workers who had suffered a pay cut. On 15 June the government forbade La Calle to print any more Castro articles (his last one had been titled 'Before Terror and Crime') and, in effect, Fidel was at last silenced. La Calle was closed by the police the following day.

Castro's next, unpublished article was to have been called 'You Cannot Live Here Any More', and it hinted heavily that he was preparing to go abroad. On 17 June Fidel instructed Raúl to seek asylum at the Mexican Embassy in Havana; there were two court warrants out against him, and an assassination was feared. On 24 June, Raúl left for Mexico, the first Movement rebel to take the long road of exile.

Before leaving, however, Raúl had attended the secret meeting on the night of 12 June at an old house on Factoría Street near Havana harbour, where the National Directorate of the 26th of July Movement was organized. Fidel, realizing he himself had to leave Cuba soon, felt it was imperative to leave behind a well-functioning organization. This was the meeting that Armando Hart would mention thirty years later when he reminisced about the foundation of the Movement; every person who had been present, he said, was either still with the revolution or dead. The eleven-member National Directorate was composed of Fidel Castro, Pedro Miret, Jesús Montané, Melba Hernández, Haydée Santamaría, José Suárez Blanco, Pedro Celestino Aguilera, Ñico López, Armando Hart, Faustino Pérez and Luis Bonito. The Moncada fighters were in the majority, but new blood had been added.

On 6 July Fidel made his final preparations to leave Cuba. A Mexican tourist visa had been discreetly obtained for his passport, and his sister Lidia sold her refrigerator so that he could travel with a small amount of cash. Then she packed his suitcases – typically, with more books than clothes. On the afternoon of 7 July Castro left the apartment in an automobile with his sisters Lidia and Emma, his son Fidelito (whom Lidia had brought from the college), and a woman lawyer. At the airport Fidel embraced and kissed Fidelito, then boarded Flight 566 of the Mexican Aviation Company. He left behind this message, published by *Bohemia* in 250,000 copies:

'I am leaving Cuba because all chance of a peaceful resistance has been closed to me. Six weeks after being released from prison I am convinced more than ever of the dictator's determination to remain in power, ruling by the use of terror and crime. But the patience of the Cuban people has its limits and, as a follower of Martí, I believe the hour has come to demand our rights and not to beg for them, to fight for them instead of pleading for them. I will temporarily make my home somewhere in the Caribbean. From journeys such as this, a man either does not return or else returns with the tyranny dismembered at his feet.'

Chapter 7

Fidel Castro arrived in exile in Mexico with the clear and privately stated purpose of organizing and training a rebel force to be landed in Cuba at some future date in order to engage in guerrilla warfare in the Sierra Maestra. This guerrilla army would defeat the Cuban armed forces, depose General Batista and proclaim a revolutionary government on the island. To achieve all this he had at his command, as he set foot in Mexico, a few friends, limitless tenacity, and tremendous powers of persuasion.

'Sitting in front of me, Fidel Castro was shouting at me in my own house, gesticulating violently, as if we were in the midst of a great quarrel: "You are a Cuban, you have an absolute duty to help us!" ' This is the recollection of the late Alberto Bayo, a one-eyed Cuban-born veteran officer and guerrilla specialist in the Republican Army in the Spanish Civil War, whom Castro tracked down in Mexico City, where the old soldier lived in self-imposed exile.

In his book about directing the training of the *Fidelista* expedition, General Bayo describes the encounter: 'The young man was telling me that he expected to defeat Batista in some future landing that he planned to carry out with men "when I have them", and with vessels "when I have the money to buy them". At that moment, however, he had not a single man nor a single dollar . . . Wasn't it amusing? He was asking me whether I would commit myself to teach guerrilla tactics to his future soldiers, when he had recruited them and when he had collected the money to feed, dress and equip them, and buy ships to transport them to Cuba. Come now, I thought, this young man wants to move mountains with one hand. But what did it cost me to please him? "Yes," I said, "Yes, Fidel, I promise to instruct these boys the moment it is necessary." Fidel Castro added, "Well, I am going to the United States to gather men and money, and when I have them – within seven or eight months, certainly by the end of this year – I'll come back to see you and we shall plan what we have to do for our military training." . . . We shook hands, but it all seemed to me quite impossible.'

Castro must have heard of Bayo's reputation through the Latin American revolutionary grapevine. When he reached Mexico City on the morning of 8 July 1955, after a night in Veracruz, he was wearing his old grey wool suit, and on meeting his brother Raúl and several other Cuban refugees the first evening, he admitted that 'I almost wept when I took the plane' from Havana. But he instantly put together a plan, as he said later, to 'reach influential persons in this country, whose friendship and sympathy could be useful'. General Bayo was among the first such persons whom Fidel went to see.

Alberto Bayo, frequently but falsely described as a Communist agent, was exactly the man Castro needed for his venture. The amateurish military training of the surviving Moncada rebels would be entirely inadequate for the invasion he was planning, and their lack of professionalism (including his own) could hardly be remedied by inspired readings of the memoirs of José Martí, or the nineteenth-century guerrilla experiences of generals Máximo Gómez and Antonio Maceo. What the 26th of July Movement had to have now was expertise in modern guerrilla warfare in tough mountain terrain against a sophisticated enemy. Bayo, an aging, white-haired man when Castro approached him in 1955, had fought with the Spanish Army against Moorish guerrillas in the North African Rif in the 1920s. He campaigned against the fabled Abd-el-Krim, went on to study guerrilla warfare at the Spanish Military Academy at Toledo, then taught his favourite subject at the Salamanca staff school. During the Spanish Civil War he had argued for the greater use of guerrilla forces by the Republicans against Franco's better-armed Nationalists. Now, in Mexico, General Bayo told Fidel Castro: 'The man of the guerrilla is invincible, provided that he can rely on the support of the peasants in place.'

The Spaniard had spent his years in exile training both leftist and anti-communist rebels throughout the Caribbean for assaults on dictatorships in Nicaragua and the Dominican Republic. In the mid-1950s he was teaching French and English at the Latin American University in Mexico, serving as professor at the Military Aviation Mechanics' School, and running a furniture factory. Bayo told Castro that he could only devote three hours daily to his rebels after finishing his normal work, but Fidel protested: 'No, General Bayo, we want from you the entire day. You must give up all your other occupations, and devote yourself fully to our training. Why would you want a furniture factory when within a short time you will be able to come with us, and together we shall be victorious in Cuba. . .' The sixty-five year old general wrote that the young Castro 'subjugated me, I became intoxicated with his enthusiasm, and he conveyed his optimism to me. Then and there I promised Fidel to resign from my classes and to sell my business.'

Bayo never collected the $6000 or so he had been promised for the sale of his factory, and lost a monthly income of around $300. Not telling his wife, Bayo said, Castro gave them $65 monthly 'to continue the fiction' that the factory produced an income, but when she discovered the truth three months later, Bayo's wife took on additional teaching duties to keep the family in food. Bayo refused further payments from the nearly destitute Cubans, and later wrote books in order to raise money to repay Castro the $195 given him at the beginning.

Despite his lack of resources Castro had a fairly precise battle plan in mind even before leaving Havana. Pedro Miret, who worked closely with Fidel throughout the whole period, says that Castro's decision to go to Mexico was already based on a plan to land a rebel force in Oriente. He recalls: 'All this had already been thought out, the landing zone as well as the place where we would go in the Sierra . . . I knew about it even before Fidel left for Mexico.' Miret explains that the concept of going to the Sierra evolved after Moncada (Castro had actually wanted to launch a guerrilla operation in the mountains above Santiago following his escape from the barracks), and that the idea of operating in the mountains presupposed 'mass activities' elsewhere in Cuba. He says: 'Without mass-support activities there would be no possibility of victory.' This was one of the lessons of Moncada.

According to Miret, he and Fidel had narrowed down the landing area to a zone between Niquero on the west coast of Oriente province where a huge peninsula juts into the sea, and the small port of Pilón on the south coast, some forty miles along the torturous seashore. After Castro departed for Mexico Miret had travelled to the Oriente peninsula, studying the terrain, the beaches and the surf along the coast between Niquero and Pilón. He was accompanied by Frank País, the twenty-year-old regional coordinator of the Movement in Santiago and one of its most influential leaders, and by Celia Sánchez, the dark-haired thirty-four-year-old daughter of a physician in the town of Media Luna, who would become Fidel's most intimate companion and associate in the Sierra afterwards.

Miret's inclination was for landing on the beaches near Pilón, and Celia obtained from the navy office there depth and tides charts for that section of the coast. Celia was one of five daughters of a patriotic and radical-minded physician named Manuel Sánchez. One day in her adolescence her father had taken her up Pico Turquino in the Sierra Maestra, Cuba's tallest mountain, to place a bust of José Martí at the peak. The Sánchezes were an *Ortodoxo* family, and at the sugar mill where he practised as a company doctor Dr Sánchez had seen enough human misery to give him very strong notions about social justice. Celia took after him politically, and she had travelled to Havana following the release of Fidel Castro from prison to see if she could be of help in the Movement. According to friends she wanted to persuade Castro that he should pursue his war in the Sierra Maestra, and she even brought maps of the area with her. She visited the *Ortodoxo* party headquarters, apparently hoping to meet Fidel, but she did not find him there. However, she met Pedro Miret, and he remembers discussing the subject with her. In September Miret and Frank País, who knew Celia very well, contacted her for assistance with the coast survey, and obtaining the charts was the first service she rendered the revolution. Miret then flew to Mexico to hand the maps, the charts and all other relevant information to Castro.

He approved the proposal to land near Pilón, but the plan remained a closely guarded secret. Miret flew back to Cuba to continue organizing the 26th of July Movement inside the country, and to begin preparations for the landing expected a year or so later. He kept in touch with Celia, and flew again to Mexico at the start of 1957 to bring Castro up to date on all the developments. Miret was able to report that in Cuba the Movement, now known by its initials, 'MR-26-7' *(Movimiento Revolucionario 26 Julio)*, was acquiring personnel and importance.

Being clandestine, the Movement was at this stage inevitably small, and potential members were carefully screened by the National Directorate which Castro had left behind in Cuba. Specific functions, from recruitment and fund-raising to propaganda and preparations to supply a guerrilla war in the mountains, were assigned to Movement members, and there were 'coordinators' on the national, provincial and municipal level. The *Ortodoxo* party, too, was perceived by Fidel at that juncture as a suitably massive political base for his revolutionary enterprise. He was careful to maintain his indentification with this party, and from Mexico he went over the heads of the leaders to the rank and file to urge commitment to armed insurrection.

Eager to appear as the legitimate heir of Eddy Chibás, in mid-August Castro sent a message to the Congress of *Ortodoxo* Militants then being held in Havana, telling them they had a central role to play in 'the struggle for national liberation'. The message was read to some five hundred delegates by Faustino Pérez, a member of the Movement's National Directorate, and it urged the party to reject the congressional elections offered by Batista as 'a peaceful solution', because they were a sham. Castro then called upon Batista to resign. For the opposition, he said, there were two alternatives: to 'cross their arms and cry like Mary Magdalene, because they lack the courage to demand their rights', or to take the road 'called revolution, the right of all people to rise up against oppression!' The delegates, on their feet, broke into chants of 'Revolution! Revolution! Revolution!' As far as Fidel was concerned the

Ortodoxos had signed up for 'armed insurrection', and his Movement was 'the revolutionary apparatus of *Chibásismo*'. Politically, he thus merged his two organizations.

The Communists still had no interest in Castro's insurrection, believing that their responsibility was to control or coordinate militant opposition to Batista in Cuba. Learning that Fidel was about to leave the country, the party had dispatched Raúl Valdés Vivó, the secretary general of Socialist Youth at Havana University, to talk him out of it. The Communists preferred Castro to stay in Cuba and work with them to organize a united political front against Batista, again under-estimating both his intelligence and his ego. Fidel replied that any mass movement had to be built around a direct confrontation with the enemy, and that he was going away to prepare the ground for a revolution. As for Raúl Castro, although a Party member since the eve of Moncada, his loyalty seemed to be first and foremost to his brother, at least until these two loyalties became fused in the aftermath of the revolution. In the meantime Raúl was in Mexico, a member of Fidel's personal circle of future invasion leaders.

Fidel's first home in Mexico City was a tiny room overlooking the courtyard of a cheap downtown hotel. He did all his reading and writing there. For lunch and dinner, he had to walk from wherever he was to the apartment of María Antonia González, a Cuban married to a Mexican wrestler named Avelino Palomo, in the old section of the city on Emparán Street. Mariá Antonia's apartment was the haven, shelter, kitchen and headquarters for all Cuban political refugees in Mexico, where Raúl Castro had gone to live on his arrival. The Castro brothers had known Mariá Antonia back in Cuba, and during the Mexican exile she became the fairy godmother of the *Fidelistas*, one more in the galaxy of Cuban revolutionary women who made the ultimate victory possible. Her generosity kept the brothers alive. Fidel was receiving $80 monthly from Cuba, and Raúl only $40.

A week after arriving in Mexico, Castro wrote to Faustino Pérez through a secret mail channel that he was studying the Mexican revolutionary process in the 1930s, under the presidency of General Lázaro Cárdenas. Cárdenas had expropriated foreign oil companies and promulgated a drastic land reform (and presently would become Fidel's protector). These moves became part of Castro's draft of a 'complete revolutionary programme' that he planned to send to Cuba as a clandestine pamphlet for mass distribution. He had to pawn his overcoat to pay for the printing of some copies of his document, remarking in a letter to a friend that 'the pawnshops here are run by the state and they charge very low interest . . . If the rest of my clothes had to go the same way, I wouldn't hesitate for a second.'

Castro caught the grippe, and despite his high fever he continued to write out in longhand his plans for Cuba after Batista's defeat. At dawn on 2 August he scribbled a note to his sister Lidia in Havana that 'although it is now five past four in the morning, I'm still writing. I have no idea how many pages I have written! I have to deliver it to the courier at 8 a.m. I have no alarm clock; if I oversleep, I may miss the courier, so I won't go to sleep . . . I have grippe with a cough, and my whole body aches. I have no Cuban cigars, and I really miss them.' In another letter that week he remarked that his life in exile was 'sad, lonely and hard'.

What his solitary writing produced was the Movement's 'Manifesto No. 1 to the People of Cuba', signed by Castro and dated 8 August 1955. Based on a fifteen-point programme, this manifesto was much more radical than his proposals two years earlier in *History Will Absolve Me*. The Manifesto was intended to reach Cubans on 16 August, the fourth anniversary of Chibás's death. Symbolism was crucial in the continued elaboration of Castro's image, and the Manifesto opened with the requisite citations from Martí and General Antonio Maceo. Castro instructed his followers at home to print 'at least 50,000' copies of the document and to start distribution at the Chibás grave in Havana cemetery. In Mexico, 2000 copies were printed by Alsacio Vanegas Arroyo, a Mexican printer who was a friend of Mariá Antonia. The orginal handwritten text of the Manifesto was smuggled out by another woman friend, the sister of the pop singer Orquídea Pino, inside *The History of the Incas*, a classic of the Spanish Conquest. That week Fidel had his twenty-ninth birthday.

While maintaining the continuity of the Moncada tradition, Castro's Manifesto was essentially designed to transform the Movement ideologically and militarily into a new streamlined structure. Enormously lengthy, as were all Castro writings and pronouncements, it was 'an open call for revoloution, and a frontal attack against the clique of criminals who trample the honour of the nation and rule its destiny counter to the sovereign will of its people . . . Our bridges have been burned: either we return in war to the fatherland so that we can live with dignity and honour, or we remain homeless.' The Movement, Castro wrote, 'is formed without hatred for anyone; it is not a political party but a revolutionary movement; its ranks are open to all Cubans who sincerely desire to see political democracy re-established in Cuba, and social justice introduced; its leadership is collective and secret, formed by new men of strong will who are not accomplices of the past . . . We defended the military when no one defended them, and fought them when they supported the tyranny, but we shall welcome them with open arms when they join the cause of liberty. . .'

The specific points of the revolutionary programme provided for: 'The outlawing of the latifundia, distribution of the land among peasant

families . . . The right of the worker to broad participation in the profits
of all large industrial, commercial, and mining enterprises . . . Immediate industrialization of the country by means of a vast plan made and
promoted by the state . . . Drastic decrease in all rents, effectively
benefitting the 2,200,000 persons who are today spending a third of their
income on rent . . . Construction by the state of decent housing to shelter
the 400,000 families at present crowded into filthy single rooms, huts,
shacks and tenements . . . Extension of electricity supplies to the
2,800,000 persons in our rural and suburban sectors who have none . . .
Nationalization of public services: telephone, electricity and gas . . .
Construction of ten children's cities to fully shelter and educate 200,000
children of workers and peasants . . . Extension of education to the
farthest corner of the country . . . General reform of the tax system . . .
Reorganization of public administration . . . Establishment of an inviolable military roster safeguarding members of the armed forces so that
they can be removed from their posts only for good reasons . . .
Elimination of the death penalty in the Military Penal Code for crimes
committed during peacetime . . . Generous and decent pay to all public
employees . . . Adequate measures in education and legislation to put an
end to every vestige of the discrimination for reasons of race or sex which
regrettably still exists in our social and economic life . . . Reorganization
of the judicial branch . . . Confiscation of all the assets of embezzlers
acquired under all past governments . . . '
   As with the History address, the Manifesto has been submitted to
endless analysis, in order to determine to what, if any, extent it either
suggested or brilliantly concealed Castro's real or attributed Marxism–
Leninism. Interestingly, those who accused him of Communism before
he publicly announced his faith in it, and today's official spokesmen who
insist that he *always* was a Marxist–Leninist, concur in judging the
Manifesto to represent Marxist views. Careful scrutiny of the text, in the
context of the period during which it was written, may lead, however, to
a different conclusion: that Castro had left his options open, enabling him
in the future to select the interpretation that best suited him politically.
Obviously, land reform, profit-sharing, rental cuts, state housing, state-
managed industrialization, rural electrification, effective education and
anti-discrimination measures were not inherently Marxist notions, even
in a Latin American country in 1955: they could in fact be conveniently
fitted either into a Communist or a socialist programme. Nationalization
of public services need not be a Marxist act (although the Eisenhower
administration might well have seen it that way). Mexico under
Cárdenas, whose policies Castro had studied so closely, had gone much
further in nationalization without being accused of Communism; though
Péron in Argentina was considered a Fascist and a thug he had recently
nationalized British and American public-service interests, and public

services of this type had been nationalized in most of Western Europe since World War Two.

Once again, then, it is an idle endeavour to search for hidden ideology in this Castro Manifesto. He knew exactly what he was saying – and how far he could and should go. In 1955, and even four years later, he retained the freedom to manoeuvre. He told Lionel Martin twenty years later that his early programmes were 'the antechamber of the socialist revolution', but this is ex post facto management of history.

Beyond question, however, were Castro's anti-imperialist or plain anti-Yankee sentiments, which were never disguised. As a student he had belonged to organizations advocating independence for Puerto Rico, and among the first friends he made in Mexico was the wife of the imprisoned Puerto Rican *independentista* leader Pedro Albizu Campos, the Peruvian-born Laura Meneses. Albizu Campos was serving a long prison term in the United States, and Castro regarded him as a hero. Laura had attended Fidel's commemoration of the Moncada attack on 26 July, and for the balance of his stay in Mexico they remained close friends, spending much time together.

In his speech on Che Guevara's death in 1967 Castro said: 'It was a day in the month of July or August 1955, when we met Che.' Fidel Castro and Ernesto Guevara met for the first time at the apartment of Mariá Antonia González in Mexico City. Hilda Gadea, a Peruvian with Incan features who was Guevara's first wife, places the meeting at 'the beginning of July' in her book on Che (Hilda died of cancer in Havana in 1974, having been divorced from him in the early 1960s). An account of Castro's Mexican exile published by the Central Political Directorate of the Revolutionary Armed Forces says he and Guevara 'established relations around the month of September'. Castro's history-keepers seem unperturbed by such imprecisions.

It happens that, through a coincidence in personal histories, Castro and Guevara began their active revolutionary careers within two weeks of each other. On 8 July 1953, as Fidel Castro was completing the preparations for Moncada, Che Guevara departed Buenos Aires for Bolivia on the first leg of another revolutionary journey. His father, Ernesto Guevara Lynch, recalls that when Che was saying goodbye to him and his mother, he explained that he was undertaking a self-appointed mission 'to fight for the liberation of South America from United States imperialism'.

'Here goes a soldier of the Americas,' Che told his parents, adding that he could help in the anti-American crusade which he believed Juan Perón, whom he greatly admired as a potential hemisphere leader, had launched from the presidency of Argentina. Che, who was two years younger than Fidel Castro, had graduated from the medical school at Buenos Aires

University on 11 April 1953, but almost instantly decided that he preferred revolution to the practice of medicine.

Considering himself a Marxist, but never formally joining the Argentine Communist Party, Che had spent much of the previous year travelling through South America with a fellow medical student, convincing himself of the colonial status of the continent's nations, and acquiring a profound distate for the United States during a month-long stay in Miami. Guevara, according to his father, had run out of money there, and had to await an Argentine plane on which he could hitch a free ride home. Living in Miami on $1 per day, the father says, Che ate poorly, and seemed never to have met any Americans he cared to remember. He was back in Buenos Aires in September 1952, resuming his studies on a crash basis in order to be able to graduate with his class.

Che was in La Paz, the Bolivian capital, the day Castro attacked Moncada, and he must have read of the attack in the local press, but there is nothing to suggest that he was especially impressed. He did not rush to Cuba, but journeyed instead in slow stages across Bolivia, Peru, Ecuador, Colombia, Costa Rica, Nicaragua, Honduras, El Salvador and finally Guatemala where, in mid-1954, he witnessed the overthrow of the leftist government of President Arbenz by rebels financed and organized by the Central Intelligence Agency. Che reached Mexico in 1955, and it was only then, on 'a cold Mexican night', as he put it, that he first met Fidel Castro, about whom he had been hearing reports through the Latin American revolutionary grapevine. From there on their revolutionary destinies became joined.

Contacts between Guevara and the Cubans first developed in Guatemala late in 1953, and early in 1954. Ñico López, one of Castro's most trusted lieutenants, had gone to Guatemala after escaping from the Bayamo affray on 26 July and he was soon introduced to Guevara and Hilda, then working for the leftist Arbenz regime. Guevara then met other *Fidelista* refugees, learning the background and details of the Moncada and Bayamo uprisings. Dedicated to the notion of great Marxist revolutions in Latin America and viscerally anti-American, he became fascinated by what he was told about Castro. After Arbenz was overthrown by his CIA-directed enemies Guevara fled the country, and reached Mexico on 21 September 1954. There he again ran into Ñico López, who kept assuring him that Castro would soon get out of prison in Cuba, and would probably come to Mexico.

By 1955 Guevara worked full time as a physician at the General Hospital of Mexico in his speciality of allergies (he was an asthma sufferer himself), and lectured unpaid at the medical school of the National Autonomous University. His salary at the hospital was so low, however, that to make ends meet he was forced to work as a news photographer for the Latina News Agency. Guevara lived in a miniscule apartment on

Napoles Street, his life-style was spartan, and his only extravagant gestures were occasional gifts of classical records and bits of silver jewellery to Hilda whom he married in Mexico in 1955. They had first met in Guatemala, and she followed him north after the Arbenz débâcle. Clean-shaven and with his hair neatly trimmed, outwardly Ernesto seemed the classic young Latin American professional with an impressive intellectual bent, what in those days was regarded as a 'parlour revolutionary'. He had the gift of fine irony in conversation, but preferred to be quietly in the background. He was well read, he wrote descriptive prose and poetry exceedingly well; his French was excellent but his English barely passable.

Ideologically, Guevara considered himself a Marxist–Leninist, and he was a serious student of the doctrine. Castro would say many years later that when they first met, 'Che already was a Marxist in his thoughts' and 'a more advanced revolutionary than I was'. Not immediately evident then was Ernesto Guevara's profound idealism, his absolute lack of political opportunism, and his passionate dedication to revolutionary causes. Upon being introduced to the freshly exiled secretary general of the Guatemalan Communist Party, which had supported the Arbenz government, Guevara chastized the Guatemalan leftists for not having resisted the American-organized attack, arguing that Arbenz should have gone into the countryside 'with a group of true revolutionaries' and kept on fighting. As Hilda recalled it, they parted coldly. Ernesto was the romantic revolutionary in search of a revolution.

When Raúl Castro arrived in Mexico in late June 1955 he was invited at once by companions from the Movement already there to meet Ernesto Guevara. The exiled Cubans knew Guevara through Ñico López and the encounter with Raúl was a great success. Hilda recalled that Guevara brought Raúl to their apartment (she and Ernesto had just begun to live together), and that it instantly became a great friendship. She wrote that Guevara and Raúl Castro met almost every day; and that Raúl introduced Che to other Latin American leftists exiled in Mexico. Of Raúl she said: 'He had Communist ideas, [was] a great admirer of the Soviet Union . . . and believed that the struggle for power should become a revolution on behalf of the people, and that this struggle was not only for Cuba, but for Latin America and against Yankee imperialism.' At the same time, Hilda recalled, 'It was stimulating to talk with Raúl: he was merry, open, sure of himself, very clear in the exposition of his ideas, with an incredible capacity for analysis and synthesis. This is why he got along so well with Ernesto.'

Around the second week of July (by Hilda's account), Raúl arranged for Fidel, in Mexico City since 8 July, to meet Guevara at María Antonia's apartment. They hit it off instantly, talking continuously for ten hours, from early evening until the morning. Hilda wrote that

Ernesto had told her when he came home that Fidel was 'a great political leader in the new modest style, a man of great tenacity and firmness who knew exactly where he was going'. And Guevara also told her: 'If anything good has happened in Cuba since Martí, it is Fidel Castro: he will make the revolution. We agreed profoundly . . . A person like him I would be disposed to help in everything.'

Afterwards Guevara wrote about meeting Castro: 'I met him one of those cold nights in Mexico, and I remember that our first discussion covered international politics. Within a few hours that night – at dawn – I was already one of the future expeditionaries.' In a letter to his father in Buenos Aires the following year, explaining what he was doing in Mexico, Guevara said: 'Some time ago . . . a young Cuban leader invited me to join his movement of armed liberation of his people and I, naturally, accepted.'

And this is Fidel's recollection: 'An Argentinian by birth, he was Latin American in spirit, in his heart . . . Much is written about all revolution-aries, and this is the case with Che. Some try to present him as a conspirator, a subversive and shadowy individual dedicated to devising plots and fomenting revolutions . . . As a young man Che had a special interest in the things going on in Latin America, a special enthusiasm for delving into detailed knowledge, and a special yen to go and see all our homelands . . . He didn't have anything more than his degree [of physician] . . . but Che wasn't Che then. He was Ernesto Guevara. It was because of the Argentine custom of calling each other Che that the Cubans began to call him Che . . . the name which he made famous later, the name which he turned into a symbol . . . It took only a matter of minutes for Che to join our small group, Cubans who were working to organize a new phase for the struggle in our country.'

After their first encounter Fidel and Che met two or three times a week, and late in July Castro went to dinner at the Guevaras. Che also invited the wife of Albizu Campos and Juan Juarbes, another Puerto Rican exile. Much of the conversation consisted of an interrogation conducted by Castro about the situation in Puerto Rico, but at one point Hilda asked him, 'But why are you here, when your place should be in Cuba?' Fidel replied 'Ah, a very good question, and I shall answer you,' and, as Hilda put it, 'His reply lasted four hours'. His main points were, she remembered, that 'the Yankee penetration of Cuba was so complete that there was no other way than to continue the road of Moncada,' and that he came to Mexico to prepare an invasion of the island 'to launch an open battle against the army of Batista, who was supported by the Yankees,' and that 'the struggle in Cuba was part of the continental struggle against the Yankees that Bolívar and Martí had already foreseen'. Castro went on to describe how the invasion was being prepared, and how important it was to maintain total security, 'always being aware that there may be infiltrators, but knowing that traitors could be detected'. The danger of treason was always on Castro's mind.

Hilda's personal impression of Fidel was 'very white and tall, big without being fat, with very black hair, shiny and curly, with a moustache, and with rapid, agile and confident gestures. At first he did not seem to be the leader he was: he could have passed for a well-turned-out bourgeois tourist; but when he spoke, his eyes lit up with passion, and with faith in the revolution . . . He had the charm and the personality of a great leader and, at the same time, truly admirable naturalness and simplicity.'

After Castro left, Guevara asked Hilda: 'What do you think of those Cubans' folly, wanting to invade a completely armed island?' She answered: 'There is no doubt that it is folly, but we must be a part of it.' Guevara embraced her and said: 'I think the same . . . I've decided to be one of the future expeditionaries . . . We shall soon begin our preparations, and I'll go as a doctor.'

On 18 August Che and Hilda were married in the village of Tepozotlán in the presence of Raúl Castro, Jesús Montané (who had just arrived from Cuba to join the conspiracy), and the Venezuelan poetess Lucila Velásquez, the bride's closest friend. Fidel joined them later for an Argentine barbecue prepared by Che; he had originally planned to be the witness, but decided against it for security reasons. He thought that Batista agents, the Federal Bureau of Investigation and the Mexican political police were watching him, and he may not have been entirely wrong. The Cubans and the Guevaras were now inseparable; on one occasion Fidel threw a party for his political friends, preparing spaghetti with seafood sauce and cheese.

Even with Che and Hilda, Castro could not resist the temptation to run everybody's lives. When Hilda told him one day that Che had earned extra money for covering the Pan American Games for his news agency, and that they could not decide whether to buy a car or take a trip, Castro counselled them 'to buy something for the house, like a record player', because there was too much red tape in Mexico connected with owning automobiles. Anyway, he said, there were friends with cars if they ever needed one. The Guevaras did buy a record player, and Fidel was delighted to see it the next time he visited them. That particular evening Castro met Lucila, and they appeared to be interested in each other. He took the poetess out several times but, as Hilda observed, 'He was so busy with his political problems that he put aside all his other interests.' On one occasion Lucila asked Hilda: 'Tell me, how did you conquer Ernesto, how did you get him to marry you?' Everybody laughed, including Fidel.

In September Guevara and Castro both grieved at the army's overthrow of Juan Perón in Argentina. To a great many Argentinians his defeat meant the end of a corrupt dictatorship and a gradual return to representative democracy, but to the two young revolutionaries it marked the end of what they perceived as an experiment in social justice. Both Che and Fidel had concluded independently that Perón's *Justicial-ismo*, a vague populist philosophy combined with a welfare state, was the beginning of liberation from capitalism and imperialism. Even though Perón was loudly anti-Communist, he had enormous support among urban workers, and he was anti-American. That was good enough for Guevara and Castro: they saw the military revolution as reactionary, and Castro always remained pro-Perón, immune to the arbitrariness and corruption of Perónismo. It was Perón who had funded Castro's trip to Bogotá in 1948 for the students' congress, and it was Perón who financed the news agency for which Guevara now worked in Mexico. In Latin America loyalties and allegiances in politics and philosophies are a most complex matter. Working closely with Fidel for a revolution, Che Guevara still found time in September to go to Veracruz to present a paper on allergies to a scientific congress.

With the Movement's top command now firmly established in Mexico, Fidel Castro proceeded to set in motion a series of new operations. He instructed Pedro Miret when he arrived with the coastal charts in September to speed up the arrival of additional Movement members from Cuba for training in Mexico; he sent a stream of detailed orders to the National Directorate on the island; and he prepared for a long fund-raising voyage to the United States. Jesús Montané and Melba Hernández had already come from Havana, so with Raúl Castro and Che Guevara they could coordinate the affairs in Mexico in Fidel's absence. Juan Manual Márquez, the forty-year-old *Ortodoxo* party leader who had been beaten savagely by the Batista police because of his friendship with the *Fidelistas*, also succeeded in reaching Mexico at that time; he too joined the leadership circle. And the rebels had a friend in Raúl Roa, the university professor who had sent them books in prison and who now lived in Mexico as co-editor of the periodical *Humanismo*.

In Cuba the key personality in preparing for the invasion was Pedro Miret. He has explained that during that period his trips to Mexico to brief Fidel were 'one part of the plan'; the other part 'was for me to send people over there' to join the military force. 'When Fidel left, I was charged with responsibility for the most delicate aspects of the con-spiracy.' With plans needed for an insurrection and, subsequently, a general strike, 'the whole country had to be organized, and this took a long time because so many people in the *Ortodoxo* party were turning towards insurrection. We had to collect money for arms for them all, make contacts to buy arms, and conceal arms.' Then, Miret recalls: 'We had to select companions to send to Mexico,' and the candidates 'had to be tested . . . we had to see how they performed under stress. For example, we would order them to paint a "26" sign (for the 26th of July Movement) on walls or somewhere, which seems easy . . . but some people painting the "26" would begin to lose respect for the authorities, and became dangerously reckless. . . '

'Men had to prove their stability,' Miret says, 'so that we could start selecting those who would be squadron leaders. When they became "burned", in the sense that the police were on to them, we undertook to send them abroad. Basically, we were sending people to Mexico at the rate they were getting "burned" . . . Sometimes we could send them out openly, it was incredible what one could get away with. But, of course, officials at the airport belong to the 26th of July . . . Since we had no money, every time a person left, a cell of the Movement in Cuba had to commit itself to send him money abroad . . . Some people got only $40 monthly, but that was plenty in Mexico.' Thus Fidel Castro's new Rebel Army grew.

And Fidel was bombarding Cuba with his bulletins. Two weeks after his Manifesto No. 1 was distributed he issued a letter to the National Directorate with its emphasis on propaganda and security. Propaganda, he wrote, 'must never cease . . . I give it a decisive importance because apart from keeping our morale high, material secretly circulating in the country does the work of thousands of activists, converting every sympathetic citizen into a militant who repeats the arguments and ideas.' On the other hand Castro demanded 'the most rigorous silence' concerning arms, persons handling them, and places where they are stored. 'If any *compañero* learns too much he must be removed from the internal front,' Fidel ordered, adding that no more than fifteen or twenty persons in Cuba should know about such matters, and none should know who the others were.

The new Movement would have 'a centralized direction', Castro said, 'that will control all the principal links, but a decentralized organization of the masses, acting in specific tasks; responsibility will be given to all members of the armed forces who sympathize with us.' In this fashion he expected that the best-known leaders of the Movement inside Cuba could be replaced gradually, without any break in the work. The main difference in strategy from the past was that whereas Moncada was conceived as a relatively rapid insurrectional war based on the cities, the new phase called for a prolonged war in the rural areas as well. The prolonged-war concept was now central to Castro's thinking.

He had come to the conclusion that a well-directed and imaginative guerrilla had a very good chance against a traditional army that operated by the book; this was the key to his decision to launch an invasion. According to Castro, different political groups should play roles of differing importance in a revolution, depending on their public record and the 'social interests' they represent; this was his first hint that in his revolutionary unity, some groups would be more equal than others (this was a point generally missed by many early *Fidelista* backers).

Modern sabotage techniques were to be taught to special combat units inside the country for follow-up action after the invasion, Castro wrote, and 80 per cent of collected funds should be spent on buying arms, against 20 per cent on organization and propaganda. Everybody could participate in the revolution, he said, young and old, men and women, providing 'useful collaboration' without necessarily having to fire a rifle. And in a letter on 4 October Fidel demanded a commitment by Movement activists in Cuba to provide systematic financial support; this would be his chief test of 'the loyalty of our militants to revolutionary principles and discipline'. Referring to himself as 'Alex' (one of his conspiracy names, derived from his middle name Alejandro), he wrote that 'Alex is convinced' that the revolutionary plan would be successful if funds were adequate. For this reason, in October Fidel undertook a speechmaking and money-raising tour of the United States, his first public political exposure on the American scene.

'I can inform you with complete certainty that in 1956 we will be free or we will be martyrs!' Fidel Castro announced before an audience of 800 exiled Cubans at the Palm Garden hall at Fifty-second Street and Eighth Avenue in New York on Sunday 30 October 1955. This was the first time Castro had publicly and formally made the specific commitment, to be repeated on many occasions in the year to come, to invade Cuba before the end of 1956. He did so in order to make his Movement more credible, and to set a deadline for himself and his companions. If the Movement were to grow inside Cuba, Castro reasoned, it had to be given something more than vague promises of a revolutionary return – some day. And he believed that a direct challenge to Batista would work psychologically to weaken him within his own government. He told his enthusiastic New York audience: 'The regime is totally at a loss with regard to our revolutionary activities . . . we have developed an invincible organization . . . Our apparatus of counter-espionage functions much better than their espionage. Whatever their agents abroad inform the government, we immediately get the same information. Batista's spies and their offices are carefully watched by us.'

The New York speech was one of the highlights of Castro's seven-week American tour. Its practical objective was to raise funds for the Movement, ideally by persuading 'Patriotic Clubs' of Cubans living in the United States to support the revolution in a sustained fashion. But Fidel made sure that the symbolism of following in José Martí's footsteps in mobilizing Cuban exile communities for the 'war of liberation' was not lost on anyone. Martí had lived in New York for years before

proclaiming the revolution of 1895, and most of the financing for
Castro's final war of independence came from Cuban businessmen and
workers in the New York area, and cigar-makers in Tampa, Florida. As
he moved along the east coast of the United States to deliver his
revolutionary exhortations the spirit of José Martí and of Eddy Chibás
went with him, their names invoked continuously. (And Chibás voice
was heard on gramophone records which Fidel had brought with him.)

Castro began his United States tour by dispatching a letter to the
Ortodoxo party executive committee in New York, promising 'a radical
and profound change in national life' as the lynchpin in the Movement's
liberation of Cuba. He expanded on this theme at the Palm Garden by
saying that 'the Cuban people want more than just a simple change of
command', and that 'Cuba longs for a radical change in every aspect of its
political and social life . . . The people must be given something more
than merely theoretical liberty and democracy; decent living conditions
must be given to every Cuban.' To his audience these were the themes of
Martí and Chibás, and they went over well; nobody read Marxist
messages into them until later.

Cubans had been emigrating to the United States since the latter part of
the nineteenth century, but additional thousands had moved in the 1950s
because of the economic crisis on the island, and they constituted the
principal target of the Castro campaign. Fidel evidently had no problems
obtaining a United States tourist visa, presumably because Washington
and the embassies in Mexico and in Havana did not consider him
sufficiently 'subversive', and the Batista regime may not have learned of
his planned trip in time to request a visa denial. Actually, Union City
police stopped the car taking Castro to his meeting there, and briefly
interrogated him and his hosts, but it appeared to be a routine check and
he was not bothered again. Another version had it that the organizers of
the Union City rally had forgotten to obtain a permit, and the police came
to find out what was happening. The New York event had been called
only on a four-day notice, possibly for security reasons.

It went very well. Imposing in his ancient dark-blue suit, Castro fired
his audience with his passionate oratory, and at the end of the meeting,
cowboy hats on the head table filled up with dollar bills. Juan Manuel
Márquez, the *Ortodoxo* leader who had now become one of Castro's close
advisers, travelled with him during most of the American tour; he had
spent some time in Miami in the past and he was well connected in the
exile community. In the New York speech Castro made an important
point in his revolutionary strategy: 'We are against violent methods. We
are radically opposed to terrorism and personal assault.' As he explained
many years later in a private conversation, Fidel had taken the view that
terrorism, apart from being immoral, is counter-productive, scaring
away moderates who otherwise might be potential supporters. During

the entire anti-Batista war the *Fidelistas* would eschew political assassination or bomb-throwing in public places (Castro says there had been
incidents of terrorist bombing in Havana at the outset, but he quickly
forbade it; sabotage of power plants, on the other hand, was considered
highly desirable).

On 20 November Castro spoke to 1000 Cubans at the Flagler theatre in
Miami; he had spent the three weeks since his New York rally in private
conversations and negotiations with exiled Cuban leaders, and seeing old
friends. His tourist visa had expired, but the Immigration Service in New
York extended it automatically. Fidel was joined in Miami by his sister
Lidia who brought Fidelito with her, and by their fairy godmother María
Antonia from Mexico. How Fidelito was able to join his father remains
unclear. According to one account, Lidia took him out of school in
Havana (and from Mirta's control) and travelled with him to Miami in
what detractors call a virtual kidnapping. Another account is that Lidia
first took Fidelito to Mexico where their younger sisters Emma and
Agustina had followed Fidel Castro during the autumn. In any event,
six-year-old Fidelito was present at the Miami speech, and when he
started playing with dollar bills being placed inside upturned *sombreros*,
his father said: 'Don't touch it, Fidelito – this money belongs to the
motherland.' In his speech Castro said: 'My son is here; if he were old
enough I would take him with me to the battle.' Cuban students in Miami
handed him a huge Cuban flag. He wound up the tour with speeches in
Tampa and Key West, Florida, traditional Cuban communities. In Key
West Fidel spent ten days resting and writing at a boarding house on
Truman Avenue.

The American expedition was a relative success. Castro never disclosed how much money he had collected, but in a letter from Miami to
Raúl Castro he said that he would have a $9000 surplus after the printing
of 10,000 revolutionary pamphlets. Everywhere he went in the United
States, he asked for funds; in the Miami speech he said: 'It does not
embarrass us to ask for alms for the motherland, because we ask for it
with honour . . . nobody will repent of having contributed. But even if
aid is insufficient, we shall still return to Cuba, with ten thousand rifles or
with a single rifle. . .'

Castro commented on public surprise over his disclosing the year he
had set for the revolution, and pointed out: 'We said which year, but we
did not say which month, which day or hour, now how or where . . .
Martí never denied his revolutionary plans when he was in exile. . .'

Politically also, the tour was worthwhile. He helped to organize
Patriotic Clubs and 26th of July Clubs in a half-dozen cities. His idea was
that every unemployed Cuban abroad should give a dollar a week, the
employed ones should contribute one day's wage, and members of his
clubs should pay two dollars a week. Although he would complain later

that Cubans in the US were not helping enough, when he finally launched the Sierra war, Miami-collected funds paid for many arms shipments.

Finally, at the end of March, Castro returned to Mexico to resume building his invasion army. In the nearly six months since his departure from Cuba he had created rebel organizations in Mexico, Cuba and the United States, and the rest of 1956 could be entirely dedicated to military preparations.

Back in Mexico, however, Castro had to cope with Cuban politics – and with Cuban politicians who were finally beginning to realize that he was emerging as the principal opposition leader. An article in *Bohemia*, coining the new expression, in the first known use of words derived from Castro's first name, said that a '*Fidelista* complex' was developing among politicians. 'They felt dwarfed,' it went on, 'by the shadow of Fidel Castro, which is becoming gigantic, and they see in him too dangerous a rival.' Although such politicians should be establishing a coherent stance against 'the revolutionary action of *Fidelismo*' and seeking a peaceful solution to the Cuban crisis, the article said, they already felt displaced by the magnitude of the *Fidelismo* phenomenon . . . Photographs of Castro and Batista illustrated the article, suggesting that the two men were the only real power contenders. Two weeks later Miguel Hernández Bauzá, a political commentator, published an article in *Bohemia* titled 'Motherland Does Not Belong to Fidel', a savage attack on Castro. Hernández warned that if Castro should ever gain power in Cuba he would become 'the only dispenser of civic, moral and spiritual grace . . . God and Caesar in one mass of flesh and bones,' and that 'all those who did not care for Fidel would be executed as immoral'. Yet the author conceded: 'nobody can claim that Fidel has profited from public funds' as had most Cuban politicians.

Hernández Bauzá must have touched a raw nerve in Castro by depicting him as an egomaniac. Fidel replied in *Bohemia* with a violent diatribe in nine columns, noting: 'four years ago nobody occupied himself with my person . . . I went unnoticed among the all-powerful masters who discussed the destinies of the country . . . Today, strangely, everybody rises against me.' But this was not, he wrote, because he had abandoned his ideals, but because 'they know my rebelliousness cannot be bought with money or position'. Fidel was furious, but he valued the attacks made on him by the Havana Establishemnt: at last he was recognized, at last everybody was paying attention to him, at last he was feared.

Inside Cuba tensions and revolutionary violence were growing in the latter part of 1955. At Havana University a group of students led by José Antonio Echeverría, who would before long die for the revolution and enter the pantheon of great Cuban heroes, formed a secret Revolutionary Directorate (DR), dedicated to armed urban struggle against Batista. The DR, however, had no direct links with the 26th of July Movement, and would remain a fairly independent revolutionary group until after Castro's triumph. In the meantime the DR came near to being destroyed while plotting to capture the Presidential Palace and kill Batista. The plan was apparently designed by former President Prío who was preparing to return to Cuba in mid-August and had arranged to have large caches of arms and ammunition concealed in downtown Havana. The DR students were persuaded to carry out the assault, but Batista's secret police seized the caches on 4 and 5 August, thereby defusing the conspiracy. The students were arrested nevertheless, and remained detained for over a month. On his return Prío announced that he was abandoning his commitment to insurrection and would combat Batista politically; this earned him a contemptuous broadside from Fidel Castro in Mexico.

Castro also denounced the efforts by a group calling itself the Society of Friends of the Republic (SAR), headed by an octogenarian politician named Cosme de la Torriente, to negotiate new elections with Batista. To Fidel negotiations were a waste of time, and he announced tht the 26th of July Movement would consider elections only if Batista resigned and left beforehand. Confrontation was the only strategy Castro regarded as plausible, and in Havana, students battled with the police in November and December, and when José Antonio Echeverría was seriously injured in a street affray, the DR responded by firing on the police, wounding a dozen policemen. On 5 December hundreds of women belonging to the Martí Women's Civic Front, an organization allied with the 26th of July, fought the police in midtown as they tried to march to a rally organized by the Society of Friends of the Republic. Scores of women were beaten, and many arrested. On 7 December the police fired on a crowd of students and workers protesting against Batista; one of the wounded that day was Camilo Cienfuegos Gorriarán, a worker who soon would be another hero of the revolution.

On 23 December nearly a quarter of a million sugar workers in the mills and plantations went on strike over a wage dispute, and they were instantly supported by the 26th of July Movement, the student's DR organization and even the illegal Communist Party. As the strike continued over Christmas, strikers and students skirmished with the police in a dozen towns; at the same time tens of thousands of leaflets with the *Fidelista* slogan 'In 1956, We Will Return Or We Will Be Martyrs' were distributed across the island, and the sign 'MR-26-7' appeared in red or black paint on walls everywhere.

In Mexico Fidel interrupted his conferences with Che Guevara and Raúl Castro long enough to celebrate Christmas Eve with his friends and fellow rebels. He prepared the traditional Cuban festive meal of rice and black beans, roast pork, nougat, apples and grapes. But no sooner had the dinner ended than Fidel launched into a night-long monologue about economic and development projects he planned for Cuba when the revolution triumphed. Hilda Guevara recalled: 'Fidel spoke with such naturalness, such certainty, that we had the impression we were already in Cuba, getting things done.' Then Fidel and Che spoke of the need to nationalize natural resources and the principal sources of wealth. Yes, Fidel told them, 'In 1956, we will return. . .'

Chapter 8

The training of Fidel Castro's invasion army started in earnest at the start of 1956, when the first serious amounts of money began reaching the conspirators in Mexico. Pedro Miret had brought about $1000 when he came to Mexico on a second visit to Fidel in December 1955, and Faustino Pérez, a member of the National Directorate, arrived with $8250 early in February. The Rev. Cecilio Arrastía delivered $10,000. This hardly represented a revolutionary bonanza but Castro had been complaining that in the first two months he had been in Mexico he had received only $85 from Cuba, and that 'each of us lives on less money than the Cuban army spends on one of its horses'. Now the Movement was able to pay the very modest living expenses of the rebels concealed in safe houses throughout the city, but the personal weekly allowance per man was eighty cents; the calculation was that it cost eight cents a day to feed a *Fidelista*. Anyone receiving $20 or less monthly from home had to turn over fifty per cent of it to the Movement's treasurer, and sixty per cent was taken from remittances over $20. When Max Lesnick, the chief of *Ortodoxo* Youth branch and an old personal friend, visited Mexico on 30 December he found an unshaven and hungry Fidel awaiting him at the Regis Hotel; they lunched on steak Milanese, a Fidel favourite.

By mid-January over forty hand-picked men arrived from Cuba and the United States to join the rebel force in Mexico; with Fidel, Raúl, Che and those already in place since the previous year the total stood at over sixty fighters – plus a group of deeply involved Movement supporters, mainly women, and several Mexican friends. To house the future *guerrilleros* six small houses were rented, each just large enough for about ten men; more houses were obtained later. Fidel Castro stayed with Melba Hernández and Jesús Montané (who were engaged to be married), and two bodyguards. From Miami Fidelito had gone to Mexico with his father's sister Lidia, where they lived with a rich Mexican–Cuban couple in a villa with a swimming pool.

Once Lidia had succeeded in flying Fidelito out of Havana, Fidel was determined to keep his son with him (though he was not certain where he expected Fidelito to be after he left on the invasion), and he saw him as often as he could. In the Havana revolutionary archives there is a photograph showing a very serious Fidelito in shirt and tie and an oversize military overseas cap, standing in a safe-house garden with his father, Raúl, Lidia, María Antonia and several friends. María Antonia's apartment remained the message centre and point of coordination, and all the new arrivals were processed there.

For reasons of security and discipline, life in the safe houses was of monastic rigour. Each house had a commander who was responsible for discipline as well as household and management problems and it was forbidden for any individual to reveal to any other Movement member his personal activities or those of his house group. Members who lived in different houses were not allowed to disclose their addresses when they met at exercises, and they could not visit with each other. Rebels were not allowed to establish outside acquaintanceships, they could not go out except with at least one companion, they could not date women alone (double dating was usually permitted), they had to be home by midnight, they could not make telephone calls, and alcohol was strictly banned. Mealtimes were on a strict schedule, the men took turns cooking and cleaning, and no excuses were accepted. Free time was used for study and lectures, especially on military and revolutionary themes. Each house commander was responsible for high morale among his men and for friendly relationships between them – on the theory that those who could not get along together would not be able to fight together. So severe were the rules that any indiscretion could be regarded as treason; Fidel Castro assumed correctly that Mexico was full of Batista spies seeking to destroy the Movement, and he was accordingly obsessive about security. Betrayal or indiscipline could – and did – result in death sentences in Castro's secret army.

When Fidel had collected enough money and gathered enough men in mid-January, he informed General Bayo, the Spanish guerrilla specialist, that he was ready to proceed with the training. At first Bayo conducted classes and drill exercises in the safe houses. He says in his memoirs: 'I was the only one to know the location of all the houses, apart from Fidel, because I had to go to all of them to teach.' He pretended to be an English teacher whenever someone in the neighbourhood asked him what he was doing there.

In training emphasis was laid on physical fitness. The fighters had to get used to day and night marches over the worst terrain in the most adverse weather, to sleeping on the ground, and to going for days with little or no food and water. Nocturnal training was particuarly important. Che Guevara decided to improve his physical condition by losing weight although he was already slim, and Hilda recalls that he gave up his Argentine habit of eating a steak at breakfast, confining himself to a sandwich at lunch and a light dinner of meat, salad and fruit.

Since walking was the guerrilla's principal means of getting about, the rebels marched for hours and hours along Mexico's streets, especially the long Insurgentes Avenue. Every morning groups of *Fidelistas* rented rowboats on Chapultepec Lake and rowed for long periods; not only was this good exercise and cheap, but Castro thought experience on the water might come in handy during the crossing to Cuba. Alsacio Vanegas, his Mexican printer friend who was also a wrestler (like María Antonia's husband), was drafted in by Fidel to teach the men hand-to-hand combat at the Bucarely Street gymnasium. They also played basketball and soccer in the suburbs to improve their agility. Then Castro and Bayo ordered mountain-climbing, beginning with Sacatenco and the higher Chiquihuite just outside the capital. Men from different safe houses converged at their meeting point in front of the Linda Vista cinema in the northern section of Mexico City to start the climb; they moved in small groups so as not to attract attention. Gradually Bayo made the men carry heavier and heavier backpacks. Some of the men, including Che Guevara, went far out of town on weekends to climb the 5280-metre Iztaccíhuatl and the 5450-metre Popocatépetl (Che considered it a point of revolutionary discipline never to let his asthma attacks interfere with these efforts).

In February Castro arranged for his group to use Los Gamitos firing range, also near the city. There were mountains around the range, and Bayo and his instructors used this terrain for guerrilla training. Armed with 30.06-calibre rifles with telescopic sights – these were the first weapons the Movement could acquire – the rebels practised firing and studied ballistics in the most professional detail: deviation rate, trajectory tension, line of fire, plan of fire, angle of fire, trajectory origin, projection line, sighting angle, range, initial velocity, correction in firing on aircraft, and on and on, hour after hour. Bayo was convinced that the individual proficiency of a guerrilla makes up for superior enemy numbers and firepower. Then he taught them compass reading and map reading, and how to transfer terrain measurements from a 1:300,000 to a 1:100,000 map, how to dig shallow trenches, and how to string communication lines. 'You men need to learn military culture if you're going to be guerrillas,' the one-eyed Spaniard kept telling them.

Fidel rarely participated in the exercises because overall organization, political contacts and fund-raising took up most of his time, but he made a point of checking periodically on the progress in the training, observing firing exercises through a theodolite. Melba Hernández recalls that Fidel spent a whole day, from dawn until late afternoon, observing the training, then decided to calibrate the rifle sights. 'We were terribly tired,' Melba says, 'having practised all day with only half an orange each for food, so most of us just took things easy. I, for example, stretched on the ground, chatting with someone. The only one of us to go on working with Fidel was Che. When they had finished on the rifles Fidel gathered us, telling us with infinite sadness that the struggle ahead was very long, that if we became exhausted so easily we wouldn't be able to keep up, and that he was very upset that Che, an Argentinian, a foreigner, hadn't gotten tired, that he had gone on training, while all of us, the Cubans, had just given up . . . He spoke with such sadness that afterwards it never occurred to us to get tired – we had no right to be tired. . .'

Castro, as seen by his closest associates, was absolutely single-minded about the revolution, but he tried very hard to be sociable, and he may even have fallen in love with a young woman in the months immediately preceding the invasion. But he was an unpredictable blend of patience and impatience – patience in the long run – a willingness to wait for the correct historical moment to act – and impatience in the short-term sense of hating to see even one revolutionary moment wasted. One morning in January 1956 Fidel burst into Melba Hernández's and Jesús Montané's bedroom at 5.00 a.m., shouting: 'But this is not possible! We came here to make a revolution, not to sleep until nine o'clock in the morning!' He had evidently concluded that an extra hour or so should be gained for revolutionary training, and he wanted instant action. From then on, when on their way to the Gamitos firing range, they started by marching for some eight or nine miles at dawn before taking the bus.

But a few days later Fidel tried to make up for his behaviour. It was 14 February, St Valentine's Day (the Cubans call it Lover's Day), and he started out by wishing Melba a happy holiday, making breakfast (he had taught her earlier how to fry eggs 'the best way'), and proposing an evening on the town. As with his military operations this was planned with equally precise mathematical calculations. 'Well,' he said to Melba and Montané, 'we have sixteen Mexican pesos [roughly $1.20]. Now, a woman, a *compañera* named Lucy has just arrived from Havana. So, we could invite her somewhere for refreshments, or go to the movies, which would be four pesos per person. But this is your day, so you decide.' Melba chose the movies, and the picture they decided to see was a Hollywood production called '*Four Feathers*' concerning Indian wars. After fetching the *compañera* whom Melba thought to be very pretty and in whom Fidel later 'became interested', they ran into Jesús Reyes, a Movement member usually assigned to protect Castro. Reyes insisted on going with them, and because he had no money at all, and they could not get rid of him, they were four pesos short for movie tickets for the five of them. Walking past a pastry shop they saw *tamales*, and realized how hungry they were. But, as Melba remarked: 'This was forbidden fruit; we were broke.' Finally the young woman said: 'Come on, tell the truth: you have no money. But you feel like eating the *tamales*, so let's eat them; I'll invite you.' Fidel refused flatly, but finally allowed himself to be persuaded to accept a loan. They ate *tamales*, and took Reyes along to see the picture, 'and really it was a much improved evening'. As soon as new money arrived, Castro rushed to repay Lucy. He saw her again, but she was not the woman he would propose to a few months later.

The problem with Fidel Castro and women was that he insisted on them being as passionately interested in politics and revolution as he was. One evening, for example, Melba, Jesús Montané and Raúl Castro persuaded Fidel to go out with two young Mexican women who were being very helpful in the invasion preparations. Fidel agreed, and Raúl said: 'Now Fidel, we are not going to talk about politics; we are going to pay attention to the girls; we're going to make it a *fiesta* evening for them. Otherwise your date will get bored.' Fidel nodded pleasantly and promised to pay attention to his date and keep her amused. They were three couples at a Mexico city nightclub: Melba and Montané, Raúl Castro with a girl named Piedad and Fidel with his date whose name was Alfonsina González. Presently Montané and Raúl and their women companions rose to dance, but Fidel did not move from the table. Melba recalls that when they returned to their seats Fidel was lecturing Alfonsina on politics. Although they kicked him under the table and he briefly changed the subject, he quickly returned to politics.

Melba says that Fidel lost interest in a girl 'as soon as he realized that she was not interested in his goals; then the relationship would grow cold'. But, she recalls, 'On other occasions, if a girl understood the Cuban situation and, especially, if she was involved in working for the revolution, I saw him very interested in her. But for various reasons he never wanted to link his life with such a person.'

Teresa Casuso, a Cuban novelist who became Castro's friend in Mexico and later a diplomat in his service (until she broke away from the regime), thinks that he fell in love there with an 'extraordinarily beautiful' eighteen-year-old girl from Havana who was her house guest. Casuso identifies the girl only as 'Lilia' (other friends say her last name was Amor), adding that she had 'an exceedingly polished liberal education . . . disconcerting frankness, and a spontaneity that enabled her to talk on every subject on the earth'. Castro often visited Teresa Casuso in the latter part of 1956 – he had convinced her to let him store weapons and ammunition in locked cupboards in her villa – and usually lingered, waiting for Lilia to come home. Casuso remembers that 'as the days and weeks went by the romance between Lilia and Fidel flowered'. Casuso says that Castro 'sought her out with a youthful effusiveness and impetuosity that both startled and amused her. The amusement gave her an appearance of imperturbability which, combined with her great beauty, enchanted him, although it may also have been the quality which finally exasperated him, for Fidel cannot suffer people to remain unconquerable before him.' According to Casuso 'Fidel made a proposal of marriage to Lilia, and she accepted', and he proceeded to obtain her parents' consent. He bought her 'a pretty bathing suit to replace her French bikini, which infuriated him'. But the engagement lasted no more than a month because Fidel could spare virtually no time at all to see her as the invasion preparations quickened; in the end Lilia decided to marry her former fiancé instead. When she informed Fidel of her decision, Casuso says, 'with that terrible pride of his, he told her she was wise to marry the other man – he was "better suited" to her'. Later, as he assembled a machine gun in Casuso's house, he told her that the revolution was his real 'beautiful fiancée'.

Fidel's obsession with his personal independence extended to his health. After agreeing to see a physician for a check-up on the insistence of his companions, he was given a sedative to slow him down a bit. Melba Hernández tried to make him take the pill every morning at breakfast at their house, but Fidel refused. Finally, he told her: 'Look, I can't start to depend on a little pill. I have to depend on myself. This is going to be a long struggle, and when we are in the midst of the war I won't be able to have any pills. If I'm forced to keep going with pills, then I'm in a very bad way. I won't be a prisoner of pills.' Once, while talking in his bedroom to Melba and Jesús Montané, Castro became depressed and his mood affected them too. Suddenly he jumped up and began pacing the room, saying: 'This is a bad example, a chief must never do this sort of thing and, besides, this is a very transitory state of mind because I have full confidence in the revolution.' Melba says Castro apologized profusely, 'promising never again to commit this very grave error'.

Early in 1956 the Military Intelligence Service (SIM) in Havana announced its discovery of a 'subversive plot, directed from abroad by Fidel Castro, to overthrow the government'. Numerous Movement members were arrested and Colonel Orlando Piedra, chief of the investigations bureau of the National Police, was dispatched to Mexico to try to uncover the conspiracy there. Castro heard from friends in Havana close to the regime that Batista had ordered his assassination: $20,000 had been offered to two hit men to disguise themselves in Mexican police uniforms, 'arrest' him in the street, and take him somewhere out of town to kill and conceal his body. A letter would be sent to María Antonia González over Castro's forged signature informing her that he had to leave Mexico suddenly, and there should be no concern about him. This operation was, according to Castro's information, conducted by the Cuban naval attaché in Mexico City, but it collapsed when the rebels were advised of the plan and announced it publicly. The Havana regime's next move against Castro would be through the Mexican authorities.

In the meantime Castro finally decided to break his ties with the *Ortodoxo* party, proclaiming the 26th of July Movement as the only real opposition to the Batista rule, 'the revolutionary organization of the humble, by the humble and for the humble'. The pretext for this rupture, announced in a long declaration issued on 19 March and published in *Bohemia*, was the *Ortodoxo* position that Castro's insurrection had not been authorized by the party's directorate council. Since the policy of insurrection and armed struggle had in fact been approved in August 1955 by the *Ortodoxo* activists' congress, Castro could now denounce the leadership for its 'infamy' in rejecting it. He accused it of cowardice and submission to the Batista regime.

The break was most convenient. His link with the party, which belonged to the traditional political establishment in Cuba, was no longer necessary in order to legitimize his growing revolutionary movement. The 26th of July Movement was ready to emerge as an independent organization controlled by Castro. He felt free, therefore, to denounce the wealthy landowner leaders of the party and charge them with betraying the Chibás heritage, and to proclaim that his Movement was 'the hope of the Cuban working class . . . the hope of the peasants living like pariahs in the motherland their ancestors liberated . . . the hope of the refugees who have had to leave their country because they could not work or live there . . . the hope of bread for the hungry and justice for the forgotten'. The Movement, Castro emphasized, was 'a warm invitation . . . extended with open arms to all the revolutionaries of Cuba, setting aside all mean-spirited partisan differences. . .' Significantly Castro was telling the nation that the removal of Batista no longer constituted the foremost or the only objective of the revolution, but that what was at stake was the nation's whole political and economic structure.

In Cuba organized opposition to Batista was rapidly growing. On 4 April the secret police uncovered plans for an uprising by a group of liberal army officers, only hours before it was to occur. It was known as the Conspiracy of the Pure, and its leaders were part of a network established in the Superior War School with contacts in all the Havana commands. The rebellion was aborted because of a spy infiltrated among the officers, and thirteen of the leaders were sentenced to prison by a court martial. Among them were José Ramón Fernández, then a lieutenant (and later a vice president of Cuba under Castro), and Colonel Ramón Barquín, a most respected army officer who subsequently helped to build the Rebel Army. On 20 April a Student Revolutionary Directorate (DR) commando seized the studios of Havana's Channel Four television station, but a student was killed in the ensuing shoot-out, and the revolutionaries were unable to get on the air. On 29 April a group of

militant members of former president Prío's political organization
assaulted the Goicuría army barracks in the port city of Matanzas, sixty
miles east of Havana, hoping to force Prío to abandon his conciliatory
attitude towards Batista and to employ his huge financial resources in
armed actions. Fourteen of the attackers were mowed down by
machine-gun fire and Prío was forced into exile in the United States. To
Fidel Castro, Goicuría was reminiscent of Moncada, and he charged the
government with deliberately staging a massacre inasmuch as it knew
beforehand that the assault was being prepared. In order to destroy the
Prío organization hundreds of people were arrested throughout Cuba in
the aftermath of this incident. A leader of the Student Revolutionary
Directorate was murdered by the police on 15 May. At the same time the
first issue of the 26th of July Movement's clandestine publication, the
mimeographed *Aldabonazo* (the *Blow*), was issued in Havana by Carlos
Franqui, a former Communist editor who had joined the Castro forces.

By mid-spring of 1956 Castro had decided that Los Gamitos firing range
was no longer adequate and had instructed General Bayo to find and lease
a ranch better suited for the organization of his small army. Bayo came
upon the perfect spot near the town of Chalco, some twenty-five miles
from the capital. Santa Rosa ranch covered ninety-six square miles,
including fields and mountains. The ranch house, large enough to
accommodate comfortably more than fifty men, was surrounded by a
nine-foot stone wall. It had four towers for protection from bandits, and
Bayo remembered that it looked like 'an ancient castle'.
    Santa Rosa belonged to Erasmo Rivera, a rich landowner in his
seventies who had once fought against Americans with Pancho Villa's
guerrillas; Bayo thought the significance was striking. Castro had
authorized Bayo to spend $240 monthly to rent the ranch, but Rivera
wanted to sell it for $240,000. After long days of negotiations Bayo
convinced the owner that he was fronting for a millionaire Central
Americal colonel who would certainly buy Santa Rosa, but the ranch
house would have to be repaired and painted first. He offered to bring
some fifty 'Salvadorians' in this colonel's employ who would work on
the house for the two or three months it would take to get it in shape – this
was the period for which Castro needed the ranch – and finally Rivera
agreed to the proposal and a nominal rent of $8 monthly during the
repairs. Bayo warned him that the arrangement had to be kept secret
because if the press in El Salvador learned about it the deal would be off. It
was necessary, he said, to maintain the Salvadorians away from the
villagers, especially from women, to avoid problems. Bayo was very
proud: he had saved Fidel $232 monthly.
    The first rebels arrived at the ranch within a day or two, and Castro
named Che Guevara chief of personnel at Santa Rosa under Bayo. Che

wrote later that the *Fidelistas* 'learned plenty' with Bayo, and that after he attended the Spaniard's first class 'my impression was that there existed a serious possibility of victory. I had considered this very doubtful when I signed up with the rebel commander [i.e. Fidel Castro], but from the beginning I had such ties of romantic sympathy and shared belief with him that it would have been worth it to die on a foreign beach for them.' Bayo worked his men day and night: they rose at 5 a.m. and trained until dark, always sleeping on the floor.

Now that the Movement's treasury was richer, the revolutionaries had twenty Johnson automatic rifles, several Thompson submachineguns, twenty hunting rifles with telescopic sights, two .50-calibre anti-tank rifles, a Mauser light machine gun and numerous smaller weapons. Uniforms and sleeping bags were sewn at the warehouse of the Mexican arms dealer. General Bayo also wrote epic, romantic poems in tribute to Fidel and several of his favourite fighters.

Fidel was so delighted with the progress of his guerrillas that he took time out to serve at the Basilica of the Virgin of Guadalupe in Mexico as godfather to the daughter of Bayo's son Alberto, a pilot who subsequently became an officer in the Cuban revolutionary air force.

Fidel Castro was armed when Mexican policemen surrounded and arrested him in the street on the evening of 20 June 1956. He pulled his pistol but the policemen pushed forward Universo Sánchez and Ramiro Valdés, whom they had grabbed seconds earlier, as a screen to prevent him from firing. Fidel was disarmed at gunpoint and forced into a police cruiser together with Sánchez and Valdés. The three of them had left their safe house on foot after being informed by a Movement member that the police were inspecting cars parked in front of it. Fidel and his two companions were taken to the Interior Ministry jail on Miguel Schultz Street, and in the course of the night the police rounded up twelve more rebels and their friends, including María Antonia González and Alberto Bayo Cosgaya, the general's aviator son. The general went into hiding for weeks, escaping arrest. Seizing documents and arms, Federal Police agents learned about the existence of the Santa Rosa ranch, and prepared to raid it. Fidel, however, insisted that he be allowed to go along with the police to avoid a bloody clash. Arriving in Santa Rosa on the afternoon of 24 June with strong police contingents, Fidel urged his companions to surrender peacefully. Thirteen men were arrested at the ranch, Che Guevara among them. But most of the weapons and ammunition had been removed to Mexico the day before. Fidel and twenty-seven of his followers were in jail; of the Movement's leadership, only Raúl Castro was at large. It seemed as if the Castro revolution had come to an abrupt end that June week, General Batista having succeeded in having the

Mexican authorities smash the 26th of July organization. Now, Havana demanded the prisoners' extradition.

Castro had not realized to what extent the Mexican Federal Police were willing to act on Batista's behalf; nor did he understand the labyrinth of Mexican politics which enabled official factions and agencies often to act independently both of each other and of the country's president. In fact, Castro had felt so relaxed about the situation that he flew to San José in Costa Rica on 10 June to meet with Cuban refugees there and Costa Rican politicians, returning to Mexico just in time to be arrested.

Since the Mexican police knew everything about the safe houses and the addresses of their Mexican friends, the assumption within the *Fidelista* camp was that they were betrayed from within by an infiltrated agent or traitor. But the first priority was to obtain the freedom of Castro and his colleagues before they were deported to Cuba. Juan Manuel Márquez, one of Fidel's top associates, rushed back from the United States where he was buying arms and collecting money, and he and Raúl Castro were able to retain two influential Mexican lawyers to defend the prisoners. On 2 July a judge ruled that the Cubans should be released, and although the Interior Ministry refused to do so, at least the judge's order prevented deportation. In the meantime Castro had found it necessary to defend himself against charges that he had Communist ties. He had been accused of planning Batista's assassination in Havana, and the Mexican police charged that Castro had come to Mexico with the help of Lázaro Peña, a Cuban Communist labour leader, and Vicente Lombardo Toledano, the Mexican Communist labour leader. Moreover the police described him as one of 'seven Communists' detained in the 20-21 June roundup.

Clearly it did not suit Castro to be identified as a Communist, and on 22 June, wasting no time, he issued a denial from prison, a denial couched in extremely careful language. Published in *Bohemia* in Havana the following week, Fidel's statement said: 'No one in Cuba is unaware of my position towards Communism, for I was a founder of the *Partido del Pueblo Cubano* (the *Ortodoxos*) along with Eduardo Chibás, who never made a pact nor accepted any type of collaboration with the Communists.' He added that his Movement had no contacts, either, with former president Prío. In a massive article in *Bohemia* on 15 July Castro went back to the Communist issue in considerable detail:

'Naturally Batista's accusation that I might be a Communist was absurd in the eyes of all who knew of my career in Cuba, which had been without any kind of ties with the Communist Party. But such propaganda is offered for the benefit of Mexican public opinion and of the international news agencies, and for the purpose of enlisting the support of the American embassy in the pressure which he has been applying to the Mexican authorities . . . Captain Gutiérrez Barros himself read me the report forwarded to the President of Mexico after a week of minute investigation; among its observations it was categorically affirmed that we had no ties whatsoever with Communist organizations . . . What moral authority, on the other hand, does Mr Batista have to speak of Communism when he was the Communist Party presidential candidate in the elections of 1940, when his electoral posters took shelter under the hammer and sickle, with pictures of him beside Blás Roca (then the Communist Party's secretary general) and Lázaro Peña, when half a dozen of his present ministers and trusted collaborators were once well-known members of the Communist Party?'

This was the first time that Castro had publicly connected the Communists with Batista and the question arises whether he was doing it because he was truly angry at the party, which was ignoring him, or as a tactical manoeuvre to save his Movement. Castro himself is not known to have returned publicly to the subject, but the fact remains that at the time of his imprisonment in Mexico Castro and the Communists were undeniably very much at odds over revolutionary strategy.

Fidel devoted the seven weeks of his Mexican detention to writing and speaking continuously on behalf of his revolution. Behaving with considerable aplomb, he received visitors in the patio of the jail (the Mexicans were lenient about his social life in detention), always wearing a suit and tie, making new friendships and sending out instructions to his underground Movement. Teresa Casuso first met him in the jail yard when she decided to pay a call on him. Describing the jail scene, she wrote: 'More than fifty Cubans were gathered in the large central courtyard . . . In the middle, tall and clean-shaven with close-cropped chestnut hair, dressed soberly and correctly in a brown suit, standing out from the rest by his look and his bearing, was their chief, Fidel Castro. He gave one the impression of being noble, sure, deliberate – like a big Newfoundland dog . . . He looked eminently serene, and inspired confidence and a sense of security.' For years Casuso belonged to the sisterhood of highly intelligent and impressive women supporters of Fidel.

Universo Sánchez remembers that he had borrowed the brown suit in which Casuso saw Castro in jail because 'Fidel had very bad clothes, and since he was put on television a lot, we wanted Fidel to look elegant'. The suit was borrowed from Armando Bayo, the Spanish general's other son, and Universo remarks that 'for Fidel to represent the group, he needed a little *cachet*. . .' It was also Universo who, with Castro's permission, tried to bribe a senior Mexican official with $25,000 for the group's release (although, as Fidel admitted later, the Movement had only $20 in its treasury at that point), triggering a shocked reaction. But the shock stemmed from the large size of the proposed bribe, and Universo says that he subsequently learned that 'because I had offered so much money they thought they must have grabbed something very important, much more important than it really was.'

In any event the bribe did not work. All the same, for some reason the Mexican authorities began releasing the Cubans. Twenty-one rebels were sprung by 9 July, including Universo Sánchez, Ramiro Valdés and Juan Almeida, and four more later that week. That left only Fidel, Che Guevara and Calixto García still in jail on charges of residing in Mexico with expired permits. In desperation the Movement lawyers succeeded in contacting ex-President Lázaro Cárdenas, the old revolutionary, and he agreed to intercede directly with President Ruíz Cortines. Because nobody in Mexico, president or not, could ever refuse any request from the legendary Cárdenas, the government released Fidel on 24 July, more than a month after his arrest. Che and Calixto García were let go on 31 July. Fidel made a point of calling on Cárdenas to thank him.

The revolution was back in business. Castro ordered the Movement reorganized, and most of the fighters and arms moved to Mérida in Yucatán (where the police seized, then returned a weapons cache) and to Veracruz and Jalapa on the south-east coast of the Gulf of Mexico. Fidel remained with a contingent in Mexico City. Che Guevara wrote later thaat the Mexican police, paid by Batista, had 'committed the absurd error of not killing [Fidel] after taking him prisoner'. Guevara also noted that when he and Calixto García were the only ones left behind in jail he had urged Castro not to delay the revolution for his sake – he did not know how much longer he would be imprisoned – but Fidel replied simply: 'I won't abandon you.' To Che this gesture touchingly subordinated Castro's revolutionary zeal to personal friendship, and he remarked:'These attitudes that Fidel has towards people whom he appreciates are the key to the fanatical loyalty that he creates around him . . . so that to an adherence to principle is added a personal adherence, making this Rebel Army an indivisible block.' Che also composed a 'Canto to Fidel'', an epic revolutionary poem, ending on the note: 'If iron halts us on our way/We ask a kerchief of Cuban tears/To cover the guerrillero bones/In transit to American history/Nothing more. . .' Guevara told his wife he would give the poem to Castro 'on the high seas, en route to Cuba'.

Fidel Castro turned thirty on 13 August, deep in revolutionary politics and invasion planning, making up for the month in prison and the loss of Santa Rosa. Forty new, carefully selected recruits arrived from Cuba and the United States, ten of them Moncada veterans. The new contingent included Camilo Cienfuegos Gorriarán, a young Havana worker who had been wounded in an affray with the police, then had emigrated to California where he married an American. His older brother, Osmany, was already in Mexico, but not as a member of the Castro Movement; he belonged to a clandestine group of Cuban Communists who maintained liaison between Havana and Mexico City.

During August, Frank País, the twenty-one-year-old Oriente co-ordinator of the 26th of July Movement and the son of a Protestant minister, travelled secretly to Mexico to confer with Fidel about the support to be given the rebels the moment they landed in Cuba. Castro, who remained determined to keep his word and land in Cuba before the end of the year despite his summer reverses, proposed that the arrival of the invasion force be accompanied by armed uprisings throughout Oriente, and that the political climate be prepared for a general strike. The idea was to distract the Batista army with multiple armed actions, making it easier for the rebels to reach the Sierra Maestra. In the meantime Castro and País agreed not to send any more men to Mexico, but to start building up the Movement militarily at home. Simultaneously Fidel instructed the Movement in Oriente to retain for itself the collected funds that were normally sent to Mexico, or eighty per cent of the total (the balance went as usual to the Movement's National Directorate).

But Castro had also concluded that the time had come for unity among the various other revolutionary movements in and out of Cuba. In Havana, where Batista was attempting to persuade the opposition to participate in congressional elections in November 1957, Castro's call for unity became the central subject of political conversations. In an interview printed in Cuban newspapers he acknowledged that the unity he now advocated represented a change in his 'tactical line', saying that it was necessary to absorb the lessons of reality. 'We can discuss later', he said, 'but now only the struggle is honourable.' Castro had broken away in March from the Ortodoxo party, privately he believed he would always remain in control, yet the summer setbacks required him to seek outside support and alliances.

The first step was a pact he worked out with José Antonio Echeverría, the twenty-four-year-old president of the University Students Feder-ation (FEU) and secretary general of the Student Revolutionary Directorate (DR). Echeverría arrived in Mexico on 29 August, meeting with Fidel for forty-eight hours, virtually without rest, at the apartment on Pachuca Street where Castro now lived with Melba Hernández, Jesús Montané and Cándido González. On 30 August they signed the 'Mexico Letter', declaring that their respective organizations had decided 'to unite solidly their efforts in order to oust the tyranny and carry out the Cuban revolution'. Castro and Echeverría added that social and political conditions in Cuba were propitious and the revolutionary preparations sufficiently advanced for liberation to be offered to the nation in 1956, and that 'insurrection backed by a general strike in the whole country will be invincible'. In principle, the 26th of July Movement and the Student Revolutionary Directorate committed themselves to armed actions throughout Cuba, both ahead of the invasion to create a revolutionary climate, and after the invasion to coordinate with Castro's rebels. However no specific plans were outlined, and the two leaders made it clear that their organizations remained independent; there was no joint command contemplated by either side. Besides, the immediate problem was that neither group had enough weapons to launch a serious operation.

In the meantime the Batista regime sought to undermine Castro by accusing him of accepting money and arms from the Dominican Republic's rightist dictator, Rafael Leónidas Trujillo, and of planning with him a joint invasion of Cuba. This was patently absurd, given Castro's involvement in the 1947 conspiracy against Trujillo and his general opposition to dictatorships. He fired off a four-column letter to *Bohemia*, declaring that 'the barrage of calumny hurled against us by the dictatorship exceeds all reason . . . It has only recently been suggested that I am a member of the Mexican–Soviet Institute and a Communist Party militant.' Castro wrote that he continued to despise Trujillo. 'We shall never change our principles, not for all the arms that all the dictators may have, put together . . . Batista, on the contrary, will never renounce the tanks, the cannon and the aircraft that the United States sends him, not to defend democracy, but to massacre our defenceless people.' Castro was once again the favourite subject of discussions and polemics in the Cuban press – to his immense satisfaction. It was propaganda at work for his cause.

The cause, however, urgently needed funds. Many of his friends at the time claimed that Castro worked out a secret arrangement with Carlos Prío, the millionaire ex-president of Cuba he had so often denounced, to secure money for the 26th of July Movement. Castro never confirmed this, but in the interview published in August he went out of his way to say that 'Batista has been merciless with Prío beyond all limits, by insults, taunts, and humiliation . . . When we were arrested in Mexico, and people spoke insistently about our deportation, Prío – a man I have fought several times – was very much a gentleman . . . He wrote in his capacity as former President of Cuba an open letter to the President of Mexico asking him not to deport us.'

Certainly, after his release from jail Castro met in Yucatán with Justo Carrillo, president of the Cuban Agricultural and Industrial Development Bank before the 1952 coup, and close to the Montecristi military anti-Batista faction. Reportedly Carillo gave Castro $5000. But a crucial source of funds was Prío, and Teresa Casuso, Fidel's new friend and widow of the famous poet Pablo de la Torriente Brau who had died in the Spanish Civil War, was also Prío's friend. Casuso says that on Castro's request she flew to Miami where she spent five days with Prío who 'was eager to talk to Fidel'. As a result, according to friends' accounts, Castro illegally entered the United States some time in September to meet Prío at Casa de Palmas Hotel in McAllen, Texas. Many published accounts claim that Castro immediately received perhaps as much as $50,000 from the former president. Casuso says 'Prío helped to sustain the expense of two years of costly expeditions . . . and secret shipments of arms and men.'

Late in the spring Castro saw in an arms catalogue a photograph of a PT boat for sale in Dover on the Delaware River. Equipped with torpedoes and 40-mm cannon, this boat was known for both its speed and manoevrability. Antonio del Conde Pontones, the Mexican arms' supplier known as 'El Cuate' and Castro's friend, was dispatched to Dover with Jesús Reyes to look over the PT boat. The craft was in good condition, and the two emissaries agreed to pay $20,000 for her, making a down payment of $10,000 in mid-June; they were to take possession of the boat and make the final payment on their return within a few weeks. However, Castro was then arrested and El Cuate was picked up by the police on his return to Mexico. In August El Cuate, Onelio Pino and Rafael del Pino, the student who went to Bogotá with Castro in 1948 and who now belonged to the Movement, were sent back to Delaware with another $10,000, to sail the boat to a Mexican port. Because everything seemed in order El Cuate was ordered to Miami to meet with Prío while the two Cubans were completing arrangements for the craft.

El Cuate says that in Miami he was introduced to Prío by Juan Manuel Márquez, who then represented the Movement in the United States, and the ex-president handed him $20,000 'which I delivered to Fidel in Mexico'. The fresh Prío money was providential at this juncture because it proved impossible to obtain an export permit for the PT boat from the United States government – normally, export licences were granted easily, but now, in view of the unrest in the Caribbean, the State Department was reluctant – and for obscure reasons its owner refused to refund the Movement's money. The revolution was now short, there-fore, of a precious $20,000, and it had no vessel either. Briefly Fidel considered buying a Catalina PBY flying boat, but he dropped the idea along with Universo Sánchez's proposal that they initiate the war by bombing La Cabaña fortress in Havana. The time limit for his promised invasion was fast approaching.

Late in September Castro and El Cuate went to the hills above the port of Tuxpán on the gulf coast between Tampico and Veracruz to test 30.06-calibre Remington automatic rifles in conditions resembling Cuban Sierras. El Cuate told Castro that he wanted to go down to the Tuxpán river to see a boat he was buying for himself, and when Fidel saw her he said: 'In this boat, I'm going to Cuba. . .' The Mexican argued that the white motor yacht was a luxury craft, too small for an expedition. But Castro said: 'If you can get it for me, I'll go to Cuba aboard this one,' and

El Cuate finally gave in. As he said later: 'You just can't say no to Fidel. . .'

The yacht was the *Granma* and she belonged to Robert B. Erickson, an American who lived permanently in Mexico City. The wooden 13-metre yacht was propelled by two diesel engines. She had been built in 1943 and could carry up to twenty-five people safely. But she had sunk during a 1953 hurricane, remaining for a time under water, and much work was required to make her seaworthy again. Erickson was willing to sell her for $20,000, providing that he could also sell a modern house he owned on the Tuxpán River, for a further $20,000. Castro decided to go ahead with both purchases, reasoning that they would need a house anyway for their men who would be working on *Granma*, and for those waiting to leave. A $17,000 down payment was made to Erickson, and work on the yacht started instantly. Two rebels were assigned to live in the house, and Onelio Pino was named *Granma*'s captain.

Fidel was optimistic now that he had acquired *Granma*, but he still kept a watchful eye on revolutionary politics. Pedro Miret, Faustino Pérez and Ñico López had arrived in Mexico to join him on the expedition; thus the entire general staff of the Movement was with their chief. The FEU student leader, José Antonio Echeverría, returned to Mexico City in mid-October for another conference with Castro, and the differences in their personalities and approaches to the revolution began to show more clearly than at their first meeting. Apart from being natural political rivals, Echeverría and Castro also saw tactics in contrasting ways, the former insisting on continuous violent, all-or-nothing action, and the latter preferring long-term, carefully coordinated operations; clearly, at stake was the ultimate leadership.

Then, a week after Echeverría had returned to Cuba, Student Revolutionary Directorate commandos ambushed and killed Colonel Manuel Blanco Rico, the SIM chief, as he was leaving the Montmarte nightclub. The attack, carried out by Juan Pedro Carbó Servía and Roland Cubela (who in the 1960s would try to assassinate Castro, on behalf of the CIA), originally had been intended for Interior Minister Santiago Rey, but when he did not turn up as expected, the colonel was shot instead. Castro was angered, saying in a newspaper interview: 'I do not condem [assassination] attempts as a revolutionary weapon if the circumstances require it. But such acts must not be indiscriminate. I do not know who carried out the assault on Blanco Rico, but I do believe that, from a political and revolutionary standpoint, his assassination was not justified. Blanco Rico was not a Fascist executioner.' In Havana, the police raided the Haitian embassy looking for Carbó, who was not there, and instead, killed ten other youths in political asylum there.

On 24 October Frank País came from Santiago to persuade Castro to postpone the rebel landing until some time the following year. As he had said in an earlier letter sent through secret channels, he had doubts about the efficiency of his armed groups in Oriente 'because they were unprotected, unprepared and uncoordinated'. País and his friend Pepito Tey had worked hard to organize a clandestine network in the province, collecting arms and readying the 26th of July units to rise in the cities while others covered the rebels' landing along Oriente's western coast between Manzanillo and Pilón. In charge of the Movement groups in the landing zone was Celia Sánchez, one of Frank País's closest collaborators. Still, País felt an immediate invasion was inadvisable. Castro remained adamant, stressing that his credibility would be destroyed if he broke his promise to return to Cuba in 1956, and that after the June imprisonments it was risky to stay much longer in Mexico. He and País spent five days arguing, and the young man finally accepted that the landing would come within the next two months.

Castro also faced a problem with the Communists. Back in mid-October, Osvaldo Sánchez Cabrera, a leader of the illegal Popular Socialist Party (PSP), had attempted to talk Fidel out of invading Cuba so soon. Speaking in the name of the party, Sánchez Cabrera had proposed that the expedition be postponed until late January, when the sugar harvest began, so that a sugar workers' strike could be launched to support the landing. Again, Fidel explained that it was vital to keep his word. In mid-November the PSP leadership met secretly in Havana to dispatch another emissary to Castro; this time it was Flavio Bravo, formerly secretary-general of Socialist Youth, university friend of Fidel and ideological mentor of Raúl.

The Communist message was that in the Party's opinion the internal situation in Cuba was 'unfavourable to military action prior to 31 December', that the invasion did not take political realities into account, and that it could easily result in a damaging failure. Flavio Bravo reminded Fidel that at one stage in the Independence War, José Martí himself had recognized the need to 'postpone military action until he had created more favourable material and subjective conditions'. But Fidel thought he understood subjective conditions better than the PSP (not to mention Martí) and he said so to Flavio Bravo. The envoy continued to insist that anti-Batista opposition was 'very disunited'. The PSP, he said, wished to bring all the young revolutionary groups together before embarking on an insurrection: otherwise the masses would not follow. Specifically, the Communists urged Castro to postpone the invasion, and then issue a short document denouncing Batista, calling for unity of the opposition and demanding general elections with guarantees for all political parties. The Communists suggested that it would be best couched as an open letter by Castro to workers, students, peasants, the youth and all the civic institutions. It would be, Flavio Bravo said, the 'final call' for a peaceful solution, and the anticipated refusal by Batista would justify before public opinion a turn to armed action against his dictatorship.

Castro patiently explained to Flavio Bravo that he had no alternative but to move soon. Not only had he a promise to keep but the Mexican police were on the offensive again. A cache of arms had been confiscated and both Pedro Miret and Teresa Casuso had been arrested. If he did not sail soon, Castro said, he could lose all his men and all his arms. He hoped that his arrival would be met by uprisings, and he was asking the Communist Party for its cooperation. Subsequent official accounts make this exchange appear as a friendly review of the situation, but for Fidel this was a tough political fight; the Communists still had no faith in him, and still intended to take over his revolution.

On that same day Fidel Castro learned that his father, Don Ángel, had died in Birán on 21 October. There is nothing known of Fidel's reaction; there are no known letters about it.

On 19 November General Francisco Tabernilla, the army chief of staff, told the press in Havana that 'there is no possibility of a landing as announced by Fidel Castro' because 'from a technical viewpoint, any landing by a group of undisciplined men without military experience or the proper equipment for combat must inevitably end in failure'. At the same time, however, Cuban warships and aircraft were patrolling the coasts from Pinar del Río in the west to Oriente in the east, and army and Rural Guard garrisons were on the alert.

Fidel Castro realized that the decision to sail had to be taken immediately, but he was delaying it mainly because *Granma* was not quite ready. As a result, much of the work on the engines and on general seaworthiness was done too quickly and carelessly. Then on 21 November, when two rebels defected from the Abasolo training camp near the United States border south of Matamoros, Castro knew that he could not wait any longer. On 23 November he travelled at night from Mexico City to the house on the river in Tuxpán to supervise the loading of arms, ammunition and supplies aboard the *Granma*; simultaneously rebel commanders at all the training camps from Abasolo and Veracruz to Mexico City were ordered to move their men to Tuxpán. They began arriving by bus and car under torrential rain.

Before leaving Mexico City Castro sent coded messages to Frank País that he would land in Cuba on 30 November, and that the chosen spot would be Playa las Coloradas below the town of Bélic, south of Niquero on the west coast of Oriente. Then, on 24 November, in his car driving to Tuxpán, he wrote his will and gave instructions for it to be sent to his friends with whom Fidelito had been staying for more than a year. He wrote: 'I leave my son in the custody of Engineer Alfonso Gutiérrez and his wife Orquídea Pino. I am making this decision because I do not want, in my absence, to see my son Fidelito in the hands of those who have been my most ferocious enemies and detractors, those who, in a base act without its equal, and using my family ties, attacked my home and sacrificed it to the interest of a bloody tyranny that they continue to serve. Because my wife has demonstrated herself incapable of breaking away from the influence of her family, my son could well be inculcated with the detestable ideas that I now fight. I adopt this measure not out of resentment, but thinking solely of my son's future. I leave him to those who can educate him best, a good and generous family, my best friends in exile, in whose house Cuban revolutionaries have found a true home. I leave my son to them and to Mexico, so that he can grow and learn in this friendly and free country . . . He should not return to Cuba until it is free or he can fight for its freedom. I hope that this just and natural desire on my part with regard to my son, the only one I have, will be fulfilled.'

(On 15 December, days after the landing of the *Granma*, Fidel's sister Emma reported to the Mexican Federal Police that 'three unknown persons, armed with pistols, intercepted the automobile in which we were travelling at the corner of Revolución and Martí avenues, seizing my nephew, Fidel Castro Díaz, seven years old. . .' In Havana, however, Foreign Minister Gonzálo Güell announced: 'The child is with his mother, which excludes the possibility that it could be considered a kidnapping. . .')

Wearing a black cape over his dark wool suit, Castro stood in the rain on the dock, watching his eighty-one men embarking aboard the small white yacht. Tuxpán harbour was closed because of stormy weather, but El Cuate persuaded his friend the harbour master to let him sail 'because I was planning a little party aboard'. Universo Sánchez asked somebody: 'When do we get to the real ship? Where is the mother ship?'

At 1.30 a.m. on 25 November *Granma* started her engines, slid out of her dock, and sailed without lights along the river, towards the sea and Cuba. El Cuate followed the yacht in his car along the river road until she reached the open sea and vanished in the darkness.

Chapter 9

Instead of the five days and nights that Fidel Castro had planned, the crossing of the *Granma* from Tuxpán on the Mexican coast of the gulf to the coast of Oriente in Cuba was a nightmare that lasted seven days and four hours. Terrifying weather whipped by a powerful *El Norte* wind, mechanical breakdowns, the yacht's staggering burden of eight-two heavily armed men instead of the twenty-five passengers she was built to carry (Castro had left a further fifty rebels behind simply because there was no more space aboard), and the presence on the boat of only three experienced sailors, all this contributed to the misery and delay. The delay, in turn, provoked tragedy ashore.

Castro's plan was risky but it was not unreasonable. In relatively good weather it should have worked. The chosen route – it added up to 1235 miles – made strategic sense, and the time allowed for it was fairly realistic. The yacht was to sail a virtually straight west–east track; from Tuxpán to the exit from the Gulf of Mexico at the tip of the Yucatán peninsula; then crossing the passage between the peninsula's tip and the westernmost point of Cuba (this was potentially the most dangerous because patrolling Cuban navy and air force units could most easily spot the *Granma* there); dipping south at a safe distance from Cuba's southern coasts; and hitting the western shores of Oriente province below Niquero. The risk of being caught in the Gulf of Mexico was minimal because operationally this was too far for Batista's air-and-sea forces, and once the vessel had entered the Caribbean, Castro would capitalize on the deception factor, sailing eastwards, far from the Cuban coast, only making a run for the Oriente coast at the very last minute. Batista ships and planes did not patrol that far south; Castro would be practically in British waters off the Cayman Islands.

Also, although the extremely foul weather made the crossing exceedingly difficult, with the *Granma* grossly overloaded, mechanically unfit and poorly steered, the conditions worked against Batista, too. The regime had begun to believe privately that Castro was mad enough to make the dash to Cuba, and its Intelligence services came up with a list of vessels in Mexican ports that the rebels might be planning to use in an invasion; the list included the *Granma*. Starting on 5 November, and in total secrecy, the air force began flying constant patrols along the north and south coasts of Oriente with one or more B-25 light bombers or C-47 transports (Cuban history had persuaded the regime, as it had Castro, that the landing *had* to be in Oriente). The regime also began deploying ground forces to Oriente, artillery units were flown from Havana to Holguín (coincidentally the day after the *Granma* sailed), and the Santiago garrison was reinforced and placed on alert. But along the southern coast the aircraft patrolled only twenty miles south of the coastline, which was what Castro had figured they would do, while he sailed 170 miles south of it. And the generally bad weather in the last days of November seriously curtailed all the Batista air and sea operations.

For the expeditionaries the horror began the instant they entered the Gulf of Mexico, just before daybreak on 25 November. They hailed the open water by singing the Cuban national anthem and the 26th of July March, and shouting '*Viva la Revolución!*' and 'Down with Batista Dictatorship!' – and then the sea attacked them. Immediately most of the men became violently seasick, throwing up incessantly and, as Universo Sánchez recalled 'shitting in their pants'. They were no longer a fighting force, just a band of desperately sick men. Guevara searched frantically for antihistamines aboard, but there were none. Che wrote: 'The entire boat had a ridiculously tragic aspect: men with anguished faces grabbing their stomachs; some with their heads inside buckets, others collapsed in the strangest positions, motionless, their clothes filthy from vomit . . . except for the two or three sailors and four or five others, the entire contingent was seasick.' Che, Fidel and Faustino Pérez were among those who did not succumb. Then the *Granma* began to take on water, the pump was found to be broken, and they had to bail with two buckets until the leak was located and fixed.

On the third day the weather improved. Castro ordered the rifles calibrated again, and some firing exercises. But it now emerged that the yacht was running at 7.2 knots instead of the 10 knots Captain Onelio Pino and Castro had calculated, and the expedition had fallen badly behind schedule. Zig-zagging to cope with the weather forced further delays, and one of the engines began to fail. With the men feeling better, they became hungry, too, and Castro had to order rationing as he realized that the *Granma* would never reach land within the planned five days. In the rush of departure from Tuxpán, they could take aboard only two thousand oranges, forty-eight tins of condensed milk, four baked hams, two sliced hams, a box of eggs, a hundred chocolate bars and ten pounds of bread; this could not keep eighty-two men adequately in food for over a week. During the last two days, there was simply no food and very little potable water.

On 29 November the *Granma* came within sight of two fishing boats, but as Castro readied their two anti-tank guns against a possible attack the fishermen disappeared. The following morning the expedition was cruising towards Great Cayman Island, only three-fourths of the way to the landing zone. But that was when Frank País and the 26th of July armed groups in Santiago thought Castro would be coming ashore so, according to the battle plan they had worked out, he ordered an uprising to coincide with their landing. He had no way of knowing that the *Granma* was running forty-eight hours late. At 7 a.m. his pathetically small detachment of twenty-eight attacked the National Police and Maritime Police headquarters as scheduled, hoping to be able to follow up with an assault on Moncada. Wearing olive-green uniforms with 26th of July red and black armbands, the rebels set fire to the National Police barracks, but lost Pepito Tey, one of the top Santiago leaders, to an enemy machine-gun barrage. At the Maritime Police they captured weapons, but were unable to move on Moncada; the army had 400 highly trained anti-guerrilla troops in the city. Though some street fighting went on for another day, the rebellion had effectively collapsed. In Havana and elsewhere on the island the Movement and the Student Revolutionary Directorate lacked sufficient means to undertake any kind of further armed action. Fidel listened to Cuban radio reports of the Santiago tragedy, gritting his teeth in impotent rage.

On the beaches between Niquero and Pilón, 26th of July Movement members also awaited Castro in vain that dawn. Celia Sánchez Manduley, the Movement's coordinator in Manzanillo, had assembled five trucks, gasoline drums and several dozen men near the town of Bélic and the Colorada beach. The plan was to transport the *Granma* expeditionaries from the beach to Niquero and Media Luna, to capture arms from the local Rural Guard garrisons, and then move with the 26th of July adherents to the Sierra Maestra, where Castro was to base his guerrilla war. Inland, the Movement's peasant supporters had prepared their mountain homes to receive and feed the *Fidelistas*. But when Castro did not land and word of the Santiago fiasco reached Celia on the evening of 1 December, she had the reception parties pulled back. Now, if and when the *Granma* force reached land, it would be on its own.

Late that night of Saturday 1 December the white yacht was still wallowing in high seas as she approached the Oriente coast. The darkness was total: no moon and no visible coastal lights. Castro ordered the rebels to change into their olive-green uniforms, and he distributed the weapons.

Climbing on to the roof of the cabin to try to spot the Cabo Cruz lighthouse for a navigational fix – Cabo Cruz is on the south-western tip of the Oriente coast – Roberto Roque, the navigator, slipped and fell overboard. Despite the darkness Castro ordered the *Granma* to undertake a search for Roque. After sailing in circles for an hour the rebels heard a weak voice from the water and, incredibly, they found him, and with just a lantern to shine out over the waves, Che Guevara and Faustino Pérez, both physicians revived the nearly-drowned Roque, and Castro proclaimed that now they were on their way to victory.

Resuming its careful progress towards the coast, *Granma* entered the Niquero channel at low tide, and as he checked the buoys Captain Pino realized that his charts were wrong, and he did not know where he was. The dawn of Sunday 2 December had begun to break when the yacht suddenly hit mud and came to a dead halt. The time was 4.20 a.m., the spot Los Cayuelos, more than a mile south of the beach where Castro had wanted to land (and just below the ironically named Purgatorio Point). The men were ordered to jump into the water, carrying only their personal weapons. All the heavy equipment and stores were left behind. René Rodríguez, slight of build, was the first to go, and the bottom held him; the much heavier Castro followed, sinking up to his hips in the mud. Che Guevara remarked later: 'This wasn't a landing, it was a shipwreck.' The yacht was stuck some hundred yards from what appeared to be the coast, and Fidel and his men managed to wade ashore. Che Guevara and Raúl Castro were the last to leave the *Granma*, trying to salvage some equipment.

When they reached the shore, however, the rebels discovered they were in a huge mangrove swamp. Gnarled tree roots rose in an appalling obstacle course, vines and razor-like leaves slashed their faces, and vast clouds of mosquitoes tried to devour them. The men's brand-new heavy boots slowed their advance; some boots and uniforms were so soaked and cut that they began coming apart; rifles and ammuniton became wet; equipment was lost. The 'general staff', consisting of Fidel Castro, Juan Manuel Márquez and Faustino Pérez (the former with the title of commander-in-chief, and the two others with the rank of captain), led the way, with men constantly tripping over submerged tree trunks, falling down, picking each other up, leaning on one another, and somehow succeeding in moving ahead. Until a man has actually tried to cross a mangrove swamp he cannot begin to understand the lung-bursting effort it demands.

It took Castro's guerrilla army over two hours to reach firm ground across the mangrove and a lagoon in the centre of it, a distance of less than a mile in a straight line; it was a frightening and exhausting experience for them after a week at sea in the overcrowded little yacht. When they finally reached firm ground they collapsed, panting, to rest. But Juan Manuel Márquez and seven other men were missing; they seemed to have been swallowed by the swamp, and their companions were immensely concerned.

Still, Fidel Castro had fulfilled his promise: he had returned to Cuba before the end of 1956, and now he was ready to open his war on Batista. Like José Martí, who had landed at Playitas in the dark with a handful of companions sixty years earlier, Fidel Castro stood on the coast of Oriente on this 2 December, anxious to liberate Cuba from her enemies.

Batista, however, was ready for Castro. A forty-five day suspension of constitutional guarantees had been decreed when Frank País rose in Santiago on 30 November, and in less than two hours after the landing the military authorities knew that Castro was back in Cuba. The sand-carrying barge *Jibarita* and a coastal craft had both observed the *Granma* stuck in the mud off Los Cayuelos, immediately informing the navy. On the afternoon of 2 December Castro had eighty-one men (Juan Manuel Márquez and the seven others had emerged from the mangrove slightly to the north, rejoining the main group) with minimal armament, no food, and no contact with the Movement ashore. The Batista regime had a standing army, navy and air force of over 40,000 men – plus the militarized Rural Guard and the National Police. It had Sherman tanks and artillery, and in mid-November, just before Castro sailed from Tuxpán, the American Ambassador in Havana, Arthur Gardner, had turned over a squadron of T-33 jet trainers (usable in combat) to the Cuban Army Air Force.

News of the landing on the south-western coast reached the commander of the Rural Guard at Manzanillo after seven o'clock in the morning, just as the rebels were reaching firm ground. A bombardment was ordered. Then a patrol was sent out, and although it returned late in the day without finding the *Fidelistas*, its commanding officer reported that local peasants spoke of 'some two hundred men, well armed, and directed by Dr Fidel Castro'.

It was Castro who had identified himself to the peasants. On the high ground above the mangrove the rebels came upon the shack of Ángel Pérez Rosabal, a charcoal burner and the first person they saw ashore. Castro said: 'Have no fear, I am Fidel Castro. We come to liberate the Cuban people.' This was exactly the sort of thing that Castro would say, but official accounts that Rosabal, a destitute and illiterate peasant living in a poor and thinly populated area, had heard of Castro beforehand are less than credible. In any event, Rosabal invited Castro and several of his men inside his hut, and shared food with them. At that moment, hearing powerful explosions along the coast, Fidel ordered a forced march into nearby hills, with Rosabal guiding the column. The explosions came from a bombardment of the mangrove by a coast guard vessel and army aircraft, and Castro feared that air attacks would be made on coastal huts as well. Most likely, a peasant there heard Castro introducing himself to

Rosabal, and passed on the word to Rural Guard soldiers. Rosabal himself returned to his home by mid-afternoon. In the hills the hungry rebels came upon two other peasants who showed them a well and raised water for them; they also found a beehive, helping themselves to honey.

While the Castro contingent halted for their first night in Cuba on a wooded hill, the regime was already claiming total victory. Rural Guard units and an artillery battalion converged on Niquero where the rebel attack was expected, and additional reinforcements were ordered to the region. Although government forces failed to locate the rebels that Sunday, General Pedro Rodríguez Ávila, the army inspector general in command of the operations in Oriente, informed the press that military aircraft had 'strafed and bombed the expeditionary force, annihiliating forty members of the supreme command of the revolutionary 26th of July Movement . . . among them its chief, Fidel Castro, thirty years old'. The general further said that the army had collected the bodies of the rebels and that, besides Fidel, the cadavers of Raúl Castro and Juan Manuel Márquez were identified by documents in their pockets. The rebels, the general reported, were 'literally pulverized' by the air attacks, and official sources indicated the bodies would be brought to Havana by navy ships. This army report was the origin of the news, disseminated worldwide by Francis McCarthy, the United Press bureau chief in Havana, that Castro had been killed, and that his identity was confirmed by the passport he carried in his pocket. At first the story was believed in Cuba and abroad, but before long the Batista regime paid a dear price in credibility for false reporting (and Castro never forgave McCarthy for prematurely announcing his death; the UP newsman had to leave Cuba when the *Fidelistas* won).

The Sierra Maestra is a massif rising along the south coast of Oriente, from the western foothills right past Cabo Cruz all the way to Santiago in the east. It runs for roughly eighty miles on a west–east line, and for some thirty miles at its broadest north–south stretch. The spine, called *el firme* in Spanish, averages 4500 feet in altitude, and its highest point (also Cuba's highest) is Pico Turquino, slightly over 6000 feet. The Sierra Maestra's terrain is forbidding – mountain peaks and valleys, forest and boulders, rivers and streams – even today the region is poor and sparsely inhabited. At the time of Fidel Castro's appearance there the area was almost wholly isolated from the rest of the country, no major paved highways, and unpaved roads often impassable because of drenching rains which turned them into deep, red mud. Tough as it was to move through these mountains, the Sierra Maestra was ideal guerrilla territory. From the moment his expedition came ashore at Los Cayuelos, and the plan to take Niquero and Media Luna had to be aborted, Castro knew he must break out of the western foothills, where the rebels were so vulnerable to air and ground attacks, into the safety of the Sierra Maestra.

As they marched east the men's orders were always to keep the low-lying sugarcane fields on the left, and the mountains on the right in order to reach the Sierra haven.

Although Castro had always planned to launch the war from the Sierra Maestra and all the preparations ashore by his local supporters were geared to this, doubt remains as to the precise strategy he had in mind when he landed in Cuba. Faustino Pérez, who was one of Fidel's two chiefs of staff, says that while they were sailing on the *Granma* 'none of us was convinced that the struggle would develop fundamentally through [the creation of] an army in the mountains'. He explains: 'The vision we had was that of a nationally organized Movement, a general strike, and also a guerrilla focus that would have a very great symbolic importance, but would never offer at any given moment the possibility of defeating the tyrant's army.' But, Faustino adds: 'What in fact happened was that the companions who stayed in the mountains began acquiring confidence, the guerrilla [force] was growing, blows were being dealt to the tyrant's army, and it became conceivable that in this way a revolutionary army could be built, capable of defeating the forces of the tyranny.' At the same time, he says, urban groups of the 26th of July Movement always believed that much could be achieved through insurrection in the cities.

Fidel Castro, on the other hand, had a different concept of the basic rebel strategy – or, at least, he has it now. In an interview twenty years after the start of the guerrilla war, he said: 'We did not arrive in the Sierra merely with the purpose of creating a centre of disturbance throughout the island. . .' This difference between Pérez and Castro in interpreting the initial strategy of the guerrilla war is extremely important in understanding the whole Cuban revolutionary process because the argument over whether the overall leadership should be centred in the Sierra or shared with the urban underground soon became the war's central political issue. Subsequently it led to the disappearane of the 26th of July Movement and the emergence of 'unity' under the auspices of Castro's 'new' Communist Party. In all fairness, however, the record shows that on numerous occasions *before* the December 1956 landing Fidel had forcefully argued that a revolution cannot be accomplished in collaboration with an existing army.

The story of how Castro was able to recover from a serious initial defeat, regroup, fight, start winning against Batista units, and form an ultimately victorious rebel army, is basically the story of the extraordinary support he received from Sierra Maestra peasants. Without this support, first from individuals and then from whole networks of people, Fidel would never have survived the initial weeks in the mountains, nor would he have been able to organize the guerrillas. Peasants and their families hid and protected the poorly-armed and famished little rebel band in the beginning, they served later as a principal channel for obtaining food and arms and ammunition from what could be found in the Sierra or brought up from the urban underground groups and, finally, they provided a source of manpower. It was not exactly a peasant revolution that gave Fidel Castro power, but certainly there would have been no revolution without the peasants. And it was Castro who knew how to inspire such a display of solidarity and sacrifice, despite the danger it presented to the peasant's lives.

The story of Fidel Castro's rebels and the Sierra Maestra peasants begins with the débâcle at Alegría de Pío on Wednesday 5 December when the Rural Guard ambushed, dispersed and nearly annihilated the expeditionary force on their fourth day in Cuba. The men had spent their second night in Cuba, the night of 3–4 December, in a clearing on another wooded hill, this one called La Trocha, after marching east all day over a boulder-strewn path, guided by Tato Vega, the son of a peasant at whose shack they had stopped at noon. The expeditionaries dined on rice and blackbeans, and had a good rest. Tato Vega left them, saying he was going home, and it never occurred to the still inexperienced guerrilla leaders that he would look for Rural Guard units and report to them the rebels' presence in the area. This was one of very few acts of betrayal in the Sierra, but one that resulted in a catastrophe. On 4 December, a Tuesday, the Castro column resumed the march east, coming to a tiny charcoal-burners' village called Agua Fina where a Spanish store-owner gave the rebels some tinned sausage and crackers. Because the terrain ahead of them was now mainly canefields where they could be spotted by aircraft, Fidel decided to march all night after a brief dinner pause. They arrived at the spot known as Alegría de Pío on the morning of 5 December in a state of absolute exhaustion; it had taken three days and two nights to cover the twenty-two miles over rocks and boulders from the landing point to the low hillside where Castro now ordered them to set up camp.

In this he committed three major errors. The first was his choice of an unprotected low hill jutting into the canefield, instead of a higher and wooded hill that was slightly further off. But the men were so fatigued that he hesitated to ask them to advance another several hundred yards; in spite of their arduous training the night uphill march over the rocks that Cubans call 'dogs' teeth' had been too much for them. The second mistake was to deploy sentries too near the camp, thereby cutting down warning time when the attack came. Thirdly, Castro had paid no attention to the trail of sugarcane debris the men were leaving behind as they sucked pieces of the cane during their march. And added to these errors was the treason of Tato Vega, their guide.

Shortly after 4 p.m. on 5 December the men awoke and were each given a piece of sausage, a cracker and a mouthful of condensed milk. Quite a few rebels had taken off their boots to wrap bandages on their bleeding feet. At 4.30 p.m., in the words of Raúl Castro, 'The great public sacrifice began . . . we were ambushed by the army.' A 100-man Rural Guard company, firing machine guns and rifles at the rebels, turned the hillside into what Raúl described as an inferno. The revolutionary contingent simply came apart.

Fidel kept firing his rifle while roaring orders for an orderly retreat, hoping his men could hide in the canefields and regroup. But, as at Moncada, the time for regrouping was past, and it had to be each man for himself. Che Guevara was hit by a bullet in the lower shoulder, and Faustino Pérez, who was next to him, thought the Argentinian had been killed. Later Guevara wrote in his diary: 'I thought of myself as dead, and I told Faustino from the ground. "they fucked me" . . . Immediately, at that moment when all seemed lost, I began to think about the best way of dying. I remembered an old story by Jack London in which the protagonist, leaning against a tree trunk, prepares to end his life with dignity, knowing he is condemned to freeze to death in the plains of Alaska. This is the only image I remember.' Actually, Che's wound was superficial and he escaped the trap, moving east with four companions, including Juan Almeida and Ramiro Valdés. Fidel, Faustino and Universo Sánchez found themselves together later that afternoon, obliged to start their odyssey on hands and knees, under sugarcane straw.

The Rebel Army was destroyed. Three expeditionaries are known to have been killed in battle that afternoon. Many of them inside burning canefields, the remaining seventy-nine men broke up, some into separate little groups, such as Fidel's and Che's, others hoping to make it to safety on their own. One of these was Juan Manuel Márquez, the second chief of staff, who was quickly captured by the army, and brutally murdered. Jesús Montané, too, was captured, but then taken to prison in Havana. Twenty-one others were also known to have been executed within the next few days, twenty-two were caught and imprisoned, and nineteen more simply vanished; some made their way out of the Sierra to return home and hide, or surrender, some were never seen again. From the eighty-two men who landed from the *Granma*, only sixteen survived Alegría de Pío to pursue the war.

Fortunately, however, the entire leadership, except for Juan Manuel Márquez and Ñico López (also captured and executed), stayed alive to fight another day. Though Fidel would not know about them for a number of days, apart from him and Che, among the sixteen survivors were Raúl, Faustino Pérez, Juan Almeida, Ramiro Valdés and Camilo Cienfuegos. Even so, as he lay under the sugarcane *paja* with his two companions, Fidel was whispering inexhaustibly about how and when they would regroup and go back into battle. As Faustino Pérez remembers: 'This was the great lesson of faith and optimism – as well as of realism – that Fidel taught us in those days.' But none of it would have helped Castro had it not been for the peasants of the Sierra Maestra.

In the aftermath of Alegría de Pío, General Batista and his government were absolutely convinced that Fidel Castro was dead and his expeditionary force completely smashed. With so many prisoners captured by the army, Batista was justified in assuming that the danger was over. Even if Castro himself had not yet been located it was obviously only a question of time before he was. Consequently on 13 December the army high command withdrew most of the combat units from the Sierra Maestra region, leaving behind normal Rural Guard garrisons in towns and villages; aerial surveillance was likewise cancelled. An official comuniqué said the command considered 'the insurrection movement' to have ended. And Fidel's relatives, friends and followers were just as certain that the great revolutionary adventure had collapsed and that Fidel and Raúl were most likely dead. Their mother, Lina Ruz de Castro, told a Holguín newspaper: 'If they let me go up the Niquero mountains, I shall make them come down with me . . . I suffer as the mother of soldiers and revolutionaries, but if Fidel and Raúl decide to die, I pray that they may die with dignity . . . I weep for my sons, and I would embrace the mothers of the companions of my sons in the same way as the mothers of the government soldiers who have died in this painful war.'

Still in mourning after her husband's death in October, Lina Ruz de Castro then travelled to Santiago with her oldest son Ramón to settle inheritance problems – including Fidel's and Raúl's inheritances. Three weeks after Alegría de Pío there was still absolutely no information about Fidel's fate. Marta Rojas, the reporter who had covered Castro's *History Will Absolve Me* speech, wrote in *Bohemia* magazine that Fidelito, now back in Havana with his mother Mirta (whose new husband was the son of Cuba's chief delegate to the United Nations), kept asking, 'Has Papa written? Where is Papa?' Mirta now insisted that she had not kidnapped Fidelito in Mexico, but that his paternal aunts, Lidia and Emma, had voluntarily surrendered him to her.

Even with crucial help from Sierra peasants, it had in fact taken Fidel and his two companions six days to reach the Cinco Palmas farmhouse of Ramón (Mongo) Pérez in Purial de Vicana on the Vicana river, some thirty-five tortuous miles north-east of Alegría de Pío. Mongo Pérez was the brother of Crescencio Pérez, one of the two key members of the 26th of July Movement's peasant underground who had vainly awaited the *Granma*'s arrival on the last day of November under the command of Celia Sánchez.

Fidel, Faustino and Universo had left their canefield hideout after dark on 10 December, five days after the disastrous battle, walking slowly and carefully in single line, with Universo usually the point man. Guided by the stars and their instincts, they covered two and a half miles that first night, moving north-east. Spending all day in another canefield, the trio resumed the march on the evening of 11 December, and reached a forest-canopied mountain called La Conveniencia after midnight. The cane-fields were behind them, the terrain was less rocky, and they could advance more rapidly. The silhouette of the Sierra Maestra now discernible in the moonlight served as the reference point. Below La Conveniencia, the mountain dipped sharply to the Toro river, with the Sierra Maestra itself beginning on the far side. Fidel spotted a peasant's thatched-roof house down the hillside, but he decided to observe it very carefully before risking a contact. In a downpour that seemed never to end, the three men watched the house for the rest of that night and much of the next day; they had no food and no water, they were drenched, and Universo was suffering with his feet, having lost his boots at Alegría de Pío. When he was convinced that the peasant family was engaged in normal activities – and that there were no soldiers around – Fidel told Faustino to go down to the house. It was 4 p.m. of 12 December, over sixteen hours after they had arrived at La Conveniencia.

The peasant couple, mountain coffee-growers, were Daniel Hidalgo and his wife Cota Coello. On Fidel's instructions Faustino requested food for twenty to twenty-five in order to give the impression that they were an important force. Their hosts slaughtered a piglet, and the three rebels feasted on meat and vegetables. Daniel Hidalgo had heard about a landing by armed men on the coast, and he told Fidel he had heard about him, too. They spent the rest of the afternoon discussing the best ways of penetrating the Sierra Maestra, and at night Fidel decided to move out again. Led by one of Hidalgo's sons, the three revolutionaries went down a narrow canyon, crossed the Toro river, climbed Copal heights and continued on several miles to Yerba heights. Now they were inside the Sierra Maestra.

On the morning of 13 December, after walking all night and covering eight miles through the Sierra forest, Castro and his companions arrived at the house of Rubén and Walterio Tejeda, brothers who belonged to the peasant network of the 26th of July Movement. At last they had made contact with the organization, and no longer had to depend on luck. Following a three-hour rest and a meal of *malanga* roots and milk, the trio continued through the mountains to a farmhouse near the village of El Plátan. This was the mountain fief of the García family, really a tribe, and it was the home of Guillermo García Frías, the childhood friend of Celia Sánchez and for nearly two years an active member of the Movement. But the first García whom Fidel met that noon in a field was Guillermo's father, Adrían García, who was carrying a bucket filled with rice, bread, coffee and milk. He had heard that there were rebels in the area, and he was looking for them with food literally in his hands. Castro had not yet realized how efficient was the Sierra communications network, and he introduced himself to the old man as 'Alejandro', his code name, only to be greeted as 'Fidel'. Later in the day, some twenty young peasants came to the farmhouse to offer their services to the Rebel Army, and Castro promised to take them as soon as he could organize such an army. However, his immediate concern was to get to the Mongo Pérez farmhouse, a planned rendezvous still further to the north-east, because he hoped to find enough of the other expeditionaries there to rebuild his original force. But, first, he had to break through the army cordon left behind around the Sierra Maestra's main massif, and this meant crossing the heavily guarded Pilón–Niquero highway. To get across he needed Guillermo García to guide him. Guillermo was somewhere in the mountains searching for lost rebels (he had watched the Alegría de Pío battle from a mountaintop). Word had gone out for him to rush home, and Fidel decided to wait for him at El Plátano, where he felt reasonably safe.

Guillermo García arrived at his *finca* at one o'clock in the morning of Friday 14 December, and he and Fidel immediately launched into an all-night conversation. It was a memorable occasion in the history of the Cuban revolution. Guillermo not only was the first peasant officially to join the Rebel Army, but he would become one of its top commanders and, later, a key member of the *Fidelista* regime. If there was a single individual in the Sierra who can be credited with helping Castro to survive and win, it certainly was this tough, squat peasant, then twenty-seven years old.

Guillermo is also one of the most interesting personages of the Cuban revolution, and his background and allegiances go far to explain why from the outset Fidel Castro was able to command such tremendous support from the mountain peasantry. He was one of eleven children in a family that barely subsisted on what it could grow in the rocky soil, and what it could earn from big landowners in the area. One peso a day ($1) was the normal pay there in the 1950s. As Guillermo recalls, the nearest doctor was in Niquero, a day's horseback journey away from the *finca* (two of his brothers had died of gastroenteritis as babies), and the doctor charged two pesos for a visit. 'My physician was my mother with her medicinal herbs from the fields,' he says. The nearest school, a multigrade elementary school, was three miles away in the mountains, and at the age of ten Guillermo quit to go to work. He helped the family in the fields, tended the landowners' cattle (becoming something of a cattleman himself), and still as a child, accompanied an uncle selling produce around the region.

He met Celia Sánchez for the first time when he was twelve years old, and went with his uncle to deliver vegetables every week to her family house in Media Luna, twenty-seven miles or twenty-four hours away on horseback. Celia, who was eight years older than Guillermo, was always politically active, he says, and she enlisted him in the 26th of July Movement in 1955, two years after Moncada. Guillermo García recalls that he was captivated by her explanations of how the Castro ideas represented the aspirations of all young Cubans, particularly given the culture of poverty in which families of his social class had to live. Cuba being a small island, historical and political traditions are important and are passed on from generation to generation, even among the poorest of the population. Peasants and slaves fought colonizers in the nineteenth-century, and Guillermo emphasizes that his grandfather, Bautista Frías Figueredo, was a veteran of the 1895 and 1898 independence wars. During the Spanish–American war over Cuba, Guillermo's ancestors fled from the plains of Oriente to the mountains 'where we constituted something of a tribe, and then we emerged as a new generation, the third peasant generation'. In this sense, Guillermo thinks it was only logical for him to join the 26th of July Movement. Three of his brothers also joined the Rebel Army. One was killed, one ascended to the rank of army general, as Guillermo had, and the third returned to the mountains.

After the Alegría de Pío battle Guillermo was invaluable. Knowing the area like the back of his hand, he coordinated the rescue of many lost rebels and picked up a half-dozen survivors personally. García says the rebels were passed 'very safely, from peasant to peasant, because there, in that area, the peasants were really well organized . . . I could enforce perfect security because I knew the political affiliation of every peasant as well as their morals. Those who had few morals, I sought to isolate totally.' But some of the men saved by Guillermo did not choose to go on looking for Castro.

Fidel and his two companions were in a terrible physical state when he met them that night, Guillermo says, and Faustino Pérez was a 'human rag' from exhaustion, hunger and deep wounds from sharp-edged mountain vegetation. Castro, however, 'was incredible: he started interrogating me about our organization, telling me about the plans he had, how we were going to collect arms for the Sierra, how many shotguns we would need, and so forth . . . It seemed like he already had an army with him . . . So I decided to stick with him.' Although he hadn't slept for forty-eight hours, Castro talked all night, wanting to know everything about army movements, the sentiments of the popu-lation in the region, and which individuals were reliable and which were not.

Late on Friday 14 December Guillermo and two of his friends escorted Fidel, Faustino and Universo down the mountain to a canefield near the village of La Manteca, stopping twice for meals at peasant's homes. The canefield was just off the highway they had to cross to enter the heart of the Sierra Maestra, and Guillermo wanted to wait for a safe moment, when there were no army patrols around. They waited there for over twenty-four hours, until Guillermo decided that the Saturday-night sound of music from the jukebox on a bar at the edge of the highway, singing and shouting, and the rumble from a nearby power plant would drown whatever noise their movements might cause. Flat on the ground, the six men dragged themselves to the mouth of a drainage culvert under the highway, traversing through the mud and rotting, stinking matter inside the pipe to the other side. Guillermo had proposed this as the safest way to cross, and Fidel approved the idea. Afterwards they marched for eleven hours up and down mountainsides, covering twenty-five miles and stopping only once to rest, finally arriving at Mongo Pérez's farmhouse at seven o'clock in the morning of Sunday 16 December. It was exactly two weeks after landing in Cuba that Fidel Castro attained safety – and the real possibility of waging his guerrilla war.

At Mongo Pérez's farm Fidel set up camp in the middle of a canefield, and now the three of them could eat, drink, rest and sleep. Castro's plan was to wait there for some of the other expeditionaries to join them, and then start moving again. Through the peasant information network he learned that there were *Granma* companions in the area the day he arrived, and he sent out the tireless Guillermo to look for them. On Tuesday 18 December Raúl Castro and four companions reached a farmhouse less than a mile from where his brother was camping; for a week now, they too had been guided and fed by Sierra peasants. Raúl made a point of leaving in every case a handwritten note, signed by him as 'Captain', to be displayed after the revolution as proof of help given to the rebels. Informed that Fidel was in the nearby canefield, Raúl sent his Mexican driver's licence via a peasant, so that his brother would know he was approaching with his men. Fidel, always careful, dispatched the peasant back with test questions for Raúl, to confirm his identity further. Just before midnight the brothers embraced in the canefield. Fidel asked Raúl: 'How many rifles did you bring?' and Raúl replied: 'Five . . .' Fidel shouted: 'And with the two I have, this makes seven! Now, yes, we have won the war!' The next day another man, a schoolteacher, Calixto Moráles, arrived unarmed. The Rebel Army was up to nine men and seven rifles.

But there was no time to waste. On 20 December Fidel sent Mongo Pérez to Manzanillo on the north-west coast of Oriente and then on to Santiago to contact Movement leaders there and inform them that the *guerrilleros* were alive and well. He also gave Mongo an enormous list of instructions concerning his needs in food, weapons, supplies and men. Raúl noted in his diary that the peasants 'have a fairly good organization, and we are perfecting it, especially in liaison and espionage . . . Any movement by anyone in these surroundings is immediately communicated to us.' In the evening Fidel moved their camp to a nearby coffee field, close to a creek where they could bathe and swim.

The group of eight rebels which included Che Guevara, Juan Almeida, Ramiro Valdés and Camilo Cienfuegos – all future revolutionary chiefs – met their first peasants on 13 December after a week of wandering aimlessly between the south coast and the foothills of the Sierra Maestra. Then, at a farmhouse sheltered by trees, the eight, so exhausted they could not take another step, spent all night in what Che described as 'an uninterrupted festival of food'. Inevitably, their stomachs un-accustomed to such excess, all eight became violently ill. Next day the peasants gave them fresh clothes to replace their torn uniforms, and the rebels split up into two groups. Except for Che and Almeida who held on to their submachineguns, the rebels left their weapons behind at the farmhouse as they resumed the march to the north-east; they already knew from their hosts that Fidel was alive and awaiting them. Hearing that the army had picked up their scent, Che, Almeida and two other rebels hid at the house in El Mamey, a few miles away, belonging to a Seventh Day Adventist lay preacher named Argelio Rosabal, another extraordinary figure from the Sierra. Not far from them Camilo Cienfuegos was concealed inside the dry well of another farmhouse.

Rosabal, who was a sugarcane field worker during the week and 'with the church on Saturdays', remembers meeting a group of four rebels three days after Alegría de Pío, near his house in the mountains just west of Pilón. He knew there had been a battle involving armed men from a ship, and he gave coffee and clean clothes to the four men, who then went on. They told Rosabal that they had come to 'liberate Cuba'. The lay preacher therupon went to his church, gathered his fellow Adventists, and told them that 'the men who claim they came with the mission to ease a little of our misery . . . must be saved'. He said that 'all of you must take an interest in their lives, and when you learn that there is one or more of them around, you must take them in . . . If you have no courage to do it, advise me . . .' A few days later Rosabal was informed that a group of eight men were hiding in the Sierra house of one of his friends: this was the group that included Che and Almeida, and at that point the lay preacher moved four of them to his house. The next step, he says, was to get them marching again. Rosabal recalls: 'As I am a man of God, I say, "The situation is not easy, so let us pray . . ." We all knelt, and I begged God to help me in this situation.' Che Guevara, who affectionately referred to Rosabal as 'The Pastor', knelt with them, probably for the first time in his life.

Led by Rosabal, Che, still suffering from his shoulder wound, and the three other men marched all that night until they reached the house of the Adventist's sister-in-law where a chicken was killed for a meal. Che threw up twice before his stomach could hold the chicken broth, then

Rosabal removed the men's boots, and stood guard over them as they slept. The next morning Che asked Rosabal if he could send 'anonymous' telegrams to their families, and The Pastor said he would try. Hiding a sheet of paper with their family addresses in a basket of red beans, he walked down the mountain to Pilón and to the house of Celia Sánchez's father, the physician, whom he knew well. He was unaware, however, that the Sánchez family belonged to the clandestine Movement, and he produced the list Che had given him only when he satisfied himself that the doctor would protect the rebels.

Returning to the farmhouse, Rosabal discovered that the army had captured one of the rebels from the original group of eight – he had been left behind because of high fever – and seized the weapons left in the peasant house. Now it was urgent to send Che and his three companions far into the Sierra Maestra, and on 16 December Guillermo García (who happened to be Rosabal's brother-in-law) arrived from Mongo's farm to be their guide. He reassembled the men hiding in the area into a group of six and at dawn on 21 December they arrived at Mongo's homestead to rejoin the Castro brothers (Raúl wrote in his diary that among the survivors was 'my inseparable friend, Ramiro Valdés'). Che reached the *finca* in the midst of an asthma attack, then overcame it. And Guillermo told Che and his companions: 'You will never know how much this man Rosabal did for you. . .'

Indeed there seemed no limit to what the peasants were willing to do for the Castro *guerrilla*. Argeo González, a storekeeper and itinerant merchant in the Sierra when the rebels arrived, explains that 'The reason all the peasants helped them was that they were told the truth about the coming struggle against tyranny . . . The landowners didn't let anybody else work the land, it was all theirs . . . Peasants had no way out without a revolution.' Argeo was among the first regular volunteer suppliers of the growing rebel army, running food and arms up the Sierra Maestra from lowland towns, and he says that although the peasants did not know Castro at the outset, 'he earned their confidence, helping them, and never mistreating them'. When a Rural Guard trooper visited a mountain house, Argeo recalls, 'He would receive bread, demand a chicken if there was one there, take a daughter if there was one there – but the rebels were different; they respected everything, and this was the basis for the confidence they gained'. When a rebel got out of line, he says, Castro would instantly punish him, sometimes have him executed. Peasant women, according to Argeo, were 'the first ones to want to join Castro, to help him'. Universo Sánchez remembers that Fidel insisted on paying ten pesos for a chicken, even if it was worth only five.

Mario Sariol, another Sierra merchant turned secret rebel quarter-master, remembers meeting Castro in a coffee field early in 1957 and being embraced by him after offering to prepare food for the rebels. He recalls that Fidel's beard was just beginning to grow and Raúl had 'a few hairs, nothing more, and they both seemed like callow youths'. Actually, Castro had decided in the beginning that the rebels should not even try to shave while in the mountains; in their Mexican training camp General Bayo had them throw out their razors and toothbrushes 'because you won't have them where you're going . . .' As Sariol tells the story peasants developed a protective feeling about the *Fidelistas*. When Sariol ran out of funds to purchase food for the rebels in the town of Las Mercedes, the local merchant told him: 'Mario, don't let these people go hungry even for one day; come here and take what you need.' He never accepted payment, and Sariol says that later Castro ordered him to keep track of all food caches, making certain there was enough for the peasants as well as the rebels. Sergio Casanova, an enthusiastic peasant volunteer, was turned down by Castro when it turned out he had six children and no income other than an occasional day's work; Fidel told him: 'You can't go with us . . . Who would look after your family?' Remembering these days Casanova says: 'To me, Fidel was a god.'

At Mongo Pérez's farm in Purial de Vicana, Fidel Castro gave his expeditionaries the rest they needed, while at the same time, he kept them at maximum readiness. The day after Che and his group rejoined him the entire contingent was relaxing on a hillside when Castro suddenly shouted: 'We are surrounded by soldiers! Take your battle positions!' The rebels responded at once, flattening themselves on the ground or hiding behind trees, their weapons at the ready, but nothing happened. Nobody moved. Then Castro informed them that this was a false alarm, a training exercise.

At this juncture the Rebel Army had twenty men, including Fidel. Sixteen were *Granma* expeditionaries and four were peasants who had formally enlisted: Guillermo García, Crescencio Pérez, his son Ignacio Pérez, and Manuel Fajardo. Subsequent propaganda emphasized that Castro resumed the war with twelve men, but this was a symbolic apostolic touch. As Guillermo García recalls that period, Castro had taken the decision 'not to fight' until his force could be adequately reorganized. While carefully selected peasants were being allowed to sign up with the rebels, 'it was not adviseable for too many people to gather because then there would be only limited mobility in the case of an enemy attack'. Besides, volunteers had to be recommended by peasants well known to the guerrilla leadership, in order to prevent infiltration by Batista agents.

Castro's greatest problem was arms. He had only twelve weapons for twenty men, and he had been furious at the group led by Che and Almeida for having left their arms behind in a farmhouse. 'To leave behind rifles in such circumstances is to risk paying with one's life . . . for such crime and stupidity,' he berated them. But Mongo's trip to Manzanillo on 20 December brought results very quickly: peasants arrived at the *finca* on the morning of 22 December with a Thompson submachinegun and eight rifles. On 23 December two men and two women (one of them Mongo's daughter) came from Manzanillo, sent by the 26th of July Movement in response to word brought down by Mongo that Fidel was alive. Eugenia Verdecia, the other woman, carried 300 submachinegun bullets and nine dynamite cartridges under her skirt.

More relaxed about arms, Fidel now turned to the politics of the revolution. His first major decision was to send Faustino Pérez to Manzanillo, Santiago and Havana for the twin purposes of informing the National Directorate of the 26th of July Movement about the rebel situation in the Sierra Maestra, and bringing newsmen – foreign newsmen if possible – to the mountains to convince the world that Castro was well and fighting. In Fidel's mind, armed struggle and propaganda were always linked.

Faustino says that he was chosen because he was a member of both the Movement's National Directorate and the military general staff, and thus in an excellent position to organize support for the Rebel Army in the mountains and provide credible confirmation of Castro's fighting presence. The immediate need was for a small group of armed fighters from the lowlands to strengthen the army, and for newspapermen to write about Fidel.

On Sunday 23 December, three weks after the *Granma* brought the *Fidelistas* to Cuba, Faustino got into the Jeep that had carried the four Movement members up the mountain from Manzanillo earlier that day. As the army had cancelled its search-and-destroy operations against Castro the week before, it was not difficult to get through to his destination. Faustino dressed like a *guajiro* with a straw hat, and Eugenia Verdecia, the girl who had concealed submachinegun bullets and dynamite under her skirt on the way up, pretended to be his fiancée. Reaching Manzanillo in the evening, Faustino saw Celia Sánchez immediately after his arrival, and now contact was formally restored between the Rebel Army and the Movement. Faustino and Celia talked all night. But first 'they gave me a meal I can never forget. I was suffering from organic hunger, and they served me some marvellous cream of asparagus soup . . .'

The following day Faustino drove to Santiago for meetings with key members of the Movement's leadership: Frank País, the provincial coordinator who had thought Fidel too precipitate in the invasion, Vilma Espín, his local associate and, from Havana, Armando Hart, Haydée Santamaría and María Antonia Figurea. It was Christmas Day when Faustino Pérez quietly slipped into Havana. It would be almost a year and a half before he returned to the Sierra Maestra.

At Mongo's *finca* the expeditionaries and their peasant friends spent Christmas Eve in a coffee field, eating roast piglet and washing it down with wine. On Christmas Day Fidel decided it was no longer safe to remain there, and that the time had come to move deeper into the Sierra Maestra. Before departing just before midnight fifteen rebels signed a letter of thanks to Mongo Pérez, drafted by Fidel, his first document of the Sierra war, declaring that 'the help that we have received from him and many others like him in the most critical days of the revolution encourages us to continue to struggle with more faith than ever, convinced that a people such as ours deserves every sacrifice . . . '

Castro could not wait to engage in military activities, and the entire night after leaving Mongo's farm was spent in exercises that ranged from an assault on a mud hut to the crossing and recrossing of the Vicana river eighteen times in the dark. Then Fidel turned south-east, moving towards the Caribbean coast through the Sierra's high mountains. On 28 December the rebel column was augmented by three expeditionaries who had been believed lost, and three peasant volunteers. They brought a rifle and, for Fidel, magazines and newspapers – the first he had seen since the *Granma* landing. Reading them, he learned that José Miró Cardona, the president of the Cuban Bar Association, and Elena Mederos, a liberal-minded member of the Society of Friends of the Republic, had met with Batista's Prime Minister Jorge García Montes to demand decent and humanitarian treatments for *Fidelista* rebels captured after Alegría de Pío. Castro filed the names away in his mind: both would be invited to join his revolutionary government.

On 29 December Eugenia Vardecia, concealing sixteen explosive charges, four submachinegun clips, three dynamite cartridges and eight hand grenades, caught up with Castro's column in the hills. Again a Cuban woman was playing a crucial revolutionary role. Her companion brought volumes on the geography and history of Cuba to be used in teaching peasants joining the Rebel Army; Calixto Morales, the school-teacher, was put in charge of education and indoctrination, a vital function in building the new army. Che Guevara received an algebra text he had requested. Then, another all-night march in cold rain with only a two-hour halt at a peasant home where a hot meal awaited the rebels. The Rebel Army, now composed of twenty-nine men (more peasants had joined it), spent New Year's Eve asleep under sentries' guard in a large shed without walls on a wood-covered hillside.

The year 1957 opened for the Castro guerrillas with a downpour of freezing rain that prevented them from advancing for two days. They had nine small nylon covers for the rifles, and nothing to protect themselves. Raúl Castro slept for one night inside a flour sack. The march resumed on 3 January and two days later the rebels stood atop Tatequieto heights on the spine of the Sierra Maestra. In the distance, five miles away, Fidel could see the triple peaks of Caracas mountain to the east. 'If we can get there,' he said, 'neither Batista nor anybody else can defeat us in this war.'

Then they were on the march again, still moving south-east, towards the coast. Castro had concluded that he could reach the centre of the Sierra Maestra more easily from the south, up the natural ridges and canyons, rather than straight east across them. This route was longer, but less punishing. Besides, he had developed the notion of seizing small coastal military garrisons in order to acquire more weapons. The march from Tatequieto to the coast, with the column advancing sometimes at night and sometimes in daytime, took eleven days, until 16 January. More peasants joined it during the first weeks of January, and now the Rebel Army had thirty-three men. On 8 January the rebels halted for two days at the farmhouse of Eutimio Guerra, a trusted peasant, in El Mulato, a village directly south of the Caracas peaks. The men ate, drank brandy with honey, then suddenly learned that their presence had been somehow reported to the army, and Castro ordered instant departure in the middle of the night. The mountains were so steep that the rebels had to climb holding on to the vegetation, sometimes moving on all fours. Ramiro Valdés fell, chipping a knee bone, and Che treated him. Valdés dragged himself as best he could. On 11 January five peasant guerrillas decided to return home, and Castro let them go. He had already resolved to attack the garrison at La Plata on the coast, and he wanted to be surrounded only by men he could fully trust. On 13 January government forces arrested eleven local peasants; all were murdered.

On 14 January the rebels came to the banks of the Magdalena river, just west of La Plata, leaving the injured Ramiro Valdés and another ailing rebel at a mountain farmhouse. Crossing the Magdalena, they ran into two beekeepers. They paid ten pesos for sixty pounds of honey, but decided to keep one of the beekeepers as hostage to protect themselves; the other beekeeper was let go, taking an oath of silence. The hostage was paid five pesos a day during captivity, and Castro let him sleep in his hammock. The next day, now guided by the beekeeper, the *Fidelistas* reached heights overlooking the estuary of La Plata river, and could see uniformed soldiers below around the post's four buildings, the military barracks and the house of the foreman of the company owning the land in the area.

In Havana General Batista announced on 15 January that the United States had sold his regime sixteen brand-new B-26 bombers. Batista was still sceptical about a Castro revolution, but now he knew that Fidel was alive somewhere in Oriente, and he thought it prudent to strengthen his armed forces. The Eisenhower administration was glad to oblige. Above La Plata that same day Fidel Castro was preparing his first attack on the Batista forces since Moncada, three and a half years ago. The little garrison on the beach consisted of five Rural Guard soldiers and five sailors under the command of an army sergeant, (a coast guard cutter sat offshore).

Castro had twenty-two men with him and, for once, numerical superiority. With a few rebels he moved on the night of 16 January to a point about three hundred yards from the barracks, awaiting passers-by who could tell him exactly what the soldiers below were doing. Four peasants told Castro that Chicho Osorio, the land company overseer, feared and detested by the local peasants, should be coming by on his way home. Presently the fifty-year-old Osorio, mounted on a yellow mule, a brandy bottle in his hand, and completely drunk, appeared on the trail. He was captured by Castro and his .45 pistol was taken away. Fidel introduced himself as an army colonel, and the overseer, putting in his false teeth, told him that 'the order is to kill Fidel Castro . . . If I find him, I'll kill him like a dog . . . You see this .45 you took away from me? I'll kill him with this gun if I catch him. . .' Then Osorio proceeded to give Fidel the names of the peasants in the region who cooperated with the army and those suspected of helping the rebels. He added: 'You see the boots I'm wearing? They belonged to one of those who came with Fidel Castro, and whom we killed around here. . .' Che Guevara wrote later that at that moment Chicho Osorio had signed his own death warrant.

Castro had Osorio's hands tied behind his back, and in the following dawn, 17 January, asked him to guide his force to the military barracks, pretending that as a colonel he wanted to surprise the slothful soldiers there. Still drunk, the overseer happily agreed. The rebels were divided into four squads – Fidel, Che and four other fighters deployed to the right of the target area, the other squads closing the circle. At 2.30 a.m. the *Fidelistas* started firing on the garrison. Simultaneously Chicho Osorio was executed on Fidel's orders by rebels guarding him. The rebels were totally unforgiving when it came to traitors and 'exploiters' of the people, men said to have killed and mistreated peasant families.

The combat was brief. Two soldiers were killed, five wounded (three of them died later), one escaped, and three were taken prisoner. The barracks and other structures were set on fire, and weapons and ammunition were collected. The booty was nine Springfield rifles and a Thompson submachinegun, plus plenty of munitions and other supplies. This was the first time since Alegría de Pío that Fidel had more weapons than men. It was his first victory, and with no losses, and he and his companions showed magnanimity. Che treated the wounded, and Fidel told the prisoners: 'I congratulate you. You behaved like men. You are free. Look after your wounded, and leave whenever you want.' The rebels left medicine for the enemy wounded before vanishing back in the Sierra Maestra. At La Plata Castro set the policy towards his enemies for

Castro and supporters in the jungle. *(Popperfoto)*

Emphasising a point during an inaugural speech, 16 February 1959. *(Popperfoto)*

With his son, Fidelito, at the Hilton, Havana. *(Popperfoto)*

With his brother, Ramon. *(John Hillelson Agency Ltd)*

At breakfast in his Havana home, with Juan Orta, Celia Sanchez, and Fidelito, trying on his father's hat. *(John Hillelson Agency Ltd)*

At a farm in Northern Chile. *(John Hillelson Agency Ltd)*

The heady days of January 1959 when Batista was ousted. *(John Hillelson Agency Ltd)*

Bienvenido Fidel. *(John Hillelson Agency Ltd)*

The Baseball Fan. *(Popperfoto)*

The historic meeting in New York on 23 September, 1960, with Nikita Krushchev. *(Popperfoto)*

Above: In Nicaragua, January 1985. *(John Hillelson Agency Ltd)*

Below left: In New York, October 1979. *(John Hillelson Agency Ltd)*

Below right: In Havana, May 1986. *(Frank Spooner Pictures)*

the rest of the war: prisoners were always sent back alive, traitors and 'exploiters' were mercilessly executed.

La Plata was a significant milestone in the guerrilla war. Pedro Álvarez Tabío, the official historian of the Sierra Maestra era, says that this battle 'demonstrated for the first time the axiom that Fidel would apply throughout the whole war: that a *guerrilla* army must live on weapons and supplies captured from the enemy [and] except for a few shipments of arms received from outside the Sierra, this would be the state of affairs during the entire war.' Exactly two hours after the start of the battle Fidel Castro ordered his triumphant men back into the heart of the Sierra Maestra. It was 4.30 a.m. of 17 January 1957, and he set the peaks of Palma Mocha as the next objective.

Chapter 10

Two weeks after the victory at La Plata, Fidel Castro's *guerrilla* barely escaped alive from an extraordinarily precise surprise aerial attack on their camp in the heart of the Sierra Maestra by B-26 bombers and P-47 fighters of the Batista army. It was sheer luck that the rebels lost no men in this raid (a bomb exploded on top of the big kitchen stove on which breakfast was being cooked that morning), but they were once more dispersed and disorganized. Only on the third day after the furious bombing and strafing of the *guerrilleros* high up on the side of the Caracas peaks was Castro able to reassemble his force; it had been divided into three groups led, respectively, by him, by Raúl and by Che.

The drama of Caracas also served to make it virtually official that Raúl and Che had now become the principal rebel leaders under Fidel. In the two months since the landing of the *Granma* they easily eclipsed their surviving fellow officers and such prominent fighters as Ramiro Valdés, Camilo Cienfuegos and Universo Sánchez. Raúl and Che had a degree of education and sophistication their present companions lacked, and they were much more politically mature than the others. Raúl had been a member of the Cuban Communist Party for nearly four years, and Che, three years older, was a serious student of Marxism–Leninism, never concealing his allegiance.

In terms of their relationships with Fidel there is no question that Raúl was the closest personally and politically. He was a practical politician and the natural number two figure in the *guerrilla* – and afterwards. Intellectually, with his erudition, fine irony and quick mind, it was Che who had the greatest kinship with Fidel. Both were superb chess players. Though Che never quite overcame his complex about being a foreigner among Cubans, he tried to be the conscience of the Cuban revolution. He was not a practical politician, his revolutionary principles were above compromise. He did not hesitate to disagree with Fidel over matters of ideology during the war in the Sierra, nor to take on the Soviet Union many years later when he thought revolutionary ideals were at stake. Che may have been naïve, but he was the purest and the most honest idealist of the revolution.

Despite outward appearances Che's relations with Raúl were not as warm as they were with Fidel. Still, they were friendly and close, after a fashion. Che taught Raúl to speak French during the long months in the Sierra but he never sought to compete with Raúl in relation to Fidel.

When men are thrown together to fight a war their relationships, character traits, strengths and weaknesses are defined more sharply and quickly than under other circumstances. This was especially true in the Cuban guerrilla war. After two months of this war it was already very clear what Fidel, Raúl and Che represented, both then and for the future. In their actions, beliefs, personal behaviour, conversations, official and private letters and, in the case of Raúl and Che, in the campaign diaries they kept, they were acutely aware of their historic roles. The campaign diaries were poetic, romantic and frankly lyrical. Fidel's literary output in the two years of the Sierra, on the other hand, was of an epistolary, order-of-the-day and political-manifesto nature. Knowing Fidel, Raúl and Che in the Sierra Maestra was to know them afterwards, even when they wielded great power. They never really changed, though the nature of the revolution that sustained them would change.

The man responsible for the bombing on 30 January 1957 was a traitor named Eutimio Guerra at whose house they had rested and prepared for the assault on La Plata and who had guided them up and down the mountain for weeks. That neither Fidel with his sixth sense about danger and betrayal, nor Raúl with his obsession about espionage and counter-espionage, were able to see through this Eutimio represented one of their great failures in the guerrilla war.

Eutimio, slim, thirtyish and ever-smiling, was in fact so highly regarded as a guide and peasant supporter of the revolution that on 20 January Fidel had granted him permission to make a quick visit to his home in El Mulato, a few miles to the north-west of the spot where the rebels were resting that day, and even gave him money. On his way back, however, Eutimio was detained by the army and given the choice of being executed for collaborating with the rebels or of betraying them. Specifically, Eutimio was offered 10,000 pesos, a major's rank in the army and a farm of his choice if he succeeded in assassinating Castro or locating the *guerrilla* so that the Batista troops could destroy it. Apparently he agreed, because he was given an army safe-conduct and sent off on 25 January. At that point Fidel's force was moving west towards the Caracas mountains, en route to the south-western rim of the Sierra for a planned conference with 26th of July Movement leaders from

the cities. Two days later Eutimio encountered the rebels in a coffee field
at La Olla, near El Mulato. He was warmly greeted by the unsuspecting
guerrillas, and told them a long story about crossing the Llanos de
Infierno battlefield, finding burned-out houses, and hurrying to warn
Fidel that the army was in the vicinity. He also brought them candy.

On the strength of his reports Castro decided to move on during the
night to a high saddle on the Caracas mountain, and to remain there.
Because the night was cold Fidel shared his blanket with Eutimio as they
lay down to sleep on the ground. The peasant had his Colt pistol and two
hand grenades under the blanket, and he proceeded to ask Fidel questions
about the locations of sentries around them. Instinctively Fidel gave him
evasive answers. Eutimio evidently hadn't the courage to shoot Castro
then and there, prefering to let the army do the job. The next morning, 28
January, Eutimio again left the rebels, this time ostensibly to look for
food and locate several *guerrilleros* who had become separated from the
main force. But he went straight to the army forward command near El
Mulato to report on the rebel's deployment. Meanwhile Fidel suddenly
had the idea of moving his men some three hundred yards higher on the
mountain from the canyon where the big kitchen stove had just been
installed; his instinct again saved his companions' lives.

In Castro's judgement their Caracas peak camp was safe from an
encirclement by the army; it was too steep and hard a climb. He
dispatched four men to Manzanillo to deliver additional instructions
concerning his approaching meeting with Movement leaders. The rebel
army on the mountain now had twenty-five fighters, seventeen of them
Granma expeditionaries (additional Alegría de Pío survivors had been
reaching Castro for weeks) and more volunteers were sent up from
Manzanillo. The little army's numbers fluctuated daily with arrivals and
departures. Ramiro Valdés and another rebel were still convalescing in a
farmhouse not far away, but hid in the forest when an army unit was
spotted approaching. The previous evening Fidel's group had rested on
their mountain. Che wrote in his diary that in the evening 'Fidel delivered
a speech to the troops to warn them about the risks of indiscipline and loss
of morale . . . Three crimes would be punished with death: insubordination, desertion and despotism. . .' At that same time Eutimio
Guerra arrived in Macho, south of the Caracas mountains, to confer with
army commanders on how best to destroy Castro. Given the terrain, the
commanders decided that air strikes would be the most effective, and
Eutimio was taken by jeep to the port of Pilón from where the next
morning he would be flown in a spotter plane to pinpoint the guerrilla
camp.

On 30 January, just after seven o'clock in the morning, Batista's
airforce struck the *Fidelistas*, and the rebel army broke up in three groups
to flee the area. Fidel's group of thirteen men crossed the spine of the

Caracas range to the south-east slopes where the aircraft could not see them through the foliage. Castro was enraged that his force allowed itself to be dispersed for the second time, just when he thought he had consolidated the *guerrilla*. But at noon of the next day he was joined by Raúl and his four-man group, and things looked better again. Che, Guillermo García and three other men got lost in the forest, and it was two more days before they caught up with Fidel. On 1 February Castro learned that three army columns were advancing on the Caracas mountains, and he ordered the rebels to resume their westward march. Guerrilla war in the mountain forests is something of a blind man's bluff: neither band can see or hear the other, unless they suddenly collide in the dark, and usually the advantage goes to those with the best scouts and the best knowledge of the terrain. Castro had this advantage and thus he again evaded the army.

Hunger and thirst now became his group's real enemy. They had virtually nothing to eat for two days. On 3 February, while crossing a forest, a rebel fighter collapsed from thirst. Castro gave him a dry lemon he had in his pocket, and the man sucked it. Another rebel drank putrid water from a beer bottle he found on the trail. Che Guevara suffered an attack of malaria, made it to the place where the column would spend the night, and collapsed. He had to stay behind the next day with two companions to look after him. Then they were found by Raúl with a patrol, bringing hot chicken broth.

Eutimio Guerra reappeared late that day, when the men were resting at a farmhouse. He was wearing new white trousers, a cream-coloured *guayabera* and a new hat, and carrying fifty tins of condensed milk. Again he was greeted with joy by the expeditionaries. Castro had decided to divide his army into two teams to make it easier to cross the Sierra to the west, and the first one, including Ramiro Valdés and eight others, left at night. Fidel with twenty men, including Eutimio, stayed behind for another day. Eutimio then asked Castro to meet with him alone in a coffee field, but Universo Sánchez accompanied them, visibly unnerving the peasant guide. Finally Fidel had become suspicious of Eutimio's frequent trips, his ability to obtain food and his constant questions. Nevertheless, unaware that both in Manzanillo and Santiago several Movement members had overheard Eutimio's name in conversations among army officers, he wanted more evidence before acting.

On 7 February Batista aircraft bombed and strafed the Caracas mountains and Eutimio recommended to Castro that they set up camp around an abandoned shed at the bottom of a deep canyon. Fidel agreed, deploying sentries around the canyon. But the planes were back the next day, and bombs fell on the *guerrilla*. Nervously Eutimio joked that 'I didn't tell them to bomb here', and Castro was almost convinced that he had a traitor on his hands. Heavy rain came on Friday 8 February and Raúl bet Fidel and Che that it was raining harder inside the shed in the canyon than outside. Eutimio returned from still another mysterious expedition, volunteering to stand guard at the entrance to the canyon. Apparently the plan was for him to let army units into the canyon, but the rain was so hard that this scheme was abandoned. Now the troops were close to the *guerrilla*. On Saturday 9 February Raúl noted in his diary that 'Eutimio's behaviour preoccupies Fidel' and Universo Sánchez came running into the house, shouting that a large army column was approaching. Eutimio had gone out again that morning, allegedly to buy food.

During the day a local peasant was detained by a rebel sentry, and told Fidel that 140 soldiers were deployed above the canyon. Fidel climbed a rock to watch the enemy positions through his telescopic rifle sight and heard the peasant say that he had seen Eutimio Guerra 'down there' that morning. At last Castro could inform his men that he was convinced that Eutimio was a traitor, and he led the rebels out of the canyon and up the Espinosa peak, which overlooked the area. Suddenly several rebels spotted Eutimio running behind a clump of bushes, and soldiers concealed by nearby ridges opened fire on the *Fidelistas*. Júlio Zenon Acosta, one of the first peasants to join the Rebel Army, was killed instantly; he stood a few steps from Fidel. Che Guevara wrote that Acosta was his first literacy pupil, and that 'we were just beginning to tell the A from the O, and the E from the I . . . This illiterate *guajiro* who was able to understand the enormous tasks the revolution would face, and who was preparing himself for it by learning the first letters, could not complete his labour. . .'

The fight went on for hours, and the rebels again divided themselves into three groups to withdraw to the next mountain. Fidel and Raúl led a group of five under intense fire, dragging themselves through high grass to avoid detection. Brambles tore at their hands. Che, Juan Almeida and ten others worked their way up the mountain from the other side, pursued by soldiers firing at them with automatic weapons. Guevara lost all his medicines, his books and his rifle: 'I was ashamed,' he wrote. Again the rebel army was dispersed, but it had not allowed itself to be surrounded. It lost one war, but the army's sustained effort in the mountains was a fiasco. By a pre-arrangement, all the rebel groups were attempting to reach a nearby mountain called Lomón, and the army, in a final effort to destroy them, sent out planes on 12 February to strafe the forest there. But the *Fidelistas* escaped unscathed, and by nightfall they were back together again, decreased in number to only eighteen men as some of them were away on missions for Fidel, and some peasants had had enough and returned to their homes. The rebels found a farmhouse in a clearing, where they were served roast pork for late dinner. Four days later Fidel Castro reached the farm at the south-western end of the Sierra Maestra where a new chapter in the political history of the revolution would soon be written. The march was easy: only a few harmless mortar attacks by the army. Still, Eutimio Guerra would not be forgotten.

The eighteen men who arrived at the farm of Epifanio Díaz and his wife María Moreno at four o'clock in the morning of Saturday 16 February for meetings with the Movement's National Directorate and a carefully prepared interview with a *New York Times* editorial writer, formed a hardship-toughened and extremely cohesive fighting group. Castro was certain they would make a very positive impression on the visitors; the meetings were important to him as an assertion of his undisputed leadership of the revolution – so much so that he had risked coming to the outer edge of the Sierra Maestra, only twenty-five miles as the crow flies from the city of Manzanillo. Despite the Batista regime's determination to destroy him, Fidel felt in control of the military situation.

'We identified completely with the natural surroundings of the mountains,' he recalls, 'we had adapted so well that we felt in our natural habitat. It was not easy, but I think we identified with the forest as much as the wild animals that live there [actually there are no wild animals in the Sierra Maestra]. We were constantly on the move. We always slept in the forest. At first, we slept on the ground. We had nothing with which to cover ourselves. Later, we had hammocks, and nylon . . . and we used plastic for covers to protect ourselves from the rain. We organized kitchen duty by teams. In the beginning we had to stop at houses to eat, but later we fed ourselves. And yet we did not know the region well. We had practically no political connections there, but we established good relations with the population . . . Batista was carrying on a fiercely repressive campaign, and there were many burned houses, and many murdered peasants. We dealt with the peasants in a very different manner from that of the Batista soldiers, and we slowly gained the support of the rural population – until that support became absolute. Many of our soldiers came from that rural population.'

Che Guevara, always more critical than the others, was more sceptical in his assessments. He wrote: 'The peasantry was not prepared to become part of the struggle, and communication with [the Movement's] bases in the cities was practically non-existent.' To him the first moments after the invasion created a 'subjectivist mentality', a phase when there was 'blind confidence in a rapid popular explosion, enthusiasm and faith in our power to liquidate Batista's might by a swift armed uprising combined with spontaneous revolutionary strikes.' Undeniably, Guevara was right in thinking that their faith was exaggerated, but the key to Fidel Castro's whole approach to the revolution *was* 'subjectivism', a belief that inspiring leadership (his) combined with skilled propaganda could rally the masses behind great national causes. Interestingly, Fidel's own fight with Cuban Communists precisely grew out of his 'subjectivism' versus the Party's classical Marxist view that 'objective conditions' must be created before an insurrection is launched.

In the third month ashore Castro had survived virtually every imaginable disaster. The shipwreck at the edge of a mangrove swamp, a major military defeat, three dispersals of his rebel force, betrayal, and now almost continuous attacks on his tiny army by the Batista air force and at least 3000 elite government troops (the figure is Castro's). Yet none of it could break his determination or his supporters' readiness to help him. What Castro understood, probably better than Guevara, with his blend of Cuban romanticism and Marxist dogma, was that revolutions are not strictly rational affairs. To be sure, the setbacks had taught Fidel the accuracy of Che's disbelief in instant and spontaneous uprisings throughout the island. But in this next phase Castro was able to use magnetism and imagination to keep the morale of his men perhaps unreasonably high and to thus expand the guerrilla war. This brand of 'subjectivism' worked very well in the mountains.

As far as the peasants in general were concerned, their fears of his men disappeared once Castro was able to demonstrate the rebels' kinship with them. Che Guevara himself recognized that the guerrillas 'were the only force which could resist and even punish the abuses' of the army. For the peasants to take refuge among the guerrillas where their lives would be protected, was a good solution for them. Castro's application of 'revolutionary justice' was applauded; whenever a Rural Guard torturer or land company overseer was executed, word spread instantly throughout the mountains. Fidel's rebels endeared themselves even more to the *guajiros* when they set their weapons aside to help with the coffee harvest in May 1957; without their assistance much of the crop would have been lost by the families who depended on it for survival, since many peasants had been removed by the army during punitive expeditions. Naturally Castro delivered a revolutionary speech to the coffee growers in the middle of the Sierra.

To maintain morale among the rebels, and especially the peasant and lowland volunteers, Fidel both enforced rigid discipline (he had decreed that insubordination and desertion were capital offences) and displayed a warm personal relationship with his rebels. Guillermo García remembers that Fidel's relations with his subordinates were a 'constant occupation in his life – talking to people, explaining things to them, listening to them, asking everybody's opinions about everything'. At the end of every march, no matter how long, Castro 'would analyse for us all that had happened that day, our problems and the enemy's problems, then he would offer an evaluation of the territory where we were'. In this fashion, García says, the men had 'a complete knowledge of everything . . . that was happening', and they responded with 'extraordinary respect for Fidel'. He remembers that 'if anyone was ill, or if anyone felt bad, it

was a matter of great concern to him, and this earns a man's respect . . .
He always asked people, "How do you feel?" "Did you sleep well?"
"How was the food last night?" . . . He cared for each soldier.'

According to García, Fidel also knew how to listen to the peasants and
how to talk to them: 'He arrived with a programme to discuss with the
peasants, hearing their opinions, asking what they thought of different
social and political problems . . . For Fidel it was fundamental that each
peasant, each child, each youth, each adult would understand the reasons
for this revolutionary struggle. . .' On the other hand, the peasants
would not listen to government officials or the army, García says,
because 'they had nothing to say to them . . . They could not keep up a
conversation for five minutes with a humble peasant, a poor worker,
because he would simply ask them, "What do you bring me?" "Whom
do you defend?" '

Fidel and his men were a rough-looking and rough-sounding band,
however. By the end of February most of them were *barbudos*, sporting
beards of varying sizes and colours, long hair and filthy and torn clothes.
Headgear ranged from captured army helmets to straw hats and green
caps like Castro's. They easily scared anyone they encountered, and their
smell was not faint. Raúl noted in February that he had just taken his third
bath (in a stream) since leaving Mexico at the end of November. And
their speech, too, was coarse. Carlos Rafael Rodríguez, the Communist
leader who spent several months with Castro in the mountains in 1958,
remarked: 'In the Sierra Maestra he developed a brutally filthy language,
if I can put it that way . . . He was living in the exaltation of battle, and his
every third or his every fourth word was . . . well, you know. . .' But
Rodríguez says, Castro always watched his language in front of women.

Shortly after five o'clock in the morning of Saturday 16 February Fidel
Castro met the woman who was to become the most important person in
his life. Celia Sánchez Manduley was thirty-six years old, unmarried,
extremely intelligent and efficient, dark-haired, attractive without being
beautiful, and wholly dedicated to the ideals of the 26th of July
Movement as defined by Castro. One of five daughters of Dr Manuel
Sánchez Silveira, a radical-minded physician at Oriente sugarcane mills
and a Cuban history buff, Celia lived in Manzanillo and Pilón in the
south-west of the province, was acquainted from childhood with just
about everybody in that tight little world, from politicians to Sierra
peasants, and was deeply involved in politics. After the 1952 Batista coup
she had visited Havana to meet *Ortodoxo* party leaders but curiously had
never come across Fidel Castro.

When Castro exiled himself to Mexico in mid-1955, after his release
from prison, Celia already had solid contacts with the nascent Movement. She obtained navigation charts for the south-western Oriente coast

for Pedro Miret, during his reconnaissance tour of the area with Frank
País. Armando Hart, a Movement founder, recalls that Celia came to
Havana afterwards to ask to be included in Castro's projected invasion.
But, he says, Frank País wanted her to stay in Manzanillo to organize
support for the landing.

In Oriente, and working with Frank País, she put together the
clandestine peasant network designed to meet the *Granma* and transport
the rebels to the Sierra; she waited over forty-eight hours for Castro to
land in her area. In the aftermath of Alegría de Pío, as a new member of
the Movement's National Directorate, Celia organized in Manzanillo the
first urban support system for the guerrillas (Frank País's Santiago group
had been demoralized by the abortive 30 November uprising). She
dispatched arms, ammunition, food, supplies and volunteers to the
mountains through her peasant network. It was not much at the start, but
for Castro even a single bullet counted then. It was Celia who received
Faustino Pérez when he came down from the Sierra at Christmas to tell
the world that Castro was alive and fighting (she had sent up a Jeep to
fetch him, after the first messenger brought word of Fidel's survival), and
she helped him to continue to Santiago and Havana. Then Celia went to
work preparing Castro's meeting with the National Directorate, and the
interview with the *New York Times* writer. She turned Manzanillo into
the rebel logistics centre, right under the noses of the Batista police, the
Military Intelligence Service, and the army garrison. Six years older than
Castro, Celia was the latest of the providential women to appear at a
crucial moment in his life.

Celia, whose clandestine code names were 'Norma' and 'Aly', left
Manzanillo with Frank País by car on the evening of Friday 16 February,
driven by Felipe Guerra Matos, a Movement member. Reaching the
point of entry into the Sierra around midnight, they walked all night with
a rebel guide, running soon after dawn into Luís Crespo, one of Castro's
top fighters, and then into Fidel and his group. He, too, had been
marching all night to the Epifanio Díaz farmhouse, and now Fidel and
Celia came face to face in the middle of a pasture several hundred yards
from the house. Castro had met Frank País on his two visits to Mexico,
but to him Celia had been a legend. Neither of them ever described this
first meeting, but the mutual attraction must have been formidable. The
pasture meeting marked the birth of a twenty-three-year association,
lasting until her death.

Raúl joined his brother in the field to meet Celia and Frank, and the
four talked until high noon when for security reasons they decided to
move to a canefield a half-mile away to lunch on 'delicacies' the visitors
had brought from Manzanillo and to continue their talk. Fidel gave Celia
and Frank a detailed account of what had happened to the rebels from the
time they left Mexico. Celia and Frank reported on the failed Santiago

uprising, the progrss in their efforts to expand the Movement, and the rumours they had heard that Eutimio Guerra was in the pay of the army. Fidel insisted on the urgent need for recruits and arms and ammunition from the cities, and together they outlined a plan for making Manzanillo a staging point en route to the Sierra Maestra under Celia's direction, and for the use of the Epifanio Díaz farm, Los Chorros, as the channel into the mountains. The farm had been chosen for this meeting because the Díaz family was completely trusted, two of the sons belonging to the Movement, and Castro realized that their farm would make an excellent gateway to the guerrilla world. By mid–afternoon the sky began to look like rain, and Fidel asked Guillermo García and two other rebels to put up a shed in the field; the four went on talking until nightfall. Castro had decided to stay away from the farm until the arrival of the other Movement leaders and the American journalist, spending the night outside.

Faustino Pérez, Armando Hart, Haydée Santamaría and Vílma Espín arrived early in the evening and were taken to the field to meet the Castro brothers and Celia and Frank. Fidel had not seen Hart and Haydée (who had since become engaged) since he left Havana in mid-1955, and this was the first time he met Vílma. The daughter of a Santiago physician and American-educated, Vílma was not a member of the National Director-ate, but she was so active in the Movement in Oriente that Frank País had made a point of inviting her. Also, Vílma spoke English and so could interpret for the newsman. She presently met Raúl whom she would marry after the revolution. There were many marriages among the top rebel leadership. Melba Hernández and Jesús Montané were already married. Divorces came later in most cases, but Raúl and Vilma would be an exception.

At dawn the *New York Times* emissary arrived at the farm, and Universo Sánchez located Castro. Fidel instructed him to tell the journalist that he was at a meeting with the general staff in one of the other camps the rebels had in the area, and that he would come over as soon as possible; Castro was determined to prevent the journalist from finding out that the rebel army consisted of only eighteen men, and he had instructed Sánchez to make the farm seem like a busy guerrilla command post.

The emissary of the *New York Times* to the Sierra Maestra was Herbert L. Matthews. He was a highly respected member of the editorial board of his newspaper, and he specialized in Latin American affairs. As a reporter for the *Times* he had covered the Italian invasion of Ethiopia, the Spanish Civil War, and World War Two, and in the 1950s he became the editorial voice of the newspaper on the Western hemisphere. When Faustino Pérez came to Havana from the Sierra at Christmas to arrange a visit to the

Rebel Army by an American journalist, the 26th of July Movement immediately contacted the local *Times* bureau. Matthews had interest in the Cuban story – at a time when most of the American press was barely aware that a story, or a Fidel Castro, even existed – and he agreed instantly.

To Mathews the assignment had great personal as well as professional significance. Scholarly and reserved, he was a romantic at heart, and the defeat he had witnessed of the Republic in Spain by the Fascist Nationalists was an emotional jolt from which he never fully recovered. A champion of Latin American democracy on the *Times* editorial page, Matthews saw the emergence of the Castro rebellion as the latest worthwhile cause in the Americas; in Fidel Castro and his Movement he sensed a vindication of the Spanish tragedy. At the age of fifty-seven Matthews felt almost paternal about this movement of young people in Cuba.

Although he had never heard of the journalist, to Castro Matthews' visit had a calculated and immediate political importance. Once more Castro was taking a page from José Martí's book. In 1895 Martí too had arranged to have an American journalist cover his guerrilla war shortly after landing in Oriente. In his diary Martí remarked that he worked with 'the correspondent of the *New York Herald* George Eugene Bryson until three o'clock in the morning', and then, next day, 'I work the entire day on the manifesto for the *Herald*, and more for Bryson.'

Now, sixty-two years later, the Bryson scenario was being replayed with Matthews in another Cuban revolution. Matthews had not been caught unawares, and in his own personal account of his involvement with Cuba he observed that Castro 'was a myth, a legend, a hope, but not yet a reality . . . and like General Gómez, he must have been saying to himself, "without the press we shall get nowhere." ' In any event Matthews and his English-born wife Nancie flew from New York to Havana on 9 February. On the evening of Friday 15 February the Matthews left by car for an unspecified destination with Javier Pazos, Faustino Pérez and Liliam Mesa; all Matthews knew was that he would meet Castro in the Sierra Maestra at midnight the next night. He did not know Faustino, who used the name of 'Luís', and posed as the husband of 'Marta', the name used by Liliam Mesa. Matthews described her as 'young, attractive . . . from a well-to-do, upper-class Havana family' and as 'a fanatical member of the 26th of July Movement, typical of the young women who risked – and sometimes lost – their lives in the insurrection'. Matthews then observed most accurately that 'the extent to which the women of Cuba was caught up in the passion of the rebellion was extraordinary, for like all Latin women they were brought up to lead sheltered, non-public and non-political lives'.

They arrived in Manzanillo sixteen hours later, in the afternoon of 16

February (Castro had reached their rendezvous spot that dawn). Matthews departed for the Sierra early in the evening, leaving Nancie behind at a Cuban family's home. The trip to the edge of the Sierra was in Felipe Guerra Matos's Jeep with Javier Pazos and two other youths; it was Felipe's third trip through army-patrolled territory that day, having first taken up Celia and Frank, then Faustino and his companions. At midnight Matthews and the others left the Jeep to begin climbing up the mountain. They got lost, and had to wait for two hours 'in a heavy clump of trees and bushes, dripping from the rain . . . crouched in the mud . . . trying to snatch a little sleep with our heads on our knees'. Then a rebel scout appeared, identified himself with two low, soft, toneless whistles, which was the *guerrillas*' signal, and led Matthews and his escort to the camp at Los Chorros where Castro was to meet him. At that point Fidel's staging of the event began. In his first dispatch to the *Times* Matthews wrote that 'Señor Castro was encamped some distance away and a soldier went to announce our arrival and ask whether he would join us or we should join him. Later he came back with the grateful news that we were to wait and Fidel would come along with the dawn.' Castro had succeeded in giving Matthews the impression that he had many camps and, as the *Times* article put it, 'had mastery of the Sierra Maestra'.

It was theatre that Castro put on for Matthews. In an official account of the Sierra war published in 1979, in the Communist Party newspaper *Granma* the authors say that 'before entering the camp [to meet Matthews], Fidel had given instructions for his companions to adopt a strictly military bearing'. But, they add, 'for some it was hard to reconcile the military bearing required by Fidel with the conditon of their clothes and their general appearance . . . Manuel Farjado, for example, had no back to his shirt, which had been torn to shreds by his knapsack harness. During the time the journalist remained in the camp, Fajardo was obliged to walk sideways.' At one point Raúl Castro brought sweat-covered Luís Crespo to where Castro and Matthews were talking, to say: '*Comandante*, the liaison from Column No. 2 has arrived,' and Fidel replied airily, 'Wait until I'm finished.'

As the *Granma* article explains: 'Finally, the journalist believed he had counted some forty fighters . . . and he left convinced that the group he had seen was part of a much larger force.' In his *Times* story Matthews observed that Castro had 'kept the government troops at bay while youths came in from other parts of Oriente . . . got arms and supplies and then began the series of raids and counter-attacks of guerrilla warfare', and that therefore 'one got a feeling that he is now invincible'.

Matthews had no way of knowing that up to then the Rebel Army had engaged in only two very minor clashes with the army, that Castro just barely made it across the Sierra to meet him, and that he controlled only the ground where they sat. He would never have belived that the Rebel

Army consisted of only eighteen men, all of whom he saw time after time during his three hours with Castro.

Matthews, however, must never be accused of being a dupe or naïve: he was in an environment totally controlled by Fidel, the Cuban leader was eminently credible, and above all he was very much alive at a time when Batista was still claiming him dead. And, in the end, Matthews was correct in concluding: 'From the look of things, General Batista cannot possibly hope to suppress the Castro revolt. His only hope is that an army column will come upon the young rebel leader and his staff and wipe them out. This is hardly likely to happen . . . '

As soon as Matthews departed the camp to be taken back to Manzanillo, Castro resumed discussions with the National Directorate. For four hours they covered the question of recruiting an armed contingent in Oriente cities to join the Rebel Army in the hills, with Fidel insisting on the Movement's support for the guerrilla war being its first priority. In so doing, Castro was addressing for the first time the differences of priority between the Sierra and the *llano* (the lowlands), differences that soon developed into a struggle over leadership roles within the Movement, and led after 1959 to the winding up of the 26th of July Movement and the consolidation of the 'new' Communists' rule in Cuba, headed by Fidel Castro. In this sense the political battle over the future fate of the revolution began only two-and-a-half months after the *Fidelistas* had landed on the island, when their strength was still limited to eighteen men.

During this conference Faustino Pérez, identified with both the Sierra and the urban insurrectional groups, proposed that a second front of guerrilla war be opened in the Escambray Sierra in the central province of Las Villas in order to lessen the pressure on the Castro force. Faustino had in mind a 26th of July Movement guerrilla comparable with the Rebel Army in Oriente, and he argued that weapons more easily available in Havana could be effectively used in the Escambray. According to the version printed in the historical account in *Granma*, this proposal was accepted 'although Fidel was not convinced by this idea because he considered that the most important thing at that moment was to concentrate available resources in the already existing *guerrillero* nucleus'. The version circulating privately was that Castro in fact vetoed Faustino's suggestion because he saw it as a threat to his overall leadership; the Escambray was much nearer than the Sierra Maestra to Havana, and it could have merged politically with the urban groups. In any event an Escambray 'second front' was not established until more than a year later, and then by the Student Revolutionary Directorate, a rival of *Fidelismo*. Che Guevara wrote that the Movement in the Sierra and in the cities was 'practically two separate groups, with different tactics and strategy'. He added: 'There was no sign yet of the grave differences that would endanger the unity of the Movement several months later, but it was already clear that we had different concepts.'

Castro concluded the Los Chorros meeting by emphasizing the importance of women in the revolutionary struggle and by announcing that he would draft a manifesto to the people of Cuba for the Directorate members to take down with them. As usual Fidel was not wasting a moment in his around-the-clock military, political and propaganda revolutionary enterprise. He even found time to demonstrate the functioning of his beloved telescopic-sight automatic rifle to Celia Sánchez; magically, he had encountered a woman who not only shared and understood his political and philosophical ideas but was also an expert with weapons. They were clearly made for each other.

In the afternon, incredibly, Eutimio Guerra turned up near the farm where the *Fidelistas* were holding their meetings, evidently in the hope that he could finally spring a lethal trap for Fidel. He did not know that he was already under suspicion. Exploring the farm, Eutimio ran into a relative who was in the Rebel Army. The relative rushed off to find Fidel, who dispatched a squad under Juan Almeida to capture the traitor. Army safe-conduct passes were found on Eutimio, and he was manacled and taken to the camp where Fidel interrogated him at length. (Raúl commented later: 'He might have given us more information if we tortured him, but we did not apply such methods even to such miserable people.') Then a relative spoke to Eutimio, with bitter recriminations. A tremendous storm exploded overhead with thunder and lightning, and at 7 p.m. Eutimio Guerra was shot to death.

Castro spent the next three days at the farmhouse drafting his 'Manifesto to the People of Cuba' to be distributed throughout Cuba at about the time the Matthews articles would appear in the *New York Times*. Fidel had calculated that the Matthews reportage would establish the fact that he was, indeed, alive – and that this in itself would be a sensation – and that the Manifesto could then be circulated with enormously enhanced credibility. Also, it would be the first formal document of the 26th of July Movement to be issued from the Sierra Maestra, making it absolutely clear that Fidel Castro was the commander-in-chief of the revolution.

The visiting Movement leaders had brought newspapers and magazines with them, and Fidel (who normally depended on his battery-powered radio for news) was able to catch up with events elsewhere. Among the events reported in the Havana press was the ceremony at which United States Ambassador Arthur Gardner had presented seven Sherman tanks to General Batista, and referred to Castro as a rabble rouser. The same week the aircraft carrier *Leyte* and four destroyers paid an official visit to Havana. American policy remained one of unquestioned support for the regime. Even before reading about this latest United States support for Batista, Castro had complained to Matthews that the regime was using American weapons not only against him, but 'against all the Cuban people . . . They have bazookas, mortars, machine guns, planes and bombs.' Diplomatically answering a follow-up question, however, Castro said: 'You can be sure we have no animosity towards the United States and the American people.'

It is understandable, then, that Castro reacted with rage upon learning that Colonel Carlos M. Tabernilla y Palmero, the head of the air force that had been bombing and strafing the rebels and Sierra peasants, had been awarded the United States Legion of Merit by Air Force Major General Truman Landon. The general flew to Havana to present the decoration to Tabernilla (whose father was the Cuban Army's chief of staff) for 'the furtherance of amicable relations between the Cuban Air Force and the United States Air Force from May 1955, to February 1957'. At the same time the US Congress was informed that between 1955 and 1957 the United States had delivered to Cuba seven tanks, a battery of light mountain howitzer artillery, four thousand rockets, forty heavy machine guns, three thousand M-1 calibre semi-automatic rifles, fifteen thousand hand grenades, five thousand mortar grenades, and a hundred thousand .50-calibre armour-piercing cartridges for machine guns.

At the farm Fidel and his men had the opportunity to read the Movement's clandestine newspaper *Revolución*, which Carlos Franqui, a former Communist and an early *Fidelista*, had been publishing in Havana on an irregular basis since mid-1956. The issue, printed late in January with the headline 'Fidel in the Sierra', had been sent to Santiago to be reprinted there, and the total circulation was said to have been 20,000 copies.

The first of Herbert Matthews's articles was published a week later, on Sunday 24 February, and its most significant part as far as the guerrillas were concerned lay in the opening sentences: 'Fidel Castro, the rebel leader of Cuba's youth, is alive and fighting hard and successfully in the rugged, almost impenetrable vastness of the Sierra Maestra . . . Batista has the cream of his army around the area, but the army men are fighting a thus-far losing battle to destroy the most dangerous enemy General Batista has yet faced in a long and adventurous career as a Cuban leader and dictator.' Elsewhere, Matthews wrote: 'The personality of the man is overpowering. It was easy to see that his men adored him and also to see why he has caught the imagination of the youth of Cuba all over the island. Here was an educated, dedicated fanatic, a man of ideals, of courage and of remarkable qualities of leadership.'

Predictably, the impact of the Matthews articles (the *Times* printed three of them on successive days) was immense. Because censorship in Cuba had been lifted that week, Matthews's stories were reprinted in the national press, instantly elevating Castro to hero status. The Batista regime made things even worse for itself when Defence Minister Santiago Verdeja issued a statement on the day after the last article claiming that Matthews had written a 'chapter in a fantastic novel', that he had not interviewed 'the pro-Communist insurgent, Fidel Castro', and that even if Castro were alive, he commanded 'no supporting forces'. This was compounded by the remark that if the interview had taken place there would have been a corroborating photograph of Matthews and Castro. The *Times*, of course, did have such a photograph and published it the following day, but even then Batista disbelieved it. In his memoirs, written in exile, Batista admitted: 'I myself, influenced by the statements of the High Command, doubted [the interview's] authenticity . . . Castro had begun as a legendary person and would end by being a monster of terror.' The Matthews visit was a major turning point in Castro's career, and subsequently a magazine in New York published a cartoon of Fidel with the newspaper's advertising slogan 'I Got My Job Through the *New York Times*'. Today Herbert Matthews is a forgotten man in Cuba: only old-timers like Faustino Pérez remember him, and Castro no longer mentions him.

Dated 20 February, Castro's 'Appeal to The People of Cuba' was a call for violent action throughout the island in support of the revolution for which, 'if necessary, we shall fight in the Sierra Maestra for ten years'. This was in fact a time of great weakness for the eighteen-man army, but Castro knew well how to appear powerful and potentially victorious.

The six-point revolutionary programme signed by Castro on behalf of the Movement urged 'intensification in the burning of sugar cane . . . to deprive the tyranny of the revenue with which it pays the soldiers it sends to their deaths and buys the planes and bombs with which it assassinates scores of Sierra Maestra familes'. He asked: 'What does a little hunger matter today if we conquer bread and freedom tomorrow?' After the cane is burned, he wrote, 'we shall burn the sugar in the warehouses. . .' The next point proposed 'general sabotage of all the public services'. Then Castro called for the 'summary execution of the thugs who torture and assassinate revolutionaries . . . and all of those who pose an obstacle to the Revolutionary Movement'. He demanded the creation of 'civic resistance' in all Cuban cities and a 'general revolutionary strike as the culminating step in the struggle'. The document was retyped, and the Movement leaders made their way home to Manzanillo, Santiago and Havana with copies of the Appeal concealed on them.

At this juncture Castro was not interested in taking ideological positions, and his Appeal steered clear of them, much more so than *History Will Absolve Me*. He was concerned with the military aspects of the struggle against Batista, with the inadequacy of his guerrilla band, and with the Movement's inability to bring other revolutionary groups into its fold (and under its control). The question of unity – and unified leadership – was increasingly on Fidel's mind, and he was careful not to upset the volatile revolutionary situation with unnecessary statements and proclamations about his future plans. Proclamations could await a more favourable political climate. This is why, for example, he chose to disassociate himself personally from a detailed programme for the Movement drafted by Mario Llerena, the organization's director of public relations in exile (chosen by Frank País, not by Castro) but not brought to him in the mountains for approval. Instead, he put all his support behind the organization of a Civic Resistance Movement along the lines of his own Appeal, and this became extremely successful. Concentrating on propaganda, fund-raising and general support activities, it was meant to attract those who were ready and able to help, but not to fight.

For Castro's Rebel Army the next three months were a period of expansion, preparation and immense hardship. In terms of the overall contest between Batista and all his opponents it was a time of stalemate. Army troops could not destroy the *guerrilla* nor could the police in the cities smash the clandestine organizations involved in sabotage, propaganda and support for the Sierra Maestra fighters. Castro's forces, on the other hand, were too weak to venture out of their constantly changing mountain hideouts. For Batista not to be winning, however, was for him to be losing; each day that the rebels continued to operate, the greater the danger to his dictatorship. As Fidel told his men in mid-March: 'We have fulfilled our promise to the Cuban people . . . We are here!'

When Frank País left the Sierra after meetings with Castro he promised to have a group of volunteers at the same farm on 5 March, or two weeks later. Fifty-eight recruits from Santiago and Manzanillo, led by Captain Jorge Sotús, reached the farmhouse on 25 March, three weeks behind schedule, and only thirty had weapons. Among them were three young Americans, sons of servicemen from the Guantánamo naval base: Charles Ryan, Victor Buehlman and Michael Garney. Now, Castro observed, the Rebel Army was almost back to its original strength of eighty-two who landed from the *Granma*. This contingent had been organized and sent up the Sierra by Celia Sánchez from the secret staging area she had set up at a small farm known as La Rosalia, a block from the Manzanillo city jail. She had the men hidden in clumps of bushes (there were no trees on the farm) for several days while small groups of them were being loaded aboard trucks belonging to a rice farmer and part-time teacher named Huber Matos, an active Movement member, to be taken to the edge of the Sierra. From there the inexperienced recruits climbed to the rebel outposts.

While Fidel and his men waited at the farm for Sotús's column they learned from radio news broadcasts on 13 March that an attack on the

Presidential Palace in Havana by the Student Revolutionary Directorate had failed. At least thirty-five DR members were killed at the palace, the DR's President José Antonio Echeverría was shot dead in an affray near the university, and scores of others were captured, tortured and then murdered. Pelayo Cuervo Navarro, too, a very well-known *Ortodoxo* party leader, was assassinated, in his luxury Havana neighbourhood.

Castro and Echeverría had clearly been rivals for national revolutionary leadership. At the same time the two young men represented different societal groups, with all the implications that carried in Cuba: Castro had chosen to lead a working-class constituency with the aid of a handful of intellectuals, while Echeverría spoke for the young generation of the Cuban middle class – with a sprinking of middle-class and intellectual veterans of the Republican armies in the Spanish Civil War.

In the context of their rivalry, Castro had made the first spectacular move when he invaded Cuba in December, and was able to survive and grow in the months that followed. The DR, meanwhile, had been unable to mobilize an uprising in Havana to support the landing. Castro's standing was then immensely enhanced by the Matthews articles in the *Times*. But it is among the many mysteries of that day in March, why this particular moment and this particular type of action were chosen for the DR and Echeverría to assert their commitment to the revolutionary bargain and to their political *machismo*. It is not absolutely certain that the idea of storming the palace and killing Batista actually came from Echeverría; he did not personally lead the assault, being instead in command of a simultaneous strike on a radio station. It remains unclear how exactly the weapons were obtained for the palace coup and by whom they were financed; it may well have been done by wealthy Cuban political exiles, who persuaded (or dared) Echeverría and his companions to kill the dictator. Certainly the DR had already engaged in selective political assassination. In any event the day's attacks were superbly planned and their executors were supremely heroic – the plan failed because Batista barricaded himself on the third floor of the palace while the students who had taken the second floor were later dislodged by powerful army reinforcements. Had the plan worked it would have left Fidel Castro in his mountains as a suddenly irrelevant factor in the revolutionary equation.

According to one of the versions of these events the DR had amassed arms in Havana not only to kill Batista but also to block Castro's attempts to seize power in the capital once the dictatorship had been overthrown. This is reasonably credible because weapons for the DR's second Escambray front established the following year came from caches in Havana, and because armed DR units did capture the Presidential Palace to prevent Castro from taking it, after Batista fled the country on the last day of 1958.

In any case Castro and the leadership of the 26th of July Movement had little use for the DR and its tactics. Fidel himself did not hide his absolute disapproval of the DR action, making it clear to his companions that he thought it was simply part of the overall struggle for control of the Movement. In a radio interview with an American reporter a month after the DR assault, he said it was 'a useless spilling of blood. The life of the dictator does not matter . . . I am against terrorism. I condemn these procedures. Nothing is solved by them. Here in the Sierra Maestra is where they should come to fight.' And Castro was consistent in his views against political assassination as a revolutionary instrument. Twenty years later, discussing the assassination of John F. Kennedy, he returned to the theme, saying: 'We have never believed in the assassination of leaders . . . We fought a war against Batista for twenty-five months, but we were not trying to kill Batista. It would have been easier to kill Batista than to assault the Moncada, but we did not believe that a system is abolished, liquidated, by liquidating its leaders . . . We were fighting against reactionary ideas, not against men.'

Castro's disparaging comments nevertheless emphasized the leadership issue. When he said the students should have come to the Sierra Maestra to fight, he obviously meant for them to be under his command. Ironically, Cuban Communists also came out against the DR attack on the palace, but putting it under the same heading as Fidel Castro's guerrilla operations. Four days after the assault, Juan Marinello, chairman of the Communist Popular Socialist Party and a minister in the Batista government in the late 1940s, wrote to Herbert Matthews that 'our position is very clear; we are against these methods'. Marinello wrote that there was no need for 'a popular insurrection', and what Cuba needed was 'democratic elections', and 'a government of a Democratic Front of National Liberation' – which the Communists would of course have hoped to dominate. Therefore Marinello informed Matthews: 'We think that [the 26th of July Movement] has noble aims but that, in general, it is following mistaken tactics. For that reason we do not approve of its actions, but we call on all parties and popular groups to defend it against the blows of tyranny. . .' The Communist position had not changed from November to March despite Castro's ability to survive, and, like Batista, they were still not taking him seriously. This is worth noting, in the light of subsequent official propaganda claims that in 1957 the Communists were already helping the *guerrilla*.

Another unanswered question, this time involving the Communists, arises from what came to be known as the 'Crime at 7 Humboldt Street'. This was the address in Havana of a safe-house apartment where the surviving leaders of the student's attack on the Presidential Palace hid during Easter Week. They were Fructuoso Rodríguez, who was elected president of the University Student's Federation (FEU) after

Echeverría's death, Joe Westbrook (who was with Echeverría at the radio station), José Machado and Juan Pedro Carbó Serví. On 20 April, Easter Sunday, the four were killed by the secret police after the location of the apartment had been given them by an inside informant. Following the triumph of the revolution, it emerged that the traitor had been a student named Marcos Armando Rodríguez (Marquito) with extremely close personal ties to the top leaders of the 'old' Communist Party – although he was not believed to be a party member at the time. In 1964 Marcos Rodríguez, who in the meantime had been favoured with a scholarship in Prague, was arrested and tried. Fidel Castro acted, in effect, as the prosecutor at the trial, and Rodríguez was found guilty of the 'Humboldt Street' treason and ultimately executed. The Communists were never specifically linked with Rodríguez's actions, but the names of all his powerful friends in the 'old' Communist Paty surfaced at the trial, Rodríguez, while in exile in Mexico, having confessed to the crime to them. As it happened, most of them were purged by Castro in 1962 for leading a 'sectarian clique' against him inside the 'new' Communist Party he was then forming. The 'old' Communists were a classic Moscow party, and it was never clearly explained why its leaders had not informed Castro earlier of the Rodríguez treason 'confession', in one of the most painful and dramatic episodes of the struggle against Batista.

In the meantime Castro was shaping his strengthened *guerrilla* into an effective fighting force, teaching new recruits the secrets of irregular warfare, making them accustomed to hard marches. He rejected Che Guevara's recommendation that they engage in immediate combat as he did not think the men were ready for a major encounter. For the time being, therefore, their life was nomadic, moving camp almost every day, marching at night, and sometimes going without sleep for days on end. Food was short and, as Che told the story, one day the rebels had to eat their first horse. It was an 'exquisite' meal for some of them, and 'a test for the biased stomachs of the peasants who thought they were committing an act of cannibalism, chewing up an old friend of man'.

Late in April Castro was joined in the mountains by Robert Taber and Wendell Hoffman of the Columbia Broadcasting System. Castro, who had asked for more American journalists after the success of the Matthews trip, did not know who Taber and Hoffman were until they arrived (he had only a brief message that American journalists were on their way up the Sierra), or how complicated it was going to be to transport them and their bulky television equipment to the Oriente hideouts. Armando Hart and Haydée Santamaría were in charge of the Havana arrangements, but Hart was arrested, and Haydée drove the Americans to Bayamo with Marcelo Fernández, the Havana coordinator of the 26th of July Movement (Haydée managed to hold onto the several thousand pesos in collected funds that Hart had been carrying). In Bayamo they met Celia Sánchez and Carlos Iglesias, a Movement leader from Santiago, and the six travelled together to Manzanillo and up to the Sierra.

The American television team and Celia and Haydée remained with the *guerrilla* for nearly two months while Castro concentrated on building a supply system in the region. Food depots were set up in peasant houses to receive shipments from the lowlands, permanent camps were built for the *guerrilleros* for use during their constant moves, and peasant liaison teams were organized to serve as couriers and as a rudimentary Intelligence service. At this stage the rebels were in control of an ever-expanding area in the Sierra that they called the Free Territory.

Then the entire column climbed Turquino peak, Cuba's highest mountain, for Castro to hold a CBS television interview in front of the bust of José Martí which Celia Sánchez and her father had erected there many years earlier. He said: 'We have struck the spark of the Cuban revolution.' Che Guevara noted that Castro, who had never been there before, checked his pocket altimeter to assure himself that Turquino was exactly as high as shown on the maps.

Castro then shifted his operations back to the central part of the Sierra Maestra where he felt he could develop a better infrastructure for what he now thought would be a protracted war. Little is known of the strategic planning by the Batista high command at that time because in the euphoria of victory the crowds were to destroy key military archives in Havana and at Bayamo.

Because Castro's presence in Cuba was becoming both an accomplished fact and a major element in all political calculations, other rivals sought to challenge his position. Former president Carlos Prío financed an expedition led by a United States Army veteran named Calixto Sánchez, to establish a separate anti-Batista guerrilla front in the mountains in the north of Oriente. Cuban politics being what they were (and Prío being as wealthy as he was), there was no real contradiction in his financing first Castro in Mexico and then a competitive operation later; Prío wanted his fingers in every pie. The group sailed from Miami aboard the yacht *Corintia* on 19 May, landed in Cuba on 24 May, and were betrayed by a peasant to the army on 28 May. Twenty-four men, including several DR members, were caught and shot.

The war continued therefore to be Castro's show, and on the same day that the *Corintia* expedition was liquidated, Fidel led his men into combat for the first time since January. This was the battle of Uvero on 28 May, when the Rebel Army moved east to take a government garrison on the Caribbean coast. Castro's principal reason for this shift was a message from Santiago that an important shipment of modern arms would be placed for him by Movement couriers at a specific point in the Sierra

Maestra, east of Turquino, for his forces to recover. But, as usual, there
were delays, and the cache was not found until 20 May. In the meantime
Che Guevara got lost for a day (discovering that a compass is not enough
in the Sierra, and that knowledge of the terrain is essential); the rebels
executed a spy; and another American journalist, Andrew St George,
joined the Castro column. Additional peasants also signed up with the
rebels (in each case Fidel interviewed volunteers at length about their
backgrounds and motivations before accepting them), so that towards
the end of May the *Fidelistas* were up to 120 men. But it was the new
weapons that gladdened Castro's heart: three tripod-mounted machine-
guns, three submachineguns, and nineteen automatic rifles, including
American M-1s. Che Guevara was issued with his own submachinegun,
becoming for the first time a full-time soldier; until then he had spent
most of his time as a physician for the troops and the peasants in the
villages they crossed, fighting only when necessary.

The Uvero battle had been extremely tough and costly: of the eighty
rebels involved, six were killed and nine wounded (including Juan
Almeida, a general staff officer); of the fifty-three government army
personnel, fourteen were killed, nineteen wounded and fourteen taken
prisoner. It was the bloodiest encounter since Alegría de Pío, starting at
dawn and lasting nearly three hours, but this time the *Fidelistas* won.
They took two machine guns and forty-six rifles, and Castro declared
that 'thus began a new phase in the Sierra Maestra'. Che looked after the
enemy wounded and, according to Fidel, left them 'in the care of their
own doctor, so that the army might pick them up and move them to their
own hospitals, thanks to which none of them died'. Pedro Álvarez
Tabío, the military historian, says that Uvero 'had a very important
strategic significance because it demonstrated for the first time . . . that
the Rebel Army could defeat the army of the tyranny, and that the seizure
of power through a military defeat was therefore possible'.

Immediately after Uvero, Celia Sánchez left the Sierra with the CBS
team, then continued on to Santiago where Herbert Matthews was
visiting on his return to Cuba. Castro wanted her to bring Matthews up
to date on rebel activities. She had taken part in the Uvero battle, the first
woman to fight with the Rebel Army. Four months would elapse before
she would return as she was needed in Manzanillo to coordinate the flow
of men, arms and supplies to the Sierra. Addressing her as 'Norma', her
underground name, Fidel wrote to her shortly after she left the mountain:
'We have such pleasant memories of your presence here that we feel your
absence has left a real vacuum. Even when a woman goes around with a
rifle in her hand, she still makes our men tidier, more decent, gentlemanly
– and even braver. And after all, they are really decent and gentlemanly all
the time. But what your poor father would say. . .' After hearing a false
report that Celia had been detained, Castro had Raúl, Che Guevara,

Camilo Cienfuegos and other top fighters signed a letter addressed to 'Norma', declaring that 'you and David [Frank País] are our pillars. If you and he are well, all goes well and we are tranquil. . .' A formal statement by the rebel commanders proclaimed that 'concerning the Sierra, when the history of this revolutionary epoch is written, two names must be printed on the cover: David and Norma'.

Frank País was killed by the Batista police in Santiago on 30 July, and Castro wrote to Celia Sánchez the following day: 'For the moment, you'll have to assume a good portion of Frank's work, especially as you know more about it than anybody else.' País had been not only the Movement's principal leader in Oriente, providing together with Celia logistics support for the Rebel Army in the mountains, but also, increasingly, a political thinker on a national scale. His death was a particularly damaging blow to the Movement because it happened to be in the midst of a fundamental political crisis.

The growth of the *Fidelista* army and the expansion of the Free Territory once again pitted Castro in the mountains against the urban wings of the Movement in rivalry for revolutionary leadership and policy-making. By July the *guerrilla* had grown to 200 men, and the earlier Sierra–lowlands frictions intensified. Castro took the view that the first and foremost priority of the Movement in the lowlands was to support the guerrilla army. This implied, of course, their acceptance of his national leadership, and Fidel was as ready to fight for this as he was to fight Batista. In letters to Celia in July and August, Castro insisted: 'The proper order should now be: *All guns, all bullets, and all supplies to the Sierra.*' In the cities, however, the feeling was growing that Castro should share decision-making with the National Directorate, ostensibly because he was too isolated in the mountains to be sufficiently informed about events in Cuba, but really because many Movement leaders thought they, too, were entitled to a voice in the country's future. Not only were they sending arms, money and supplies to Castro, they argued, but the 26th of July Movement and the Civic Resistance were also assisting him through sabotage against the economy, and scores of these clandestine fighters were being killed, arrested and tortured in the cities.

Having barely consolidated his military position in the Sierra Maestra after the Uvero battle, Fidel now had to turn his attention to the emerging political struggle within revolutionary ranks. Although Castro knew what was coming, it was Frank País who had finally forced him to face the political problem. País wrote Castro a long letter early in July, shortly before his death, informing him that because of the chaos and confusion reigning in the Movement throughout Cuba, he and Armando Hart had 'decided on an audacious move to revamp the Movement in its entirety'.

The significant aspect of this decision was that Castro had not been consulted beforehand, which in itself was a challenge to his authority. Though País spoke of poor coordination within the Movement as the reason for the changes, it was clear that his concept was to divide power between the mountain and the cities; he said, for example, that the National Directorate would include the six provincial coordinators, and the Rebel Army would be represented by only one delegate. Moreover he stressed that one of the 'defects' of the Movement was the 'lack of a clear and precisely outlined programme, which is, at the same time, serious, revolutionary, and within the realm of possibility'. País then informed Castro that he had already ordered the drafting of such a programme by a group of intellectuals. Finally he urged the creation of nationwide armed Movement militias. Again Castro saw prerogatives taken away from him by the twenty-two-year-old Santiago leader, even though País respectfully told Fidel that 'you will decide on this, but I ask that your opinion be communicated to this directorate as rapidly as possible'.

Whether or not Castro saw in Frank País a potential rival for leadership, even before País's communication he had summoned to his side two respected moderates of an older generation, Raúl Chibás and Felipe Pazos, and used their prestige to enhance his own political standing in the country. A great tactitian, Castro chose that moment to form a highly visible alliance with the political centre.

Chibás, an unassuming, quiet but courageous man, recalls the circumstances of his arrival in the Sierra on 4 July. He was guided to a house in the mountains to await Castro who then arrived with his column of men, followed by Che Guevara with a contingent of wounded rebels. The scene, he says, 'was like something out of the movies, watching them coming, taking positions all around, and all in complete silence. Everything there was said in whispers. I spent a month speaking in whispers: it was their discipline, the difference between the Rebel Army and the Batista army. The Batista army always arrived shouting, and it was easy to surprise them because it was known they were there.'

In his long talks with Castro, whom he had known for nearly ten years, Chibás insisted that elections be called in Cuba within a year of the victory over Batista. He told him that with control over the Congress 'all the necessary revolutionary laws can be passed'. Chibás emphasizes that Castro agreed with the electoral concept and that 'nobody forced him' to accept it. The Sierra Maestro Manifesto, issued on 12 July, was a result of Castro's meetings with Chibás and Pazos, and was signed by all three, thus declaring that within a year 'we want elections, but with one condition: truly free, democratic and impartial elections'. It constituted Castro's firm and formal commitment to 'free, democratic elections' as the central point of the Manifesto that he intended to be the Movement's programme. Two years later, Castro would break that commitment in

the climate of revolutionary euphoria on the island, offering rationalizations as to why no elections were needed in Cuba.

   According to Chibás, Castro drafted the Manifesto 'totally by
himself', without being influenced by him or Pazos. But, Chibás says,
Pazos did push Castro into proposing in the Manifesto the creation of a
'civic-revolutionary front with a common strategy of struggle' and the
immediate designation of 'a person to preside over the provisional
government, whose election will be left to the civic institutions'. Castro
liked the idea of the 'civic-revolutionary front' because it would
transcend the 26th of July Movement and, being proposed by him, could
be controlled by him from the Sierra. The notion of a provisional
government was likewise appealing to Fidel: it would be a prestigious
front for his own revolutionary activities, and he expected to be able to
choose its president. Although both Chibás and Pazos were given the
impression that they would be considered for the chairmanship of the
provisional government, Castro all along planned to name a figurehead.

   A product of Castro's imagination and manipulative talents, this latest
Manifesto had the desired effect of at least temporarily resolving the
political crisis in the Movement by invoking 'national unity' under his
leadership. Patronizingly the document said that 'it is not necessary to
come to the mountains to discuss this; we can be represented in Havana,
in Mexico, or wherever may be necessary,' which however gave the
Fidelistas an appearance of moderation and reason. Concerning the
endless debate as to whether the tone of the Manifesto shows that Castro
was a Marxist–Leninist at the time or not, probably the best judgement
was provided by Che Guevara in writing subsequently about these
events. To him the Manifesto was a compromise and he concluded that
'we were not satisfied with the compromise, but it was necessary; it was
progressivist at that moment . . . We knew it was a minimal programme,
a programme that limited us, but we also knew that it was not possible to
impose our will from the Sierra Maestra and that we had to count for a
long period on a whole series of "friends" who would try to utilize our
military force and the great confidence the people already felt in Fidel
Castro for their macabre manoeuvres . . . to maintain the domination of
imperialism in Cuba. . .' Castro never disputed the substance of
Guevara's interpretation of the Manifesto, and later that year he would
again take the offensive to assure his absolute leadership of the revolution.
The Movement was given a new National Directorate, but it remains
unclear who named the members.

   Fidel also had personal problems. During the summer he wrote to
Celia: 'When are you going to send me the dentist? If I don't receive
weapons from Santiago, Havana, Miami or Mexico, at least send me a
dentist so my teeth will let me think in peace. It's the limit; now that we
have food, I can't eat; later, when my teeth are all right, there won't be

any food . . . I really feel that I'm just not lucky when I see that so many people have arrived here, and not one dentist.' But Celia had sent him a new uniform, and he wrote to her that 'I'm going to begin the fourth campaign in it . . . And you, why don't you make a short trip here? Think about it, and do so in the next few days . . . A big hug.'

During the remainder of 1957 the Rebel Army went on consolidating its control of the Sierra Maestra, expanding the Free Territory further to the east. Che Guevara, promoted by Castro to the rank of *comandante* (major, which was the highest rank in the guerrilla force), moved south-east with his own column, taking the small Batista garrisons at Bueycito and El Hombrito, and capturing weapons. In the El Hombrito area Guevara set up an armoury, a bakery, and his column's newspaper, *El Cubano Libre*. But the wider anti-Batista opposition suffered reverses. An uprising by the navy in the port of Cienfuegos on 5 September was smashed by loyalist armoured units and the airforce and thirty-two officers and sailors were killed. The Cienfuegos rebellion was part of a larger military conspiracy extending to Havana, Santiago and the port of Mariel, but at the last moment the plans for organized revolt were cancelled; because of a breakdown in communications the navy there was not informed and they moved alone.

The timing of this military conspiracy came as a surprise to Fidel Castro, and it strengthened his suspicions that schemes were being developed to bypass his Rebel Army and remove Batista by other means. What he feared most was the defeat of the dictator by a military coup d'état, shifting the power to a military junta, and making him irrelevant.

For all these reasons Castro reacted with fury when he was belatedly informed that in November seven opposition groups had signed a pact in Miami to create a Cuban Liberation Junta and, among other steps after Batista's fall, to incorporate Fidel Castro's revolutionary forces into the regular army. Not only he had not been consulted beforehand, but the Miami Pact was signed on behalf of the 26th of July Movement by Felipe Pazos and two other Movement leaders, without a specific authorization from the National Directorate. In a scathing communication on 14 December Castro announced that the Movement 'did not authorize any delegation to discuss such negotiations', that 'the 26th of July Movement claims for itself the function of maintaining public order and reorganizing the armed forces of the republic', and that 'while the leaders of the other organizations who endorsed the pact are abroad fighting an imaginary revolution, the leaders of the 26th of July Movement are in Cuba, making a real revolution'. He said the Movement 'will never relinquish its leadership of the people . . . and we alone know how to overcome or to die . . . To die with dignity, one has no need of company.'

Castro's rejection of the Miami Pact meant the death of the Liberation

Junta even before it could be officially born because clearly without the Rebel Army it would be a wholly meaningless organization. At the same time Castro acquired new enemies, notably in the Student Revolutionary Directorate (DR) whose new leaders had signed the Miami document. The DR's leader, Faure Chomón, wrote 'No organization can, or should, as Dr Castro has done in a sectarian fashion, claim for itself the representation of a revolution being made by all of Cuba.' Castro would have further problems with the DR and the 26th of July Movement the following year, but for now he was again in full control. He also regained the confidence of Che Guevara who, strangely, had assumed at first that the Miami Pact was signed with Fidel's authorization. Upon learning that Castro rejected it, Guevara wrote to him that now he was filled 'with peace and happiness'. He said it was clear 'who is pulling the wires behind the scenes', adding that 'we may unfortunately have to face Uncle Sam before the time is ripe'.

Uncle Sam, meanwhile, was engaged in a number of actions in Cuba that were both contradictory and mysterious. On one hand the US continued to supply the Batista regime with weapons to fight the rebels; on the other hand it secretly channelled funds to the 26th of July Movement through the Central Intelligence Agency.

The story of CIA financial support for the Castro rebellion is interesting – although it is unclear whether such support was formally authorized by the Eisenhower administration or undertaken by the agency entirely on its own. It is not even certain that Castro himself knew some of the money reaching him or his Movement came from the CIA. A new analysis of this United States involvement with Castro shows that between October or November of 1957 and the middle of 1958 the CIA delivered no less than $50,000 to a half-dozen or more key members of the 26th of July Movement in Santiago. The amount was large, relative to what the Movement itself was able to collect in Cuba. The entire operation remains classified as top secret by the United States government, and therefore the reasons for the financing of the Movement cannot be adequately explained. It is a sound assumption, however, that the CIA wished to hedge its bets in Cuba, and purchase goodwill among some members of the Movement, if not Castro's goodwill, for future contingencies. This would have been consistent with CIA policy elsewhere in the world where local conflicts affected United States interests.

These funds were handled by Robert D. Wiecha, a CIA case officer attached to the United States Consulate General under the cover of vice consul who served in Santiago from September 1957 to June 1959. The late Park Fields Wollam, who as consul general was Wiecha's superior in Santiago, had told State Department colleagues at that time of the CIA role in dealing with the Castro organization. Correspondence now in Cuban official archives shows furthermore that Wiecha had tried hard to arrange a meeting with Fidel himself from the moment he arrived in Santiago. The CIA officer's contact was with the Frank País group, and some time early in July País wrote to Castro that a United States diplomat wished to meet him (Wiecha's CIA identity was unknown to País). Castro replied: 'I don't see why we should raise the slightest objection to the US diplomat's visit. We can receive any US diplomat here, just as we would any Mexican diplomat or a diplomat from any country.'

Castro went on: 'It is a recognition that a state of belligerence exists, and therefore is one more victory against the tyranny. We should not fear this visit if we are certain that no matter what the circumstances may be, we will keep the banner of dignity and national sovereignty flying. And if they make demands? We'll reject them. And if they want to know our opinions? We'll explain them without fear. If they wish to have closer ties of friendship with the triumphant democracy of Cuba? Magnificent! This is a sign that they acknowledge the final outcome of this battle. If they propose friendly mediation? We'll tell them . . . no mediation is possible in this battle.'

On 11 July Frank País wrote to Castro: 'María A. told me very urgently at noon today that the American vice-consul wanted to talk with you, in the presence of some other man, but she didn't know who.' This was the first direct reference to Wiecha and País added: 'I told her I would consult with you, but that we would first have to find out who the other man is and where they wanted to go and what they wanted to talk about.' País's letter also showed that secret contacts existed as well with the United States Embassy in Havana: 'I'm sick and tired of so much backing and forthing and conversations from the embassy, and I think it would be to our advantage to close ranks a bit more, not losing contact with them, but not giving them as much importance as we now do; I see they are manoeuvring but I can't see clearly what their real goals are.'

On 1 August, the day after Frank País was buried, a new American ambassador, Earl E.T. Smith, a political appointee in Cuba to replace Arthur Gardner, went to Santiago. There, 200 women clad in black had gathered to request United States intervention against the terror practised by the regime. When the women started to chant, 'Libertad! Libertad!' the riot police charged them with truncheons and water cannon. At a news conference that followed, Smith delivered his protest against the 'excessive use of force'. Raúl Chibás, who was in the Sierra with Castro that week, recalls that the news of Smith's statement caused 'a moment of happiness among the troops . . . People were saying, "You see, the ambassador has already changed, it looks like he isn't supporting Batista." ' Chibás says that even Castro said that American policy could change, 'and people there talked about it as a thing that would help the struggle . . . Anti-Americanism did not exist among those rebels.'

On 16 October Armando Hart wrote to Castro: 'I have been in contact with people close to the embassy. These contacts have told me that people who are on our side – but who may not appear to be – have had conversations with the ambassador himself. I think this is the best policy, since we are kept up to date about everything happening there and of all the possible US plans, and at the same time the Movement does not officially commit itself.' In all probability Hart's contacts were officers in the CIA station at the American Embassy; this would be consistent with Robert Wiecha's efforts in Santiago to meet Castro, and with his handling of agency funds for the Movement. Robert Taber, the CBS reporter who had visited Castro in the mountains, wrote in his book about the Cuban revolution that 'Wiecha rendered invaluable and humanitarian service to the Batista opposition'. Taber, who was unaware that Wiecha worked for the CIA, identified him as the vice consul who made searching inquiries about Armando Hart, Javier Pazos and Antonio Buch who had been arrested in Santiago, 'with the result that General Chaviano was compelled to produce the prisoners, unharmed, to prove that they had not been tortured or killed'. Hart's unwitting contact with the CIA began with this intervention by Wiecha, and the agency's secret relationship with the rebels may have started there.

The meeting between Castro and Wiecha never took place, however, for reasons that Castro never learned. It may have been blocked by senior United States officials, particularly when Ambassador Smith himself expressed the firm hope that Batista would proceed with elections acceptable to Cubans. Curiously, official American support for Batista seemed to grow just as Castro's power was increasing, and it would be withdrawn only when it no longer mattered. The Wiecha episode suggests that the United States may have missed an extraordinary opportunity to establish a dialogue with Castro when he was still in the hills and, theoretically at least, open to a positive future relationship. But it is idle to second-guess history.

The Americans did not come to Fidel Castro's mountain in 1957, but the Communists did – even though in great secrecy. The visitor was Ursinio Rojas, a sugar worker and member of the Communist Party's Central Committee, and he was the first senior Communist leader to see Castro since Flavio Bravo's visit to Mexico a year earlier to try to dissuade him from the invasion. (Gottwald Fleitas, a low-ranking Party leader from Bayamo, went up the Sierra in the spring, supposedly to tell Castro that Communist activists among the peasants had been instructed to co-operate with the guerrillas). Rojas had been in prison in Havana early in 1957, with Armando Hart, Faustino Pérez and Carlos Franqui, and in long chats there with the Movement's men he maintained his party's official line that Castro was running a 'putschist' operation in the Sierra. But by the end of the year the Communists were beginning to think over their policy, and Rojas told Castro in October that certain party members would be authorized to join the Rebel Army as individuals. One full year after Castro had established himself in the Sierra Maestra this was still only as far as the Communists were prepared to go. *El Campesino*, the party's underground newspaper, declared: 'There exists a great difference between the level of the struggle in the Sierra Maestra . . . and the rest of Cuba, that is almost all of Cuba.' Fidel Castro seemed unable to convince either the United States or the Communists that he should be taken seriously.

But before the year ended Castro received a permanent visitor: on the verge of being caught by the police, Celia Sánchez abandoned her operations in Manzanillo to go up the Sierra. She would stay there with Fidel through the year of victory.

Chapter 11

It was not a happy time for military dictators in Latin America. On 23 January 1958, after nearly ten years in power, General Marcos Pérez Jiménez in Venezuela was overthrown by the armed forces as the climax of a revolt by the civilian population led by students, intellectuals and businessmen. The previous year General Gustavo Rojas Pinilla had been ousted by the military under roughly similar circumstances – with the Roman Catholic Church playing a major role in the rebellion – after a three-year rule. General Juan Péron in Argentina and General Manuel Odría in Peru departed, respectively, in 1955 and 1956 (Odría stepping down voluntarily in an unprecedented fashion in Latin American history). It was, indeed, a twilight of the tyrants, yet in Cuba General Batista seemed impervious to the possibility that a hemispheric trend was under way. So was the Eisenhower administration in the north.

What was understood even less in Havana and Washington, as 1958 opened, was the character of the struggle being conducted in the Sierra Maestra by Fidel Castro and his steadily growing Rebel Army. Whereas the ending of dictatorships in the four South American nations had led simply to the restoration of representative democracy in the standard, modern, liberal mode, Castro was preparing a fundamental social revolution. Even though he had continued to insist publicly that Batista's removal would be followed by 'free, democratic elections' within a year, he would soon inform Cubans that free elections were incompatible with a social revolution – and strictly speaking his assessment was politically and ideologically accurate.

An article published under Fidel Castro's byline in the February issue of *Coronet* magazine in New York (and most likely written by him) went to astonishing and exaggerated lengths to portray him and his 'armed campaign on Cuban soil' as the way to pure liberal democracy under which free enterprise could flourish. Even if he applied Martí's and

Marx's concept of 'historical justification' to conceal his real purpose until the right moment in the interests of a higher cause, and even if this were justifiable, the *Coronet* article borders on intellectual dishonesty.

In any event, in the opening months of 1958, Castro still believed that he was facing a protracted war against Batista. He acted accordingly in the military field by establishing three new battlefronts in the Sierra Maestra. Politically he made it clear that he welcomed a longer war because it would give him more time to prepare the Rebel Army and the country for the wider revolution he had in mind. (In a letter to Celia in July 1957 Castro wrote: 'I feel that the fall of the regime in a week's time would be far less fruitful than four months from now . . . Here, as a joke, I usually assure the comrades that we don't want to give birth to a *seven-month* revolution.'

The Rebel Army, in particular, was being turned into the cutting edge of the revolutionary process, to later become the ideological and operational centre in implementing great changes, thus assuring Castro's control of the entire Cuban political picture then and in the future.

For the Rebel Army to play this political role successfully, a myth had to be built around it, and to Fidel Castro this was a high priority. This myth, preserved thirty years later in the Revolutionary Armed Forces, was based as much on the army's function as a social revolutionary force as on its military prowess. Because rebel soldiers increasingly concerned themselves with awarding land to the peasants who worked it in the Free Territory of the Sierra, as well as with help to farms (as in the 1957 coffee harvest), the protection of peasant families from landowners' overseers and the Rural Guard, the application of 'revolutionary justice' to rapists and 'exploiters', and the opening of a few schools and clinics, they became firmly identified as friends of the population. Guevara, who ran his own zone fairly independently from the autumn of 1957, remarked that 'we came to overthrow a tyrant, but we discovered that this immense peasant zone, where our struggle is being prolonged, is the area of Cuba that needs liberation the most'. To a greater extent than Castro, the commander-in-chief always on the move, Guevara soon engaged in political education for the peasants as well as his own troops: he was not yet preaching Marxism, but land reform and other structural changes required in Cuba. His newspaper, *El Cubano Libra*, printed the comment that Communists 'are all those who take up arms because they are fed up with poverty. . .'

As self-appointed social revolutionaries the Rebel Army evoked peasant support far beyond the initial response that had made it possible for Castro to survive during his first months in Cuba. Again, this support was crucial in the guerrilla war as it entered a new phase in 1958. The *guajiros* brought food for the rebels, helped them to obtain weapons, provided free labour for the construction of armouries and warehouses (they would not accept payment), served as an early-warning system when Batista army forces penetrated the mountains, and acted as couriers among rebel groups and between Castro and the *llano* Movement leaders; some of the best couriers were women. And the peasants remained the principal source for recruitment for the Rebel Army; they knew their way around, they were tough, they were believers in *Fidelismo*, and it was easier to integrate them in the *guerrilla* than the urban volunteers. And now Castro needed the best fighters available to expand the war.

On 10 March 1958, the sixth anniversary of the Batista coup, Raúl Castro left with sixty-five men from Fidel's camp to establish a new front, or rebel war theatre, in the Sierra Cristal along the north coast of Oriente. It was directly east of the Castro brothers' birthplace at Birán, and north-east of Fidel's principal operational area. The idea was to create a second 'liberated zone' in Oriente, extending the war and increasing the strain on the Batista forces. Always myth-conscious, Fidel named this second front after Frank País. Raúl's force was designated as Column No. 6, to create the impression that the Rebel Army was composed of many units. About the same time Juan Almeida was dispatched with another column to set up a third front in the eastern range of the Sierra Maestra, immediately north-west of Santiago. In April Camilo Cienfuegos moved north towards Bayamo to harass the Batista army there. Guevara had been operating in the central Sierra Maestra around El Hombrito since August 1957. By mid-spring 1958, therefore, the Rebel Army occupied or controlled most of the mountain regions in Oriente. Fidel's strategy became one of denying the enemy more and more territory. But Fidel also believed in prudence; in a note he sent to Guevara in February he recommended that a planned attack be cancelled if support was not available from other rebel units. 'I do not belive anything suicidal should be done, as we shall be risking too many casualties', Castro wrote. 'I strongly recommend that you be careful. Take charge. Lead the men well.'

Gradually the guerrilla army was developing into a more conventional and better-equipped force. In April Fidel acquired a brand-new Toyota general purpose vehicle, and the rebels held enough teritory in the area for him to need to drive rather than walk; most of the mountain paths were passable for the Toyota, and even a few roads were now under Castro control. Colonel Arturo Aguilera, who served as Fidel's first driver and aide-de-camp, recounts that they moved from place to place every two or three days for security reasons; Castro still exercised enormous caution. Because of possible detection by aircraft they drove at night without lights, 'with Celia or Fidel carrying a lantern along for use when necessary'. Aguilera says that they always travelled without an escort because they were in rebel-held areas. Late in April and early in May,

Castro spent his time inspecting his forces in preparation for what he was certain would soon be a large-scale enemy offensive. He ordered fortifications to be built at the approaches to the spine of the Sierra Maestra, believing that he would lose part of his territory, but would triumph in the end so long as he continued to dominate the main crest of the mountain chain.

Morale was high everywhere. A hospital for the seriously wounded was established in the mountains in Guevara's territory, well concealed by vegetation from aerial observation, but hard on patients because of the extreme humidity. Another hospital was set up on the western slopes of the Sierra Maestra, and small medical installations were strung through-out the rebel territory. Medicine arrived regularly from the lowlands, if not always of the desired volume or type. A radio transmitter was installed in Alto de Conrado in Guevara's territory in February, but it was of low power and could be heard only by a few patrols and peasant families in the immediate vicinity. Guevara began manufacturing explosive devices, known as 'M-26'; he also set up a slaughterhouse for captured cattle and a small cigar-making plant.

High morale stemmed in part from the rigid discipline imposed by the commanders, but also from their personal example. Fidel, Raúl, Che and the others always were in the vanguard, never asking the men to take risks they would not accept themselves. When a peasant officer acci-dentally shot dead a soldier who had been subject to disciplinary action, the troops demanded the officer's execution. After Fidel and Che argued for hours that he did not deserve the death penalty, the men grudgingly agreed – mainly out of personal respect for the commanders. Guevara never sat down at a meal until he was satisfied that all his soldiers had the same quantity and quality of food. Universo Sánchez recalls sharing a chicken-and-rice meal with Fidel on the same metal plate; after each had consumed exactly one-half, a single piece of meat was left, and neither of them would eat it. As Guevara recalls, the only thing almost never in shortage was coffee: one could always get a cup at a peasant's hut. Little escaped Che's sharp eye; he was the most complete, if sharp-tongued, chronicler of the Sierra war – as one can appreciate from his campaign diary and subsequent writings. Much of these writings touch bitterly and violently on the political dissensions tearing asunder the 26th of July Movement.

It was the question of the general strike that brought the Movement's political crisis to a head, forcing a fundamental confrontation among its leaders. This, in turn, had a critical impact on the course the Cuban revolution would ultimately take. The idea of a general strike in support of a national rebellion against Batista certainly was not a new one, and Castro had first planned one to be timed with his landing in Cuba. In July

1957 Frank País informed Fidel that a National Workers' Front (FON) had been established throughout the country to be followed by the creation of strike committees so that a general strike could succeed. In his December communication to the Cuban Liberation Junta rejecting the Miami Pact, Castro singled out a general strike as being among 'concrete acts . . . useful in the overthrow of the tyranny', to be carried out through 'the effective coordination of the efforts of civic organizations in conjunction with the 26th of July Movement'.

There are nevertheless reasons to believe that in Castro's mind support for his Sierra war was far more important at this point than anything the Movement could and would do in the *llano*, the lowlands and their cities. His stream of complaints about not receiving enough arms, ammunition, supplies and money from the *llano* finally led Armando Hart, a co-founder of the Movement, to write to him from Santiago in October that 'our comrades here have always considered the Movement there and here as one single entity . . . Supplying you up there is so vital for us that we consider it our foremost and fundamental revolutionary obligation.' But in early December Hart wrote in desperation to Celia in the Sierra Maestra that if the Movement's work in the cities were regarded as unnecessary, 'then that raises the question of whether we should consider ourselves members of the present directorate solely as instruments for supplying the Sierra . . . We think we have a duty to organize the workers, to strengthen the civilian resistance, to build provincial and municipal cadres with real revolutionaries, who, together with the revolutionary army of the Sierra Maestra, will guarantee the accomplishment of our programme. We must also help the militia which, outside the Sierra Maestra, without resources or arms (all that we had were sent to you) have heroically succeeded in extending the revolution beyond the frontiers of the Sierra Maestra and have created an organization that you, as much as ourselves, are duty-bound to protect.'

René Ramos Latour, who replaced Frank País as coordinator in Oriente (and whose underground name was 'Daniel'), wrote to Castro expressing surprise 'at the note signed by you, which essentially was an expression of mistrust towards us, tacitly accusing us of responsibility for the state of neglect in which our forces in the Sierra found themselves, as well as of holding back for the cities the supposed newly arrived weapons destined for you . . . No, we have never belittled the Sierra. But we think the battle ought not to be limited solely and exclusively to the mountains; we must fight the regime on all fronts.'

Against this background of rising tensions between Fidel Castro in the mountains and the Movement's Directorate below, the problem of the general strike returned to the fore in March. Neither side would admit that a political power contest was developing, but it was evident that Castro did not care for rivals. When the DR had established a guerrilla front on the Escambray mountains in central Cuba late in 1957, Castro acknowledged it grudgingly and only belatedly, in February 1958, remarking in a message that 'regardless of the revolutionary militancy of your group, we have given instructions to the Movement to give you all possible help'. As for the DR, they had even less use for the Rebel Army, and soon the two would be embroiled in bitter disputes. And the issue of a general strike had to be faced by Castro in the context of his overall relationship with the *llano* revolutionaries. It was inevitable that other anti-Batista groups would engage in operations of their own. The creation of the DR front in the Escambray mountains was one example; another was the murder in Holguín, a garrison city in nothern Oriente, of Colonel Fermín Cowley Gallegos, one of the most hated and brutal Batista army chiefs, by a Civic Resistance action commando at the end of 1957.

For Castro the general strike thus became one way of imposing revolutionary unity. In his capacity as delegate of the Movement's National Directorate in Havana, Faustino Pérez had returned to the Sierra early in March, and after conferences with Castro and other members he joined him in signing a manifesto titled 'Total War Against Tyranny' calling for a general strike. Pérez pushed for the strike as soon as possible, believing that Castro lacked 'first-hand information on the existing conditions in Havana', and that his duty was to provide it. After all, he saw himself as one of Castro's closest associates: a companion aboard the *Granma*, one of Fidel's two companions during the desperate days and nights after Alegría de Pío, and the first emissary from the Sierra to Santiago and Havana. He was certain that Castro would listen to his assessments.

The twenty-two point 'Total War Against Tyranny' manifesto that Castro agreed to from 'the camp of Column 1, General Headquarters of the Rebel Forces', started out by proclaiming that 'the struggle against Batista has entered its final stage' and that 'the strategy of the final blow is based on a general revolutionary strike, to be seconded by military action'. The strike, it said, 'will be ordered at the proper time', and would continue along with the armed struggle 'if a military junta should try to take over the government'. Again, Castro was determined to prevent any deal behind his back by the military and the civilian opposition in the *llano*. As a further step to guarantee Castro's control, the new manifesto reaffirmed the Movement's choice of Manuel Urrutia Lleó as the head of a provisional government to be formed upon Batista's fall with the mission of preparing national elections. Castro had first proposed Urrutia in his December letter to the Cuban Liberation Junta, but now he and Faustino Pérez felt that the future appointment should be formalized as soon as possible.

Urrutia was the fifty-eight-year-old presiding judge of the Court of

Appeals of Oriente who cast the dissenting vote when his two colleagues on the bench had found guilty numerous captured *Granma* expeditionaries and Movement activists arrested during an abortive uprising in Santiago on 30 November 1956. The verdict condemned the rebels to eight-year prison terms. Urrutia wrote later that to him the defendants were 'models of dignity and patriotism' and that the basis for his dissent was 'the "sacred right of resistance against oppression" consecrated by Article 40 of the Cuban Constitution of 1940'. He added: 'I held that armed action by the accused men was legitimate because it was an attempt to end oppression in Cuba.' Four years earlier Urrutia had been the investigating judge in Santiago who certified the deaths of Castro's rebels involved in the Moncada attack on 26 July, and his sympathies with the Movement dated back to that bloody Sunday.

When Castro first conceived the notion of a provisional government, either Raúl Chibás or Felipe Pazos, co-signers with him of the Sierra Manifesto in July 1957, were his prime candidates for president. But Chibás refused the candidature, and Castro concluded that Pazos was too much involved in traditional politics. He then thought of Urrutia as the perfect apolitical candidate, and in November sent emissaries to the judge in Santiago to offer him the presidency on behalf of the Movement. Urrutia agreed, resigned from the judiciary, and left for the United States at the end of December to wait upon Batista's disappearance. His mandate was 'to lead our country to democracy, freedom, and a regime of law'.

Urrutia, a liberal and an anti-Communist jurist, added prestige to the Castro cause, another of Fidel's immediate needs, and he was received in Washington by senior State Department officials dealing with Latin America. His concern at that point was to persuade the United States to halt arms deliveries to Batista, and he may have played a role in the Eisenhower administration's eventual decision on 14 March 1958 to suspend these on the ground that American weapons were being used for internal security and not for hemispheric defence as provided by law. Arms shipments were indeed stopped, but Batista's bombers were still allowed to refuel at the Guantánamo naval base between strikes against the rebels.

The 'Total War' Manifesto declared that from 1 April all highway and railway traffic in Oriente was prohibited and that moving vehicles would be fired on, and that after that date it was forbidden to pay any taxes in Cuba – payment of taxes would be considered 'unpatriotic and counterrevolutionary'. At that stage the Rebel Army barely had 300 men under arms, but Fidel Castro's sense of drama and propaganda impelled him to announce that 'from this moment, the country should consider itself in total war against the tyranny . . . The entire nation is determined to be free or perish!'

The general strike date 9 April was secretly set as Movement representatives were ordered to speed up their clandestine efforts, and the Rebel Army readied itself for coordinated attacks. The *Fidelistas* were strengthened by the arrival in late March of one of the first aircraft to land in the Sierra Free Territory. A twin-engined C-47 transport flew from Costa Rica with a load of arms and ammunition – and two very important officers. One was Castro's principal military adviser Pedro Miret, who had been under arrest in Mexico when the *Granma* sailed for Cuba, and now was finally able to join his companions, and the other was Huber Matos, the rice planter whose trucks took up volunteers from Manzanillo to the Sierra Maestra. Matos, who organized the flight and delivered a letter from Fidel to Costa Rica's president, was instantly given a troop command. Pedro Miret recalls that Castro was waiting for them at the meadow where the plane landed at twilight, smashing a propeller, and he immediately named him to the general staff. Faustino Pérez, in the meantime, had gone back to Havana to coordinate the strike activities. Action groups in the capital were busy exploding bombs, scores of them every night throughout March, in order to create the psychological climate for a general strike. The effect was enhanced by the spectacular kidnapping of world car-racing champion Juan Manuel Fangio of Argentina on the eve of a major Havana race. In an operation engineered by Faustino Pérez, Fangio was released the next day, announcing that he had been well treated. The regime was properly humiliated. In the 26th of July Movement, optimism was soaring.

Yet the strike was a terrible failure. Fidel Castro described it as the 'hardest blow suffered by the revolution during its entire history' because 'the people had never had as much hope as on that day, and we had never had so many illusions as we had on that occasion'. What happened was that for a long chain of reasons – poor planning (notably in Havana), a breakdown in coordination among various groups, bad timing, and less than adequate response and participation among the population – Castro's hopes of a precipitous revolution in the cities were skewered. The regime, which had again suspended constitutional guarantees and drafted an additional 7000 men for the army, had been ready to smash the strike. At least a hundred Cubans were killed by the police throughout the island that day, and many hundreds were arrested. General Batista allowed himself to believe that the tide had turned, and that in the aftermath of the strike fiasco the rebels in the Sierra Maestra would be demolished by a major military offensive.

One of the long-standing arguments about the general strike concerns the role of the Communist Party and its relationship with the 26th of July Movement's leaders in Havana prior to the event. Because of their basic opposition to the Castro rebellion the Communists had been charged with sabotaging the strike to provoke a débâcle of the Movement, leading to a rise in their revolutionary influence and the adoption of their strategies. However, the Communist story is much more complex. No comprehensive account of the general strike drama has ever been published – it remains an acutely sensitive topic in Cuba and therefore the reconstruction of this whole occurrence and its consequences is bound to be incomplete. There is no question, however, that the failed general strike marked a fundamental turning point in the history of the revolution. The political influence of the Movement's moderates in the *llano* vanished and the assumption of total revolutionary power by Fidel Castro and his radical 'militarists' in the Sierra became paramount.

As for the Communists, the Movement's National Workers' Front (FON) avoided contact with the party's labour leaders, particularly influential among sugar workers, and for all practical purposes failed to include them in strike planning. FON did not give the Communists the date of the strike because it did not trust them. Although the Communist Party was certainly aware of what was going on, according to them the Movement's vision of a general strike was an appeal to the population instantly to join the stoppage and participate in armed attacks on pre-selected targets in Havana – without any preparation in plants, offices and other work places. In early April the party had concluded that the strike should be aborted if the procedures were not at once improved, and it dispatched Osvaldo Sánchez, a Central Committee member, to the Sierra to inform Castro of their decision. Sánchez reportedly told Castro that the Havana leaders had overestimated their strength, failed to work at organizing the strike at work centres, refused to cooperate with the Communists, and trusted too much in a spontaneous response to strike appeals.

Six years later, on 9 April 1964, the Communist Party's newspaper *Hoy* published for the first time a statement issued by Castro on 26 March 1958 to the effect that 'in summoning the nation to the final struggle against tyranny, our Movement makes no exclusions of any kind . . . All Cuban workers, whatever are their political or revolutionary allegiances, have the right to belong to strike committees at their places of work. The National Workers' Front is not a sectarian organism . . . The Front's leadership will coordinate with the worker's sections of political and revolutionary organizations that fight the regime, and with all the organized factions that struggle for economic and political revindications of their class, so that no worker can be severed from this patriotic effort.' However, the Communists claim, the Movement never publicized Castro's instructions, continuing their unilateral activities. On 2 April the Party's underground *Carta Semanal* publication called for a general strike, while noting that 'the forces of disunity remain present'.

In any event Fidel Castro did not call off the strike. At ten o'clock on the morning of 9 April three Havana radio stations seized by the revolutionaries broadcast an appeal by the Movement for a 'general revolutionary strike' to begin at once. It said: 'Today is the day of liberation . . . all thoughout Cuba at this very moment the final struggle to overthrow Batista has begun!' From the Sierra the radio called: 'Strike! Strike! Strike! Everyone on strike! Everyone into the streets!' Another broadcast urged patriots to 'throw stones at all strikebreakers from your windows . . . throw ignited Molotov cocktails at the patrol cars. . .' But very little happened in way of work stoppages, mainly because workers were taken by surprise, and the police were out in force. In Havana there were acts of sabotage, and heavy fighting developed in Sagua la Grande, a town in the central province of Las Villas. But the following day it was all over.

On 13 April Faustino Pérez and his Movement associates dispatched a communication to their committees in exile to acknowledge the failure, and the errors committed by the urban leadership. They said the gravest error was to keep secret the date of the strike, and then to broadcast an appeal to stike 'at an hour when only housewives listen to the radio'. Fidel was much tougher: in a letter to Celia on 16 April he said: 'The strike experience involved a great moral rout for the Movement . . . the revolution is once again in danger and its salvation rests in our hands . . . we cannot continue to disappoint the nation's hopes . . . No one will ever be able to make me trust the organization again . . . I am the supposed leader of this Movement, and in the eyes of history I must take responsibility for the stupidity of others, and I am a shit who can decide on nothing at all . . . I don't believe that a schism is developing in the Movement, but in the future we ourselves will have to resolve our own problems.' Four days later he told Celia 'We have not renounced the general strike as a decisive weapon against tyranny . . . A battle was lost but not the war.'

Now the time came for a final confrontation within the revolutionary ranks. Castro began with a letter on 25 April to Raúl Chibás and Mario Llerena, leaders of the Movement's Committee-in-Exile in Miami, charging that 'the Movement has failed utterly in the job of supplying us' and that 'egotism, and at times trickery from other sectors, have combined with incompetence, negligence and even the disloyalty of some comrades . . . The organization has not managed to send us so much as one rifle, not one bullet from abroad . . . But apart from all moral considerations, once again the task of saving the revolution in one of its most profound crises falls on our men.' Castro warned: 'The danger of a military coup reaffirms the thesis that only the military can overthrow dictatorships, just as they first put them into power, a thesis that bogs down the populace in fatalistic apathy . . . all this is now in the forefront as a result of the failure of the strike. *And the failure of the strike was a matter not only of organization but also of the fact that our own armed action is not yet strong enough. . .'*

All this set the stage for Castro's evisceration of the Movement as a political force outside his personal control. The Movement in the *llano* was dramatically accused of denying him resources from Cuba and abroad (it is impossible now to determine how accurate were the charges; for one thing, the first aircraft from Florida were beginning to land in the Sierra with war material). The spectre of a military coup and junta, Castro's constant fear, was raised anew. Finally, Castro washed his hands of any responsibility for the collapse of the strike he had approved in advance.

The actual confrontation between the two wings of the 26th of July Movement came at a meeting of the National Directorate on 3 May at a farmhouse at the Mompié heights in the heartland of the Sierra Maestra. Lasting from early morning until two o'clock in the morning of the next day, the session was presided over by Fidel Castro and attended principally by the Movement's *llano* leaders – Faustino Pérez and Marcelo Fernández from Havana, the Santiago coordinator René Ramos (Daniel) Latour, and the labour leader David Salvador – and Fidel's closest personal associates in the Directorate, Celia Sánchez, Vílma Espín from Santiago and Haydée Santamaría. Che Guevara was not a member of the National Directorate, but he was invited at the request of Faustino Pérez and Latour because they had been the target of his violent criticism in the wake of the failed strike. It marked Guevara's formal entry into the top Cuban revolutionary policy-making circles. Guevara was also the best chronicler of what he called the 'Decisive Reunion'.

More honest and outspoken than his companions, Guevara wrote: 'The division between the Sierra and *llano* was real . . . Differences of strategic concepts separated us.' Prior to the strike, Guevara noted, 'the comrades from the *llano* constituted the majority' in the National Directorate, and they were inclined 'towards certain "civilist" actions, a certain opposition to the *caudillo* who was feared [to exist] in Fidel, and the militarist faction represented by us, the people in the Sierra'. As a result of the Mompíe meeting, where Faustino Pérez, Latour and Salvador were virtually on trial, the 'guerrilla concept' of direct military action became 'triumphant, with the consolidation of the prestige and authority of Fidel [who] was named commander-in-chief of the forces, including the militias, that until now had been subordinated to the *llano* Directorate'. After what Guevara described as 'an exhaustive and often violent discussion', Faustino Pérez, Latour and Salvador were removed from their posts in the leadership of the Movement. He wrote: 'Politically, the National Directorate was shifted to the Sierra Maestra where Fidel took the post of Secretary General, and a Secretariat of five members was created.'

In Havana, Marcelo Fernández was made the Movement coordinator under Castro, and Faustino Pérez was replaced as a national *llano* leader by Delio Ochoa Gómez, a Fidel military man. Faustino, Latour and Salvador were transferred to the Sierra where Castro gave the first two men important responsibilities. He was not a personally vindictive man, except when he sensed a betrayal, and he thought that Faustino's and Latour's talents and loyalty should be fully used. Faustino, who says that he was regarded at the time as part of the right wing of the Movement, has remained with Castro in the revolutionary establishment for thirty years; Latour was killed in battle four months later. Urrutia, already designated as provisional president of Cuba, was put on a salary while awaiting the summons and now in exile in Caracas (he was the only salaried Movement leader), and Haydée Santamaría was sent to Miami to coordinate fund-raising in the United States. Carlos Franqui was recalled to Cuba to take over the Radio Rebelde station that was beginning to broadcast to the rest of the island from the top of the Sierra Maestra in the spot where Castro's permanent headquarters were being set up. Radio Rebelde immediately became one of Fidel's most important psychological warfare weapons. For Che Guevara the most important outcome of the Mompíe confrontation was that now 'the war would be conducted militarily and politically by Fidel in his double capacity as commander-in-chief of all the forces and secretary general of the organization.'

But Guevara, despite his oft-repeated declarations of allegiance to Marxism–Leninism, remained unhappy with Cuban Communists. In 1958 he wrote that there were 'mutual fears' between the Movement and the Communist Party, 'and, fundamentally, the party of the workers had not perceived with sufficient clarity the role of the *guerrilla* nor Fidel's personal role in our revolutionary struggle'. Che recalled having told a Communist leader: 'You are capable of organizing cadres that are allowed to go to pieces in the darkness of a dungeon without saying a word, but you are not capable of forming cadres that can capture a machine-gun nest in an assault.' No matter what was said and what happened later, the top *guerrilla* leaders, with the possible exception of Raúl Castro, resented the Communists during most of the Sierra war. Whether or not this was part of his tactical line at that stage, Castro made a point of saying in a 1958 *Look* interview that 'the Cuban Communists . . . have never opposed Batista, for whom they have seemed to feel a close kinship'. He said that Americans 'should know more about Latin American movements that are democratic and nationalist . . . Why be afraid of freeing the people, whether Hungarians or Cubans?'

Fidel Castro would go on criticizing Communists, sometimes savagely, in public and in private, but in reconstructing the events of 1958 in terms of his own political evolution, it appears that the trauma of the aborted strike led him to at least a preliminary decision to go the Marxist–Leninist route. The strike revealed to him the political un-reliability of the 26th of July Movement liberals and moderates from a revolutionary viewpoint as well as from an organizational one. From men and women who lived that period with Castro, the consensus emerges that he had resolved, as a practical matter, that Marxist–Leninist strategies, procedures and techniques would be the best suited to the future of his 'real' revolution. That the traditional Communist Party still denied him support, these witnesses say, mattered little to Castro who was already thinking of fashioning his own Communist Party, a pretension more absurd than his original determination to overthrow Batista single-handed. His early Marxist sympathies evidently played a role in turning him towards this decision, as did his resentments against the United States. More to the point, however, he judged that what he thought to be Communist organizational talents and experience with mass organizations – unlike the 26th of July Movement – could be harnessed to the revolution with him in command. In this sense, then, there was never an ideological struggle for Fidel's soul, as some commentators have suggested. But, unquestionably, the entire process was irreversibly set in motion as a consequence of the April 1958 general strike.

But now it was General Batista who decided to launch a total war. An offensive late in 1957, designed to isolate the Sierra Maestra from the outside, produced no meaningful results, so the Havana high command elaborated a different strategy for its May 'summer offensive'. This new concept provided for encircling the Sierra, gradually closing the circle, and then launching the final definitive blow against Castro at his headquarters in La Plata high in the heart of the Sierra Maestra. The campaign left Raúl Castro's Liberated Zone to the north-east at first under little more than air attacks, with the assumption that once Fidel was liquidated, the younger brother's forces would collapse sooner or later. In June, however, Raúl came under powerful air and ground attack. The Batista blueprint called for advances on the central Sierra Maestra from the south where troops were landed on the coast, from the north-west and from the north. As many as 10,000 men were deployed in Operation FF (*Fin de Fidel*, or End of Fidel) in three battle groups; they were supported by artillery, helicopters, aeroplanes, and navy frigates firing on the coast from the sea.

Fidel Castro's Column No. 1 in the centre of the Sierra had 280 armed men, including Che Guevara's force to the east, and was later reinforced by Juan Almeida's column of several dozen rebels recalled from the easternmost front. Batista possessed crushing superiority in numbers and firepower, but Castro had turned the mountains into a fortress he could defend with a much smaller force of men, men who knew every path in the forest, every turn of the road, and every peasant's house. Both sides recognized that this would be the decisive battle of the war, and Castro was prepared to cede territory up to a certain line protecting his La Plata headquarters, and then to hit back with ambushes, and fight to the death. 'Every entrance to the Sierra Maestra is like the pass at Thermopylae,' Fidel told Venezuela newsmen, 'and every narrow passage becomes a death trap.'

When the government forces began their final attack on 20 May, Castro had entered what Guevara described as a 'sedentary phase', expanding La Plata headquarters, and consolidating and organizing the Free Territory administratively and politically. Not far from La Plata, Che Guevara set up a Rebel Army recruits' school at Minas del Frío where new volunteers were trained by a former Batista army captain. The headquarters, called *comandancia* in Spanish, was a large forest clearing on the crest of the Sierra Maestra that could be reached only up a tortuous, narrow path, studded with rocks and boulders, and usually covered with mud. It was an extraordinarily tough climb, and mules could be used only a part of the way.

Wooden buildings erected in La Plata were concealed by branches from above, and each structure was so cleverly located in the trees at the edge of the clearing that one could not spot it even in daylight until coming very close to it. Castro's house was built solidly against the side of a ravine over a creek, and it had an escape route down a long ladder to the creek if it were frontally attacked. The house consisted of a bedroom with a double bed for Fidel and Celia, a room serving as an office for Celia, a deck where Castro often received visitors, and a kitchen. Nearby was the building where Faustino Pérez ran his civil affairs office for 'liberated territories', then a hospital, a guest house, and a large shed for the women's combat regiment. The women had a score of sewing machines on which they worked on uniforms, but they dropped their sewing when necessary and grabbed their rifles to go into battle.

The first house on the clearing was the office of a dentist who became a guerrilla officer, responsible for the men's teeth and for ammunition stores; Castro, who has bad teeth, was a frequent customer of the bearded dentist, and more than once he received visitors and battle reports while a pedal-activated drill worked in his mouth. Several hundred feet above the clearing were the studio and antenna of the rebel radio, which served both as a broadcasting station and as a radio link for Castro with Caracas, Mexico, Miami and places in Cuba. Finally, a field telephone network was established between La Plata and a number of outlying rebel positions, lessening the dependence on couriers for every message.

The Batista offensive lasted seventy-six days before being decisively beaten back by the *Fidelistas*. The rebels came several times very close to defeat when the army had captured most of their positions around La Plata. Castro said that 19 June was the 'most critical day'. He had gambled everything on preventing the Batista soldiers from dislodging his forces from the spine of the Sierra Maestra. So long as he held it, his rebels could fire down on the enemy and keep them in check. Repeatedly, army battalions attempted to cross a river near Santo Domingo and scale the range, but each time they were beaten back by the rifles, machine guns and mortars of no more than forty rebels deployed along the crest. Castro, who raced with Celia and his aide Arturo Aguilera by Jeep or on foot from spot to spot, was at times so close to enemy troops that he could count individual soldiers as he stared down at them with his binoculars. He also employed psychological warfare for the first time in the Sierra war during this battle by installing loudspeakers that blared the national anthem, patriotic songs and revolutionary exhortations at the exhausted Batista soldiers. He believes that it helped to sap their morale. In any event, the offensive ended.

It was a violent and vicious war, but Castro and some of the Batista commanders developed an old-fashioned gentlemanly relationship that Fidel, in particular, enjoyed. At the outset of the enemy offensive he received a communication from General Eulogio Cantillo, the chief of the Batista forces in the region, inviting him, in effect, to surrender. Castro answered instantly: 'I think highly of you. My opinion is not incompatible with my having the honour of recognizing you as an adversary . . . I appreciate your noble feelings towards us, who are, after all, your compatriots, not your enemies, because we are not at war against the armed forces, but against the dictatorship . . . Perhaps when the offensive is over, if we are still alive, I will write you again to clarify my thinking and to tell you what I think you, the army, and we can do for the benefit of Cuba. . .' Che Guevara took a dim view of this exchange.

Earlier in July, too, before the rebels repulsed the Batista offensive, when Castro defeated a battalion led by Major José Quevedo that had been landed on the coast with orders to storm the Sierra up La Plata river, he first wrote to the major, whom he knew from Havana University as a fellow law student. It had been difficult to imagine, he said, 'that some day we would be fighting against each other, even though we perhaps do not even harbour different feelings about our fatherland . . . I have used harsh words in judging the actions of many, and of the army in general, but never have my hands or those of my companions been stained with blood by the mistreatment of any soldier taken prisoner . . . I write these lines on the spur of the moment, without asking you for anything, only to greet you and to wish you, very sincerely, good luck.' Five days later Castro sent Quevedo another message that 'your troops are surrounded, they have not the slightest hope of being saved . . . In this situation, I offer you an honourable, dignified surrender . . . All your men will be treated with the greatest respect and consideration. The officers will be permitted to keep their weapons.' But Quevedo kept fighting, and on 19 July Castro sent one of his men to ask him to surrender to save lives on both sides; he broadcast a radio appeal to the Quevedo battalion to give up, promising them special treatment; then he went to meet the major. When Quevedo finally surrendered on 21 July the rebels took 220 prisoners. Castro entered the camp, and ordered Ramiro Valdés: 'Have all the officers keep their sidearms. Make sure that nobody tries to take them away from them.' Then he sent a message for Guevara to 'try to have them prepare lunch' for the prisoners at the Mompíe hill before their release. The prisoners were turned over to the International Red Cross three days later, and Che Guevara arrived on a little mule to watch it. Castro meanwhile had raced across the mountains to fight at Santo Domingo.

On 12 August both Fidel and Che were at Las Mercedes to observe the delivery to the Red Cross of some hundred prisoners from another Batista unit. They met the army colonel representing his side at the ceremony, and they had coffee together and chatted amiably. The colonel said he thought the rebels would win in the end, 'but you will find a destroyed Cuba'. When Castro showed interest in the colonel's heli-copter parked outside, the officer invited the rebels to fly around with him. With Che, Celia and a rebel captain, Fidel flew over the Sierra for fifteen minutes, having a marvellous time and spotting from the air places he knew. It was his first time aboard a helicopter, and his aides were horrified for his safety: 'It was a Fidel-type thing to do,' Colonel Aguilera said. From there, Castro returned to the *comandancia* to plan the rebel counter-offensive – which would turn out to be the final offensive of the war.

As Aguilera remembers, 'Celia never left him, Celia was always with him.' The only times they separated was when Castro wanted her for some specific Rebel Army problem at La Plata when he had to make a dash to a unit caught up in sudden combat. Others remember Celia with her slacks and blouse pockets full of Castro's and Rebel Army papers and documents; Fidel would dictate any time, anywhere, receive briefings whenever and wherever he could, and Celia operated, in effect, a portable office.

Batista lost the summer offensive and close to a thousand men in dead and wounded, plus the prisoners the rebels kept returning as they captured them. Castro took over five hundred modern weapons, including two tanks. It was calculated later that 321 men beat back the huge Batista offensive, and it was calculated at the time by politicians and senior officers in Havana that the regime could not last much longer. Castro's Radio Rebelde broadcast to all Cuba every detail of the victories, his ringing battle reports read by Violeta Casal, the first woman announcer in the mountains.

Late in June, Raúl Castro had forty-nine American citizens kidnapped in eastern Oriente, in a desperate attempt to force the Batista air command to halt bombing his units and the peasant families spread throughout the Sierra Cristal war zone. Without consulting Fidel, who was fighting off enemy troops in the central Sierra Maestra, Raúl ordered the kidnappings when he obtained proof that Batista planes were not only being refuelled but also loaded with bombs at the Guantánamo US naval base; he had obtained photographs showing Cuban aircraft receiving ordnance there, and a rebel agent at the Cuban embassy in Washington had forwarded to the Sierra documents showing that 300 rocket warheads had been delivered to the Batista command through Guantánamo. The Eisenhower administration's excuse, three months after arms deliveries to Cuba were officially suspended, was that the warheads were replacements for defective ones sent earlier; it was also explained that the replacement was done more easily in Guantánamo. In Washington, nobody was thinking politically.

At a time when they were nearly out of ammunition, Raúl's forces were being badly hurt by the intensive bombings, rocketing and strafing. In a lengthy operational report on 2 June Raúl informed Fidel of 'our lack of all kinds of ammunition . . . This offensive worries me.'

On 26 June, therefore, Raúl's commandos raided the American-owned Moa and Nicaro nickel mines and the United Fruit Company's sugar mill at Guaro in the north of Oriente, capturing twenty-five American managers and employees. Simultaneously another commando on the south coast of the province captured a bus taking twenty-four US marines back to the base. The rebels also took tractors and trucks from the nickel mines 'as strict war necessities'. American Consul General Park Wollam from Santiago went up to the Sierra to negotiate with Raúl for the release of the hostages, and was shown fragments of American-manufactured bombs and the Guantánamo photographs. Earlier, the hostages had been taken to see damage caused by the bombing, and the victims of napalm firebombing. Though Wollam and the other Americans were well treated and even given a Fourth of July party by the rebels, Raúl released the hostages only after Fidel had ordered it in an adroit broadcast from La Plata on 3 July; even so, the last hostage was freed only on 18 July. During the entire time of the Americans' captivity Raúl was spared air attacks (presumably Washington suggested to Batista that this would be a good idea) and he was able to resupply and reorganize his *guerrilla*.

As for Fidel, he used the kidnapping incident to assert his war leadership, to please the United States and to affirm his support for his brother's actions. Though his broadcast came a full week after the initial kidnapping, Fidel could make the excuse that his headquarters had received no reports on it because of the distance and the absence of radio transmitters with Raúl's forces, but such an occurrence was 'possible . . . as a reaction to the recent delivery of 300 rockets from the North American naval base at Caimanera [the Cuban name for the base] to Batista's planes, with which civilian populations are being bombed in the territory occupied by the rebels'. Then he grandly announced that 'despite all this, today I am publicly ordering [the hostages'] release . . . If it is true that these North Americans are being held by some revolutionary troops, my orders will be received and carried out, because I believe that these North American citizens cannot be blamed for the shipment of bombs to Batista by the government of their country. I feel certain that no rebel forces would make hostages of United States citizens so that they could observe the results of the inhuman bombings of Cuban civilians with weapons sent by the United States . . . The 26th of July Movement is fighting for the respect of human rights. We believe that individual freedom is one of the inviolable rights of every human being and therefore no one should be arrested without a just cause. We hope that the United States government will, in like manner, respect the lives and liberty of Cubans . . . This is the necessary condition for the continuation of the present friendly relations between our two countries.'

Castro, behaving more and more like a statesman, handled the next incident with the United States, late in July, with equal diplomacy. As Batista had withdrawn army guards protecting the aqueduct from Cuban territory to the Guantánamo naval base (which depended completely on water from Cuba), US marines took over this responsibility and the rebels protested against this immediately, as an act of American intervention. Rebel emissaries, including the journalist Carlos Franqui, entered into quiet negotiations with American diplomats in Santiago – more and more, reality forced American officials to deal with the *Fidelistas* – and rejected a proposal that the aqueduct area be regarded as a neutral zone. Thereupon Castro issued a formal declaration that 'the presence of North American forces . . . is illegal and constitutes aggression against Cuban national territory', but 'we are ready to give guarantees that the water supply will not be interfered with because our objective is not to attack that facility. . .' This was both a firm and conciliatory message, and Castro's language was carefully making the point that while he wished no disputes with the United States, he would make no concessions whenever in his view Cuban sovereignty was infringed by the *Yanquís*. This would remain his consistent policy towards the United States.

Apart from the fact that Raúl did not consult Fidel over the kidnapping of the Americans, which he probably could have done given his practice of sending long operational reports to rebel headquarters, there is no question that, much more than his brother, he was emphasizing Marxist ideological indoctrination in his zone. It is also a fact that the Communist Party's contacts with his rebels were much stronger than with Fidel's units. Interestingly, whereas Fidel chose to deal with the Communists almost exclusively on a high policy level before and during the war years, Raúl concentrated on forging discreet but effective operational links, politically and militarily. This may have been a deliberate division of political labour between the brothers, aimed at protecting Fidel's democratic image before international public opinion, but the different ways in which their commands were run does suggest that Raúl took or was given the freedom to do what he pleased in this area. A similar situation would develop later in Che Guevara's command in the final stages of the war. Even guerrilla dress differed: Raúl and Che wore black berets with a star for rank insignia; Fidel preferred his olive-green cap with no stars.

Jorge Risquet Valdés-Saldaña, in 1986 a full Politburo member and Castro's chief trouble-shooter in Africa as well as in labour affairs, was another young Communist whom Raúl put in charge of his Department of Revolutionary Instruction and the José Martí School for Troop Instructors at the Sierra Cristal village of Tumbasiete. This school became the model for post-revolutionary military indoctrination centres as it taught selected fighters 'ideological formation' along with other aspects of education. At Tumbasiete Communist instructors introduced for the first time a Cuban history text based on Marxist interpretations. By the end of 1958 all the Rebel Army instructors in Raúl's territory were Tumbasiete graduates, and the ideological influence spread to the peasants in the well-populated regions of northern Oriente. Raúl likewise organized a Corps of Rebel Intelligence Officers (a forerunner of the Army's G-2 Intelligence Service) and a Committee of Revolutionary Peasants as an 'information' branch.

When Carlos Rafael Rodríguez, one of the top Communist Party leaders, finally travelled to the mountains late in July as part of the Communists' changing attitude towards the rebels, he first stopped to see Raúl. He was subsequently quoted as saying: 'In the Sierra Cristal, where Raúl Castro commanded, all was harmony with the Communists; but when I arrived at Fidel Castro's in the Sierra Maestra, harmony was converted into suspicion.' This was Rodríguez's first trip to Fidel's headquarters; there would be others.

In the meantime Fidel Castro was emphasizing unity and moderation. On 20 July, while he was directing operations against the Quevedo battalion above the coast, Radio Rebelde broadcast from the mountain the text of the 'Unity Manifesto of the Sierra Maestra', also known as the

Caracas Pact (because it was signed in the Venezuelan capital). It was issued jointly by the 26th of July Movement and eight other Cuban opposition political parties and revolutionary and action organizations, including the rival Students' Revolutionary Directorate, but not including the Communists. Castro said later that this was on account of objections to the Communists by all the other groups (which he accepted without public protest). Having long resisted pacts with other Cuban revolutionaries and politicians, Castro was evidently willing to sign the Caracas document because he was now dealing from a position of military strength. At the same time the pact further improved his statesman's image: he was the undisputed leader of the revolution, and the other signers of this 'Unity Manifesto', all of them political moderates, implicitly recognized this.

The Manifesto was not a revolutionary programme, but an agreement 'to create a large revolutionary, civic coalition, made up from all of Cuba's people'. It provided for 'a common strategy to defeat the dictatorship by means of an armed insurrection' and 'the popular mobilization of all labour, civic, professional and economic forces, culminating in a great general strike on the civilian front'. On the military front, it said, 'action will be coordinated throughout the country'. Concerning the future, only two points were made: 'a brief provisional government will be formed to establish full constitutional and demo-cratic rights'; and 'a minimum government programme will be formed to guarantee workers' rights, the punishment of those who are guilty of crimes, fulfilment of international agreements, public order, peace and freedom, as well as the economic, social and political progress of the Cuban people'. The Manifesto then asked the United States 'to cease all military and other types of aid to the dictator'. José Miró Cardona, the exiled president of the Cuban Bar Association, was the coordinator of the pact; it was understood that Manuel Urrutia, the president-designate who was in New York when the Manifesto was issued, would soon be flown to the Sierra Maestra.

It was to discuss the post-Batista Cuba in the light of the Manifesto that Carlos Rafael Rodríguez had gone to see Fidel late in July, remaining there until 10 August, when he returned to Havana to report to the Communist Party leadership. It is unclear whether Rodríguez had Fidel in mind when he spoke of the 'suspicion' he encountered at La Plata, and there is no evidence to suggest that an actual agreement for subsequent collaboration emerged from these preliminary discussions. According to Rodríguez, Castro said that it would be a grave tactical error to alert the enemy prematurely by defining with excessive clarity the revolutionary objectives, but this did not necessarily commit him to an alliance with the Communists. Rodríguez was replaced at La Plata by Luís Más Martín, another ranking Communist leader and an old friend of the Castro brothers, arriving there on 6 September. Más Martín told an interviewer later that Fidel, while reminiscing with him about obtaining books from the Communist Party's bookshop in Havana, remarked that 'when the revolution triumphs, we'll have Marxist books coming out of our ears'. Again, this is hardly a statement of political intent. Much more relevant was the Communist Party's decision to maintain from then on a permanent presence with Castro, and his evident acceptance of it. Thus Rodríguez came back to La Plata in mid-September, remaining with the rebels until the end of the war. No other Cuban political group sought or had such representation.

The likelihood is that Castro made the final decision to strike a deal with the Communists during the time of Rodríguez's residence on the mountain, culminating a very pragmatic process that had begun with the collapse of the April general strike. This would explain the ease with which Castro slid into a relationship with the Communists immediately after his victory. It is important, however, to understand that Castro's plan was to use the 'old' Communists merely for his instant needs, and in the absence of any other organization in the cities that he could trust, including his own 26th of July Movement. The Rebel Army was his revolutionary vanguard, but it was not prepared to run the country for him when it came down from the Sierra. Chances are that, except for Carlos Rafael Rodríguez, the 'old' Communists did not comprehend Fidel's strategy until he finally swallowed them. Raúl Chibás, who flew to the Sierra for a second visit in August 1958, says that his nearly daily discussions with Fidel over long weeks covered every subject except the question of Communism; in exile from Cuba for over a quarter of a century, he still thinks Castro is a 'Fidelista, not a Communist'.

Perhaps the greatest insight into Castro's politics and ideology was expressed by Régis Debray, the French intellectual who knew him better than any foreigner: 'A Leninist is an opportunist with principles. Fidel is a Leninist. His principles remain firm, but the opportunities change. The unique thing about him is his combination of great realism in the evolution of the means available, and his final goal.' In his 1967 book, *Revolution in the Revolution?*, Debray remarked that the stronger the revolutionary nucleus in Cuba, 'the more it could permit itself to seek alliances'. He also underlines the Castro novelty the 'old' Communists missed: 'Eventually, the future People's Army will beget the [political] party of which it is to be, theoretically, the instrument: essentially the party is the army . . . [it] already existed in embryo – in the form of the Rebel Army. Fidel, its commander in chief, was already an unofficial party leader by early 1959.'

On 10 October 1958, however, Fidel Castro signed in the Sierra Maestra an agrarian reform law, as Revolutionary Law No. 1, that preserved his moderate image. Drafted by the Rebel Army's Advocate-

General Humberto Sorí-Marín, but approved by Castro, it turned over to tenants, renters and squatters the land they worked; it said nothing about breaking up the great estates. This agrarian reform did not affect 58 per cent of Cuba's land area in private hands though it benefited 64 per cent of all the farmers. Coming after the bland Sierra Manifesto and the communication to the Cuban Liberation Junta in 1957, the revolutionary documents of 1958 were equally devoted to moderation, despite (or because of?) the Rebel Army's victories.

It has been argued for over a quarter of a century whether Castro and his movement were secretly more radical than they admitted in public, but this is an increasingly barren theme. Official histories in Cuba cite Castro's *History Will Absolve Me* address in 1953 as an example of Marxist thought – and, taken at face value, even this is debatable – but no serious explanations are provided for the moderate sounds from the Sierra, apart from Che Guevara's comment that the rebels had to live with 'a minimum programme'. In the end the public record must stand, and the Cuban exiled scholar Nelson P. Valdés is probably correct when he says that 'the Cuban revolutionary leadership ached for truly radical credentials, but could not produce any'. The truth may be in the pragmatic opportunism elaborated in the Sierra Maestra as the Rebel Army's final offensive began, and transformed into official radicalism after the victory a half-year later.

Karl E. Meyer, then an editorial writer for the *Washington Post*, visited Castro at La Plata for three days just as the rebel offensive was getting under way, and he found him relaxed, 'sprawled across a bed' and expressing views that 'as he described them to me are suprisingly moderate'. Meyer wrote that 'his social views are vague, but incline to a kind of welfare-state liberalism'. When Meyer arrived, Castro was reading a book titled *Kaput* by Curzio Malaparte, one of Mussolini's favourite journalists, and he quoted from Il Duce that 'you can make a coup with the army or without the army, but never against the army'. Flourishing his cigar, Castro observed: 'We are proving Mussolini wrong. We are winning here in Cuba against the army.' Castro complained that Israel was sending arms to Batista now that the United States had finally suspended deliveries, saying: 'Why should they do such a thing? We have nothing against the Jewish people.' Meyer says that on his return to Washington he passed it on to an Israeli newspaper correspondent who used it in a story, 'which in turn provoked a challenge in the Knesset and I believe brought an end to the shipments'. Finally, Castro informed Meyer that 'in three months, three-fourths of the island will be in rebel hands'. During Meyer's visit a portrait of Fidelito in a gilt frame was delivered to Castro, and he exclaimed beamingly, 'This is my son.' Fidelito must just have returned to Havana with his mother after attending school for one year in Queens, New York, where they went shortly following the boy's kidnapping from his aunts' care in Mexico City.

In making his military prediction to Meyer, Castro was not too far off the mark. Camilo Cienfuegos, leading the Antonio Maceo Column with eighty-two men, was ordered to march from the Sierra Maestra to the westernmost province of Pinar del Río, and Che Guevara at the head of the Ciro Redondo Column with 148 men was assigned to take the central province of Las Villas, including the Escambray mountains. They left in the third week of August. It may have appeared to be a demented plan, considering that the rebels were leaving the safety of the Sierra for the lowlands where Batista still had tens of thousands of soldiers and policemen, but Castro was convinced that Cienfuegos and Guevara would triumph. They were to act as military governers as well as setting up revolutionary authority as they advanced. Castro himself planned to attack Santiago later in the autumn.

Incredibly, Cienfuegos and Guevara made it to Las Villas, marching, fighting and starving under the most adverse conditions – and creating new myths for the Rebel Army. It took the first column nearly six weeks to cross western Oriente and Camagüey province to reach Las Villas, walking through swamps and swimming through rivers, usually without food. The second column under Che made it in seven weeks. They had extremely few casualties, and it had never occurred to the commanders or the men to doubt the wisdom of Castro's orders to seize most of Cuba with a total of 230 men. But, astonishingly, the government was pulling back, volunteers were joining the invaders from the Sierra, and the rebels kept advancing. The plan was modified for Cienfuegos and Guevara to work together to reach the north coast of Las Villas and thereby sever the island into two parts; the march on Pinar del Río was set aside. In the Escambray mountains the *Fidelista* chiefs encountered four other separate revolutionary forces: the Student Revolutionary Directorate (DR), a spin-off from DR known as the Second National Front of Escambray, a Communist Party unit, and one organized by former President Prío. Che Guevara wrote that it took 'laborious negotiations' to create an approximately common strategy in regard to the enemy, the problems being of both political and ideological differences. The DR and Second Front fighters were convinced that Guevara and Cienfuegos were Communists, and at first refused all cooperation. Enrique Oltusky, the provincial coordinator for the 26th of July Movement, had a bitter clash with Che Guevara over ideological matters. The Communist unit, the only fully Communist guerrilla group in the whole war, worked well with the Sierra rebels. Still, during November and December the fighting against the Batista troops for the control of the province's capital of Santa Clara went on.

Fidel Castro moved out of his mountain haven in mid-September at the head of Column No. 1, José Martí, initiating an offensive designed to capture most of Oriente, then surround Santiago and force its capitulation. Raúl's forces in the east fanned out to attack Batista forces from the rear. Castro now had military momentum going for him as well as the financial resources he had lacked in the past: landowners, industrialists and businessmen were contributing on such a scale to the 26th of July Movement that Fidel could instruct Major Juan Almeida in October to pay as much as $1 for a single semi-automatic rifle bullet, if necessary. The Rebel Army could not afford to run out of ammunition as it raced to crush Batista. On 6 December Castro's column won a tough battle for the town of Guisa, opening the way into the heart of Oriente. And on the same day Manuel Urrutia landed on a secret field in the western outskirts of the Sierra Maestra, to become Cuba's provisional president. On his flight from Caracas, Urrutia brought a shipment of arms and ammunition sent to the rebels by Venezuela's provisional president, Admiral Wolfgang Larrazábal. This was the first delivery of arms from a foreign government, but Larrazábal had ousted his country's dictatorship less than a year before, and he felt close to Castro; he was not the kind of traditional military officer the Fidelistas so feared at home as an alternative to Batista.

From Guisa, Castro kept up the pace, seizing the towns of Baire, Jiguaní, Maffo and Contramestre, firing daily broadships of communiqués, proclamations and ultimata. His victories were particularly spectactular because at the outset his column had consisted mainly of rough recruits from the Minas del Frío basic-training school. On 19 December Fidel established his command post outside of Jiguaní, receiving there for the first time President-Designate Urrutia at a meeting also attended by Celia, Raúl, Vilma Espín and Juan Almeida. Urrutia wrote later that Castro greeted him coldly, which seems unlikely in those euphoric days. The next morning Colonel Aguilera, his aide, had to hold back Fidel physically to prevent him from advancing at the head of his column through enemy fire in the next town they were attacking.

Palma Soriano, directly north-west of Santiago, fell on 20 December, and Castro found himself retracing, now as military chief, his steps of more than five years earlier as a conspirator en route for Moncada. At that point Batista began preparations to flee Cuba. His armed forces were psychologically disintegrating, with only a few battalions still willing to go on fighting. The people in Havana and the other cities, as well as in the countryside, were openly against him. The ship was sinking. In Havana a Castro agent was contacted secretly by a faction of senior army officers proposing a peace settlement which included the replacement of Batista with a civilian–military junta composed of General Eulogio Cantillo, an anti-Batista army officer now in prison with whom Fidel had exchanged letters during the summer offensive, Manuel Urrutia, and two other civilians chosen by the revolutionaries. The agent was further informed that the United States would immediately recognize such a junta. This was the military-coup trap which Castro had suspected and feared all along, and he shot back a brief message: 'Conditions rejected. Arrange personal meeting between Cantillo and me.'

Released from jail, Cantillo met Castro near Palma Soriano on 28 December, and the rebel commander repeated his rejection of a junta; power, he said, had to be vested in the revolutionary army. With Santiago surrounded, Cantillo agreed to lead a mutiny on 31 December and unconditionally turn over his troops to Castro. Celia Sánchez and Vílma Espín were present, along with Raúl Chibás and Major José Quevedo who had just arrived at Fidel's new headquarters at the Oriente sugar mill outside Palma Soriano. Quevedo was the superb Batista troop commander whom Castro had defeated in July and brought over to the Rebel Army (in the 1980s Quevedo was the Cuban Military attaché in Moscow). However, Cantillo broke his word, informing Batista of the junta plan, and giving him until 6 January to leave the country. Then he asked Castro for a week's postponement of their deal, instantly arousing his suspicions. But events moved very fast. Che Guevara finally captured Santa Clara on 30 December, putting an armoured train out of action, and the regime had nothing left to shore it up. Just after midnight of New Year's Eve, Batista, his family and closest associates drove to Camp Columbia's airfield and took off for the Dominican Republic. His final act was to appoint General Cantillo as head of the armed forces.

Fidel Castro quietly spent New Year's Eve at the sugar mill with Celia and his commanders, learning from radio broadcasts at dawn what had just occurred in Havana. Carlos Rafael Rodríguez was in Palma Soriano too, but apparently he did not see Castro that night; Chibás, who was summoned by Celia to join Fidel in his room, says that Fidel seemed annoyed over Rodríguez's presence. It was bad for his image, Chibás thinks. (Errol Flynn was in Palma Soriano too, as it happened, filming a movie.) That morning, in the capital, Cantillo formed a junta chaired by Carlos M. Piedra, a Supreme Court judge, and Castro instantly moved into action. Speaking over Radio Rebelde from its new location in Palma Soriano, Castro first issued an ultimatum for the Santiago garrison to surrender by 6 p.m. saying: 'The events of 1898 will not be repeated', an allusion to the fact that American forces had not allowed Cuban independence fighters to enter the city at the end of the war with Spain. Then he issued a proclamation to the nation denouncing the junta as 'accomplices of the tyranny' and calling a general strike for the next day. He ordered Camilo Cienfuegos and Che Guevara to march on Havana to seize, respectively, Camp Columbia and La Cabaña Fortress. 'The Rebel

Army will continue its campaign,' Fidel shouted. 'Revolution, *yes*; military coup, *no!*'

In Havana the junta collapsed before nightfall. At noon a diplomatic delegation, which included the American ambassador, Earl Smith, had met with General Cantillo at the Presidential Palace, but by the afternoon Camp Columbia was turned over by its officers to Colonel Ramón Barquín, who had just been released from prison on the Isle of Pines where he was serving a sentence for conspiring against Batista. Barquín placed Cantillo under house arrest, and by midnight a plane arrived from the Isle of Pines bringing other officers who had been imprisoned there, including Captain José Ramón Fernández, and such civilian leaders as Armando Hart. Cienfuegos and Guevara would reach Havana only by the afternoon of 2 January, and for three days the capital was without government or authorities; but there was no violence in the city, only joy, chanting and singing long into the night. Cubans had taken to heart Castro's broadcast appeals not to take justice into their own hands.

Fidel Castro and his entourage entered Santiago on 2 January, surrounded by a joyful explosion of popular feeling. Symbolically, he took possession of the Moncada Barracks where he had launched the revolution on 26 July 1953. He named Manuel Urrutia to be the Provisional President of Cuba, declared Santiago to be the provisional capital of Cuba, and that evening delivered his first speech as the victorious chief of the revolution to a deliriously happy crowd. Immediately he set the tone for the future, the future that had already arrived: 'The revolution begins now. The revolution will not be an easy task. The revolution will be a very difficult undertaking, full of danger. This time it will not be like 1898, when the North Americans came and made themselves masters of our country. This time, fortunately, the revolution will truly come to power. At this moment we must consolidate our position before anything else . . . The revolution will not be made in two days, but now I am sure that the revolution *will* be made, that for the first time the republic will really be entirely free, and that the people will have what they deserve . . . This war has been won by the people!'

Part Four

The Revolution
1959–1963

Chapter 1

Fidel Castro took over Cuba and launched his great revolution in January 1959, to the thunderous applause of an overwhelming majority of his compatriots. Within eighteen months he had guided the country to the threshold of a Marxist–Leninist society and into an alliance with the Soviet Union. In the words of his closest Communist associate, Carlos Rafael Rodríguez, 'the democratic-bourgeois period in Cuba really ended in August 1960', and Castro himself said at the time that 'we are entering a new stage' of the revolution. He also explained that the revolutionary movement had to be the work of 'New Communists . . . because they were now known as such'. The same month the Central Intelligence Agency in Washington formally approved top-secret plans to assassinate him.

Castro set out from his first day in power to destroy every vestige of the old social order in Cuba. He accomplished this through the extraordinary procedure of operating for well over a year, until his revolutionary controls were fully consolidated, with two parallel governments in Havana, one that was overt and staunchly non-Communist, and the other, concealed from his own cabinet ministers, to say nothing of his fellow Cubans, that was laying the foundations of the future Marxist state. In an equally secret fashion he negotiated a pact with the old Communists, and separately entered into the first conversations with a Soviet emissary over caviar and vodka in a Havana hotel suite in the autumn of 1959.

The inside story of the origins of the present Communist state in Cuba has never before been published, and its substance remains unknown to Cubans in general. It has been reconstructed here from interviews held in Havana during 1985, with those who were personally involved in the running of Castro's 'hidden government' and in such related activities as the creation of special schools where 'old' Communists taught

Marxism–Leninism to the 'new' Communists among top *Fidelistas*, at first in total secrecy. Publicly, Castro savagely rejected domestic and foreign accusations that Communism was creeping into his 'humanist' revolution, imprisoning on treason charges those of his wartime companions who resigned their posts over this issue. Castro's Ariadne thread remained invisible while the Maximum Leader, basking in national adulation, put together his real revolutionary structure.

In peace, as in war, Castro was a master both of strategy and of timing. Looking back at the events of the first year of the revolution with the benefit of inside knowldedge, it is clear that he knew exactly what he was doing, that his apparent improvisations had been carefully thought out, and that nothing was left to chance. Castro understood above all else that his own personality was, as a purely practical proposition, the key to the success of his entire enterprise. Having always insisted that propaganda was vital in mobilizing the masses for a revolution, Castro immediately seized on television, which was already quite well-developed in Cuba in 1959, as the ideal publicity vehicle for himself and the revolution. He was a natural television personality and, literally, he sold the revolution on TV. Antonio Nuñez Jiménez, the erudite geographer and writer who was the coordinator of Castro's inside team and has remained at his side for nearly thirty years, says that in terms of a leader's relationship with his nation 'the case of Fidel is unique in modern history . . . Lenin did not have radio and television and, moreover, Lenin never had the ascendency over the Soviet people that Fidel has had over Cubans.'
   Politically, Castro conducted himself with remarkable acumen from the moment power came within his reach. Having forced the collapse of the junta that attempted to replace Batista in Havana by calling a general strike and threatening a military attack on the capital and Santiago, he kept up political pressure for a full week. He maintained the work stoppage for two more days as a guarantee against new coup attempts (the strike also constituted a victory holiday, with Castro as the centre of national attention) and, on 3 January, he organized a slow, triumphal march from Santiago to Havana, in the Roman manner. That morning, however, he first conferred with Camilo Cienfuegos who had flown from Havana to brief him on the security situation in the Capital, and instructed Raúl to stay behind in Santiago to protect his rear. The advance to Havana lasted five days and nights, with Fidel surrounded by his *bárbudos* riding atop a tank or in a Jeep, receiving wild acclaim from the population, every step of the way relayed to the rest of the island by live television. His semi-automatic rifle (now an American M-2) slung over his shoulder and his horn-rimmed spectacles perched on his Roman nose, Castro now presented the image of a warrior-philosopher king. This was precisely the way he intended to be seen and remembered for ever. The

famous beard, the cigar clenched in his teeth, and the olive-green combat fatigues (with a small medallion of the Virgin of Cobre on a chain around his neck conveniently visible under his open-collar blouse), these were the symbols of the Fidel Castro personality. Inching ahead through thick crowds, he halted repeatedly to greet or embrace somebody he had recognized, to shout a slogan, to deliver a few words, even to make a speech. When his final offensive had begun back in the autumn Castro commanded 300 men, and when he entered Santiago he had a total of 3000 armed rebels. Marching to Havana he was like the Pied Piper, attracting more and more followers.

It was unquestionably a risk for Castro, physically and politically, to be on the road for five days, but he had calculated that his trusted commanders throughout the island would ensure that nothing went amiss; he was in permanent radio and telephone contact with them. Concerning the danger of assassination Castro was always fatalistic, not prepared to sacrifice his relationship with the masses to security requirements. And the idea of the march to Havana the length of the Central Highway represented such potent political exposure, and proof of his absolute sway over the nation, that it simply could not be forfeited. Castro was even able to control the politics of the revolution from the road despite the maddening chaos and confusion that surrounded his progress. With Celia Sánchez firmly in charge of communications, Fidel managed to conduct private conferences with the men he wanted to serve him in key posts. (For example, Raúl Chibás, who was the treasurer of the 26th of July Movement, flew from Santiago to Camagüey where he caught up with the Maximum Leader in order to say he was *not* interested in the Finance Ministry being offered to him.) At the same time, Celia busily sent out messages around Cuba and abroad to summon old friends whom Fidel wanted to see as soon as possible.

In Cotorro, at the approaches to Havana, Castro finally encountered his son Fidelito whom he had not seen since leaving Mexico over two years earlier. Fidelito, now nine years old, was brought out by relatives to meet his father; Mirta, his mother, evidently did not oppose the reunion, and soon Castro would take him out of his Havana private day school and put him in a public boarding school, making sure he could see him as often as possible. By then Mirta and her husband and children would have left for Spain for good; Castro's old friend Naty Revuelta took it upon herself to find the school for Fidelito.

Whatever Castro was planning for the long-term future of Cuba, his instinct had convinced him that a smooth transition was politically advisable. For this reason he let his hand-picked Provisional President, Manuel Urrutia, select the prime minister and the cabinet in Santiago that first week, though naturally he kept a watchful eye on them. For himself Fidel reserved the title of Military Commander-in-Chief that he had already held in the Sierra Maestra, knowing that his real power lay in the totally loyal Rebel Army. Urrutia, who had arrived in the Sierra the preceding December (but saw Castro only twice), named an exceptionally talented cabinet. Drawn mainly from the 26th of July Movement's moderate wing, it included only three guerrilla companions as ministers, one of them being Faustino Pérez, a veteran mountain fighter but an ideological moderate. The other *barbudos* were Augusto Martínez Sánchez as Defence Minister and Humberto Sorí-Marín, who had drafted the Sierra agrarian reform law, as Agriculture Minister. From the founders of the 26th of July Movement after Moncada, only Armando Hart was invited to the cabinet and named Education Minister. The only ideological leftist was Osvaldo Dorticós Torrado, the Minister of Revolutionary Laws, who had belonged in the late 1930s to the university committee of the illegal Communist Party, joining the Castro movement in the late 1950s and serving for a time as chairman of the Cuban Bar Association. That same chairmanship had also been held by José Miró Cardona whom Urrutia appointed as Prime Minister. Urrutia wrote later that he had proposed to Castro 'the desirability of appointing a centralized cabinet representing all the revolutionary sectors, but Castro opposed it, asserting that the government should be as homogenous as possible'. At that juncture Castro wanted this homogenous group to be along the lines of the 26th of July Movement, which already enjoyed worldwide respect.

But even more to the point, Castro needed instant competence. His Rebel Army, peasant-based and overwhelmingly illiterate, could not provide government adminstrators on any level, certainly not ministerial (Faustino Pérez, Martínez Sánchez and Sorí-Marín were pre-guerrilla intellectuals with university degrees, and all three were identified with the 26th of July Movement). While Castro explained later that the revolution had to turn to 'old' Communists while the Sierra rebels lacked government expertise, he could not actually be open about this for at least two years without triggering lethal opposition from large segments of the Cuban population, and from the United States. By the end of 1960 his police and political controls were strong enough to cope with domestic opposition, and his relations with the United States had deteriorated to such a stage that he no longer had to take the American factor into account in formulating his defiant policies. At that point Castro could afford to ally himself openly with the Communists of the Popular Socialist Party (PSP).

Keeping the Communists out of the cabinet in 1959 (Dorticós whose past Communist ties were generally unknown was easily accepted by Urrutia) meant that the Maximum Leader – as Fidel was now known – had to keep out the Student Revolutionary Directorate (DR) as well, in order to maintain the 'homogenous' character of his provisional government; besides, the DR had challenged him by occupying the Presidential Palace in Havana and the university with armed guerrillas before the Rebel Army reached the capital. To avoid opposition Fidel also deliberately gave his brother Raúl and Che Guevara very low public profiles. But although Raúl simply had his military command in Santiago, and Che was no more than the chief of La Cabaña fortress in Havana, their actual power and influence far exceeded their job descriptions. They participated in all the secret revolutionary policy decisions, and they were instrumental in placing Communist-orientated Rebel Army personnel from their wartime commands in strategic middle-level positions throughout the country. With the impressive facade of the 26th of July Movement cabinet studded with such internationally recognized economic specialists as Rufo López-Fresquet as Finance Minister and Felipe Pazos as President of the National Bank, thus providing the new regime with respectability, Castro and his collaborators used the time this bought to discreetly construct the Marxist–Leninist edifice.

Characteristically, while the rest of the core leadership were content to labour behind the facade, Che Guevara insisted on being frank and outspoken. Enrique Oltuski, who was the regime's first Minister of Communications (and at the age of twenty-three the youngest minister) before being fired and imprisoned, later recalled this frankness. In his encounter with Guevara during the Las Villas campaign in the autumn of 1959, when he was in charge of the 26th of July Movement in that province, and Oltuski urged caution in order not to provoke the United States, Che told him: 'So you are one of those who think that we can make a revolution behind the back of the Americans . . . What a shit-eater you are! We must make the revolution into a struggle to the death against imperialism from the first moment. A true revolution cannot be disguised. . .'

But it was on Fidel Castro's activities that the attentions of Cuba and much of the fascinated outside world were focused in these first months of the Year of Liberation (Castro liked the French Revolution's concept of designating years by its own calendar, as if to erase the past). He was mesmerizing. His entrance into Havana on 8 January was an apotheosis, marvellously staged. As Fidel drove into the ancient colonial city at the head of his Column No. 1, church bells tolled, factory whistles blew, and ships' sirens sounded. The first stop was the harbour, and he stepped aboard the *Granma* moored there – it had been recently brought to Havana – to the proud crashing of navy frigate's cannon salutes. The Castro motorcade then eased its way through the dense mob to the plaza in front of the Presidential Palace, where the commander-in-chief wished to call on the civilian president, Manuel Urrutia, and the cabinet. Urrutia had been able to move into the palace earlier in the week when the Rebel

Army persuaded the rival DR guerrillas to leave the building, but the armed students were still occupying the university, and now Castro was facing his first major crisis. He chose to solve it through rhetoric rather than through force, and this won him new acclaim and support.

Night had fallen when Fidel reached the army's Camp Columbia headquarters in north-western Havana to deliver his great victory speech before the tens of thousands of Cubans who had been waiting for many hours. His main theme was the Rebel Army's responsibility for the success of the revolution then being launched, and this led him to emphasize the need for revolutionary unity, and finally to bring out into the open the seizure of weapons by the DR. Turning to Camilo Cienfuegos, the Rebel Army's chief of staff and the second most popular revolutionary figure, Castro asked: 'Am I doing all right, Camilo?' and Cienfuegos replied to the roar of the crowd: 'You are doing all right, Fidel!' – and a new revolutionary slogan was born.

Letting his voice drop, Castro announced he had a question for 'the people', and thereby he inaugurated a new approach to the art of government: dialogue with the masses through which they would affirm his policies by chanting responses to his 'questions'. Soon he would call it 'direct democracy . . . of the market place', cleaner and more honest than old-fashioned corrupt electoral procedures of the past. But on that first night the questions were: 'Why hide arms in different places in the capital? Why smuggle arms at this moment? For what? . . . Arms, for what? To fight against whom? Against the revolutionary government that has the support of the whole people [shouts of: NO!] . . . Is it the same with Judge Urrutia governing the Republic as it was with Batista governing the Republic? [shouts of: NO!] . . . Arms, for what? Is there a dictatorship here? [shouts of: NO!] . . . Will they fight against a free government that respects the peoples' rights? [shouts of: NO!] . . . Arms, for what, when elections will be called in the shortest time possible? . . . Hide arms, for what? To blackmail the President of the Republic? . . . Arms, for what? . . . So I must tell you that two days ago, members of a certain organization went to a military base and took five hundred weapons and six machine guns and eighty thousand bullets! [shouts of: LET'S GET THEM!]'

'Arms, for what?' became the latest revolutionary expression, and later that night the DR guerrillas, watching Castro on television, surrendered the weapons to the Rebel Army, ending the crisis without bloodshed. Shortly, key DR leaders joined Fidel's circle, becoming the mainstay of his Security services as he ushered socialism into Cuba. Back at Camp Columbia, Castro had consulted the crowd as to whether he should accept the 'petition' addressed to him by the provisional government to serve as commander-in-chief of land, sea and air forces and to reorganize the armed forces, and there was a unanimous 'Yes!' He then informed the nation that while 'decent soldiers who have not looted and who have not committed murder' would have the right to continue in the army, 'I'm also telling you that those who have committed murder will not be saved by anybody from the firing squad'. This was his way of serving notice that trials and executions of Batista 'war criminals' would soon start. Castro ended his first great public performance as the leader of Cuba with these words: 'For us, principles are above all other considerations, and we do not struggle because of personal ambition. I believe we have demonstrated sufficiently that we have fought without personal ambition. I believe no Cuban can have the slightest doubt of that!'

As he finished speaking, the spotlights bathing him illuminated a pair of white doves that suddenly came to rest on his shoulders. Although apparently unstage-managed, this astounding piece of symbolism touched off an explosion of 'FIDEL! . . . FIDEL! . . . FIDEL!' as the sky was caressed by the first colours of the dawn. Cubans are a people of powerful superstitions, going back to the Afro–Cuban traditions of the slaves and that night in January the white doves confirmed their faith. And, as it happened, for some strange reason doves again and again would alight on Fidel's shoulders as he faced his people. The deification of Fidel Castro became a phenomenon in Cuba in the aftermath of his victory, so greatly had he touched the hearts and souls of Cubans. Soon *Bohemia* magazine published an immensely controversial portrait of the thirty-one-year-old Maximum Leader with a Christ-like halo subtly drawn above his bearded countenance. Some Cubans thought it was overdoing political allegiance. But Raúl Chibás, who travelled with Castro a part of the way from Oriente to Havana, recalls that between Santiago and Bayamo 'elderly ladies embraced him as he went along . . . Every five minutes, at every intersection of the highway, women stopped him, the old women kissed him, telling him he was greater than Jesus Christ.'

Castro himself must have felt a profound kinship with Christ. Antonio Nuñez Jiménez says that later in 1959, in a 'secret speech' before officials of the new Agrarian Reform Institute, Castro said: 'The revolution . . . ceased to be a romantic thing, becoming instead that in which there is only room for those who are suffering conversion into revolutionaries, and are in accordance with Christ's precept when He said: "Leave all that you have and follow me." This is the reality.' In a televised speech in December delivered in defence of the revolution, Castro said he made a point of attending a Roman Catholic congress in Havana because 'our revolution is in no way against religious sentiment . . . our revolution aspires to strengthen the noble desires and ideas of men . . . When Christ's preachings are practised, it will be possible to say that a revolution is occurring in the world . . . Because I studied in a religious school, I remember many teachings of Christ, and I remember that He was implacable against the Pharisees . . . Nobody forgets that Christ was persecuted; and let nobody forget that He was crucified. And that His preachings were very much fought against. And that these preachings did not prosper in high society, but germinated in the heart of the humble of Palestine. . .' Even twenty-five years later Fidel Castro would continue to invoke Christ as his role model, and Christianity as the philosophical basis of the Cuban socialist revolution.

This socialist revolution was set in motion in secret through Fidel Castro's hidden government and his clandestine dealings with the 'old' Communists within days of his arrival in Havana. Being 'simply' the military commander-in-chief, with no ostensible government responsibilities in the first six weeks of the new regime, Castro could engage in these enterprises without attracting undue attention. In any event his whirlwind activities in and out of Havana were a perfect cover. During the month following his arrival in the capital on 8 January Fidel delivered at least twelve speeches, some of them major policy statements before huge crowds; held five major news conferences, mainly for foreign journalists, and made two lengthy television appearances (the speeches and press conferences were televised, too). At the end of January he flew to Caracas on his first foreign trip as the victorious revolutionary leader, to thank Admiral Larrazábal and the ruling Venezuelan government junta for dispatching arms to the Sierra in 1958; he also called on President-Elect Rómulo Betancourt despite the contempt he had for him as a reformist (and not a revolutionary) of the Latin American 'democratic left'. Venezuelans, liberated from dictatorship a year earlier, gave Castro a deliriously happy reception. He made a quick visit to Artemisa in Havana province and to Pinar del Río, the two areas from which most of his Moncada companions hailed, and spent four days in Oriente in foothill towns of the Sierra Maestra telling people about the plans for land reform. And on 9 February he announced the revolutionary regime's decision to declare Argentine-born Che Guevara a *native* Cuban citizen as an act of gratitude and as the legal step required to allow him to hold office in Cuba. All in all, it was hard to keep up with Fidel as he burst in and out of his suite on the twenty-third floor of the Havana Hilton Hotel that served him at the outset as main office and occasional home.

Meanwhile his secret political operations continued. That the decision to seek Communist collaboration was made by Castro before Batista's fall is corroborated by Fábio Grobart. Now in his eighties, the co-founder of the Cuban Communist Party and presently its historian and oldest member of the Central Committee, the Polish-born Grobart recalls that these consultations began 'in the first few days' of the new regime. However the secret conversations between Castro, his associates and the Communist leadership were not a shortcut to a power-sharing deal, but highly complex debates on how a unified revolutionary party could be fashioned into a Marxist–Leninist force and, in the meantime, how best Communist talents could be used in running the country and preparing the transition. Castro insisted from the outset that the 'old' Communist Party be absorbed into a 'new' Communist Party under his leadership, requiring the actual delivery of the party to him, an unprecedented act in Communist history.

It goes without saying that Castro engaged in this process in the belief that the moderate regime under Urrutia was a transitory affair, unaccept-able in the long run as an instrument of the revolution. This is why he had to create his hidden government to move the nation rapidly along the revolutionary road while unity with the Communists was being ironed out. Moreover, the consultations had to be conducted in absolute secrecy because of deep resentments and mistrust between the Communist Party and the 26th of July Movement. Not to mention what might be expected from the United States if it became known that the Maximum Leader was in business with Communism. This caution was expressed in a private wartime remark by Castro that 'I could proclaim socialism from the Turquino peak, the highest mountain in Cuba, but there is no guarantee whatsoever that I could come down the mountain afterwards.'

As Fábio Grobart put it in a long discussion of the Castro–Communist relationship: 'A process, taking months and years, was necessary to prepare public opinion for the necessity of having a unified Communist Party, and that Communism is not so earnest, so dangerous, so bad. . ,' But in 1959 the orthodox Communist Party was not ready for Castro, either. Although on 11 January the party's Executive Bureau issued a declaration urging the defence of the revolution and the maintenance of revolutionary unity, it was not until August of the following year that the party formally recognized its long-standing 'errors' in minimizing and misunderstanding Castro's movement. Pending this act of contrition, the top leadership had to tread very carefully. Even after the decision to form a unified Communist Party under Castro was announced, important 'old' Communist leaders sought to sabotage it – even to the point when one of them had to be imprisoned for 'conspiracy'.

Castro held most of his secret encounters with the Communists at a hilltop house in the fishing village of Cojímar some ten miles east of Havana. This house was lent to him in March for an indefinite period by Agustín Cruz, a former *Ortodoxo* party senator. The large Cojímar villa overlooking the sea was under heavy Rebel Army guard, affording maximum privacy. Fidel used it as a residence during the first years of the revolution, alternating it with Celia's Vedado apartment and the Hilton penthouse. In his meetings with the Communists, Castro was always accompanied by Che Guevara, Camilo Cienfuegos, Ramiro Valdés, and often by Raúl, who commuted between Santiago and Havana. Cienfuegos, the army chief of staff, appears to have been a closet Communist during the war, finally identifying himself with Marxism during the Las Villas campaign the previous autumn. His brother Osmany, an architect who sat out the war in Mexico, belonged to the party. Ramiro Valdés, veteran of Moncada, the prison, the *Granma* and the Sierra, had been Che Guevara's deputy at the end of the war, and now he was chief of the Rebel Army's investigations department, the G-2 (the secret police). He was an unabashed admirer of Communism and the Soviet Union. Raúl Castro had been a Party member since 1953, and Che Guevara was far to the left of all the Communist parties. Fidel, then, was the only one in this group without open Communist commitments. The Party's negotiators were led by Blás Roca Calderío, a sturdy mulatto and its secretary general since 1934, and included Carlos Rafael Rodríguez and Aníbal Escalante of the Executive Bureau. All of them were considerably older than the *Fidelistas*, and they were held in some awe by the young rebels – except by Fidel.

Blás Roca, who was seventy-seven years old and well recovered from a stroke when he agreed in 1985 to reminisce about the past, was the first one to meet with Castro after the revolution, keeping up personal exchanges in addition to the group discussions. He says: 'We began to hold meetings as soon as Fidel, Che and Camilo arrived here', and laughingly remembers Castro exclaiming, 'Shit, we are the government now, and still we have to go on meeting illegally.' On another occasion there was great merriment when Che remarked, 'Yes, things have really changed now that we have an agenda before us.' Blás Roca says that in those days the party's rank and file were not being told that the top leadership had come to regard Castro as Cuba's principal revolutionary leader: 'We were not informing the militants, only a small group in the leadership.' Likewise, according to Blás Roca, the party leadership refrained from informing the rank and file that Castro was being regarded as a socialist and a Marxist: 'The success [of the negotiations] was linked to the need to prevent the Americans from having an excuse for intervention, as they had in Guatemala.' However, top party leaders, he says, began educating party organizations to accept Castro's decisions on government appointments, stressing that membership of the Communist Party did not confer special rights in the revolution, contrary to the belief of many activists. Blás Roca says that at labour union conferences he made a point of telling the workers: 'A new leader of the Cuban working class has been born, and this new leader is Fidel.'

Fábio Grobart recalls that, in time, the meetings between the *Fidelistas* and the Communists became institutionalized. 'There was,' he says, 'a coordination of activities and a collaboration. This was the beginning.' Late in 1959 or early in 1960 Castro and the Communists concluded that the time had come to move ahead with the organization of a unified

Communist Party, but Fábio Grobart points out that the first step was to set up Integrated Revolutionary Organizations – the ORI – by bringing together the 26th of July Movement, the Popular Socialist Party (the Communists' offical name) and the Students' Revolutionary Directorate (DR). Each party maintained its identity and 'autonomy', he says, though Castro's overall leadership was recognized. In 1961 the three organizations were formally fused as a prelude to the establishment of the 'new' Communist Party in 1965, But its real birth had been in 1959, in the villa in Cojímar, the same fishing village where Ernest Hemingway had found his old man and the sea.

Among the first decisions taken together by Castro and the Communists was the creation of special schools to teach Marxism–Leninism to the *Fidelistas*, particularly those with an obvious political future, in preparation for the ultimate transition to Communist rule on the island. They were called Schools for Revolutionary Instruction (EIR), and initially they disguised their Marxist teachings behind the pretence of simply showing officials how to run revolutionary institutions. In fact they were the counterpart of the military political education centres set up at the Havana commands by Camilo Cienfuegos and Che Guevara, and subsequently expanded to all the rebel army units. These centres grew out of Raúl Castro's Troop Instructors' School conducted by Communist officers in 1958, and they were run by members of the Communists' Popular Socialist Party and officers with membership in the party. This was consistent with Castro's principle that the Rebel Army must play the leading ideological role in the revolution, and the basic military text for it was the *Civic Preparation Manual* issued late in 1959. This was used in the Rebel Army's literacy programme, and its language was essentially Marxist, stressing 'anti-imperialist struggles'.

On the civilian side the first Revolutionary Instruction School was established late in 1959 in a house on Primera Avenida in the Playa section of western Havana, and the full network of these schools was officially inaugurated in December 1960.

With the unveiling of the Integrated Revolutionary Organizations in 1960, Marxist–Leninist schools became crucial in equipping the 'new' Communists for their tasks in the unified party to be set up soon. In Grobart's words: 'The person graduating from this school is a *cadre* prepared in multiple ways to be a political leader of the revolution.' Over the years these schools became centralized under the Ñico López Central School of the Cuban Communist Party, which is in effect a Marxist–Leninist university offering everything from three-month basic courses to a five-year doctorate in the social sciences. All top Cuban officials must be Ñico López graduates (J.R. Fernández, Cuba's vice president and education minister, for example, went back to school in his fifties to earn this degree), and the curriculum includes scientific Communism and atheism, Party construction, ideological struggle, universal history, Cuban history, philosophy, the political economy of socialism and the political economy of capitalism. By late 1961 over 30,000 students had gone through the indoctrination schools, but the elite were a class of fifty-three of the most promising young leaders who, starting in January 1962, were given exhaustive nine-hours-a-day courses in Marxism, economics and philosophy. In March Fidel Castro came to the school to pick from this class a secret task force of twenty young officials who would supervise the as yet unannounced shift from Integrated Revolutionary Organizations to the United Party of Cuban Socialist Revolution (PURSC) that would constitute a transitional stage to the new Communist Party. By the end of 1960 there were still no Communists in the Cuban Council of Ministers, but Marxism–Leninism had made immense inroads.

In case questions should be asked, Fidel Castro's hidden government in 1959 carried the innocent-sounding name of the Office of Revolutionary Plans and Coordination. Operating as a secret task force carrying out fundamental policy assignments for Castro, it had Antonio Nuñez Jiménez as its chairman, and Che Guevara, Alfredo Guevara, Vílma Espín, Oscar Pino Santos and Segundo Ceballos as its members. Nuñez Jiménez, who knew Castro slightly from their university days, had joined Che Guevara's column in Las Villas during the autumn 1958 offensive and later, as a Rebel Army captain, became his deputy at La Cabaña fortress. Ardently committed to Marxist–Leninist thought, Nuñez Jiménez was brought into Castro's personal entourage by Che Guevara, immediately becoming a full-time companion and trusted planner; as a geographer, geologist and historian he was [and is] very familiar with Cuba's problems – just the man Castro needed intellectually and ideologically for the transition.

Alfredo Guevara was Fidel's Communist friend from the university, his companion at the 1948 Bogotá uprising, and the victim of torture by the Batista police in Havana in the last year of the war. He then went to Mexico, and Fidel had his sister Lidia summon him from Matanzas, where he had just returned from exile, in the first week of January. Alfredo Guevara, who had become a movie-maker, had hoped to launch a revolutionary motion-picture industry, but Fidel told him he was urgently needed for other tasks. Vílma Espín was the MIT-educated young woman from Santiago who had joined Raúl Castro's Second Front in 1958, then married him in January 1959, at an Oriente wedding which Fidel was too busy to attend. Raúl's presence with the army in Santiago was still required, but he was nevertheless deeply involved with the hidden government as he commuted between the two cities. Oscar Pino Santos, a Communist economist, and Segundo Ceballos, an elderly journalist specializing in agrarian problems, were advisers, and never participated in policy decisions. Pedro Miret was Fidel's aide-de-camp, and he was increasingly involved in the secret planning as the initial group evolved into a full-fledged hidden government. Celia Sánchez was part of the operation as Fidel's principal assistant.

The task force met at a house at the beach resort at Tarará where Che Guevara was convalescing from illness and fatigue; two years of asthma attacks and malaria bouts during the Sierra war had ravaged him. Tarará is a half-hour's drive from Havana, a few miles east of Cojímar where Fidel moved during March. The main assignment of the Tarará team was to draft a new agrarian reform law, much more drastic than the one Castro had signed in the Sierra the previous year, as well as additional revolutionary laws, and to become familiar with crucial areas of government operations in preparation for the ultimate takeover. Nuñez Jiménez says: 'For two months, we held meetings during the night in Tarará where Che was recovering his health.' Castro, he says, kept track of the drafting of the agrarian reform law, the centrepiece of the revolutionary legislation, 'suggesting ideas and modifications'. According to Nuñez Jiménez the drafting was kept secret until Castro presented it to Revolutionary Laws Minister Dorticós for a review, by-passing the rest of the cabinet; in any case, Dorticós was a Castro ally.

Alfredo Guevara offers the best description of the latitude and mandate enjoyed by the task force: 'We met every night until dawn at Che's house, then Fidel would come and change everything [in the land reform bill], but we also prepared a merchant marine law, and we had to become specialists in the craziest things; for example, we began to work in the National Bank.' Felipe Pazos was the regime's new National Bank President (he and Raúl Chibás had joined Castro in drafting the first manifesto from the Sierra in 1957), but, as Alfredo Guevara recalls, 'Castro wanted us to start going to the bank, and we went there once a week . . . Fidel kept saying: "We don't know what a bank is, and we must know what a bank is." ' Subsequently Che Guevara would replace Paz as National Bank President.

The activities of the hidden government changed and grew when Castro persuaded President Urrutia to obtain the resignation of José Miró Cardona as prime minister and to appoint Castro himself in Cardona's place on 13 February, an easy undertaking. Circumstances had not allowed Miró Cardona to be effective in the premiership, mainly because most ministers privately cleared their projects first with Castro at the Havana Hilton penthouse suite. Urrutia wrote before his death in exile that Castro had visited him several times early in February to say he would agree to be prime minister 'but since he would be responsible for the policy of the government he would need sufficiently broad powers to enable him to act efficiently'. Carlos Rafael Rodríguez, writing many years later about these events put it more brusquely: 'The government that emerged on 1 January could not be considered a true revolutionary government in the light of its composition or its procedures . . . Revolutionary power at that moment resided outside of the government – in the Rebel Army headed by Fidel Castro. His designation as prime minister served to fuse together revolutionary power and the government.' But Castro still wanted to keep all the ministers in the cabinet, and rejected Urrutia's offer of resignation. But he obtained from Urrutia and the cabinet a change in the new Cuban constitution, vesting in the prime minister full power to direct government policy; that constitution had been approved by the cabinet only six days earlier on 7 February.

Urrutia's power as president was reduced to the signing of laws – as he wrote, Castro 'conceded me veto power but asked that I use it as seldom as possible'. From thereon Castro began to preside over cabinet meetings at the Presidential Palace, with Urrutia in mute attendance, and with the Tarará task force acting as invisible coordinator of policy. Alfredo Guevara says that Castro put him in charge of summoning the cabinet and helping him to run it. Shortly thereafter Castro moved to Cojímar and the task force set up its headquarters there, with still greater secret power. Che Guevara had recovered completely, and Tarará could be left behind. The first stage in the conduct of the Cuban revolution had been completed with Castro's open assumption of total power, and he and his teams prepared for the next phase.

Chapter 2

The immediate and overwhelming reality facing Fidel Castro was Cuba's relationship with the United States, only ninety miles away. And the antagonism between the new Cuban revolution and the Americans next door was instant, implacable, powerful – and inevitable. What Castro had touched off on both sides of the Straits of Florida was an explosion of nationalisms, historical resentments and misunderstandings, sharply differing perceptions of national interests, and an earth-shaking cultural shock for which neither side was even remotely prepared.

This antagonism, soon turning into open mutual hostility, predated the great Cuban–American clashes, the questions of ideology, and the ultimate Cuban–Soviet military alliance. Seen from the perspective of more than a quarter of a century, it is evident that the antagonistic relationship was, in effect, foreordained by the forces of history, and there was virtually nothing either side could have done within the parameters of the politically possible to avoid it. Put in a nutshell, Fidel Castro obsessively feared that his revolution would be stolen from the Cubans by the United States, as independence had been stolen at the end of the Spanish–American War in 1898, while Americans (and not only the Eisenhower administration) saw in the *barbudo* cry of defiance ominous threats to their national and economic interest.

These fundamental attitudes, then, defined from the very beginning the behaviour of the big and the little neighbours towards each other. No lasting compromise was ever possible, and it is demonstrably incorrect to believe that American actions pushed Castro towards Communism or that, obversely, the United States resolved to try to oust him only after he had moulded his revolution into an anti-American and pro-Communist instrument.

There is abundant evidence that Castro's aim in the immediate aftermath of victory was to forge revolutionary unity around his own

Communist Party when practicable, and there is no reason to doubt his comments on this theme twenty-seven years later: 'We were carrying out our programme little by little. All these [United States] aggressions accelerated the revolutionary process. Were they the cause? No, this would be an error. I do not pretend that the aggressions are the cause of socialism in Cuba. This is false. In Cuba we were going to construct socialism in the most orderly possible manner, within a reasonable period of time, with the least amount of trauma and problems, but the aggressions of imperialism accelerated the revolutionary process.'

And in Washington the mind-set was equally firm. Even before Eisenhower policy-makers began to understand what was happening in Cuba (and they never really succeeded in understanding it, as the Bay of Pigs invasion two years later would show), a top-level decision had been taken to get rid of Castro. Specifically, the agenda of the National Security Council meeting on 10 March 1959 – two and a half months after Batista's defeat and with President Urrutia and a moderate cabinet still ostensibly governing Cuba – included as a principal topic the possibility of bringing 'another government to power in Cuba'. The Cubans had not yet seized or nationalized any American property on the island, and the United States had no reason thus far to complain about any Cuban actions. In fact the official policy was to *appear* to be friendly to Castro, the United States being on 7 January the second country in the world (after Venezuela) to recognize the revolutionary regime; the Soviet Union had no diplomatic relations with Havana anyway, and it had seemed to ignore altogether Castro's struggle against Batista. Philip W. Bonsal, a career diplomat with a liberal reputation, excellent knowledge of Latin America and fluency in Spanish, was immediately named ambassador to Cuba to replace Earl T. Smith, the friend of Batista. Bonsal (who had served in Cuba as a young diplomat and whose father was a war correspondent in 1898), met Castro at Cojímar on 5 March, a day after presenting his credentials to Urrutia, and their first conversation was pleasant. The ambassador wrote later: 'I was encouraged to believe that we could establish a working relationship that would be advantageous to both our countries' and 'Castro had gone out of his way to express a warm desire for frequent meetings with me.' The following day Castro spoke during a television speech of his 'cordial and friendly conversations with the Ambassador of the United States', and disclosed his plans to visit the United States the next month as a guest of American newspaper publishers (but in December 1961 Castro offered a different version in another TV speech, accusing Bonsal of 'a style of someone who came to deliver instructions').

It remains a mystery why the National Security Council discussed Castro's liquidation within five days of his first encounter with the American ambassador (Bonsal was not informed of it) – unless the

Eisenhower adminstration had a secret second track designed to derail the revolution as a matter of principle. A similar approach had worked in Guatemala in 1954, under the same White House and CIA leadership, and it may have seemed easy to re-run the operation in Cuba five years later. That such a policy undermined Bonsal as ambassador in Havana posed no problems to the policy-makers: it was par for the course in this type of situation.

However, as it now turns out, the Intelligence community was split on Cuba. Late in March, for example, a special panel on Cuba in the CIA's Board of Estimates concluded in a secret review that Castro was not 'a Moscow-oriented Communist', a correct estimate in which Bonsal in Havana had concurred. The full board rejected that conclusion under pressure from CIA director Allen W. Dulles, architect of the Guatemala approach, even though as late as 5 November 1959 General C.P. Cabell, the agency's deputy director, testified before the Senate Internal Security Subcommittee that even the Communists in Cuba did not consider Fidel Castro 'a Communist Party member, or even pro-Communist . . . We know that the Communists consider Castro as a representative of the bourgeoisie, and were unable to gain public recognition or commitments from him during the course of the revolution.' In retrospect it is likely that these opinions were culled by the Havana CIA station from low-ranking Party members unaware of the secret talks between the *Fidelista* command and their leadership. In any event it was not until March 1960 that the United States government formally decided to mount a paramilitary operation against Castro. Admittedly, in the latter part of 1959 the CIA had begun to arm the first anti-*Fidelista* guerrilla bands appearing in the Escambray mountains in central Cuba, but just as these bands started posing a problem for Castro, the CIA abandoned them.

In the spring of 1959, as Fidel Castro prepared to go to the United States in triumph, the tensions developing between the two countries had to do with mere daily irritants rather than with broad government policies. Again, emotional and psychological factors coloured the relationship – and the gulf of cultural misunderstanding grew. The problem was that Americans insisted on judging Cuban attitudes by American standards, and Cubans responded by judging Americans by Cuban standards, in a quickening and damaging vicious circle. Nowhere was this more vividly demonstrated than in the case of the trials of Batista 'war criminals' by revolutionary justice.

Reduced to its simplest terms, the issue – in the eyes of Fidel Castro and masses of Cubans – was that while the United States government had never protested against the killing and torture of thousands of the old regime's opponents by the Batista police and soldiers (and public opinion took hardly any notice), now that the victorious revolutionaries were punishing their opponents with executions and lengthy prison sentences Americans were indignant. The climax in this tragedy of misunderstandings came when Wayne Morse, the great liberal from Oregon, rose on the Senate floor to denounce the Cuban 'blood bath' and to urge that executions be halted 'until emotions cool'. Castro, who saw a threat to his revolution in any and every criticism of Cuba, shot back that the trials would go on 'until all criminals of the Batista regime are tried', and that 'if the Americans don't like what's happening in Cuba, they can land the marines and then there will be 200,000 *gringos* dead. . .' That was an off-the-cuff remark to a crowd of newsmen, and Castro had the sense to apologize for it, but the threat made worldwide headlines, and the atmosphere became even more poisoned. It was only January, less than a month after the revolutionary triumph.

There is no question that Castro used the trials issue, an immensely emotional one to thousands of families who over the years had found on their doorsteps at dawn the mutilated corpses of their sons, brothers and husbands, to focus Cuban public opinion against the United States. In this sense, Americans were playing into his hands, but it is just as important – historically – to place the episode of the trials in persepective. The first point is that in the normally accepted meaning of the expression, no blood baths occurred in Cuba after Batista fell. No vengeful crowds took revenge into their own hands, and former ambassador Bonsal, a most objective observer, wrote afterwards that 'thirty years earlier, the hirelings of the Machado regime deemed guilty of similar crimes were simply ferreted out by the mob and killed . . . The Castro procedure of setting up special tribunals to try the cases of people who, on the basis of the Nuremberg principles, were accused of serious crimes, could have been an improvement over the earlier method . . . [Admittedly] these special courts were subject to all sorts of pressures including those generated by the circus-like atmosphere in which many of them were conducted.'

Castro acknowledges that around 550 persons were executed after summary trials in 1959 and 1960. Whatever can be said of the procedures at these trials, defendants were not picked at random, but because they were believed to have committed crimes and brutalities on a large scale, and they were punishable under the provisions of revolutionary laws proclaimed from the Sierra in 1958. Cuban revolutionary trials, then, bore no resemblance to the real blood baths that followed the Mexican, Russian and Chinese social revolutions in the twentieth century – or the the vengeance in the streets that erupted in Cuba after Machado, in France and other Nazi-occupied nations after liberation in World War Two, in Venezuela following the deposition of the dictator Pérez Jiménez in 1958, and in the Dominican Republic after Dictator Trujillo was murdered in 1961. By the same token the Cuban revolution refrained from institutionalized mass killings such as those perpetrated against hundreds of thousands of Chinese in Indonesia in the aftermath of the 1965 army anti-Communist coup, or those attributable in the thousands to Chilean military authorities when they overthrew the Marxist president, Salvador Allende Gossens, in 1973. Considering that in the first few days of revolution, public order in most of Cuba was assured by 26th of July Movement local militias, boy scouts and the advance units of the Rebel Army, it is quite remarkable that violence-prone Cubans remained so unviolent.

Castro's worst mistake, however, was to hold a show trial in Havana's sports stadium in January for three exceedingly brutal Batista ex-commanders. He may have thought that such public televised proceedings would both defuse the temptation to exact private enforcements of justice and show the people that Batista crimes were being swiftly judged, but from the international public-opinion viewpoint, it was an unmitigated disaster, creating the legend of 'circus-like atmosphere' to which Bonsal alluded (in fact, only that one trial was held in the sports stadium). The principal defendant was ex-Major Jesús Sosa Blanco, charged with scores of murders in Oriente and famous for his brutality. This was not a kangaroo court, however. The three judges were Agriculture Minister Humberto Sorí-Marín, a Catholic lawyer who was the Rebel Army's judge-advocate (later shot for counter-revolutionary activities); Raúl Chibás, the moderate treasurer of the 26th of July Movement (who fled Cuba two years later); and Castro's wartime companion, Universo Sánchez. Sosa Blanco and his co-defendants had defence attorneys, and he himself contributed to the theatrical atmosphere by shouting that he was being subjected to a 'Roman circus' procedure. He was sentenced to death, then re-sentenced later, at a more tranquil trial in a military courtroom.

Castro's next error, in March, was to demand a new trial when a revolutionary court in Santiago had acquitted forty-four aviators from the Batista army for bombing peasants in the Sierra and he announced on television that 'revolutionary justice is not based on legal precepts, but on moral conviction'. Major Manuel Piñeiro Losada, a founder of the Castro secret police, was named chairman of the tribunal, and on this second time round all the fliers were sentenced to prison terms.

There remains a philosophical aspect to the question of the trials. The central point is that Castro believes that the revolution had every right to hold them on the basis of wartime revolutionary laws while the American view in 1959, a sanctimonious view ignoring Cuban emotions and demanding Anglo–Saxon legal procedures, denied the Cubans this right. Apart from the fact that Cuban law is based on the Napoleonic Code, which (contrary to the English common law) places on the defendant the burden of establishing his (or her) innocence, Castro takes the view that 'in the Sierra Maestra, when we were an embryo state, we wrote a penal code to punish war crimes . . . once the revolution had triumphed, the courts of the land accepted these laws as applicable laws, validated by the victorious revolution, and the tribunals tried many war criminals.' Castro says that 'this started the first campaigns abroad against Cuba, especially in the United States, which realized quickly that we had a different government here, not a very docile government. . .'

Rufo López-Fresquet, the moderate and pro-American Treasury Minister during the first fourteen months of the Castro regime, has written that 'the foreigner, especially the North American, put his emphasis on the legal aspects of the revolutionary trials, [but] the Cuban was interested in moral justice . . . When a man who has boasted of killing dozens of men while protected by his Batista uniform was executed, the Cubans believed justice was served. The rest of the world concentrated on criticism of the revolutionary judicial process. Perhaps both were right, but they were miles apart. Not many calm voices dedicated themselves to explaining these differences.'

(The trials should not have surprised Cubans or Americans: early in February 1958, a year before the war ended, *Look* magazine in New York and *Bohemia* in Havana published a photo-reportage on 'Justice in the Sierra', showing Castro sitting informally on the ground while interrogating prisoners charged with murder and rape before 'revolutionary tribunal' trials lasting twelve days, and Raúl Castro commanding a firing squad.)

Consequently an anti-Cuban campaign did begin to shape up in the American government, Congress and segments of the media, and Castro let nothing escape his attention. Convinced that a 'Plattist mentality' still existed among many Cubans and Americans – the belief in the applicability of the long-abrogated Platt Amendment granting the United States the right to intervene in Cuba – he saw conspiracies and his self-fulfilling prophecies coming true. When Americans condemned the trials Castro reacted with accusations that the United States had granted asylum to the worst Batista 'war criminals', which was true, and that they would plot against the revolution, which also was true.

From his first week in Havana, Castro used every speech to tell the United States as plainly as possible that it no longer had a say in Cuba. Before the Lions Club on 13 February he reminded his hosts that 'the Platt Amendment is finished', that the revolution was already being attacked in the United States, and that Cubans had the right to trace their own destiny and 'do things better than those who spoke of democracy while sending Sherman tanks to Batista'. Two days later he told the Rotarians: 'Nobody can intervene here because sovereignty is not a favour granted us, but our inalienable right as a nation.' The following afternoon he touched off approving roars from hundreds of thousands attending a rally at the Presidential Palace when he warned that if the United States wished to have good relations with Cuba, 'the first thing they have to do is to respect her sovereignty'. Back at a palace mass rally five days later, Castro reopened the question of the validity of the trials by demanding the huge crowd to raise their hands 'if you agree that the murderers must be executed' – a forest of hands rose over the plaza, and Fidel said: 'A jury of one million Cubans of all opinions and all the social classes has voted!'

During March, if he was truly aiming at a favourable shift in United States public opinion, Castro engaged in political activities that were to say the least contradictory. By accepting an invitation from the American Society of Newspaper Editors to speak at their annual meeting in Washington (allowing him to visit the United States without an invitation from the Eisenhower administration) and launching Operation Truth for American newsmen willing to visit Cuba as official guests, Castro appeared to be courting the Americans. But at the same time he 'intervened in' the American-owned Cuban Telephone Company, which meant that its management was taken over by his regime in order to investigate its operations. This might have been consistent with Castro's statements dating back to Moncada about the need for Cuba to operate its own utilities, but the political timing was tactless in terms of his approaching United States trip. Next he publicly embarrassed José Figueres, the former president of Costa Rica and one of his early supporters, by accusing him of intolerable 'imperialist' tendencies for having suggested at a rally that in the Soviet–American struggle there could be only one place – alongside the United States. With that Fidel Castro departed for the United States.

Normally, new Latin American leaders made a pilgrimage to Washington as soon as possible to win official favour and seek emergency economic aid. However, Fidel Castro turned out to be an exception, refusing to ask for money, or even talk about it. Rufo López-Fresquet, the Finance Minister, who was among the hundred-plus Fidel entourage on the trip, recounted in his memoirs in exile this conversation with Castro: 'I don't want this trip to be like those of other new Latin American leaders who always come to the US to ask for money. I want this to be a goodwill trip. Besides, the Americans will be surprised. And when we go back to Cuba they will offer us aid without our asking for it. Consequently we will be in a better bargaining position.' López-Fresquet replied that 'the reasoning was not completely illogical' although at that point the government's cash reserves were below $1 million. The American visit, to Fidel's mind, had to underscore the absolute independence of the Cuban revolution from the United States, mainly because he saw himself as the great hemispheric leader.

Castro's visit to the United States was primarily a brilliant exercise in public relations. But for all his anti-Americanism, Castro had also come to seek, consciously or not, North American approval for the person and the deeds of Fidel Castro. His visit began on the evening of 15 April, amidst the confusion characterizing all his travels: he was two hours late in boarding his special *Cubana* airline plane for Washington, keeping everybody waiting on both sides, and he told a nervous adviser: 'We are going to be in the US fifteen days; what difference does an hour or two make?' Clearly Fidel was savouring his moment. His last visit to the United States had been nearly four years before, when as an impecunious and rather obscure revolutionary he had asked Cuban communities for cash contributions to finance the promised war against Batista, and had been obliged to humbly request an extension of his visitor's visa.

In the United States Castro was both lionized and continuously lectured by American government officials, congressmen and editorial writers on the dangers of Communism and the beauties of democracy in that lovingly patronizing fashion Americans apply to foreigners. Having a marvellous time, he went along with this game, being the modest charmer, saying what he knew Americans wanted to hear, basking in the applause and the huge national attention he was commanding, drawing additional sympathy from the presence of nine-year-old Fidelito whom he took almost everywhere, and keeping his private contempt for his hosts to comments among his friends. President Eisenhower arranged to be out of town (playing golf) during the five days Castro spent in Washington – not precisely a slight since the Cuban was not a head of state and not an official guest, but it might have been a useful gesture to receive him at the White House. None the less the olive-green-fatigues-clad Castro enjoyed red-carpet treatment elsewhere in Washington: a lunch given by Acting Secretary of State Christian Herter; a two-hour-and-twenty-five-minute private meeting with Vice President Nixon at his office in the otherwise deserted Capitol (they met there on Sunday afternoon after Fidel had refused to go to the vice presidential home) which was notable for an absolute lack of mutual understanding and for Nixon's conclusion that the Cuban was controlled by Communists; a lunch at the National Press Club where he treated newsmen to twenty-minute answers to questions in his surprisingly fluent if heavily accented English; a Meet the Press television interview; visits with key senators and congressmen; and the hosting of a reception at the Cuban Embassy on Sixteenth Street where he was staying. On that occasion Castro appeared for the first time in a formal military uniform with tie and jacket, and had a brief conversation with the Soviet Ambassador, Mikhail A. Menshikov. It was his first known encounter with a Soviet official.

In his free time Castro went to see the Lincoln and Jefferson memorials, and walked for an hour around the grounds of Washington's home at

Mount Vernon. At Jefferson's Memorial he was asked whether he thought governments should ever be overthrown, and he was ready with appropriate words: 'I am not an advocate of frequent changes in laws and constitutions, but laws and constitutions must go hand in hand . . . this *is* a revolutionary principle for . . . progressive changes of institutions as the minds of men change.' Saturday night, after the embassy reception, Castro playfully reverted to his Havana practices, disappearing for four hours from the surveillance of the enormous American Security apparatus to tour Washington in a private automobile with five Cuban companions. He dined in a downtown Chinese restaurant and debated with a group of university students at nearby tables, finally making it home at three o'clock in the morning.

Politically, Castro was most adroit in Washington. On the issue of Communism in Cuba, endlessly raised with him in Washington, he repeated time after time that 'we are not Communists', that if there happened to be any Communists in his government 'their influence is nothing', and that he did not agree with Communism. To reassure Americans during the post-victory transition period, pending ultimate consolidation, Castro announced that Cuba would not confiscate foreign-owned private property (which meant mainly American-owned concerns), and indeed would seek additional investments to provide new jobs. And addressing the lunch of the newspaper editors who had invited him to the United States, Castro said: 'The first thing dictators do is abolish the free press and establish censorship. There is no doubt that a free press is the first enemy of dictatorship.'

It was during a Washington appearance that Castro for the first time publicly ruled out elections in Cuba in the foreseeable future, telling television interviewers that at least four years would have to elapse before the revolutionary regime could 'establish conditions for free elections,' and that in the meantime, 'real democracy is not possible for hungry people'. Previously Castro had been saying that the delay before holding elections would be no more than two years, and he had not been attaching conditions to the timing.

Almost imperceptibly, Castro had changed the rules of the Cuban political game as he smiled disarmingly before television cameras in a Washington studio. The 'conditions' for free elections – and Castro certainly was not saying there would be no elections – sounded eminently sensible, and after all, he clearly had the trust of 90 per cent of the Cuban population at that point. Advancing along several fronts, including invisible fronts, the Prime Minister of the Revolution had his overall strategy well in hand. Very soon the slogan of 'Revolution First, Elections Afterwards!' would begin to be heard in Cuba, Fidel could say he was simply responding to *vox populi*, and by mid-year, elections (like anti-Communism) would have become counter-revolutionary.

Secure in the knowledge that the situation at home was under control with Raúl Castro fully in charge (though Defence Minister Martínez Sánchez was the acting prime minister), Fidel could enjoy his North American tour and quietly prepare to extend his travels to South America. He also became involved in an extraordinarily bizarre episode. Either to test his non-Communist protestations or to profit from his Communist experiences, the CIA arranged to have Castro receive its supposedly leading expert on Communism in Latin America, a cigar-smoking wartime German refugee named Gerry Drecher who used the pseudonym of Frank Bender. He had no Latin American experience whatsoever. Castro had refused to see him in Washington, but relented and agreed to a meeting at his hotel suite in New York where he arrived by train (after a speech en route at Princeton University) on 21 April.

The contact was arranged in all good faith through Finance Minister López-Fresquet (pressed by his American friends) who wrote afterwards that Castro and Bender talked privately for more than three hours. Then Bender 'returned to my suite in a state of euphoria . . . he asked for a drink, and with great relief exclaimed, "Castro is not only not a Communist, but he is also a strong anti-Communist fighter." ' Bender next informed López-Fresquet that he 'had arranged with Castro an exchange of Intelligence information on the activities of the Communists and that I was to be the Cuban contact'. López-Fresquet wrote that 'the following month, during a reception at the French Embassy in Havana, a high US official approached me and gave me an oral message for Castro from Mr Bender. At the next cabinet session I gave Castro the intelligence. He didn't answer me, and he never gave me any information to pass on to Mr Bender.' What López-Fresquet did not mention was that Bender–Drecher was already preparing for his role as one of the chief architects of the Bay of Pigs invasion two years later; he would be the chief of political action of the operation. It was a strange encounter: did Bender really expect Castro to be his informant on Communism? (He had no way of knowing about the Cojímar sessions with the Communists.) Did Castro suspect that he was receiving the arch-plotter-to-be? (Probably not.) And yet Castro apparently said to López-Fresquet, who still had his illusions, 'Look, Rufo, I am letting the Communists stick their heads out so I will know who they are. And when I know them all, I'll do away with them, with one sweep of my hat.'

In New York Castro spent four days as a conquering hero, touring the United Nations, addressing a night-time crowd of 30,000 in Central Park, visiting the Coffee and Sugar Exchange and City Hall, and speaking at luncheons and dinners to publishers, businessmen and financiers. He made a superb impression, and little attention was paid to his remark at the United Nations that Cubans were 'unanimously' opposed to immediate elections because they would risk the return of 'oligarchy and tyranny'. (Likewise scant attention was paid to a page one dispatch in the *New York Times* from its Havana correspondent, Ruby Hart Phillips on 23 April, that 'the Communist Popular Socialist Party is organizing every town and village . . . the Communist influence in unions is rising . . . leaders of the 26th of July Movement are combating these Communistic efforts, but the youthful rebels are amateurs at organization compared with the Communists'.) From New York Castro travelled by train to Boston and a speech at Harvard University, then to Montreal. There he let it be known that he would go on immediately to Buenos Aires to attend an inter-American economic conference.

Fidel Castro's decision to fly to South America at the end of his North American tour resulted from his determination to reach out instantly for wider Latin American leadership – it was his first Bolivarian gesture – and to emphasize his independence from the United States. At the same time Castro was evidently eager to clarify his stand on the question of Latin American revolutions and any possible Cuban assistance to them in the light of his own pronouncements on the subject and a series of odd events occurring during his stay in the United States.

Castro's principal pronouncement in this context had been that Cuba would provide 'hospitality', the opportunity to work, and help to exiles from Latin American countries who hoped to overthrow dictatorships at home. This was, in effect, his first declaration of what has become known as Castro's 'internationalism', but, as he would keep repeating for the next thirty years, 'the Cuban revolution was not for export' because revolutions must stem from internal conditions. None the less he must have been aware of nervousness in the region following reports that Nicaraguan, Panamanian and Haitian rebels were on the verge of invading their countries from Cuban bases. In fact he was clearly embarrassed by them, and there were strong suspicions at the time that these expeditions had been authorized by Raúl Castro in Fidel's absence. Be that as it may, on 18 April over a hundred Nicaraguans were arrested at a camp in the province of Pinar del Río, and their arms seized, by the provincial Rebel Army commander who declared that Fidel had forbidden invasions from Cuba. Even so, that same day a Panamanian opposition leader named Ruben Miró said in Havana that his armed groups would land in Panama within a month; on 21 April Dame Margot Fonteyn, the ballerina, was arrested in Panama and expelled while her politician husband, Roberto Arias, went into hiding after they had circled in a yacht off the coast in a peculiar fashion. López-Fresquet, who was in Boston with Fidel, remembered overhearing an angry telephone conversation between him and Raúl on the day the Panamanian government announced the capture ashore of three rebels, two of them

Cubans; Fidel was apparently chastizing his brother. Then, there were rumours of Haitian exiles planning an invasion from Cuba.

When Fidel stopped in Houston, Texas en route from Montreal to South America on 27 April, Raúl flew up from Havana for a half-hour conference with him at the airport. It was never explained publicly why Fidel had summoned Raúl, but the next day he broadcast from his aircraft flying over Cuba a denunciation of 'irresponsible' Cubans landing in Panama, damaging the prestige of the revolution. At the Organization of American States in Washington the new Cuban ambassador, Raúl Roa García, also denounced the Panamanian venture – and Fidel was widely applauded for being so statesmanlike. True to his 'internationalism', however, he never actually refused sanctuary to a single Latin American revolutionary. Which shows yet again Castro's talent for having the best of all worlds.

Castro devoted ten days to his South American *tournée*, another triumph for him and his revolution, attracting vast crowds, wild applause, and the undivided attention of local leaders. In Port of Spain he was greeted by Prime Minister Eric Williams; in São Paulo he announced that 'our aspirations are the same as those of all Latin America', then flew to the site of the future capital of Brasília to confer with President Juscelino Kubitschek; in Buenos Aires he met President Arturo Frondizi; in Montevideo he was welcomed by the Uruguayan government and spoke at a huge street rally; back in Brazil he conferred again with Kubitschek, addressed a mass rally, and appeared on the television programme *This Is Your Life*, loving the exposure. But the high point of his journey was the economic conference in Buenos Aires where Castro sat in his olive-green fatigues among the hemisphere ministers of economy (the United States sent only an assistant secretary of state, a sad comment) to proclaim that 'the hour has come for the people of Latin America to make daily efforts to find a true solution to those of our problems that are economic in character'. In this 2 May speech before the Committee of 21, Castro urged the United States to grant Latin America $30 billion in economic aid over a decade, an idea immediately derided in Washington as ridiculous and demagogic. But less than two years later President John F. Kennedy would offer $25 billion to Latin America's development under the Alliance for Progress programme, over which Castro later chuckled, seeing it as an attempt to steal his thunder. In fact Castro had a sense of Latin American needs and moods that no United States administration in the decades to come would ever equal.

Mixing with crowds everywhere he went – in the United States, in Canada and in South America – Castro was always an easy target for assassination, and yet no public attempt was ever made against him. This did not stop Fidel from displaying *guerrillero* fatalism. Shown in New York a headline about an assassination plot, he smiled and said: 'I'm not worried. I will not live one day more than the day I am going to die.'

Back in Havana on 7 May, Fidel Castro wasted not a moment in launching the next major phase in the Cuban revolution. The very next day, conscious of the need for contact with the masses, he convened a rally of tens of thousands on the vast Civic Plaza (now Revolution Plaza) to pledge 'The revolution will never renounce its human principles . . . nor the existence of social justice in Cuba.' Then he drove off in his motorcade of Oldsmobiles to his seaside house at Cojímar to present his ministers with the text of the agrarian reform law that his inside team had secretly drafted at Che Guevara's residence in the previous months. On 17 May the law was signed by the entire cabinet and Castro announced on television that 'Cuba is beginning a new era.'

On the page, the new law (replacing the 1958 Sierra agrarian law) did not seem breathlessly radical, not abolishing private property but instead limiting land ownership to 400 hectares per individual; while sugar, rice and cattle holdings could be as large as 1375 hectares. For practical purposes, however, since the law inevitably led to state consolidation of nationalized lands so that great plantations and pastures could go on operating efficiently, the *latifundium* was abolished in Cuba as an economic and political phenomenon. In this sense, agrarian reform marked the first real revolutionary milestone; as Castro said afterwards: 'It established a break between the revolution and the richest and the most privileged sectors in the country, and a break with the United States, and with trans-national companies.' As Castro noted, some American companies each owned as many as 200,000 hectares of Cuba's 'best land'. Not surprisingly the law was immensely popular among Cubans, especially the peasants, and the already finely honed internal propaganda apparatus instantly produced the slogan 'The Agrarian Reform Works!' to be repeated endlessly by radio and television, and by every telephone operator in the country answering a call.

Politically, by creating the National Institute of Agrarian Reform – INRA – which, in effect, provided the structure for his hidden government, the law handed Castro his greatest instrument of unchecked power. He became the president of INRA in addition to his premiership and his post as commander-in-chief, and Antonio Nuñez Jiménez, the coordinator of the Tarará secret task force, was named executive director. A nexus was immediately established between INRA and the Rebel Army, the latter executing the economic and political decisions of the former: it was a logical step in the unfolding of Castro's determination that a strong and modernized Rebel Army be the revolution's power centre and its vanguard. INRA and the Rebel Army became, in fact, indistinguishable – the ministerial cabinet at the Presidential Palace that Castro attended less and less was no more than an adornment.

Looking back at that first year, Nuñez Jiménez says that under Castro INRA 'was the bastion where the revolution occurred in those initial months . . . the organism that dealt the real blow to the bourgeoisie and imperialism.' He remarks: 'It would not have been good tactics to change suddenly the council of ministers . . . our people were not yet prepared ideologically for an open battle between the revolution and the counter-revolution within the government itself.' Therefore Nuñez Jiménez recounts, 'Fidel duplicated in INRA the most important functions of the revolutionary government.' One of these duplications was the creation within INRA of a Department of Industrialization headed by Che Guevara, which became the de facto ministry of industries; when Guevara subsequently became President of the National Bank, Nuñez Jiménez was named its executive vice president to assure INRA's voice there; the old Commerce Ministry was transformed into INRA's Department of Commercialization.

Gradually ministries and INRA departments overlapped 'until the Council of Ministers,' Nuñez Jiménez says, 'was formed totally by revolutionaries.' Next INRA created its own armed 100,000-man militia units with the aid of Raúl Castro, and 11 million pesos in INRA funds were used to organize an army artillery school and the first anti-aircraft and anti-tank artillery units. Likewise INRA financed the construction of most of the highways in Cuba in the first revolutionary period, built peasant housing and tourist resorts. Rebel Army officers were given the power to seize private land and to run farms as cooperatives under INRA, and Che Guevara ordered that the new industrialization projects should be directed by Rebel Army 'companions'. Thus a hidden government was indeed formed, but strangely, most Cubans even in senior positions were unaware of it.

Using the tall INRA building (erected by Batista to be Havana's city hall) as his principal office, Castro speeded the process of revolution in regular secret meetings with top officials and administrators. Late in 1959, for example, he announced that all sugarcane fields would be seized from individual small owners after the 1960 harvest, and turned into cooperatives; this violated the May agrarian law, but behind INRA's closed doors only Fidel's orders counted. And at that stage he proposed to go on running Cuba from INRA, declaring in another secret speech that the Institute was 'a political instrument and the apparatus for activating the country's masses to carry out a task and to defend this task . . . INRA will be a gigantic apparatus with extraordinary powers to mobilize [the people], especially if we organize the peasants in social military groups . . . An armed people is the definitive guarantee of the revolution. . .'

Thus, as he kept reminding his companions, the revolution had to move carefully and gradually while he consolidated power from his INRA 'bastion'. Fidel's sensitive political antennae were attuned to disturbing signals in the air. He was uncertain of the revolutionary loyalty of his own 26th of July Movement, particularly of its 'bourgeois right wing', as he called it, and although he had finally succeeded in bringing the Revolutionary Directorate (DR) to his side after the past rivalries, and to attract DR's chief, Faure Chomón, to the government, he still felt uncomfortable with this middle-class organization. Then, there was the problem of the strutting *barbudos* (some of whom had actually fought in the mountains) demanding rank and privilege, a request driving Fidel to paroxysms of fury. In rage, he denounced 'the stupidity, the demagogy, the opportunism and the politicking of all those who today give the appearance of being more revolutionary than anyone else'.

And, finally, there were the Communists. Though he continued the long-range unity talks with the party's leaders, Castro was aware that the Communist leadership was split, and many old-timers resented him. The party as a whole (possibly because Moscow remained unconvinced) had still failed to recognize his revolutionary genius, triumphing in *his* way instead of in the orthodox Marxist–Leninist way. Pragmatic as they may have tried to be, key party leaders found hard to swallow Castro's denials in the United States of Communist influence in the Cuban revolution, and his occasional outbursts of private impatience with the arrogance of some party members.

Externally, Castro increasingly feared an American intervention, especially after the signing of the land-reform law. Bonsal, the American ambassador in Havana, wrote afterwards: 'In the spring of 1959 Castro believed it probable that the Cuban revolution as he envisaged it would sooner rather than later come into irreconcilable conflict with American interests on the island and that the United States government would respond with a full-scale invasion of Cuba.' But Bonsal also commented that 'Castro's scenario at this time did not contemplate the massive help in the form of economic aid and weapons that he later received from the Soviet Union . . . [he] became oriented towards dependence on the Soviet Union only when the United States, by its actions in the spring and summer of 1960, gave the Russians no choice other than to come to Castro's rescue.' This is a complex proposition, and set forth by a diplomat of Bonsal's acuity it is worth examining.

If Bonsal's assessment is correct – and, in the end, only Fidel Castro knows the truth – then my own impression is that the American determination to prevent Cuba from acquiring arms anywhere in the world during 1959 and 1960 was the decisive factor, even before Eisenhower launched economic and covert action warfare against the revolutionaries. It is certainly arguable that if the United States had not threatened his survival Castro might have chosen domestic Marxist solutions without becoming wholly dependent on the Russians economically and militarily – Yugoslavia and China are not such far-fetched analogies. Moreover, at least a year elapsed before Soviet assistance began arriving on the island, and before that Washington need not have closed off all the alternatives. Finally, a study of the record will show that Castro had begun to move steadily towards his version of a socialist revolution long before Moscow promised or gave him help.

Immediately after victory, Castro made the modernising of the Rebel Army – and subsequently of the new people's militia – a top priority. The militia was particularly important because Castro, much as he believed in the Rebel Army as the chief instrument of revolutionary power, did not want the army to become an elite organization that, even theoretically, could some day turn into a political threat. But Castro also knew that it would be costly to maintain a large standing army, even though he daily feared an American invasion, and that a well-trained militia, which could be mobilized for action within hours, would be the perfect complement to a smaller though heavily armed professional army. Finally, he considered that the militias, as part of 'an armed nation', represented an additional dimension of popular revolutionary commitment. In mid-1959 Castro was telling INRA associates in his secret speeches that he wanted 100,000 peasant militias (in addition to workers' and students' militias), being trained at a rate of one thousand every forty-five days in the use of weapons – up to .50 calibre tripod machine guns. What guns Batista had left behind, however, were not suitable to the modern mobile forces Castro had in mind, and by mid-May trusted emissaries had fanned out overseas to try to buy arms.

Rufo López-Fresquet, the revolution's first Finance Minister, recalls being summoned to Castro's hotel penthouse late in January to be asked if there were funds available for 'an immediate purchase of arms'. Castro told him he was concerned about an invasion from the Dominican Republic where Batista had found haven with Trujillo, and that Cuba was poorly armed because 'the generals stole the money, and, in spite of the heavy expenditures on armaments, these are nowhere to be found'. López-Fresquet was able to track down $5.3 million of Cuban military funds in European banks, and the regime purchased 25,000 light automatic FAL rifles (including 2000 weapons with grenade-throwing attachments), 50 million rounds of ammunition and 100,000 grenades from Belgium. The United States had not yet begun pressing foreign governments to refuse arms to Cuba, and the first FAL shipment reached Havana in September, just in time for the fresh militia units (though the militias' creation was announced by Castro only on 26 October).

Soon, however, the Europeans, under pressure from Washington, declined to sell armaments to Cuba. Britain, honouring an American request, refused to supply Hawker Hunter jet fighters to the Cuban Air Force. Yugoslavia, approached secretly by the Cubans in 1959, decided on its own not to sell arms to Castro, presumably to avoid antagonizing the United States with which it maintained a delicate relationship.

Announcing in October the creation of the militias because, as he put it, of the growing danger of attacks from the United States, Castro told a million Cubans at a Presidential Palace rally that 'if we cannot buy planes, we shall fight on land, when the time comes to fight on land . . . we shall immediately start training peasants and workers . . . If they don't sell us planes in England, we shall buy them wherever they will sell to us; and if there is no government money for warplanes, the people themselves will buy the warplanes. . .' Turning to army Chief-of-Staff Juan Almeida, Castro exclaimed: 'And right here, I hand you a cheque from the President of the Republic and the Prime Minister as a contribution for the purchase of the planes.'

J.R. Fernández says that the first arms from Czechoslovakia and the Soviet Union began arriving late in 1960, months after the final breach in Cuban–American economic ties. As Castro had said, Cuba would buy arms wherever possible (or accept them as gifts) but the record suggests that Castro had first tried Western sources, and Ambassador Bonsal is right that the revolutionaries were forced into dependence on the Soviet bloc. According to Fernández, the first Czech shipments were automatic M-52 rifles, BEZA-792 machine guns that could be used for anti-aircraft fire, and 82-mm mortars. Czech instructors accompanied the weapons. Soviet arms came next.

If Castro feared an invasion from the United States in 1959 he also feared an attack from the Dominican Republic by his arch-enemy, the generalissimo Trujillo, who remembered Fidel's involvement in the abortive Cayo Confites expedition against him twelve years earlier, was just as concerned with the threat of a Cuban invasion, directly or through Haiti. Both rulers therefore devoted themselves to preparations for pre-emptive blows though neither seemed to understand the political situation in the other's country. Trujillo started out by organizing a 'Foreign Legion', including Caribbean mercenaries, anti-Castro Cubans, Fascist Blue Division veterans from Spain, Germans and right-wing Croatians. It was never clear whether Trujillo planned to use this 'legion' to defend Haiti from Cuba or to attack Cuba, but Castro, who had been training anti-Trujillo Dominicans in his camps, struck first. At dusk of 14 June a C-46 twin-engine transport plane provided by Venezuela landed in Constanza in the central mountains of the Dominican Republic with fifty-six rebels aboard. Ten of them were Cubans, and the commander was Major Delio Gómez Ochoa, the former 26th of July Movement coordinator in Havana. The Dominican Army rapidly destroyed the invading force, capturing Gómez and six days later Trujillo's air force and warship sank two yachts filled with additional Dominican rebels trying to land at La Plata on the north coast. This marked the end of Castro's only attempt to tangle with Trujillo. Perhaps he had again been practising 'internationalism' or perhaps he was simply hoping to discourage the old dictator from assaulting him.

In any event Trujillo would not give up, and immediately after Constanza his top Intelligence agents resumed plotting with two Rebel Army *comandantes* whom they considered ready to betray Castro. One was an American mercenary named William Morgan and the other was a Spaniard named Eloy Gutiérrez Menoyo who had participated with his brother Carlos in the 1957 attack on Batista's palace by the Revolutionary Directorate. Carlos was killed, and Eloy joined the DR guerrillas in Escambray the following year, meeting Morgan who seemed to be fighting there strictly for the money. Trujillo supposedly offered Morgan and Gutiérrez Menoyo one million dollars to start a rebellion in the Escambray mountains that would then be supported by landings on the coast by the Cuban exiles and Dominican 'legion'. Inasmuch as there was bad blood between the DR factions and Castro, Morgan and his Spanish friend appeared to the Dominicans as perfectly plausible traitors, and the American actually collected $500,000 as a down payment.

What Trujillo did not know was that Morgan and Gutiérrez Menoyo had informed Castro of the conspiracy, allowing the Cubans to tape radio traffic between the two *comandantes* and the Dominican capital. It is entirely possible that the two men were playing a double or triple game, depending on the most favourable outcome, but on 12 August they radioed Ciudad Trujillo on Castro's instructions that 'rebel guerrillas' had taken the port of Trinidad and now awaited reinforcements. Castro and his bodyguards sat inside a mango grove off the airfield listening to the radio exchanges all night, then watching a Dominican plane land munitions and depart, and finally coming out from behind a mango tree to capture the ten Cubans disembarking from a second plane from the Dominican Republic at dawn of 13 August. It was his thirty-third birthday treat. The area was surrounded by several Rebel Army battalions, but Fidel proudly relived his guerrilla days when he personally captured the pilot, Lieutenant Colonel Antonio Soto, who had flown Batista to exile on 1 January. It is strange that Trujillo had fallen into the Castro trap, considering that only four days earlier the Cuban Security forces had rounded up a thousand ex-Batista soldiers and others with Dominican connections, but then, logic never was a prevailing wind in the Caribbean. As to Morgan, he was shot two years later for involvement in a 'counter-revolutionary' conspiracy, and Gutiérrez Menoyo was captured in 1965 after landing clandestinely from a CIA boat from Florida. He was still in prison in 1986, despite entreaties by Spain's socialist government.

For Fidel the Trinidad incident was a welcome and exhilarating distraction from the rigours of managing a revolution, living behind a microphone and juggling all his political balls. His temperament required constant movement and change, and he succeeded reasonably often in pleasing himself. In Havana he had the choice of working at either of his offices at INRA (he disliked the Presidential Palace and he never set foot at the nearby official quarters of the prime minister), at the hotel penthouse suite, at the seaside house in Cojímar, at Celia Sánchez's apartment on Eleventh Street, or at another house set aside for him next to the Chaplin theatre in Miramar. He also had his secret military command post in the Vedado residential district.

Though Castro commuted continuously between all these places he was still restless. Occasionally he turned up at the Cerro stadium in the evening to pitch a few balls at Sugar Kings' batters; or his motorcade would appear at Carmelo's terrace café in Vedado across the street from Alicia Alonzo's ballet school for Fidel to eat ice cream and chat with the patrons; or he would drop in at a foreign embassy reception. One night, after a midnight steak dinner in the kitchen of the Habana Libre Hotel (the Hilton's new name), he took Herbert Matthews and me to a suburban beach in the small hours to have a Coke and show us the resorts the revolution had built for the people; afterwards we chatted until mid-morning in the hotel cafeteria, Fidel being the only one of us who was not sleepy. Sometimes he spent several days at a military camp, usually in Oriente, chatting with the troops, reading and writing. Caught by three days and nights of rain in one such camp, he avidly played dominoes and chess for hours on end, strangely showing no impatience. His torso bare, he did chin-ups, shot basket balls, or played with his alsatian dog, Guardián. Celia Sánchez was usually along on these trips, but Castro seemed to enjoy military camaraderie with his friends and bodyguards: his physician René Vallejo, his chief bodyguard Jesús Yañes Pelletier (his Santiago jailer who had saved his life) until he was fired for improper behaviour, his friend Nuñez Jiménez, and Raúl Castro and Che Guevara if they happened to be around. Fidelito visited his father at the Cojímar house, but he was a boarder at school and their contacts were infrequent. During the spring of 1959 Fidelito was in an automobile accident near Matanzas, perforating his spleen, and it took hours for Castro to be located and brought to the hospital.

Always looking for the new and the unusual, Fidel Castro discovered and invaded the Bay of Pigs two years before the Americans thought of it. Moreover, when the CIA decided to surprise him in the great southern swamp, its planners had no idea that Fidel knew the Ciénaga de Zapata like the back of his hand, making it even easier for him to win the battle. It was one of those coincidences of history. The Ciénaga de Zapata is the immense, virtually uninhabited marshland stretching far inland along the southern coasts of Havana and Matanzas provinces – the domain of quick sand, charcoal-burners, crocodiles and mosquitoes. Probably because it was the only geographic challenge left for him in Cuba after the conquest of the Sierra Maestra – and assuredly because it was even poorer than the Sierra – Castro became fascinated with the Ciénaga, and in March 1959 began visiting the area regularly. At least twice he nearly lost his life in the immensity of the treacherous swamp.

The Ciénaga was the classic example of Castro's enthusiastic, sweeping, generous and often impractical approach to socio-economic development. His idea was that a great drainage system would turn the 200,000 hectares of western Ciénaga into an immense rice field, that the destitute charcoal-burners' families would prosper through rice cultivation and the expansion of tourism, and that canals, roads and resorts should be built at once to make it all possible. More than a quarter of a century later, however, no huge rice plantations have followed Castro's original experimental station, tourism has remained marginal and only the crocodiles and sea-cows have been saved. It was the usual sad story of insufficient resources, know-how and follow-up that has so often diluted the revolution's most ambitious plans.

On one of Fidel's first visits to the swamp the motor vessel taking him, Celia Sánchez, and Nuñez Jiménez and his wife down a canal suddenly went under, and only the agile commander-in-chief managed to jump to a bank. When his wet companions joined him, Castro was relaxedly reading Giovanni Papini's *The Remote Past*, which he had happened to be carrying in his pocket. The next few days brought even greater dangers. First the pilot of Castro's helicopter, Air Force Commander Major Pedro Luis Díaz Lanz, told him he lacked sufficient fuel for the planned tour of the Ciénaga. He left Castro, Nuñez Jiménez and Pedro Miret on Playa Girón, one of the future Bay of Pigs landing beaches, to pick up petrol at a sugar mill in the north, and was to return within a few hours. The three men spent the afternoon in rifle practice on the beach, but Díaz Lanz did not return, and they slept in a fisherman's shack. In the morning, the weather worsening, Castro and his companions walked ten or more miles to a military post to telephone the sugar mill – and to learn that the helicopter had never made it. After summoning search aircraft from Havana Castro climbed into a single-engine light plane with a pilot, taking off in driving rain to look for Diáz Lanz; landing an hour later, he reported spotting the crashed chopper with no sign of survivors.

Meanwhile, Raúl Castro, Che Guevara and other top rebel commanders had arrived aboard Fidel's personal plane *Sierra Maestra* from Havana, followed by two helicopters. Fidel took off in one of these helicopters, with the storm still raging, and four light planes went after him in a search pattern; Raúl was flying one of them. While Fidel's helicopter landed at the main tourist resort, near the crashed craft, the light plane with Raúl vanished in the rain clouds. Díaz Lanz was found late that day at the far end of the swamp where he had reached help, but Raúl was still missing. The following morning Raúl's plane was located in the pancaked mud near the coast. Raúl and two pilots were lost in the marshland, but were rescued by a search party and placed aboard a navy flying boat on the beach. Flying to Havana, the Catalina's landing gear collapsed but the pilot made a successful crash landing at the airfield.

The Ciénaga's pitfalls and adventures did not discourage Fidel. The marshland had become his pet project, and he kept referring to it rhapsodically in his speeches. 'We have rediscovered the Bay of Pigs, broad and deep,' he said in December in a speech the CIA must have missed. On Christmas Eve Castro and Nuñez Jiménez drove from Havana to the Laguna del Tesoro resort in the centre of the Ciénaga, then flew by helicopter to the charcoal-burners' village of Soplillar, joining local families at a dinner of roast pig and revolutionary songs. A contemporary photograph shows a smiling Fidel, his rifle in his left hand, looking down at a table surrounded by children and covered with a machine gun on a tripod, an ammunition belt, bottles of wines and rum, glasses and sweets. After Christmas he had a small aluminium house-and-office structure erected at the Laguna del Tesoro: for a time it was Castro's favourite hideaway and a place to receive special guests.

In Havana the Castro revolution and its enemies, both foreign and domestic, were becoming increasingly confrontational. In June 1959 Castro felt powerful enough to force the resignation of Foreign Minister Roberto Agramonte, a pro-American politician of the old school, replacing him with Raúl Roa, the vociferously revolutionary ambassador at the Organization of American States who only two years earlier in a series of articles had bitterly denounced the Soviet intervention in Hungary. Now Roa had joined the *Fidelista* camp. Four other 'moderate' ministers were also dismissed, and Castro now prepared to get rid of President Urrutia. The basic issue on which the internal battle had focused was Communism: the charges from one side were that Communism was taking over the revolution, and the response from the Castro camp was that anti-Communism was the principal instrument of the 'counter-revolution' in general, mainly forged in Washington. This was exactly two months after Castro had proclaimed in New York that 'I have said in a clear and definitive fashion that we are not Communists . . . The doors are open to private investments that contribute to the industrial development of Cuba . . . It is absolutely impossible for us to make progress if we do not come to an understanding with the United States.'

By June, however, not even Castro and Ambassador Bonsal seemed to understand each other. Following the signing of the new agrarian law,

Bonsal had sent a note to the Cuban government, pointing to the problems it posed for American investors in Cuba, and the next day, 12 June, the ambassador was invited to visit Castro in Cojímar. It was their first formal meeting, despite repeated requests, since Bonsal's get-acquainted call on the prime minister in March. Bonsal has written that Castro was 'cordial' and replied with 'an emphatic affirmative' to the ambassador's question whether American interests still had a role in the development of revolutionary Cuba. According to Bonsal, Castro also denied in the press that 'my approach to him [was] . . . a proconsular attitude'. In a speech in December 1961, however, Castro had a different recollection of his overall relations with Bonsal: 'From the first moment, shocking disputes began over criteria and view points, and these meetings became intolerable . . . this gentleman's statements were simply intolerable . . . He kept asking for an interview until, in the end, there was no way of not granting it.' Bonsal's comment in his book twelve years later was that all this 'is far from a unique example of the manner in which the Maximum Leader's flexible memory permits him statements contrary to the truth of the event he is recalling'. Certainly Castro did not seem to realize at the time that Bonsal was virtually putting his own career on the line by arguing in Washington for maintaining a dialogue with Cuba.

The removal of President Urrutia in July was dictated by the logic of Castro's revolutionary politics: the naive, patriotic judge from Santiago he had named in the Sierra to be provisional president was now turning out an obstacle to the revolution. With his power curtailed since February to the signing of laws prepared by Castro or the cabinet, by mid-spring Urrutia had rashly made himself even more vulnerable by staying away from cabinet sessions chaired by Castro and by delaying law-signing. Even López-Fresquet, the finance minister, wrote that Urrutia's actions were 'a mistake' and 'his conduct disrupted the functioning of the government . . . When Castro had an interest in the legislation in question, his animosity towards Urrutia increased . . . By his actions Urrutia succeeded only in alienating the cabinet, which later offered no opposition to his overthrow.' Then Urrutia began to make anti-Communist speeches and television statements as if to force a confront-ation with Castro. Playing blindly into Castro's hands, he offered to go on a 'leave of absence', from which he did not propose to return, on the day in June when the first batch of moderates was fired from the cabinet; Urrutia did not realize that in Castro's mind a resignation was an attack on him and the revolution, but he let himself be talked out of leaving. Fidel intended to control events himself.

On 29 June air force chief Major Díaz Lanz, who had piloted Castro's helicopter in the Ciénaga the previous month, defected to the United States, appearing before a Senate subcommittee in Washington to denounce Communism in Cuba and thereby quickening the crisis in Havana. That same week Urrutia went on television to say: 'I do not believe in Communism and I am ready to debate these questions with anyone.' Castro, now ready to go for the kill, responded publicly: 'I consider it not entirely honourable that if we are to avoid being called Communists we must embark on campaigns against the party; no honourable government would do this. . .' On 13 July Urrutia went back on television to feed Castro more rope by saying that 'the Communists are inflicting terrible harm on Cuba'. In retrospect it is clear that Urrutia would have accomplished much more in his confrontation with Castro if he had resigned at the moment of his choice over the Communist issue. But he was no match for the chief of the revolution.

And when Fidel Castro was ready to strike, he marshalled the full panoply of revolutionary drama. On the evening of 16 July Cuban radio and television announced that Castro had resigned as prime minister (but not as commander-in-chief) because of Urrutia's blocking of revolutionary laws and other government measures. He then dropped out of sight for the next twenty-four hours. As it happened Castro had ordered that all the peasants of Cuba, as many as wished it be brought to Havana for the celebrations of the sixth anniversary of the Moncada assault, and they began arriving massively in the capital as the Urrutia guerrilla theatre began to unfold. On 17 July the cabinet was summoned to the Presidential Palace, surrounded by troops and a growing crowd, but Urrutia was not to be seen. Defence Minister Martínez Sánchez appeared to be in charge as the minister awaited further developments. In the evening Castro went on television for a two-hour speech to explain that he had had to resign because of Urrutia's attitude in the presidency, then went on to link him with the Díaz Lanz defection, exclaiming: 'This has come close to treason, companions; we have been on the brink of treason!' He charged Urrutia with fabricating a Communist legend in Cuba in order to provoke foreign aggression, and finally mentioned that the president had bought a house 'for thirty or forty thousand dollars'.

With crowds outside chanting demands for Urrutia's resignation, the president signed it while Castro was still on television. The ministers accepted the resignation, and named Osvaldo Dorticós, the Minister for the Drafting of Revolutionary Laws, to be the new president. The proposal was made by Education Minister Armando Hart, one of Castro's close associates. Dorticós would be Castro's loyal collaborator. But the drama was still running its course, Fidel requiring an overwhelming national show of support. He attended a textile workers' rally at the sports stadium to hear pleas for him to return to the premiership, and on 23 July an hour-long general strike was called by revolutionary labour unions to insist on his return. Castro had carried out a *coup d'état* by television, and now *habaneros* and the visiting peasants, straw hats on their heads and sharp machetes inside brown leather sheaths, joined in parading around the city to hail their chief, songs about Fidel and the agrarian reform rising in the warm evening air. On 26 July Castro addressed a million of his supporters on the Civic Plaza, agreeing to be prime minister again, and warning that 'to attack Cuba is to attack all of Latin America'.

He had to continue mending revolutionary fences at home, however, to defuse rising criticism of Communist inroads in his regime and the Rebel Army. As we have already seen, he considered all politically-motivated resignations acts of treason, and he acted accordingly when Major Huber Matos Benítez, military governor of Camagüey and a top Sierra fighter, prepared his resignation over the Communist issue. Tipped off on 20 October that Matos had sent him a resignation letter and that twenty of his officers would likewise resign, Castro dispatched Rebel Army Commander Camilo Cienfuegos to arrest the major. He rushed personally to Camagüey and on the morning of 21 October led a revolutionary crowd in a march on the provincial military headquarters to pre-empt whatever rebellion may have been brewing. The Matos episode held immense dangers for Castro, questioning as it did the unity and loyalty of the Rebel Army. Díaz Lanz, the former air force commander, had flown over Havana that same day in a light plane from Florida, dropping anti-Castro leaflets and allegedly machine-gunning the city, and Fidel immediately linked him to the Matos affair as part of a larger American-based conspiracy likewise involving the hapless Urrutia. On 26 October Castro again gathered an enormous crowd – around a million people – in Havana to protest against these counter-revolutionary plots, to announce officially the creation of the armed militia, and to consult his supporters on the restoration of the death penalty and revolutionary tribunals. The crowd shouted its approval, chanting, *'Paredón! Paredón!'* (To the Wall! To the Wall!) In December Matos was sentenced to twenty years in prison after Castro's impassioned prosecutorial speech. Castro would not trust anyone else with the defence of the revolution at such a crucial moment.

At the same time he went on consolidating revolutionary power. The day before the Matos incident Raúl Castro was named Minister of Revolutionary Armed Forces, making official his control of the army. On 26 November Che Guevara took over the presidency of the National Bank while remaining in charge of national industry. Guevara's wartime deputy Ramiro Valdés became the head of DIER, military Intelligence and secret police, assisted by Manuel Piñero Losada, the red-bearded ideologue. But late in October the revolution lost its second most popular leader after Fidel when Camilo Cienfuegos disappeared on a solo flight aboard his light plane from Camagüey to Havana. Despite a land and sea search personally coordinated by Castro, no trace of his aircraft was ever found, Camilo joining the ever-expanding pantheon of revolutionary heroes upon whom today's myths still repose.

The Cuban revolution's growing orientation towards socialism or Communism was not matched at the outset by Soviet support. In fact there are convincing indications that Castro had to sell the Soviets on himself and his revolution when it became obvious that he needed them in order to survive economically and militarily in the light of United States antagonism. It can even be argued that Castro, taking advantage of the international situation, pushed Moscow into a relationship faster and to a greater degree than the Russians desired. If nothing else, the Kremlin had long shared the Cuban Communists's view that Fidel Castro was an unreliable customer. By the end of 1959, however, Castro had the Russians pretty much where he wanted them – as an antidote to the Americans

The Cuban revolutionary government was recognized by the Soviet Union on 10 January 1959, three days after the United States, but this was basically meaningless. Batista had broken diplomatic relations with Moscow in 1952, and neither side proposed to restore them at that stage. Fidel had never been an uncritical admirer of the Soviet Union like Raúl, Nuñez Jiménez and Che Guevara (until he soured on the Russians), and relations with Moscow were not a priority. Nevertheless in the course of a television interview on 19 February he said Cuba was prepared to sell sugar to the Soviet Union, not a startling idea considering that the Russians were traditional buyers anyway. During 1959 Moscow contracted to buy 500,000 tons of sugar, roughly the volume purchased in 1955. China bought 50,000 tons. Together, it was less than 10 per cent of the Cuban harvest.

A Soviet labour union delegation had been invited for May Day celebrations in Havana, but visas were not issued in time. Three Soviet trade unionists did appear, however, in November – though the CIA station in Havana was much more interested in the visit in May and again in October of one Vadim Vadimovitch Listov who was reported to be a top Soviet Intelligence operative. At the same time the Americans learned that four top Cuban pilots had gone secretly to Czechoslovakia to prepare a MiG jet training programme: their leader was Captain Victor Pina Cardoso, a wartime Royal Air Force flier.

Officially Moscow was not encouraging a close relationship with the Castro regime during 1959, possibly not to interfere with the Spirit of Camp David born from Premier Nikita Krushchev's visit to President Eisenhower in September. Deputy Premier Anastas I. Mikoyan, a powerful Politburo member, had gone to Mexico to open a Soviet trade fair, but nothing was said about hopping over to Havana to meet Castro. A more subtle method of making contact was devised instead. On 16

October, ten days before he disappeared with his plane, Camilo Cienfuegos told Nuñez Jiménez that he had had a long conversation at a Havana hotel with Aleksandr Alexeiev, a correspondent for the Soviet TASS news agency who had come to Cuba after awaiting a visa for eight months and who would like to meet Castro. It is not known how Alexeiev was able to meet Cienfuegos, the army commander.

Nuñez Jiménez passed on the word to Castro, and Alexeiev was informed that he would be received for a 'friendly' conversation at the prime minister's office on the top floor of the INRA building. Wearing a black suit and a grey necktie, the Soviet correspondent was brought from his hotel by two bearded Rebel Army soldiers, finding Castro and Nuñez Jiménez in olive-green fatigues. Greeting Castro, Alexeiev handed him a package wrapped in a Moscow newspaper: it contained a bottle of vodka, several tins of black caviar and an album of photographs of Moscow. Opening the conversation, the Russian told Castro of the 'great admiration' of the Soviet people for him and the Cuban revolution. The Soviet government and the Communist Party, he said, held his work for Cuba's social progress in great esteem. Castro responded pleasantly that his revolutionary regime would be disposed to enter into trade relations with the Soviet Union at the proper time.

Nuñez Jiménez mentioned having met Mikoyan at a Soviet fair in New York in July, and a conversation developed about such an exhibit being brought to Havana, too. Castro then said that it would produce a 'great impact' if Mikoyan came to Cuba to open the fair. At one point Alexeiev noticed a silver medallion around Castro's neck, and the prime minister told him: 'Don't worry, it's the image of a Christian saint that a little girl in Santiago sent to me when I was in the Sierra Maestra.' Then Fidel said: 'So long as you've brought the caviar and the vodka, let's taste it.' Conchita Fernández brought crackers, and the three men leaned back to enjoy the feast. Turning to Nuñez Jiménez, Fidel remarked: 'What good vodka, what good caviar! Nuñez, I think it's worth establishing trade relations with the Soviet Union? What do you think?'

'Very well, Fidel,' Alexeiev said, 'we can now count on re-establishing economic relations, but what about the most important one, the diplomatic relations?' Castro replied: 'Ah! . . . I can see why you came dressed so formally . . . But it's better that we go on talking. We'll have to do it this way for the moment because we need time to create the [proper] conditions. Do you remember an article by Lenin in which he was saying that to apply a new policy or to introduce new ideas it is necessary to persuade the masses, make them participate in these decisions? We shall do that . . . The idea of bringing the trade fair is excellent . . . It's an opportunity to show Cuban people the progress of the Soviet Union. At the present time, everything said about the Soviet Union is negative, and we must see to it that this type of information does not continue. The fair and a visit by Mikoyan could be a successful beginning, don't you think? We've already started with caviar and vodka.' The three men clinked glasses and Castro said: 'The fundamental question now is not diplomatic relations. The most important point is that Cubans and Russians are already friends.'

Within three months Mikoyan was in Havana to launch the immensely far-reaching relationship with Cuba. Aleksandr Alexeiev soon became the Soviet ambassador in Cuba. But five successive Soviet rulers – from Krushchev to Gorbachev – would learn in the ensuing quarter of a century the massive frustrations of dealing with Fidel Castro as an ally.

Chapter 3

Fidel Castro and Nikita Krushchev, two of the greatest political actors of our time, warmly embraced in a Harlem hotel in New York on 20 September 1960, signalling the sealing of an alliance that two years later would push the world to the brink of a nuclear war. The sixty-six-year-old Soviet Premier called on the thirty-four-year-old Cuban Prime Minister, whom he dubbed a 'heroic man', as his first public appearance after arriving in New York to attend the United Nations General Assembly. Thus he created the impression that Cuba was the number one foreign-policy priority for the Russians. So delighted was Castro with this attention that he was the first delegate in the huge hall to leap to his feet to applaud fervently Krushchev's address to the General Assembly later that week. The Castro–Krushchev New York act was magnificent political theatre, leaving no further doubt that Cuba had exchanged the American influence sphere for the Soviet sphere with all the political implications attendant in the Western hemisphere and in East–West relations.

The immediate backdrop for the cordiality betwee Krushchev and Castro was the catastrophic deterioration in Cuba's relations with the United States; the two nations separated by ninety miles of blue Caribbean water were now on an accelerating collision course. During the summer Castro had nationalized $850 million worth of United States property on the island, from sugar mills and cattle ranches to oil refineries and utilities companies, while the Eisenhower administration had deprived the Cubans of their vital quota in the high-premium American sugar market. Moreover the United States had taken two secret decisions: to train and equip a Cuban exile force to invade Cuba, and to have the American Mafia assassinate Fidel Castro on the CIA's behalf.

At the same time the overall international situation had changed radically during 1960, making Cuba and its *Fidelista* revolution much more attractive and interesting to the Soviet Union. Both Krushchev and Castro being calculated-risk gamblers, they joined forces to exploit the new situation – though it must be assumed that as a matter of principle they had a healthy distrust of each other. From the Kremlin's viewpoint the previous September's Spirit of Camp David had been replaced by the ugly tensions growing out of the shooting down in May over Soviet territory of the CIA's U-2 spy plane and by the cancellation of the Krushchev–Eisenhower summit that spring. Simultaneously the long-simmering ideological feud between Moscow and Peking had finally boiled over in public view, and the two great Communist nations became rivals for the affections and allegiances of the emerging Third World. In this suddenly changed context Cuba acquired desirability for the Russians and evidently Krushchev was not about to let China become the prime champion of the Cuban revolution. The Soviets must have been aware of the attraction China initially had for many young Cuban revolutionaries, seeing parallels between their two countries' 'peasant' revolutions, and even for ranking PSP members such as the party's Secretary-General Blás Roca, who was cordially received by Mao Tse-tung as late as April 1960. It had been from Peking that Roca had gone on to Moscow to meet Krushchev for the first time.

The Chinese were courting the Cubans while deliberately ignoring the Krushchev leadership. When Krushchev was in New York (meeting Castro, among his other activities), the Chinese official news agency Hsin Hua gave his two-hour General Assembly speech, for example, only one paragraph in its daily world report. At that juncture, however, Castro obviously had already made the logical decision that the Soviets possessed the means to assist him greatly in his revolutionary en-deavours, whereas the still totally impoverished Chinese did not. This did not stop him, for the next two years, striving to navigate between the Communist giants, even coming up with the astonishing notion that he could mediate in this vast Marxist-Leninist dispute. Castro and his principal advisers acknowledge privately that the Sino–Soviet split, reaching the degree it did in 1960, has to have been the overriding element in Krushchev's decision to go all-out for Cuba. Observing the rising hostility of the United States, Krushchev also reached the conclusion that Cuba was a priceless strategic asset for the Soviets in those days of relatively limited nuclear arms range and technology. Becoming avail-able to Moscow as it did in the aftermath of the U-2 incident with *its* strategic overtones, Castro's island was too much of a target of opportunity for the Soviet premier – with his penchant towards adventurism – to resist the temptation of a full commitment. For Krushchev, in effect, this was the moment of 'the buying of Cuba', as a senior Cuban official commented privately and with certain bitterness not long ago, and the premier presumably knew what he was doing.

It is less clear, on the other hand, whether Castro fully understood the geopolitical process upon which he was embarking in New York in his bear hugs with Krushchev. Yet it was he who pushed for the marriage.

Castro and Krushchev were among the heads of state and government at the 1960 United Nations General Assembly, marking the fifteenth anniversary of the birth of the world organization. It was an un-precedented gathering of notables – President Tito of Yugoslavia and President Nasser of Egypt, Premier Jawaharlal Nehru of India and Prime Minister Macmillan of Britain, and President Eisenhower were there – but the tall, bearded Cuban and the rotund, bald Russian instantly emerged as the most vivid, even aside from their personal eccentricities. And Krushchev's visit to Castro at the Theresa Hotel in Harlem, where the Cuban and his entourage had moved in pique from a midtown Manhattan hotel earlier in the week, was designed to publicly crown their new alliance.

This alliance had first taken shape when First Deputy Premier Mikoyan, one of the few surviving 'old Bolsheviks' of the Russian Revolution, alighted in Havana seven months before, back on 4 February 1960, for a nine-day visit with plenipotentiary powers to strike a complex and far-ranging deal with Fidel Castro, a deal which has never been made public in its entirety. Castro and Che Guevara, who greeted Mikoyan at the airport, were the principle Cuban negotiators, the Argentinian in his capacity as National Bank President. After Mikoyan had inaugurated the Soviet Science, Technology and Culture exhibit at Havana's Bellas Artes Museum, the ostensible reason for his trip to Cuba, he delivered a speech at the government-controlled labour-union confederation (strangely handing Castro a cheque for $90,000 for the purchase of planes and arms). Then he was taken to see land cooperatives in Pinar del Río, Camagüey and Oriente, and visited Fidel's beloved Ciénaga de Zapata, and the Isle of Pines where he was shown the prison cell once occupied by the chief of the revolution. On 13 February a joint Cuban–Soviet communiqué was issued, emphasizing that the consolidation of world peace depended largely 'on the inalienable right of every nation to decide freely on its own political, economic and social road', which was the first Soviet commitment, indirect as it may have sounded, to the protection of the Cuban revolution. The other political aspect of the communiqué was the agreement to discuss, when convenient, the resumption of Cuban–Soviet diplomatic relations; it obviously was found to be convenient very quickly, since this resumption 'on the level of embassies' was announced on 8 May. Cuban officials say that Castro sought to obtain some form of explicit security guarantees from Mikoyan, but the communiqué does not touch upon this theme; it is known, however, that the deputy premier informed Castro that Soviet arms would be delivered to Cuba as soon as possible; indeed, they began arriving late that year, immediately after the initial Czech shipments. In this broad sense, therefore, a strategic security understanding was reached.

Economically the results – as outlined in the communiqué – were not particularly impressive, but this relationship had to develop gradually. The arrangement worked out by Mikoyan with Castro and Guevara was called a trade agreement, a term that would always be applied in the future to all the economic dealings between the two countries; 'assistance' was not a word the Cubans desired to see in print. Specifically, the Russians agreed to buy 425,000 tons of Cuban sugar during the balance of 1960, in addition to the 345,000 tons they had already bought during the spring (the total exceeded somewhat the 1959 purchases, but it was still less than one-fifth of the current Cuban crop). Because the communiqué did not mention price, it was assumed that Moscow was paying the very low prevailing world price, roughly one half of the per-pound subsidized price paid by the United States under its quota system in which Cuba still participated. Additionally the Soviets committed themselves to buy one million tons of sugar annually (the 1960 total was 770,000 tons) for the next four years, certainly not enough to meet Cuban foreign-exchange requirements. Basically a barter transaction with payment in kind, for the 1961–64 period the Soviets thus offered Cuba $100 million in credits 'for the acquisition of equipment, machinery and materials' and for technical assistance.

Contrary to Cuban assertions this was not a phenomenal deal for Havana – actually it was a better one for Moscow – but it did trap the Soviets even deeper in trying to assure the survival of the Cuban revolution. If this was Castro's and Guevara's long-term objective they had undeniably outfoxed the Armenian-descended Mikoyan. On the other hand their official explanation of the agreement showed that they either did not understand world economics or were wilfully misleading the citizenry. In a speech a month after signing the Mikoyan accord, Guevara argued that it did not matter that only 20 per cent of the Cuban sugar harvest going to the Soviets under the trade agreement would generate actual dollars because 'the dollar is nothing more than an instrument for purchasing, the dollar has no value other than its purchasing power, and when we receive manufactured goods or raw materials [from the Soviets] we are simply using sugar as if it were dollars'. A quarter of a century later, when 80 per cent of all Cuban exports went as barter to the Soviet bloc, Castro was desperate because the high technology he now needed could be obtained only in the West and only for dollars which he did not possess.

Curiously, one person Mikoyan specifically asked to meet in Cuba was Ernest Hemingway, who had lived on and off since 1939 at Finca Vigía, a hilltop property in San Francisco de Paula, a south-eastern Havana

414   FIDEL

suburb. Hemingway had spent the first half of 1958, the last year of the war, in Cuba but his ample published correspondence shows little interest in the revolution. In a letter to his son Patrick from Idaho in November he wrote, for example, that 'Cuba is really bad now . . . living in a country where no one is right – both sides atrocious – knowing what sort of stuff and murder will go on when the new ones come in – seeing the abuses of those in now – I am fed on it. . .' Hemingway was away from Cuba all of 1959, but shortly before returning to the island early in 1960 he wrote to his friend, General Charles T. Lanham: 'I believe completely in the historical necessity of the Cuban revolution. I do not mix in Cuban politics but I take a long view of this revolution and the day by day and the personalities do not interest me . . . In the present situation there is nothing I can say that would not be misinterpreted or twisted. I have a terrible amount of work to do and want to be left alone to do it.' Nevertheless Hemingway found time to receive Mikoyan at Finca Vigía; a photograph shows him smilingly pouring a drink for the deputy minister and Vladimir Bazikin, then the Soviet Ambassador in Mexico. Castro did not accompany Mikoyan, and the only time Hemingway and Fidel met was in May at Havana's Barlovento yacht club where both attended the Hemingway Fishing Tournament. Castro had won the individual championship that day, catching the biggest blue Marlin. One wonders why Castro never sought out Hemingway while he still lived in Cuba in 1960, given his admiration for the writer and Hemingway's support for the revolution; this may be the only time when Fidel was uncomfortable imposing on someone, in this case a man he regarded as a genius.

After the Mikoyan visit and the establishment of Soviet–Cuban diplomatic relations (Sergei Kudryatsev, specialist on Latin America, came as the first ambassador to Havana and Faure Chomón, the former Student Revolutionary Directorate leader, went to Moscow), the new alliance's growth was a direct function of the now rapidly rising open hostility between Cuba and the United States. In retrospect it does appear that at this stage both Castro and Krushchev were keen on exploiting this hostility – Castro probably more than Krushchev – and that the United States did not know what to make of the emerging Havana–Moscow axis, other than being scared of it. Bonsal wrote that the Mikoyan trade agreement in his opinion 'did not in itself jeopardize the American economic position in Cuba', but that 'the pleasantries exchanged by Mikoyan and Castro in February had been given the most alarming significance in some Washington quarters. The economic arrangements between Cuba and the Soviet Union seemed intolerable to people long accustomed to a dominant American position in Cuba.'

Then a ship blew up in Havana harbour, and with it the last chance for an accommodation between Fidel Castro and the Americans. It was *La*

Coubre, a French freighter that docked in Havana's inner harbour on 4 March with seventy tons of ammunition and explosives from Antwerp, which was the balance of matériel purchased from Belgium the previous year. The first explosion, killing and maiming mainly crewmen and stevedores, came around 5 p.m., and a second one about an hour later killed and injured Cuban soldiers, militiamen and firemen. The death toll was eighty-one. Castro was soon on the scene, directing rescue operations and instantly accusing the United States of 'sabotage'. No proof of sabotage was actually produced by the Cubans, and the cause of the explosion was never officially established through inquiries. The United States angrily rejected Castro's charges, making the point that to dock an explosives-laden ship inside a busy harbour violated international safety rules anyway. In any event *La Coubre* rallied Cuban masses around Castro at a time when he was beginning to face growing internal political problems, and at funeral services the next day at Colón cemetery Castro delivered an immensely emotional oration, declaring that 'today I saw our nation stronger than ever, today I saw our revolution more solid and invincible than ever' and vowing that 'Cuba will never become cowardly, Cuba will not step back, the revolution will not be delayed . . . The revolution will march ahead victoriously!' He ended the speech using for the first time his great revolutionary slogan *Patria o Muerte, Venceremos!* (Motherland or Death, We Shall Win!) Since that day every revolutionary speech in Cuba ends with this phrase that the audience picks up and repeats with rising fervour.

La Coubre was a milestone in many ways. For a majority of Cubans the explosion confirmed all the dire Castro predictions that the United States was determined to stamp out the revolution; they believed him that this tragedy was the work of 'enemies of the revolution . . . who do not wish us to receive arms for our defence'. For Castro it was another useful confirmation of his premise that external danger strengthens the revolution through the powerful impact of nationalism on popular reactions. And the United States, of course, was always happy to oblige in this, from the first year of the new regime to the 1983 invasion of Grenada.

For the United States Castro's accusations over *La Coubre* became, in the words of Ambassador Bonsal, the factor that 'perhaps . . . tipped the scales in favour of Washington's abandonment of the policy of non-intervention in Cuba.' Likewise 1960 was an election year and, as Bonsal put it, 'the American posture of moderation in the face of Castro's insulting and aggressive behaviour was becoming a political liability'. Bonsal was never informed of it officially, but he believed that 'the new American policy . . . was one of overthrowing Castro by all the means available to the United States short of the open employment of American armed forces in Cuba.'

Indeed, on 17 March President Eisenhower approved a basic policy paper on the subject: A Program of Covert Action Against the Castro Regime. Developed by the CIA and the White House 'Special Group' (Deputy Under Secretary of State, Deputy Secretary of Defense, Director of Central Intelligence and the Special Assistant to the President for National Security Affairs), the plan's principal feature was 'the development of a paramilitary force outside of Cuba for future guerrilla action'. Before long the concept of the paramilitary force for guerrilla warfare grew into one of a fully-fledged invasion brigade. It is now known that Vice President Nixon was the chief advocate of the 17 March plan – not only had he met Castro in Washington the previous year and concluded that he was dealing with a Communist, but he also was a presidential candidate in a race in which Cuba loomed big.

Even so, it is not really credible to suggest that *La Coubre* tipped the scales in the US decision to go for Castro. Such a programme could not have been elaborated in only twelve days, there is ample evidence that the initial idea to remove Castro already had the force of top-secret policy in March of *1959*, and almost any excuse would have served for the presidential approval of the anti-Castro program. After all, the regime, and most notably INRA's Rebel Army officers running the land reform, were seizing American property in absolute disregard of Castro's own law, anti-American propaganda was unbridled, and the revolutionary government felt much more secure now that Mikoyan had given it Moscow's blessings.

Bonsal, the astonishingly patient ambassador in Havana, had concluded in mid-spring that there really was no future in Cuban–American relations though he neither favoured violent action against Castro nor was being kept posted by the Eisenhower administration on its latest secret plans. In a private conversation one afternoon, he remarked: 'You know, it's a no-win situation . . . It's damned if we do, and damned if we don't . . . You just can't please Castro.' Bonsal and Castro had not met since the previous September and official Cuban propaganda bad-mouthed the Ambassador frequently. He was attacked in the press when, for example, he chose to see off at the airport the Spanish ambassador, Juan Pablo de Lojendio, whom Cuba had ordered expelled on twenty-four hours' notice. Lojendio was ejected because he had the temerity to erupt into a TV studio while Castro spoke – to protest against attacks on the Franco regime which the prime minister had made earlier. The Spaniard had seen them on television at his residence and, full of indignation, had rushed to the station to confront Fidel. The ambassador was a short, balding man, and there was a touch of the grotesque in his brief shouting duel with the towering Castro before he was bodily removed. This was not classic diplomacy, Castro had never before been publicly interrupted, and the televised scene was the clash of two very hot-blooded Spaniards.

Economic warfare in earnest broke out in May when Che Guevara informed two American companies and one British company, each owning an oil refinery in Cuba, that henceforth they would have to process crude petroleum to be imported from the Soviet Union. The companies had traditionally shipped to Cuba the oil they were themselves producing in Venezuela as part of the worldwide production-shipping-marketing-refining system then practised by the multinationals. Guevara argued that Cuba had the sovereign rights to import the cheaper Soviet crude – the Soviets chose to make it cheaper, and besides, Cuba would be paying for it with sugar, instead of dollars, under the Mikoyan accord – and additionally warned the three companies that the government would not pay them $50 million owed for earlier imports. Acting on the direct advice of the Treasury Department (the State Department not having been consulted), the US companies decided to reject the Cuban demand without any serious negotiations, and on 29 June Castro seized all three refineries while the Soviets assembled enough tankers to transport from Black Sea ports all the crude needed by Cuba, and Soviet technicians adjusted the plants for processing the new oil.

The arrival of the *Andrey Vishinsky*, the first tanker, is now a revolutionary anniversary. Castro portrayed Cuba as an aggrieved party in the dispute, and Bonsal wrote: 'The Cuban revolution had won a great victory and had had a powerful ally thrust into its arms.' That day a US aircraft carrier sailed past Havana, two of its jets roaring over the refineries. Both Eisenhower and Krushchev were, in effect, doing Castro's bidding.

On 6 July it was again Eisenhower's turn to make a move. He announced that the United States would not allow the import of the balance of the Cuban sugar under the 1960 quota. It was roughly one-quarter of the total for the year of some three million tons, but Eisenhower also made it clear that the United States would not buy *any* Cuban sugar until further notice. The White House acted immediately after Congress had authorized the administration to re-allocate the sugar quotas of foreign producers, a law that Fidel Castro immediately described as the Dagger Law, the dagger in the back of the revolution. Bonsal, who had opposed the ending of the quota, rejects the suggestion that Eisenhower acted simply in reprisal for the oil refineries' seizures: 'The suspension of the sugar quota was a major element in the programe for the overthrow of Castro.' As to Castro, he had warned in a television speech two weeks earlier, when the Dagger Law was about to be passed, that 'if we lose our entire sugar quota, they could lose all their investments in Cuba' – plus the huge annual trade surplus. The loss of the quota, Castro said in a five-hour speech, which was a treatise on the history of sugar and Cuban–American trade relations over a century, 'would cost Americans in Cuba everything, down to the nails in their shoes'.

However Castro waited a full month before striking back. Always concerned with strategy and tactics, he first sought to extract maximum political advantage from the sugar affair by portraying Cuba as the victim of 'economic aggression' by the United States in violation of the Charter of the Organization of American States (for which he otherwise had no use), and then to obtain overwhelming Soviet public support for the Cuban cause. Fidel had always understood the immense importance of Third World solidarity with his revolution, and as early as mid-1959 he had dispatched Che Guevara to Africa and Asia to look for friends. Early in May 1960 President Achmed Sukarno of Indonesia, a virtual ally of the Soviet Union, became the first foreign chief of state to visit Cuba; the Marxist Prime Minister of British Guyana, Cheddi Jagan, came twice that year. At the end of August the Cuban delegation walked out of an inter-American foreign ministers' conference in San José, Costa Rica where a resolution criticizing Cuban meddling in Latin America was approved; on 2 September Castro convened one million Cubans in Havana to hear his denunciation of the San José conclave and to 'approve' the First Declaration of Havana, condemning man's exploitation by man in the impoverished world. In those days Washington was not taking the Third World very seriously, but Castro was already reaching out for Third World leadership, knowing that his natural allies were there.

As soon as Eisenhower chopped off the sugar quota, Nikita Krushchev came through generously. Moscow announced it would buy (though only at world prices) the 700,000 tons that would have gone to the United States, in addition to the 770,000 tons already purchased in 1960. This meant that over one-fourth of that year's sugar harvest was going to Russia. Though Castro and Guevara still could not make up their minds whether Cuba should remain a major sugar producer or concentrate (as Che urged) on industrialization, the Soviets were saving the Cuban economy – becoming, in effect, the guarantors of the island's economic viability. Krushchev clearly had already taken the strategic decision to form an alliance with Castro, and his most significant commitment to Cuba came on 9 July when he declared in a speech that 'the Soviet Union is raising its voice and extending a helpful hand to the people of Cuba . . . if it became necessary, the Soviet military can support the Cuban people with rocket weapons. . .'

In a display of high drama, Castro spoke on television from his sickbed the next day (his illness was never explained) to thank the Soviets for their expressions of support, but he repeatedly stated that the Krushchev offer was 'absolutely spontaneous'. Typically, Fidel appeared to be trying to avoid the impression in Washington that *he* had requested the Soviet rockets while at the same time magnifying the scope of the Soviet commitment to suit himself. In July 1960 it was crucial for Castro to be able to print in his newspapers the Soviet promises of rockets even though a joint communiqué issued in Moscow when Raúl Castro met with Krushchev early in August would mention no rockets of any kind.

But now Fidel was ready to punish the United States for taking away his sugar quota. The Cuban cabinet had passed a Law of Nationalization immediately after Eisenhower had acted on sugar, and on 5 August he was ready to implement it. Much land, chiefly from the United Fruit Company, had already been seized, but now Castro moved on the bulk of American investment on the island. Conchita Fernández, his secretary at INRA, recalls that late in the evening he called her into his fourth-floor office and told her: 'Call Che and call that Mexican named Fofo, because I'm now going to nationalize all these foreign companies: Shell, Standard Oil, Esso . . . right now, at midnight.' Then Castro instructed her to summon Carlos Franqui, then editor of *Revolución*, so that the announcement of the nationalizations could be published the following morning. Conchita Fernández says that Castro had remained three days and nights at his INRA office, preparing the nationalizations with Che Guevara, then, suddenly, announced that he was ready to sign the documents. He told Conchita: 'Right now, we'll give the back of our hand to these imperialist companies.' Then he went to a Latin American youth meeting at Havana stadium to announce what he had done. In all, Cuba nationalized thirty-six American-owned sugar mills, two oil refineries and two utilities companies (two nickel mines were taken in October). It took months to nationalize all the American property in the country. It was the end of an era – and the start of a new one for Cuba, at home and internationally.

It was in the context, therefore, of a nearly total break with the United States and a strongly nascent Soviet alliance that Fidel Castro flew to New York in September to address the United Nations and, as much as anything else, to meet Nikita Krushchev on American turf. Fidel felt very strong and self-assured, having successfully weathered his great confrontation with the United States, and consolidated his domination at home. Finance Minister Rufo López-Fresquet, the last moderate in the cabinet, had resigned in March, and Castro no longer needed to rule with a hidden government. He and his companions were fully and openly in charge of all that mattered in Cuba, and what remained of relatively independent life – such as culture – would soon be regimented as well. The Cuban Workers' Confederation (CTC) had tried to keep the Communist leadership at bay, but Castro put an end to the CTC in November 1959 when he forced its convention to drop a democratically chosen non-Communist slate; the force of his personality always won the day. The CTC's secretary general, David Salvador, a top 26th of July Movement leader, was dismissed and briefly joined the anti-Castro underground, before being arrested.

Propaganda and the control of public opinion were fundamental Castro concerns, and were given special attention as soon as sufficient revolutionary consolidation was attained. Superficial observation of Castro's seemingly wildly uncoordinated activities and his chaotic life-style might suggest that he was running Cuba from whim to whim. In retrospect, however, it is evident that Fidel knew exactly what he was doing – and how and when. Every step logically followed the previous one, and the timing was impeccable. Castro unfailingly sensed what the nation was prepared to accept, his preacher-like speeches fitted perfectly into the concept of revolutionary indoctrination, and his improvisations were in reality carefully thought-out chessboard moves. When outsiders commented on Castro's 'rantings', they failed to perceive that he was engaged in a campaign to educate the masses in his beliefs and in his political and economic analyses.

It was logical, then, to subordinate the media to the revolution. During the first year he was basically served by *Revolución*, the organ of the 26th of July Movement, and the Communist Party's newspaper *Hoy* reopened shortly after the victory with Carlos Rafael Rodríguez, who was Fidel's principal Communist ally, as editor. From the outset Castro acted as *Revolución*'s super-editor, visiting its offices, conferring almost daily with Carlos Franqui who was paper's editor and chief propagandist, and seeing to it that the revolutionary line was expressed in precisely the way he wanted it. The two principal TV channels, CMQ and Mundo, were put instantly under official control though for a time their private ownership was left untouched. Radio stations were joined in a network called FIEL, always available to broadcast Fidel's words.

Early in 1960 it was time to curtail the independent press, and Castro invented the notion of the *coletilla*, a postscript note appended at the end of every article, news dispatch, editorial or photograph which happened to disagree with the official line. Castro-controlled journalists' and printers' unions drafted and published these *coletillas*, or simply refused to work for the newspapers they disliked. It was a lethally subtle form of censorship-cum-intimidation, all in the name of the revolution, and by mid-1960 the so-called 'bourgeois press' went out of business because editors could no longer control the contents of their publications, and the rapidly shrinking private sector of the economy could no longer provide the necessary advertising. But Castro's view was that only the revolution brought real freedom of the press to Cuba, replacing the right-wing biases of the bourgeoisie. His propagandists went the absurd extra mile by banning Santa Claus as a Christmas symbol, with a revolutionary figure named *Don Feliciano* taking his place, and with the popular tune re-emerging equipped with new lyrics: 'Jingle Bells, Jingle Bells, Always With Fidel!' It did not catch on (nor did that other revolutionary jingle, 'Ping-Pang-Poong! Viva Mao Tse-tung!')

Astonishingly it was the old Communist Party that went on giving Castro trouble, notwithstanding Nikita Krushchev's fervent July support of the Cuban revolution. Castro and his group and the 'old' Communist leaders had begun meeting secretly eighteen months earlier to plan an ultimate merger, but the party still resisted the 'exceptionality' of the *Fidelista* triumph as Marxist dogma. Only Castro personally was trusted by the PSP old guard, to the extent they trusted anyone, and Pedro Miret recalls that on many occasions when Raúl Castro made a proposal, Blás Roca, the secretary general, would ask: 'But have you cleared it with Fidel?' At the PSP's Eighth Congress in August 1960 Blás Roca seemed out of touch with Cuban reality when he described the revolutionary regime as a power that 'represents and executes the policy of the coalition of the proletariat, the peasantry, the petty bourgeoisie.' Aníbal Escalante, another top PSP leader, opposed the confiscation of all private property because of the 'national bourgeoisie's strong fear of revolutionary changes', adding that 'we maintain the strategy of the alliance of classes with which the revolution originated'. This was historical nonsense, but as subsequent events would show, the 'old' Communists appeared to be holding out for key posts in the regime, something Castro was not about to grant.

Only Carlos Rafael Rodríguez was Castro's unconditional ally (he seemed to be better attuned to Moscow's thinking than his colleagues were), and he was largely responsible for the October 1960 merger between the party's Socialist Youth and the 26th of July Movement's youth division. Recalling those days, Pedro Miret says that the first step for the *Fidelistas* was to 'dilute' the Movement without most Cubans realizing it because 'we had to create our own little group'. Castro was setting the stage for the Integrated Revolutionary Organizations, but through most of 1960 the 'old' Communists were still dragging their feet. Finally, Aleksandr Alexeiev, back in Cuba ostensibly as the permanent TASS correspondent, delivered a private message from Krushchev to Castro to the effect that the Soviet government considered that there was 'no intermediary party' between them, and that Fidel was the 'authentic leader' of the revolution. Anticipating meeting Castro in New York, Krushchev was careful not to make him feel like the head of an Eastern European satellite country.

Unlike Cuba's 'old' Communists, Krushchev had the sense to accept Castro for what he was at that stage in history – although afterwards he learned that Fidel could not be easily manoeuvred into going along with the Kremlin dogmas. In any attempts to reconstruct Castro's ideological evolutions – and to dispel the persistent impression in successive

American governments that he always was a Soviet tool – it is useful to consider his comments on the subject of Marxist interpretations in conversations with the French writer Régis Debray in the mid-1960s. Castro said: 'I am accused of heresy. It is said that I am a heretic within the camp of Marxism–Leninism. Hmmm! It is amusing that so-called Marxist organizations, which fight like cats and dogs in their disputes over possession of revolutionary truth, accuse us of wanting to apply the Cuban formula mechanically. They reproach us with a lack of under-standing of the Party's role; they reproach us as heretics within the camp of Marxism-Leninism.' Debray explains that the great difference between Castro and the dogmatists accusing him of heresy was his belief that Marxist–Leninist parties are not necessarily the only or the best 'vanguard' leadership in launching revolutions. The *Sandinista* victory in Nicaragua in 1979 would prove Castro right, but in the meantime he had to keep protecting his heresies.

Fidel Castro arrived in New York on 18 September, the day after signing decrees nationalizing three American bank branch offices in Cuba. Four days before he reached the city, a CIA-organized plot to assassinate him was formally set in motion at a meeting at a New York hotel with a key figure in the Mafia whom the agency wanted to handle the assignment. The decision to murder Castro was an outgrowth of the Program against him approved by Eisenhower in March, and it was to coincide with intensive guerrilla warfare to be triggered on the island; the first guerrilla operations had, in fact, already begun in the Escambray mountains.

An internal CIA memorandum states: 'In August 1960 [Deputy Director] Mr Richard M. Bissell approached Colonel Sheffield Edwards to determine if the Office of Security had assets that may assist in a sensitive mission requiring gangster-type action. The mission target was the liquidation of Fidel Castro.' Bissell, who was also in charge of preparing the Bay of Pigs invasion, briefed CIA Director Allen Dulles who 'gave his approval'. What remains unknown is whether Dulles acted on his own authority to order the assassination of a foreign head of government or whether he obtained President Eisenhower's explicit assent. In the 1960s, however, the White House practised the concept of 'plausible denial' in risky and potentially embarrassing operations in order to protect the prestige of the president, and usually the CIA Director and the National Security Adviser took it upon themselves to keep Eisenhower in the dark about specific enterprises so that he could claim ignorance without actually lying if the agency was caught red-handed. Authority for such operations was derived from overall policy directives by the president – such as the March decision to oust Castro. 'Plausible denial' was invoked for Eisenhower in May when the U-2 spy plane (another Bissell undertaking) was shot down over the Soviet

Union, and chances are that the same principle was applied to the Castro assassination plots.

Castro says that he had assumed all along that he was on an American hit list, but he had also concluded that in this sense he was safer in the United States than at home; he did not think the CIA would risk the awesome political fallout that would result from murdering him in Manhattan. According to the CIA memo, a former agent of the Federal Bureau of Investigation, Rober A. Maheu, was asked if he could develop 'an entrée into the gangster element' as the first step towards organizing the murder. Maheu therefore met at the Hilton Plaza Hotel in New York on 14 September with Johnny Roselli who was described as 'a high-ranking member of the "syndicate".' An offer of $150,000 to kill Castro was conveyed on behalf of 'businessmen' who had suffered financially in Cuba because of the revolution, and Roselli put Maheu in touch with Mafia chiefs Momo Salvatore Giancana and Santos Trafficante in Miami. On the gangsters' suggestion the CIA's Technical Services Division developed and produced pills with 'elements of rapid solubility, high lethal content, and little or no traceability'. The CIA says that 'several attempts without success' were made to make Castro take the pill in some fashion, and 'the project was cancelled shortly after the Bay of Pigs episode'. Subsequent testimony at Senate hearings into anti-Cuban Intelligence operations disclosed that the murders of Raúl Castro and Che Guevara were also contemplated because in the opinion of the CIA's Western Hemisphere Division chief unless the three top leaders 'could be eliminated in one package – which is highly unlikely – this operation can be a long-drawn-out affair and the present government will only be overthrown by the use of force'.

This then was the atmosphere prevailing towards him in the United States government when Castro arrived at very short notice in New York to lead the Cuban delegation to the UN General Assembly. The great unwitting irony of his reception was that the United States government confined him and his entourage to the island of Manhattan 'to ensure his personal safety', and that during his ten-day stay in the city the special 258-man police detail guarding him was nearly as large as Castro's Rebel Army of 300 when it launched its final offensive in 1958. The Police Department obviously had no way of knowing that another United States official agency was planning to kill elsewhere the man they were guarding in New York, and the State Department (also unaware of the CIA plot) was desperately searching for a city hotel willing to accept the Cubans. To complicate matters the *Cubana* airlines plane that brought Castro to New York had to race home to Havana to avoid being seized by American creditors; another *Cubana* airliner had been placed under lien at the airport two days earlier. Castro's presence in New York was turning into a tragi-comedy, a mass of misunderstandings, plenty of American harassment, dangers to Fidel from Cuban exiles, and – secretly – the shadow of official assassination. Castro may not have known about Maheu, Roselli and poison pills, but he was thriving on the rest of it. In Havana, where Raúl Castro was Acting Prime Minister, the American ambassador's movements were restricted to the Vedado residential section in reprisal.

Nikita Krushchev had planned to meet Fidel Castro even before he boarded the liner *Baltika* in Kaliningrad for the crossing to New York for the UN General Assembly. Arkady N. Shevchenko, then a junior diplomat travelling as an adviser with the Krushchev group, recalls that the premier began talking to him about Cuba one day on *Baltika*'s deck (Shevchenko, who later rose to the rank of Under Secretary General of the United Nations, defected in 1978, writing down his memories in *Breaking with Moscow*). Shevchenko recorded Krushchev's remarks that 'I hope that Cuba will become a beacon of socialism in Latin America' and that 'Castro offers that hope, and the Americans are helping us'. Krushchev said that the United States was trying to drive Castro to the wall instead of establishing normal relations with him, adding: 'That's stupid, and it's a result of the howls of zealous anti-Communists in the United States who see red everywhere, when possibly some things are only rose-coloured, or even white . . . Castro will have to gravitate to us like an iron filing to a magnet.'

In New York Krushchev took immediate steps to accelerate this gravitation by visiting Castro in Harlem – and the Cuban having chosen black-inhabited Harlem as his headquarters made the visit even more interesting politically to the Russian premier. The day Krushchev landed in New York, Castro had abandoned the Shelburne Hotel on Lexington Avenue and Thirty-seventh Street, a comfortable hotel near the United Nations, in protest against what he described as the management's 'unacceptable cash demands' for advance deposits; he may not have realised that the Shelburne had rented the Cubans the twenty suites (at $20 each) only because the State Department had pleaded with it to do so. Whoever was right in the cash-deposit argument, twenty-four hours after coming to the Shelburne Castro led his fifty Cubans in the descending dusk eight blocks to the United Nations Secretariat Building on First Avenue to confront Secretary General Dag Hammarskjöld. In his olive-green combat fatigues, having piled into a black Oldsmobile with seven companions for his rush to the United Nations, followed by other Cubans in cars or on foot, by police and by hundreds of newsmen, Fidel informed Hammarskjöld that his delegation would stay there until the housing problem was solved. He said the Cubans were prepared to march to Central Park, remarking that 'we are mountain people, we are used to sleeping in the open air'.

Turning down an offer of free accommodation at the fairly luxurious Commodore Hotel, just three blocks from the United Nations, Castro then directed his wild-looking motorcade to the eleven-storey Theresa Hotel at Seventh Avenue and 125th Street in Harlem where the management were evidently ready to accept the Cubans. They took forty rooms there, finally moving in at 12.30 a.m. Having totally over-shadowed all other United Nations-related activities with his nocturnal skirmishes around the city, Castro announced that he had wanted all along to stay in Harlem because blacks would be more sympathetic to the Cuban revolution. Then he stayed up most of the night, receiving black journalists and the black Muslim leader, Malcolm X.

And now enter Nikita Krushchev. His account of the events appears in his memoirs, *Krushchev Remembers*, and the premier reports his indignation upon learning that the Cubans 'were thrown out' of their hotel and invited to Harlem. The next morning he drove to Harlem to 'shake Castro's hand as a gesture of sympathy and respect', after having the Cuban advised by telephone that he was on his way. Krushchev writes that Castro had offered to call on him instead because 'he thought that, the Soviet Union being a great country and his a young revolutionary government representing a small country, it would be proper for him to pay a visit to me first'. But, Krushchev goes on, 'I felt it would be better for me to make the first visit, thereby emphasizing our solidarity with Cuba, especially in the light of the discrimination they were being subjected to . . . By going to a negro hotel in a negro district, we would be making a double demonstration: against the discriminatory policies of the United States of America towards negroes as well as towards Cuba.'

At noon of Tuesday 20 September Fidel Castro greeted Krushchev at the entrance of the Theresa Hotel in one of the most improbable diplomatic encounters of the postwar years. Krushchev himself describes it best: 'He made a deep impression on me. He was a very tall man with a beard, and his face was both pleasant and tough at the same time. His eyes sparkled with kindness towards his friends. We greeted each other by embracing. When I say "embrace", I'm using the word in a rather specialized way. You have to take into consideration my height as opposed to Castro's. He bent down and enveloped me with his whole body. While I'm fairly broad abeam, he wasn't so thin either, especially for his age.' The two men went up to Castro's ninth-floor suite for a twenty-two minute conversation through interpreters, and Krushchev writes that the Cuban 'expressed his pleasure at my visit, and I repeated my sentiments of solidarity and approval of his policy. The meeting was very brief; we exchanged only a few sentences . . . You can imagine the uproar this episode caused in the American press, and elsewhere as well.' The *New York Times* reported: 'It was the biggest event on 125th Street since the funeral in 1958 of W.C. Handy, who wrote "St Louis Blues".'

Back at the Soviet residence on Park Avenue and Sixty-eighth Street, Krushchev told reporters he was 'very much pleased with the conversation I've had with Dr Castro', whom he described as 'an heroic man who has raised his people from the tyranny of Batista and who has provided a better life for his people . . . I salute Fidel Castro and wish him well.' But this was not the end of Krushchev's courtship of the revolutionary chief. At the afternoon session of the General Assembly he walked from his seat almost at the rear of the hall to the front, across the rostrum and over to the front row of the other side where Castro sat with his diplomats. Castro then rose to his feet, and the two men embraced repeatedly and beamingly for the benefit of photographers. Three days later Castro dined with Krushchev at Soviet headquarters on Park Avenue for four and a half hours, and it was evidently then that they held their substantive talks – among other things, on the scope of Moscow's military backing for Cuba. Breaking up at midnight, Krushchev walked arm in arm with Castro to the Cuban's car. Their next meeting would be two and a half years later when they tried to make up at the Kremlin after their bitter dispute over Soviet nuclear missiles in Cuba.

Apart from his meetings with Krushchev, the Cuban Prime Minister saw only Czechoslovakia's President Antonin Novotny and Bulgaria's Premier Todor Zhivkov, and, from the neutralist group, President Gamal Abdel Nasser of Egypt, Prime Minister Nehru of India, and President Kwame Nkrumah of Ghana. Yugoslavia's Marshal Tito declined to see Castro despite efforts by Foreign Minister Raúl Roa. Fidel treated the General Assembly to a four-and-a-half-hour speech on 26 September, speaking from only a single sheet of notes, and accusing the United States of aggression against Cuba. Krushchev was present through the entire address, often interrupting for smiling applause.

While in New York, Castro also chaired by telephone a cabinet meeting in Havana to decide on diplomatic relations with the People's Republic of China and North Korea. But he spent much time in his suite at the Theresa Hotel, presumably because there were not enough diplomatic contacts available for him to fill the ten-day stay in New York. He had brought over from Havana Major Juan Almeida, army chief of staff, who is black, to meet with United States black leaders, but little came of this. He worked with Celia Sánchez and Captain Nuñez Jiménez to keep track of developments in Cuba, and many of his meals were chicken-and-rice dishes delivered to the hotel from a nearby restaurant. One evening he invited the Theresa black employees to a steak dinner at the hotel with him and Major Almeida; on another evening Castro received leaders of the Fair Play for Cuba Committee, including the poets Langston Hughes and Allen Ginsberg. After a few days the novelty of his presence in Harlem wore off, the crowds thinned out, and only the police maintained a heavy presence. A police horse named

Bangle collapsed in front of the Theresa from a kidney ailment resulting from exhaustion.

On 29 September Castro finally flew home aboard a Soviet Ilyushin-18 turboprop airliner, in order not to risk the loss of another Cuban plane to American creditors. At the airport he declared: 'The Soviets are our friends . . . Here you took our planes – the authorities rob our planes – Soviets give us planes.' Back in Havana he was greeted by 150,000 cheering fellow citizens, telling them that the United States was a 'cold and hostile nation' and New York was 'a city of persecution'. But on balance Castro had achieved what he went to seek in New York: a great deal of public attention and a solid understanding with Nikita Krushchev concerning all forms of assistance for Cuba. It would be urgently needed – and very soon.

On his return to the island Fidel Castro instantly discovered the plethora of problems he had to face. And most of them were related to American pressures now that the Eisenhower administration was absolutely determined to bring down his revolutionary regime. On 18 October Ambassador Bonsal was recalled 'on extended consultations', knowing perfectly well that this marked the end of his Cuban assignment; the United States no longer wanted any dealings with Castro. The following day the administration banned exports to Cuba of any American goods, except non-subsidized foodstuffs, medicines and medical supplies. This was the embargo, or 'blockade' as Castro calls it, and it was still in force twenty-six years later. It has complicated the Cuban economy, and made Cuba totally dependent on the Soviet Union, but has failed completely to demolish the revolution.

Cuba's perilous internal security situation too, at that time, was linked to American efforts to oust Castro. By September he simply had to accept that the rebel guerrilla centres in the Escambray mountains in central Cuba (and to a much lesser extent in Oriente) were air-supplied by the CIA, even if most of the drops never actually reached the rebels, being recovered, instead by his army and by the militia. But he knew from his own experience how tough it was for a conventional army to deal with guerrillas – and now *he* had a conventional army – if they were allowed to grow and expand.

Castro's principal advantage was that these rebels had no centralized command and therefore no coordination. On 8 September, shortly before he flew to New York, his army had organized special militia battalions in the Escambray Clean-Up Operation, surrounding the mountains with as many as 50,000 militiamen in a deliberately massive search-and-destroy effort. By the time of Fidel's return to Havana the regime was able to announce a victory over a rebel unit in Escambray – the first public admission that there was fighting in the central Sierras. At

428 FIDELFIDEL

the same time the first heavy Soviet arms – 82-mm mortars and 120-mm howitzers – began arriving on the island to bolster its defences. The first Soviet tanks came early in 1961.

Vice President Fernández, then one of the few professional military commanders serving under Castro, says that the most dangerous moment in Escambray was between December 1960 and February 1961. That was why Castro had assumed personal command of the operations on his return from the United Nations, spending days and nights with the militia battalions and showing himself to the troops and the local population. Again, his *guerrillero* experience was handy. Fernández recalls that the Escambray strategy devised by Castro was to place a militiaman permanently every forty or fifty yards along a road or a ridge, to live in his trench, with food being delivered three times a day. In this fashion the mountains were completely sealed off, while other units were moving into the hills to pursue the rebels. The enemy bands, Fernández says, never had more than twenty men each, moving rapidly from spot to spot, but never forming a strong group. Castro's and Fernández's best estimates are that the total guerrilla numbers may have reached 5000 at one point; in a single operation, for example, 500 rebels were captured. They were a mix: small landowners who feared the agrarian reform, ex-Batista soldiers, disgruntled Rebel Army fighters, and pure adventurers; much of the combat by them was in the name of anti-Communism.

According to Fernández the last band in Escambray was liquidated as late as 1965, which meant that militiamen were tied down there, in greater or lesser numbers, for over five years. To deal with these uprisings without denuding other Cuban defences, militiamen were given twenty-one days of basic training before being sent off to war. Around six thousand men were being trained at any given time and, in time, the militias became the backbone of the Cuban defences. They were to be crucial, for example, at the Bay of Pigs.

Another vital Castro weapon was his Intelligence service under the command of Ramiro Valdés and Manuel (Redbeard) Piñeiro. The revolutionary army's Intelligence arm had an astonishing degree of infiltration inside rebel and anti-revolutionary groups, making it possible for Castro to hold at bay all his enemies, including the CIA, for nearly three decades. Castro says that at one stage there were as many as 300 'counter-revolutionary organizations', each expecting American support, and that 'we knew more about what they did than they knew themselves'.

Full-time Security services, however, were not considered sufficient, and on 28 September, the day he came back from New York, Castro announced the creation of Committees for the Defence of the Revolution (CDR) as a people's system of collective vigilance. The CDRs were Castro's invention – nothing on such a scale exists even in the Soviet

Union – and their immediate function was to keep the police and Security services informed of strangers appearing in their neighbourhoods (there is a CDR for every urban block and in every plant and farm), citizens voicing criticisms of the regime and so on. Castro estimated in 1986 that 80 per cent of the population belonged to the CDRs, an unparalleled security network. And nowadays the CDRs are also responsible for the vaccination of children and other community tasks.

For all practical purposes the first major phase of the Cuban revolution was completed at the end of 1960, a two-year period. In the words of Carlos Rafael Rodríguez, the nationalization of foreign companies as well as Cuban industry, farms and businesses brought the finish of capitalism in Cuba. Ties with the United States had been broken, and an alliance with the Soviet Union created. Internal security was firmly in hand, with the militias and the new CDRs, and the revolutionary government was free of 'liberal' or 'moderate' influences.

On 13 October Castro ordered the expropriation of 382 large industrial and commercial companies 'belonging to the Cuban bourgeoisie', and all Cuban and foreign banks (except Canadian banks). On 15 October he went on national television to say that his revolutionary programme outlined in *History Will Absolve Me* had been fulfilled – he had in mind nationalizations of foreign companies and the agrarian reform – and that the revolution had entered a new stage. In the same speech, however, Castro pledged that the revolution has 'no need' of liquidating small private businesses, such as shops and small factories. To set up People's Stores in the cities, he said, would create 'an obstacle to the revolution', and the revolution had no interest in retail distribution mechanisms. In 1968, when Castro felt the time was right for still another revolutionary stage, he went back on his word, and nationalized everything, from the corner coffee-shop to taxis in the cities. Not even street vendors were permitted to exist while Castro was experimenting with 'pure Communism', one of his greatest errors, as he would say much later.

When Castro presented the ideological programme to the first congress of his new Communist Pary in 1975, he declared that during the second half of 1960 'the Cuban Revolution had entered its era of socialist construction'. Back in October 1960, of course, he had omitted the word 'socialist' in announcing the new revolutionary phase. Cuba was not quite ready yet for the 'construction of socialism'. But on 31 December 1960 Castro ordered general mobilization in Cuba to defend the nation from an imminent military attack 'by the troops of Yankee imperialism' that he insisted President Eisenhower was planning as his last act at the White House.

Fidel Castro could not know that when the attack came he would be dealing with John F. Kennedy, now the president-elect and already partially briefed on the Bay of Pigs plans. In fact the new phase in Cuban life would be more complex and explosive than Castro seemed to realize as he was ordering his New Year's Eve mobilization.

Chapter 4

Fidel Castro and John F. Kennedy belonged to the same generation. Both had superb minds and a broad vision of history. They never met, but were fascinated by each other – as adversaries and as national leaders. I know this from discussing Castro with Kennedy in the short years when they were simultaneously in power in their respective countries, and discussing Kennedy with Castro over a quarter of a century. Each was intensely interested in everything concerning the other. There was an intellectual respect between them. Historically, they had an immense impact on one another and their nations: Castro's existence pushed Kennedy into the tragedy of the Bay of Pigs and, in a strangely contradictory manner, into launching the Alliance for Progress programme for Latin America. Kennedy's existence, still feared by Castro after the Bay of Pigs, led to Cuban requests for Soviet military guarantees and to the installation of Soviet nuclear weapons on the island in the great crisis of 1962, the closest the world has ever come to a nuclear war.

In this sense, Castro and Kennedy shared a common destiny. To this day Castro believes that had Kennedy lived they would have, sooner or later, settled intelligently the basic Cuban–American dispute. To Castro, himself an assassination target, Kennedy's death came as a tremendous blow, and he frequently returns to the theme of it. Whether Kennedy would have wished a settlement that left Castro in power, however, is inevitably a question without an answer; even the best informed American historians hold differing opinions on the subject.

Nominated by Castro as the Year of Education, 1961 was the third year of the revolution – and its ideological turning point, the year in which it openly embraced the Marxist–Leninist doctrine.

For the United States it was the year when Fidel Castro was to be liquidated as the Kennedy adminstration proceeded with the invasion plans first secretly formulated by the Eisenhower administration. Eisenhower's farewell gesture towards Cuba had been to break off diplomatic relations on 3 January, the day after Castro demanded in his revolution anniversary speech that the American Embassy in Havana be reduced to eighteen diplomats – the same number the Cuban Embassy had in Washington. The United States had over sixty diplomats in the Cuban capital, principally because American interests on the island were so sizeable, and Eisenhower chose to regard Castro's request as a provocation and as justification for severing diplomatic ties. Now the United States felt even freer to pursue every conceivable course of action that might oust Castro. Even as John Kennedy was being inaugurated in Washington, Cuban exiles were being trained for the invasion at the CIA's secret camps in Guatemala. Castro, for his part, used the anniversary celebrations to warn that imperialism remained a mortal danger despite the change of administration in the United States, and he underlined his fears by presiding over the first revolutionary military parade in Havana. Revolutionary soldiers and militia units, no longer rag-tag *guerrilleros*, happily displayed new Soviet, Czech and Belgian weapons.

This display, of course, also symbolized the nature of Castro's essential dilemma. Because he really did face a lethal danger from the United States, he was forced to divert much manpower, resources, energy, attention and leadership to defence – and away from 'revolutionary construction', the simple dismantling of the pre-1959 economic and social order. On the other hand, as he has often said himself, external danger was necessary to keep alive the revolutionary spirit, particularly when tough realities of daily life replaced the romantic euphoria of the victory days. To compound matters Castro had no clear economic policy in the first years of the revolution. Moreover, after having dispensed with the 'moderates' by the mid-1960s, he lacked economists and managers on the policy level. For years the Cuban economy was conducted from INRA by Castro personally with advice from Che Guevara, Captain Nuñez Jiménez who was a geographer and an ideologue, and, later, Carlos Rafael Rodríguez, a charming intellectual and the best politician Cuban Communism has produced.

The events in Cuba directly involving Castro during just one week at the start of 1961 illustrate the pressures on him. During 1960 Fidel had made up his mind that Cuba's principal priority was to make the population literate. When the revolution triumphed, roughly 40 per cent of the six million Cubans were illiterate (as was most of the Rebel Army), and Castro calculated that there was a shortage of 10,000 elementary school teachers in the rural zones. In the course of the first two years in power the Castro regime had added 10,000 classrooms to the educational system, but it lacked teachers for them. The notion of a crash literacy campaign was born from these realities and, beginning in mid-1960, the government formed 'literacy brigades' from university students and high-school seniors in the cities who fanned out all over the countryside. Training teachers would be the next step, and Castro's plan therefore was to make 1961 the Year of Education, himself directing the literacy campaign along with defence and the economy. This, then, was Fidel's week:

On New Year's Eve he dined with 10,000 elementary teachers at the old army Camp Columbia in Havana, converted earlier into a school complex, to launch the literacy campaign, and to warn the nation at the same time that imperialist aggression was imminent. A few hours earlier he had gone downtown to direct firemen in efforts to put out a fire that destroyed the vast La Época hotel, and that in his opinion was an act of sabotage. He had also ordered that day general mobilization against an American invasion. On 1 January Castro official inaugurated the National Literacy Campaign, declaring that Cuba needed 'a revolutionary awareness that it is shameful not to know how to read and write'. On 2 January he attended the military parade on Plaza Cívica, and demanded the cutback in the staff of the American Embassy. On 4 January Fidel donned his battle fatigues and brown beret to join, rifle in hand and compass on his left wrist, the militiamen fighting the bands in the Escambray, having first signed in Havana documents creating a National Culture Centre. On 5 January word reached Castro, now back in Havana, that Conrado Benítez Garcia, a volunteer student teacher participating in the literacy campaign, had been assassinated by 'counter-revolutionaries' in an Escambray village where he had just begun working with the local peasants.

Benítez now also belongs to the pantheon of the martyrs of the revolution, and his murder, too, was put at America's door by Castro – the Escambray bands being CIA-supported. Wherever he now went Fidel heard the chant 'Cuba Sí, Yanqui No!' the latest revolutionary slogan. Then came 'Fidel, For Sure, Hit the Yankees Hard!' that schoolchildren still chanted in 1985, to greet Castro. He sheepishly explained to an American friend when they went together to visit a Pioneer children's camp that 'they don't know that *you* are American. . .' A local teacher said: 'Yes, we're supposed to teach it to the kids,' but, strangely, there was no hate at all in the children's voices or the teacher's explanation. It simply was revolutionary folklore, turned into living history twenty-five years later; the teacher had not been born when the slogan first sounded in Cuban streets.

But slogans and revolutionary fervour could not shore up the economy as it foundered in 1961, improvised from day to day, and brutally severed from the American economy of which it had always been an appendage.

The central problem was that Castro desired to rapidly refashion the Cuban economy, but had no real idea of how to do this. As René Dumont, a leading French agronomist whom Castro consulted in the early 1960s, wrote later: 'Cuba in 1959–60 confusedly searched for truly original socialism', but in the next decade it committed 'an impressive series of economic errors'. In fact this 'truly original socialism' degenerated into ill-conceived imitations of orthodox Soviet central planning, administrative and managerial chaos, new vested ideological and bureaucratic interests, hauled hither and thither by brusque course corrections.

By claiming late in 1960 that the Moncada Program contained in the *History Will Absolve Me* discourse had been fulfilled, Castro led the nation to mistake his decision to carry out the programme for actual programme results. Nationalizations and the agrarian reform laws simply meant that the revolutionary regime had embarked on a new approach to industrial, trade, banking and farming segments of the Cuban economy. What this approach would lead to remained to be seen. Che Guevara wrote, for example in the October 1960 issue of the army publication *Verde Olivo*, that 'the laws of Marxism are part of the development of the Cuban revolution', but he offered no clue as to what these Marxist laws were supposed to be or what they portended for the third year of the revolution.

In terms of fundamental economic policy, which should have been practical as well as ideological, Castro and Guevara, the principal planners, long could not make up their minds, for example, about the role of sugar in the Cuban economy. Though sugar had always been Cuba's mainstay, the revolutionary chiefs developed during 1959 and 1960 the daring notion that the island should end its dependence on sugar – presumably because it was a bitter reminder of the American-dominated 'colonial' past. Consequently, plantings were reduced and production dropped sharply in the harvests between 1962 and 1964. Then, economic realities – the fact that Cuba had only sugar to pay even in part for the mounting Soviet aid and that nothing had yet replaced cane-cutting as a gainful rural occupation at a time of endemic national unemployment – forced Castro and Guevara to abandon the idea that industrialization could overnight be the new fountainhead of wealth. In 1965, therefore, the Cubans (possibly under Soviet pressure) returned to sugar as their main production priority, then went to the other extreme of aiming for record harvests, which also turned out to be a painful error.

Fidel Castro, ever the great teacher, kept the nation informed of this shifting course through a formidable array of declaimed statistical data, lengthy projections and interpretations. He always concluded on the note that whatever decision was being announced or explained by him on a given day represented the collective wisdom of the revolution, and the adoring crowds cheered and chanted, 'We Shall Win!' Fidel's word was never questioned by the masses, and there was anyway not enough expertise around for anyone to do so. Colossal errors, as Castro later acknowledged, were committed by INRA's military administrators of nationalized lands, especially on the cattle ranches where their absolute inexperience and politically directed demand for immediate increases in meat production combined to destroy the herds and the industry.

Castro had launched from the outset a series of grandiose but nevertheless rational and promising food-production and diversification schemes, ranging from much higher rice yields and a huge increase in vegetable farming (as China had done successfully at about the same time) to a fowl industry on a national scale that would rapidly provide cheap and abundant protein supplies from chickens and eggs. In 1959 – as in 1986 – Castro was convinced that the latest state-of-the-art technology in agriculture or anything else could alone solve great economic problems. But he lacked the resources, personnel and patience to transform his dreams into reality. Thus nothing serious was accomplished, and Fidel rushed restlessly from a rice experimental station to a new stand of eucalyptus trees, exploding with bursts of impatience and bursts of new ideas the length and width of his island.

Above all, it was the obsession of Fidel Castro to do away with social and economic underdevelopment in Cuba. To understand Castro and his revolution it is essential to comprehend this concept of underdevelopment as a crucial psychological attitude in Cuba, probably even more crucial than elsewhere in the Third World. To Fidel and the revolutionary generation, underdevelopment means illiteracy and disease, economic inadequacy, dependence on the West under the shackles of 'neo-colonialism', and above all, the thinking patterns of people in poor countries. To him and his disciples, underdevelopment is shame, it is a mental prison, it is third- or fourth-class citizenship in the world. In Cuba this word has been used constantly in speech and print since the birth of the revolution: it expresses degradation, it provides justification for failures and insufficiencies of systems and of individuals, but also a sense of defiance in response to criticism.

From the beginning, to eradicate underdevelopment in all these meanings was indeed Fidel Castro's magnificent obsession, and this was what the social-justice aspects of the Moncada programme were all about, long before he chose to apply Marxist language to them. Once in power, social improvement goals were paramount to Castro, and from the first day they commanded an enormous share of the revolution's time and attention. Clearly, decisions on sugar and industry were vital, but such was the mood in those early days that what really captivated him as a human being were the literacy campaign, the classrooms in the Sierra

Maestra, the creation of a public health network (including forty-five new hospitals built in one year), decent peasant housing, country roads, and a new Cuban sense of pride that really meant more to Fidel than anything else. He had spoken of racial equality and of the 'new Cuban man (or woman)' long before he turned to 'the new socialist man (or woman)', and naturally the masses adored him. Through the first agrarian reforms Castro gave the peasants land (before, in effect, taking it away again), and through urban reforms he halved the rents and banned ownership of more than one dwelling per person (before the state went massively into the city landlord business in a subsequent revolutionary paroxysm). It all was marvellous, but it cost money, and it required the functioning economy that Cuba simply lacked at that revolutionary stage.

Castro, therefore, turned to improvisations – and to an ever-increasing dependence on the Soviet Union. He was economically vulnerable, and he knew that direct armed confrontation with the United States, now under President Kennedy, was both inevitable and imminent. To put his house in order in anticipation of the great clash, Castro tried to tighten up the economy at home through the creation in February of three new ministries: Industry under Che Guevara who gave up the presidency of the National Bank (after delightedly signing new banknotes with his nickname Che), Foreign Trade and Internal Trade. Guevara had just returned from a lengthy visit to Eastern Europe and the Soviet Union – his first trip to Moscow – where he joined the Soviet leadership at the Kremlin in reviewing the October Revolution military parade and signed a new trade agreement providing for Russian purchases of half of the Cuban sugar crop (2.7 million tons) at a price above the world market. Guevara sold another 1.3 million tons to other Eastern European countries, also Cuba's new allies. Nuñez Jiménez, too, had gone to Moscow, heading the first Cuban trade mission to the Soviet Union and returning with a commitment that thirty Soviet industrial plants would be installed in Cuba. This was the Cuban leadership's technique for industrializing the island – but sugar had to be grown to pay for the plants and oil and everything else being sent by Moscow.

Castro made no secret of his dependence on Soviet aid: in an interview on 1 February 1961 with Jiřy Hochman, the correspondent of the Czech Communist Party organ *Rude Pravo*, he remarked that 'if it were not for the intervention of imperialism, the Cuban revolution would have developed without difficulties . . . The solidarity and the aid given revolutionary Cuba in this situation by the socialist countries have played a decisive role for the definitive victory of our people. If the socialist camp and its supportive attitude did not exist, we would pay very dearly for our revolutionary laws . . . Thanks to arms that we have received from socialist countries, we have been able to create a defensive force capable of arousing the respect of the mercenaries and the respect of the aggressive circles of imperialism. . .'

The stage was now set for the Cuban-American confrontation. Castro felt secure that he could defend Cuba from anything short of an all-out American attack, and in Washington the new president was being urged by the CIA not to delay the invasion because, according to the CIA Havana station, Cuban pilots in Czechoslovakia were about to complete their training and would be returning home any day to fly the MiG jets that the Soviets were expected to provide (none had yet arrived).

In the meantime the United States banned travel to Cuba by Americans, which Castro took to be another sign of approaching hostilities. Still concerned about the Escambray bands that he suspected of having been instructed by the CIA to support in some fashion the invasion, he therefore went back to the mountains on 1 March. Again he appeared in battle gear, chatting with militiamen and their officers, joking with local peasants — all these activities being televised, photographed and reported in detail. In fact, the CIA had lost interest in the Escambray bands and was concentrating on the planned landing on the shores of the Bay of Pigs.

But now events were picking up momentum. On 2 March the Kennedy administration announced that it planned to prohibit all imports from Cuba. On 11 March Kennedy blocked the sales of United States farm products to Cuba. And in the days and weeks that followed, Kennedy and Castro engaged in a chain of simultaneous activities affecting each other's country — sometimes in surprising and contradictory ways. Such a day was 13 March.

Speaking in inspired tones, President Kennedy invited Latin America to join the United States in an Alliance for Progress to ameliorate people's lives and achieve economic advancement, pledging $25 billion over a decade as the American contribution to this goal. Having turned a deaf ear for long years to Latin American urgings for a large-scale economic development programme, the United States under a younger man's administration finally was at last offering to do exactly what Castro had proposed in Buenos Aires two years earlier. The irony, however, was that even as Kennedy spoke in Washington the training of his invasion brigade was being perfected in Guatemalan camps. Still that same day, rockets were fired from a high-speed boat at the oil refinery in Santiago, killing one sailor and injuring a militiaman; this was part of the CIA-organized pre-invasion softening up of Cuba. And in Havana, Castro went to the great staircase of the university to commemorate with a fighting speech the fourth anniversary of the assault on Batista's palace by the Student's Revolutionary Directorate.

We now know that Kennedy approached the Alliance for Progress with much greater enthusiasm than the supposedly secret plans for the

Bay of Pigs. Both enterprises, however, were responses to the Castro revolution, one to prevent its repetition elsewhere in Latin America, and the other to liquidate it. The rationale in the administration, to the extent that any coherent rationale existed at all, was that the Alliance would build a bright future for Latin America on the ruins of the Cuban revolution. It evidently had not occurred to the planners that in the aftermath of the Bay of Pigs the great gesture of the Alliance might have been regarded in Latin America as something other than pure altruism.

Castro was impressed, however, with Kennedy's idea for creating the Peace Corps. What he saw in it was an American version of what he called 'internationalism', that is, direct involvement in the development process of other countries through assistance teams or individuals. In a way, Cuba's assignment of thousands of Cuban doctors, nurses, teachers and technicians in Africa and Nicaragua is an imitation on a vast and political scale of Kennedy's Peace Corps: Kennedy and Castro both understood the need for establishing person-to-person contacts in the Third World as a factor of influence. So aware was Castro of what he calls 'Third World internationalist solidarity' that in the spring of 1960, when Cuba herself lacked resources, he had dispatched a shipload of medicine, foodstuffs and clothing aboard the freighter *Habana* for the victims of a terrible tidal wave that had hit Chile.

Both Castro and Kennedy thought in guerrilla terms, too, concerning the Third World. From the outset the Cubans trained young Latin Americans and Africans for future guerrilla operations in their countries (aid shipments to Chile included copies of Che Guevara's *The War of Guerrillas*, his manual on rural insurrection and warfare). There was Cuban support for Venezuelan urban and rural guerrillas in 1960, and the leaders of the movement that grabbed revolutionary power in the British colony of Zanzibar in 1963, had been trained in Cuba. (Zanzibar later merged with Tanganyika to form the republic of Tanzania whose leadership has cordial ties with Cuba.) Much more such guerrilla training came later, and it continued into the late 1980s. Kennedy responded to the threat of the Cuban subversion by creating a special warfare school at Fort Bragg, North Carolina, the home of the US Army's 82nd Airborne Division, now known as the John F. Kennedy Special Warfare Center, and Guevara's *War of the Guerrillas*, hurriedly translated into English, became one of its principal textbooks. US Army Special Forces Detachments (or the Green Berets) as they now exist were born at the JFK School, and one of the first units assigned overseas was sent to Panama to aid Latin American armies in counter-insurgency. Ironically, it is quite probable that American advisers who helped the Bolivian Army to track down Che Guevara and kill him in 1967 had studied Guevara's manual.

Between the end of March and mid-April 1961 tensions went on rising. Kennedy ordered the suspension of the Cuban sugar quota for the year (the law gave the president the authority to 'suspend' or cut quotas, but not to abolish them altogether), and on 3 April the administration issued its 'White Book' on Cuba that decried the denial of democracy under the revolution. It was, in effect, Washington's intellectual justification for the coming invasion, and this was certainly the way Castro read it. Now he addressed the Cubans daily with warnings of an imminent attack: he spoke to thousands of construction workers who had organized Committees for the Defence of the Revolution at the Public Works ministry, to labour union delegates preparing May Day celebrations, to another labour rally to protest the flight abroad of Cuban workers, intellectuals and technicians, and to the nation over television to discuss revolution and education. He also found time to dispatch a message to Krushchev to congratulate the Soviet Union on the first manned space flight.

That an attack was about to happen was no secret to Castro and his highly efficient Intelligence apparatus, and in his April exhortations, determined to have the nation psychologically ready for the attack when it came, he blended sarcasm with dire warnings to his foes. Speaking of the Democratic Revolutionary Front (FRD), the CIA-constructed political organization in whose name the invasion was being prepared – and its chairman José Miró Cardona who had been the first revolutionary prime minister – Castro asked: 'Are those the men who will come to overthrow the armed people? Don't make us laugh! . . . This mercenary government will not last twenty-four hours in Cuba. . .'

Fidel's Intelligence and Security networks were functioning to perfection. Ramiro Valdés, who was Interior Minister until 1986, and had created the Security services as one of the first endeavours of the revolutionary regime in 1959, says that Cuban Intelligence was able to track invasion preparations step by step, from Miami, to the training camps in Guatemala. 'It was an open secret,' Valdés adds. Because of the traditional indiscretion of Cubans, he recollects, the Little Havana district of Miami was so full of invasion talk that Cuban Security's biggest problem was to sort out truth from rumours in the mass of information streaming from the mainland.

Based on information from Miami, Central America and from within Cuba, on 1 April State Security Services began rounding up people suspected to be CIA-linked or involved in clandestine anti-regime activities. As Valdés says: 'We knew who everybody was, what weapons they carried, how much ammunition they had, where they were going to be, how many of them, at what time, and what they proposed to do . . . We were very successfully infiltrated into the counter-revolutionary bands.' Clearly, according to Valdés, the CIA acted correctly in not informing the anti-Castro underground beforehand about the date and place of the invasion because the information would have fallen at once into the hands of Cuban Intelligence. However, the invasion made absolutely no sense without instant and massive support from the underground, and for this reason the invasion was doomed to failure from the outset.

Meanwhile the Security services arrested members of six separate anti-regime groups in the first week of April, mainly men and women involved in CIA-aided sabotage acts, and in Oriente, 145 members of 'counter-revolutionary bands' were captured. In several instances shoot-outs preceded the arrests. And neighbourhood Revolution Defence Committees in the cities were crucial in ferreting out suspicious persons. Nevertheless Havana's El Encanto department store was torched and burned.

On 12 April President Kennedy offered assurances at a Washington news conference that United States forces would not intervene in Cuba. Castro reasoned – correctly – that Kennedy would not make a point of excluding American participation unless an attack, presumably from exiles, was in the offing. He took Kennedy's comment therefore as a confirmation that *an* invasion was on its way, and he based his defensive strategy on the assumption that he would be fighting only exiled Cubans. He was not certain exactly where and when the main landing would be made, but he thought it would come with simultaneous attacks in the south and the north of Oriente and in Pinar del Río in the west. On the eve of the battle Castro had the relative planning advantage of being ready for a number of alternatives whereas the CIA and its Pentagon advisers, as it soon turned out, had no real idea what they were facing; a board of inquiry discovered subsequently that the planners believed Castro had 'no doctrine' of any kind. Once more, he had the luck of being underestimated.

To defend the island with his clear policy of main-force deployments and mobility by tactical units, Castro had his regular army of about 25,000 well-trained and equipped men plus around 200,000 militias organized in battalions and stationed throughout the country in strategic areas. The army was divided into three tactical regional commands, and Castro's battle plan provided for Raúl Castro to command forces in the east (Oriente and Camagüey), Che Guevara in the west (western Havana province and Pinar del Río), and Chief of Staff Major Juan Almeida in the centre with headquarters in Santa Clara. Fidel, as commander-in-chief, would coordinate all operations from a secret command post in the Neuvo Vedado section of Havana (he also commanded directly the troops in the capital) although he was prepared to move rapidly from place to place as required. As he explained later: 'Every time there was talk of an invasion from the United States we dispensed ourselves around the country.' Under this defensive doctrine, no main-force units would move from their assigned areas unless battle developments made it necessary; early tactical operations were assigned to the militia battalions. Thus Castro would not be trapped by any diversions and deceptions that the CIA might plan.

About two weeks before the invasion Castro had paid one of his periodic visits to the Ciénaga de Zapata, and at one point strolled along the Girón beach at the entrance to the bay to see how a tourist village construction was coming along. Suddenly he turned to a Cuban journalist accompanying him and, pointing to a one-storey concrete house, said: 'You know, we should place a .50-calibre heavy machine gun there, just in case.' The day before the invasion Juan Almeida had toured the Bay of Pigs area, and decided to send a militia company there, dividing it among three principal beaches, because he thought communications were inadequate there. At that moment the invasion fleet was already sailing from Puerto Cabezas in Nicaragua (where the brigade had been moved from Guatemala) under a US Navy escort. The first ship of the invasion force left on 11 April, and the last one on 13 April: the landings were set for the post-midnight hours of 17 April.

Fidel Castro spent the night of 14–15 April awake at his emergency command post known as Punto Uno (Point One), a two-storey house at Forty-seventh Street in the residential district of Nuevo Vedado in Havana, near the Zoological Gardens. Major Sergio del Valle, his chief of staff who had been a guerrilla physician in the Sierra Maestra, and Celia Sánchez were with him. Castro had had so many signals in recent days saying that 'something' was about to happen that he made Punto Uno his temporary home; it was principally a communications centre with the rest of the country. Specifically, Fidel was informed on Friday 14 April that a suspicious-looking ship had been spotted off the coast of Oriente, not far from Guantánamo, and he had to conclude that it could be the vanguard of a major invasion force. Oriente *was* the traditional gateway to 'liberations' of Cuba. Castro's information was correct, but the ship, a freighter named *La Playa*, was carrying a diversionary force – not the main one. The CIA's idea was that diversionary activities at various points on the island forty-eight hours before the Bay of Pigs landing would confuse Castro and force him to improvise. *La Playa* therefore was to land 164 men commanded by Major Nino Díaz at the mouth of the Mocambo River, some thirty miles east of Guantánamo, in the small hours of 15 April, after steaming three days from Key West, Florida. Niño Díaz had fought under Raúl Castro in that same area of Oriente, but he turned against the revolution, and now was willing to fight there again. However, a reconnaisance party from *La Playa* aboard a rubber boat reported back that there were militia units on the Mocambo beaches, and Díaz decided to abort the landing, sailing for home.

Fidel Castro had no way of knowing about the failure of this planned diversion, but a few minutes after six o'clock on that same morning, Saturday 15 April, two B-26 light bombers with his air force's FAR insignia fired rockets from low altitude at the runway at Ciudad Libertad, the former army camp that had been transformed into a school, but where a military landing strip was still operational, less than a half-mile from Castro's command post. Then the planes came back for bombing and strafing runs, hitting houses in the densely inhabited neighbourhood. Within minutes Castro was informed that air force bases at San Antonio de los Baños, his principal base, near Havana, and at Santiago in Oriente, were being attacked simultaneously by two B-26s each. Castro's first thought was that the aerial attacks signified the start of the invasion, but there was no follow-up, and a few hours elapsed before it became clear what had happened.

The air strike at the three Cuban bases was designed to destroy Castro's airforce and thus ensure full control of the air on invasion day two days later. The planes had actually flown from Puerto Cabezas in Nicaragua, and they were part of the CIA's exile brigade, but the CIA believed it could create the impression that the B-26s belonged to the FAR, and that their pilots were defecting to the United States after destroying other aircraft on the ground. The agency believed there were political and propaganda advantages in making the world believe that Castro's pilots were defecting; Castro obviously knew within seconds that there were no such defections. The strike was as ill-conceived as everything else in the invasion: whereas sixteen B-26s were supposed to fly the mission, Kennedy had had the number cut in half the day before (he was uneasy about the whole proposition, and this was a compromise). Out of the eight bombers in the sortie, only six participated in the attacks (one being shot down by teenage militiamen firing Czech-made anti-aircraft guns at San Antonio) and two flew directly on to Florida, instead of returning to Nicaragua. As a result, the political deception collapsed when news photographs of the B-26 that had landed in Miami were presented that night to the Political Commitee of the UN General Assembly meeting in an emergency session in New York at Cuba's request. They showed that this particular B-26 had a solid metal nose whereas the B-26s Castro had inherited from Batista had Plexiglass noses. This was a detail the CIA had forgotten but the Cubans immediately called to the Political Committee's attention.

Castro's tiny air force lost five planes on the ground in the raids, including two B-26s, an AT-6 propeller trainer, a DC-3 transport and one T-33 jet trainer – leaving it with four British-made Sea Fury light attack bombers, one B-26 and three T-33s as the only operational aircraft. As Fidel remarked later, he had eight planes and only seven pilots. But the CIA had never understood Castro's special talent for turning seeming defeats into triumphs. Apart from the fact that the Saturday attacks warned him of the real imminence of an invasion – all the military units went on high alert and the seven pilots took turns sitting inside cockpits or sleeping on cots under aircraft wings – Fidel was handed a great political victory. Seven persons were killed and fifty-two wounded as a result of the raid on Havana, and he turned the funerals into a stirring act of patriotic nationalist mourning and revolutionary defiance.

A quarter of a century later, Castro could still be emotional and indignant about the attack, telling a foreign visitor: 'One of those who were dying there, a wounded man, was bleeding to death, and he wrote my name with his blood on a wall . . . It showed the attitude of the people: a young militiaman who is dying, and his protest was to write a name with his blood.'

In his funeral oration at Colón cemetery on Sunday 16 April, Castro compared the air raid to Pearl Harbor except, he said, that it was 'twice as treacherous and a thousand times more cowardly'. He proclaimed that 'yesterday's attack was the prelude to the aggression of the mercenaries' paid by the United States, and that the American government could be called liars for pretending that the attacking pilots were defectors. He reminded the audience of soldiers and militiamen and women that the previous year the Eisenhower administration had also initially lied about the U-2 spy plane shot down over the Soviet Union, and went on to compare the 'admirable' Soviet achievement of putting man into space with the American achievement of 'bombing the installations of a country that has no air force'. His voice roaring to a climax, Fidel Castro then issued his ideological indictment: 'Because what the imperialists cannot forgive us . . . is that we have made a socialist revolution under the noses of the United States . . . and that we shall defend with our rifles this socialist revolution!'

This was the first time Castro had publicly described the Cuban revolution as a 'socialist revolution'. Since then Castro and other Cuban leaders have said on many occasions that he had to unveil the revolution's socialism on 16 April because men had the right to know for what they would be dying in the now inevitable confrontation. But such top leaders as Armando Hart, a member of the party's Political Bureau, and Blás Roca, former secretary general of the 'old' Communist Party, told me in separate conversations in mid-1985 that Castro had long planned to proclaim the socialist revolution in his 1961 May Day speech. In which case the proclamation came two weeks ahead of schedule, but under the circumstances Castro's decision was absolutely logical: the patriotic passion aroused by the air raids created the perfect conditions to make the new official ideology fully acceptable. As Fidel always said, Martí and Marx are inseparable in the Cuban revolution, and he told the irate cemetery crowd that Cubans would defend this revolution 'of the humble, by the humble and for the humble to the last drop of blood'.

And even as Castro spoke in Havana on Sunday 16 April, John F. Kennedy was giving the final authorization for the invasion in a telephone call from the Virginia estate of Glen Ora to the CIA headquarters in Washington. But he simultaneously signed the invasion's death warrant when he forbade air strikes by Cuban exiles' B-26s against the remainder of Castro's aircraft in support of the landings. The president feared that such missions, which would have to be flown from Nicaragua or Florida, would publicly compromise the United States in the eyes of the world. Cubans, he told the CIA, could fly combat missions the moment they secured a field on Cuban territory. The invasion might have failed even if Kennedy had allowed the D-Day strikes: without them it did not have a hope of success. Fidel had both a secret weapon and quite a few other surprises for his foes.

The secret weapon and the other surprises were produced by Fidel Castro, a master at the game of letting his enemies trap themselves, within five hours or so of the first landing of the exiles' invading force on the beaches of the Bay of Pigs. The men of Brigade 2506 (so named after the serial number of its first volunteer to die during training in Guatemala) began coming ashore first on Playa Larga (Red Beach) deep inside the bay and then on Playa Girón (Blue Beach) near to its eastern entrance at about 1.15 a.m. of Monday 17 April, in landing craft launched from ships that had brought them from Puerto Cabezas. The force of approximately 1500 men was under the command of José Pérez (Pepé) San Román, a young career officer who had been trained in the United States, and had fought in the Batista army against Castro. As the Havana regime kept emphasizing later, the brigade included nearly 200 ex-Batista officers, soldiers and officials, sons of rich or middle-class families, and over 100 of what it contemptuously called 'lumpen'. Nevertheless the brigade was well trained and equipped, and when word of the landings reached him just before 2.30 a.m., Castro took them very seriously.

Militia patrols had spotted the invaders immediately and began to fire on them, but it took messengers in jeeps almost an hour to reach the town of Jagüey Grande to the north where the nearest telephone was located. From there, reports on the landings were phoned to the Punto Uno command post in Havana and instantly relayed to Fidel, that night at Celia Sánchez's Eleventh Street apartment, less than ten minutes away. Castro's instinctive reaction was that the Bay of Pigs would be the principal invasion area, and he proceeded at once to unveil his strategic surprises: on the land and in the air – where his secret weapon would be mobilized.

The first telephone call Castro made was to his trusted friend Captain José Ramón (Gallego) Fernández at his commander's quarters in the Managua army cadets' school just south of Havana, to pass on the information he had received, and to order him to the Bay of Pigs. Castro told him to pick up on the way the elite Militia Officers' School Battalion headquartered in Matanzas – 870 men – and assume operational command in the whole battlefield region; the other unit immediately available to Fernández was Militia Battalion 339 from Cienfuegos, which had detachments throughout the great swamp. At that stage Castro had no idea of the size or composition of the invading army, but his political judgement was that he had to prevent at all costs the consolidation of a beachhead large enough to allow the exiles to set up a provisional government and request international recognition. As it happened, such a beachhead was exactly the centrepiece of the CIA's masterplan.

While Fernández raced south in his green Toyota Jeep, Castro was despatching artillery units from Managua and Havana urgently to the battle zone and also ordering Soviet-built T-34 tanks placed on flatbed trucks to be transported there. He was careful, however, not to denude Havana of its army and militia troops: he could not yet rule out landings on the north coast.

Now operating from Punto Uno, Castro made his next telephone call to the air-force base at San Antonio de los Baños where the exiles' B-26s had attacked on Saturday. Poised on the runway were two Sea Furies, two B-26s and three T-33 jet trainers. And the T-33s were Fidel's secret weapon in the context of a very imaginative overall aerial strategy. He had decided that the rocket-equipped Sea Furies would concentrate on attacking the eight-vessel invasion fleet to sink as many ships as quickly as possible while the T-33s were to neutralize enemy aviation. CIA and Pentagon planners had assumed that Castro's small air force of fighting planes would be destroyed on the ground, and the ships therefore had no anti-aircraft weapons. As to the jet trainers, the Americans never suspected that Castro had them armed with two .50-calibre machine guns each. With this armament and a jet's manoeuvrability and speed, the T-33s were vastly superior to the lumbering B-26s that at first daylight began to fly exhausting round-trip combat missions between Nicaragua and the Bay of Pigs. Thus the little jets played a key role in Castro's victory, depriving the invasion force of air support, and allowing the Sea Furies to go unchallenged after the ships. Testifying in May before a presidential inquiry board, the Air Chief of Staff, General Thomas White, would remark: 'Well, I really believe that the Cuban Air Force had a whale of an effect on the bad outcome . . . I was surprised to find that [the T-33s] were armed.' He acknowledged that the Joint Chiefs of Staff did not consider the T-33s to be 'combat aircraft'. National Security Adviser McGeorge Bundy wrote in a formal statement to General Maxwell Taylor, chairman of the inquiry board: 'One startling omission . . . is the failure of any of the president's advisers to warn of the danger of the T-33s.'

Castro made a point over the telephone of personally urging his pilots to find and destroy the ships, impatient over every minute elapsing. He knew the pilots from earlier visits to the base, and he wanted to impress on them how vital it was to deprive the invaders of back-up supplies – weapons, ammunition, food and stores. This was consistent with his goal of isolating the brigade on the beach and then smashing it. His greatest concern was that the exiles might succeed in establishing positions on the high ground in the Zapata swamps beyond the beach and thereby control the three paved highways linking the Bay of Pigs with firm land in the north and east. If they achieved this and continued to be supplied from the sea, it might have become impossible to dislodge them. Again Castro had correctly guessed the enemy plan.

At 4.30 a.m. Fidel called the air base and demanded to talk to Captain Enrique Carreras, the senior pilot, who had been sitting strapped inside the cockpit of his single-seat Sea Fury. Carreras raced to the phone to hear Castro tell him: '*Chico*, you must sink those ships for me!' At first light Carreras took off in his Sea Fury armed with rockets and four 20-mm cannon, followed by another Sea Fury and a B-26. Reaching the Bay of Pigs, Carreras saw landing craft moving towards the beaches, and a large freighter approaching Playa Larga. He missed on the first pass, but on the second his rockets hit the freighter, which was in fact the *Houston*, carrying the brigade's Fifth Battalion and its equipment, and seconds later the second Sea Fury scored too. At 6.30 a.m. the *Houston* went aground five miles south of Playa Larga, and the battalion never landed. *Barbara J*, a Landing Ship Infantry (LCI) serving as a CIA command vessel, was damaged by Sea Fury machine-gun fire, began to take water, and fled for the open sea. Carreras returned to San Antonio to refuel and rearm, and was back over the bay at 9.30 a.m., this time hitting and sinking the freighter *Rio Escondido*, which carried ten days' supply of ammunition for the brigade and essential communications gear. At that juncture other invasion ships steamed out of the bay, leaving some 1350 brigade men stranded ashore.

Not even Castro was yet aware of the truth, but the battle of the Bay of Pigs was won by the Sea Furies only eight hours after the first landings. Captain Carreras' plane was hit by fire from a Brigade B-26, but he limped home safely to San Antonio. Meanwhile the T-33s had taken to the air to cope with the exiles' B-26s, shooting down four of them during the day. Castro lost two Sea Furies and two B-26s, but strategically this no longer mattered. His aerial secret weapons had accomplished their mission.

Proceeding south from Matanzas with his militia officers' battalion, Fernández halted in Jovellanos where he was intercepted by a phone call from Castro who wanted to check on his progress. Fernández and his battalion reached the Australia sugar mill on the outer perimeter of the Zapata swamps around 8 a.m. and now Castro ordered him to take Palpite, a village just three miles north of Playa Larga, one of the two planned brigade beachheads. Palpite was some twelve miles from Australia by paved highway. Advancing in buses and trucks under enemy air bombardment, the militia battalion had occupied the village by noon while another unit raced a few miles south-east to take the village of Soplillar where there was a landing strip. Fernández was just in time to prevent brigade units from Playa Larga from reaching Palpite and the south–north highway. He was helped by the fact that paratroops earmarked to support this mission were dropped too far away to be of any assistance, and they were quickly captured by the militias. Another paratroop unit took San Blas to the east of Girón, but the village had no strategic importance at that point, and the men came immediately under fire from the Cienfuegos battalion.

When Fernández telephoned Castro in Havana to report the capture of Palpite, Fidel exclaimed: 'We've already won the war! . . . Our air force has sunk three or four ships, and it continues in action . . . You are to attack Playa Larga with the militia battalion. . .' Castro had also triumphantly shouted that 'we've won the war' back when he and the two other survivors of Alegría de Pío had encountered Raúl Castro and his few companions after the 1956 débâcle in the foothills of the Sierra Maestra, but this time his assessment was rather more immediately accurate. With the invasion fleet eliminated and the invaders bottled up on the beaches, even though much heavy combat still lay ahead, Castro faced what was essentially only a clean-up operation.

Fernández's attack on Playa Larga, using 500 militiamen armed with mortars, machine guns and rifles, was repulsed at 2 p.m. after suffering considerable casualties. Castro now felt that his presence might energize his troops (and, anyway, he wanted to be in the thick of the action), so he arrived by car at Australia at 3.15 p.m. – a three-hour drive at break neck speed. He did not take a helicopter because it would be vulnerable to air attack. At the sugar mill he informed Fernández that artillery, anti-aircraft guns and tanks were on their way, and that the attack on Playa Larga must be resumed immediately. He wanted to go to the front at Palpite, but Fernández talked him out of it. The first photograph of him in the combat area – walking in battledress and brown beret, rifle in left hand and cigar in teeth as he listened to Fernández a step behind – was taken there and immediately circulated around the world. The other famous Castro war picture, showing him jumping off a tank at Playa Larga, was shot the following day; it has since appeared on millions of heroic posters.

That Castro appeared personally in the war zone that very first afternoon served to emphasize how militarily and politically secure he felt. The troops and militias he had left behind in Havana were totally loyal, the seaside Malecón boulevard was ringed with artillery and anti-aircraft guns, and in the capital alone about 35,000 people suspected of anti-regime sentiments were detained during the morning by State Security, the police and the Revolution Defence Committees. Havana's Roman Catholic Auxiliary Bishop was among the detainees. Sixteen thousand of these were placed in Havana prisons, 10,000 in the sports stadium, and 4000 in the huge Blanquita theatre. In case the CIA had really ever hoped for anti-Castro Cubans to rise in support of the invasion, Fidel made sure that they did not have any leadership. And before leaving Havana he had drafted an appeal to 'The People of America and the World', signed by him and President Dorticós, for 'solidarity' with Cuba in her struggle against 'the imperialism of the United States' and its 'mercenaries and adventurers who have landed in our country'.

There was tough combat for two more days. Notwithstanding the hopelessness of its situation, the brigade fought a brave rearguard action, even in Castro's opinion. Despite heavy artillery bombardment it defended Playa Larga until the morning of the next day, 18 April, when additional militia units arrived. That morning Fidel returned to Havana because of reports that enemy troops were landing in Pinar del Río in the west, but this turned out to be another CIA deception, this time involving electronics gear aboard small boats well off shore, and he was back on the battlefield early on Wednesday the 19th – in time to see final victory. He was with Pedro Miret's artillery batteries east of Girón when San Blas was retaken and the noose tightened around the Blue Beach. Brigade B-26s, which had inflicted heavy casualties on Fernández's militias as they moved towards Girón on Tuesday, could no longer operate because their Cuban pilots were totally exhausted from the seven-hour round-trip flights from Nicaragua. Four CIA-recruited American pilots from the Alabama Air National Guard died when their two B-26s were shot down by Castro's T-33s. Kennedy had authorized one-hour morning sorties by American jets from the carrier *Essex* on Wednesday to help protect the evacuation from Girón Beach, but unexplainedly they appeared too early to be of any help. The last efforts at resistance ended at 5.30 p.m.

Considering that he had no radio or telephone communications within the vast battle region of the Zapata – handwritten messages were rushed by Jeep or motorcycle or even on foot – Castro maintained a remarkable control of the events as they unrolled for three days. Celia Sánchez was at the Havana command post, keeping him informed by radio and telephone of developments elsewhere. And, above all, his strategic instinct was unerring. When Fernández reported to him on the 19th that two US destroyers were approaching the beach at Girón in what might be the prelude to a new landing, Castro replied: 'What you're seeing are not landings but evacuations. . .' He wanted the rubber boats with escaping exiles pinned down, but cautioned Fernández not to fire on the US destroyers, even though they were within Cuban territorial waters. He assumed correctly that the warships would fire back, and if a clash with the United States erupted the consequences were unforeseeable.

Castro spent Thursday the 19th at the beach in Girón, satisfying his curiosity by inspecting the enemy positions and talking to the prisoners. There were so many prisoners that quite a few had not yet had their weapons taken from them as they surrounded Fidel to answer his questions. Fernández who knew most of the brigade officers personally from old days, says that the prisoners first feared immediate execution by their captors, then 'were surprised that they were treated with total correctness . . . Human dignity was scrupulously observed.' It took several days to round up the remnants of the brigade; in the end 1189 prisoners, including the entire high command, were taken as prisoners to Havana and interned at the Naval Hospital near La Cabaña fortress. Castro lost 161 dead in the battle, and the brigade lost 107.

Castro's victory at the Bay of Pigs defined for the future Cuba's basic relationship with the United States as well as with the Soviet Union. He proved both that he had an extremely high military defensive capacity, and that the Kremlin was prepared to act in Cuba's defence. As Krushchev said in a note to Kennedy on 18 April: 'We shall render the Cuban people and their government all necessary assistance in beating back the armed attack on Cuba.' And eighteen months later Krushchev showed how far he was really prepared to go: unquestionably the Bay of Pigs affair led directly to the Cuban missile crisis in 1962.

There is also little question, although it was Castro's use of the air that was the decisive factor from the outset, that Soviet and Czech weapons, including artillery and tanks, made his triumph quicker and easier – even though the weapons were so new, Fernández says, that some of the tank crews were learning how to fire the weapons en route from the depots to the battlefield.

There is nothing to suggest, on the other hand, that the Soviet advisers who had begun arriving in Cuba with the equipment late in 1960 had anything to do with the victory. The revolutionaries won because Castro's strategy was vastly superior to the CIA's; because the revolutionary morale was high; and because Che Guevara as the head of the militia training programme and Fernández as commander of the militia officers' school, had done so well in preparing 200,000 men and women for war.

The report of the Taylor board of inquiry, parts of which remained classified twenty-five years later, freely recognized that Castro had been totally underestimated. Richard Bissell, the CIA's architect of the invasion, testified that among the wrong judgements were 'the under-estimation of Castro's capability in certain specific respects, mainly his organization ability, speed of movement and will to fight . . . Contrary to our opinion, the T-33s were armed and flown with skill, loyalty and determination.' Finally, the board agreed that the notion that if they were defeated, brigade troopers might join guerrillas in the Escambray (an idea pushed by the CIA), was pure fantasy.

To Ambassador Bonsal the Bay of Pigs 'was a serious setback for the United States . . . It consolidated Castro's regime and was a determining factor in giving it the long life it has enjoyed . . . It became clear to all concerned in Washington, in Havana and in Moscow that for the time being the Castro regime could be overthrown only through an overt application of American power.' A quarter of a century later,, a huge billboard overlooks the Girón tourist beach, proclaiming: 'GIRÓN – THE FIRST IMPERIALIST DEFEAT IN AMERICA!' On a sunny day in the summer 1985 a group of Soviet sailors from a visiting warship in Cienfuegos had their pictures taken in front of the billboard; most of them probably had not yet been born when that event occurred.

Having 'defeated imperialism', Fidel Castro lost no time in extracting from his victory glory for the revolution, political advantage for his revolutionary regime, and inevitably an enormous boost to the Cuban sense of national pride. He did this primarily by staging an extraordinary revolutionary passion play, running from spring to autumn. On 23 April, victory Sunday, he opened the show with a four-hour appearance on *Popular University*, his favourite television programme, to narrate the saga of the invasion and revolutionary triumph, using maps, a pointer and captured documents. Fidel blended humour, sarcasm, scorn, defiance and rousing explanations of revolutionary strategy to narrate the tale of Girón, and his voice soared as he proclaimed that 'our men know how to die, and they have demonstrated this abundantly in recent days!' Practically the entire population of Cuba watched Fidel on television that Sunday, streets and plazas and parks everywhere becoming deserted, and his popularity seemed even greater than on the day of his first victory, in 1959. Girón had unified the nation behind him, no matter what, as Castro would say later, 'our Marxist–Leninist party was really born at Girón; from that date on, socialism became cemented for ever with the blood of our workers, peasants and students'.

At the same time Castro began producing captured prisoners on television to explain their backgrounds and involvement in the invasion brigade. In what became a veritable television serial for days on end, the exiles either repented their participation in the Bay of Pigs expedition, or stolidly confined themselves to their story in an equally self-incriminatory fashion. Some were defiant, asking why Castro held no elections if he was so popular. But under questioning, fourteen of them confessed to murders and other crimes while serving in the Batista forces after the 1952 coup – and, again the 'imperialists' were shown up as the assassins' masters. The following week Castro had the prisoners assembled at Havana's Sports Palace where, also on television, he questioned the men, and argued and discussed with them – another act in the passion play.

Castro had decided while the battle was still progressing that he did not wish to damage the revolution's image of purity and generosity with brutality, summary executions or a mass trial. Instead, much more subtly – and practically – he demanded ransom from the United States for the overwhelming majority of the men, including all the commanders, and had revolutionary courts try only the fourteen prisoners accused of pre-revolution crimes. Five of them were executed, and nine sentenced to thirty years in prison. Seven of the nine had their terms shortened, and in 1985 only two were still imprisoned.

The negotiations for the release of the brigade prisoners took twenty months – Castro had first asked for 500 tractors in exchange for them, which the Kennedy administration had balked at – and Fidel came up with another sensation in his drama when he allowed ten of the men to fly to the United States on 20 May, to support his demands. The prisoners were personally told by Castro that ten of them, chosen by the whole group, could go to Miami and Washington for the negotiations, on their word of honour as officers and gentlemen that they would return to Cuba. He made his offer when he visited the captives after being awarded the Lenin Peace Prize at the Soviet Embassy, a touch of Fidel's ironic timing. And another Fidel touch was that he had them travel in their brigade camouflage battle uniforms, clean and shaved, a gesture of military honour which he always applied to his enemies in war. They took mail with them for the families of those left behind and, when they flew back to Havana a week later they were allowed to carry 660 pounds of gifts for their fellow prisoners. Though Eleanor Roosevelt agreed to chair a 'tractors committee' (and Castro immediately announced his willingness to negotiate with 'the widow of the great president') no accord could be reached, mainly because the United States refused to let the Cubans make the exchange appear as a form of indemnification for the invasion. Only on 23 December 1962 were the prisoners released – and then against the delivery of $53 million worth of medicines and food.

On two widely separated occasions I had the opportunity of discussing the Bay of Pigs – and President Kennedy – with Fidel Castro. The first time was in June 1961, less than two months after the invasion, when I joined Castro in a tour of the battlefield. He was the guide, the victorious commander, and the military historian, as he pointed to sites where crucial events had occurred. Describing the second day's battle for Playa Larga, he said: 'The attack was incessant, and we counter-attacked incessantly.' On Girón beach Castro rested his boot on the wreckage of a brigade B-26 bomber and said, expansively waving his long cigar with his hand, that 'they underestimated us and they used their own forces incorrectly'. He went on to say that the invaders had been fatally surprised by his mastery of the air, and that they should have engaged in multiple landings, instead of a single one.

'That was their first error,' he expounded. The second major error, he said, continuing his critique, was the brigade's failure to prevent his tanks from reaching the Zapata area on flatbed trucks from Havana; this failure was due to the fact that paratroopers were dropped too late on D-Day morning: by then road communications were already controlled by his militiamen. The paratroopers, he said, were used 'too conservatively', but when he was asked how *he* would have used them, he wagged his finger laughingly, remarking: 'I am not going to tell *you* that.' Furthermore, Castro commented, troops were not landed fast enough after the first wave came ashore at Playa Larga, so that when the *Houston* was sunk a whole battalion was still aboard.

'Their problem,' Fidel said, clearly enjoying the lecture, 'was that they did not have the guerrilla mentality, as we do, and they acted like a conventional army. We used guerrilla tactics to infiltrate their lines, while attacking steadily from the air and on the ground. You must never let the enemy sleep.' He thought, however, that the brigade had first-rate equipment and excellent firepower. His own error, he added, was to have let a militia battalion advance on the second day on the open road that rises above the quicksand of the marshes where they were an easy target for enemy aircraft. Yet, the CIA planners' greatest miscalculation, Castro concluded, was to believe that the air strike on the three Cuban bases on 15 April had destroyed most of his planes. This was the key to the 'imperialist' defeat and his victory.

The next time Castro spoke to me of the invasion was at his offices at the Palace of the Revolution in Havana late in January 1984 – almost twenty-three years later. We had not seen each other in the intervening period, and the conversation picked up where, in effect, we had left it off on Girón beach. I mentioned to him that in November 1961, seven months after the Bay of Pigs, I had been summoned by President Kennedy for a private discussion of Cuba in the Oval Office, and that I had been stunned when he asked me: 'What would you think if I ordered Castro to be assassinated?' I told Castro that my reply had been that the United States should not be involved in political assassinations, and the president said: 'I agree with you completely.' Kennedy had added, I informed Castro, that he was under pressure from some of his advisers to have the Cuban leader killed, but was 'glad' that I opposed the idea because, indeed, he felt that for 'moral reasons' the United States must not be party to assassinations. Richard N. Goodwin, then assistant to the president, who was present at this conversation, testified in 1975 before a Senate committee that when he asked Kennedy several days later about this discussion, the president replied: 'We can't get into that kind of thing, or we would all be targets.' I made a point of mentioning this to Castro, too, and my story started him on the subject of John Kennedy. Castro, of course, knew in 1984 that numerous attempts had been made by the CIA in the 1960s to murder him but, as he said, he could never bring himself to believe that President Kennedy would have authorized them.

'Well, what you tell me is really very interesting,' Castro said. 'I've never heard it before, and it's very interesting for me because, in the first place, there's a strong connection between what you have described . . . and Kennedy's idea of having a dialogue [with Cuba].' Castro went on to tell me that on 23 November 1963, the day Kennedy was assassinated in Dallas, he was meeting in Cuba with Jean Daniel, a French magazine editor, who had brought him a secret message from the president. This was a year after the Cuban missile crisis. Kennedy, according to Castro, had asked Daniel to come to Havana and ask him how he felt about 'discussing the possibility of a dialogue with the United States . . . to find some channel of contact, of dialogue, to overcome the great tensions that existed'. Castro said that the radio flash about Kennedy's death came just as he and Daniel were discussing the presidential message to him over lunch. 'For this reason,' Castro said thoughtfully, 'I have always had the impression that Kennedy was seriously considering the question of relations with Cuba.'

Castro then alluded to a speech Kennedy had made in the spring of 1963, at American University in Washington, proposing nuclear arms control negotiations with the Soviet Union. 'It was really a peace speech,' Castro said, 'and, in my opinion, it marked a change in the position of the United States in relation to international problems.' Coming back to the subject of Cuba, he remarked: 'I always had the impression that Kennedy was capable of rectifying US policy [towards Cuba] . . . I have considered him to have sufficient valour to put that policy right. That's why I consider that for us, for Cuba, and for relations between Cuba and the United States, the death of Kennedy was a great blow. . .'

Turning again to the question of his proposed assassination, Castro said that my account of the Kennedy conversation 'fits well with the idea I've always had of Kennedy's character. . .' But, he went on, 'I still see Kennedy at the root of everything that has happened between America and Cuba, beginning with Girón. I do not hold Kennedy wholly responsible for Girón because the idea of Girón had appeared much earlier . . . Once we proclaimed the Agrarian Reform Law in May 1959 the United States had decided to liquidate the Cuban revolution, one way or another. I understand that after my conversation with Nixon at the Capitol in 1959 – what had been a frank and amiable conversation – in which I spoke very openly to Nixon about the problems in Cuba – Nixon was convinced I was a Communist and that it was necessary to liquidate the Cuban revolution. In reality, from what I said to Nixon, it could not be deducted that Castro was a Communist . . . It is possible that, initially, it was thought the economic blockade, with the suspension of sugar purchases and sales of equipment and spare parts from the United States, would be sufficient to force the collapse of the Cuban revolution.'

But two years later, Castro continued, there was the convergence of the Bay of Pigs and the Alliance for Progress. 'Clearly,' he said very emphatically, 'Kennedy had inherited the whole plan of Girón from the Eisenhower government. At the time Kennedy was, in my opinion, unquestionably a man full of idealism, of purpose, of youth, of enthusiasm. I do not think he was an unscrupulous man. He was, simply, very new, you might say – besides, very inexperienced in politics although very intelligent, very wise, very well prepared, with magnificent personal qualities. I can speak of experience and inexperience in politics because when we Cubans compare ourselves now with what we knew then about politics – the experience we had in 1959, 1960 and 1961 – we are really ashamed of our ignorance at that time. Twenty-five years have elapsed [for us], and Kennedy only had a few months in the government.'

Addressing the question of the invasion, Castro said: 'I am convinced that he had doubts . . . but he did not decide to cancel it because so many forces were committed: prestigious institutions in the United States, the Pentagon, the CIA, the tradition of [keeping] government decisions. So, with many doubts, he decided to move ahead with the invasion of Girón. And even though he launched the invasion, I think that Kennedy had great merit. If it had been Nixon, I am convinced that he would not have resigned himself to the defeat of the invasion, and there would have been an escalation, and that in this country we would have been trapped in a very serious war between North American troops and the Cuban people, because the people, without any doubt, would have fought. The revolution, without any doubt, would have resisted. At that moment we already had tens of thousands of weapons, we had them distributed in the mountains, we had them everywhere. We had hundreds of thousands of men, even if not very well trained . . . Because when we saw that a military threat was hanging over us, we did everything possible to acquire arms, especially infantry weapons, and there would have erupted in our country a war that would have cost us tens of thousands, hundreds of thousands of lives. And I think that the man who had the personal qualities, who had the personal courage to recognize that a great error had been committed, to calm himself and to hold himself back – this man was

Kennedy. So, if we had an invasion that was prepared by Nixon and Eisenhower, we also had the luck that a Nixon was not elected to the presidency, and that at that moment it was a Kennedy, who was ethical, who was president . . . Thus we recognize that Kennedy had the moral valour to assume the responsibility for what had been done . . . For this reason, I place these plots for my physical elimination in the same context as Girón – something he had inherited. I have never had an attitude of resentment about them, even if he had considered the idea, because it has always been hard for me to believe that Kennedy would have given a direct order of that nature – not because he is dead, but analysing it with calm and in cold blood. I can add that I really felt a profound pain the day I received the news of his death – it shocked me, it hurt me, it saddened me to see Kennedy brought down.'

And Fidel Castro was remembering John Kennedy in this fashion so many years after not only in the light of the Bay of Pigs, but also of the great confrontation with the president that had occurred the following year.

Chapter 5

The Cuban missile crisis of October 1962 was a historically inevitable consequence of the Bay of Pigs events. The dynamics on both sides of the straits of Florida had to force a new confrontation – it was like a law of physics – and this time the conflict was enlarged, raised to superpower level. Never before, or since then, has the world come so near a nuclear war. But by then Cuba and Castro had become simply the pretext and the trigger, a crucial point that this globally minded leader somehow failed to grasp at the moment of crisis. This intellectual lapse on Castro's part served, in turn, to lock him with seeming finality into the Soviet power system – even though he had resisted a subtle Soviet takeover campaign for over six years, its full extent being his deepest political secret.

No sooner had the blood dried at the Bay of Pigs than a new process of polarization developed between Washington and Havana, John Kennedy and his advisers and Fidel Castro equally sharing the blame and responsiblity for the results. In Washington, Kennedy received in mid-June the conclusions of the Taylor board of inquiry on the Bay of Pigs disaster: 'There can be no long-term living with Castro as a neighbour', the Cuban situation should be reappraised 'and new guidance be provided for political, military, economic and propaganda action against Castro'. Studies on how best to execute such action were provided by the National Security Council staff and the CIA, and on 30 November Kennedy sent a memorandum to Secretary of State Dean Rusk to inform him of his decision to 'use our available assets . . . to help Cuba overthrow the Communist regime'. In Havana, meanwhile, Castro had proclaimed that after the April invasion 'the struggle in this country is for socialism', and he proceeded to accelerate this socialization in every possible way. Inevitably he was inviting fresh violent responses from the United States, but for Castro it was a matter of revolutionary principle – now that it was no longer 'counter-revolutionary' to regard the revolution as simply the socialist stage in the march towards Communism. Before Girón, men went to prison for saying that was so.

The post-invasion acceleration of the revolutionary process spotlighted the immense transformations in Cuban society. As the country experienced the third year of Castro's rule, the new realities were the very considerable improvement in the living, health and education conditions of the population, especially in the impoverished countryside; a painful deterioration in the national economy for reasons ranging from chaotic planning to defence requirements and the US's economic warfare; and an almost total political, intellectual and cultural regimentation. Put more crudely, a revolutionary dictatorship had been established by the end of 1961.

Having declared that this was a socialist revolution and that the next step would be the creation of the United Party of the Cuban Socialist Revolution (PURSC) as the ruling political organism under his guidance, Castro moved to eradicate all forms of opposition (loyal or not) and every vestige of independent thought. Always insisting that these measures were aimed at the absolute national unity required for the revolution's survival, he urged Cubans to join him in joyfully greeting the new age of regimentation. In the course of his 26th of July speech at Havana's Revolution Plaza, Fidel asked those who belonged to the militia, to the Revolution Defence Committees, the Revolutionary Workers' Confederation and the Cuban Women's Federation to raise their hands – and a hurricane of applause and shouted approval swept the huge crowd. It was another 'consultation' with the masses, and Castro exclaimed: 'The Revolution has organized the people! . . . Even children are being organized in the associations of Rebel Pioneers!' And Cubans now addressed each other as *compañeros* in this brotherhood of the revolution.

Notwithstanding the Bay of Pigs invasion, the threat of new American thrusts, the Escambray anti-revolution guerrillas who managed to regroup in mid-1961, and relentless economic difficulties, Fidel never deviated from his blueprint for step-by-step political consolidation and control. In fact, the greater the pressure and the dangers, the more determined he became to carry out his basic programme. Nothing could disturb his sense of priorities or interfere with his painstaking and often convincing rationalizations.

Castro's handling of Cuban intellectuals, writers and artists, forcing the country's cultural community into an ideological straightjacket and depriving it of the last ounce of freedom in the sense accepted in the non-totalitarian world, was one of his more masterful exercises in power, intimidation and manipulation. Because the revolution's wisdom could not be questioned and because of Fidel's skills, Cuba's best and richest minds would give him an ovation when he had concluded his lethal surgery on them. He produced, in effect, a cultural wasteland in Cuba, and a quarter of a century later creativity is not even beginning to be reborn – at least not visibly.

The events which occurred in the conference room of the José Martí National Library in Havana on three consecutive Saturdays in June 1961 brought about this state of affairs, and they provide a special insight into the workings of the amazing mind of Fidel Castro. Familiar with the writings of Antonio Gramsci, the Marxist thinker who propounded the view that the control of popular culture is needed to win (or retain) the support of the masses, Castro approached the Cuban problem from this premise. Much earlier, he had acquired full control over the mass media, establishing at the same time a high-quality cinema institute, directed by his old friend Alfredo Guevara, to produce feature films, documentaries and newsreels with heavy revolutionary content. Now came the turn of the writers, poets, journalists, artists, composers, movie directors (as individuals), playwrights and ballet masters.

Actually, the June crisis was precipitated by a more-or-less ideological dispute involving a mildly controversial twelve-minute documentary film and the decision by the Castro-created National Culture Council not to exhibit it, but it was instantly clear that what was at stake was the definition of cultural freedom under the revolution.

Incongruous as it may appear, the real issue was the unhappiness of Castro and Edith García Buchaca, the council's head and a ranking member of the Communist Party, with the weekly literary supplement of the newspaper *Revolución*, which was still the official organ of Fidel's own 26th of July Movement. Published on Mondays and therefore called *Lunes de Revolución*, it had been launched in March 1959, and it was probably the best and most interesting literary publication in Latin America. Its problem, however, was defined in its first editorial's statement that while the revolution had broken 'all the barriers of the past', *Lunes* 'has no defined political philosophy although we do not reject certain systems [such as] dialectic materialism, psychoanalysis and existentialism'. *Lunes* therefore published whatever its editors (who were leading writers, most of whom had lived abroad during the Batista era) considered interesting: it ran the full gamut from Raúl Castro's and Che Guevara's war diaries to articles about Marx and Lenin (annoying moderate *Fidelistas*), Trotsky and Djilas (annoying the Communists), Proust, Chekov, Hemingway, and American beatnik writers. At the outset nobody seemed to mind, and Fidel occasionally dropped in at *Lunes* offices late at night for *café con leche*, one time bringing along Jean-Paul Sartre and Simone de Beauvoir. This was still the romantic phase, and Fidel enjoyed being the bohemian intellectual. In 1961, however, the revolution was no longer romantic, Castro had publicly chosen a dogmatic ideology, and hard–line Marxists ran the Culture Council. *Lunes* no longer belonged.

At the National Library, Castro patiently listened for two Saturdays to lengthy debates among the writers and artists on the meaning of cultural liberty under the revolution; the sessions were made even livelier by a few favour-currying writers accusing some of their best friends in Fidel's presence of being 'counter-revolutionaries'. On the third Saturday, 30 June, Fidel Castro laid down the revolution's intellectual and cultural laws in one of his most important speeches, known as Words to Intellectuals (two hours of them). Apart from Gramsci's dictum about popular culture, Castro defined in the clearest fashion to date the philosophy of the revolution and the limits of its tolerance, or rather the total rigidity of its intolerance.

Too intelligent and sophisticated to spout Marxist slogans to such an audience (he refrained from mentioning socialism even once in his Words), Castro put the situation very plainly: 'We believe that the revolution still must fight many battles, and we believe that our first thought and our first preoccupation must be what to do to make the revolution victorious . . . The fear expressed here in this room is that the revolution will drown liberty [of expression], suffocate the creative spirit of writers and artists . . . The most polemical point is whether liberty in artistic expression must or must not exist . . . [But] the revolutionary places something above even his own creative spirit; he places the revolution above all else, and the most revolutionary artist will sacrifice even his own artistic vocation for the revolution . . . This means that within the revolution [there is] everything; against the revolution – nothing. Against the revolution nothing because the revolution also has its rights, and the first right of the revolution is the right to exist . . . What are the rights of writers and artists, revolutionaries or not revolution-aries? Within the revolution: everything; against the revolution, nothing.'

In this manner Castro established the policy principle that the revolution (or the revolutionary bureaucracy or himself) would interpret – arbitrarily – what *was* and what *was not* 'within the revolution', with no right of argument or appeal. It implied the censorship of ideas, and it encouraged self-censorship – presumably on the lowest denominator level of averting ideological risks. Should writers or artists have doubts, however, about what belonged 'within the revolution', Castro offered them the National Culture Council as 'a highly qualified organ to stimulate, promote, develop and orient – yes, orient – this creative spirit. . .' Reassuringly, Fidel added that 'the existence of authority in the cultural realm does not mean that there is reason to be preoccupied by abuses of that authority.'

Having unveiled his revolutionary concept of cultural freedom, Castro proceeded to implement it by calling a congress to organize an association of writers and artists – one more revolutionary unity organization – and by proposing that this association publish a 'cultural magazine' open to all, instead of many different literary and artistic publications that would tend to provoke disunity. The message was understood clearly: on 16 November 1961 *Lunes de Revolución* published its last issue. As one of its editors put it later, *Lunes* vanished unlamented in the climate of revolutionary conformity and submission. The magazine, as well as the more obscure literary supplement of the Communist newspaper *Hoy*, was presently replaced by the new association's 'cultural magazine'. It is still, even today, as uninspiring as the rest of the Cuban press.

Fidel, the only truly cultured man in the *guerrilla* leadership, would irately regret the notion that his island has been transformed into a cultural wasteland (Che Guevara, another cultured man, was cynical enough to have acknowledged it had he lived to see the ravages). But culture is a matter of perception as well as definition. It is only the traditional Western concept of cultural liberty that has been erased by the Castro revolution. Instead, he offered Cuba mass culture.

Castro has convinced himself that true culture for the people does exist in Cuba, on account of the near-miracle of having made the whole nation literate: by 1986, over *50 million* books were being printed annually, and ballet, music, quality theatre and cinema were available to the masses. It did not seem to trouble him that, between 1968 and 1976, the best Cuban writers of his own generation were blacklisted without explanation by Cuban publishers, and that twenty-five years after Castro delivered his Words to Intellectuals, the most widely read authors are Hemingway (so admired by Fidel) along with Mark Twain, Dashiell Hammett and Raymond Chandler.

Finally, in its cultural travail the revolution is responsible for the persecution of homosexuals – among them some of the most talented writers and artists with the freest minds – which reached a peak in the 1960s and 1970s, when hundreds were forcibly enroled (along with common criminals) in the so-called Military Units for the Support of Production (UMAP). These forced-labour units have since been abolished, but there is no explanation of why a man of Fidel's humanistic and intellectual orientation should have tolerated them in the first place. Surely not to assert the *machismo* of the fiery fighters of the Sierra Maestra?

To proclaim his revolutionary defiance at home and abroad regardless of the possible consequences was part of Fidel Castro's nature. As a permanent *guerrillero*, he loved to taunt his enemies, the 'imperialists', as if anxious for another confrontation and another test of his militarized society. In his speech on 26 July 1961 he preached the necessity of always keeping weapons to hand 'because the imperialists do not forgive us our successes, and the more we become organized, the more they become filled with ire.' He spoke after awarding the newly created Order of Girón to his guest of honour, the Soviet cosmonaut Yuri Gagarin, whom he laughingly told: 'You can fly twice around the world while I'm delivering my speech.'

Castro's defiance included his willingness to accept the serious brain-drain affecting the Cuban economic structure as tens of thousands of middle-class physicians, engineers, managers and professors left the country. As many as 250,000 Cubans out of a population of six million had fled in the first three years of the revolution, but Fidel saw them as 'parasites' and potential counter-revolutionaries, and he preferred them in the United States. It was a calculated long-range risk: he would do without a management class he did not trust anyway, and educate his own revolutionary elites, and he has been vindicated. Now, twenty-five years later, Cuba can train enough physicians to assign thousands of them to work throughout the Third World, after achieving at home one of the highest doctor/patient ratios in the world.

Fidel Castro's moment of supreme challenge came on the evening of 1 December 1961 when he informed Cuba and the world that the new united revolutionary political party will have 'a Marxist-Leninist programme adjusted to the precise objective conditions of our country', that this would no longer be 'a secret', and that 'today we shall see to it that it is a proud thing to be a Communist'. This statement culminated three years of revolution, and it established once and for all Castro's ideological identity.

Typically he chose to announce the advent of Marxism-Leninism on the *Popular University* television programme, using the format not of a formal speech but of a chat about the history of his revolutionary movement, back to his own youth, and badinage with others on the panel. He speculated about how little Lenin and Marx could have achieved if they had lived in the eighteenth century, to make the point that nothing exists in a vacuum, and that the Cuban revolution was made when the necessary conditions developed. Of Marx and Lenin he said: 'One cannot be the intellectual of a class that did not exist or the creator of the doctrine of a revolution that could not occur.' Describing the early phases of his movement, Castro acknowledged that at the time of Moncada 'certain proposals were made with the intention of not damaging the scope of the revolutionary movement . . . If we hadn't drafted this document carefully, and we had made it more radical, the revolutionary movement of struggle against Batista would not have acquired the momentum that made victory possible.'

Rhetorically, he asked himself: 'Do I believe absolutely in Marxism? I believe absolutely in Marxism . . . Did I understand it [in 1953] as I understand it today after ten years of struggle? No, I didn't understand it then as I understand it today . . . Did I have prejudices concerning Communists? Yes. Was I influenced by the propaganda of imperialism and reaction against Communism? Yes . . . Did I think Communists were thieves? No, never . . . I always thought Communists were honourable, honest people. . .'

In declaring Cuba to be embarked on the Marxist–Leninist road Castro knew that he was increasing by a vast order of magnitude the risk of a new United States intervention. His announcement hit the Kennedy administration like a bombshell. The great crisis was less than a year away, but neither Kennedy in Washington nor Krushchev in Moscow had yet comprehended where Fidel Castro was pushing them.

And the Soviets may also have had difficulty in reconciling Castro's ever-growing economic and military assistance, especially as a new crisis with America was obviously approaching, with his ruthless treatment of 'old' Communists with close Moscow ties who dared to challenge his leadership at home. This power battle was over the issue of 'sectarianism' that erupted early in 1962, and Castro dealt with these Communists as if they were the 'bandits' of Escambray.

After Castro had sealed his alliance with the 'old' Communists in the secret Cojímar meetings back in 1959, and had decided to merge the 26th of July Movement, the Student Revolutionary Directorate (DR) and the Communists' Popular Socialist Party into a single political organization, it became necessary to weld the whole thing together. As a first step the three groups were joined in the ORI (Integrated Revolutionary Organizations) in preparation for the emergence of the United Party of the Cuban Socialist Revolution (PURSC) with Castro as the secretary general. The 'new' Communist Party would be the final step. Given Castro's respect for the 'old' Communists' supposed political skills, Aníbal Escalante, an old-line leader, was given the task of organizing the ORI. It seemed like a fine idea until Castro indignantly realized that Escalante and his associates were packing the whole organization with their own party people on every level and, in effect, carrying out a classicial Communist takeover from the inside. It was a quiet attempt at a coup d'état, which would have placed the revolution in the hands of orthodox Communists, and presumably turned Fidel into a magnificent figurehead.

Castro himself has not said publicly whether or not this notion had originated in Moscow, but there are valid reasons not to exclude this possibility. The Russians still regarded Fidel as a loose cannon, and may have wished to exercise some form of control over a regime whose upkeep was becoming increasingly onerous. It is also possible that at least a faction among the 'old' Communists may have concluded that it was they who should run Castro, and not the other way around, and that they might find allies among ideologically sympathetic Rebel Army officers who would agree to elevate him to the rank of an exalted statesman of the revolution, but with reduced authority. The only certainty is that Aníbal Escalante could not have invented it all by himself; too many other Communist old-timers were involved. How these Communists came to believe that they could outwit Fidel Castro is still a mystery. Their conspiracy was elegantly called 'sectarianism', but to Castro it was pure and simple counter-revolution.

With his superb sense of timing Castro waited for the right moment. Thus he said nothing publicly when the composition of the twenty-five man National Directorate of ORI was announced – evidently with his approval – on 9 March 1962, with him, Raúl Castro and Che Guevara leading the list as chiefs of the 26th of July Movement. But of the twenty-five members, ten were 'old' Communists (who had played no serious role in the war), and even among the thirteen men from Fidel's Movement, at least three had strong Communist leanings. The Student Directorate, which fought against Batista in Escambray, received only two seats. Theoretically, then, as Fidel knew, the orthodox Communist faction could assemble a majority in the ORI leadership. Four days later he exploded in unprecedented public fury but tangentially, when at anniversary commemorations of the Directorate's 1957 attack on the Batista palace, a Communist Party orator omitted the invocation to God in the text of the 'testament' of the student leader José Antonio Echevarría. He shouted that the memory of a dead companion was being censored and falsified.

It was entirely in character for Castro to do this as a matter of principle. Nevertheless, those who knew him well, believed that Fidel was sending the Communists a message. If he was, they missed it altogether. Castro waited two more weeks, and on 26 March (his favourite day of the month in his private superstitions), he staged one of his great dramatic television productions. In a previous television appearance earlier in March Castro had announced a depressingly sharp programme of food rationing (agriculture under the revolution was not keeping up with consumer needs), but now he focussed the national attention on the 'sectarian' plot. Aware that political dramas must be personalized in order not to be abstract to the masses, Castro singled out Aníbal Escalante for some of the most withering accusations in his formidable arsenal of sarcastic invective. He informed Cubans that Escalante had created 'a counter-revolutionary monstrosity' in ORI, that he had built up his own 'machine' to take over the party and the government, and that *Fidelista* veterans from the Sierra Maestra were losing troop commands to Communist officers (who may have been part of the Escalante affair). Escalante was suffocating Cuba, Castro said, to the point that when 'a cat had four kittens, one had to go to the ORI office to resolve the matter' of the kittens' fate.

However, Fidel had the political sagacity not to declare war on all the 'old' Communists, having made his point with the public political execution of Escalante. Only a few other party leaders were purged along with Escalante, among them the cultural chief, Edith García Buchaca, and her husband Joaquín Ordoqui, an executive bureau member of the PSP. Others in the party leadership quickly realized they could not confront Castro, and were delighted to let Aníbal Escalante be the principal sacrificial lamb (his brother César Escalante joined in the rites and thus remained in the leadership). Once more Carlos Rafael Rodríguez rose to the occasion to mediate between his friend Fidel and his old comrades – negotiating from a position of power towards the party since Castro had named him President of INRA only the month before. With the farm crisis raging, Castro preferred to concentrate on other matters and resigned from the INRA presidency, leaving agricultural problems to Rodríguez and Che Guevara. Others fell instantly into line. The PSP's secretary general Blás Roca wrote in the party newspaper *Hoy* that Castro was 'the best and the most efficient Marxist–Leninist in our country' and Marxism–Leninism's 'insuperable guide and chief', remarkable praise for a man who had formally embraced this doctrine only five months earlier. A quarter of a century later, Escalante's 'sectarianism' remains a sore topic with the 'old' Communists; both Blás Roca and Fabio Grobart uncomfortably called it 'simple measles' in separate interviews in 1985.

The Soviets stayed out of this internal affray, preferring to let nature take its course and not assuming positions prematurely. That Castro was angry at them for unspecified reasons was made obvious when he refused to receive Soviet Ambassador Kudryatsev for a farewell audience (apparently he had requested his removal, and had said to friends that Kudryatsev 'tires me more than Bonsal did') in a typical display of displeasure. Still, Moscow chose to maintain the friendship with Havana, and it is probable that the mounting schism with China played a role in the decision. Thus Aleksandr Alexeiev, the young 'journalist' who had drunk the vodka toast with Fidel in 1959, was named as the new Ambassador to Havana, to the Cubans' great satisfaction. Alexeiev had accompanied Mikoyan in 1960 for the signing of the first trade treaty, and now he came from his ambassadorship in Argentina. *Pravda* wrote an editorial on 11 April praising Castro and denouncing the unfortunate Escalante, and Deputy Foreign Trade Minister I.I. Kuzmin turned up in Havana to conclude a new trade treaty for 1962. It increased the two-way trade (in reality, Soviet deliveries to Cuba) from $540 million to $750 million.

A trade accord with China, though on a much smaller scale, had been signed a month earlier, and the Peking official journals hailed Castro for opposing 'sectarianism'. Krushchev obviously did not believe that the

Cubans would go over to the Chinese side, but the bare thought of even-handedness towards China was troublesome to him in the midst of the rising Soviet battle for control of the world Communist movement as well as the sympathies of the increasingly important Third World. Castro had his way, and now he was in the best possible position to extract Soviet guarantees of military protection from the United States. In a June speech he was happy to describe Krushchev as 'that great and dearly beloved friend of Cuba'. Again, Fidel was demonstrating that strategy and tactics must never be confused.

Foremost on his mind was still the threat from the United States. Although there were in fact no plans afoot by the Kennedy adminstration, as far as is known, to launch an American invasion of Cuba, Castro (and possibly Krushchev) believed that a direct attack was in the offing. Certainly this misperception produced dire results, but even without it Castro could not have afforded to rule out an invasion, and so he had to be ready for one. His subsequent accords with the Soviets are consistent with an overall precautionary stance, but it remains unclear even a generation later how exactly Castro and Krushchev arrived at the notion of deploying Soviet nuclear weapons on the island. Nor is it comprehensible how the two of them could have expected that the United States would fail to discover the presence of these weapons – and sit still for it.

Castro, however, was absolutely right in assuming that the Kennedy administration was attempting by all non-invasion means to remove him from power, and his Intelligence services were providing him with growing evidence of such subversive activites. What he was witnessing, early in 1962, was the start of Operation Mongoose, authorized by the president the previous November, 'to help Cuba overthrow the Communist regime'.

General Edward Lansdale, a counter-insurgency specialist, was named to head Mongoose, and the operational plan he presented at the White House in mid-January 1962 called for a six-phase effort by the entire United States government to undermine Castro from inside. It was designed to culminate – ironically, as it turned out – in October 'with an open revolt and overthrow of the Communist regime'.

As it happened, Operation Mongoose never even came close to attaining any of its anti-Cuban goals (although 400 CIA officers in Washington and Miami were attached full-time to this enterprise). The best it could do was to run minor Intelligence infiltration missions, carry out minimal sabotage and, as far as the CIA was concerned, revive plans to assassinate Castro. Having attempted an assassination plot through Mafia figures in 1960, the agency, acting on its own, dusted off these plans when Mongoose was created. Richard Helms, at the time the CIA's

Deputy Director for Plans (covert operations), testified before a Senate committee in 1975 that he had assumed that the 'intense' pressure exercised by the administration to oust Castro had given the agency authority to kill him – although assassination was never formally ordered. As Helms said: 'I believe it was the policy at the time to get rid of Castro and if killing him was one of the things that was to be done in this connection, that was within what was expected.'

Historians have been debating for many years whether or not the Kennedy adminstration's efforts to oust Castro after the Bay of Pigs fiasco were *directly* responsible for the Soviet deployment of nuclear weapons in Cuba. All the available evidence suggests that an affirmative answer is possible only if it is accepted that the Cubans and the Russians did really believe that an actual invasion, as distinct from Mongoose, threatened the island in 1962. Since it is now known that Kennedy entertained no invasion thoughts, the debate over American responsibilities for the *nuclear* crisis is couched in false terms. The nuclear issue in 1962 was strictly a matter of Soviet strategic decision-making. Naturally, Castro had every right to seek maximal Soviet protection because he was facing great uncertainties, but it may never be known whether Fidel used Krushchev to escalate the nuclear crisis with the United States – or vice versa. The existing record is fragmentary and contradictory.

There is no question, however, that Cuban–Soviet negotiations over significant Kremlin support for the revolutionary regime began in earnest in the spring of 1962, just as Castro had completed liquidating the Escalante 'sectarian' Communist challenge to his leadership. Not only did Castro see imminent military dangers from the United States, but in January the Organization of American States expelled Cuba from membership under Washington's pressure at the hard-fought foreign ministers' conference at Punta del Este in Uruguay. This was seen in Havana as political preparation for an invasion, the idea being to present Cuba as the Communist enemy of the entire Western hemisphere, not only of the United States.

Castro fought back politically by issuing the Second Declaration of Havana in an exceptionally emotional speech on 4 February, charging that at Punta del Este 'Yankee imperialism gathered the ministers together to wrest from them – through political pressure and un-precedented economic blackmail in collusion with a group of the most discredited rulers of this continent – a denial of the national sovereignty of our peoples and a consecration of the odious Yankee right to intervene in the internal affairs of Latin America.'

Always on the offensive, Fidel responded further to Cuba's expulsion from the OAS with the kind of challenge calculated to make Washington even more hysterical about him. Addressing a vast crowd in the Revolution Plaza, he said: 'The duty of every revolutionary is to make the revolution . . . The revolution will triumph in America and throughout the world, but it is not for revolutionaries to sit in the doorways of their houses waiting for the corpse of imperialism to pass by. The role of Job doesn't suit a revolutionary.'

At home Castro also had cause for concern, with the reappearance of guerrilla bands in the Escambray mountains and, to a lesser degree elsewhere in Cuba, after the successful clean-up operations late in 1960 and early in 1961. This clean-up had neutralized Escambray as an area of operations in support of the Bay of Pigs landing, but in 1962 the guerrillas were again a serious problem. Strangely, the CIA provided no help to these bands in the context of Mongoose, but the situation was grave enough for Raúl Castro to describe it as 'the second civil war'. In any event, Escambray was a costly drain on Cuba's defence resources, adding to the regime's overall vulnerability. The Castro brothers and men like Che Guevara realized that the existence of the guerrillas was intolerable to the regime – they knew it from their own experience as mountain rebels – and they watched with great concern as the bands grew to approximately 3000 men by mid-1962. This was ten times as many men as Fidel had had in the Sierra at the end of the war but, fortunately for him, there was no unified leadership and no real leader, and the guerrillas were split up into scores of groups without communication.

Politically it was embarrassing for Castro to admit that so many men were up in arms against him, even if they did not constitute a coherent force, but initially nothing on the subject was published in Cuba until well into the 1960s, when the last remnants of the guerrillas were being finally destroyed. Most of the *guerrilleros* were small landowners – the Cuban rural middle class – and former estate managers, foremen and workers, but also rural merchants and quite a few ex-officers of Castro's Rebel Army and the Student Revolutionary Directorate. This was a group to whom revolutionary socialism had nothing to offer and, in fact, these men had lost much privilege in the wake of the revolution. Unlike Castro in the 1950s they had no support in the cities, and they did not present ideological or political positions. According to a Cuban specialist on this subject, the Escambray bands 'were not a true danger for the revolution if we acted in time and in silence, and we did not convert them into a national preoccupation'.

At a strategy meeting in Havana Fidel suddenly interrupted one of his commanders who was referring to the new rebels as *guerrilleros* to say: 'Don't ever again say that they are *guerrilleros* – they are bandits.' The counter-insurgency units that were then being trained were consequently given the name of Battalions of Struggle against Bandits, and the description of 'bandits' caught on. Castro had understood the psychology of the situation facing him. Many years later Castro would explain at great length in a confidential speech befor Angolan officers that he had defeated the 'bandits' through a combination of throwing great military resources against them and secret negotiations with guerrilla chieftains for surrender on generous terms, and for encouraging others to surrender. Still, these were costly operations, and Castro's casualties reached over three hundred killed in Escambray alone; economic losses were calculated at around $1 billion in ruined crops, burned houses, destroyed rolling stock, roads and bridges – not to mention the military cost of the 'anti-bandit' operations. Castro, despite his other concerns, was always in overall command of this war; on one occasion during a trip, he personally captured a number of 'bandits' when with several soldiers he climbed a wooded hill above the Cienfuegos highway where he was told a guerrilla band was hiding. But the last of the Escambray 'bandits' were not caught until 1966.

Things were bad for Castro in the spring of 1962, when he turned to Moscow for military protection. There were guerrillas in the mountains, 'old' Communists were trying to undermine him, the farm economy was collapsing, and the Americans were after him with Operation Mongoose on one level and diplomatic isolation in Latin America on the other. There is no single event that seems to have triggered Castro's requests to Moscow, but indications are that he raised the issue for the first time when S.R. Rashidov, an alternate member of the Soviet Politburo, came to Havana late in May. He was the highest-ranking Soviet government official to visit Cuba since Mikoyan's trail-blazing presence two years earlier. There must have been continuing secret talks during June because Castro disclosed in a subsequent speech that negotiations for 'the strengthening of our armed forces and the dispatch of strategic missiles to our country' occurred that month. They may have been conducted through Alexeiev, who had just arrived as the new ambassador, or through Carlos Olivares, the new Cuban ambassador in Moscow. But a secret channel is more likely.

At this stage Fidel turned once more to public drama. On 15 June he departed with great fanfare for the Sierra Maestra, wearing his battle fatigues and carrying his rifle, and he spent eight days there, reliving the glories of the *guerrilla* and being ostentatiously absent from Havana. Castro's mountain meanderings were covered in detail in the press and on television, including his statement that 'once more I have raised the banner of rebellion'. The symbolism must have been meant for Kennedy and Krushchev as well as for Cubans who had to be prepared for a new crisis. On 1 July the Communist newspaper *Hoy* started publishing daily reports on US 'violations' of Cuban air space and territorial waters.

This sequence of events continued with a two-week visit to Moscow early in July by Raúl Castro and a delegation of his officers. Official announcements reported that Mikoyan and Marshal Rodion Malinovsky, the Soviet Defence Minister, received Raúl on 3 July, but the Soviet historian Roy Medvedev writes that the military talks lasted a week. Medvedev, who always had access to official Soviet sources, also adds in his biography of Krushchev that 'he attended the talks on 3 and 8 July'. And according to Medvedev these discussions centred 'on the provision of military aid to Cuba and the secondment of a number of Soviet military specialists', and 'it was presumably during that week that the decision was taken to send to Cuba medium-range missiles with nuclear warheads and bombers capable of carrying atomic bombs'. This is most likely accurate, although there may well have been follow-up conversations through secret channels between July and early September when the Soviets began secretly to ship the missiles to Cuba.

There may have also been secret contacts before Raúl Castro's *official* visit to Moscow in July. Thus Fidel had said to a visitor a year after the crisis that 'in June 1962 my brother Raúl and Che Guevara went to Moscow to discuss ways and means of installing the missiles'. If Fidel's dates are correct . . . and despite his prodigious memory he occasionally has problems with precise dates when he talks about past events involving his activities or interests – Raúl and Che would have gone to Moscow secretly even as he was waving the rebellion banner in the Sierra Maestra.

There is no known record of an actual Soviet-Cuban agreement on the missiles, and it is possible that nothing was ever put on paper in order to protect Krushchev as well as Castro in the future. Raúl Castro mentioned in a little-noticed speech late in August that 'Soviet troops' had begun to arrive in Cuba, but he offered no details, and it was unclear whether he referred to advisers, combat units or rocket forces specialists who came to prepare missile sites. Simultaneously, MiG jet fighter-bombers began arriving for the Cuban Air Force.

Che Guevara and Major Emilio Aragonés, who was very close to the Castro brothers, visited Krushchev at his vacation *dacha* in the Crimea, but it was not announced. Guevara was in the Soviet Union for the ostensible purpose of signing an agreement on modernizing Cuban steel plants, and he may also have finalized the missile arrangements with the premier.

A Soviet-Cuban military agreement on 2 September announced that as a result of 'imperialist threats' Cuba had asked the Soviet government 'for help by delivering armaments and sending technical specialists for training Cuban servicemen', and Moscow had responded affirmatively. However, this text had to be designed to explain publicly the arrivals of Soviet military personnel and conventional equipment, and even possibly to allay any American fears over missiles. That same week Anatoly Dobrynin, the new Soviet ambassador, conveyed to Attorney General Robert F. Kennedy a message from Krushchev to the president to the effect that no 'offensive weapons' were among the equipment being sent to Cuba. On 12 September TASS issued a statement to stress that the Soviets had 'no need' to deploy retaliatory 'defensive weapons' in any other country, adding, 'Cuba, for instance'. This was a reply to a Kennedy warning that the United States would not tolerate the installation of ground-to-ground missiles in Cuba. Krushchev had now set in motion his incredible attempt to deceive the US about nuclear weapons in the Caribbean.

Twenty-five years after the Cuban missile crisis it remains a matter of debate whether it was Krushchev or Castro who first proposed the Soviet nuclear deployment on the island. There are also subtleties in various accounts concerning the fashion in which the two leaders decided on this risky course of action. However, Castro is still most anxious for his interpretation of the events of October and November 1962 to form the historical record. In the course of an all-night conversation in his office at the Palace of the Revolution in Havana, I touched on the missile crisis, and Castro said: 'Are you interested in my opinion about that moment?' He then proceeded to narrate for hours the origins, the development and the aftermath of the crisis in the context of his relationship with Krushchev. For reasons of clear chronology I have rearranged here the order in which Castro told me the story – it was a conversation with many questions and answers and backing and filling – but this version is based on a transcript of our taped Spanish-language talk.

I asked Castro where and how the idea of deploying the Soviet missiles in Cuba had emerged, and he replied:

'Look, I shall tell you with much precision how the idea surfaced. After Girón, the United States government indubitably was very irritated, very dissatisfied with what had happened, and the idea of solving the Cuban revolution through force, of liquidating it through force, was not abandoned. But it was not considered possible to go back and repeat the Girón experience, and the idea of a direct invasion of Cuba was being seriously considered and analysed. And we, through various sources, had news of the plans being elaborated, and we had the certainty of this danger.'

Castro said that at the meeting between Kennedy and Krushchev in Vienna in June – two months after the Bay of Pigs – the Cuban question was discussed, and 'Kennedy spoke with much irritation there'. Castro went on to say: 'From the terms in which Kennedy expressed himself, it could be deduced that he considered he had the right to use the armed forces of the United States to destroy the Cuban revolution. He referred to different historical events, [and] on that occasion made a reference to Hungary. Having received information about that conversation, we reached the conclusion, as did the Soviets, that the United States persisted in the idea of an invasion.'

Evidently the Soviets were Castro's source for accounts of the Krushchev–Kennedy sessions, and the suggestion has been made by many historians that they had set out to convince the Cubans that Kennedy was planning an invasion, although they knew it was not true, in order to provoke Castro into demanding far-reaching military protection. In another conversation Castro has said that Kennedy had pointedly reminded Krushchev that the United States remained neutral when the Soviets invaded Hungary – and that this should be considered a hint that, in terms of reciprocity – the Russians should not interfere if there was an American attack on Cuba. In his own memoirs Krushchev does not even mention Cuba in the chapter on the Vienna meeting with Kennedy, but this does not necessarily disprove the Castro version. What matters is that Fidel chose to accept Soviet reports on Vienna as confirmation of his own suspicions about a US invasion, and he behaved accordingly. Finally, the decision on the missiles may have been triggered by Krushchev's impression in Vienna that Kennedy was indecisive – he had allowed himself, for example, to be defeated at the Bay of Pigs – and therefore would live with missiles in Cuba once they were an accomplished fact.

'We were then in discussions with the Soviets,' Castro continued narrating the 1962 events. 'At that moment the Soviets were already committed to us. They were giving us a maximum of help, they had responded with the purchase of Cuban sugar when [our] market in the United States was totally closed, they supplied petroleum when all our sources of petroleum were suspended – which would have annihilated our country. They, I say, had accepted a heavy commitment towards us, and now we were discussing what measures should be taken. They asked our opinion, and we told them in so many words – we did not speak of missiles – that it was necessary to make it clear to the United States that an invasion of Cuba would imply a war with the Soviet Union. We told them: it is necessary to take steps that would imply, in a clear manner, that an aggression against Cuba is an aggression against the Sovet Union. These were the statements we made . . . as a general concept.'

'It was then,' Fidel Castro told me, 'that they proposed the missiles. As a result of all these discussions, our position was that steps were needed to demonstrate that an aggression against Cuba was equivalent to an aggression against the Soviet Union – it could be a military pact, it could be just that. And then, among the measures that were looked at, the installation of medium-range missiles was analysed. We were thinking fundamentally about the political inconveniences we might incur. At that time we were not thinking so much of actual dangers because, you know, we had come down from the mountains, we had come from a war, we were very irritated with all the things that had happened, all the aggressions of which we were the vicitims, and so we examined the political inconveniences we faced.'

Speaking of the missiles deployment, Castro said that 'we analysed [the fact] that this, besides being convenient for us, could also be convenient to the Soviets from a military viewpoint. This is to say that we analysed what advantages there were for us and what advantages for them . . . from the strategic viewpoint – we understood this. We reached the conclusion that [the missiles] were mutually beneficial.' Castro then explained at length that it would have been 'morally incorrect' for Cuba to 'expect for a country to support us, even to the point of going to war, but – for reasons of prestige or to avoid military-type commitments, or for strictly political reasons – for us to fail to do what we could might also be convenient for the other side.' Therefore, he said, 'it seemed to us equitable, it seemed to us just, for us to accept these measures that implied safety even though they also implied a cost from the political viewpoint – the political results of installing these missiles here.'

'Then, after analysing it according to truly serious, just and honourable criteria, we took the decision of communicating to the Soviets that we were agreed to the installation of missiles here,' Castro said. 'That is, it was not pressure by them – it does not emerge as the consequence of them coming over to us one day and saying to us, "We want to install the missiles because it is convenient for this and for that." Basically, the initiative of soliciting measures that would give Cuba an absolute guarantee against a conventional war and against an invasion by the United States was ours. But the idea of the missiles, concretely, was Soviet.'

Castro's words convey the impression that he was easily persuaded by the Soviets to accept the missiles as a quid pro quo for Soviet military protection once Krushchev made the case, that as he put it in his memoirs, there was 'no other way of helping [the Cubans] meet the American threat except to instal the missiles'. But Krushchev himself claimed that he had to overcome considerable Castro resistance to the missiles. He wrote: 'When Castro and I talked about the problem, we argued and argued. Our argument was very heated. But, in the end, Fidel agreed with me. Later on, he begun to supply me with certain data that had come to his attention. "Apparently what you told me was right," he said. That in itself justified what we then did.' Krushchev's reference to their 'heated . . . argument' also raises the question of where they argued, unless he meant it figuratively as exchanges through Raúl Castro, for example, or some other channel. The record does not show any Krushchev–Castro meetings since New York in 1960. It is possible, of course, that Castro secretly visited Krushchev in the Soviet Union during June (when he was supposedly raising rebellion flags in the Sierra Maestra and was out of sight for several days), but this has never been mentioned even as speculation.

Most historians tend to agree that, indeed, Krushchev was the author of the missiles idea, although its evolution into a military agreement between the two governments is entirely sketchy. More interesting is the Soviet official line at the time of the crisis, both for Kennedy's benefit and for Soviet public opinion, which portrayed Castro as the party asking for the missiles. In his letter to Kennedy on 26 October, at the height of the crisis, Krushchev insisted that concerning Soviet missiles in Cuba, 'All the means located there, and I assure you of this, have a defensive character, are on Cuba solely for the purposes of defence, and we have sent them to Cuba at the request of the Cuban government.' On 6 November Deputy Premier Aleksei N. Kosygin told a gathering of Soviet Communist Party leaders that the Cubans had requested the missiles to protect their national security. This speech was printed in *Pravda*, but strikingly not in the Cuban press – most likely because it also justified the withdrawal of the missiles under American pressure and without consulting Castro. Krushchev repeated it before the Supreme Soviet on 12 December. But then, the record shows that Krushchev had lied to both Kennedy and Castro on numerous occasions during the crisis period.

Absent from official Soviet and Cuban pronouncements on the origins of the October crisis is any hint of how Krushchev and Castro imagined Kennedy would react to the missile deployment. The assumption is that Krushchev had hoped to get away with completing the installation before being discovered, and then make Kennedy blink with a Soviet ultimatum. Nowhere are there any indications of any consideration that no matter when the missiles' presence became known, Cuba would then be even more vulnerable to a United States attack than it had been before. Therefore I asked Fidel Castro how he thought Kennedy would react to the deployment.

'I was convinced,' Castro replied, 'that a very tense situation would be created, and that there would be a crisis.' Then he offered me a rationale for the missile gamble, which was pure Castro in terms of his calculated-risk instinct blended with his sense of principle, and which in the light of his own history is entirely believable. Contrary to common belief, Castro's gamble succeeded better than Krushchev's: he won a non-invasion guarantee from the United States at no cost to himself whereas the Soviets were simply humiliated by Kennedy. But it took Castro a few months to realize it in his fury at Krushchev for making a missile-withdrawal deal with Kennedy behind his back. Being Fidel, he had wanted more than just survival from the crisis.

In the meantime, he said to me, 'Put yourself in my place – between a situation of impotence facing a very powerful country that could at any moment decide to invade Cuba, costing the lives of millions of Cubans who would have resisted, and a situation of running a risk from a more secure position, a risk of a world nature, but not a risk of conventional war.' Castro's calculation was that, in effect, the threat of nuclear conflict would save him from a non-nuclear attack by the United States.

'We preferred the risks, whatever they were, of a great tension, a great crisis,' he said, 'to the risks of the impotence of having to await a United States invasion of Cuba . . . At least they gave us a nuclear umbrella, and we felt much more satisfied with the response we were giving to the policy of hostility towards our country. From the moral point of view I never had and I shall never have doubts that our attitude was correct. From a strictly moral as well as strictly legal viewpoint, as a sovereign country we had the right to deploy the type of arms we considered gave us the best guarantee. And, just as the United States had bases in all parts of the world around the Soviet Union, we, as a sovereign nation, considered we had the absolute legal right to deploy such weapons in our country.'

Thus the only relevant issue was 'political', Castro said, and the United States 'acted according to political attitudes and formulas and according to force' to prevent the Soviet deployment. However, he volunteered the comment that at that time 'the balance of forces in the nuclear realm favoured the United States', adding that it was a fact he had ignored in 1962. Castro was thus saying that he had engaged in the missile confrontation without being adequately informed by the Soviets of the superpowers' relative nuclear strength. Too elegant diplomatically to spell it out, Castro was nevertheless giving me a very clear impression that Krushchev had led him astray with his missile proposals – leaving one to wonder what Fidel would have done had he known the truth. This was unprecedented insight into the secrets of Soviet–Cuban relations.

'At that time,' Castro said, 'I did not know how many nuclear weapons the Soviets had and how many nuclear weapons the North Americans had. I did not know it, and it did not occur to me to ask the Soviets about it, it did not seem to me I had the right to ask: "Listen, how many missiles do you have, how many do the North Americans have, what is the balance of strength?" We simply trusted that they, for their part, were acting with knowledge of the entire situation. We did not have the information to be able to make a complete evaluation, we only received a part of the information.' As it turned out, Castro never really forgave the Soviets for keeping him in the dark about the world nuclear balance of power when he put Cuba's life on the line on the basis of Krushchev's assurances. So confident were the Cubans of the Soviet's good judgement that President Dorticós told the United Nations General Assembly in New York on 8 October, when the missiles were already being clandestinely deployed, that 'we warn that if an error is committed, aggression against Cuba can become, to our great regret and against our desires, the start of a new world war.'

Among other continuing controversies about the 1962 nuclear crisis is the question of how close the world really did come to war – atomic or, at least, conventional. The accepted wisdom is that war might have begun if Soviet ships bound for Cuba had not halted on Wednesday 24 October. If instead, they had crossed the quarantine line drawn by Kennedy, they would have been forcibly stopped by United States warships and planes – an act of war presumably followed by a Soviet response, and then unpredictable rounds of escalation. The danger still persisted until the morning of 28 October, a Sunday, when the crisis was settled through the final Kennedy–Krushchev exchange of letters. A nuclear duel was certainly possible during that week inasmuch as Soviet medium-range missiles in Cuba had become operational on 23 October, and it had to be assumed that they were armed with nuclear warheads.

However, as Fidel Castro recounted the history of the crisis, Saturday 27 October was a most critical day, not only because Soviet-operated surface-to-air (SAM) batteries had shot down a high-flying United States Air Force U-2 reconnaissance plane that morning, but because the Cubans also were trying to shoot down American aircraft. Castro insisted that, contrary to published allegations, the Russians and not the Cubans, had brought down the U-2 because they had the exclusive control of the SAMs, but he was just as vehement in saying that he was determined to destroy any low-flying American plane his anti-aircraft artillery could reach – regardless of consequences. For him it was again a matter of principle and sovereignty, and days after the crisis was settled he had still ordered that any American aircraft to appear over Cuba be fired upon – even if it reopened the confrontation. And he was aware that Kennedy had resolved to bomb Cuba if a second American aircraft was shot down after the loss of the U-2.

'The [SAM] rockets were in the hands of the Soviets, and the anti-aircraft batteries – all the conventional ones – were in our hands,' Castro recounted. 'We had hundreds of batteries. The Soviet rockets were effective above one thousand metres, but they could not fire below one thousand metres. In the days of the crisis the North Americans began flights at a very low level, in addition to the U-2s. They began flights at two hundred or three hundred metres. I realized that the SAMs as well as intermediate-range [ground-to-ground] missiles were impotent, threatened with destruction by these low-level attacks.'

Castro continued: 'I ordered the deployment of all the anti-aircraft batteries we had, some three hundred batteries. I submitted to the Soviets that we could not permit the low-level flights and we were going to use the batteries. We had installed batteries around all the SAM bases and around all the missiles, and that day we issued the order to fire. It was me who gave the orders to fire against the low-level flights. This is rigorous historical reality.'

On the morning of 27 October, Castro said, 'A couple of planes, or several couples of planes, appeared in low-level flight over different places, and our batteries began to fire.' Official United States records confirm that on that morning two low-flying reconnaissance aircraft were fired upon, but not hit, around 10 a.m., when the U-2 was shot down by an SA-II rocket. Castro said: 'The inexperience of our artillerymen, who had only recently learned to operate these weapons, probably made them miss as they fired on the low-flying aircraft.' When the U-2 was crossing Cuba and flew over Oriente, Castro said: 'A Soviet surface-to-air rocket battery fired on the plane and hit it.'

Fidel told me: 'It is still a mystery why it happened; we had no jurisdiction, no control over Soviet anti-aircraft weapons. We had simply presented our decision [to the Soviets], our opposition to low-level flights, and we ordered our batteries to fire on them. We could not fire against the U-2. But a Russian there – and for me it is still a mystery, I don't know whether the Soviet battery chief caught the spirit of our artillerymen and fired, too, or whether he received an order – did fire the rockets. This is something we do not know ourselves, and we didn't want to ask too much about it.'

I commented that the downing of the U-2 could have triggered a world war. Castro replied: 'I don't know what would have happened if the U-2s had flown over again, but I am absolutely certain that if the low-level flights had been resumed, we would have shot down one, two, or three of these planes . . . With so many batteries firing, we must have shot down some planes. I don't know whether this would have started a nuclear war.' He said the planes did not return the following day because the Soviet–American agreement was reached, but they did come back several days later in low-level flights.

Castro said that Soviet Deputy Premier Mikoyan was already in Havana 'to explain all this to us, and we warned him that we did not accept low-level flights under any circumstances. We told the Soviets that although the accord had been reached, we would still fire against low-flying aircraft, and we gave orders accordingly to our batteries. A contact between the Soviets and the Americans may have occurred that day, in which they suggested to them not to fly. I was at the San Antonio air force base, where we had some batteries, and that was where every day at 10 a.m. American planes had flown over. I went there, and I waited for the planes. I knew there would be a counter-strike if we fired, and that possibly we would have many casualties. I thought it was my duty to be there, in a place that surely would be attacked, but the planes did not come that day.'

Fidel sounded almost wistful. But he lived up to his concept of military honour: four days after the U-2 was shot down by the Soviet battery, Castro ordered that the body of the pilot, Major Rudolph Anderson, be returned to the United States for dignified burial at home. Ironically, Major Anderson was one of the two U-2 pilots who, on 14 October, had brought back the first photographs of the Soviet missile deployment in Cuba; the crisis was set in motion by these photographs.

Fidel Castro never concealed his 'irritation', as he put it, with the Soviet Union for having struck a deal with the United States to repatriate the missiles without consulting him. The rancour was still there when he was telling me the crisis story twenty-two years later, remarking that 'it had really never crossed my mind that the expedient of withdrawing the missiles was conceivable'. Although Castro said that in the end he understood why Moscow had removed the missiles – because of their nuclear inferiority of which he had not been aware – and that the Russians had been right, 'we were irritated for a long time'. He then volunteered the further remark, never before publicly uttered by him, that 'this incident, in certain ways, damaged relations between Cubans and the Soviets for a number of years – many years elapsed'. Despite surface displays of friendship and mutual high-level visits, relations remained tense, difficult and fragile until 1969 – six long years – and they never really returned to the situation of trust which Castro had had in the Soviet Union prior to the October crisis. And Soviet failure to react meaningfully to the United States invasion of Grenada in October 1983, twenty-two years later, when American and Cuban troops found themselves in combat for the first time in history, produced a new explosion of Castro's rage against the Russians.

Recalling his reaction to the missile crisis settlement, Castro said: 'I never considered the withdrawal solution. Perhaps in the revolutionary fervour, passion, the fever of those days, we did not consider possible the removal of the missiles once they were established here.' Yes, he added, 'there certainly were some communications between us and the Soviets, but in the last two days, after the plane was shot down, events moved so rapidly that it was not possible for prior discussions to be held between us about their decision to withdraw the missiles. But we were really very irritated that an agreement was reached without our participation, or any consultation with us . . . We were informed when the accord had already virtually been concluded.' Castro told me that had he been consulted, 'I think I would have understood the necessity of finding a solution, but we would have demanded at least three things: the cessation of aggression against Cuba, the cessation of the [economic] blockade by the United States, and the disbanding of the Guantánamo naval base. These would have been conditions that were perfectly understandable and acceptable.'

What Castro did not know at the time – as he told me – was that a secret part of the Kennedy–Krushchev deal in 1962 provided for the removal of US Jupiter nuclear missiles from Turkey in exchange for the Soviet repatriation of its missiles from Cuba. All Castro knew was that Krushchev was taking away his nuclear weapons to avert a global war and in return for guarantees from President Kennedy that the United States would not invade Cuba. Inasmuch as the entire missile adventure had been undertaken by Krushchev and Castro to protect Cuba from an American invasion, it had achieved its objective. Fidel nevertheless took the view that so long as his fate was being negotiated, he was entitled to try for political bonuses. As he told me, 'An honourable accord could have resolved once and for all the questions that would continue to poison relationships between the United States and Cuba for a long time.' Castro's point was well taken, but the Soviets at that stage had become more interested in getting the Jupiters out of Turkey, and were not prepared to press Kennedy for more concessions.

Castro said that all the terms of the October agreement, including the secret clauses on the Turkish missiles and a formal no-invasion guarantee for Cuba, are contained in documents exchanged between Kennedy and Krushchev. But, he remarked, 'nothing was said about the Turkish missiles in the weeks following the crisis. It was kept behind a mantle of silence, and we did not know that the withdrawal of missiles from Turkey was part of the accord.'

I asked how long he had been kept in the dark, and Castro replied that it was until he had gone to visit the Soviet Union in late April 1963. He said: 'One day, Nikita is reading to me all the documents that had been exchanged between the United States and the Soviet Union. Then he says: "In the American document they say they have made such and such commitments, and, besides they have made the commitment to withdraw their missiles from Turkey." And this was when I learned that the missiles in Turkey were in the agreement, and that they had actually been removed. But this was never discussed because the Americans had asked the Soviets not to make public this part of the compromise.' Castro was right. The Jupiter missiles, which were obsolete, were removed from Turkey during late April 1963 without any public announcement. Over the years the pull-out became generally known, but the United States government did not declassify the pertinent documents until 1985 – nearly two years after Castro told me the October story. The full exchange of documents with the Kremlin on the settlement of the crisis is expected to remain classified indefinitely.

In the meantime, although there is nothing on the public record to confirm the existence of an *explicit* commitment by Kennedy not to invade Cuba, Castro insists that the commitment is 'explicit, not implicit', and that the proof of its validity is that there has never since been an invasion attempt against Cuba. Under the Kennedy-Krushchev agreement the withdrawal of the missiles from Cuba was to be subject to United Nations inspection, but Castro furiously rejected this on the ground that it violated Cuban sovereignty. U Thant, the UN Secretary General, was unable to budge Castro during a special trip to Havana and, in the end, the inspection was carried out by United States aircraft from Guantánamo flying low over Soviet ships displaying the missiles on their decks. Castro's refusal to accept United Nations inspection led the Kennedy administration to become publicly vague on the non-invasion pledge; as Arthur M. Schlesinger Jr, the historian of the Kennedy era, has written, 'the guarantee never went into formal effect'. After Krushchev brought back home his IL-28 bombers from Cuba (another source of anger for Castro) in November, Kennedy stated 'If all offensive weapons are removed from Cuba and kept out of the hemisphere in the future, under adequate verification and safeguards, and if Cuba is not used for the export of aggressive Communist purposes, there will be peace in the Caribbean.'

While the missiles were being shipped out of Cuba, Castro contrived to balance his private ire at Krushchev with public assurances that all was well between the two countries. His economy was in appalling shape (there had even been anti-regime demonstrations over food shortages earlier in 1962), he needed to raise sugar production very substantially, and he had to have fresh resources for the first four-year economic plan that had just been launched with a commitment to invest $1 billion in industrial and farm development. Krushchev's deal with Kennedy brought Castro unsolicited support from China, Cuba being portrayed as a victim of Soviet betrayal, but it was on Moscow that he depended for basic assistance. Therefore Castro went before the television cameras on 1 November to proclaim: 'We are Marxist–Leninists . . . There will be no breach between the Soviet Union and Cuba.' But Anastas Mikoyan who arrived in Havana on 2 November to pacify Castro, received bitter recriminations from the Maximum Leader. Fidel greeted him at the airport, but refused to see him for weeks, until finally the elderly deputy premier had to plead for a meeting so that he could return to Moscow for his wife's funeral. He stayed in Havana for over three weeks. And so unhappy was the whole mood that Ambassador Alexeiev, who considered himself Castro's friend, is said to have wept during conversations with him.

Although the relationship with the Kremlin had to be the centrepiece of Castro's foreign policy, he never lost sight of the possibility of some form of accommodation with the United States. Castro has said that the settlement of the missile crisis could have included adjustments in Cuban–American relations and, indeed, it may have been a lost opportunity. In our 1984 conversations he remarked: 'The removal of the missiles should have permitted Kennedy to make some small concessions to Cuba that would have eliminated many of the obstacles that ever since have remained in the way of good relations between the United States and Cuba.'

Speaking of the message from Kennedy brought to him by Jean Daniel on the day of the president's assassination, Castro told me: 'Kennedy would not have received a rebuff from us . . . I was meditating and thinking very seriously, and I was considering a constructive and positive answer . . . At that moment we could perhaps have begun a dialogue, an exchange of impressions . . . After the 1962 crisis Kennedy had the authority, he had the will. . .'

Fidel's judgement was perceptive. The crisis led to the dismantling of Operation Mongoose (though the CIA went on for years attempting to assassinate Castro), and until his death Kennedy maintained interest in a possible peace overture to Cuba. Even before Jean Daniel went to Havana the president was considering sending a secret emissary of his own to see Castro, and the National Security Council staff was exploring possible 'channels of communication with Castro'. As Arthur Schlessinger has observed, in 1963 'the White House [was] drifting towards accommodation. But John Kennedy's death in November froze prospects for Cuban–American diplomacy for nearly fifteen years. Through an incredible irony, the CIA officer in charge of planning the current attempt to kill Castro had met with the prospective murderer in Paris on the day Kennedy was assassinated in Dallas. The president had never been apprised of the continuing plot against Fidel.

If the Soviet Union was vital for Cuba's economic survival, the Russians needed the Cubans politically – and even militarily. In the light of the deepening ideological conflict with China and its impact on Soviet standing in the Third World, the Kremlin could not afford a break with revolutionary Cuba. The removal of the missiles had already caused the Russians considerable embarrassment internationally, and a reaffirmation of friendship with Cuba was now a top priority for Krushchev. The marriage of convenience between Castro and Krushchev had reached such extraordinary importance that in the name of 'internationalist and socialist solidarity' they staged an unprecedented spectacular around the Cuban leader's visit in the spring of 1963 to the Soviet Union. His visit lasted forty days, unquestionably a record in the annals of international travel by chiefs of governments.

Left behind in Cuba in charge of the country were Raúl Castro and the Revolutionary Armed Forces, now better trained and equipped than ever. A military consolation prize for the Cubans after the departure of the nuclear missiles was SAM batteries (enabling them to shoot down marauding U-2 spy planes, if they wished) to which the United States did not object because of their strictly defensive character. What the United States did not know at first (and managed to forget afterwards) was that a Soviet Army combat brigade remained on the island following the repatriation of some 20,000 other troops who had accompanied the missiles. The brigade was meant as a symbol of continuing Soviet commitment to the active defence of Cuba, and Castro described it to a visiting American journalist in 1964 as 'a solid Russian combat force'.

Actually, this force numbered between 4000 and 5000 men (in addition to military advisers, also in the thousands), and nobody seemed to pay much attention to it until the brigade was 'discovered' by the Carter administration in 1979, causing such executive disarray that the president was too scared to submit the new strategic arms limitation treaty (SALT II) with the Soviets to Senate ratification. Cuba seemed able to affect American policies in the most obscure ways, and Castro told me with a chuckle when I asked him about the brigade during one of our conversations in Havana in January 1984 that 'this is only the brigade the Russians left behind in 1962'. It must have been the second or third generation of Soviet soldiers stationed in Cuba.

To set the tone for Castro's trip to the Soviet Union, Krushchev had delivered a speech in Moscow at the end of February, declaring that an 'imperialist' attack on Cuba or any other socialist country would mean the start of World War Three. On 26 April Castro and a vast entourage boarded the giant Soviet TU-114 turboprop airliner for the non-stop flight from Havana to Murmansk, the northern Russian port This was a regular Aeroflot route inaugurated in January, but this time Fidel almost did not make it. When the TU-114 reached Murmansk the following day, the fog was so dense that the airport had to be closed. There was not enough fuel left to look for alternative fields, however, so the pilot was forced to land at the Murmansk airport in zero visibility, and with inadequate instrument-landing-system facilities. But he did it perfectly and, once more, Fidel Castro had embarked on a new adventure in a dramatic fashion. Mikoyan, for whom Cuba and Castro had become practically a full-time occupation, was on hand to welcome the visitor – and Fidel, now wearing a fur hat, went directly from the plane to a mass rally. His speech (in Spanish) was short – he said that 'we've encountered temperatures to which we are not used: lots of cold outside, but plenty of warmth inside our hearts!' – and the people of Murmansk naturally loved it.

During his forty days in the Soviet Union Castro visited fourteen cities, from Central Asia to Siberia, from the Ukraine to Georgia, and from Moscow to Leningrad; inspected the Northern Fleet and a strategic forces rocket base; delivered countless speeches at sports stadiums, factories, battlefields and town squares; reviewed the May Day Parade from the top of the Kremlin Wall, received the title of Hero of the Soviet

Union, the Order of Lenin and the Gold Star; attended the Bolshoi Ballet
in Moscow and an open-air concert; and spent scores of hours publicly
and privately with Nikita Krushchev. The two of them spoke at a special
mass rally in Red Square, an unusual honour for a foreigner, but Castro
also had the opportunity of meeting quietly other top Soviet leaders. At a
dacha near Moscow he joked and chatted with Leonid Brezhnev, the man
who would oust and replace Krushchev the following year – in part
because of the Cuban missile humiliation. A photograph at the *dacha*
shows Krushchev and Brezhnev in stodgy suits and ties, with rows of
medals on their lapels, and Castro in his usual olive-green battle fatigues.
    The tour was a phenomenal success: no foreigner had ever been
received in such a grandiose fashion since the Great Patriotic War. The
crowds and television audiences were fascinated by the romantic guerrilla
fighter from the far-away Cuban mountains, and they all adored the
spectacle. Krushchev accompanied him to Murmansk for the flight home
at the end of May. Fidel had never before received such attention and on
such a scale. But he never lowered his political guard, quietly conveying
to his hosts his economic aid requirements, insisting on his independence,
and neatly keeping off balance the revolutionary factions at home. On the
one hand, as if to enhance the *Fidelismo* of the revolution, he had made
sure not a single 'old' Communist accompanied him on the Soviet tour
(not even the ever-mediating Carlos Rafael Rodríguez). On the other
hand he launched a savage public attack on *Revolución*, the organ of the
Fidelista movement, for the way it reported his Soviet trip. He criticized it
for an article comparing him to Lenin in terms of the adulation he found
in the Soviet Union, and for reporting 'amusing' details that he thought
detracted from the significance of the visit, and his message was clear
when he stated in all seriousness that *Pravda* was the best newspaper in the
world. Clearly, it was a warning to the remaining 'moderates' of the
revolution grouped around the *Fidelista* newspaper. The following year
Revolución was merged with the Communist paper *Hoy* to become the
regime's chief mouthpiece under the name of *Granma* and under hard-line
Communist editors. *Granma* now rivals *Pravda* in quality, especially
through the generous use of red ink.

After five years of the revolution, Fidel Castro had established himself as
the undisputed, powerful, ruthless, imaginative and unpredictable leader
of a country now edging towards a Communist system of life and
government. He continued to command great national support – often
national adoration. At the time of the exiles' invasion, Cubans had rallied
around their country's flag – and their Maximum Leader – as American
warplanes roared over the countryside.
    Above all, Castro knew how to keep the nation's faith alive and
engender hope in the midst of hardship and sacrifice. When Hurricane

Flora, one of the worst hurricanes of this century, flattened and flooded the island during 1963, Fidel Castro was everywhere, directing rescue operations, taking chances, leading and inspiring. Despite massive Soviet aid, the economy was performing appallingly below standard, but what Castro made his people remember was that they were being educated, fed, housed, protected and cared for by the revolution as Cubans had never been before. Therefore they were in the main loyal to the revolution, grateful to the commander-in-chief, and ready to ferret out counter-revolutionary 'worms', patrol the cities and the farms at night, and be indoctrinated to the point of numbness in the mysterious phrases of Marxism–Leninism.

When at the end of 1963 Castro told Cubans that not only would the economy be geared again to sugar production, but that a ten-million-ton harvest (the 1963 production was 3.8 million, and the all-time record 6.7 million) was planned for 1970, the people trusted his judgement. It would mean 'voluntary' work on weekends for students and city dwellers to help their peasant brethren, but it would be for the good of the revolution, and therefore it was the proper thing. Besides, it was unwise to complain or shirk revolutionary duty: one's fellow revolutionaries had sharp eyes and keen ears.

As the first quinquennium of the revolution drew to a close, Castro and Cuba were essentially set on a firm course. Fidel, now thirty-seven years old, knew precisely where he was leading the nation. Having survived the Bay of Pigs and the missile crisis, the revolutionary regime was as secure from external threat as any government in the world – or more so. Survival in the long run was, in effect, guaranteed by the Soviet Union because history and Fidel Castro left the Russians no political alternatives in a rivalry-ridden world.

His own life was still that of a *guerrillero*, restless, impatient, eager to conquer, unorthodox, sharp-shooting. Celia Sánchez was succeeding in making his activities more orderly, but even so he despised schedules and hated office work. He was still hugely enjoying himself. Fidelito, at sixteen, was preparing for the university and then for studies in the Soviet Union. In August 1963 Fidel's mother, Lina Ruz de Castro, died at their family home in Birán, and the clan gathered for the funeral. Afterwards Castro addressed a rally on Birán's main street.

In the next two decades Fidel Castro would maintain the rhythm of revolutionary life he had imposed on Cuba, but with few great surprises ahead in terms of his own behaviour and attitudes – or in organizing the new society. He would strive to consolidate Cuba ideologically under the banner of a ruling Communist Party that he would head. He would continue with reforms where anything was left to be reformed (the third agrarian reform in October 1963 limited individual holdings to 168 acres, with the state owning 70 per cent of the land), he would practise

'internationalism' throughout the Third World by helping revolutionaries everywhere and dispatching Cuban combat troops across the seas,
and he would seek for himself the role of a world statesman. And he
would lose Che Guevara.

Part Five

The Maturity
(1964–86)

Chapter 1

The death of Ernesto Che Guevara in the Bolivian jungle on 8 October 1967, climaxing the destruction of his guerrilla movement there, was a central drama in the history of the Cuban revolution in the 1960s. Despite the many unresolved mysteries surrounding Che's presence and death in Bolivia, his ultimate disappearance had a profound impact on the evolution of Fidel Castro's domestic and international policies. It even helped Castro to settle his disputes with the Soviet Union, festering since the 1962 missile crisis, inasmuch as in the name of romantic revolutionary purity Che had become an inconveniently severe critic of the Russians for their 'internationalist' timidity and their 'imperialist' way of managing economic aid to the Third World. Finally, Che Guevara was the last totally independent spirit in the increasingly rigid power structure built by and around Castro. He had vanished from Cuba in the early part of 1965, for reasons never adequately explained, and therefore did not participate in the final stages of formalizing the establishment of Communist rule in Cuba through the creation of the new party under Castro.

There must be powerful reasons for Castro's refusal, even now, nearly twenty years after the fact, to throw any light on Che's decision to sever his ties with Cuba and therefore with Fidel himself. The only explanation offered is Che Guevara's letter to him saying that 'other hills of the world demand the aid of my modest efforts' and renouncing all his positions in Cuba, as well as his Cuban citizenship, that Castro read before a stunned assembly of the 'new' Communist leaders in Havana on 3 October 1965. The occasion was the presentation of the membership list of the Central Committee of the freshly-organized Cuban Communist Party – the creation of the party had been announced only the day before – and there was an awkward silence after Fidel said that the only deserving name missing from the roster was Che's and then proceeded to read the letter.

Cuban newsreels show Castro immensely ill at ease and clearly unhappy
as he reads; this turned out to be the last thing Fidel would say publicly
about Guevara's whereabouts until 15 October 1967 – two years later –
when he went on television to announce that the news of Che's death was
'unfortunately true'.

That Guevara had left the Cuban scene had been confirmed by Castro
as early as 20 April 1965, when he tersely told foreign newsmen that
'*Comandante* Guevara is where he is most useful to the revolution'.
Guevara had returned on 15 March from his latest tour of Africa and Asia,
being received at the airport by Castro and President Dorticós, but he was
not seen again, and journalists began inquiring about his whereabouts. It
is therefore unknown exactly when he left Cuba, as well as when he
wrote his farewell letter to Fidel. But there is no reason to doubt the
authenticity of this missive, with its assertion that 'I feel that I have
fulfilled the part of my duty that tied me to the Cuban revolution in its
territory, and I bid farewell to you and the *companeros*, your people who
are already mine' and that 'my only serious shortcoming was not to have
trusted in you more from the first moments in the Sierra Maestra and not
to have understood soon enough your qualities as a leader and a
revolutionary'. Not only is the style pure Guevara, but it was also in
character for him to mention, in the revolutionary spirit of self-criticism,
his Sierra 'shortcoming', which was his doubt, expressed in a letter,
about Castro's honesty in his dealings with exiled anti–Batista politicians
late in 1957. Finally, there would have been no need to forge such a letter
at that time, two years before Che's death.

Simultaneously, Che had written to his parents in Buenos Aires that
'once again I feel beneath my heels the ribs of Rosinante . . . I return to the
road with my lance under my arm.' He reminded them that over ten years
earlier he had written 'another letter of farewell' – leaving Argentina he
wrote, 'Here goes a soldier of the Americas' – and that now 'my Marxism
has taken deep root and become purified . . . I believe in armed struggle
as the only solution for those people who fight to liberate themselves . . .
Once in a while, remember this small *condottiere* of the twentieth century.'
Ernesto Guevara Lynch, Che's father, told me in Havana in 1985 that he
had taken the letter at face value, understanding his son's restlessness.
But, he said, that was all he knew, not having seen Che since 1961. Most
probably, Fidel Castro is the only person who knows the full truth.

Castro knows, for example, why Che chose Bolivia for his new
guerrilla enterprise, improbable as the choice was, given the fact that he
fought in terrible mountain and jungle territory where he did not speak
local Indian languages (Andean peasants seldom know Spanish), instead
of in Salta province in his native Argentina where we know he had
originally hoped to start a revolution. The Bolivian mission was more
suicidal even than the *Granma* landing a decade earlier, but Fidel evidently

went along with the idea, at least to the extent of assigning Rebel Army fighters to Che's guerrilla detachment, equipping and financing the expedition, and maintaining regular radio contact with Guevara until the end. And perhaps Castro should have guessed that Che would, indeed, be betrayed by the Moscow-oriented Bolivian Communist Party, which virtually delivered Guevara to the Bolivian Army rangers and its CIA advisers.

In retrospect it is understandable that there really was not much left for Che to do in Cuba after the consolidation of the revolution. He remained Minister of Industry, but on fundamental issues of economic development in a Marxist context he was very much at odds with Castro. In an oversimplified fashion their difference was centred on Che's idealistic belief in moral incentives for the population and Castro's more practical conclusion that material incentives, such as higher wages and bonuses, were more effective. For a time in the early 1960s Che's view prevailed, but then Fidel, in effect, overruled him. None of this, of course, has ever been publicly debated or reported in Cuba, but Castro has provided the best clue to the ideological convulsions of those days in a reply he gave me during a conversation in 1984, when I asked him what errors the revolution had committed. He was surprisingly candid as he talked during that Havana dawn in his office about the trajectory of the revolution, and the awesome problems of creating a new society. He was pensive, stroking his beard slowly as he spoke.

'At the outset of the revolution,' he said, 'when we had to assume all the functions of the state and all the functions of the economy . . . we began this task without experts, just ignorant people who did not know what had to be done . . . Our economic development had highs and lows, but it was sustained development, reaching an average of 4.7 per cent in twenty-five years. It was slow in the first years, when our objective was fundamentally to survive rather than to develop, but it accelerated in subsequent years. We passed through different stages. We suffered the consequences of different errors. Let us say that one error we committed was to want to jump stages, wanting to arrive at Communist forms of [wealth] distribution, jumping over socialist forms of distribution – and it is impossible to jump stages. The Communist formula is: each must give according to his capacity and receive according to his needs. The socialist one is: each must give according to his capacity and receive according to his work . . . We were marching too rapidly towards Communist formulas. It was a jump, and it created problems. But we rectified it in time.'

Castro then went on to explain how, in the 1980s, a blend of Communism and socialism existed in Cuba, and 'many things are distributed in a Communist form'. This was his definition of Cuban Marxism–Leninism: 'I think that salaries are paid according to work and personal capacity. But education, for example, universal and generalized is free, and is a Communist type of service. The same possibilities for education are offered to the son of an engineer and the son of a worker, the son of a father who works hard, and the son of a father who works little . . . Medical services are received in an egalitarian form by the whole population, that is, a Communist-type service . . . We start from the belief that, according the ideas of Marx, Engels and Lenin, Communism is the final objective, but there is the stage of socialism. This formula is not applied in a chemically pure fashion . . . In salaries, what is paid a worker is *not* according to the needs he has. There are workers who have one or two children, and they may earn twice what is earned by a worker who has three, four or five children because their contribution through work and their capacities are greater. So, this is not Communist distribution. The Communist system would be to pay more to the worker who has seven children than the worker who has one child . . . In the socialist formula, the worker who has more capacity, even though he has less necessity, is paid more. In a harbour, a worker who can load, say twenty tons in a ship receives more than the worker who can load ten tons. There was a time when we paid the same to the worker who carried twenty tons and the one who carried ten or five tons. This was an error. It doesn't really stimulate work.'

Castro never suggested that Che Guevara might have inspired such errors, but they were 'rectified', as he put it, in the mid-1960s. This coincided with Che's gradual withdrawal from economic policy-making, and his growing concentration on contacts with the Third World, evidently in concurrence with Castro. Guevara seemed to enjoy this mission, seeing it through the prism of revolution-making, and the contribution Cubans could offer. This was the impression I gained when I spent some hours with him – for the last time – in December 1964, in New York when he came to address the United Nations General Assembly. After we appeared together on a television interview programme, we chatted for several hours about Cuba and the Third World; the next day Che left for Africa and Communist China in what would be his farewell world tour on behalf of the Cuban revolution.

This was a time of continuing – as well as of additional – tensions between Fidel Castro and the Soviet Union, and the 'old' Communists at home.

Nevertheless, a public display of fraternal love was maintained by both sides. In December 1963 Nikolai Podgorny, a powerful member of the Soviet Politburo, came to Cuba for a two-week visit, the highest-ranking Kremlin figure to appear in Havana up to then. On 12 January Castro flew with Podgorny to Moscow where he conferred at length with Krushchev and Leonid Brezhnev: ten days later the Russians signed an agreement with him to purchase the bulk of the Cuban sugar harvest for the next five years with a guaranteed minimum price – above the world market. Then Che Guevara signed an accord on technical assistance, and the two Cuban leaders went home, apparently satisfied with their achievements.

Two months later, however, Fidel Castro orchestrated the trial of Marcos Rodríguez, the pro-Communist student who, in 1957, had betrayed four of his companions in a conspiracy against Batista. They were murdered by the Batista police in the famous Humboldt Street Crime, and it later developed that Rodríguez was, in effect, being protected by key members of the 'old' Communist party. It was Faure Chomón Mediavilla, formerly the leader of the Students' Revolutionary Directorate to which the four assassinated youths belonged, who produced the evidence against Rodríguez, a fact rendered especially interesting because he was currently Cuba's ambassador to Moscow. In terms of internal Cuban politics a Rodríguez trial inevitibly revived all the *Fidelista* resentments against the Communists and the Russians, and Castro chose to let it happen. He may have decided to use the Rodríguez affair as another warning to the 'old' Communists not to try to repeat their previous 'sectarianism' as the new party was about to be launched; in any event, the trial, held during March 1964, was a Byzantine event highlighted by an immensely confusing courtroom speech by Castro. He succeeded in clearing the party of actual guilt, but left enough of its officials besmirched; Rodríguez was sentenced to death on two occasions (the second time on appeal, suggested by Fidel) and executed.

During the summer of 1964 Castro threw out hints – mainly through newspaper interviews – of his interest in improved relations with the United States, inaugurating a pattern that was to continue for the next twenty years, a pattern of always leaving the door open to some accommodation with Washington while keeping his reliance on the Soviets for military and economic survival. In mid-1964, for example, Fidel was showing this new interest in dealing with the United States even though he was investing resources in revolutionary conspiracies around Latin America (though not very successfully) and simultaneously being the target of harsh pressures by the Johnson administration. American U-2 spy planes were again overflying the island, and the CIA was back in the assassination business.

(Ramiro Valdés told me in an interview in mid-1985, when he still served as Interior Minister, that 1964 and 1965 were the years when most of the CIA assassination attempts, perhaps as many as thirty, had occurred. He said that the only attempt that nearly succeeded was the occasion in 1964, when Fidel stopped, as he often did, for a milkshake at the cafeteria at the Habana Libre Hotel. The CIA had discovered this habit, and suborned a cafeteria employee to put cyanide in the milkshake from a capsule it had delivered to the man. The next time Castro arrived

at the cafeteria and ordered the milkshake, the employee took the capsule
out of the refrigerator where he kept it to put it in the drink, But, Valdés
said, 'the capsule was frozen and it broke, and the man couldn't slip it into
the milkshake. It seems he was very nervous. And, you know, cyanide is
lethal poison; it would have instantly killed Fidel . . . This was the closest
it ever came.')

Castro's overtures to the United States led nowhere, but in October
1964, he was suddenly faced with a new set of partners in Moscow. Just as
President Dorticós was visiting Moscow, Nikita Krushchev was fired by
the Central Committee and replaced by Brezhnev as general secretary of
the Communist Party, Alexei Kosygin as Premier, and Nikolai
Podgorny as Chief of State. In November Che Guevara flew to Moscow
for what turned out to be his final visit there as well as the confirmation of
his growing suspicions that the Soviet Union no longer stood for real
revolution. But for Castro, who had the immediate responsibility of
keeping Cuba afloat, the question was whether the Brezhnev leadership
would continue Krushchev's policy of supporting the Cubans at all costs,
and he reasoned correctly that there was no reason for any change.

While failure to consult adequately his Politburo colleagues during the
Cuban missile crisis was one of the fifteen formal counts of charges
against Krushchev, and the whole Cuban adventure was one of the
principal reasons for his removal, it would make no sense to penalize
Castro who remained an extremely valuable ally and client in terms of
Soviet strategic interest. As Fidel remarked once in a private conversation, it was Krushchev's humiliation by Kennedy in Cuba that led to the
Soviet decision to embark on a crash programme of nuclear armament to
catch up with the United States. Krushchev wrote in his memoirs that
'the experience of the Caribbean crisis also convinced us that we were
right to concentrate on the manufacture of nuclear missiles . . . When we
created missiles which America and the whole world knew could deliver
a crushing blow anywhere on the globe – that represented a triumph in
the battle . . . in defending the security of our homeland.'

Meanwhile, Castro decided to demonstrate his independence by not
rushing to Moscow to congratulate Brezhnev on his elevation to power;
such hurry befitted Communist satellite leaders in Eastern Europe and
Asia, not a Cuban revolutionary chief. In fact, Fidel waited eight years
before his next voyage to Moscow. As he had told me, many years
elapsed before Cuban–Soviet relations were restored to the genuine
cordiality that had preceded the missile crisis. Instead, Raúl Castro was
given the job of conducting the high-level contacts at the Kremlin; he saw
Brezhnev for the first time on 2 April 1965, and went on visiting Moscow
on average twice a year. President Dorticós went there four times
between 1964 and 1971, and Premier Kosygin visited Havana in 1967 and
1971. But after 1965 permanent contact between Cuba and the Soviet

Union was established only on the level of deputy premiers; Carlos Rafael Rodríguez has had this responsibility for over twenty years, and Deputy Premier Vladimir Novikov finally replaced Mikoyan. More recently, Deputy Premier Ivan Arjipov inherited this responsibility.

Throughout the 1960s one underlying issue between the Cubans and the Soviet Union was that of Third World revolutions. It was in this area that Che Guevara had played a crucial intellectual and inspirational role, convinced that the responsibility of a triumphant revolution is to spawn revolutions elsewhere (Che being too subtle, however, to imitate Trotsky's 'permanent revolution' rhetoric). Guevara and Castro had shared this view from their first meeting in Mexico, and together sought to put it into effect as soon as they had seized power.

To Guevara the concept was ideological, romantic and mystical. To Castro it was more practical, at least partly motivated by his awareness that the Cuban revolution would be more secure if it were successfully repeated elsewhere in Latin America. But when he solemnly declared on 2 December 1961 that 'I am a Marxist–Leninist and I shall remain it until the last day of my life', he was committing himself to the revolutionary propagation of Marxism–Leninism throughout the Third World. In the early 1960s this was the significance of Castro's support for the emerging guerrillas in Venezuela (after the failure of his earlier revolutionary expeditions around the Caribbean) and of Che Guevara's advice to the leftists in Congo-Brazzaville and to the Frelimo guerrillas of Mozambique.

None of this, however, pleased the Soviet leadership. Thinking in cautious superpower terms, they prefered traditional 'unified front' coalitions of local Communists with the 'progressive bourgeoisie' in the Third World rather than unpredictable revolutions. Curiously, the Soviets were applying moderate 'Euro-Communism' political tactics to the Third World, always careful not to excessively challenge the United States. Moreover, they were concerned that sudden successful revolutions might be taken over by China, the Kremlin's newest arch-enemy. In the case of Cuba, therefore, the Soviets discouraged its revolutionary impulses in the direction of Latin America or Africa; most ironically, Moscow disliked Cuba's 'export of revolutions' quite as much as Washington feared it.

To show their displeasure the Russians harassed Castro with long delays in the signing of annual economic aid agreements (they were called 'trade agreements') as well as in the delivery of such vitally needed commodities as petroleum. The Soviet intention was to bring Castro back to his senses if not to his knees – and Fidel responded with typical gestures of independence, such as his creation of new mechanisms for encouraging revolutions, and his refusal to visit Brezhnev in Moscow.

But it was Che Guevara who took it upon himself to deliver a public attack on Soviet behaviour. In his last public speech, an address on 24 February 1965 to the Economic Seminar of Afro–Asian Solidarity in Algiers, Guevara, in effect, accused Moscow of being as bad as the 'imperialists' in its treatment of the struggling new countries.

Che's first point was that 'the development of countries which start on the road of liberation must be underwritten by socialist countries', and he took the Russians to task for imposing excessively harsh terms on the recipients of their largesse. 'There should be no more of the talk of developing mutually beneficial trade based on prices, that the law of value and unequal international trade relations imposes on backward countries,' Guevara said. 'If we establish that type of relationship between the two groups of nations, we must agree that the socialist countries are, to a certain extent, accomplices in imperialist exploitation . . . It is a great truth, and it exposes the immoral character of the exchange. The socialist countries have a moral duty to end their tacit complicity with the exploiting countries of the West . . . There must be a great change of priorities on the level of international relations. Foreign trade must not determine politics, but on the contrary, it must be subordinated to a fraternal policy towards the people.'

This was not language that the Soviets would normally accept from a client state, but they could not afford an open break, and Guevara received no public response to his charges. Cuban support was important in the Soviets' rivalry with China, and clearly they were not going to make an issue of Che's maverick attitudes. Whatever Fidel thought of them, he made a point of greeting Che at the airport in Havana on 15 March, which was as much a gesture for the Soviets' benefit as for home consumption.

It was as this point, of course, that the thread was broken and Che was never again seen – except dead in Bolivia two and a half years later. What went on between Castro and Guevara is a mystery. Was there a breach in their friendship as has been alleged, and did Che really leave of his own volition? Given Fidel's character, it is unlikely that he would turn for political or ideological reasons against as loyal and intimate a companion as Guevara. Che certainly was not a rival. It is true, however, that in 1965 there really was no more place for him in the Cuban revolution. Fidel had opposed his plans for the economy, moving at the same time to resume his personal control of agriculture by returning to the presidency of INRA. Internationally, Che was losing his usefulness to Castro because the Communist community now regarded him with suspicion. In the absence of conclusive evidence to the contrary, it must be assumed that they jointly agreed on Guevara's permanent departure from Cuba. Apparently it happened on 1 April. And, indeed, it would be difficult to imagine Guevara today as an aging revolutionary, approaching the age of sixty in a position subordinate at least to Fidel and Raúl. Such a thought may well have crossed Che's proud and sensitive mind.

It would be wrong, however, to conclude that with Guevara's disappearance Fidel became more tractable in his relations with Moscow and its local friends. In November 1964, for example, he had fired Joaquín Ordoquí, an 'old' Communist leader, from the post of Deputy Defence Minister, and had him arrested with his wife, Edith García Buchaca. Both were involved in the 'sectarian' purge in 1962, and in the Rodríguez trial in March 1964, but Castro struck at them immediately after the change in leadership in the Kremlin, as if to remind the new men there not to interfere with Cuban Communist politics. The trade agreement for 1965 was signed on 17 February, well behind schedule, only a week before Che Guevara's denunciations in Algiers. Guevara was still abroad when Castro engaged in his own criticism of the Russians for not helping North Vietnam more effectively, and not reacting more forcefully against the American bombings that had begun there in February. 'We are in favour of giving Vietnam all the aid that may be necessary, we are in favour of this aid being arms and men, we are in favour of the socialist camp running risks that may be necessary for Vietnam,' he said in a speech on 13 March. And Castro abandoned his pro-Soviet stand in the Moscow–Peking dispute to protest, saying that 'even the attacks on North Vietnam have not had the effect of overcoming the divisions within the socialist family'.

Fidel naturally was helpless when the United States landed troops in the Dominican Republic in April 1965, intervening in the civil war there on the side of the local generals against left-of-centre defenders of constitutional government. President Lyndon Johnson had ordered the invasion to stem what he claimed to be a Communist threat, probably inspired from Cuba, but as usual it was Castro who derived the most political profit. He had nothing to do with the civil war (though the defeated constitutional leaders later established close links with him), and the spectacle of American troops fighting Dominicans had superb propaganda value for his 'anti-imperialist' strategies at home and abroad.

Both Vietnam and the Dominican Republic were most convenient as revolutionary arguments when Castro convoked the Tricontinental Conference in Havana in January 1966, to reach out for Third World leadership. The conference spawned OSPAAAL (Solidarity Organization of the Peoples of Africa, Asia and Latin America) and OLAS (Latin American Solidarity Organization), both with headquarters in the Cuban capital. Among those attending the conference was an Angolan rebel leader named Antônio Agostinho Neto, a poet who headed the Popular Movement for the Liberation of Angola (MPLA) in the independence war against Portugal. Neto, a remarkably gifted and intelligent man, became friends with Castro, and soon MPLA guerrillas began to be trained secretly on the Isle of Youth (Pines) along with a growing number of other African and Latin American revolutionary groups. These were the beginnings of Cuba's subsequent and massive military involvement in Angola and, later, Ethiopia. From Brazil the Cubans brought Francisco Julião, the leader of peasant leagues, demanding land reform in the drought-parched Brazilian north-east, but he never emerged as a great revolutionary.

A month after the Tricontinental Conference, the Soviet Union, swallowing its distaste for Castro's costly new revolutionary instruments, signed the 1966 trade agreement, bringing two-way commerce that year to $1 billion, a record figure, and granting Cuba $91 million in fresh credits. And shortly thereafter, in the course of 1967, Fidel had the satisfaction of denouncing the Soviet Union and being courted by it at the same time.

In a speech on 13 March, he attacked the Venezuelan Communist Party, which was loyal to Moscow, for its failure to help the guerrillas fighting the country's elected democratic government; the guerrillas were being betrayed, he charged. In April a session of the reconvened Tricontinental Conference in Havana received a message from Che Guevara, radioed from his Bolivian jungle hideout, with this exhortation: 'How close our bright future would be, should two, three, or many Vietnams flourish throughout the world with their share of deaths and their immense tragedies, their everyday tragedies, their everyday heroism and their repeated blows against imperialism.' In an implicit message to the Soviets Che remarked: 'The solidarity of all progressive forces of the world with the people of Vietnam is today similar to the bitter agony of the plebeians urging on the gladiators in the Roman arena. It is not a matter of wishing success to the victim of aggression, but of sharing his fate; one must accompany him to his death or to his victory.'

Undaunted, Soviet Premier Kosygin landed in Havana on 26 June, 1967, immediately after his summit meeting with President Johnson in Glassborough, New Jersey, to spend four days with Castro, a remarkable gesture of courtesy. But in his speech on 26 July Fidel informed the world that in the case of aggression, Cuba would fight alone and never accept a truce, an obvious allusion to the Soviet–American settlement of the 1962 missile crisis. Early in August, too, Castro presided over an OLAS conference of Latin Americans, repeating his attacks on the Venezuelan Communist Party, and charging that the Soviet Union was aiding and supporting reactionary governments in Latin America. He specifically mentioned Venezuela and Colombia (both with elected democratic governments and both fighting Cuban–inspired guerrilla movements), exclaiming indignantly that 'if internationalism exists, if solidarity is a word worthy of respect, the least that we can expect of any state in the socialist camp is that it refrain from giving any financial or technical aid to those regimes'. A resolution approved by the OLAS conference warned that revolutions and armed insurrection would occur even without Communist parties, and that, in effect, it was not necessary that revolutionary leadership be in Communist hands.

Now Fidel was clearly provoking the Russians – mainly, it seems for the sake of proving his revolutionary theory. He had nothing to gain from confrontation: he had already made his point so many times, the Russians had demonstrated patience they never had had with anyone else, and therefore there was no need to bait the bear. Yet it is a Castro trait to see how far he can go; first he had dared the Americans, now the Soviets.

On 9 October, Castro learned that Che Guevara had been killed and his body mutilated by Bolivian rangers. He proclaimed official mourning in Cuba, and one should not doubt his grief: he *was* immensely attached to Che notwithstanding whatever differences they might have had. Whether or not Guevara's death had any influence on the relations between Cuba and the Soviet Union, they hit rock bottom that autumn. Castro, in effect, ignored the fiftieth anniversary of the Russian Revolution by refusing to accept an invitation to go to Moscow, and sending instead a delegation headed by the Health Minister, José R. Machado Ventura (the previous year, Raúl Castro and President Dorticós had gone to Moscow for the anniversary). Fábio Grobart, the Polish-born co-founder of the old Cuban Communist Party – and not Castro – delivered the main speech at the Soviet anniversary celebrations in Havana. The Castro brothers, Dorticós and the rest of the leadership deigned to attend the reception at the Soviet embassy on 7 November, but they were greeted by the chargé d'affaires; the ambassador happened to be away in Moscow. Possibly the Soviets had decided that the time had come to teach Fidel Castro a lesson.

For Castro and for Cuba, 1968 was the worst year since the revolution: everything seemed to be coming apart, and only through the sheer force of his personality and the efficiency of his Security mechanisms was he able to prevent a complete collapse. In their own way, the challenges of 1968 were greater and more complex than the Bay of Pigs and the missile crisis because they dealt with the essence of revolutionary rule. Curiously, however, the Johnson administration was unaware of how extremely vulnerable Castro had become. Perhaps it was too distracted by the Tet Offensive in Vietnam and its aftermath to pay much attention to the little island in the Caribbean, hardly an imminent threat to the United States.

In tribute to Che Guevara, 1968 was designated as the 'Year of the Heroic *Guerrillero*,' and this was exactly what Fidel had to be at that juncture to survive. He had the worst of all possible worlds; while the

Cuban economy was tottering on the edge of catastrophe (the problem being that Castro had no coherent planning at all in the economic realm, only grandiose ambitions), he was antagonizing the Russians who were Cuba's last hope for saving the revolution. And, presumably to be consistent, he also crushed the supposedly pro-Soviet faction of the 'old' communists now incorporated in his brand-new Cuban Communist Party. In a conversation in August 1967 with K.S. Karol, a French left-wing journalist, Fidel said that 'in a year or two' Cuba could be self-sufficient economically because its exports would expand to the point where it would no longer depend on a single market and a single supplier. For this reason, Castro told Karol (whose name and books are banned in Cuba because of his 'leftist' criticisms of Fidel), he did not need to fear the loss of Soviet support as a consequence of his ideological independence. Reality, however, turned out to be quite different – and very painful.

The first reality was the state of the economy. Though Castro created JUCEPLAN, a central planning organ based on the Soviet model, as far back as 1960, he was personally responsible for its failure to plan adequately, since his impatience led him into continuous shifts between short-medium-and long-term planning as well as into endless improvisations. No policy was given reasonable time to produce results (or to be proved unsatisfactory), and political or visionary pressures pushed Castro into grandiose projects the economy could not possibly handle. The attempt to produce the largest sugar harvest in history in 1970 was a case in point. At the same time, large capital investments in development programmes that had not been adequately studied cost Cuba precious resources diverted from normal economic activities. Inevitably production dropped in all sectors, shortages became even more acute than before, and Cubans were exhorted (or forced) to sacrifice even more for the revolutionary future.

By 1968, Castro had personally taken over the planning and execution of economic policies, shutting off all alternative ideas and, naturally, brooking no argument. It was an intriguing turning point in his career. Now in his early forties, and no longer the young man of the Sierra, Fidel had become a total dogmatist, disregarding absolutely the experiences of other men and other societies, and also rejecting many Marxist views (to say nothing of Soviet views). When the Russians finally chose to impose their will on him, Fidel knew how to bend with the wind, suspending his displays of independence for as long as appeared prudent, but never abandoning his personal dogmatism, ever ready to reassert it. Meanwhile the economy approached bankruptcy. The ravages of Hurricane Inez in 1967, and of the great drought in 1968, aggravated the situation. Production everywhere in Cuba nearly ground to a halt: as René Dumont, the French agricultural specialist who was the most perceptive foreign observer of the Cuban scene in the late 1960s, remarked later;

'There was nothing to buy, for which reason there was no stimulus to work.' Elsewhere in the Communist world, notably in Hungary and Czechoslovakia, planners were just then beginning to experiment with market economies so that there would be something to buy. In Cuba, Castro seemed determined to prove that to go backward in Marxist economic history represented progress.

On 13 March 1968, the anniversary of the students' attack on the Batista palace, Castro proclaimed a new radical revolution in Cuba, which in a sense was his equivalent of the Chinese Cultural Revolution that was just then beginning to wind down. Although Cuba had no Red Guards and no blood was shed, Fidel moved to nationalize the entire retail trade sector still in private hands – businesses ranging from auto mechanics' repair shops to small stores, cafés and sandwich and ice-cream street vendors – for reasons of ideology. Like Mao Tse Tung, Castro must have felt that revolutionary fervour was fading among his people, and that a powerful injection of radicalism was needed to make the juices flow again. He called his policy the Great Revolutionary Offensive, imposing revolutionary purity by eliminating the remnants of the 'bourgeoisie' he so despised, and mobilizing Cuban manpower on a gigantic scale (voluntary extra work by everybody) for agricultural production, and especially the record sugar harvest he was planning for 1970.

This latest milestone of the revolution was unveiled by Fidel in one of his most intricate (and long) speeches, a discourse he delivered at Havana University before an audience of hundreds of thousands. He listed, mostly from memory, massive statistics on milk production and imports, province-by-province rainfall measurements, the price of sugar over the past sixteen years, rising egg production, population growth, fish catch, gross national product comparisons worldwide, per capita incomes, economic development investments, food distribution from schools to workers' dining rooms, education and sports. This economic state-of-the-union message, emphasizing the impressive revolutionary conquests in the social realm, then turned into a bitter indictment of 'those who do not work, the loafers, the parasites, the privileged, and a certain kind of exploiter that still remains in our country'.

Castro is a master at the use of big and obscure facts and statistics to score political points, heaping scorn and ridicule on the objects of his attacks, and vastly amusing his audience in the process. On this ocasion he reported that in Havana 'there still are nine hundred and fifty-five privately owned bars, making money right and left, consuming supplies', which he described as 'an incredible thing' after nine years of the revolution. He went on for nearly an hour reciting the results of investigations of these bars and other private businesses, offering such conclusions as that 'the data gathered on hot dog stands . . . showed that a

great number of people who intend to leave the country are engaged in
this type of business, which not only yields high profits but permits them
to be in constant contact with *lumpen* and other anti-social and counter-
revolutionary elements'. Pursuing this linkage between hot dogs and
counter-revolution, Fidel informed his listeners that 'the greatest
percentage of those not integrated into the revolution was among the
owners of hot dog stands; of forty-one individuals who answered this
item, thirty-nine, or 95.1 per cent, were counter-revolutionary'. As the
crowd laughed and applauded, Castro exclaimed: 'Are we going to
construct socialism, or are we going to construct vending stands?. . . We
did not make a revolution here to establish the right to trade! Such a
revolution took place in 1789 – that was the era of the bourgeois
revolution, it was the revolution of the merchants, of the bourgeois.
When will they finally understand that this is a revolution of socialists,
that is a revolution of Communists . . . that nobody shed his blood here
fighting against the tyranny, against mercenaries, against bandits, in
order to estabish the right for somebody to make two hundred pesos
selling rum, or fifty pesos selling fried eggs or omelettes. . .'

Then the crowd roared its approval when Castro announced that
'clearly and definitely we must say that we propose to eliminate all
opportunities for private trade!' He made the point that through the 1968
nationalizations Cuba had firmly advanced towards true 'socialism', and
that it would continue to move relentlessly down the ultra-revolutionary
road. While the relationship between prices and wages is a subject that has
bedevilled Marxist economies for decades, Castro was prepared to tell
K.S. Karol in 1967 that 'it is absolutely necessary to de-mythicize money
and not to rehabilitate it. In fact, we plan to abolish it totally.'

At the start of 1968, Fidel Castro's immediate concern was to prevent a
serious breakdown in the Cuban economy resulting from Moscow's
refusal to increase petroleum shipments. This was the first sign of the
Soviet decision to bring Castro politically and ideologically under
control; when the Cuban foreign trade minister arrived in Moscow in
October 1967 to open talks for a new commercial agreement, he was told
that fuel deliveries would not be raised to match the 8 per cent growth in
the annual Cuban demand. Moreover, the Russians rejected the Cuban
proposal for extending the annual trade agreement into a three-year pact –
Castro at that stage was keen on a longer Soviet aid commitment to him –
and they became very vague about the date the 1968 agreement would be
signed. Fidel reacted with an explosion of private fury at the news, and on
2 January went on television to announce petrol rationing and to order
sugar mills to use alternative fuels. Cuba depended on the Soviet Union
for 98 per cent of its oil needs, but in his television statement on rationing
Castro said that there was only a 'limited possibility' of increased Soviet

deliveries, and that in any event the 'dignity' of the revolution prevented Cuba from begging for more oil.

Ten days later Fidel showed the Russians that not only would he not be intimidated by them, but also that he was determined to remain outspokenly critical about their policies. Addressing the closing session of a week-long International Cultural Congress in Havana, a meeting organized to enhance Cuba's prestige and attended by five hundred intellectuals from seventy countries (including Jean-Paul Sartre, Lord Russell and Julio Cortázar, the leading Argentinian novelist), Fidel Castro was at his oratorial best, urging his guests to help him to define how best intellectuals can serve the revolution. It was a most elegant appeal for world public opinion to understand the 'real' value of the Cuban experiment, but Castro minced no words in saying what he thought about orthodox Communist parties that 'remained completely removed from the struggle against imperialism'. He alluded to the fact that at the time of the 1962 missile crisis European Communist parties had failed 'to mobilize the masses' in Cuba's support, implying that they preferred to obey Soviet instructions rather than engage in 'just combat.' Finally, Fidel chastised 'these groups' for not raising high 'the banner of Che' after his death; they would 'never be able to die like him', he said, 'nor to be true revolutionaries like him'.

On 25 January Castro lowered the boom on the so-called 'micro-faction' in the new Communist Party who were the same old-line leaders whom he had purged for 'sectarianism' six years earlier, but later reinstated. Again, going for the 'old' Communists was a thinly disguised assault on the Russians. Aníbal Escalante, the alleged chief of the 'sectarian' movement, was once more the main target of Castro's purge, but this time he and thirty-six others were arrested, tried on charges of conspiracy against the revolution, and given prison sentences; Escalante was sentenced to fifteen years. Sensitive as was this whole matter of intramural Communist struggle, the regime never spelled out fully in public what exactly was the Escalante conspiracy. Nevertheless word circulted immediately that the 'microfaction' had taken upon itself to persuade Moscow to suspend all economic aid to Cuba, in order to force Fidel's removal and to put in power a 'loyal' Communist regime. While it is impossible to ascertain precisely how valid these charges were – an interpretation of attitudes is the key to Communist demonologies – Castro is not likely to have invented the entire episode. The Russians are not above staging coups d'état against their best allies if it suits their interests, and Castro was becoming almost intolerable in demanding both ideological independence and massive economic support.

In his 'revolutionary offensive' speech on 13 March 1968, Fidel said that the party's Central Committee had resolved not to publish the 'microfaction' closed-door court proceedings for the time being (they were never published). However, he made a point of noting that the Escalante group, while it lacked significance as 'a political force', engaged in actions 'of a very serious nature . . . as a political intention and as a tendency within the revolutionary movement, a frankly reformist, reactionary, and conservative current'. In presenting the case to the Central Committee Fidel spoke from noon until midnight – his longest speech.

Castro said later that in dealing with the group 'the revolutionary courts were not as severe as some would have wished . . . but unnecessary severity has never been a characteristic of this revolution'. Unfortunately this judgement is unlikely to be shared by a great many Cubans who were tried by these courts and, twenty or twenty-five years later, still remain imprisoned on obscure charges.

The only authoritative account of the Escalante affair that I know to exist was given to me in Havana in 1985, in a conversation with Fábio Grobart, a co-founder of the original Cuban Communist Party and now Chairman of the Historical Institute of the Marxist–Leninist Movement in Cuba. Grobart's account is important because he is close to Castro and because he reopened for me, as Fidel had done earlier, crucial aspects of the Cuban–Soviet disputes in the context of the missile crisis of 1962.

The Escalante group, Grobart told me, 'had its own discipline, its own purpose, and its own policy in struggling against the leadership of the party, which is the leadership of Fidel Castro . . . It was a line that could even have led to the destruction of the revolution, a division within the revolution.' Specifically, Grobart continued, Escalante's conspiracy 'coincided with the problems we had at the time of the introduction of nuclear weapons in Cuba in October 1962'.

'At that time,' he said, 'the Soviet Union committed errors, withdrawing these missiles without consulting the Cuban government. And Escalante, as a saboteur, took advantage of [Cuban] disagreements with certain aspects of the Soviet Union's methods to make himself appear as a friend of the Soviet Union, and to throw garbage and mud at the revolution, saying, "You know, they [Fidel Castro] are anti-Soviet," and so on . . . He tried to present himself as the true defender of the Soviet Union, which is what Fidel has never ceased to be. He attempted to gain supporters, to demoralize the party, to weaken the unlimited trust that the party and the people have in Fidel Castro. This was the error, this was the crime Aníbal Escalante had committed.' Escalante served part of his sentence, then died while working as a farm administrator.

Having disposed of Escalante and his group, Castro proceeded to display further annoyance with the Soviet Union by refusing to send a Cuban delegation to the conference of world Communist parties that Brezhnev had organized in Bucharest in February to deal with the divisions inside the Communist movement caused by the split with

China. This was a direct slap at the Soviets; Castro mentioned in his March speech the decision not to attend the Bucharest conclave, remarking, however, that 'for the moment this is not a fundamental question'. The Kremlin retaliated by signing on 22 March a relatively modest 1968 trade agreement with Cuba. Whereas the volume of trade (which is largely a euphemism for Soviet aid) had risen 23 per cent from 1966 to 1967, the increase in 1968 was to be only 10 per cent. Moreover, the accord provided for interest payments by Cuba on a $330 million Soviet credit that financed her adverse trade balance. To make matters worse, this debt would rise very soon since although Cuba was committed to deliver five million tons of sugar to the Soviet Union during 1969, its entire 1968 harvest had been only 5.3 million (three million below the target and one million less than in 1967), and Castro knew that the 1969 harvest would be below even that. He also knew that without considerably increased Soviet assistance all his ambitious economic development plans would have to be dropped. While the regime's official newspaper *Granma* had proudly asserted on 2 February that 'no one can call us a satellite state and that is the reason we are respected in the world', in the end Fidel Castro had little choice but to fall into line, abandoning for at least a time his exhortations for armed revolutionary struggle throughout the Third World.

Relations between Havana and Moscow were now very tense. A tough Soviet diplomat, Aleksander A. Soldatov, was transferred from London to Havana to try to deal with Castro. *Pravda* in Moscow published an editorial denouncing 'reactionaries who follow the writings of men who call for revolutionary changes in the entire social system', which seemed to be addressed as much to Fidel as to anybody else. But neither side could risk a complete break, and in late August a new rapport began to take shape between them.

Chapter 2

Just before midnight of 20 August 1968 Soviet, East German, Polish, Hungarian and Bulgarian military forces invaded Czechoslovakia to grant it 'fraternal' assistance against the reformist Communist regime headed by Alexander Dubček.

Three days later Fidel Castro – a disputatious ally and client of the Soviet Union and victim of an invasion engineered by the United States – went before television cameras in Havana to explain his and the Cuban revolution's reaction to the occupation of the territory of one socialist nation by the armies of fellow socialist states. He was to discuss as well his views on the suddenly ended Prague Spring, which was the Czechoslovak Communist Party's experiment with Marxism With a Human Face – liberal and non-repressive Marxism.

I happened to be in Prague on the invasion night, and given my journalistic coverage of the Bay of Pigs and the Dominican intervention – I was immensely curious as to where Castro would situate himself in the rising dispute between pro and anti-Soviet Communist parties around the world over the application of the Brezhnev Doctrine. This doctrine murkily vested in the Soviet Union the right (because Brezhnev, in effect, said so) to invade neighbouring Communist countries if Communism was in danger. For Cuba this loomed as a very uncomfortable doctrine if the United States chose to apply it to protect or assure representative democracry in *its* sphere of influence; theoretically, it could legitimize a new and better Bay of Pigs. Thus Castro's reaction to Prague was extremely relevant to his own destiny – just as it was relevant to the Soviet Union also, which most certainly expected solidarity and understanding from its extraordinarily costly Caribbean ally. It was a superb intellectual challenge for Fidel, and he handled it magnificently.

Most artfully, he landed on all sides of the issue. Although Czechoslovakia's sovereignty and international law were unquestionably violated, Castro said: 'We accept the bitter necessity that required the dispatch of these forces to Czechoslovakia, we do not condemn the socialist countries that took this decision' because it was 'imperative to prevent at all costs' Czechoslovakia's drift towards 'capitalism and into the arms of imperialism'. But, he went on, 'As revolutionaries . . . we have the right to demand that a consistent position be adopted towards all the questions affecting the revolutionary movement in the world.' In other words, Fidel explained, if Warsaw Pact armies had acted to prevent socialism from being destroyed in Czechoslovakia, 'will Warsaw Pact divisions be sent to Cuba if Yankee imperialists attack our country, or if our country is threatened by an attack by Yankee imperialists?' In this manner Castro had demonstrated his solidarity with the Soviet Union and the principle of 'socialist intervention' while at the same time recognizing that international law had been violated by the Russians. Moreover, he made his 'acceptance' of the Prague invasion conditional on a new Soviet guarantee of military action to protect Cuba from the United States – on top of the guarantees he believed were made by President Kennedy to Krushchev as part of the settlement of the great missile crisis.

In a way, Castro was the only real beneficiary of the destruction of the Prague Spring. By backing the Kremlin when scores of Communist parties condemned it for the invasion, he established a new claim on Soviet largesse in economic aid for Cuba, and used the crisis to end his own dispute with the Russians without losing face. Fidel was also helpful to Brezhnev by announcing that Cuba opposed 'all the liberal economic reforms that were occurring in Czechoslovakia and also in other countries of the socialist camp'. In this area, however, he was quite sincere – because of his dedication to the most rigid forms of Marxist economics, not to say of Stalinist planning. He went so far as to express the hope that the Soviet Union would reject the temptation to fall for market economy ideas. He delivered a savage attack on Yugoslavia for sponsoring 'bourgeois liberal policies' and being an 'imperialist tool' while pretending to be a Communist state. Castro denounced the Yugoslavs for refusing to sell Cuba arms in 1959, and this fury against them led ultimately to ugly personal clashes between him and Marshal Tito in the Non-Aligned Movement.

Soviet–Cuban relations did not return to normal overnight, however. There were still deep mutual suspicions, and the Soviets were still holding back on oil and other deliveries to Cuba, pending the solution of a variety of outstanding problems. In fact, such was the fuel shortage in the autumn of 1968 that Raúl Castro had to array his tanks along beaches as stationary artillery positions because he lacked fuel for them. As Fidel told me many years later, it was not until late in 1968 that all the misunderstandings and resentments dating back to the October crisis were finally resolved.

Perhaps the last sticking point between Moscow and Havana was their dispute over Manuel Piñeiro Losada, the red-bearded Deputy Interior Minister in charge of the State Security Department (political secret police). During the investigations of the Escalante affair early in 1968, Piñeiro accidentally found Escalante himself in a concealed meeting with a Soviet secret police adviser from the KGB (the Soviet State Security Committee). A corps of KGB advisers was attached to the Interior Ministry, and its chief took umbrage over Piñeiro's failure to report the incident to him. Raúl Castro, who directed the overall 'mini-faction' investigation, told this astonishing story in his account to the Central Committee, lifting a corner of the secrecy mantle over the rivalry between the two secret police organizations. Raúl said he had brought up the matter of Escalante's clandestine meeting with the Soviet adviser in conversations with Ambassador Soldatov and the chief KGB adviser, only to discover that the latter was furious at Piñeiro; the Russians were naturally disturbed that their man had been spotted with Escalante. Talking to the chief adviser, Raúl said: ' "You are almost asking me to arrest Piñeiro because he failed to show you respect, and I don't propose to do it." So the chief replied: "We are Piñeiro's bosses, not you . . . and how can you think that we would. . ." and I broke in to say: "We don't think so, but if you did not reason so obtusely you would interpret this as a warning that for us it would be rather painful to find a Soviet official here, diplomatic or not, involved in matters of an internal nature." ' It is unclear how this dispute was settled, but Piñeiro soon ceased to be Deputy Interior Minister, becoming the head of the Central Committee's Department of the Americas instead, one of the most powerful political positions – and still closely tied to Cuban Intelligence operations.

Even so relations were still cool in November. Pedro Miret went to Moscow for the revolution anniversary (Fidel, Raúl and President Dorticós again would not go). Faustino Pérez, the least ideologically-minded of Fidel's old companions, was picked to speak at the celebrations in Havana, and Raúl was the ranking Cuban guest at the Soviet Embassy reception; his big brother was still sulking.

Foremost on Fidel Castro's mind towards the end of 1968 were the centennial observation of the start of the first Independence War, the current state of Cuba's economy, and a new drive to tighten domestic political controls. The latter appeared to stem from concerns about possible contagion from the Prague Spring, and late in the year Raúl's Revolutionary Armed Forces Ministry initiated an attack on 'bourgeois' intellectuals and 'counter-revolutionary' literature. The word was that no 'softening' in the revolutionary spirit would be tolerated, and in March

1969 the ministry organized a National Forum on Internal Order for its own officers, Interior Ministry specialists, party officials and Revolutionary Defence Committee.

All these new efforts were consistent with the 1968 Revolutionary Offensive, but quite obviously events in Czechoslovakia had a big impact. In a conversation in 1984 Fidel Castro told me he had thought all along that Dubček and the other 'liberal' Communist leaders were acting in deep error. Then we spoke of the recent events in Poland, and Castro said that the Polish Communist Party had mismanaged the situation, largely because of corruption, with the resulting emergence of the Solidarity free trade-union movement. Fidel clearly disliked the Solidarity idea – other Cuban officials hinted that there had been some concern in 1980 and 1981 that it might start catching on in Cuba – and he suggested that General Wojciech Jaruzelski, the Communist premier had saved Poland from a Soviet invasion by imposing martial rule and outlawing Solidarity. The official viewpoint had quickly spread to the Cuban cinema industry: I heard Cuban directors in private conversation angrily criticizing the Polish director Andrzej Wajda for producing *Man of Iron*, his inspirational picture about Solidarity, which won the Cannes Festival award.

Among a great many things about revolutionary Cuba that had developed disturbingly in the first Castro decade – and have continued in ensuing decades – was that very same Communist Party mismanagement and deadening bureaucracy which Fidel had observed with such alarm in Poland in the pre-Solidarity years. And there also was the stolid conformity in thought and word that, for example, made Cuban film-makers denounce Wajda for his Solidarity film only because that followed the official line. Even by 1968 it was already commonplace for Castro and *Granma* to deplore periodically and liturgically the excesses of bureaucracy, without achieving the slightest progress. In truth, the revolution and the creation of the new Communist Party had spawned a privileged new ruling class built around and below Fidel by the party and Security apparatus and the military – and inevitably this new class reposed on a faithful bureacracy. The Castro cult of personality was derived from this form of political organization and it instantly raised the question whether Fidel had become isolated from the realities of his people.

His initial method of government was to commune with the masses through the 'dialogue' mechanism of preaching and teaching, then asking the crowds for approval for policies he was proposing, and then assuming that a revolutionary consensus had been achieved. Clearly, however, this was not a process of consultation in any sense of the word, and before long Castro no longer could know what people thought and what bothered them (having abolished the 'liberal bourgeois freedom of the press' in the early 1960s, he could not learn much from reading his own newspapers and magazines, and palace courtiers do not normally generate bad news). In the first years of the revolution a favourite Fidel occupation was to bounce around the countryside in his Jeep, stopping here and there, chatting with people, and asking with genuine interest what they did and what problems they had. This too had its limitations, but it gave Castro some sense of his people. When I asked him about this old practice one day in January 1984, when we were driving on the outskirts of Havana, he turned around from the front seat of the Jeep where he sat next to the driver, shaking his head sadly. 'No, I don't get to do that very much any more,' he said. 'You know, now I have all the responsibilities of running the state, attending meetings, receiving ambassadors and so on – there is no time.'

Already in 1976 visitors from abroad who spent much time with Castro – such as Frenchmen K.S. Karol and René Dumont – began to wonder whether he insisted on running everything personally because he hungered for total power or because he was simply the victim of the system he had devised. The real issue was, was there anyone else in Cuba he could (or would) trust to make certain decisions and assume certain responsibilities? But looking at Castro more than a quarter-century after the revolution, the clear conclusion is that both judgements are correct, and that, really, he is his own prisoner for life.

This is so because for Fidel Castro the revolution is a permanent struggle, not necessarily a Marxist, socialist or Communist struggle, but a Cuban national struggle. On 10 October 1968 he flew to Oriente to deliver in a downpour a patriotic speech commemorating the hundreth anniversary of the first Cuban uprising against Spain, and his theme throughout was 'one hundred years of struggle', with the emphasis on it being only the beginning for Cuba. Not once that day did Castro mention Marxism–Leninism, socialism, the Communist Party or the Soviet Union: his text was dedicated to Céspedes and Martí and all the other heroes of liberation struggles – and to sugar production. Two days earlier he said proudly, as applause soared around him, that Cubans had planted exactly 33,230 acres of sugarcane across the island in one single day in tribute to the independence anniversary and the memory of Che Guevara. In Fidel's mind the record sugar harvest he was planning for 1970 would represent the start of the second 'hundred years of struggle', and he knew that the inspiration for the great effort had to be patriotic and not ideological.

To achieve the goal of ten million tons of sugar in 1970, a goal Castro had linked to the 'honour of the revolution', the nation was mobilized for this enterprise as if it were war, and he named 1969 as the Year of the Decisive Effort. At the same time Fidel ordered changes in harvest methods so that actual harvesting would start in July 1969 and end in July

1970. Normally, the harvest lasts only the three months of the winter, but the unprecedented magnitude of the planting and the acreage had made it necessary to devote the whole year to it. Cane-cutting thus became the principal and the most obsessive economic effort in Cuba during 1969, reducing everything else to an absolute minimum. Industrial and commercial workers, students, old people and children as well as 'brigades' of foreign visitors were assigned to cut cane weekdays and weekends, and holidays were abolished. The army was drafted for cane-cutting as well, and Fidel and all his top companions were televised and photographed cutting cane as an example to the nation. However this is an activity requiring skill, endurance and strength, and the inexperienced 'volunteers' may have been in the way of the quarter-million professional *macheteros*. Nevertheless 'voluntary' work was a political requirement to justify the economic near-paralysis of the country, the harvest lasting 334 days. Drought being a menace to the crop, Castro announced that 'We have made a pact with the rain.' And the rain kept its word in 1969, providing just the right pattern.

Fidel was an incurable optimist about the revolution, never discouraged by initial failures. Not only did he want that record sugar crop in 1970, but speaking on the tenth anniversary of his victory he pledged that Cuba's overall farm production would increase by no less than 15 per cent annually over the next twelve years – the highest growth rate in world history. Given the sharp drop in farm production in the first decade of the revolution, which Castro was the first to acknowledge, his promise seemed totally lacking in reality. His word was not questioned. Still, Fidel said that to meet his objectives, Cuba had to import 8000 tractors annually for ten years, train 80,000 tractor operators, and 180,000 farm workers with mechanization skills. And when it came to imports, Castro had to rely almost entirely on the Soviet Union and other Communist countries. In 1969, fortunately, the Russians, having had their way, were ready to resume large-scale aid – and to think again of the strategic importance of Cuba.

The Cuban–Soviet economic relationship was based principally on the theory that deliveries of Cuban sugar would pay at least in part for Soviet shipments of petroleum, machinery, automotive equipment, industrial goods and just about everything else a modern economy required (weapons were a grant). But even though Moscow calculated the value of the sugar at prices well above the world market (following the example of the United States quota), Cuba was ten million tons in arrears by 1969 because the crop had been so low in past years. Therefore Castro opened the year by announcing to his people the rationing of sugar at home so that more would be available for export. He provided the nation with a series of most convincing explanations for the rationing.

Meanwhile, the entire national relationship with the Soviets was improving. Deputy Premier Novikov, the Kremlin's full-time expert on Cuba, was on hand for the tenth-anniversary celebrations, and Castro in his speech was full of praise for the Soviet Union. In February a very favourable trade agreement was negotiated. In April the love feast continued with a Castro speech on the anniversary of Lenin's birth and praise for the Soviet Union for helping Cuba to become the 'first socialist state' in Latin America. The same day Fidel presided over a ceremony inaugurating the Soviet–Cuban Friendship Association. In June Carlos Rafael Rodríguez led a delegation of the Cuban Communist Party to Moscow for a international conference boycotted by the Chinese, North Korean, Albanian and North Vietnamese parties (the Cubans evidently quietly setting aside their professed friendship with Vietnam). Rodríguez, the 'old' Communist who became a top *Fidelista* in the new Caribbean Communism, pleased his hosts when he declared that 'Cuba is convinced of the importance of the unity of action of the Communists' in order to develop 'a broader offensive against imperialism and the forces of reaction and war'.

Having led Castro back into the ideological and economic fold, the Russians now turned their attentions again to the strategic equation in Cuba. A Soviet eight-ship naval squadron arrived in Havana on 20 July, and the Castro brothers along with the entire top leadership attended a reception given by Rear Admiral Stepan Sokolan, the task-force commander. Then Fidel and his government went on a cruise on the flagship *Groznig*; Fidel and the admiral celebrated the 26 July anniversary together, cutting cane near Havana along with a contingent of sailors from the cruiser – probably an unforgettable experience. The Soviet Defence Minister, Marshal Andrei A. Grechko, was the next Soviet military chief to wield the *machete* during a November visit with Fidel and Raúl. On 30 December the entire staff of the Soviet Embassy in Havana spent a day cutting cane in what had become an act of courtesy for foreigners comparable to the laying of wreaths at national monuments. As the 1960s came to a close, Cuban–Soviet friendship was stronger than ever – with Fidel Castro frequently expressing his gratitude for economic and military assistance from Moscow. By the end of 1969 the Cubans owed the Russians $4 billion, this debt representing the difference between the value of Soviet deliveries to Cuba and Cuban deliveries to the Soviet Union. Castro himself calculated that during the decade Castro had received free $1.5 billion in military equipment, including jet aircraft.

Nineteen Seventy was called The Year of the Ten Million Tons – but it was not. Despite good weather and the incredible effort expended by the whole nation on Fidel Castro's orders, Cuba fell short of the goal, producing 8.5 million tons. Actually, it was a record crop (the previous record was seven million tons in 1952), but even this volume was not commensurate with the social and economic cost to Cuban society. Castro had repeated the same error with milk when he promised in December 1968 that production would quadruple within two years; but in 1970 production was running 25 per cent below 1969 levels (probably because the energies of the peasants were channelled into sugarcane cutting.).

However, Castro was painfully honest about the failures. Describing the agricultural shortcomings he said in a speech on 26 July 1970: 'The unquestionable inefficiency of all of us . . . signified that we were incapable of waging what we called the simultaneous battle on all fronts of production.' He admitted: 'The heroic effort to increase the sugar production led to imbalances in the economy, in diminished production in other sectors and . . . in an increase in our difficulties.' Then he somberly warned that the next five years would be even more difficult, adding: 'I want to speak of our inability in the overall work of the revolution . . . We must face our responsibility in these problems, and my [responsibility] in particular . . . Our apprenticeship as leaders of this revolution has cost too much.' Earlier, Fidel had observed: 'The battle of the ten million was not lost by the people, it is us, the administrative apparatus, the leaders of the revolution who lost it . . . Our ignorance of the problems of the sugar mills prevented us from remedying in time all the difficulties.' However, as René Dumont has remarked, sugar experts who had attempted years earlier to call Castro's attention to these problems 'were simply sent away'.

Still, no reverses could slow down Fidel or diminish his interest in everything, everybody, everywhere. He refused to settle for any kind of status quo, and in the second half of 1970 turned away from the depressing domestic scene and its economic problems, to international problems and controversies on which he thrived.

Two such situations developed in September 1970, and Fidel found himself involved in both of them, directly and indirectly. The first was the victory of his friend Salvador Allende Gossens in a three-way race for the presidency of Chile on 4 September. Allende, a frequent visitor to Havana, was of Marxist persuasion and headed the Chilean Socialist Party, and this was the fourth time he had run for president. In 1970 the CIA and American corporations invested in vain tens of millions of dollars in secret support for Allende's right-wing opponent, Jorge Alessandri, and in anti-Allende propaganda. However Allende obtained only a 36.3 plurality, and a run-off with Alessandri the following month was required under the Chilean constitution.

The Nixon administration's reaction to the idea of a democratically elected Marxist president in Latin America was naturally one of alarmed revulsion, and the immediate fear in Washington centred on the nightmarish scenario of a Castro–Allende revolutionary axis. Fidel, just as naturally, was delighted – but he exercised great care to avoid any gloating that might have given Nixon justification to intervene in some way (it was only two years before that application of the Brezhnev Doctrine to Czechoslovakia had contributed to a certain legitimacy for invasions). While the administration drew overt and covert plans to defeat Allende in the 24 October run-off in the Chilean Congress, a sudden new crisis erupted over Cuba.

About a week after Allende's first victory a U-2 spy plane brought back photographs showing new barracks, communication towers and anti-aircraft sites being constructed near the naval base of Cienfuegos in southern Cuba. Also appearing on the photographs was a new soccer field, and inasmuch as the Cubans do not play this game, CIA photo interpreters concluded that the field was being prepared for the Russians, who do play it. As it happened, a Soviet naval squadron arrived on a visit in Cienfuegos on 14 May, and another one on 9 September. The second squadron included a submarine tender, a 9000-ton *Ugra*-class vessel, two towed barges that the CIA believed were storage for radioactive wastes from reactors on nuclear submarines. Finally, a Soviet nuclear submarine was spotted in the general area of Cuba. Instantly Nixon and National Security Adviser Henry A. Kissinger concluded that the Russians were establishing a nuclear-submarine base in Cienfuegos. Given the memories of the 1962 missile crisis, this was not an unreasonable suspicion, even though the Russians had committed themselves at the time to keeping offensive weapons out of the Western hemisphere.

Nixon and Kissinger kept the U-2 discovery and their conclusions a secret, planning to deal with the Soviets through quiet diplomatic channels. On 16 September Kissinger summoned Soviet Ambassador Anatoly Dobrynin and confonted him with aerial photographs. Then he held a press briefing to discuss the dangers of the Allende victory in Chile and to warn the Soviets against 'operating strategic forces out of Cuba, say, Polaris-type submarines'. He added: 'We are watching these events in Cuba.' Now Castro and Allende seemed to form part of an interlocking crisis, but neither of them chose to polemicize with Kissinger. In October the Soviet Union privately assured Kissinger that it was building no bases in Cuba, and TASS subsequently repeated this as a public statement. Castro has never said a word on the subject in public, and this Cuban mini crisis served chiefly to reassert the 1962 'under-standing' between the superpowers over their mutual guarantees on Cuba. Still, the Americans thought that Brezhnev might have been 'testing' them over Cuba by dispatching naval squadrons there and openly engaging in military construction in Cienfuegos. Fidel certainly would not have minded such a test. And on 24 October he learned with vast pleasure that Allende had been confirmed as president by the Congress in Chile. He saw it as the beginning of a long and profitable relationship, and promised to visit Allende the following year.

When in June 1961 Fidel Castro told a group of writers, artists and intellectuals that there was full creative freedom in Cuba 'within the revolution', but nothing 'against the revolution', he was establishing a fairly relaxed set of cultural standards. It took the hard-line ideological offensive of 1971, evidently also inspired by Castro, to demonstrate how brutally these standards had changed in a decade.

The onslaught on supposedly 'counter-revolutionary' intellectuals had begun around 1965, when the regime began arresting those it considered as 'anti-social elements', especially if they were homosexuals, and putting them in the UMAP forced-labour army battalions. It was part of a broader ideological offensive against homosexuals in general during the political power struggles of the 1960s. In 1968, when the political climate turned unusually harsh, specific writers became targets of the party ideologues. The award of a poetry prize to Herberto Padilla and a theatre prize to playwright Antón Arrufat that year by the official Union of Cuban Writers and Artists (UNEAC), a Castro creation, led to an internal ideological clash typical of the changing cultural environment. As a compromise the UNEAC decided to publish the prize-winning works along with a note from the union's editorial board expressing its disagreement with them because 'they are ideologically contrary to our revolution'. In the murky Marxist ideological jargon, Padilla was accused of 'ambiguity' and 'anti-historical attitudes', and Arrufat of disseminating an 'imperialist-type' reality. Shortly thereafter a Writers and Artists Congress was held in Cienfuegos, approving a resolution that urged every writer to 'contribute to the revolution through his work and this involves conceiving of literature as a means of struggle, a weapon against weaknesses and problems which, directly or indirectly, could hinder this advance'. No Cuban author knew what it meant.

Late in 1969 a prize-winning novelist José Lorenzo Fuentes was expelled from UNEAC because of his connections with a Mexican diplomat allegedly employed by the CIA. It seemed as if the party ideologues in charge of culture were determined to absorb Marxism–Leninism to the point of turning Cuba into a tropical replica of an Arthur Koestler novel about Communist police states. In 1970 the most prestigious Cuban novelists and poets suddenly discovered that without explanation no publishing house or magazine would publish their work. This mysterious ban would last into the mid-1970s.

The new official line was proclaimed in a 'Declaration' issued by the First National Congress of Education and Culture held in Havana in April 1971, and its ideological monstrosity in terms of Cuban cultural life can be gleaned from the published text. Thus 'cultural development' in Cuba, it said, must be aimed at the masses, 'contrary to the tendencies of the elites . . . Socialism creates objective and subjective conditions that render feasible a true creative freedom while rejecting as inadmissible those tendencies that are based on a criterium of libertinage and aimed at concealing the counter-revolutionary poison of works that conspire against revolutionary ideology. . .'

Rambling for page after page, this cultural edict provided that in hiring personnel for universities, mass communications media and literary and artistic institutions, the candidates' 'political and ideological conditions be taken into account'. Selectivity in invitations to foreign writers and intellectuals was recommended to avoid the 'presence of persons whose work and ideology are at odds with the interests of the revolution'. Moreover, the congress declared that 'cultural channels may not serve for the proliferation of false intellectuals who plan to convert snobbism, extravagance, homosexuality and other social aberrations into expressions of revolutionary art, alienated from the masses and from the spirit of our revolution'. Again, it seems incomprehensible that Fidel Castro could intellectually tolerate such insults against his beloved revolution on the part of his own ideologues.

Yet Castro evidently approved of the crackdown on Cuban intellectuals because the arrest of the poet Herberto Padilla in March 1971 had to have been authorized by him. The arrest led an impressive group of European and Latin American intellectuals, including Sartre and García Márquez, to write to Castro demanding Padilla's release. He was freed thirty-seven days later, after reading a statement of self-criticism and urging other writers to do likewise. His friends regarded him as a 'traitor', but Padilla remained in Cuba for a decade, working as a translator of foreign literature. He finally left in 1981, after García Márquez had made another personal appeal to his friend Fidel. Even the obedient UNEAC protested in a letter to Castro the lengthy detention of homosexuals in the military forced-labour units, and they were finally sprung. Yet it left an ugly scar on Cuban society. Overall, Castro's oppressive cultural policies have dealt a lethal blow to creativity in his country; even in 1986 the island was a wasteland of ideas beneath a reign of strict self-censorship. It may take generations for Cuba to return to the free cultural age of José Martí.

In any event, Castro was extremely busy with Cuban foreign relations during 1971, probably lacking the time to supervise cultural life personally. Ties with the Soviets were being strengthened daily, but Fidel was not yet ready to visit Moscow. Instead he dispatched President Dorticós to attend the twenty-fourth congress of the Soviet Communist Party in March, preferring himself to meet in Havana with top Soviet officials. Nikolai Baibakov, the chief Soviet economic planner, came in April, and Soviet Premier Kosygin spent five days in Cuba in October, his second visit to Fidel.

On 10 November Castro flew non-stop to Santiago, Chile, aboard a Soviet IL-18 jet airliner equipped with a bed and an office for him, on a ten-day visit that became a three-week stay. It was his first trip abroad in seven years, since his last journey to Moscow, and he enjoyed it hugely. It was also the first time he was returning to Latin America in twelve years, and that, too, pleased him greatly, as he told his aides. From the airport Fidel drove into the city, standing up in a convertible next to Allende, and waving at the huge crowds that cheered him in the streets. After several days in Santiago, Fidel embarked on voyages to the north and south of the long and narrow Chilean territory, visiting schools and plants, delivering speeches, granting interviews, meeting young and old Chileans, and visibly having a good time. In the northern city of Antofagasta he joined a group of folklore musicians for a picture, a guitar in one hand, and a pat on the head of the musician next to him.

Nathaniel Davies, then the United States Ambassador in Santiago, described Castro's visit as 'an extraordinary display of high-level tourism, thinly disguised meddling, and shrewd commentary on the Chilean scene; it was a circus'. Fidel stayed longer in Chile than his hosts had expected, almost running out of things to do, but he evidently wanted to have a solid look at Allende's socialist experiment. He went to nine provinces, from the seaport of Valparaíso and the copper mines in central Chile to Rio Blanco high up in the Andes and Tierra del Fuego across the Magellan Straits. He talked to workers everywhere, conducted endless dialogues with university students in sports stadiums, discussed theology with 'revolutionary priests' in Santiago, donned straw hats and hard hats, kept warm in colourful wool *ruana* blankets, and played a rousing game of basketball in Iquique, wearing a Number Twelve shirt, and showing that at the age of forty-five he was still in great physical shape.

En route home, Castro stopped in Lima to meet Peru's military rulers with whom Cuba was developing cordial relations, then in Guayaquil, Ecuador, to converse with the aging president, José María Velasco Ibarra, who once upon a time had been a dictator. In all three Pacific-coast countries, Castro offered Cuba's support for their controversial claim to a 200-mile territorial-water limit to protect their fisheries, winning warm applause in exchange. In Havana Fidel received a hero's welcome after the long absence, but he was already thinking of more foreign travel the following year.

Recalling the South American trip many years later, Castro said he knew the CIA tried to assassinate him first in Chile, then in Peru and Ecuador. He told an interviewer that weapons for the assassins, who posed as Venezuelan journalists with Venezuelan credentials, had come from the American embassy in La Paz, Bolivia. These arms, he added, ranged from rifles with telescopic sights to machine guns and a television camera with a hidden gun: 'It was straight in front of me, but they didn't shoot.'

On 3 May 1972 Fidel Castro left Cuba aboard his IL-62 jet airliner on a two-month voyage to ten countries on two continents, climaxing it with his first visit to the Soviet Union in eight years. In Moscow Castro came face to face with the nascent Soviet–American détente, arriving there exactly one month after the departure of his arch enemy, Richard Nixon. While Nixon's visit to the Kremlin had resulted in the signing of the SALT I nuclear arms limitation agreement, Castro's sojourn resulted in Cuba's membership in the Council for Mutual Economic Assistance (CMEA), the Communist common market, better known as the Comecon. By joining CMEA Cuba became fully integrated into the worldwide Communist economic system, which included the Soviet Union, the six European Communist countries, Outer Mongolia and Vietnam. Fidel also received a Soviet marshal's sabre as a special accolade and, of course, he volunteered no public comments about the Brezhnev–Nixon embrace the previous month. He had become a very sophisticated revolutionary and a fine practitioner of personal diplomacy.

Castro's re-alignment with Soviet foreign policy included his accept-ance of the view (at least overtly) that the time for guerrilla warfare on the Sierra Maestra model had run its course, and that social change in Latin America had to be accomplished by less violent means, which had all along been argued by the Russians. They still thought that Fidel's 1958 victory had been basically an aberration due to his personality and special Cuban conditions, and that it could not be repeated elsewhere. The chances are that Castro had not in fact given up his personal revolutionary dogmas, yet he too had to recognize new realities in the hemisphere. After Che Guevara's death the aura of romantic revolutions had paled (Camilo Torres, the Colombian revolutionary priest whom Castro had met in 1948, had also been killed in his own guerrilla war, and the Peruvian rebel poet Hugo Blanco had been captured. Allende's election in Chile and the emergence of the left-wing reformist generals in Peru confirmed the new trend. Castro was too intelligent to ignore it, deciding on the route of Cuban statesmanship and the giving of aid to insurgents only in situations where revolutionary conditions already existed.

Consequently, the 1970s saw Castro concentrating on ending the diplomatic and political isolation imposed on him by the United States, and he was doing well. The Chile, Peru and Ecuador visits produced new friendships for Cuba on the west coast of South America. Argentina, Colombia and Venezuela resumed diplomatic relations with Cuba, leading the Venezuelan guerrilla chief Douglas Bravo to accuse Fidel publicly of betrayal (the way Fidel had earlier accused Venezuelan Communists of betraying Bravo). Relations developed with Panama, Jamaica, Barbados, Bahamas, and Trinidad and Tobago in the vital arc of Central America and the Caribbean, when Castro realized that at this point his thirteen-year-old revolution no longer required a surrounding cordon of other revolutionary states to afford it protection. Soviet protection was more weighty, anyway. Gradually Castro began re-entering Latin American organizations, such as the United Nations Economic Commission for Latin America (ECLA) and the Organization of American States prepared to lift the diplomatic and trade sanctions against Cuba established in the early 1960s. Finally, the Cubans played an important part in organizing SELA, a new regional economic entity. They were no longer pariahs.

Now Castro set out to expand his friendships in Africa, his first time there, with visits to Guinea, Sierra Leone and Algeria. Cuba has had considerable involvement in Africa since the first days of the revolution, with Che Guevara as the principal emissary to the continent until he vanished from the political scene in 1965. The Cubans had championed the cause of Algerian independence since 1959, sending military and medical supplies to the National Liberation Front (FLN), then fighting the French in 1960, and dispatching a Rebel Army combat battalion to help freshly independent Algeria in its border war with Morocco in 1963. In the 1960s there were Cuban military missions in Algeria, Ghana, Congo-Brazzaville and Guinea, and later in Equatorial Guinea, Somalia and Tanzania. Castro's visit to Sierra Leone was followed by the arrival of a Rebel Army mission to train the national militia.
    Along with Che Guevara, Castro believed that Africa was the future scene of great revolutionary changes, with Cuba as its guide and mentor. With much of Africa either recently decolonized or peacefully preparing for independence (or fighting for it as liberation movements were doing in the Portuguese colonies), Castro saw an extraordinary potential for Cuban revolutionary influence. And African nationalists, mainly of leftist persuasion, welcomed the Cubans: Cuba's cultural origins were partly African, and the Afro–Cuban tradition was powerful; the Cubans offered a perfect alternative to either American or Soviet imperialisms, and finally Cuba was a sister Third World nation with a triumphant revolution.
    By the time Castro set foot in Africa there was no African left-of-centre government or liberation movement that did not have Cuban ties of some sort. Africans were being trained by Cubans in everything from medicine to military organization in their own countries or in schools and camps in Cuba. Fidel was planning for the future, knowing intuitively

that Cuba had a perhaps decisive role to play in parts of Africa; this, in turn, gave him and his country international importance beyond Latin America. In addition to his Bolívarian dream in his own hemisphere, Castro now aspired for Third World leadership.

In Conakry he found a fellow revolutionary in Guinea's President Ahmed Sekou Touré, who told a crowd greeting Castro at a sports stadium that 'Cuba is the light in Latin America'. Their conversations served to coordinate Cuban support for guerrilla movements against Portuguese colonial rule and South Africa, Guinea being a natural transit point from Cuba to the African continent. Active backing for African guerrillas fitted Castro's (and the Russians') thinking because anti-colonial 'national liberation' movements were involved; Krushchev had been a foremost advocate of such movements. Fidel started his Guinean tour clad in his usual olive-green fatigues, but on the second day changed into the national dress of white trousers and a white short-sleeved tunic buttoned at the neck; he kept on his black combat boots, his green cap and the military webbing belt for an arresting overall effect. He always delighted in trying on the attire of countries he visited which, in turn, delighted the local audiences. Sekou Touré awarded Fidel the Order of Fidelity to the People. The *compañeros* whom Castro took along to Africa suggested his interests in the region: Juan Almeida, the black vice president and former Rebel Army Chief of Staff; Manuel Piñeiro Losada, his closest adviser on Intelligence and contacts with revolutionary movements; Arnaldo T. Ochoa Sánchez, a new-generation officer who would soon command Cuban combat troops in Angola; and Raúl E. Menéndez Tomassevich, once Raúl Castro's deputy in the guerrilla war and the principal insurgency and militia expert.

In Sierra Leone, Castro spent one day with President Siaka Probyn Stevens, a relatively moderate politician, then returned to Conakry for more talks with Sekou Touré. In Algeria for ten days, Fidel was back in a warm revolutionary environment, visiting the country Cuba had helped in its independence war. His old friend Ahmed Ben Bella had been overthrown by Hourari Boumedienne, but Castro established a good relationship with the new president. As a socialist and revolutionary state, Algeria was Cuba's oldest and best ally as well as a key link both to Africa and the Arab world. Similarly the Algerians had a military rapport with the Soviet Union, which equipped their armed forces, so Castro and Boumedienne could share their Third World views on the Russians – not always flatteringly. Algiers was a revolutionary planning and plotting centre for Africa, and Fidel devoted much time to this topic, refining his ideas on 'anti-colonialist struggles', as he said in speech after speech. Finally Boumedienne was immensely important to Castro as a key leader in the Non-Aligned Movement which Fidel hoped to dominate.

From Algiers, Castro's Soviet jet took him directly to Sofia, Bulgaria, over the length of the Mediterranean, and across Italy, the Adriatic and Yugoslavia. This was his introduction to non-Soviet European Communist states, called satellites by their detractors, and presumably an instructive experience for a man representing the Cuban variety of Soviet-supported Communism. He instantly fell into the mandatory 'fraternal' practice of warm embraces with local leaders, but in Bulgaria and throughout the rest of Eastern Europe, Castro evoked genuine interest and excitement among the crowds that did not need to be summoned to greet him in the streets and squares of the old cities. He was different, he was a legend, and he was informal – he appeared to be all the things the traditional Communist leaders were not. For his part, Fidel was fascinated to discover old cultures in new but distinctly designed Marxist mantles.

In Sofia his host was Todor Zhivkov, the Bulgarian leader who never questioned Soviet wisdom and had been in power longer than any other Communist in Europe (except for the self-isolated Enver Hoxha of Albania). Castro was in gala uniform for official functions and a concert, but seemed even happier in a grey tracksuit playing basketball with an army team against a civilian team. He dutifully observed military manoeuvres, and was presented with a Bulgarian-made AK-47 sub-machinegun and an antique Bulgarian partisan pistol; his private weapon collection grew as he travelled the world.

From Sofia, Castro flew to Bucharest to meet Rumanian President Nicholae Ceauşescu, also a Communist master in the art of survival, but a maverick in foreign policy. It had to intrigue Fidel to see how Ceauşescu, a next-door neighbour of the Soviet Union, had succeeded for so long in defying the Russians on just about everything: he refused to break relations with Israel after the 1967 Middle East war (unlike the rest of the Soviet bloc), he remained pointedly friendly with the Chinese and Yugoslav Communist heretics, and he roundly condemned the Soviet invasion of Czechoslovakia, which came five days after his visit to Prague (he also declined to let his own Rumanian troops participate in the 'fraternal' action). Defying Moscow had not been Castro's signal success, but he had in common with Ceauşescu his dedication to total internal regimentation and the inability to make workers produce well. Fidel may not have learned Ceauşescu's foreign policy secrets; he did learn, however, that Rumania produced excellent wine (a matter of interest to him) when he tasted it, drinking from a wineskin.

In Hungary there was still another subtle Communist experience for Castro. He came to Budapest a quarter-century after Soviet tanks had destroyed the anti-Communist 'freedom fighters' (this expression was born in Budapest in 1956) to find the country with a considerable degree of autonomy from the Russians in internal affairs and remarkable prosperity stemming from market-economy reforms. These were the reforms Czechoslovakia had sought to imitate and expand before the 1968 invasion, and that Castro had so violently denounced in his speech. Whatever may have been the impression left on Castro by the Hungarian achievements, he would remain just as opposed to market-economy ideas in 1986, when he banned the experiment in farmers' markets. Under Janos Kadar, who had ruled Hungary since the rebellion, the country lived in remarkable political and cultural relaxation in the context of a Communist system. Evidently Castro did not wish to imitate these practices, either. From Budapest he carried home a sabre used in the 1848 independence war and an AK-47 automatic rifle.

Then it was Poland – and still another facet of European Communism. This was a nation with viscerally anti-Russian (now anti-Soviet) traditions, powerful nationalism, a formidable Roman Catholic Church, a Western European culture, memories of terrible destruction in its opposition to the Nazis in the war – and with a shockingly corrupt and inept Communist Party. The party had so thoroughly antagonized the workers that despite the very real advances in education, public health and living standards for the impoverished population under the socialist system, there had been violent popular uprisings. The most recent had occurred only two years earlier in Gdansk, the seaport, where the army and the police had been obliged to fire on rioting workers, killing and maiming scores.

When Castro reached Warsaw the nation was living in the relative calm between storms. Poland was the only Communist country with an articulate – and tolerated – internal political opposition, and a lively and rich cultural life largely stemming from this phenomenon. Naturally this opposition had no access to Castro, and he would probably have disapproved of writers and artists to whom the building of socialism was not the only creative ambition. Fidel's rich mind notwithstanding, the political and cultural barrier between the two nominally Communist states was too deep for him to bridge. Thus the visit was a standard affair, though, as usual, Fidel brightened it with his personality and attitudes. One evening he took a walk to Warsaw's Old Town Square, stopping to chat with a flower vendor, and dropping in at a basement nightclub called Krokodyl where he promised the young patrons he would send them a stuffed crocodile from the swamps of the Zapata in Cuba. The youngsters loved it. That evening a news story had been sent out from Warsaw by an American wire service that Castro had suffered a heart attack, and Fidel sputtered in fury that it was another CIA provocation designed to destabilize Cuba – which was probably true.

In the coal region of Silesia, Castro put on the traditional black gala uniform of the miners and received the miners' medal. 'If this tour continues at this rate, I'll wind up with as many medals as a hero of labour,' he told the miners, winning laughter and applause. He raised considerably less enthusiasm when he cried 'Long Live Red Silesia!' Still in the miner's uniform, Fidel paid a visit the same day to Oświęcim and Brzezinka Nazi concentration camp sites. At Oświęcim (Auschwitz), he wrote in the visitors' book: 'Capitalist and imperialist ideology was capable of such extremes . . . What I have seen today reminds me of what the Yankees are doing now in Vietnam.' In Cracow Fidel played basketball with the university team. In Gdansk he toured the Lenin shipyards (where Solidarity would be born eight years later), then joined General Jaruzelski, the Defence Minister (who would liquidate Solidarity), at military manoeuvres in the coastal area.

On 13 June Fidel Castro arrived in East Berlin, but it is unlikely he knew it was the nineteenth anniversary of a bloody uprising there by East German workers and students against Communist rule. Soviet tanks had put down that first postwar rebellion in Eastern Europe, in 1953, now a forgotten date. Met by East German leader Erich Honecker, Castro was visiting a very prosperous Communist country. He was taken to the Brandenburg Gate, which stands astride the line between the two Berlins, and he could not have missed the Berlin Wall the East Germans had erected in 1961 to prevent their fellow citizens from fleeing to the West. He did not mention the wall in a speech to East German frontier guards, but he compared the Berlin border zone to the United States naval base at Guantánamo as a foreign enclave. In Merseburg Fidel walked down a street holding hands with schoolchildren, and at Moritzburg Castle he was the guest of the commander of the Soviet Army division stationed near East Berlin. There his speech chronicled the use of freshly arrived Soviet arms in the Bay of Pigs battle.

In Czechoslovakia, the invasion of which by Warsaw Pact armies four years earlier Castro had rationalized and praised, he was most warmly greeted by Communist Party Secretary General Gustav Husak, the man in charge of 'normalizing' the situation to suit the Kremlin. Husak awarded Castro the Order of the White Lion. The venerable Charles University, among whose philosophers the liberalizing spirit of the Prague Spring had been born, granted him the degree of Doctor *Honoris Causa* in Juridicial Sciences. In black robes and cap, and amidst medieval splendor, Castro, the philosopher of the revolution, used the opportunity to lecture his audience on the ideological history of his Movement. Confusing the matter once more, he explained that the Moncada Manifesto in 1953 'was not yet a socialist programme' although it had been officially described as such in Cuba ever since Fidel had announced in 1961 that his revolution *was* socialist in character. However, he said, 'the revolutionary process of Cuba is a confirmation of the extraordinary force of the ideas of Marx, Engels and Lenin'. And for the next hour this man of great gifts of intellect and oratory rewarded one of the world's greatest universities with his recitation of Marxist–Leninist banalities, praise of the Soviet Union, and denunciations of imperialism.

Castro landed in Moscow on 26 June, his third time there, for a relaxed two-week visit. It marked the official end of a decade of Cuban–Soviet misunderstandings, a fact underlined by the presence of Brezhnev, Kosygin and Podgorny at Vnukovo-2 airport, and the award to Fidel the next day of the Order of Lenin. Apart from his meetings with the Kremlin leadership, Castro conferred with Defence Minister Grechko and the Soviet General Staff, again emphasizing the importance of Cuban–Soviet military ties. He visited four Soviet cities, the space centre, an aircraft plant and agricultural stations, seemingly completely at home now in the Soviet Union. He flew home on 5 July, and Cuba's membership in the CMEA, the Communist common market, was announced six days later.

International relations continued to keep Castro busy for the balance of 1972 and much of 1973, while the fragile economy at home seemed to be receiving less of his attention.

In December 1972 Salvador Allende came to Cuba to see Fidel, and they spent pleasant days in the sun chatting and sailing in a cabin cruiser. This was their last meeting.

On 18 December Castro was again in Moscow for a week's stay to celebrate the fiftieth anniversary of the foundation of the Soviet Union. During that week he was able to put the finishing touches to five major economic and technical assistance agreements with the Russians. Thus the Cuban debt of some $4 billion was deferred altogether until 1986 – virtually a fifteen-year moratorium – and the Cubans would then have twenty-five years over which to repay it. The anticipated Cuban trade deficits in 1973 and 1974 (still not enough sugar was being produced) were to be covered by separate credits. The volume of two-way trade between 1973 and 1975 was increased sharply, although no precise figures were given, which simply meant more Soviet aid to the limping Cuban economy. Additional credits of $390 million were earmarked for economic development. And Moscow agreed to pay still more for Cuban sugar and nickel so that the debt would rise more slowly. Back in Havana, Castro outlined these accords in a speech on 3 January, 1973, commenting that Cuban–Soviet relations were 'a model of the truly fraternal, truly internationalist and truly revolutionary'.

This was not hyperbole. By the mid-1970s Cuba was receiving about one half of total Soviet economic aid to all of the Third World (including Vietnam) as well as probably one half of Soviet military aid to these countries. Because Soviet and Cuban foreign policies were increasingly on the same track in the light of changing world conditions – and not because Moscow was forcing Castro to follow its line as it did in 1968 –

Fidel could conduct his relations with the Third World as he pleased, free to enhance the international standing he had lost quite perceptibly after the 1962 missile crisis and after Che Guevara's death. Therefore he literally had the best of all worlds.

In this sense it should not surprise Americans, as it seems to, that Castro has no intention of ever trading his Soviet relationship for a relationship with the United States. He knows that no American administration (to say nothing of Congress) would provide him with the kind of massive economic and military aid he receives from the Soviets – with relatively few questions asked. Moreover, he realizes that the United States would require that he shed his Communist system and his Third World policies to qualify for even the most minimal assistance. In repeated public statements and in private conversations Castro insists that apart from political and 'moral' considerations it would simply make no practical sense for him to sever his friendship with the Russians – even if this friendship has its trying moments. It would certainly suit him to have easy trade with the United States as well as other arrangements helpful to the island's economy, but not at the price of renouncing his Soviet alliance. He marvels privately that serious American officials and politicians are so naïve as to believe that Washington would be doing him a favour by establishing relations with Havana with basic pre-conditions. It is simply a question of perspective that continues to elude most Americans, and this is why all the past attempts at negotiations by Washington have led nowhere – except for non-political accords of mutual convenience.

With a free hand in the Third World, Castro began to concentrate on it (aside from his Latin American interests) with great seriousness in the early 1970s, making it a centrepiece of Cuban foreign policy in the ensuing years. On his way to Moscow in December 1972 he stopped in Morocco to meet King Hassan; for his purposes, friendship with socialist Algeria did not preclude a rapport with the Moroccan monarchy. In September 1973 Fidel attended the Fourth Conference of Non-Aligned Nations in Algiers where he became acquainted with most of the Third World leaders, making new friends and a very good impression – even though he was criticised for defending the Soviet Union from accusations that it was as imperialist as America.

Then Castro flew to bomb-ravaged Hanoi on his first visit to Vietnam, with which he felt a special kinship as a fellow victim of the United States. Vietnam peace treaties had been signed in January, and America was now out of the war. This was also his first time in Asia, but Fidel had no desire to go to China, an enemy of his Soviet and Vietnamese friends. He was in Hanoi on the day when Salvador Allende's regime was ousted by the military coup and the Chilean president was killed in his palace. In Allende, Castro lost a personal friend and a vital Latin American ally.

Fidel Castro received the ultimate accolade from the Soviet Union – and further recognition of his international standing – when Leonid Brezhnev arrived in Havana on 28 January 1974. Never before had the highest Soviet leader visited Latin America, and this was a special trip to Cuba, not part of a larger tour.

Brezhnev was Castro's guest for a week, paying him the special tribute of going to Santiago to see the former Moncada barracks (now a school) which Fidel and his rebel band had attacked on 26 July 1953, setting in motion the Cuban revolution. Then he drove with Fidel to the nearby El Siboney farm where the rebels had assembled the night before the assault. This was Castro's final vindication: the Russians, recognizing the Marxist correctness of the *Fidelista* enterprise, would never again speak of Moncada as a *putsch* or adventure. In Havana, Brezhnev and Castro addressed a million Cubans at a rally on Revolution Square under the statue of José Martí, then signed a grandiloquent Soviet–Cuban Declaration of .principles. In his speech addressed to Brezhnev, Castro did, in effect, confirm the belief that he was the Kremlin's spokesman in the Non-Aligned Movement: 'As we have emphasized at the conference of non-aligned countries in Algeria, the very existence of the Soviet Union constitutes a brake on the militarist adventures of the aggressive forces of the imperialist world, without which they would already have launched a new effort to divide the planet, and would not have hesitated to invade countries possessing petroleum and other basic raw materials.'

A great turning point in the history of the Third World, Africa and revolutionary movements, was the overthrow of the dictatorial regime in Portugal by left-of-centre military officers in April 1974. One of the first moves by the young officers was to announce the end of Portugal's hopeless and ruinous colonial wars, and to promise independence as soon as possible for Angola, Mozambique, Guinea-Bissau and the Cape Verde Islands. The most important of these wars was fought in Angola, and in January 1975 the military government and the three rebel factions signed the Alvor Agreement (named after the Portuguese town where they met) providing for Angolan independence on 11 November.

Because Fidel Castro had had the foresight to support the Marxist MPLA (Popular Movement for the Liberation of Angola) since he first met Agostinho Neto early in the 1960s, Cuba found itself in an extraordinary position to exercise a decisive influence on Angolan events. This, in turn, made the Cubans the most important outside force in African military politics, first in Angola and then in Ethiopia – a state of affairs that continued to prevail in the 1980s. And Fidel Castro was consequently elevated to the status of an unquestioned world leader, calling the shots in Africa and Central America, assuming the responsibility for formulating Third World economic policies towards the industrialized countries and, of course, becoming more than ever an accursed obsession for the United States. At the same time he stood on the threshold of formally transforming his revolution into a permanent and constitutional Communist institution. He was barely fifty years old.

Chapter 3

Contrary to widespread belief, it was Fidel Castro's idea – certainly not the Russians' – to engage Cuban combat troops in the civil war in Angola on an absolutely open-ended basis. A second decade of a large-scale Cuban military presence there began in 1986; over 200,000 Cuban troops have been rotated through Angola during the first decade, and Castro has pledged to rotate 200,000 more Cubans there, if necessary. But contrary to Fidel's own assertions it was *not* South Africa's armed intervention in that civil war which forced him to rush his forces to Angola. The truth is that Castro beat everybody to it by entering the Angolan conflict quite spontaneously, in an impressive display of instinct, imagination and daring.

After the Alvor Agreement on independence, the Angolan civil war broke out among the MPLA and two rival movements. They were FNLA (National Front for the Liberation of Angola) led by Holden Roberto and backed by the United States, Zaire, China and South Africa, and UNITA (National Union for the Total Liberation of Angola) headed by Jonas Savimbi and supported by the United States and South Africa. FNLA and UNITA obviously were anti-Communist. Curiously, the Soviet Union withdrew its support for the MPLA, not trusting it politically and militarily, leaving Castro as its only friend. He had trained MPLA guerrilla officers in Cuba, and when the internal power struggle erupted he quietly dispatched 250 Cuban combat advisers in May 1975 to organize MPLA forces. Simultaneously Flavio Bravo, one of the oldest Communist friends of the Castro brothers and now a top regime official, met in Brazzaville with the MPLA president, Agostinho Neto.

In July the MPLA requested additional aid as both the FNLA and UNITA began to acquire great new strength from United States equipment and advice (the CIA was reported to have spent $31 million in helping the anti-Communist factions in 1974 and 1975, until Congress stopped this covert aid). In August, South African and Portuguese mercenary units crossed from Namibia into southern Angola to protect a border hydroelectric station from the MPLA. Now everybody seemed to be involved in Angola against the MPLA, the Cubans being its only, but increasingly effective, defenders. Late in September and early in October, three Cuban freighters delivered military detachments and arms to Angola and, belatedly, Soviet arms began arriving through Brazzaville. In early October there were about 1500 Cuban Army personnel in Angola. On 23 October South Africans in force entered Angola in Operation Zulu, and Cuba responded with a troop airlift under its Operation Carlota. It was a fully fledged Cuban expeditionary force, rushing units aboard Cubana Airlines transport planes through Conakry in Guinea (with Fidel's friend, President Sekou Touré, coordinating the operation). At first the Cuban aircraft tried to refuel without permission in Barbados and Trinidad, then Guyana authorized their action.

There is no question that the Cubans saved the MPLA. They helped it to defeat its enemies in the crucial battle for the railway terminal port of Benguela on 5 November, and assured its capture of the capital of Luanda – threatened by Holden Roberto's FNLA – in time for Angolan independence on 11 November. In February 1976 Castro had 15,000 troops in Angola, and the Organization of African Unity recognized MPLA as the government. Castro said that Cuban forces would remain in Angola as long as the MPLA needed them – they would be there ten years later as the Angolan regime remained unable to survive alone the onslaughts of Jonas Savimbi's UNITA, massively and openly backed by South Africa. As part of all the ironies of Angola, Cuban units, because of their discipline, were assigned to guard the oil-producing installations of the American-owned Gulf Oil Corporation in the Cabinda enclave in the north. Then, the Soviets quietly purchased this oil from Gulf on the high seas (through a broker in Curaçao), and the tankers from Angola sailed to Cuba; it was much cheaper for the Russians to ship at least some of the oil to Cuba from Cabinda rather than from the Black Sea. The final irony came in 1985, when South African commandos tried to blow up Gulf's installation, Castro exploded in terrible public rage.

The Angolan operation proved that Cuba and the Soviet Union can smoothly coordinate overseas military undertakings in Africa and presumably elsewhere in the Third World through rapid deployments of lightly armed Cuban personnel and simultaneous (or pre-positioned) deliveries of heavy Soviet arms. It is nonsense, however, to suggest that the Cubans are the 'Ghurkas of the Soviet empire' (as American administrations have charged), and that their troops were ordered into Angola by the Russians. While it is true that in Angola, and later in Ethiopia, Cuban and Soviet interests have coincided, it is not plausible that Moscow even attempted to 'order' Cubans there. It would not work as a practical proposition and, above all, there is ample evidence that it was all Fidel's idea in the first place.

There is no reason to doubt Castro's veracity when he told Barbara Walters in a television interview in 1977: 'You should not think that the Soviets were capable of asking Cuba to send a single man to Angola . . . That is totally alien to Soviet relations with Cuba and to Soviet behaviour. A decision of that nature could exclusively be taken by our party and our government on our own intitiative at the request of the Angolan government . . . The Soviets absolutely did not ask us. They never said a single word on that subject. It was exclusively a Cuban decision.' He added: 'We decided to send the first military unit to Angola to fight against South African troops. That is the reason why we made the decision. If we had not made that effort, it is most likely that South Africa would have taken over Angola.'

Castro's denial that Moscow had pushed him into Angola is corroborated by Arkady Shevchenko, a senior Soviet diplomat who defected to the United States in 1978. He wrote in his memoirs that when he asked Deputy Foreign Minister Vasily Kuznetsov some time in 1976, 'How did we persuade the Cubans to provide their contingent?', Kuznetsov 'laughed'. Shevchenko added: 'After acknowledging that Castro might be playing his own game in sending about 20,000 troops to Angola, Kuznetsov told me that the idea for the large-scale military operation had originated in Havana, not Moscow. It was startling information. As I later discovered, it was also a virtual secret in the Soviet capital.'

When I raised the question of Angola in a conversation with Castro in January 1984, he said that 'the Angolans asked us for help, and we sent them help, with great effort and great sacrifice . . . Angola was invaded by South Africa [which] has the moral condemnation of the entire world . . . Therefore we could never have done anything more than just to help Angola against an external invasion . . . In the instances in which we have provided help, outside of Latin America, it has been to countries that have been attacked. It is not the case of actions against governments there, regardless of what the governments are. We helped the people of the Portuguese colonies as everybody was helping them everywhere, and when the United Nations helped them. We fight against South Africa when the United Nations condemns South Africa for its aggression in Angola; we helped Ethiopia when it was the target of an external invasion aimed at disintegrating the country.' Castro also makes the point that, as in Nicaragua, the Cubans provide extensive medical, educational and technical assistance to Angola in a blend with military help. It is a unique formula, and it is accepted by the Angolans, Ethiopians, Nicaraguans and others in the Third World because it comes from a fellow Third World country.

Just as Cuba was becoming engaged in Angola, the Ford Administration decided that the time might have come to improve relations with Fidel Castro. The idea came from Secretary of State Henry Kissinger who did not think that the emerging rivalry in Angola should prevent him reaching some understanding with Cuba. Kissinger had succeeded in negotiating an overture to China (and a Nixon trip to Peking) in the midst of the Vietnam war, and he reasoned that it should be possible to establish a dialogue with Castro. The Soviet–American détente was in full bloom, and this loomed as another favourable factor in approaching the Cubans. Besides, Kissinger had valid reasons to think that Castro would be interested. What he could not predict was the ultimate degree of Cuban involvement in Angola.

Before any action was taken the State Department undertook a series of confidential conversations with Cuban diplomats at the United Nations to assess Havana reactions to possible talks, obtaining encouraging replies. Castro was known to be flexible on certain aspects of relations with the United States when it suited him – he had allowed the resumption of emigration to the mainland in 1965, over an air shuttle, and worked out an anti-hijacking 'understanding' with Washington in 1973 – and now Kissinger wanted to know how far the Cuban leader might go. In a speech in March 1975 he pointedly said there was 'no virtue in perpetual antagonism' with Cuba. In May he approved a 'secret advance probe' policy through which Castro was informed that the United States was considering selectively lifting sanctions against Cuba and would suspend RB-71 spy plane flights over the island during preliminary contacts.

On 29 July the United States joined a majority of OAS members at a conference in San José, Costa Rica, to abolish the collective embargo on economic and political ties with the Cubans. This followed fairly detailed secret conversations conducted with Cuban emissaries, who had step-by-step instructions personally from Castro; the American negotiator was Assistant Secretary of State for Inter-American Affairs William D. Rogers, a highly respected international law practitioner, and his cloak-and-dagger meetings with the Cubans ranged from the Pierre Hotel in New York to coffee shops at La Guardia airport in New York and National airport in Washington. The most promising aspect of this effort was that both sides agreed in principle that there should be no pre-conditions to actual negotiations, everything being negotiable. Ramón Sánchez-Parodi, the Cuban emissary, was able to advise Rogers that Castro did not insist on the lifting of the United States economic embargo before negotiations began, a very major change in his stand. Rogers told the Cubans that the fate of the Guantánamo naval base was negotiable as well.

When on 9 August Castro returned to Southern Airways the $2 million ransom it had paid three years earlier for a hijacked plane, the administration read it as a positive signal. Ten days later the State Department announced that American firms based in foreign countries would be allowed to do business with Cuba for the first time in twelve years. This measure had been under consideration for some time, but now was offered as a firm diplomatic gesture towards Castro. Late in September, Rogers announced that the United States was prepared 'to improve our relations with Cuba' and 'to enter into a dialogue'. But then the whole effort went off the track. In Angola the Cuban military presence assumed large proportions, eliciting public criticism by Kissinger. In Havana, Castro chose that particular period to sponsor a Puerto Rican Solidarity conference, urging Puerto Rican independence as 'a matter of principle', knowing perfectly well that it was an issue calculated to provoke United States anger. At the United Nations, Cuban Ambassador Ricardo Alarcón de Quesada tied it all together in an October speech, declaring: 'Cuban solidarity with Puerto Rico is non-negotiable' and 'it is Cuba's duty to give effective support to MPLA in Angola'.

Late in November Rogers and Sánchez-Parodi had their last secret meeting. The diplomatic enterprise had collapsed and traditional hostility returned. The American side claims the Cubans decided to break off the preliminary negotiations without providing a clear explanation; the suspicion is that Castro felt it was impossible to enter into fully fledged negotiations with Washington while the war in Angola was raging. The Cubans say that it was the Americans who severed the contacts out of anger over the Puerto Rico episode in Havana, but they do not explain why Castro had so blatantly reopened this extremely controversial issue if, indeed, he was serious about talks with the United States. Fidel frequently chooses not to explain his actions even to his closest associates, but late in 1985 he told an American visitor that the Kissinger diplomatic effort ten years earlier had come nearest to a real breakthrough in the whole history of post-revolutionary developments between the United States and Cuba.

The first great milestones of Fidel Castro's revolution were the victory in 1959, and the creation of the new Communist Party in 1965 as the ruling political body in Cuba. The next milestone was the 'institutionalization of the revolution', as Castro called it, through the promulgation of a new Cuban constitution on 24 February 1976. Over the previous seventeen years the Fundamental law drafted immediately after victory by the first revolutionary government and literally thousands of laws and regulations had formed the judicial framework of the Cuban state – though no doubt ever existed as to where actual power reposed.

Nevertheless laws had to be refined, revised and codified and, as much as anything else, full legitimacy had to be granted to the socialist character of Cuba and its objective of attaining Communism. Consequently Blás Roca, the secretary general of the 'old' Communist Party and a member of the Politburo of the new party, was named in October 1974 as chairman of a commission charged with the task of drafting the new constitution. The draft was published six months later, and it was submitted for discussion by millions of Cubans in party and military organizations, labour unions, and youth and women's groups. Predictably, no basic changes resulted from the discussions that Castro regarded as 'direct democracy', but – quite surprisingly to the regime – the people wanted that democracy to be even more direct.

An innovation in the constitutional draft was the creation of a Popular Power structure of local self-government (no such thing exists in other Communist countries) capped by a National Assembly with legislative functions described as the 'supreme organ of state power'. Over the method of electing deputies to the National Assembly a profound division developed, however, between those advocating direct elections and those favouring choice by municipal assemblies of Popular Power. In the first instance, voters would at least potentially have a voice in the formulation of main national policies, and the decision-making process would have to be made reasonably visible to the public. In the second instance, membership in the National Assembly could be determined through political manipulation on the local level with candidates nominated from the municipal assemblies or by party and government officials. Inasmuch as the draft also provided for National Assembly deputies 'to explain the policy of the state and periodically render account to [the electors]', it could have been disastrous for the central government to tolerate direct elections. So bitter was the internal dispute over this point that the constitution, on which a popular referendum was held on 15 February 1976, failed to spell out the method of election. Only *after* 97.7 per cent of the voters had approved the charter did the Central Preparatory Commission headed by Fidel Castro insert the provision that 'The National Assembly . . . is composed of deputies elected by the Municipal Assemblies'. This was the end of the first and last major attempt to democratize Cuban Marxism.

The constitutional referendum was preceded in December 1975 by the First Congress of the Cuban Communist Party, chaired by Castro and attended by Mikhail Suslov, the chief Soviet Communist ideologue and one of the most powerful members of the Politburo. Castro's report to the Congress was a 248-page document (in book form) chronicling the history of Cuba, the *Fidelista* revolutionary movement, its transformation into socialism, the first ten years of the Communist Party, the achievements of the revolution, and the Cuban struggle against 'imperialism' and in support of 'liberation movements'. Although Cuban troops were fighting in Angola even as Castro addressed the Congress, his report made no mention of them; it simply alluded to 'the recent constitution of the independent republic of Angola, under the direction of the MPLA, in the midst of strong and heroic struggle against imperialism'. The Angolan war was not yet a public event as far as Cuban opinion was concerned.

The constitution itself defined Cuba as a 'socialist state of workers and peasants and all other manual and intellectual workers', with the Communist Party being 'the highest leading force of the society and of the state, which organizes and guides the common effort towards the goals of the construction of socialism and progress towards a Communist society'. It first hailed José Martí who 'led us to the people's revolutionary victory', then Fidel Castro under whose leadership the 'triumphant revolution' was to be carried forward.

Thus enshrined in the constitutional text Castro was, in effect, named leader for life as a matter of law; the corollary was that it would be unconstitutional (and not just 'counter-revolutionary') to challenge him. Pursuant to constitutional provisions, the National Assembly then elected a thiry-one member Council of State, including Fidel Castro as its president and Raúl Castro as first vice president. As president of the Council, Castro became 'the Head of State and Head of Government'. Total power was therefore legally vested in him as President of Cuba and Chairman of the Council of Ministers as well as First Secretary of the Communist Party and military Commander-in-Chief.

There was no specific succession procedure, but Raúl was the first vice president of both Council of State and ministers, the Second Secretary of the Communist Party (no other Communist Party in the world has such a post) and Defence Minister; the rank of General of the Army was also created for him. Succession was thus automatically resolved and, as Fidel remarked once in absolute seriousness, 'the creation of the institutions has assured the continuity of the revolution' after his death. He added straight-facedly that he was not really needed any more, explaining that Raúl was his successor (automatically) because he had the leadership qualities – not because he was his brother. The faithful Dorticós was demoted from the presidency of Cuba to a ministerial post (he later committed suicide).

The 1976 constitution and the Communist Party's First Congress established the permanent character of the Cuban revolutionary state, ruling out any basic structural or ideological changes in the future, barring cataclysms. Evolution would simply reflect normal societal requirements as time went on, never affecting the existing structure or philosophy. In this sense the future of Cuba was set in granite. By 1986, after two more quinquennial congresses of the Communist Party, everything had remained the same, with Fidel Castro the only and final author and arbiter of every decision taken in Cuba. The National Assembly held two annual sessions as prescribed by the constitution, but each session lasted only two or three days.

The decade between 1976 and 1986, the year when Fidel Castro celebrated his sixtieth birthday and the twenty-seventh anniversary of his revolution, was devoted to immense activity in foreign policy areas, to ever-frustrated efforts to energize and organize the Cuban economy, and to improve the quality of life of the island's ten million citizens, after meeting equitably their basic needs of health and education. In the international realm Castro scored more successes than defeats, remaining as defiant as ever and gaining a considerable degree of world acceptability and respectability. In fact, his only defeats since the 1970s when Allende was overthrown in Chile, were the electoral defeat of his friend Prime Minister Michael Manley in Jamaica, and the American invasion of Grenada – where Castro had great hopes to expand his influence in the eastern Caribbean. With the United States, as always, there were gains and losses.

Negotiations with the Carter administration led to the establishment of diplomatic 'interests sections' by the Cubans in Washington and the Americans in Havana in 1977; in the absence of actual diplomatic relations the 'sections' were euphemisms for embassies, and they provided instant channels of communication between the two governments. The Carter and Reagan administrations kept the chief of the Cuban interests section at arms' length, but Castro made a point of giving quasi-ambassadorial treatment to the senior American diplomat in Havana, inviting him to palace receptions. When he was informed in 1985 that a new chief of the American interests section was appointed for Havana, he showed great curiosity, asking visiting Americans and diplomats what sort of a person was the new *Americano*. Talks with the United States in 1978 led to an agreement allowing Cubans exiled on the mainland to visit their families on the island, and tens of thousands took advantage of it (this was suspended in 1985, when Castro became annoyed with the Reagan administration over the inauguration of the anti-regime Radio Martí operated by the Voice of America). Attempts at political negotiations with the Carter administration, personally orchestrated by Castro, fizzled out, and the exodus of over 100,000 Cubans to Florida in small boats from the port of Mariel put an end to the contacts; Castro encouraged this invasion out of anger at Carter over an unguarded remark that the United States awaited Cuban political refugees with 'open arms'.

Castro's great moment in the international sun came when he was elected Chairman of the Non-Aligned Movement for the 1979–82 period, assuming the formal Third World leadership to which he had so

long aspired. He hosted the Non-Aligned Movement's summit conference in Havana in September 1979, at which ninety-two heads of state or
their representatives were present – from the Communist octogenarian
Marshal Tito of Yugoslavia to the deeply religious Islamic President
Mohammad Zia ul-Haq of Pakistan and Prime Minister Indira Gandhi of
India – and he succeeded in keeping the spotlight on himself. Things were
going his way everywhere. In March of that year a pro-Cuban regime
was established on the tiny island of Grenada in the eastern Caribbean by
his friend Maurice Bishop, a leftist lawyer and politician of vast personal
appeal. In July the Sandinista Liberation Front rebels ousted the Somoza
dictatorship in Nicaragua; Castro was well acquainted with Carlos
Fonseca, the founder of the Sandinista movement, who had been killed in
1966, and he provided considerable assistance to the rebels after forcing
them to unite in a common front. Now Cuba had revolutionary allies in
Central America and on the outer fringes of the Caribbean, just a hop
away from strategic Venezuela.

In October Fidel Castro returned to New York for the first time in
nineteen years to address the United Nations General Assembly as
chairman of the Non-Aligned Movement. It was a moment of vindication he savoured: in 1960 he had sought refuge in a hotel in Harlem, and
now he spent his three days in New York at the twelve-storey
headquarters of the Cuban mission to the United Nations (complete with
living quarters and a school) which Cuba had just purchased in midtown
for $2.1 million. The Cuban mission had the largest number of officials
after the United States and the Soviet Union. Reminiscing about this visit
to New York and the reception he held at the Cuban mission, Fidel told
me with immense satisfaction: 'That first time in 1960, we lived on
chicken . . . This time I brought my own lobsters, my own rum. . .' In
his two-hour speech at the General Assembly on 12 October Castro –
acting as the spokesman for the destitute Third World – urged the United
States and other 'wealthy imperialists' to grant the underdeveloped
nations $300 billion over ten years. 'If there are no resources for
development, there will be no peace', he said, 'and the future will be
apocalyptic.' The fate of the Third World, including its monumental debt
to the industrial nations, became the centrepiece of Castro's foreign
policy in the 1980s: he fervently championed it at the 1982 Non-Aligned
Movement's summit in New Delhi, and in the extraordinary anti-debt
offensive he mounted in Havana in 1985.

Economic issues were one aspect of Castro's ever-growing 'internationalism'. The other was his military participation in revolutionary
confrontations across the globe. From the initial involvement in Angola
in 1975, Castro moved on to Ethiopia in 1978, dispatching nearly twenty
thousand combat troops to assist the new Marxist regime of Lieutenant
Colonel Mengistu Haile Mariam in repulsing an attack by Somalia on the

contested Ogaden region. As in Angola, the Soviet Union provided arms and advisers. In Third World policies, Castro and the Russians were totally on the same wavelength. When the Soviet Union invaded Afghanistan in December 1979 to save 'socialism' in an Asian re-run of the Czechoslovakia application of the Brezhnev Doctrine, Castro stood foursquare behind them. He rationalized their action even though fierce Afghan resistance to the Russians made the whole affair most embarrassing, especially with Muslim nations, to Castro as the Non-Aligned Movement's chairman. But Castro could also rationalize switching his early support for the Eritrean secession movement from Ethiopia to the other side once President Mengistu became his ally. And again Castro's activities threatened to create a Soviet-American confrontation. The presence of Soviet-supported Cuban forces in the crucial Horn of Africa nearly led the Carter administration to break off strategic arms limitation talks with the Soviet Union.

Castro has never made a secret of his support for the Sandinista movement, either before or after its triumph. He has given Nicaragua, his revolutionary junior partner, military advisers and civilian technicians. He fully supports the leftist guerrillas in the civil war in El Salvador (he also supports the M-19 guerrillas in Colombia), but he knows perfectly well that Cuba cannot protect these two Central American countries from a direct United States attack (and he realizes that the Soviet Union would not commit itself to a military defence of Nicaragua in the way it is committed in Cuba). He believes that political settlements are possible both in Nicaragua and El Salvador because endless stalemate is the alternative. But he is also aware that in a total crisis the United States might try to annihilate him, a possibility increased by the Reagan administration's early threats to go 'to the source' of Central American upheavals which it believes to be in Cuba – and by the invasion of Grenada in 1983.

In a conversation early in 1984, about possible American military action in Central America and beyond, Castro told me: 'We have no means with which to decide militarily the events there. All our means are defensive. We have no fleet and no air force capable of neutralizing or breaking a blockade by the United States. It's not a question of options, it's entirely a practical matter . . . Besides, from a political viewpoint it would be improper for us to attempt a military involvement under such circumstances because it would be a justification before American public opinion for a United States aggression.' Replying to my question whether he was concerned about an American invasion, Castro said: 'We have made great efforts to strengthen our defences. After Grenada we have made even greater efforts. We are increasing our defence and resistance capability considerably, and preparing our people for a prolonged, indefinite war. If the United States deterrent, as the Reagan government has said, is the nuclear force, our deterrent is to make it impossible for this country to be occupied, for an occupation army to be able to maintain itself here. First, it would be necessary to fight very hard to occupy Cuba. But the occupation of our country would not be the end, only the beginning of a much harder and much more difficult war, in which we would – at whatever cost – be victorious sooner or later.'

In Castro's Third World policies, doctors and teachers are as important as combat troops, and he takes immense pride in explaining that Cuba is the only developing nation willing and able to help others. He says that the new Cuban generation has an 'internationalist' spirit not found elsewhere. In a conversation about this internationalism, he told me: 'Look: when after the triumph of the revolution in Nicaragua we were asked for teachers, there were twenty-nine thousand volunteers . . . In the beginning, we had no doctors to send to the interior of our country. Today, we have doctors in more than twenty-five countries of the Third World – more than fifteen thousand doctors working in the Third World. And there will be more because we are graduating two thousand annually. It is a new culture, a new morality . . . It is amazing: you go to our universities, and one hundred per cent volunteer for any task. When we needed volunteers to go to Angola, three hundred thousand responded. They were civilian reservists. Now hundreds of thousands of Cubans have fulfilled internationalist missions. People ask why there are two thousand Cuban teachers in Nicaragua, but who else will do the work that Cubans perform there? How many [people] in Latin America are prepared to go where our teachers go, to live with the poorest families, to eat what the poorest families eat, to teach there? You won't find such people . . . We have more people disposed to go to any place in the world as doctors, as teachers, as technicians and as workers than the Peace Corps of the United States and all the Churches together – and we are a country of only ten million inhabitants.'

In the economy, Castro stubbornly refuses to relax his harsh enforcement of totally centralized planning (even when most of the Communist world has discovered the merits of relative decentralization). In his ideological inflexibility, Castro sees heresy in any attempt to experiment with market forces. The chronic and alarmingly deficient performance of the economy seems to strengthen his resolve to be faithful to orthodoxy. In June 1986 – sounding as he did during the revolutionary offensive in 1968 – Castro rose to denounce 'certain concepts [proposed] by persons, supposedly very Marxist and very versed in Marxism, but really with capitalist or petit-bourgeois souls'. And ideological and political controls over what must be the world's most indoctrinated society tend to tighten rather than relax after the twenty-seven years of revolution.

Even some of Castro's close associates are at a loss to understand the reasons for the new hard-line attitude of the mid-1980s. After the Mariel exodus in 1980 Castro appeared to have concluded that the nation required a certain relaxation of tensions – the Mariel experience was a trauma because the regime was taken aback by this proof of internal resentments – and that it must be allowed a degree of consumer freedom. Accordingly, many food items were freed from rationing and made available in 'free stores' at extremely high prices, and uncontrolled farmers' markets were authorized for the sale of produce in the cities. It was far from a bonanza because foodstuffs remained in short supply as a result of inadequate production, but it seemed like a small step towards liberalization of the economy within Marxism.

As preparations were made during 1985 for the Third Congress of the Communist Party, many senior economic planners hoped for still more liberalization and a new policy of decentralization. There was talk about turning over taxis to private owners operating through cooperatives to take the government out of the business of running all the cabs in Cuba, and about ending the kind of rationing of clothes and footwear that had created a state monopoly over shoddy products at an immense cost to the treasury (Cuban women increasingly preferred to have private seam-stresses make their dresses). Ideas circulated about abandoning the ideologically-designed youth work brigades whose weekend activities cost more in blankets, boots, mosquito screens, food and transportation than they brought in farm production. But Castro evidently would have none of it, emerging again as the fierce apostle of the revolution, even as the economy kept deteriorating.

Presumably because Castro was unable to formulate an economic plan for the next quinquennium – in part because he was busy presiding over international conferences on Third World debts – the party congress was postponed to February 1986. But even then Castro still was not ready to deal with the key issues, and the most important part of the congress was put back to the end of 1986. According to Castro, the most significant achievement of the first part of the congress was to rejuvenate the leadership and bring in new blood. Even this, however, was an illusion. Although several cosmetic changes were made, the Politburo remained the same old faces. The new Central Committee turned out to be an assemblage of middle-aged men and women drawn from the bureauc-racy, party organizations, the armed forces and Security services. In a nation where more than one half of the population was born after the revolution, only 9 per cent of the Central Committee membership were below the age of thirty-five; more than 50 per cent were over the age of forty-six. There were only 18.2 per cent women. And 78.1 per cent had university education, all of which suggests that the party created a new ruling elite, heavy on bureaucrats and administrators (27.5 per cent) and full-time party officials (27.1 per cent). Twenty per cent of the seats went to the armed forces and Interior Ministry Security services.

What Fidel Castro had imposed in 1986 under the guise of keeping revolutionary fires burning was an ossification of the regime and society. Almost immediately after the first session of the party Congress ended, Castro ordered the closing of the farmers' markets on the grounds of illicit enrichment and corruption. It was strangely reminiscent of his discovery in 1968 that privately owned hot dog stands were hotbeds of counter-revolution. At the same time Castro moved even further ahead with the militarization of Cuban society through the expansion of Territorial Troop Militias, a highly trained reserve organization exceeding one million people – 10 per cent of the population. The militias' 340-page illustrated *Basic Manual* is required reading in Cuba (it sells for one peso in bookstores), and exercises and manouevres are conducted continuously in 'defence zones' into which the island has been divided. The ever-present threat from the United States has always justified a high degree of preparedness in Cuba, especially after the Grenada invasion, but the militarization in the mid-1980s looms as much as anything as a political move to strengthen the cohesion of the revolutionary society under Castro's extremely strict leadership.

Who is Fidel Castro at the age of sixty? In the immediate sense, he is the undisputed and still enormously popular (and even loved) leader of an extremely volatile nation which he has raised over more than a quarter-century to a place in the sun in world affairs and towards what he himself has called 'a life of decency'. Himself a grandfather, he sees to it that everywhere in Cuba children are healthy and clean and educated. It is a great accomplishment in any society. Thanks to Castro's revolution, no Third World country approaches Cuban standards in the area of that 'decent life'.

But there are other levels, and they are disturbing when Castro's intelligence and experiences are taken into account. His behaviour since roughly 1980 suggests that he has few fresh ideas for his aging revolution. Curiously, this man of astonishing daring and imagination and romanticism is allowing – or forcing – his beloved social and human experiment to be locked into obsolete ideological orthodoxy and deadening bureaucratization. His sallies against 'bourgeois' tendencies sound quaintly antiquated, if not actually caricatures in a world that has changed so much since the days when such expressions of ideology were still in vogue. Considering the extent to which creativeness has been blunted – one hopes not buried – in the name of revolutionary conformism, Castro faces the danger that his revolution may be decaying.

Certainly in a physical sense much of the early revolutionary construction is already in decay: paint is peeling off and windows are broken at the great and admirable Camilo Cienfuegos school complex at the foot of the Sierra Maestra, and masses of costly imported equipment are destroyed by the Caribbean weather because the regime remains unable to solve the problem of unloading ships and loading trucks. These are obvious examples: there are others. Mismanagement discourages work and production, and resulting shortages aggravate the problem of low productivity and high absenteeism. It becomes a vicious circle. Bureaucratic corruption and black marketeering in the streets are re-emerging in Cuba, a cancer on the body of a revolution that was born so pure, and Fidel Castro inveighs in rage against 'vile money'. Young people drink too much because there is little else to do in their spare time, and they are not touched by the the mystical mystery of the revolution as their fathers and mothers were.

Does Fidel Castro have doubts and fears, and can he share them with another human being: Celia Sánchez died in January 1980, and her passing away was not only a personal and emotional tragedy for Fidel, but it deprived him of a safe haven – the opportunity to be occasionally himself as Fidel and not as commander-in-chief. Watching him hour after hour, almost motionless as he listened to hundreds of speeches at conferences on the external debt he had organized in Havana during 1985, it seemed as if in this environment he was finding a refuge from pressures elsewhere; perhaps it was an illusion. Still, seen in a variety of surroundings, Fidel Castro is a lonely man – frustrated one day, triumphant the next, but lonely, and still seeking something that is impossibly elusive. He might be pondering about the past and the future – and about verdicts of the generations to come. Indeed, he expressed it all at two very crucial moments of his life:

Addressing the judges trying him for the assault on Moncada, the moment of the revolution's birth in 1953, Fidel Castro said: 'Condemn me. It does not matter. History will absolve me!'

Speaking about creation to Cuba's artists and writers in 1961, the year he triumphed at the Bay of Pigs and declared himself a Marxist-Leninist, Fidel Castro said: 'Do not fear imaginary judges here . . . Fear other judges who are much more awesome, fear the judges of posterity, fear the future generations who in the end, will be responsible for saying the last word!'

Epilogue

It is imperative – for the sake of perspective – to take a long look at the island where Fidel Castro's revolution recently entered its twenty-ninth year. How is it faring, and what sort of example does it offer?

The answer, conveyed above all through Castro's own startlingly candid recent public admissions, is that his revolution now faces the greatest and deepest crisis in its history. And, in effect, Cuba's day-to-day economic survival depends more than ever on continued, but seemingly no longer entirely adequate, Soviet economic assistance (worth over $4 billion annually).

Never before had Castro so fully and bitterly acknowledged how truly flawed his revolutionary society has become, a generation after victory. In speeches before the Third Congress of the Cuban Communist Party (which has officially ruled Cuba for twenty-one years with Castro as its First Secretary), he bluntly talked about 'anarchy and chaos' – labour force absenteeism, with many Cubans working no more than four hours a day for full-day pay, all forms of production sinking into disarray, people caring for money more than revolutionary principles, and corruption rearing its ugly head even in party ranks.

Inevitably, Castro had to act on this dismal state of affairs and on 26 December 1986, he proclaimed a new era of austerity for his already austere and deprived nation. The twenty measures he announced before the National Assembly ranged from tightening the already limited consumption of rice, milk, meat and gasoline to the curtailment of television programming in order to conserve electricity.

The consumption of rice, a basic staple of the Cuban diet, had to be cut by 18 per cent, Castro said, because the Russians would not increase shipments (he did not explain why), and Cubans therefore should instead eat potatoes with their black beans. Castro likewise left unexplained why Cuba, traditionally a rice producer, is unable to produce enough for domestic needs, nearly three decades after a revolution that emphasized the creation of a rationally developed agriculture on such a fertile island.

Castro made it clear in these pronouncements that revolutionary Cuba is caught up in a systemic crisis – and not simply in temporary difficulties, attributable to bad weather, adverse international economic conditions, or United States economic pressures (all of which happened to coincide in the last few years, though the American sanctions go back a quarter of a century).

Castro's fundamental problem appears to be that his revolution has come to a dead end as, in his words, 'workers do not work' and 'students do not study'.

What infuriates him the most is that the great 'revolutionary spirit' of the Sierra Maestra has faded away despite incessant ideological indoctrination of the youth. He sees the nation sliding back into the pre-revolutionary capitalist penchant for material profit, cheating, stealing and cultivating 'bourgeois attitudes'. Even Communist Party leaders were scolded for tolerating bribery. He sounded genuinely surprised as he remarked in his National Assembly speech that one would have thought that 'the years of lean cows would have served to teach Cubans to be more efficient and thrifty, eliminating negligence and other bad habits lingering from the pre-revolutionary era.'

Castro, however, may be unjust in blaming his fellow Cubans for revolutionary lapses. The fault may lie even more with his eccentric and over-centralized style of government and management, with virtually every aspect of decision-making held by him personally, and many of the decisions and innovations being purely capricious – such as suddenly rewriting the annual national economic plan as he did late in 1984. The consequence is that ministers and managers never know what to expect, that they shy from taking routine decisions, and that in the end the whole apparatus of government has finally come to a standstill.

These faults had existed all along, but, for at least a quarter of a century, Castro's nation was carried by the momentum of the revolution. The turning point seems to have been reached early in 1985, and it has been moving downhill faster and faster every since. On the surface, the Castro revolution still commanded international attention, even acceptance, as democratic Latin American leaders visited him in Havana, and the US-encouraged international diplomatic isolation was eroding. At home, however, the cracks in the revolutionary edifice were deepening.

During 1986, Castro carried out a far-ranging purge in the highest ranks of his regime, firing without explanation some of his oldest and closest associates, and proclaiming a 'strategic revolutionary offensive' to recapture the evanescent fervour. Political controls and repression against all forms of dissent were further strengthened, and Cuba went on war footing as people's militia units were trained and kept on the alert against an American invasion Castro insisted to be imminent.

But the economy kept worsening. Unable to produce enough sugar to meet export commitments to the Soviet Union, the Cubans had to buy it for precious dollars from the Dominican Republic. Unemployment (supposedly impossible in a communist country) rose to the point where the state had to pay seventy per cent of their salaries to tens of thousands of furloughed workers, a state of affairs Castro himself found highly alarming when he discussed the economy at the Party Congress.

That some 30,000 Cuban soldiers are serving abroad, mainly in Africa, does not seem to alleviate unemployment, and last fall Havana and Moscow signed an unprecedented agreement providing for Cubans to exploit a huge forest area in frozen Siberia, allegedly to meet Cuba's lumber needs. The announcement failed to say how many Cubans would actually work in forest areas near the Chinese and North Korean borders, but the plans are for 'four forestry enterprises'. In 1980, of course, Castro allowed some 100,000 Cubans to flee from the port of Mariel to Florida, lessening unemployment pressures. Curiously, Cuba, a nation of 10 million, seems to be exporting people rather than revolutions.

Still, Castro finds that the Cuban crisis is moral – in the revolutionary sense – not structural or managerial. His current political offensive aims, therefore, at changing human attitudes while hardening the system in contrast with other communist societies – even including the Soviet Union – where the new accent is on liberalizing and relaxing their systems. The Kremlin last year allowed minimal private enterprise for the first time in sixty years, whereas Castro moved to liquidate peasants' free markets, the only vestige of market economy in Cuba, in the name of revolutionary purity.

Then he rose before the closing session of the Party Congress in December to denounce 'negative trends' that, he said, 'encompass the whole activity of the Revolution'. Exhorting his communist comrades to turn away from the profit motive and back to idealism, Castro was the voice of Marxist–Leninist apostles of yesteryear. 'We must demonstrate to the capitalists,' he cried, 'what we socialists, we Communists are capable of doing with pride, honour, principles and consciousness. We must demonstrate that we are more capable than they of solving the problems posed by the development of a country . . . that a Communist spirit, a revolutionary will and vocation . . . will always be a thousand times more powerful than money!'

NOTES

In writing *Fidel, A Critical Portrait,* I have relied on four categories of source material, which are discussed here in detail. The four categories are: interviews and conversations in Cuba; interviews and conversations in the United States; Cuban newspapers and periodicals, before and after the revolution; and books and other texts published in Cuba and elsewhere.

I believe that an explanation of the sources and material will be more useful to readers and other researchers than the mass of footnotes that would otherwise have been required. Moreover, some passages and sections are composites of two or more interviews or conversations, occasionally incorporating information from published sources, and it would be neither practical nor helpful to try to identify individual references and quotations. Except for specific identification in the actual text, no data are provided on Castro's speeches to which references or allusions are made; given the extraordinary number of speeches he has delivered in his life (plus the fact that some of his texts are not available at all, and some only in the form of fragments), it would have been an onerous and pointless task to catalogue all the references.

Finally, the Chapter Notes are provided as a general guide to the *Portrait* in terms of identifying types and groups of source material.

I. Inteviews and Conversations in Cuba

The bulk of the original material in *Fidel, A Critical Portrait* came from tapes as well as informal interviews and conversations I conducted in Cuba in 1984 and 1985 – including long discussions with President Castro in both years. In his case, I have also drawn on my notes from interviews and conversations we had during 1959, and in the course of a tour of the Bay of Pigs battlefield in his company in June 1961.

Formal, taped interview sessions were held during 1985, with seventeen close associates and comrades of Fidel Castro; seven of them were interviewed on two or more occasions. All of the interviews were conducted in Spanish, and I translated into English from tape transcripts the portions and quotations appearing in this book. Following is the list of these interviews, with the identification of subjects:

José R. Fernández, Vice-President of the Council of Ministers; Minister of Education; Alternate Member of the Political Bureau of the Cuban Communist Party

Carlos Rafael Rodríguez, Vice-President of the Councils of State and Ministers; member of the Political Bureau

Vílma Espín Guilloys, President of the Federation of Cuban Women; member of the Council of State and Political Bureau (wife of Raúl Castro)

Pedro Miret Prieto, Vice-President of the Council of Ministers; member of the Council of State and Political Bureau

Armando Hart Dávalos, member of the council of State; Minister of Culture; member of the Political Bureau

José R. Machado Ventura, member of the Council of State; member of the Political Bureau and of the party secretariat

Jorge Enrique Mendoza Reboredo, editor of the Communist Party organ *Granma*; member of the party's Central Committee

Ramiro Valdés Menéndez, Commander of the Revolution (one of three Rebel Army officers honoured with this title); member of the Central Committee; until 1986, Vice-President of the Councils of State and Ministers, Interior Minister, and member of the Political Bureau; demoted without explanation by the Third Party Congress

Guillermo García Frías, Commander of the Revolution; member of the Central Committee; until 1986, Vice-President of the Councils of State and Ministers, minister of transport, and member of the Political Bureau; demoted by the Third Party Congress

Fábio Grobart, co-founder of the Cuban Communist Party in 1925; member of the Central Committee; Chairman of the Institute for the study of the Marxist–Leninist Movement in Cuba; Hero of the Cuban Revolution

Blás Roca Calderío, member of the Central Committee; until 1986, Vice-President of the Council of State and member of the Political Bureau; retired because of age by the Third Party Congress; Secretary General of the Popular Socialist Party (Communist) until the creation of the new Cuban Communist Party under Fidel Castro in 1965

Melba E. Hernández, member of the Central Committee; Heroine of the Cuban Revolution (one of two women participating in the Moncada attack)

Faustino Pérez Hernández, member of the Central Committee; cabinet minister in the first revolutionary government; one of Fidel Castro's two companions after the Alegría de Pío defeat

Universo Sánchez, director of the Environment Protection Office; one of Fidel Castro's two companions (with Faustino Pérez) after the Alegría de Pío defeat

Antonio Nuñez Jiménez, Vice-Minister of Culture; former executive director of INRA; chronicler of Fidel Castro's postwar years

Alfredo Guevara, Cuba's Ambassador to UNESCO; Fidel Castro's university friend; companion at Bogotá uprising in 1948

Conchita Fernández, Fidel Castro's private secretary in the postwar years

Additionally, interviews were taped with Norberto Fuentes, a Cuban journalist and chronicler of the revolution, and with seven citizens in the village of Sierra Maestra who played central roles in assuring the survival of Fidel Castro and his companions during the first year of the guerrilla war (these accounts total 210 pages of transcript).

All the above tapes and transcripts were donated to the University of Miami in Coral Gables, Florida.

Taped interviews with President Castro were conducted in and near Havana in January 1984, and the transcripts total 315 pages. Interviews and conversations in February and May 1985 were of an informal nature, not being taped. In every case I made detailed notes after these meetings. Transcripts of the 1984 Castro interviews are also at the University of Miami. Taped interviews conducted in Cuba added up to 1964 pages. Apart from the 1985 conversations with President Castro, literally scores of other informal discussions with Cuban personalities would have provided thousands more pages of transcripts; the material was preserved in my notes – some of which must remain confidential.

Among these informal conversations mention should be made of many meetings with Eugenio Rodríguez Balari, President of the Institute of Consumer Affairs; Pedro Álvarez Tábio and Mario Mencía, historians of the pre-1959 period of the revolution; Ernesto Guevara Lynch, the father of the late Che Guevara; Manuel Moreno Fraginals, a leading Cuban historian who knew Fidel Castro as a student; Pastor Vega, a major Cuban cinema director; Luis Baez and Gabriel Molina, editors of *Granma*; and Lionel Martin, an American author and journalist who has lived in Cuba since 1961. Many conversation partners to whom I am greatly in debt for their time and patience will not be mentioned here in order to respect their privacy. Among my American friends Henry Raymont, a colleague and an outstanding expert on Cuba, was a very special adviser.

I have dwelt so much on interviews and conversations in Cuba because they are crucial in any historical or biographical undertaking about the revolution and its figures. This is because no coherent or comprehensive body of revolutionary literature or history exists in Cuba. As will be seen in the section on books in these Notes, the available works are fragmentary, and historical objectivity is not their best facet. Within the senior ranks of the Cuban bureaucracy there is strong opposition to a historical reconstruction of the revolution, particularly when it is attempted by foreigners. Ironically, an example of such resistance is the Historical Division of the Council of State, under the Council's secretary, Dr José M. Miyar Barrucco. For this reason interviews become absolutely essential, and it must be emphasized that in my case the access resulted from personal instructions by President Castro.

II. Interviews and Conversations in the United States

As in Cuba, interviews in the United States, principally with Cuban exiles, were essential in reconstructing much of the life of Fidel Castro. Most of them were conducted in Miami, touching chiefly on Castro's youth.

José Ignacio Rasco and Juan Rovira provided important insights on young Fidel at the Belén College in Havana. Rasco, Enrique Ovares, and Max Lesnick contributed information on Castro's university days. Ovares was an invaluable source on Castro's involvement in the Cayo Confites expedition and the Bogotá uprising (he was there with Fidel and Alfredo Guevara). Max Lesnick's recollections and interpretations formed a bridge between Castro's activities at Havana University and the start of his revolutionary career. Raúl Chibás, the brother of the late Eddy Chibás, the founder of the *Ortodoxo* party in 1947, spent several days with me in Miami, sharing his memories of Fidel Castro. He knew Castro as a political leader at the university, a young *Ortodoxo* politician, and then as the chief of the revolution. Chibás was twice in the Sierra Maestra with Castro, serving as the treasurer of the 26th of July Movement, and later, as director of Cuban Railways.

There are 329 pages of transcripts of these taped interviews as well as tapes at the University of Miami.

Other important interviews in Miami and Washington DC were informal in character, and the material was consigned to my notebooks. Most of these conversations were confidential.

III. Cuban Newspapers and Periodicals

The Cuban press before the revolution was extremely important not only in re-creating the political mood of the era, but also for tracking Fidel Castro's public career. The first reference to him in a Havana newspaper appeared in 1944, and news stories about him and articles by him became increasingly frequent over the years, up to the eve of his victory.

This material is identified in the *Portrait* whenever it is relevant; it did not seem useful to include it in the Chapter Notes. The best Cuban press sources were the weekly magazines *Bohemia* and *Carteles*, and the newspapers *Diário de la Marina, El Mundo, El País, La Calle,* and *Alerta*. Nearly complete collections of these publications are at the Library of Congress in Washington, the University of Miami, and other universities in the United States. Pre-revolutionary university publications, such as *Saeta* and *Mella*, are very difficult to locate. Newspaper collections from the pre-revolutionary period are to be found at the José Martí National Library in Havana, but they are very incomplete, and access is controlled by the authorities. Moreover, no copying equipment is publicly available in Cuba; research in this area is incomparably easier in the United States. Pre-revolutionary university publications seem to have been lost, and the Cuban researchers seek to obtain copies from the United States.

For the first revolutionary period the principal Cuban newspaper sources are *Revolución* of the 26th of July Movement and *Hoy*, the Communist organ; they were merged into *Granma* in 1965. All the other Cuban daily newspapers had disappeared by 1961. *Revolución, Hoy* and *Granma* are useful as repositories of speeches by Castro and other revolutionary figures, and for official news, reportage and editorials. *Bohemia* is the most interesting magazine, publishing fragments of revolutionary history. *Verde Olivo* of the Ministry of Revolutionary Armed Forces and *Moncada* of the Ministry of the Interior provide much of the ideological line. References to items from these publications are made in the *Portrait* when relevant. Fairly complete collections of Cuba's post-revolutionary press exists at the Library of Congress, the University of Miami, etc.; in Havana access to this material is rather difficult. The few extant collections of *Lunes de*

Revolución, the first-rate literary supplement launched in 1959 and stopped in 1961, are in private hands in Cuba. They exist in the United States.

IV. Books

A bibliography at the end of this volume lists the most helpful and interesting Cuban, American and European books on Fidel Castro and Cuba. Most of them are obtainable at the Library of Congrress and university libraries in the United States.

As noted above, however, there is an astonishing paucity of serious and useful and up-to-date books about the Cuban revolution – and especially about Fidel Castro. His own speeches are available in a large number of incomplete or excerpted editions in Cuba and the United States, but none of these are much help to a biographical researcher.

Most of the material about Castro is confined to the pre-victory period. In my opinion the most valuable book is *Moncada: Premier Combat de Fidel Castro,* by the French biographer Robert Merle, published in 1965 (and sadly not available in English). Merle interviewed the Castro brothers and most of the survivors of the Moncada attack when their memories were still fresh. Lionel Martin, the American journalist who knows Castro as well as any foreigner, has written a helpful account of his youth and war years in *The Young Fidel,* but historians may find problems with Martin's ideological interpretations, especially on Castro's relations with the Communists; still, it is the only chronicle of this kind. The very long introduction to Castro's *Selected Works, 1947–1958* is a helpful sketch of Fidel against the background of his time.

Fidel Castro himself tells interesting tales about his childhood and youth in *Diary of the Cuban Revolution* by Carlos Franqui, the first editor of *Revolución,* who taped a series of interviews with him in 1959. Franqui's volume, which is essential for the study of the Sierra War, also contains important correspondence of Fidel, Che Guevara, Raúl Castro, Celia Sánchez and others. In 1985 Fidel Castro gave a series of extremely lengthy interviews to a Brazilian Dominican friar, Frei Betto, on the subject of religion. Published in book form in Havana and Rio de Janeiro, these interviews provide fascinating glimpses of Castro's young life as seen by him; references to this text are identified in the *Portrait* and the Chapter Notes.

Mario Mencía, the Cuban revolutionary chronicler, is the author of two very readable books: one, the account of the preparations for the attack on Moncada, and the other, the story of Fidel Castro in prison (the latter is available in English as *Time Was on Our Side*). Inevitably they reflect a strong ideological bias, but nothing better is available. Mencía's third book, covering the period between Fidel's imprisonment and the landing in Cuba, has not been issued as of 1986, although it is completed. Marta Rojas, a Cuban journalist who covered Castro's trial in 1953, has written three books on Moncada and the judiciary proceedings that offer useful facts and impressions. Antonio Nuñez Jiménez describes selectively Castro's first year in power in *En Marcha con Fidel,* but the book's sycophancy makes it almost unreadable. In terms of Castro's personality, interviews with him by Lee Lockwood in *Castro's Cuba, Cuba's Fidel,* published in 1967, may be the best material of this kind.

Important insights into Castro appear in books by the French journalist K. S. Karol in *Los Guerrilleros en el Poder,* and by the late French agrarian scientist René Dumont in *Cuba est-il Socialiste?* These critiques are from the left, and even mention of these books is banned in Havana. Comments on Castro by US Ambassador Philip W. Bonsal in *Cuba, Castro and the United States* remain very valid.

So fallow, however, is the field of biographical work on Fidel Castro that the researcher is forced back to original interviewing, with its advantages and its drawbacks.

CHAPTER NOTES

Book One: The Man

CHAPTER 1

3–4   The account of Fidel Castro after the Alegría de Pío battle is taken from interviews with Faustino Pérez and Universo Sánchez.

4–5   The author's conversations with Castro, January 1984; February 1985.

5   The visits by Communist emissaries to Castro in Mexico are discussed in detail in Book III.

5   Castro brought up nationalism and patriotism in his speech on 10 October 1978, the hundredth anniversary of the first independence war.

6   In *Fidel y la Religión,* published in Havana in 1985.

CHAPTER 2

9–13   Faustino Pérez and Universo Sánchez interviews.

CHAPTER 3

15   The Soviet aid figures are calculated at this level by the US government, and not questioned by Cuban officials.

16   Castro's discussion of 'internationalism' in taped interview with the author in January 1984.

17   Castro discussed concealing his Marxism–Leninism in the course of his report to the First Congress of the Cuban Communist Party in 1975.

17   The statistics in Castro's speeches on public health appeared in articles in *Granma* in July 1985.

18   Castro discussed speech-making in interviews with Carlos Franqui in *Diary of the Cuban Revolution.*

19   On Castro's furies, sources included Ramiro Valdés, and on foul
      language, Carlos Rafael Rodríguez.
19   Wayne Smith, former chief of the US Interests Section in Havana, in
      an interview on the reasons for Mariel.
19   The author's private interviews on Mexican trip.

CHAPTER 4

20–21   Castro's concerns with his men were discussed in interviews with
        Melba Hernández and Pedro Miret. Also in Robert Merle's book on
        Moncada.
21   Castro discussed the chaplain with Frei Betto.
21–22   The author accompanied Castro to the hospital.
22   Armando Hart's account of the meeting was in an interview with the
        author in May 1985.
22   The strike fiasco was discussed with the author by Castro in an
        informal meeting and by Faustino Pérez in a taped interview in 1985.
26   For March 1959 NSC meeting, see Pamela S. Falk's *Cuban Foreign
        Policy*, published in 1986.
26–27   The best estimates on Cuban political prisoners come from Amnesty
        International and the Americas Watch Committee. Castro's
        comments were in a conversation with the author in 1985.
27–28   The reconstruction of the Sorí–Marin episode is based on the
        author's interviews in Miami and Havana.
28   The Cubela story was reconstructed from the author's interviews in
        Havana and Washington.
29–30   Castro discussed 'institutions' in interviews with the author in 1984.

CHAPTER 5

33–34   Correspondence between Fidel and Che appears selectively in Carlos
        Franqui's *Diary of the Cuban Revolution;* it is kept in its entirety in the
        Historical Division of the Council of State, in wartime archives
        established by Celia Sánchez.
34   Castro talked about loneliness in a 1977 television interview with
        Barbara Walters; he repeated some of it to the author in 1984.
36   Piñeiro told the author about his New York days in a conversation at
        the presidential palace in 1985.
38   Castro brought up the question of personality cult in conversations
        with the author in 1984 and 1985.
39–40   Castro explained his information systems in a conversation with the
        author in 1985.
42–43   The vignettes on Castro's activities came from the author's inter-
        views with Conchita Fernández in 1985.

Book Two: The Young Years

CHAPTER 1

59–60   Castro discussed his mother's religious devotion in interviews with Frei Betto in 1985.

CHAPTER 2

62   Castro discussed his age in a conversation with the author in 1985.
63   Castro told the story about the 'Jew' bird to the author in 1985.
69   Castro told stories about his appendicitis in interviews with Carlos Franqui in 1959, and in a conversation with the author in 1985.
70   Raúl Castro is quoted by Robert Merle.

CHAPTER 3

72   The Avellaneda Literary Academy story comes from an interview with José Ignácio Rasco.
74   Castro discussed his family origins in his letters from prison.
75–76   Castro discussed the Bible in interviews with Frei Betto.

CHAPTER 4

87   The relationship between Castro and Alfredo Guevara was described by the latter in an interview with the author in 1985.

CHAPTER 5

95   The birth of the *Ortodoxo* party, with Castro in attendance, is chronicled by Luis Conte Agüerro in *Eduardo Chibás*.
105–106   Alfredo Guevara told the Demajagua bell story in an interview with the author in 1985.

CHAPTER 6

110–111   Moreno Frajinals discussed Fidel's revolutionary impulses in conversation with the author in 1985.
117–124   Castro's initial involvement and participation in the *Bogotázo* is described in this book in a narrative section constructed from four main elements. The first two are an account by Fidel included in Arturo Alape's *El Bogotázo: Memorias del Olvidio*, and a separate, lengthy interview he granted Alape. The other two are interviews conducted by the author with Alfredo Guevara in Havana in 1985, and with Enrique Ovares in Miami in 1984. Castro, Guevara and Ovares were the principal Cuban delegates to the Bogotá student congress.

CHAPTER 7

126–127   The account of Castro's early married life is based on conversations in Havana with personal friends and acquaintances who asked not to be identified.
131–133   The material on Fidel's denunciation of the gangsters and his escape from Havana is based on the author's interviews in Miami with Max Lesnick in 1984 and 1985, and on conversations in Havana in 1985 with Castro's personal friends, who have requested anonymity.
134–137   The material on Castro's law practice is based on interviews conducted by Mario Mencia with Jorge Aspiazo, and on the author's conversations with Fidel's personal friends in Havana.
141–145   The section on Castro as candidate is based on interviews in Miami with Raúl Chibás and Max Lesnick, and in Havana with Conchita Fernández, Lionel Martin and Moreno Frajinals.

Book Three: The War

CHAPTER 1

150–152   The material on the incipient period of the organization of Castro's revolutionary Movement is based on the author's interviews in Havana with Melba Hernández, Pedro Miret and Ramirez Valdés.
156–165   The section covering the first phase of the revolutionary Movement is based on lengthy interviews conducted by the author in Havana with Melba Hernández and Pedro Miret; Mario Mencia's interviews with Jorge Aspiazo; Mencía's *El Grito de Moncada*, Robert Merle's *Moncada*, and Lionel Martin's *The Young Fidel*.

CHAPTER 2

168–171   Pedro Miret and Melba Hernández were the principal sources for the section on the development of the military wing of the Movement. They discussed it in interviews with the author in Havana in 1985. Additional material came from Mencía, Merle, and Martin books.
174–179   The best material on the preparations for Moncada is found in Merle and Mencía books, in the transcripts of Castro's trial, and in Marta Rojas's accounts. Pedro Miret and Melba Hernández supplied eyewitness details in interviews with the author.

CHAPTER 3

180–188   The story of the days and hours preceding the attack on Moncada is best documented by Merle and Mencía. In interviews with the author, Melba Hernández provided additional recollections – such as Castro's determination to organize weddings.

188–189   The Movement's ideology at the time of Moncada was explained by Castro to Frei Betto in their 1985 interviews. He makes a clear ideological separation between himself and his comrades at that stage.

189–190   Haydée Santamaría's recollections are contained in a documentary filmed by the Cuban Cinema Institute. A tape of the soundtrack is at the University of Miami along with other tapes related to the production of my book.

CHAPTER 4

199–211   The best account of the Moncada and Bayamo attacks and their aftermath is contained in Robert Merle's book. Useful material is also found in Marta Rojas's *La Generación del Centenário en el Juicio del Moncada*, in Castro's trial testimony, and his newspaper and radio interviews after being captured. Melba Hernández, Pedro Miret and Ramiro Valdés offered me valuable eye-witness accounts in interviews in 1985.

CHAPTER 5

211–228   Material on Castro's imprisonment, trial and incarceration is best culled from Merle's *Moncada*, Marta Rojas's *La Generación del Centenário* and *La Cueva del Muerto*, Mencía's *Time Was on Our Side*, Fidel Castro's own *History Will Absolve Me*, and Conte Agüerro's *Cartas del Presidio*. I found much fresh descriptive material in my interviews with Pedro Miret and Melba Hernández, and in a conversation with Raúl Castro – all in Havana in 1985. Fidel contributed anecdotes about his prison life when I accompanied him to the Isle of Youth (Pines) in May 1985.

224–226   The text of 'History Will Absolve Me' as it is now widely known, was reconstructed by Fidel from memory during his imprisonment. Marta Rojas, who attended the trial and wrote about it for *Bohemia*, took some notes, but they are very fragmentary. Inasmuch as Castro quotes himself in the written version, it is really irrelevant whether it is a verbatim rendition of his actual words before the judges. Though immensely articulate and equipped with an amazing memory, Castro is a stylist and a perfectionist, and one must assume that he has polished considerably the written and now official version. No substance changes are known to exist.

CHAPTER 6

231–239   The incarceration period is best covered by Mencía and in Fidel's prison correspondence appearing in Conte Agüerro's book and in the appendix in Merle's *Moncada*. Again, Pedro Miret and Melba Hernández provided new material in their 1985 interviews with the author. Ramiro Valdés added details.

240–241   Castro's friends were the principal sources for the account of his
          divorce proceedings and the custody fight over Fidelito.
245–248   Fidel's reorganization of the Movement is chronicled in a series of
          articles by Mario Mencía, appearing in *Bohemia* in Havana during
          1985; and in original news stories and articles in *Bohemia* and *La Calle*
          in May–July 1955. Additional information was provided in the
          author's interviews with Pedro Miret, Melba Hernández, Ramiro
          Valdés and Armando Hart in Havana in 1985, and with Max Lesnick
          in Miami.

CHAPTER 7

249–262   Fidel Castro's stay in Mexico is chronicled in Mario Mencía's
          Bohemia articles in 1985; in *De Tuxpán a La Plata*, an account
          published by the Historical Section of the Central Political Director-
          ate of the Revolutionary Armed Forces in 1979; in General Bayo's
          memoirs; and in the author's interviews in Havana in 1985 with
          Pedro Miret, Melba Hernández, Ramiro Valdés, Faustino Pérez, and
          Universo Sánchez. Also, Max Lesnick was interviewed in Miami, as
          was Ben S. Stephansky in Washington, DC.
256–261   Most of the material on the early relations between Fidel and Che
          Guevara is based on *Che Guevara: Años Decisivos* by Hilda Gadea,
          Che's first wife; Ernesto Che Guevara's own recollections in Volume
          I of his *Escritos y Discursos,* published in Havana in 1977; Mencía's
          Bohemia articles; the *Tuxpán* book; and the author's interviews with
          Pedro Miret, Melba Hernández, and Universo Sánchez.
263–266   Castro's tour in the United States is described in Mencía's *Bohemia*
          articles in 1985, and in Havana newspapers in 1955. The question of
          Fidelito was discussed with the author by Fidel Castro's friends in
          Havana in 1985.

CHAPTER 8

269–287   Material on the preparations for the invasion appears in Mencía's
          articles; the *Tuxpán* book; General Bayo's memoirs; Teresa Casuso's
          Cuba and Castro (including Fidel's romantic interests); and the
          author's interviews with Pedro Miret, Melba Hernández, Universo
          Sánchez, Faustino Pérez and Ben S. Stephansky.
285–286   Castro's dealings in Mexico with Communist emissaries from Cuba
          are reported by Lionel Martin in connection with the Osvaldo
          Sánchez Cabrera visit; the visit by Flavio Bravo, much more
          important, is contained in an unpublished interview by Mario
          Mencía.

CHAPTER 9

288–292   The voyage of the *Granma* is described in the *Tuxpán* book and in
          Volume I of Che Guevara's *Escritos y Discursos*. New details came in

the author's interviews with Universo Sánchez and Ramiro Valdés. To gain a visual impression of the landing area, I visited the 'shipwreck' spot and crossed the mangrove (now a narrow causeway makes crossing it infinitely easier) to the shore during a tour of Oriente with my wife in May 1985. Pedro Álvarez Tábio, a historian of the Sierra war at the Council of State, who accompanied us, described the landing and the mangrove in a taped interview there.

292–309   The section of the Rebel Army's first six weeks in Cuba is based largely on the author's interviews with Faustino Pérez and Universo Sánchez, who were with Fidel after the Alegría de Pío débâcle, and on interviews with Pedro Álvarez Tábio, the historian. Invaluable material came in an interview in Havana with Guillermo García. In the Sierra Maestra I interviewed Ángel Pérez Rosabal, Mario Sariol, Argelio Rosabal and Argeo González who were among the first peasants to meet and help Fidel's band. My wife and I toured the Alegría de Pío battlefield, and followed part of Fidel's route into the Sierra Maestra by car and Jeep and on foot; it is impossible to understand the Castro war in the mountains without becoming acquainted with the terrain, even slightly. The battle of Alegría de Pío is described in some detail in Che Guevara's and Raúl Castro's war diaries.

CHAPTER 10

310–335   The military history of the first full year of the Sierra war is fairly well documented; the political and ideological history less well. Probably the most complete and objective chronological account of the crucial period between *Granma's* landing on 2 December 1956 and 20 February 1957, when Castro's guerrilla army became consolidated, was published in four consecutive special issues of the newspaper *Granma:* 3 January, 17 January, 23 February and 27 February 1979. The accounts were written by Pedro Álvarez Tábio and Otto Hernández, incorporating material from Raúl Castro's and Che Guevara's war diaries and other sources, Additional material on this period appeared in a special anniversary issue of *Bohemia* on 3 December 1976. Álvarez Tábio and Hernández described the battle of Uvero in *El Combate de Uvero,* published in Havana in 1980. Much important material came from the author's interviews with Faustino Pérez, Universo Sánchez, Guillermo García, José R. Machado Ventura, and Ramiro Valdés. Carlos Franqui's *Diary of the Cuban Revolution* contains significant Sierra correspondence (including operational orders and reports) of Fidel and Raúl Castro, Che Guevara, Celia Sánchez, Frank País and others. The full body of this correspondence is in the archives of the Council of State.

The political and ideological aspects of the revolutionary struggle during 1957 are inadequately explained in published sources – such as Lionel Martin's *The Young Fidel* or the Bonachea-Valdés Introduction to the *Selected Works of Fidel Castro, 1947–1958.* Important correspondence throwing some light on many acute political problems affecting the Movement is included in the Franqui *Diary*. A useful discussion on this topic is found in *The Unsuspected Revolution* by Mario Llerena. Herbert L. Matthews touches lightly on it in *The Cuban Story* in the context of his visit to Castro in the Sierra in February 1957; his book incorporates the text of his dispatches to the *New York Times*, which were the first direct reports on the *Fidelista* guerrillas. Che Guevara comments on many political aspects of the war in his *Escritos y Discursos* volumes.

Fresh material on the politics of the war resulted from the author's interviews with Faustino Pérez in Havana in 1985, and Raúl Chibás in Miami in 1984. Communist Party attitudes towards the Sierra war were discussed with Blás Roca and Fábio Grobart in the author's interviews with them in Havana in 1985.

336–339   The story of the secret CIA involvement in the Sierra war was reconstructed from my own knowledge as a *New York Times* reporter in Cuba in 1959; the information was considered privileged by me at the time. It was subsequently confirmed in Washington by senior CIA and State Department officials on a confidential basis.

CHAPTER 11

341–365   The military history of the victory year – 1958 – is amply documented in sources ranging from Franqui's *Diary* to war diaries by Raúl Castro, Che Guevara and Camilo Cienfuegos. The author obtained additional, detailed information in interviews with Faustino Pérez, Guillermo García, Vílma Espin, Universo Sánchez and José R. Machado Ventura. To gain a visual impression of the war my wife and I climbed to the Castro wartime command post at La Plata with Pedro Álvarez Tábio, the historian, and Colonel Arturo Aguillera, Fidel's wartime adjutant, who provided a running historical commentary as we went up and down the Sierra Maestra.

343–352   As in the case of the previous years, very little is available from public sources on the politics of the war – notably on the dissensions within the 26th of July Movement, the still-painful controversy over the failed general strike in April 1958, and Castro's relations with the Communists. All these remain sensitive subjects in Cuba; Ramiro Valdés, the former Interior Minister, remarked in a speech in 1977 that it would be harmful to the revolution to bring the full strike story into the open while many of the *compañeros* linked with it were still alive. A bitter denunciation of the strike was written by Che Guevara; it appears in *Escritos y Discursos*. These questions are discussed by Mario Llerena and by the late Manuel Urrutia Lleó, revolutionary Cuba's first president, in *Fidel Castro and Company, Inc.*

Fidel Castro was still angry about the failure of the 1958 strike when the subject came up in a conversation I had with him in February 1985. I was able to gain insights into many of the political problems of the last year of the war in interviews in Havana with

Faustino Pérez, Armando Hart, Jorge Enrique Mendoza and Ramiro
Valdés, and in Miami with Raúl Chibás. I discussed the Communist
Party's attitude towards Castro during 1958, and in conversations
with Blás Roca and Fábio Grobart in Havana in 1985.

352–365   Aside from published sources, material on the Batista final offensive
and the Castro counter-offensive came from interviews by the author
with Colonel Arturo Aguilera and Pedro Álvarez Tábio in the Sierra
Maestra. Raúl Chibás told me of attending the meeting between
Castro and General Eulogio Cantillo, the Batista commander in
Oriente, on 28 December.

Book Four: The Revolution

CHAPTER 1

369   The quotation by Carlos Rafael Rodríguez is from *Letra con Filo*,
published in 1983.
   The decision to assassinate Castro is reported in an internal CIA
memorandum submitted to Director of Central Intelligence Allen
W. Dulles in August 1960.

370   Nuñez Jiménez made comments on Castro and Lenin in a conversation with the author in 1985.

373   Enrique Oltuski reported his conversations with Che Guevara in an
article in *Lunes de Revolución* in June 1959.

376–380   Secret negotiations with the 'old' Communists by Castro and his top
associates were described for the author in taped interviews in
Havana in 1985 by Blás Roca, Fábio Grobart and Alfredo Guevara.

380–382   The creation, existence, and activities of the 'hidden government' in
1959 are discussed in taped interviews with the author in 1985 by
Alfredo Guevara, Antonio Nuñez Jiménez, Jorge Enrique Mendoza
and Conchita Fernández.

CHAPTER 2

383–385   Material on the initial phase in the relations between Castro and the
United States is drawn from Ambassador Bonsal's *Cuba, Castro and
the United States* as well as from my own reporting at the time in
Havana and Washington for the *New York Times*. In 1959 and 1960 I
had numerous 'background' conversations with Bonsal, and I have
retained my notes.

392   The episode on Castro's meeting with the CIA official was first
reported by Finance Minister López-Fresquet; I heard further details
from my CIA sources in Washington.

396   Nuñez Jiménez is the source for quotations from Castro's secret
speeches.

398   Nuñez Jiménez and Vice-President J. R. Fernández are the sources for
the account on the modernization of the Rebel Army and the militia.

401   Castro's activities and movements were described in an interview by
        Conchita Fernández in 1985; much of the material is first-hand from
        the author's own reporting in Havana at the time.

401–403 Nuñes Jiménez is the source for Castro's visits to the swamps.

404–407 Most of the material on Urrutia's demise comes from the author's
        own reporting in Havana in 1959.

407–409 On the first Soviet contacts with revolutionary Cuba, material comes
        from the author's own notes at the time. Nuñez Jiménez is the source
        for the story on Castro's vodka-and-caviar meeting with Alexeiev.

CHAPTER 3

414   Castro talked about Hemingway in an interview with the author in
        1984.

CHAPTER 4

431   Castro's comments about John F. Kennedy, expressed at great
        length, were part of an interview with the author on 28 January 1984.

433   The author was Castro's American companion on a visit to the
        Pioneers' camp.

437–438 Castro discussed the Alliance for Progress in interviews with the
        author on 28 and 29 January 1984.

439   Ramiro Valdés discussed the pre-invasion Security precautions in an
        interview with the author in 1985.

444–449 Vice-President J. R. Fernández, then the military field commander,
        described the unfolding of the battle and his own and Castro's
        movements in interviews with the author in Havana in 1985.

CHAPTER 5

457–460 Castro's dealings with Cuban intellectuals were reconstructed from
        numerous conversations in Havana in 1984 and 1985, and from the
        text of his 'Words to the Intellectuals' on 30 June 1961.

467–468 Valuable material on the Escambray fighting came from interviews
        with Norberto Fuentes, a noted Cuban journalist, who has studied
        this period in depth.

470–480 Castro's account of the October crisis was the central part of an
        interview with the author on 28 and 29 January 1984. I believe it to be
        the most comprehensive version ever supplied by Castro to a foreign
        writer.

Book Five: The Maturity

CHAPTER 1

489–490 Castro discussed the 'errors' of the revolution in an interview with
        the author on 29 January 1984.

CHAPTER 2

506   Raúl Castro's report on the investigation appears in *Bohemia* in November 1968.

515   Nathaniel Davis's comments on the Castro visit to Chile are contained in *The Last Two Years of Salvador Allende*.

CHAPTER 3

526–528   Apart from Castro's own public and private statements to that effect, reliable information from the United States, Portugese, French and Eastern European diplomatic sources corroborates the claim that the intervention in Angola was a Cuban idea.

529–530   Partial material on US–Cuban secret diplomacy comes from the author's interview with William D. Rogers, at the time Assistant Secretary of State for Inter-American Affairs. Additional information is from Cuban diplomatic sources.

535–536   Castro discussed Central America and 'internationaliam' in an interview with the author on 29 January 1984.

Bibliography

1. Books

Aguirre, Sergio. *Raices y Significación de la Protesta de Baragua*. Le Habana: Editorial Politica, 1978.

Alape, Arturo. *El Bogatázo: Memorias del Olvidio*. La Habana: Casa de las Américas, 1983.

Alba, Victor. *Los Sudamericanos*. Mexico City: Costa-Amic, 1964.

Álvarez Tábio, Pedro and Otto Hernández. *El Combate de Uvero*. La Habana: Editorial Gente Nueva, 1980

Argenter, José Miró. *Crónicas de la Guerra*. La Habana: Instituto del Libro, 1970.

Artime, Manuel F. *Traición!* Mexico City: Editorial Jus, 1960

Baez, Luis. *Camino de la Victoria*. La Habana: Casa de las Américas, 1975.

Baez, Luis. *A Dos Manos*. La Habana: Unión de Escritores y Aristos de Cuba, 1982.

Baez, Luis. *Guerra Secreta*. La Habana: Editorial Letras Cubanas, 1978.

Baliño, Carlos. *Documentos y Articulos*. La Habana: Instituto de Historia del Movimiento Comunista y de la Revolucion Socialista de Cuba, 1976.

Barnet, Migue. *Gallego*. La Habana: Editorial Letras Cubanas, 1983.

Batista, Alberto Reyes, ed. *Cuentos Sobre Bandidos y Combatientes*. La Habana: Editorial Letras Cubanas, 1983.

Batista, Alberto Reyes. *Los Nuevos Conquistadores*. La Habana: Instituto Cubano del Libro, 1976.

Bayo, Alberto. *Mi Aporte a la Revolución Cubana*. La Habana: Ejército Rebelde, 1960.

Benjamin, Jules Robert. *The United States and Cuba*. Pittsburgh: University of Pittsburgh Press, 1974.

Bethel, Paul D. *Cuba y los Estados Unidos*. Barcelona: Editorial Juventud, S.A., 1962.

Betto, Frei. *Fidel y la Religión*. La Habana: Publicaciones de Consejo de Estado, 1985.

Bonsal, Philip W. *Cuba, Castro and the United States*. Pittsburgh: University of Pittsburgh Press, 1971.

Brennan, Ray. *Castro, Cuba and Justice*. Garden City, NY: Doubleday and Company, 1959.

Brzezinski, Zbigniew. *Power and Principle*. New York: Farrar, Straus and Giroux, 1983.

Buckley, Tom. *Violent Neighbors*. New York: Times Books, 1984.

Cantor, Jay. *The Death of Che Guevara*. New York: Alfred A. Knopf, 1983.

Carrillo, Justo. *Cuba 1933*. Miami, Fla.: Institute of Interamerican Studies, University of Miami, 1985.

Castro Ruz, Fidel. *El Pensamiento de Fidel Castro*, Vol. 1, Books 1 and 2. La Habana: Editorial Política, 1983.

Castro Ruz, Fidel. *History Will Absolve Me*. New York: Lyle Stuart, 1961.

Castro Ruz, Fidel. *Informe de Comité Central del Partido Comunista Cubano al Primer Congreso*. La Habana: Comité Central del Partido Comunista de Cuba, 1975.

Castro Ruz, Fidel. *La Revolución de Octubre y la Revolución Cubana*. La Habana: Departmento de Orientación Revolucionária de Comite Central del Partido Comunista de Cuba, 1977.

Castro Ruz, Fidel. *Political, Economic and Social Thought of Fidel Castro*. La Habana: Editorial Lex, 1959.

Castro Ruz, Fidel. *Revolutionary Struggle 1947–1958: Selected Works of Fidel Castro*, eds. Roland E. Bonachea and Nelson P. Valdés. Cambridge, Mass.: The MIT Press, 1972

Castro Ruz, Fidel. *The World Economic and Social Crisis*. Havana: Publishing Office of the Council of State, 1983.

Casuso, Teresa. *Cuba and Castro*. New York: Random House, 1961.

Christian, Shirley. *Nicaragua*. New York: Random House, 1985.

Collins, John M. *American and Soviet Military Trends*. Washington, DC: Georgetown University, 1978.

Conte Aguërro, Luis. *Cartas del Presidio*. La Habana: Editorial Lex. 1959.

Conte Arguërro, Luis. *Eduardo Chibás*. Mexico City: Editorial Jus, 1955.

Crankshaw, Edward and Jerrold Schecter. *Khrushchev Remembers*. Boston: Little, Brown and Company, 1974.

Crassweller, Robert D. *Trujillo: The Life and Times of a Caribbean Dictator*. New York: The Macmillan Company, 1966.

Cross, James Eliot. *Conflict in the Shadows*. Garden City, NY: Doubleday and Company, 1963.

Cuba. *Constitution of the Republic of Cuba*. Havana: Editorial Política, 1981.

Cuba. Fuerzas Armandas Revolucionarias. *Manual Básico del Miliciano de Tropas Territoriales*. La Habana: Editorial Orbe, 1981.

Cuba. Fuerzas Armadas Revolucionarias. *Moncada 26 de Julio*. La Habana: Ediciones Yara, Julio, 1971.

Cuba. Fuerzas Armadas Revolucionarias. Sección de História de la Dirección Política Central. *De Tuxpán a La Plata*. La Habana: Editorial Orbe, 1979.

Daniel, James and John G. Hubbell. *Strike in the West*. New York: Holt, Rinehart and Winston, 1963.

Davis, Nathaniel. *The Last Two Years of Salvador Allende*. Ithaca, NY: Cornell University Press, 1985

Debray, Régis. *The Chilean Revolution*. New York: Pantheon Books, 1971.

Debray, Régis. *Revolution in the Revolution?* New York: Monthly Review Press, 1967.

Djilas, Milovan. *Conversations with Stalin*. New York: Harcourt, Brace and World, Inc., 1962.

Donovan, John. *Red Machete*. Indianapolis: Bobbs-Merrill, 1962.

Draper, Theodore. *Castroism: Theory and Practice*. Frederick A. Praeger, 1965.

Draper, Theodore. *Castro's Revolution: Myths and Realities*. New York: Frederick A. Praeger, 1962.

Dreier, John C. *The Organization of American States and the Hemisphere Crisis*. New York: Harper and Row, 1962.

Dubois, Jules. *Danger over Panama*. Indianapolis: Bobbs-Merrill, 1964.

Dubois, Jules. *Fidel Castro: Rebel Liberator or Dictator?* Indianapolis: Bobbs-Merrill, 1959.

Dumont, René. *Cuba est-il Socialiste?* Paris: Éditions du Seuil, 1970.

Duncan, Raymond W. *The Soviet Union and Cuba*. New York: Praeger, 1985.

Einaudi, Luigi R., ed. *Latin America in the 1970s*. Santa Monica, Calif.. Rand, 1972.

Ely, Roland T. *Cuando Reinaba Su Majestad el Azúcar*. Buenos Aires: Editorial Sudamericana, 1963.

Erisman, H. Michael. *Cuba's International Relations*. Boulder, Col.: Westview Press, 1985.

Falk, Pamela S. *Cuban Foreign Policy*. Lexington, Mass.: Lexington Books, 1986.

Fernández, Manuel. *Religión y Revolucion en Cuba*. Miami, Fla.: Saeta Ediciones, 1984.

Fraginals, Manuel Moreno. *El Ingenio* (3 Vols.) La Habana: Editorial de Ciencias Sociales, 1978.

Franco, Victor. *The Morning After*. New York: Frederick A. Praeger, 1963.

Franqui, Carlos. *Diary of the Cuban Revolution*. New York: Viking Press, 1980.

Franqui, Carlos. *Family Portrait with Fidel*. New York: Random House, 1984.

Franqui, Carlos. *The Twelve*. New York: Lyle Stuart, Inc. 1968.

Fuentes, Norberto. *Hemingway in Cuba*. Secaucus, NJ: Lyle Stuart, Inc., 1984.

Gadea, Hilda. *Che Guevara: Años Decisivos*. Mexico City: Aguilar, 1972.

García, Manuel Rodriguez. *Sierra Maestra en la Clandestinidad*. Santiago de Cuba: Editorial Oriente, 1981.

Gerassi, John, *Fidel Castro*. Garden City, NY: Doubleday and Company, 1971.

Gerassi, John. *The Great Fear*. New York: The Macmillan Company, 1963.

Gómez, Máximo Baez. *Invasión y Campaña de las Villas*. La Habana: Editorial Militar, 1984.

Gonzalez, Edward, and David Ronfeldt. *Post Revolutionary Cuba in a Changing World*. Santa Monica, Calif.: Rand, 1975.

Goodsell, James Nelson. *Fidel Castro's Personal Revolution in Cuba: 1959–1973*. New York: Alfred A. Knopf, 1975.

Goodsell, James Nelson. *Grenada: The World Against the Crime*. La Habana: Editorial de Ciencias Sociales, 1983.

Gray, Richard Butler. *José Martí, Cuban Patriot*. Gainesville: University of Florida Press, 1962.

Guevara, Ernesto Che. *Che: Selected Works of Ernesto Guevara*, eds. Roland E. Bonachea and Nelson P. Valdés. Cambridge, Mass.: The MIT Press, 1969.

Guevara, Ernesto Che. *El Diario del Che en Bolivia*. La Habana: Instituto del Libro, 1968.

Guevara, Ernesto Che. *Escritos y Discursos*, Vols. 1-9. La Habana: Editorial de Ciencias Sociales, 1977.

Hageman, Alice L. and Philip E. Wheaton, eds. *Religion in Cuba Today*. New York: Association Press, 1971.

Haig, Alexander M., Jr. *Caveat*. New York: The Macmillan Company, 1984.

Harris, Richard. *Death of a Revolutionary*. New York: WW Norton and Company, Inc., 1970.

Hart, Armando Dávalos. *Cambiar las Reglas del Juego*. La Habana: Editorial Letras Cubanas, 1983.

Haverstock, Nathan A. and Richard C. Schroeder. *Dateline Latin America*. Washington, DC: The Latin American Service, 1971.

Hemingway, Ernest. *Selected Letters 1917-1961*. New York: Charles Scribner's Sons, 1981.

Huberman, Leo and Paul M. Sweezy. *Cuba: Anatomy of a Revolution*. New York: Monthly Review Press, 1960.

Instituto de História del Movimiento Comunista y de la Revolución Socialista de Cuba, Anexo al Comite Central del PCC. *Cuba y la Defensa de la Republica Española (1936-1939)*. La Habana: Editorial Política, 1981.

James, Daniel. *The First Soviet Satellite in the Americas*. New York: Avon, 1961.

Johnson, U. Alexis. *The Right Hand of Power*. Englewood Cliffs, NJ: Prentice-Hall, Inc., 1984.

Judson, Fred C. *Cuba and the Revolutionary Myth*. Boulder, Col.: Westview Press, 1984.

Karol, K.S. *Los Guerrilleros en el Poder*. Barcelona: Seix Barral, S.A., 1972.

Kemp, Geoffrey. *Some Relationships Between US Military Training in Latin America and Weapons Acquisition Patterns*. Cambridge, Mass.: The MIT Press, 1970.

Kenner, Martin and James Petras. *Fidel Castro Speaks*. New York: Grove Press, 1969.

Kern, Montague *et. al*. *The Kennedy Crises*. Chapel Hill: University of North Carolina Press, 1983.

Lewis, Oscar, Ruth Lewis and Susan M. Rigdon. *Four Men*. Urbana: University of Illinois Press, 1977.

Lewis, Oscar, Ruth Lewis and Susan M. Rigdon. *Four Women*. Urbana: University of Illinois Press, 1977.

Light, Robert E. and Carl Marzani. *Cuba vs the CIA*. New York: Marzani and Munsell, Inc., 1961.

Llerena, Mario. *The Unsuspected Revolution*. Ithaca, NY: Cornell University Press, 1978.

Lockwood, Lee. *Castro's Cuba, Cuba's Fidel*. New York: The Macmillan Company, 1967.

López-Fresquet, Rufo. *My Fourteen Months with Castro*. Cleveland: The World Publishing Company, 1966.

Mallin, Jay, ed. *'Che' Guevara on Revolution*. New York: Dell, 1970.

Martí, José. *Obras Completas*. La Habana: Editorial de Ciencias Sociales, 1975.

Martin, Lionel. *El Joven Fidel*. Barcelona: Ediciones Grijalbo, S.A., 1982.

Massó, José Luis. *Cuba: 17 de Abril*. Mexico City: Editorial Diana, S.A., 1962.

Matthews, Herbert L. *The Cuban Story*. New York: George Braziller, 1961.

Mazlish, Bruce. *The Meaning of Karl Marx*. New York: Oxford University Press, 1984.

Medvedev, Roy. *Khrushchev*. Garden City, New York: Anchor Press/ Doubleday and Company, 1983.

Mella, J.A. *Documentos y Artículos*. La Habana: Instituto Cubano del Libro, 1975.

Mencía, Mario. *El Grito de Moncada*. La Habana: Editorial Política, 1983.

Mencía, Mario. *Time Was on Our Side*. La Habana: Editorial Política, 1982.

Méndez, M. Isidoro. *Martí*. La Habana: Fernández y Cia., 1941.

Merle, Robert. *Moncada: Premier Combat de Fidel Castro*. Paris: Robert Laffont, 1965.

Mesa-Lago, Carmelo. *Cuba in the 1970s*. Albuquerque: University of New Mexico Press, 1974.

Mesa-Lago, Carmelo. *The Economy of Socialist Cuba*. Albuquerque: University of New Mexico Press, 1981.

Mesa-Lago, Carmelo, ed. *Revolutionary Change in Cuba*. Pittsburgh: University of Pittsburgh Press, 1971.

Miller, Warren. *90 Miles from Home*. Boston: Little Brown and Company, 1961.

Mills, C. Wright. *Listen, Yankee*. New York: McGraw-Hill Book Company, Inc., 1960.

Ministerio de Fuerzas Armadas (Cuba), Dirección Política. *Moncada 26 de Julio*. La Habana: 1971.

Molina, Gabriel. *Diaria de Girón*. La Habana: Editorial Política, 1984.

Monahan, James and Kenneth O. Gilmore. *The Great Deception*. New York: Farrar, Straus and Company, 1963.

Montaner, Carlos Alberto. *Fidel Castro y la Revolución Cubana*. Barcelona: Plaza and Janes, S.A., 1984.

Moreno, José A. *Che Guevara on Guerrilla Warfare: Doctrine, Practice and Evaluation*. Pittsburgh: University of Pittsburgh Press, 1970.

Morray, J.P. *The Second Revolution in Cuba*. New York: Monthly Review Press, 1962.

Nolan, David. *The Ideology of the Sandinistas and The Nicaraguan Revolution*. Coral Gables, Fla: University of Miami Press, 1984.

Nuñez Jiménez, Antonio. *Cuba, Cultura, Estado y Revolución*. Mexico: Presencia Latinoamericana, 1984.

Nuñez Jiménez, Antonio. *En Marcha con Fidel*. La Habana: Editorial Letras Cubanas, 1982.

Nuñez Jiménez, Antonio. *Geografía de Cuba*. La Habana: Editorial Lex, 1959.

Oswald, J. Gregory and Anthony J. Strover, eds. *The Soviet Union and Latin America*. New York: Frederick A. Praeger, 1970.

Padilla, Heberto. *Fuera de Juego*. Rio Piedras, P.R.: 1971.

Partido Comunista de Cuba. *El Movimiento Obrero Cubano: Documentos y Artículos*. Vol. I: 1865–1925. La Habana: Editorial de Ciencias Sociales, 1975.

Peñabaz, Manuel. *Girón 1961*. Miami, Fla.: Daytona Printing, 1962.

Pérez, Louis A., Jr. *Cuba Between Empires*. Pittsburgh: University of Pittsburgh Press, 1983.

Petras, James F. and Robert La Porte, Jr. *Cultivating Revolution*. New York: Random House, 1971.

Pflaum, Irving P. *Arena of Decision*. Englewood Cliffs, NJ: Prentice-Hall, Inc., 1964.

Phillips, R. Hart. *Cuba: Island of Paradox*. New York: McDowell, Obolensky, 1960.

Phillips, R. Hart. *The Cuban Dilemma*. New York: Ivan Obolensky, Inc., 1962.

Plank, John, ed. *Cuba and the United States*. Washington, DC: The Brookings Institution, 1967.

Pritchett, V.S. *The Myth Makers*. New York: Random House, 1979.

Ranelagh, John. *The Rise and Fall of the CIA*. New York: Simon and Schuster, 1986.

Reckord, Barry. *Does Fidel Eat More Than Your Father?* New York: Frederick A. Praeger, 1971.

Riding, Alan. *Distant Neighbors*. New York: Alfred A. Knopf, 1985.

Ripoll, Carlos. *Harnessing the Intellectuals: Censoring Writers and Artists in Today's Cuba*. New York: Freedom House, 1985.

Rivero, Nicolas. *Castro's Cuba*. Washington, DC: Luce, 1962.

Roa, Raúl. *Aventuras, Venturas y Desventuras de un Mambi*. La Habana: Instituto del Libro, 1970.

Rodríguez, Carlos Rafael. *Letra con Filo*. La Habana: Editorial de Ciencias Sociales, 1983.

Rodríguez, Carlos Rafael. *Palabras en los Setenta*. La Habana: Editorial de Ciencias Sociales, 1984.

Rodríguez, Gerardo Morejón. *Fidel Castro*. La Habana: P. Fernandez y Cia., 1959.

Rojas, Marta. *La Cueva del Muerto*. La Habana: Unión de Escritores y Artistas de Cuba, 1983.

Rojas, Marta. *El Que Debe Vivir*. La Habana: Casa de las Américas, 1978.

Rojas, Marta. *La Generación del Centenário en el Juicio del Moncada*. La Habana: Editorial de Ciencias Sociales, 1979.

Rojas, Ursinio. *Las Luchas Obreras en el Central Tacajó*. La Habana: Editorial Política, 1979.

Ruíz, Hugo. *Angola*. La Habana: Editorial de Ciencias Sociales, 1982.

Sánchez Arango, Aureliano. *Reforma Agraria*. La Habana: Frente Nacional Democrático, 1960.

Sandford, Gregory and Richard Vigilante. *Grenada: The Untold Story*. Lanham, Md.: Madison Books, 1984.

Sarabia, Nydia. *Voisin: Viajero de la Ciencia*. La Habana: Editorial Científico-Técnica, 1983.

Sartre, Jean-Paul. *Sartre on Cuba*. New York: Ballantine Books, 1961.

Sauvage, Léo. *Autopsies du Castrisme*. Paris: Flammarion, 1962.

Sauvage, Léo. *Che Guevara*. Englewood Cliffs, NJ: Prentice-Hall, Inc.,1973.

Schlesinger, Arthur. M. Jr. *Robert Kennedy and His Times*. Boston: Houghton-Mifflin Company, 1978.

Scott, Peter Dale, Paul L. Hoch and Russell Stetler, eds. *The Assassinations*. New York: Random House, 1976.

Shevchenko, Arkady. *Breaking with Moscow*. New York: Alfred A. Knopf, 1985.

Sowell, Thomas. *Marxism: Philosphy and Economics*. New York: William Morrow and Company, 1985.

Suárez, Andrés. *Cuba: Castroism and Communism, 1959-1966*. Cambridge Mass.: The MIT Press, 1967.

Suchliki, Jaime. *The Cuban Revolution*. Coral Gables, Fla.: University of Miami, 1968.

Suchliki, Jaime. *University Students and Revolution in Cuba*. Coral Gables, Fla.: University of Miami, 1969.

Suchliki, Jaime. *Cuba from Columbus to Castro*. New York: Charles Scribner's Sons, 1974.

Taber, Robert. *M-26, Biography of a Revolution*. New York: Lyle Stuart, 1961.

Thayer, Charles W. *Guerrilla*. New York: Harper and Row, 1963.

Thomas, Hugh. *História Contemporánea de Cuba*. Barcelona: Ediciones Grijalbo, S.A., 1982.

Thomas, Hugh S., Georges A. Fauriol and Juan Carlos Weiss. *The Cuban Revolution 25 Years Later*. Boulder, Col.: Westview Press, 1984.

Tomasek, Robert D., ed. *Latin American Politics*. Garden City, N.Y.: Doubleday and Company, 1966.

Torras, Jacinto. *Obras Escogidas*. Vol I. La Habana: Editorial Política, 1984.

Ungar, Sanford J. *Estrangement: America and the World*. New York: Oxford University Press, 1985.

Urrutia Lleó, Manuel. *Fidel Castro and Company, Inc*. New York: Frederick A. Praeger, 1964.

US Commission on CIA Activities Within the United States. *Report to the President*. Washington DC: US Government Printing Office, 1975.

Valdés, Nelson P. and Edwin Lieuwen. *The Cuban Revolution*. Albuquerque: University of New Mexico Press, 1971.

Valenta, Jiri and Herbert J. Ellison, eds. *Grenada and Soviet/Cuban Policy*. Boulder, Col.: Westview Press, 1986.

Volman, Sacha. *¿Quién Impondra la Democracia?* Mexico City: Centro de Estudios y Documentación Sociales, 1965.

Wald, Karen. *Children of Che.* Palo Alto, Calif.: Ramparts Press, 1978.
Weyl, Nathaniel. *Red Star over Cuba.* New York: Devin-Adair Company, 1960.
Wilkerson, Loree. *Fidel Castro's Political Programs from Reformism to 'Marxism-Leninism'.* Gainesville: University of Florida Press, 1965.
Wyden, Peter. *Bay of Pigs.* New York: Simon & Schuster, 1979.

Yevtushenko, Yevgeny. *A Precocious Autobiography.* New York: E.P. Dutton and Company, 1963.
Yglesias, José. *Down There.* New York: The World Publishing Company, 1970.

Zeitlin, Maurice and Robert Scheer. *Cuba: Tragedy in our Hemisphere.* New York: Grove Press, Inc., 1963.

II Hearings, Reports, Pamphlets

Centro de Estudios Sobre América. *Cuadernos de Nuestra America: Enero-Julio de 1984.* La Habana: Ediciones Cubanas, 1984.
Communist Party of Cuba. *Cuba-Chile.* La Habana: Ediciones Políticas, 1972.
Communist Party of Cuba. *The Invasion of Grenada: Statements of the Party and the Revolutionary Government of Cuba Concerning the Events.* Havana: 1983.
Douglas, Maria Eulalia. *Guía Temática del Cine Cubano.* (Producción ICAIC) 1959-1980. La Habana: Ministerio de Cultura, 1983.
Greer, Germaine. *Women and Power in Cuba.* Granta, 1985.
Grobart, Fabio. *El Cincuentenario de la Fundación del Primer Partido Comunista de Cuba.* La Habana: Comité Central del Partido Comunista de Cuba, Julio 1975.
Institute of Interamerican Studies. *The Cuban Studies Project: Problems of Succession in Cuba.* Coral Gables, Fla.: University of Miami, 1985.
Johns Hopkins University School of Advanced International Studies. *Report on Cuba: Findings of the Study Group on United States–Cuban Relations.* Boulder, Col.: Westview Press, 1984.
National Bipartisan Commission on Central America. *Report to the President.* Washington, DC: 2201 C St NW, 1984.
Organization of American States. *The Situation on Human Rights in Cuba. Seventh Report.* Washington, DC: Secretariat General of the Organization of American States, 1983.
Publicaciones de Consejo de Estado. *Celia, Heroína de la Revolución Cubana.* La Habana: Editorial Política, 1985.
Smith, Wayne S. *Castro's Cuba: Soviet Partner or Nonaligned?* Washington, DC: The Wilson Center, 1984.
Smith, Wayne S. *Selected Essays on Cuba.* Washington, DC: John Hopkins School of Advanced International Studies, 1986.
Unión de Escritores y Artistas de Cuba. *Ponencias: Forum de la Narrativa-Novella y Cuento.* La Habana: Unión de Escritores y Artistas de Cuba, 1984.
US Central Intelligence Agency. *Cuban Chronology.* Springfield, Va.: National Technical Information Service, April 1979.

US Central Intelligence Agency. *Directory of Cuban Officials*. Springfield, Va.: National Technical Information Service, January 1979.
University of Miami. *The Miami Report: Recommendations on United States Policy towards Latin America and the Caribbean*. Coral Gables, Fla.: University of Miami, 1984.

III. Documents and Speeches

Communist Party of Cuba. *2nd Congress of the Communist Party of Cuba*. Havana Political Publishers, 1981.
Foreign Broadcast Information Service. *3rd Congress of the Communist Party of Cuba*. Washington, DC: US Department of Commerce, 7 and 10 February, 1986.
Partido Comunista de Cuba. *Informe del Comité Central del PCC al Primer Congreso*. La Habana: 1975

IV. Congressional Hearings

US House of Representative. Committe on Internal Security. *The Theory and Practice of Communism. Part 5: Marxism Imposed on Chile–Allende Regime*. Washington, DC: US Government Printing Office 1974.
US Senate. Foreign Relations Committee. *Executive Sessions, Vol. XIII, Parts 1 and 2*. Washington, DC: US Government Printing Office, 1961. (Made public December 1984.)
US Senate Select Committee on Intelligence Activities. *Alleged Assassination Plots Involving Foreign Leaders*. Washington, DC: US Goverment Printing Office, 1975.
US Senate. Select Committee on Intelligence Activities. *Covert Action*. Washington, DC: US Government Printing Office, 1976.
US Senate. Select Committee on Intelligence Activities. *The Investigation of the Assassination of John F. Kennedy: Performance of the Intelligence Agencies. Book V: Final Report*. Washington, DC: US Government Printing Office, 1976.
US Senate. Select Committee on Intelligence Activities. *Supplementary Detailed Staff Reports on Foreign Aid and Military Intelligence*. Washington, DC: US Government Printing Office, 1976.

INDEX